MCITP Microsoft® Exchange Server 2007 Messaging Design and Deployment

Study Guide

Rawlinson Rivera

Wiley Publishing, Inc.

Acquisitions Editor: Jeff Kellum
Development Editor: Brenda Frink
Technical Editor: Rodney R. Fournier
Production Editor: Elizabeth Campbell
Copy Editor: Candace English
Production Manager: Tim Tate
Vice President and Executive Group Publisher: Richard Swadley
Vice President and Executive Publisher: Joseph B. Wikert
Vice President and Publisher: Neil Edde
Media Associate Project Supervisor: Laura Atkinson
Media Assistant Producer: Josh Frank
Media Quality Assurance: Angie Denny
Book Designers: Judy Fung and Bill Gibson
Compositor: Craig Woods, Happenstance Type-o-Rama
Proofreader: Amy McCarthy
Indexer: Ted Laux
Anniversary Logo Design: Richard Pacifico
Cover Designer: Ryan Sneed

Copyright © 2008 by Wiley Publishing, Inc., Indianapolis, Indiana

Published simultaneously in Canada

ISBN: 978-0-470-18146-1

No part of this publication may be reproduced, stored in a retrieval system or transmitted in any form or by any means, electronic, mechanical, photocopying, recording, scanning or otherwise, except as permitted under Sections 107 or 108 of the 1976 United States Copyright Act, without either the prior written permission of the Publisher, or authorization through payment of the appropriate per-copy fee to the Copyright Clearance Center, 222 Rosewood Drive, Danvers, MA 01923, (978) 750-8400, fax (978) 646-8600. Requests to the Publisher for permission should be addressed to the Legal Department, Wiley Publishing, Inc., 10475 Crosspoint Blvd., Indianapolis, IN 46256, (317) 572-3447, fax (317) 572-4355, or online at http://www.wiley.com/go/permissions.

Limit of Liability/Disclaimer of Warranty: The publisher and the author make no representations or warranties with respect to the accuracy or completeness of the contents of this work and specifically disclaim all warranties, including without limitation warranties of fitness for a particular purpose. No warranty may be created or extended by sales or promotional materials. The advice and strategies contained herein may not be suitable for every situation. This work is sold with the understanding that the publisher is not engaged in rendering legal, accounting, or other professional services. If professional assistance is required, the services of a competent professional person should be sought. Neither the publisher nor the author shall be liable for damages arising herefrom. The fact that an organization or Website is referred to in this work as a citation and/or a potential source of further information does not mean that the author or the publisher endorses the information the organization or Website may provide or recommendations it may make. Further, readers should be aware that Internet Websites listed in this work may have changed or disappeared between when this work was written and when it is read.

For general information on our other products and services or to obtain technical support, please contact our Customer Care Department within the U.S. at (800) 762-2974, outside the U.S. at (317) 572-3993 or fax (317) 572-4002.

Wiley also publishes its books in a variety of electronic formats. Some content that appears in print may not be available in electronic books.

Library of Congress Cataloging-in-Publication Data

Rivera, Rawlinson, 1976-

MCTIP : Microsoft Exchange Server 2007 messaging design and deployment study guide (70-237 and 70-238) / Rawlinson Rivera.

p. cm.

ISBN 978-0-470-18146-1 (pbk. : CD-ROM)

1. Microsoft Exchange server. 2. Client/server computing. 3. Telecommunication--Message processing. I. Title. II. Title: Microsoft Exchange Server 2007 messaging design and deployment study guide.

QA76.9.C55R58 2007

005.7'1376--dc22

2007043722

TRADEMARKS: Wiley, the Wiley logo, and the Sybex logo are trademarks or registered trademarks of John Wiley & Sons, Inc. and/or its affiliates, in the United States and other countries, and may not be used without written permission. Microsoft is a registered trademark of Microsoft Corporation in the United States and/or other countries. All other trademarks are the property of their respective owners. Wiley Publishing, Inc., is not associated with any product or vendor mentioned in this book.

10 9 8 7 6 5 4 3 2 1

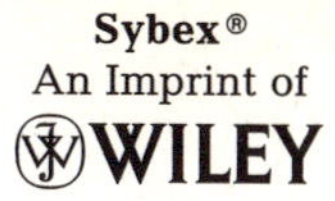

Dear Reader,

Thank you for choosing *MCITP: Microsoft Exchange Server 2007 Messaging Design and Deployment Study Guide*. This book is part of a family of premium quality Sybex books, all written by outstanding authors who combine practical experience with a gift for teaching.

Sybex was founded in 1976. More than thirty years later, we're still committed to producing consistently exceptional books. With each of our titles we're working hard to set a new standard for the industry. From the paper we print on, to the authors we work with, our goal is to bring you the best books available.

I hope you see all that reflected in these pages. I'd be very interested to hear your comments and get your feedback on how we're doing. Feel free to let me know what you think about this or any other Sybex book by sending me an email at `nedde@wiley.com`. Or, if you think you've found a technical error in this book, please visit `http://sybex.custhelp.com`. Customer feedback is critical to our efforts at Sybex.

Best regards,

Neil Edde
Vice President and Publisher
Sybex, an Imprint of Wiley

This book is dedicated to the loving memory of the people who have made a big impact on my life by providing me with advice and guidance and by believing in me. To Aurelio Rivera, Joe Lopez, John Camejo, and Frank Yautz, thanks for the opportunities and excellent advice. All of your help and guidance has made me a better person and more efficient and successful in profession.

Acknowledgments

I never thought that I would enjoy writing and teaching as much as I do now. In fact I love it. I enjoy writing about existing technology, sharing my experiences with students and colleges everywhere. I've trained people all around the world and it's been a great experience, so great that I plan to continue doing it for as long as I live. There is no question that technology is my passion and I'm very fortunate to live my passion.

I want to thank Chris McCain, my mentor for showing me the way and giving me the opportunity to take part in so many great projects including writing this book. Now I can share my passion with the rest of the world. Because of you, I had the privilege of being involved in different capacities with Microsoft Learning in the development of the certification and the courseware development for Exchange Server 2007, Windows Server 2008, Windows Vista, WSS 3.0, and SharePoint Server 2007.

I learned during this project that writing a book of this magnitude is not easy and is time-consuming. Writing books is never the product of a single person, but rather the collective effort of many. I want to thank all the people who were involved with this project, Joel Stidley, Andy Schan, Ilse Van Criekinge, Siegfried Jagott, Bob Lawler, and Tariq Azid. Your work, sacrifices, and efforts are greatly appreciated. I'd like to thank the developmental editor Brenda Frink and the technical editors, Rodney R. Fournier and Randy Muller, for providing constructive feedback and detail suggestions. My thanks also go to the copy editor, Candace English; the production editor, Elizabeth Campbell; the proofreader, Amy McCarthy; and to the compositor, Craig Woods.

A special thanks to Jeff Kellum and the staff at Wiley for the patience and the opportunity.

—Rawlinson Rivera

About the Author

Rawlinson Rivera, an 11-year veteran of the IT consulting and training field, has worked with a variety of technologies ranging from IBM to VMware to Microsoft. He has developed a specialization in architecting secure messaging and collaboration infrastructures with Windows Server 2000/2003, Office SharePoint Server 2007, Exchange Server 2000/2003/2007, and VMware Virtual Infrastructure 3.

Rawlinson is a senior consultant of RawlsNet Technologies, LLC, a firm he founded that focuses on consulting, training, and developing industry-leading content. He has authored content for Microsoft Learning for various technologies, including the latest release of Microsoft Exchange Server 2007.

Rawlinson also delivers VMware's Virtual Infrastructure classes around the world. He is the co-author of *Mastering VMware Infrastructure 3*, published by Sybex, an imprint of Wiley Publishing, Inc.

Rawlinson holds the following technical certifications: MCT, MCSE: Messaging, MCSE: Security, MCITP: Enterprise Messaging Administrator, and VMware Certified Professional.

Contributing Authors

Joel Stidley is a senior solutions engineer at Terremark Worldwide, Inc. who has been working with Microsoft Exchange Server since the 5.0 beta release. He led an engineering team to create a shared Exchange 2000 hosting platform before Microsoft provided an official solution. He is a member of the Microsoft Exchange 2007 TAP program. Joel started an Exchange community and blog website called ExchangeExchange.com. Joel also has worked on several non-Exchange-related projects, including engineering large hosted VMware ESX environments and Microsoft server-based products. Joel has an upcoming book titled *Professional PowerShell for Exchange 2007 SP1*, which will be published by Wrox, an imprint of Wiley Publishing, Inc.

Ilse Van Crickinge is currently a consultant, trainer, and business development manager at Global Knowledge Belgium bvba. Her previous experience has focused on Exchange migrations and deployments, and she has been an Exchange trainer for more than five years. Being an MCT, Ilse offered several companies guidance in their Exchange and MOM deployments, and audited the disaster recovery capabilities in their mail environment. As one of the five Exchange mentors chosen worldwide, she also has helped other trainers to become familiar with Exchange 2003. During the last year, she has ignited many IT professionals with the power of Exchange 2007 by delivering training and by cofounding a new user group in Belgium, Pro-Exchange, focused on Exchange Server. Ilse lives with her husband, Serge, and their son, Robin.

Andy Schan has been an MCSE since 1996 and holds the MCSE: Messaging and Exchange Server 2007 Technical Specialist certifications. He has been working with Microsoft Exchange in enterprise-level deployments since Exchange 4.0, and he worked on MS Mail prior to that. He was the senior engineer on the first deployment of Exchange Server 2003 in the Canadian federal government, and acted as a technical advisor to that department's CIO for the Canadian Anti-Spam Task Force. He has been working with Exchange Server 2007 since Beta 1. Andy's current position is as senior consultant with Titus International in Ottawa, Canada, where he engages with large enterprise customers in the public and private sector in both the United States and Canada.

Siegfried Jagott works as a senior systems architect and team lead for the Messaging and Collaboration team in Siemens IT Solutions located in Munich, Germany. He is part of the Siemens central architecture team that works closely with Microsoft to plan future enhancements of Windows, Exchange, and other products. He hosts a monthly column for *Windows IT Magazine*, “Exchange & Outlook UPDATE: Outlook Perspectives” and writes about Outlook 2007 topics. He is a frequent writer for various international magazines and speaks at conferences on Windows and Exchange topics. He holds an MBA and a diploma in management from Open University in England, and has been an MCSE since 1997.

Tariq bin Azad has been working in the IT industry for the past 15 years, 8 years of which have been spent as a system analyst/consultant. Throughout his career, Tariq has had the opportunity to work on a diverse set of technical projects and to participate in the development of several business solutions. Some projects involved in-depth technical knowledge, while other projects took advantage of his soft skills. During the latter portion of Tariq's career, he has been concentrating mostly on Microsoft Windows 2000/2003, Exchange 2000/2003/2007, Active Directory, Microsoft Virtual Server, VMware, and Citrix implementations. Tariq currently holds MCT, MCSE 2003, CCEA, VCP, and numerous other certificates from other vendors.

Contents at a Glance

Contents

Table of Exercises

Introduction

Microsoft has recently changed its certification program to contain three primary series: Technology, Professional, and Architect. The Technology Series is intended to allow candidates to target specific technologies and is the basis for obtaining the Professional Series and Architect Series certifications. The certifications in the Technology Series consist of one to three exams, focus on a specific technology, and do not include job-role skills. By contrast, the Professional Series focuses on a job role and is not necessarily focused on a single technology, but rather on a comprehensive set of skills for performing the job role being tested. The Architect Series offered by Microsoft includes premier certifications that consist of passing a review board consisting of previously certified architects. To apply for the Architect Series of certifications, you must have a minimum of 10 years of industry experience.

When you've obtained a Technology Series certification, you are recognized as a Microsoft Certified Technology Specialist (MCTS) on the specific technology or technologies that you have been tested on. The Professional Series certifications include Microsoft Certified IT Professional (MCITP) and Microsoft Certified Professional Developer (MCPD). Passing the review board for an Architect Series certification will allow you to become a Microsoft Certified Architect (MCA).

This book has been developed to give you the critical skills and knowledge you need to prepare for the exam for obtaining the MCITP: Enterprise Messaging Administrator certification (Exams 70-237 and 70-238).

The Microsoft Certified Professional Program

Since the inception of its certification program, Microsoft has certified more than 2 million people. As the computer network industry continues to increase in both size and complexity, this number is sure to grow—and the need for *proven* ability also will increase. Certifications can help companies verify the skills of prospective employees and contractors.

Microsoft has developed its Microsoft Certified Professional (MCP) program to give you credentials that verify your ability to work with Microsoft products effectively and professionally. Several levels of certification are available based on specific suites of exams. Microsoft has recently created a new generation of certification programs:

Microsoft Certified Technology Specialist (MCTS) The MCTS can be considered the entry-level certification for the new generation of Microsoft certifications. The MCTS certification program targets specific technologies instead of specific job roles. You must take and pass one to three exams.

Microsoft Certified IT Professional (MCITP) The MCITP certification is a Professional Series certification that tests network and systems administrators on job roles, rather than only on a specific technology. The MCITP certification generally requires completion of one to three exams, in addition to obtaining an MCTS-level certification.

Microsoft Certified Professional Developer (MCPD) The MCPD certification is a Professional Series certification for application developers. Similar to the MCITP, the MCPD is focused on a job role rather than on a single technology. The MCPD certification generally requires completion of one to three exams, in addition to obtaining an MCTS-level certification.

Microsoft Certified Architect (MCA) The MCA is Microsoft's premier certification series. Obtaining the MCA requires a minimum of 10 years of experience and requires the candidate to pass a review board consisting of peer architects.

How Do You Become Certified as an MCITP: Enterprise Messaging Administrator?

The MCITP: Enterprise Messaging Administrator certification requires an individual to pass two examinations and have an MCTS: Exchange Server 2007 Configuring certification. The two exams are the 70-237 and the 70-238, and they require extensive training in Exchange Server 2007 to complete.

Attaining a Microsoft certification has always been a challenge. In the past, students have been able to acquire detailed exam information—even most of the exam questions—from online "brain dumps" and third-party "cram" books or software products. For the new generation of exams, this is simply not the case.

Microsoft has taken steps to protect the security and integrity of its new certification tracks. Prospective candidates must complete a course of study that develops detailed knowledge about a wide range of topics. It supplies them with the true skills needed, derived from working with the technology being tested.

Make sure you take a Microsoft Skills Assessment for Exchange Server 2007 to help you focus your exam preparation. You can find the assessments at `http://assessment.learning.microsoft.com/test/home.asp`.

The new generation of Microsoft certification programs is heavily weighted toward hands-on skills and experience. It is recommended that candidates have troubleshooting skills acquired through hands-on experience and working knowledge.

Fortunately, if you are willing to dedicate the time and effort to learn Exchange Server 2007, you can prepare yourself well for the exams by using the proper tools. By working through this book, you can successfully meet the exam requirements to pass the Designing Messaging Solutions with Microsoft Exchange Server 2007 and Deploying Messaging Solutions with Microsoft Exchange Server 2007 exams.

This book is part of a complete series of Microsoft certification Study Guides published by Sybex, which together cover the new exams and the core MCSA and MCSE operating-system requirements. Please visit the Sybex website at `www.sybex.com` for complete program and product details.

MCITP Exam Requirements

Candidates for MCITP certification on Exchange Server 2007 must pass three Exchange Server 2007 exams (in the case of this book, the Microsoft Certified IT Professional: Enterprise Messaging Administrator, Exams 70-237 and 70-238). For a more detailed description of the Microsoft certification programs, including a list of all the exams, visit the Microsoft Learning website at `www.microsoft.com/learning/mcp`.

The Microsoft Certified IT Professional: Enterprise Messaging Administrator Exams

The Microsoft Certified Enterprise Messaging Administrator exams cover the concepts and skills related to designing messaging solutions with Microsoft Exchange Server 2007 and deploying messaging solutions with Microsoft Exchange Server 2007. It emphasizes the following elements of Exchange Server 2007:

- Designing and planning messaging services
- Designing and planning server high availability
- Designing and planning coexistence and migration
- Defining policies and security procedures
- Planning Microsoft Exchange Server 2007 upgrades and migrations
- Planning for high-availability implementation
- Planning the Exchange topology deployment
- Planning messaging security and compliance implementation
- Planning for messaging-environment maintenance

These exams are quite specific regarding Exchange Server 2007 designs and deployment settings. They also focus on fundamental concepts of Exchange Server 2007 operation. Careful study of this book, along with hands-on experience, will help you prepare for this exam.

Microsoft provides exam objectives to give you a general overview of possible areas of coverage on the Microsoft exams. Keep in mind, however, that exam objectives are subject to change at any time without prior notice and at Microsoft's sole discretion. Please visit the Microsoft Learning website (`www.microsoft.com/learning/mcp`) for the most current listing of exam objectives.

Types of Exam Questions

In an effort to refine the testing process and protect the quality of its certifications, Microsoft has focused its newer certification exams on real experience and hands-on proficiency. There is a greater emphasis on your past working environments and responsibilities and less emphasis on how well you can memorize. In fact, Microsoft says that certification candidates should have hands-on experience before attempting to pass any certification exams.

Microsoft will accomplish its goal of protecting the exams' integrity by regularly adding and removing exam questions, limiting the number of questions that any individual sees in a beta exam, limiting the number of questions delivered to an individual by using adaptive testing, and adding new exam elements.

Exam questions may be in a variety of formats. Depending on which exam you take, you'll see multiple-choice, select-and-place, and prioritize-a-list questions. Simulations and case study–based formats also are included. You may also find yourself taking what's called an *adaptive format exam*. Let's take a look at the types of exam questions and examine the adaptive testing technique so you'll be prepared for all of the possibilities.

Multiple-Choice Questions

Multiple-choice questions come in two main forms. One is a straightforward question followed by several possible answers, of which one or more is correct. The other type of multiple-choice question is more complex and based on a specific scenario. The scenario may focus on several areas or objectives.

Select-and-Place Questions

Select-and-place exam questions involve graphical elements that you must manipulate to successfully answer the question. For example, you might see a diagram of a computer network, as shown in the following graphic taken from the select-and-place demo downloaded from Microsoft's website.

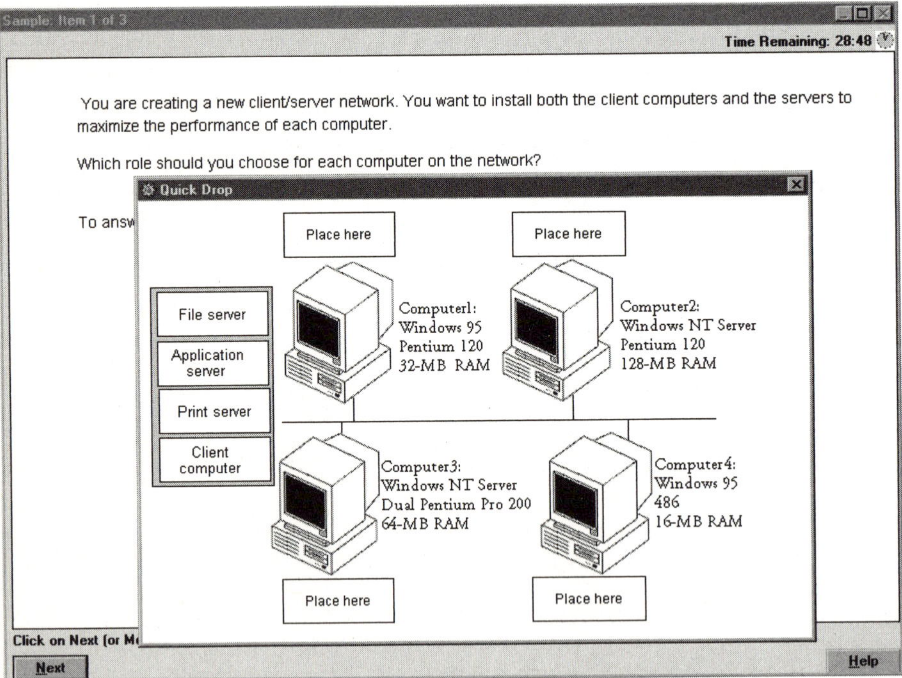

A typical diagram will show computers and other components next to boxes that contain the text "Place here." The labels for the boxes represent various computer roles on a network, such as a print server and a file server. Based on information given for each computer, you are asked to select each label and place it in the correct box. You need to place *all* of the labels correctly. No credit is given for the question if you correctly label only some of the boxes.

In another select-and-place problem, you might be asked to put a series of steps in order by dragging items from boxes on the left to boxes on the right, and placing them in the correct order. One other type requires that you drag an item from the left and place it under an item in a column on the right.

For more information on the various exam question types, go to `www.microsoft.com/learning/mcpexams/policies/innovations.asp`.

Simulations

Simulations are the kinds of questions that most closely represent actual situations and test the skills you use while working with Microsoft software interfaces. These exam questions include a mock interface on which you are asked to perform certain actions according to a given scenario. The simulated interfaces look nearly identical to what you see in the actual product, as shown in this example:

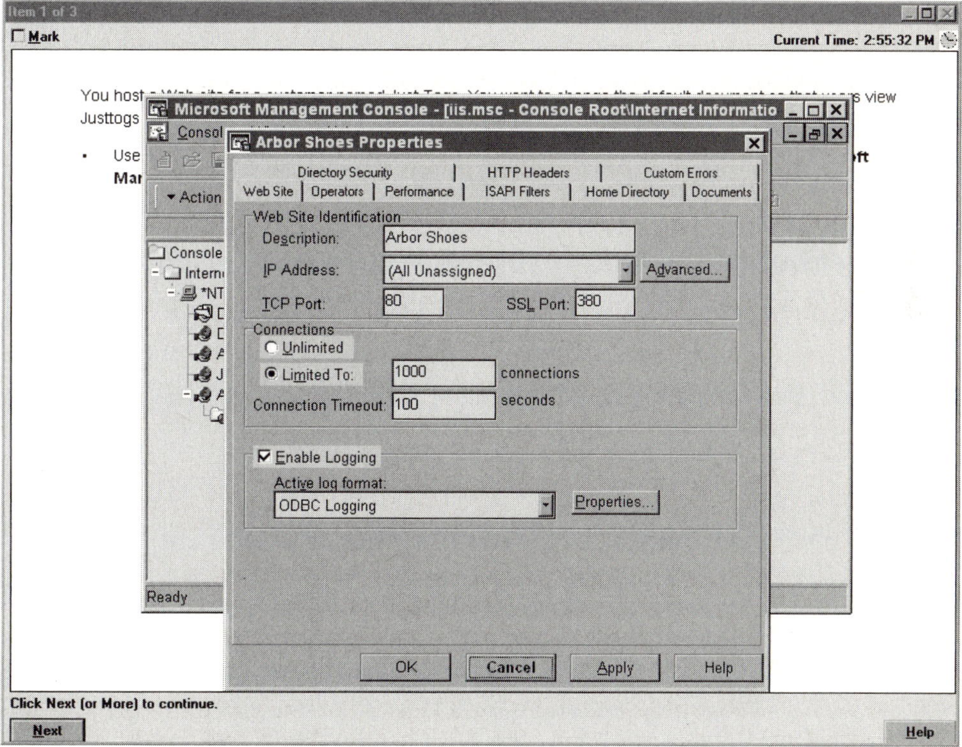

Because of the number of possible errors that can be made on simulations, be sure to consider the following recommendations from Microsoft:

- Do not change any simulation settings that don't pertain to the solution directly.
- When related information has not been provided, assume that the default settings are used.
- Make sure that your entries are spelled correctly.
- Close all the simulation application windows after completing the set of tasks in the simulation.

The best way to prepare for simulation questions is to spend time working with the graphical interface of the product on which you will be tested.

Case Study–Based Questions

Case study–based questions first appeared in the Microsoft Certified Solutions Developer MCSD program. These questions present a scenario with a range of requirements. Based on the information provided, you answer a series of multiple-choice and select-and-place questions. The interface for case study–based questions has several tabs, each of which contains information about the scenario. At present, this type of question appears only in the design exams.

Microsoft will regularly add and remove questions from the exams. This is called *item seeding*. It is part of the effort to make it more difficult for individuals to merely memorize exam questions that were passed along by previous test-takers.

Tips for Taking the Microsoft Certified IT Professional: Enterprise Messaging Administrator Exams

Here are some general tips for achieving success on your certification exam:

- Arrive early at the exam center so that you can relax and review your study materials. During this final review, you can look over tables and lists of exam-related information.
- Read the questions carefully. Don't be tempted to jump to an early conclusion. Make sure you know *exactly* what the question is asking.
- Answer all questions. If you are unsure about a question, then mark the question for review and come back to the question at a later time.
- For questions you're not sure about, use a process of elimination to get rid of the obviously incorrect answers first. This improves your odds of selecting the correct answer when you need to make an educated guess.
- On simulations, do not change settings that are not directly related to the question. Also, assume default settings if the question does not specify or imply which settings are used.

Exam Registration

You may take the Microsoft exams at any of more than 1,000 Authorized Prometric Testing Centers (APTCs). For the location of a testing center near you, call Prometric at 800-755-EXAM (755-3926). Outside the United States and Canada, contact your local Prometric registration center.

Find out the number of the exam you want to take, and then register with the Prometric registration center nearest to you. At that point, you will be asked for advance payment for the exam. The exams are $125 each, and you must take them within one year of payment. You can schedule exams up to six weeks in advance or as late as one working day prior to the date of the exam. You can cancel or reschedule your exam if you contact the center at least two working days prior to the exam. Same-day registration is available in some locations, subject to space availability. Where same-day registration is available, you must register a minimum of two hours before test time.

You also can register for the exams online at `www.prometric.com`.

When you schedule the exam, you will be provided with instructions regarding appointment and cancellation procedures, ID requirements, and information about the testing center's location. You also will receive a registration and payment confirmation letter from Prometric.

Microsoft requires certification candidates to accept the terms of a non-disclosure agreement before taking certification exams.

Is This Book for You?

If you have a solid foundation with Exchange Server 2007 and your goal is to prepare for exams by learning how to design and deploy enterprise messaging solutions with Exchange Server 2007, this book is for you. You'll find clear explanations of the fundamental concepts you need to grasp and plenty of help to achieve the high level of professional competency you need to succeed in your chosen field.

If you want to become certified as an MCITP, this book is definitely for you. However, if you just want to attempt to pass the exam without knowing and understanding Exchange Server 2007, this Study Guide is *not* for you. It is written for people who want to acquire hands-on skills and in-depth knowledge of Exchange Server 2007.

What's in the Book?

What makes a Sybex Study Guide the book of choice for hundreds of thousands of MCPs? We took into account not only what you need to know to pass the exam, but how to take what you've learned and apply it in the real world. Each book contains the following:

Objective-by-objective coverage of the topics you need to know Each chapter lists the objectives covered in that chapter.

The topics covered in this Study Guide map directly to Microsoft's official exam objectives. Each exam objective is covered completely.

Assessment test Directly following this introduction is an assessment test that you should take. It is designed to help you determine how much you already know about Exchange Server 2007. Each question is tied to a topic discussed in the book. Using the results of the assessment test, you can figure out the areas where you need to focus your study. Of course, we do recommend you read the entire book.

Exam essentials To highlight what you learn, you'll find a list of exam essentials at the end of each chapter. The "Exam Essentials" section briefly highlights the topics that need your particular attention as you prepare for the exam.

Glossary Throughout each chapter, you will be introduced to important terms and concepts that you will need to know for the exam. These terms appear in italics in the chapters. At the end of the book, a detailed glossary gives definitions for these terms, as well as other general terms you should know.

Review Questions, complete with detailed explanations Each chapter is followed by a set of review questions that test what you learned in the chapter. The questions are written with the exam in mind, meaning that they are designed to have the same look and feel as those you'll see on the exam. Question types are just like the exam, including multiple choice, exhibits, and select-and-place.

Hands-on exercises In most chapters, you'll find exercises designed to give you the important hands-on experience that is critical for your exam preparation. The exercises support the topics of the chapter, and they walk you through the steps necessary to perform a particular function.

Real-world scenarios Because reading a book isn't enough for you to learn how to apply these topics in your everyday duties, we have provided real-world scenarios in special sidebars. These explain when and why a particular solution would make sense, in a working environment you'd actually encounter.

Interactive CD Every Sybex Study Guide comes with a CD complete with additional questions, flashcards for use with an interactive device, a Windows simulation program, and the book in electronic format. Details are in the following section.

What's on the CD?

With this new member of our best-selling Study Guide series, we are including quite an array of training resources. The CD offers numerous simulations, bonus exams, and flashcards to help you study for the exam. We also have included the complete contents of the Study Guide in electronic form. The CD's resources are described here:

The Sybex e-book for Exchange Server 2007 Many people like the convenience of being able to carry their whole Study Guide on a CD. They also like being able to search the text via computer to find specific information quickly and easily. For these reasons, the entire contents of this Study Guide are supplied on the CD, in PDF. We've also included Adobe Acrobat Reader, which provides the interface and search capabilities for the PDF contents.

The Sybex test engine This is a collection of multiple-choice questions that will help you prepare for your exam. There are three sets of questions:

- Four bonus exams (two for each Microsoft exam) designed to simulate the actual live test-taking experience
- All the questions from the Study Guide, presented in a test engine for your review
- The assessment test

Sybex flashcards for PCs and handheld devices The "flashcard" style of question offers an effective way to quickly and efficiently test your understanding of the fundamental concepts covered in the exam. The Sybex Flashcards set consists of 100 questions presented in a special engine developed specifically for this Study Guide series. Here's what the Sybex Flashcards interface looks like:

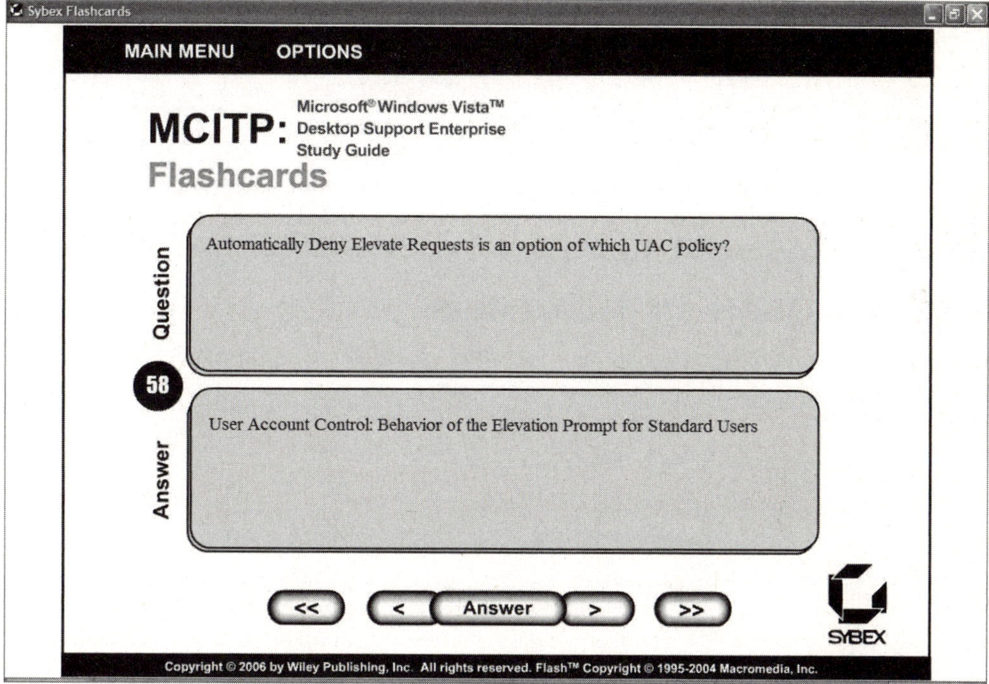

Here is a sample screen from the Sybex test engine:

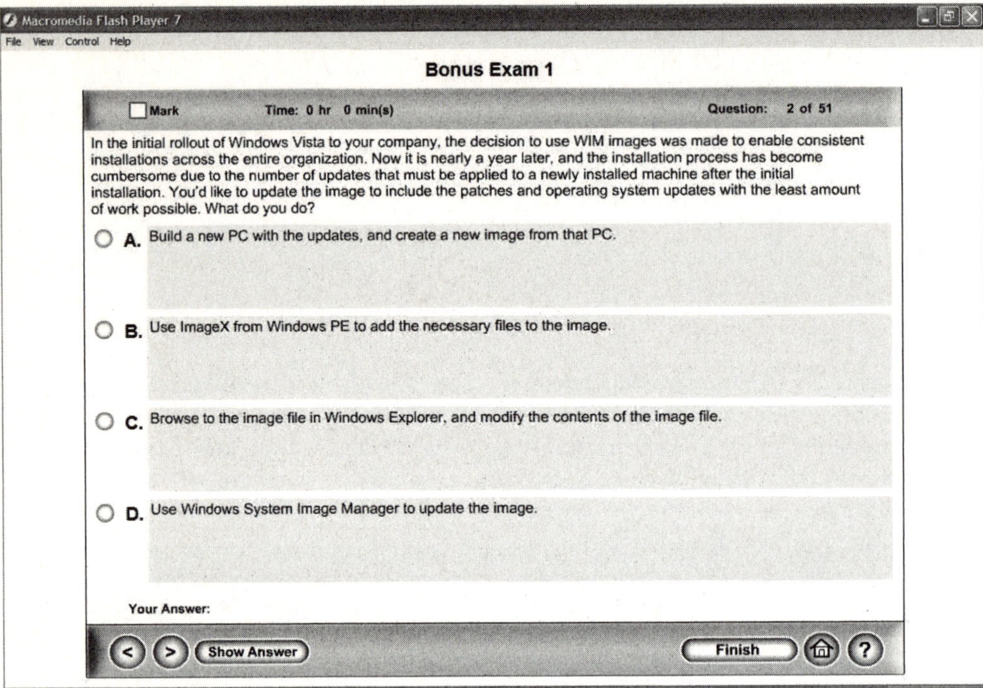

Because of the high demand for a product that will run on handheld devices, we have developed, in conjunction with Land-J Technologies, a version of the flashcard questions that you can take with you on your Palm OS PDA (including the PalmPilot and Handspring's Visor).

Hardware and Software Requirements

The exercises in this book assume that your computer is configured in a specific manner. Your computer should have at least a 20 GB drive that is configured with the minimum space requirements and partitions. Other exercises in this book assume your computer is configured as follows:

- 20 GB C: partition with the NTFS file system
- Optional D: partition with the FAT32 file system
- 1 GB or more of free space

Of course, you can allocate more space to your partitions if it is available.

Contacts and Resources

To find out more about Microsoft education and certification materials and programs, to register with Prometric, or to obtain other useful certification information and additional study resources, check the following resources:

Microsoft Learning home page

`www.microsoft.com/learning`

This website provides information about the MCP program and exams. You can also order the latest Microsoft Roadmap to Education and Certification.

Microsoft TechNet Technical Information Network

`www.microsoft.com/technet`

(800) 344-2121

Use this website or phone number to contact support professionals and system administrators. Outside the United States and Canada, contact your local Microsoft subsidiary for information.

PalmPilot Training Product Development: Land-J

`www.land-j.com`

(407) 359-2217

Land-J Technologies is a consulting and programming business specializing in application development for the 3Com PalmPilot Personal Digital Assistant. Land-J developed the Palm version of the EdgeTests, which is included on the CD that accompanies this Study Guide.

Prometric

`www.prometric.com`

(800) 755-3936

Contact Prometric to register to take an MCP exam at any of more than 800 Prometric Testing Centers around the world.

Microsoft Certified Professional Magazine Online

`www.mcpmag.com`

Microsoft Certified Professional Magazine is a well-respected publication that focuses on Windows certification. This site hosts chats and discussion forums and tracks news related to the MCSE program. Some of the services charge a fee, but they are well worth it.

Windows IT Pro

`www.windowsitpro.com`

You can subscribe to this magazine or read free articles at the website. The study resource provides general information on Windows 2000, XP, and .NET Server.

Assessment Test Questions

1. You are an Exchange administrator, and your manager requests that you investigate possible high-availability solutions for your Exchange servers. You currently have one Exchange Server 2007 server and you are allowed to buy additional hardware if needed to make sure that the failure of one server does not imply mail-service loss. What options can you include in your disaster-recovery plan?

   A. Network load balancing

   B. Windows clustering

   C. Backup

   D. DNS round-robin

2. You are an Exchange administrator and you are required to design a disaster-recovery plan. You need to choose what kind of backup software program your backup administrators should include to be able to successfully back up your Exchange servers. What kind of backup software solution would you recommend?

   A. Open file backup agent

   B. File-level backup agent

   C. Exchange-aware backup agent

   D. Outlook backup agent

3. You are an Exchange administrator, and you are required to make a backup of the configuration of your Exchange organization. What data should you include in your backup plan?

   A. Active Directory

   B. Exchange database files

   C. Active Directory Application Mode

   D. Windows Registry of every Exchange server

4. You are an Exchange administrator, and you are investigating the possibilities you have to secure your mail environment against spam. What filters can be useful to control spam? Choose all that apply.

   A. Sender ID filtering

   B. Sender filtering

   C. Recipient filtering

   D. Content filtering

   E. Connection filtering

5. You are an Exchange administrator, and you are required to investigate the requirements for messaging records management. What should you include in your design? Choose all that apply.

   A. Legal requirements

   B. Regulatory requirements

   C. Personal requirements

   D. Exchange requirements

6. You are an Exchange administrator, and you are required to make sure that all mailflow between your Exchange organization and a partner organization is secured without requiring your users to do anything. How can you configure this?

   A. Implement sealing between your organization and your partner's mail environment.

   B. Implement signing between your organization and your partner's mail environment.

   C. Implement Transport Layer Security (TLS) between your organization and your partner's mail environment.

   D. Implement Information Rights Management (IRM) between your organization and your partner's mail environment.

7. You are an Exchange administrator responsible for a mixed Exchange 5.5-Exchange 2000 organization. You are investigating the possibilities to transition to Exchange 2007. What action should you take before installing your first Exchange 2007 server?

   A. Remove all Exchange 5.5 servers

   B. Remove all public folders

   C. Remove all routing groups

   D. Remove all connectors

8. You are an Exchange administrator responsible for an Exchange 2000 organization. You are investigating the possibilities to transition to Exchange 2007. What tool can help you discover potential issues before transitioning to Exchange 2007?

   A. ExMerge

   B. Exchange Best Practices Analyzer

   C. `PFMigrate.wsf`

   D. ESEUtil

9. You are an Exchange administrator responsible for an Exchange 2000 organization. You are investigating the possibilities to transition to Exchange 2007. You would like to prepare you Active Directory forest for Exchange 2007 by extending its schema for Exchange 2007. Which command should you run?

   A. `Setup.exe /forestprep`

   B. `Setup.com /forestprep`

   C. `Setup.exe /schemaprep`

   D. `Setup.com /schemaprep`

10. You are an Exchange administrator responsible for an Exchange organization that contains one Exchange 2007 Mailbox server and one Exchange 2007 Hub Transport/Client Access server. Your users are currently using Microsoft Office Outlook 2003, running on Windows XP Professional SP2, but you would like them to be able to use the new Autodiscover feature available in Exchange 2007. What should you do prior to configuring the Autodiscover service in Exchange 2007?

    A. Upgrade the client workstations to Windows Vista

    B. Upgrade the client workstations to Windows Server 2003

    C. Upgrade to Microsoft Office Outlook 2007

    D. Upgrade to Windows Mail

11. You are an Exchange administrator responsible for an Exchange organization that contains one Exchange 2007 Mailbox server and one Exchange 2007 Hub Transport/Client Access server. Your users are currently using Microsoft Office Outlook 2007, running on Windows XP Professional SP2. How do your users gain access to free/busy information of other users in your Exchange organization?

    A. Public folders

    B. System public folders

    C. Exchange Web Service: Availability service

    D. Exchange Web Service: Out-of-Office service

12. You are an Exchange administrator responsible for an Exchange organization that contains one Exchange 2007 Mailbox server and one Exchange 2007 Hub Transport/Client Access server. Your users require the ability to use a mobile device to gain access to their mailboxes, and they should be able to access Windows SharePoint Service and file servers using the mobile device. What kind of device should you consider configuring?

    A. Windows Mobile 4

    B. Windows Mobile 5

    C. Windows Mobile 6

    D. Windows Mobile 2003

13. System folders are required in an Exchange Server 2007 and Outlook 2007 organization.

    A. True

    B. False

14. Which of the following tools can be used to migrate public folders between two Exchange organizations?

    A. Exchange Server 2003 Exchange System Manager

    B. Exchange Server 2007 Exchange Management Shell

    C. Active Directory Users and Computers with the Exchange Server 2003 extensions

    D. Inter-Organization Replication tool

15. What is the first step in preparing your Exchange 2000 Server or Exchange Server 2003 environment for Exchange Server 2007?

    A. Extending the Active Directory schema

    B. Configuring Exchange Server 2007 objects and groups in Active Directory

    C. Preparing legacy Exchange permissions

    D. Installing Exchange Server 2007 on the first computer

16. What is the most important component of your email compliance implementation?

    A. Corporate email policy

    B. Messaging records management

    C. Message classification

    D. Managed folders

17. What component in messaging records management processes mailbox content?
    - A. Managed content settings
    - B. Managed folders
    - C. Managed Folder Assistant
    - D. Managed-folder mailbox policies
18. Message classification is a function available in Exchange Server 2007 for encrypting email messages and providing persistent content protection.
    - A. True
    - B. False
19. In the change-management process, what types of changes are approved automatically, without undergoing a formal review process?
    - A. Low-priority changes
    - B. Standard changes
    - C. Minor changes
    - D. Emergency priority changes
20. What process or solution helps you ensure that you are meeting your Service Level Agreements (SLAs)?
    - A. Change management
    - B. Patch management
    - C. Monitoring and reporting
    - D. Windows Server Update Services
21. What process or solution will have the most positive effect on the stability and availability of your Exchange Server 2007 environment?
    - A. Change management
    - B. Patch management
    - C. Monitoring and reporting
    - D. Windows Server Update Services
22. You want to implement Exchange 2007 Domain Security using mutual TLS. What kind of certificate is needed on your server to make this work? (Select all that apply.)
    - A. A Windows PKI-generated certificates
    - B. A certificate that has been purchased by a third-party certificate authority (CA) like VeriSign
    - C. A self-signed certificate created during Exchange 2007 set up
    - D. No certificate is needed on the server.

23. What statements regarding transport rules are correct? (Select all that apply.)
    A. Edge rules are used to apply compliance and policy-based rules.
    B. Transport rules are used to apply compliance- and policy-based roles.
    C. Edge rules are used to manage antispam and antivirus protection.
    D. Transport rules are used to manage antispam and antivirus protection.
24. In Exchange 2003, journaling meant that a copy of the message was sent to the journal mailbox. In Exchange 2007, a journal report is now generated with the original message attached. Is this a correct statement?
    A. Yes
    B. No
25. One of your non-clustered Mailbox servers has had a database failure. The database may take hours to restore or repair. The business requires that you allow users to be able to send and receive email as quickly as possible. Which option will provide for the business requirement?
    A. Streaming database restores
    B. A recovery storage group
    C. Database portability
    D. A dial-tone database
26. Your company has a plan to deploy centralized Mailbox servers. These servers need to be redundant and minimize data storage on the SAN because of budgetary constraints. What server configuration would meet these business needs?
    A. Local continuous replication (LCR)
    B. Single-copy clustering (SCC)
    C. Cluster continuous replication (CCR)
    D. Network load balanced servers
27. You need to design a redundancy solution for your company's three Edge Transport servers. You need to create a design so that each server is used equally. Which of the following are supported options?
    A. Create MX records with the same preference weight for the host name of each server.
    B. Create MX records with the sequential preference weights for the host name of each server.
    C. Create a network load balanced cluster with each server with a single MX record pointing to the host name of the cluster.
    D. Create MX records with the same preference weights for an alias record of each server.
28. You have been asked to design a backup solution. The business requirement is that a maximum of eight hours of data can be lost and that a minimal number of restore sets are used. Which schedule would meet this need?
    A. Full backup nightly and incremental backups every eight hours
    B. Copy backup nightly and incremental backups every eight hours
    C. Copy backup nightly and differential backups every eight hours
    D. Full backup nightly and differential backups every eight hours

29. You are planning a disaster-recovery solution for the Mailbox server role at one of your company's locations. The Mailbox server is configured as a continuous-copy replication cluster, assuming the appropriate backup was performed. Which are viable options for completing a restore?

    A. Streaming restore of the active databases

    B. Streaming restore of the passive databases

    C. Volume Shadow Copy Service (VSS) restore of the active databases

    D. VSS restore of the passive databases

30. You are designing a Mailbox server will host three different business units' mailboxes. You need to maintain separate SLAs for each of the business units. Assuming that the restore speed is not a problem, what is the minimum number of storage groups and databases your design should include?

    A. 1

    B. 2

    C. 3

    D. 4

31. Which of the following is a valid configuration of a CCR cluster?

    A. One storage group and fifty databases

    B. Fifty storage groups and one database in each

    C. Two storage groups and three databases in each

    D. One storage group and five databases

32. When planning to deploy a Mailbox server with local continuous replication and only one storage group, what is the minimum number of volumes needed to meet the recommended configuration?

    A. 2

    B. 4

    C. 6

    D. 8

33. What tool will simulate Exchange database disk I/O load without needing to have Exchange installed?

    A. Exchange Load Simulator

    B. Jetstress

    C. Exchange Server Stress and Performance

    D. Performance Monitor

34. You are planning deployment of Exchange services to a new location for your company. In what order would you deploy the following server roles?

    A. Unified Messaging

    B. Client Access

    C. Mailbox

    D. Hub Transport

35. You are planning to deploy a new Exchange Server 2007 messaging system in your company's domain. What forest functional level must the forest be in before Exchange Server 2007 is installed where trusts will not be maintained with other forests?

A. Windows 2000 native

B. Windows 2000 mixed

C. Windows 2003 interim

D. Windows 2003

36. Which of the following roles can be installed on a CCR cluster?

A. Hub Transport

B. Unified Messaging

C. Client Access

D. None of the above

Answers to Assessment Test Questions

1. B. By configuring Windows clustering, you implement high availability for your mail services. If a cluster node goes offline, the other node will provide mailbox access to your users. You cannot deploy the Hub or the Client Access server (CAS) role on a clustered Mailbox server; therefore, you will need to buy additional hardware to deploy the Hub and CAS roles.

2. C. An Exchange-aware backup tool will tell Exchange that it is going to make a backup of its database files and log files. It will check every page of the database file for corruption. After finishing the backup, the backup tool will make sure that the database files are marked as being successfully backed up and all log files that are redundant will be purged automatically!

3. A. Exchange stores almost all of its configuration information in the Active Directory configuration partition.

4. A, B, C, D, and E. All of the above are effective filters to use to control spam

5. A and B. Email is a means of communication that is very easy to use, and very easy to abuse to exchange business and private information among people. It is very important that an Exchange administrator can control the message flow inside the organization and the message flow between the Exchange organization and the outbound messaging environments to prevent confidential information from being exposed. You must understand all legal and regulatory requirements that might require you to set up any policies.

6. C. Transport Layer Security, as defined by RFC 2246, is a protocol that establishes a secure connection between a client and a server. TLS requires both client and server to have a valid certificate. TLS uses the certificates to authenticate client and server, and to encrypt all data that are exchanged between client and server. Configuring and enabling TLS will ensure that, in your Exchange organization, every SMTP connection that is initiated will be authenticated and encrypted.

7. A. You can transition only a native Exchange 2000 or Exchange 2003 organization to Exchange 2007.

8. B. The Exchange Best Practices Analyzer (ExBPA) version 1.0 was first released in September 2004 as a free tool that could be downloaded from the Internet. In Exchange Server 2007, it is built in as a configuration-management tool inside the Exchange Management Console. The main goal of ExBPA is to analyze an existing Exchange environment and give you a report on what can and should be changed to make it run smoother. All recommendations are based on Microsoft's best practices. Starting with version 2.7, there is an Exchange 2007 Readiness Check.

9. D. `Setup.com /schemaprep` will extend your Active Directory schema with Exchange 2007–specific attributes.

10. C. Microsoft Exchange Server 2007 introduces a new service, Autodiscover, that allows Microsoft Office Outlook 2007 to automatically discover the configuration information needed to successfully access Exchange Server 2007 features such as Offline Address Book, Unified Messaging, Out-of-Office, and Availability.

11. C. The Microsoft Exchange Server 2007 Availability service provides access to free and busy information and Out-of-Office information for clients running Microsoft Office Outlook 2007.

12. C. Windows SharePoint Services and Windows file share document access is supported only by mobile devices equipped with Windows Mobile 6.

13. B. In an Exchange Server 2007 organization with no previous versions of Exchange installed and Outlook 2007 used as the messaging client, system folders are not required. Free/busy functionality is provided with the Availability service, and the offline address book is provided via web-based distribution rather than system folders.

14. D. The Inter-Organization Replication tool is the only one that can replicate public folders between two separate Exchange organizations. It is supported only with Exchange Server 2003 public-folder servers in both the target and source forests, however.

15. C. The first step in preparing the legacy environment for Exchange Server 2007 is to configure Exchange permissions in each domain containing Exchange 2000 Server or Exchange Server 2003 computers before updating the schema for Exchange Server 2007. This ensures the Recipient Update Service functions correctly after the Active Directory schema is updated for Exchange 2007.

16. A. Corporate email policy is the most important component of any email compliance implementation. Without it, your implementation will likely be a failure in the long run.

17. C. The Managed Folder Assistant configures managed folders in users' mailboxes and processes mailbox content based on the messaging records management (MRM) configuration created by the administrator. Managed content settings are defined on managed folders, while managed folder mailbox policies are collections of managed folders that are assigned to users.

18. B. Message classification adds metadata and visual labels to email messages to designate the intended use of the message. Rights Management Services (RMS) can encrypt email and provide persistent content protection.

19. B. Only standard changes are automatically approved and go directly to the planning and release phases. Minor changes can be approved by the change manager without being referred to the Change Advisory Board (CAB); emergency changes are approved by a subset of the CAB called the Emergency Committee.

20. C. Monitoring helps to detect issues before they affect your users and provides you with a means of determining whether your SLAs are being met.

21. A. The purpose of change management is to introduce required changes into the IT environment in a disciplined manner to ensure minimal disruption to ongoing operations. How change is introduced, including patches, has the most influence on the uptime of your environment.

22. A, B. Exchange 2007 Domain Security uses mutual TLS to authenticate the partner and encrypt the traffic. A certificate from a trusted CA is required. Also, you can use Windows PKI–generated certificates if both partners trust the root CA. Using self-signed certificates does not work with mutual TLS.

23. B, C. Transport rules apply to compliance and policy rules. Edge rules are to prevent spam and virus outbreaks.

24. A. Yes, that's correct. Exchange 2007 changes the journaling format to the new journal report format that includes the original message unaltered as an attachment in the Transport Neutral Encapsulation Format (TNEF).

25. D. A dial-tone database will allow the users to get back online quickly and allow for mail to be recovered in the background.

26. B. A single-copy cluster provides for redundant services and minimizes the data stored on the SAN.

27. A, C. To equally balance loads among the servers, create an MX record for each of the server's host records. Another supportable option is to use network load balancing with a single MX record.

28. D. A full backup every night will purge the logs, and then the differential backup every eight hours will capture the changes since the full backup. The restore would require two backup sets: the full and the last differential that was made.

29. A, C. Restores can be done only against active databases or to a recovery storage group.

30. C. Three storage groups would need to be created so that backups and restores for each of the business groups would not affect any of the other storage groups

31. B. A CCR cluster can have only storage groups with a single database in each. No other configuration is valid.

32. B. To keep the transaction logs and database files separate, two volumes would be required. To keep both the active and passive copies separate, two more volumes would be required, for a total of four.

33. B. Jetstress is used to simulate database I/O without having to install Exchange.

34. B, D, C, A. The deployment order should always be Client Access, then Hub Transport, then Mailbox, then Unified Messaging.

35. A. Windows 2000 native mode is all that is required.

36. D. You cannot install any other role on a clustered Mailbox role.

70-237 Pro: Designing Messaging Solutions With Microsoft Exchange Server 2007

Designing and Planning Messaging Services

MICROSOFT EXAM OBJECTIVES COVERED IN THIS CHAPTER:

- ✓ Evaluate and recommend Active Directory configuration
- ✓ Evaluate and plan server deployment based on best practices, budget, and other business factors
- ✓ Evaluate network topology and provide technical recommendations
- ✓ Design and plan for new Exchange features
- ✓ Design organization configuration to meet routing requirements

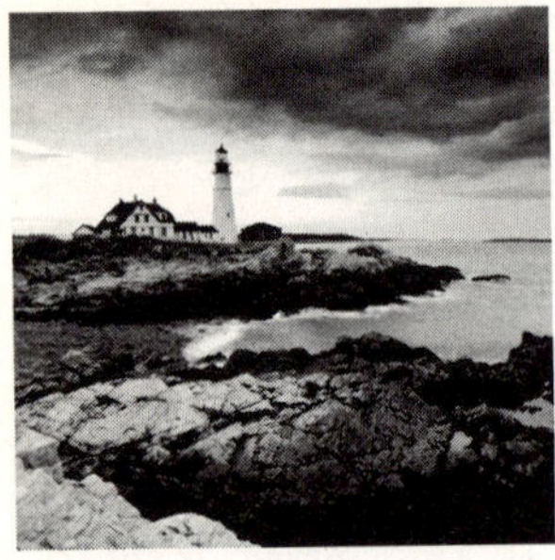

Designing and planning Messaging Services is one of the most important tasks of a messaging IT pro and needs careful considerations in many areas. This chapter introduces you to important Exchange design topics: Active Directory (AD) requirements, server placement, and message-routing considerations.

The main subjects of this chapter are as follows:

- Defining Active Directory prerequisites
- Designing an administrative model
- Planning Exchange Server 2007 placement
- Understanding Exchange Server 2007 roles
- Reviewing the current and planned network topology and providing technical recommendations
- Understanding new Exchange features
- Understanding internal and external message routing

Evaluating and Recommending Active Directory Configuration

As an Exchange Server 2007 message professional, your responsibilities normally will not include a single domain with a single Exchange Server installation. The Active Directories and Exchange organizations you plan, manage, or support will be highly complex as well as dispersed around the world. To cover this exam requirement, this section will teach you some specific commands and considerations that are special to medium-to-large organizations. Here you will learn about all the requirements of Active Directory for Exchange Server 2007.

Defining Active Directory Prerequisites

The following section will teach you about Exchange Server 2007 and how it uses Active Directory to store configuration data. It starts with the high-level basics of Active Directory and Exchange data and continues with explanations of software version requirements as well as Active Directory preparation for Exchange.

Exchange Uses Active Directory to Store Information

The Active Directory database is divided into logical partitions, namely the schema partition, the configuration partition, and a domain partition for every domain. Here's how Exchange Server 2007 uses each of these partitions.

The Schema Partition

Before Exchange Server 2007 can store information in Active Directory, this partition needs to be modified so Exchange-related objects (e.g., connector or mailbox information) and attributes (e.g., Exchange Mailbox server or a user object) can be stored there. The schema partition stores the general layout of all Active Directory objects and its attributes. It includes two types of information:

Schema classes: The objects that can be created

Schema attributes: The properties that can be used for each object

Each and every domain controller and global catalog server in the Active Directory contains a complete replica of the schema partition. Thus it is important to plan the Exchange Server 2007 schema extension accordingly—it will initiate a full replication on all domain controllers and global catalog servers in your forest.

It is true that the Exchange Server 2007 schema extension also includes the Exchange 2003 schema extension. However, if you are ever planning on installing an Exchange 2003 server, you must install it as the first server and install Exchange Server 2007 afterwards. Once you have installed an Exchange Server 2007 server, you will not be able to install Exchange 2003 anymore.

The Configuration Partition

As the name implies, the configuration partition stores information about the forest-wide configuration. For example, the configuration of AD sites and site links is stored here. Therefore, it is available on every domain controller and global catalog server throughout the forest.

Exchange Server 2007 stores information like global settings, address lists, connections, and so on to the configuration partition. You can take a look at what information Exchange Server 2007 stored in the configuration partition by following Exercise 1.1.

EXERCISE 1.1

Looking at the Exchange Configuration

To look at the Exchange configuration, follow these steps:

1. Click Start ➢ All Programs ➢ Administrative Tools ➢ Active Directory Sites and Services.

EXERCISE 1.1 *(continued)*

2. Click on View ➤ Show Services Node.

3. Expand Services to find Microsoft Exchange container, as shown below.

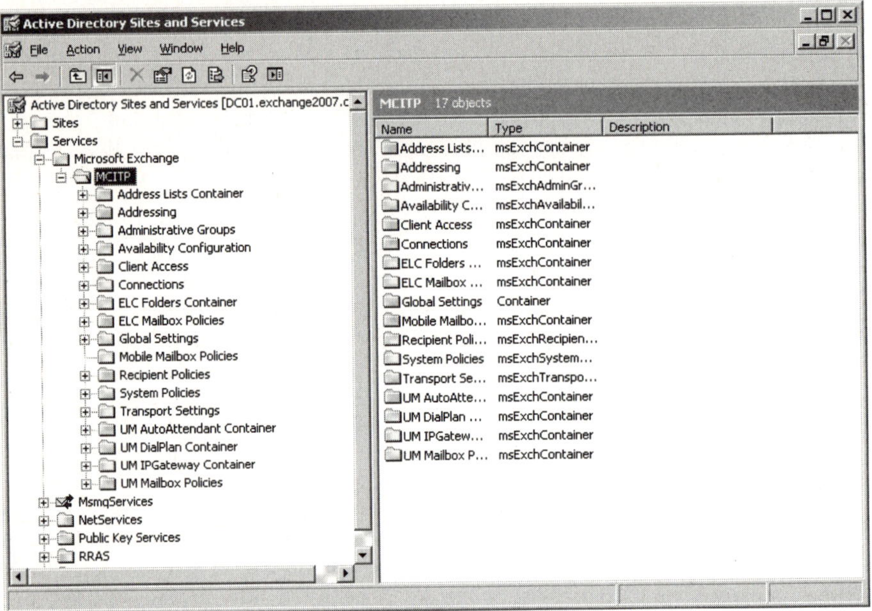

Important: Please be aware that any modification in this container directly impacts the Exchange Server 2007 configuration and thus might crash your system!

The Domain Partition

The domain partition holds domain-related information in containers as well as organizational units (OUs). It includes information about users, groups, and computers in that domain. Exchange Server 2007 creates for every domain-prepared domain (which means that the Exchange `Setup /PrepareDomain` has been run for the domain) an OU called "Microsoft Exchange Security Groups" where it will store Exchange related management groups.

The domain partition is stored on every domain controller of that specific domain. Every global catalog server has a subset of information from every domain partition in the forest, as well as the complete partition from its own domain. For example, a global catalog server in a different domain will contain information of the individual user, such as the user's display name or its SMTP addresses, but not its password.

Active Directory Requirements

For Exchange Server 2007 there are several requirements that Active Directory and domains must meet. Consider the following when evaluating your current Active Directory design:

- The server on which the Schema Master role runs must have at least Windows Server 2003 SP1 installed.
- You need to run Windows Server 2003 SP1 or later on global catalog servers in every Active Directory site where you plan to install Exchange Server 2007. I recommend that you upgrade all your domain controllers to prevent any problems.
- All domains that will include Exchange Server 2007 servers or recipients must have an Active Directory domain functional level Windows 2000 Server Native or higher; Windows Server 2003 functional level is recommended.

Windows Server 2008 (formerly code-named Longhorn) is supported only with Exchange Server 2007 Service Pack 1 or later. You cannot install Exchange Server 2007 in any AD site that contains Windows Server 2008 domain controllers, nor can you install it on a Windows 2008 member server!

Preparing Your Active Directory and Domains

This section walks through the steps required to prepare your Active Directory and domains to run Exchange Server 2007.

Preparing the Schema Only

If you need to extend the schema of your Active Directory *separately* from the Exchange Server 2007 installation, you can run the following from a command prompt from the Exchange Server 2007 setup directory: `Setup /PrepareSchema`. Especially in larger organizations where Active Directory and Exchange administration are separated, you will need to plan well ahead to do this.

You must be a member of the Schema Admins group and the Enterprise Admins group and run the `/PrepareSchema` command on the server that is in the same Active Directory domain ad site as the Schema Master role. I strongly recommend doing this directly on your Schema Master server.

However, this command is not needed, as it is part of the Preparing Active Directory switch `/PrepareAD`.

Preparing Your Active Directory

To prepare your Active Directory for Exchange Server 2007, you must run the following command: `Setup /PrepareAD`. Please consider the following when running this command:

- You need to run it on a server in the root domain.
- You must be a member of the Enterprise Admins group, and if the schema also needs to be extended you also need to be part of the Schema Admins group.
- If you have Exchange Server 2003 servers, you must have Exchange Full Administrator permissions.

Exchange Server 2007 setup does the following tasks preparing your Active Directory environment:

1. Extend the schema if it was not done already.
2. Configure global Exchange objects in the configuration partition. These include Exchange Administrative Group (FYDIBOHF23SPDLT), Exchange Routing Group (DWBGZMFD01QNBJR), and so on.
3. Create an OU in the root domain called Microsoft Exchange Security Groups, which includes the following universal security groups (USGs):
   - Exchange Organization Administrators
   - Exchange Recipient Administrators
   - Exchange View-Only Administrators
   - Exchange Servers
   - ExchangeLegacyInterop
4. Prepares the root domain as mentioned in next section.

If your Active Directory site topology is complex, you have to check before you continue to make sure that replication to all domain controllers in your forest took place. Tools like the Active Directory Replication Monitor (`replmon.exe`) that is part of the Windows 2003 Resource Kit Tools can assist you with monitoring the progress.

Preparing Domains

If you are in larger environment where your Active Directory consists of multiple domains, you also need to prepare every domain for Exchange Server 2007. Your domain preparation will do the following things to the domain:

- Set permissions on the Domain container for the Exchange Servers, Exchange Organization Administrators, Authenticated Users, and Exchange Mailbox Administrators.
- Create an OU called Microsoft Exchange System Objects and set permissions on this container for the Exchange Servers, Exchange Organization Administrators, and Authenticated Users.
- Create a global group called Exchange Install Domain Servers and add it to the Exchange Servers USG in the root domain.

There are two possible ways to prepare domains: you can prepare them all together or you can run the command domain by domain. Preparing all domains together might seem like the easiest way to prepare all domains, but sometimes you might not be able to do this. Consider the following situations:

- You have a regional Active Directory domain design; no central administration is available.
- Permissions for the Enterprise Admin group were removed from some domains.

- Not all domains can be contacted; Exchange Server 2007 setup needs to contact at least one domain controller from every domain to make the changes.
- Firewalls prevent some locations from communicating to each other directly.

For each command, you must consider the requirements in Table 1.1.

TABLE 1.1 Exchange Server 2007 Setup—Domain Preparation Considerations

Setup Command	Consideration
`Setup /PrepareAllDomains`	Requires Enterprise Admin permission, Domain Admin permission in all domains, and network access to every domain.
`Setup /PrepareDomain:<FQDN of domain>`	Requires Domain Admin permission in the domain that you want to prepare. If it is a domain that did not exist when you ran `/PrepareAD`, you also need to be a member of the Exchange Organization Administrators group.

You must prepare every Active Directory that will host Exchange Server 2007 servers or Exchange-specific objects like mailboxes, distribution lists, contacts, or public folders. You do not need to prepare the root domain, as this was done during the "Preparing Your Active Directory" section.

Isolating Exchange Server 2007 from your Active Directory

To completely separate your Exchange Server 2007 installation from your Active Directory implementation, you have the option to create an Exchange resource forest. A *resource forest* is a completely different Active Directory environment created for the sole purpose of serving Exchange Server 2007. For example, I've seen this strategy in hosting (or outsourcing) environments where the company managed the user accounts but they outsourced their mailboxes to a hosting company. To configure this, the following is required:

- The minimum forest functional level of both forests must be Windows Server 2003
- A forest-to-forest trust needs to be established

Designing an Administrative Model

It is important to consider a thoroughly planned administrative model for your organization when you integrate Exchange Server 2007 into your Active Directory. Generally there are three ways to organize your administrative roles:

- A single administrative team manages both Windows Server and Exchange Server.
- Permissions are split between Windows and Exchange administrators.
- The Exchange administrator role is isolated by using an Exchange resource forest.

Using the first or last option, you don't need much extra configuration in Exchange Server 2007. However, splitting permissions is a more complex story. After offering some background in the following sections, I will explore this topic in detail under the heading "The Split-Permissions Model."

Exchange 2003 was based on an administrative role model of two layers: organization– and administrative group–based. This model has proven to be insufficiently flexible, especially for medium-to-large organizations. Thus, Exchange Server 2007 uses a more granular administrative roles model similar to the built-in Windows Server security groups.

Administrative Roles

Exchange Server 2007 uses the following predefined roles to manage permissions:

- Exchange Organization Administrators
- Exchange Recipient Administrators
- Exchange View-Only Administrators
- Exchange Server Administrators

All roles expect Exchange Server Administrators provide you with permissions to any domain that was prepared for Exchange (i.e., `Setup /PrepareDomain`). You cannot change the scope of them.

To assign a role to a group or account, you can either use the Exchange Management Console (EMC) and configure it in the Organization Configuration pane, or use the `Add-ExchangeAdministrator` command in the Exchange Management Shell (EMS). Figure 1.1 shows the Exchange Management Console where you can view and modify all administrative roles.

FIGURE 1.1 Exchange administrative roles in the Exchange Management Console

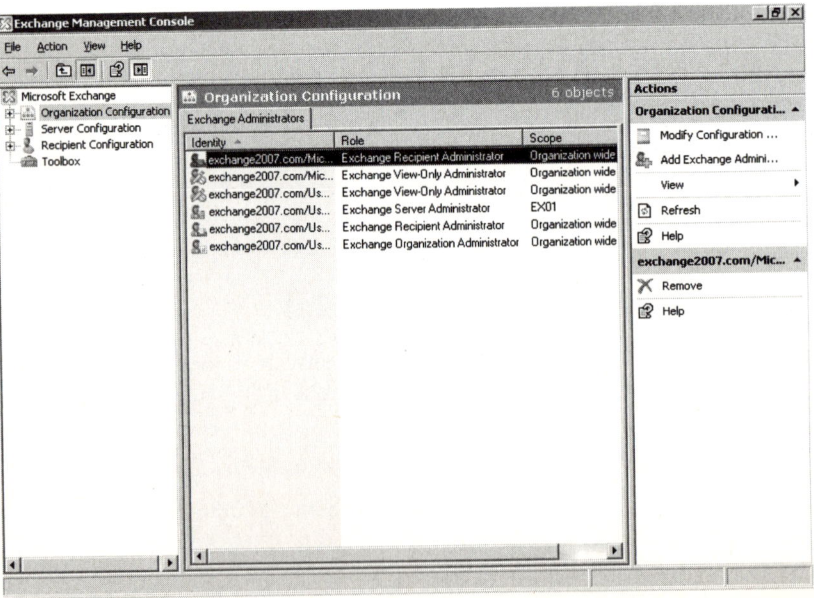

During the initial Exchange setup in the root domain (i.e., `Setup /PrepareAD`) all groups (except Exchange Server Administrators) are created as a security group in the Microsoft Exchange Security Groups container. You can see those using Active Directory Users and Computers.

Exchange Organization Administrators

The Exchange Organization Administrators role is the most powerful role in Exchange Server 2007. As in Exchange Server 2003, you get full access to all Exchange-related servers and objects in your organization. You need this role for any configuration that impacts all your Exchange servers, like connectors or global settings.

The following list provides an overview of what permissions you receive when you are part of this role:

- Owner permission to the Exchange organization in the configuration partition of Active Directory
- Read access to all domains that were prepared for Exchange
- Write access to all Exchange-specific attributes in all domains that were prepared for Exchange
- Membership in local Administrators group of all Exchange servers in your organization

Because this role automatically gets write permissions on the Exchange-specific attributes in all domains that where prepared for Exchange, Exchange Organization Administrators can assign or remove a mailbox from any user account in the forest—no need to be a full Domain Admin or an Account Admin!

Exchange Recipient Administrators

The Exchange Recipient Administrators manage mailboxes, contacts, groups, dynamic distribution lists, and public folder objects. They can add or remove SMTP addresses, enable or disable specific groups for mail, or create a contact. This role also lets you manage Unified Messaging and Client Access settings on mailboxes. Basically, you can think of the Exchange Recipient Administrators as the Exchange user management team.

You receive the following permissions when you're part of this role:

- Read access to all domains that have been prepared for Exchange
- Write access to all Exchange-specific attributes in all domains that have been prepared for Exchange
- Membership in the Exchange View-Only Administrators group—thus the ability to view the complete Exchange configuration

Exchange View-Only Administrators

As an Exchange View-Only Administrator you will receive read-only access to the Exchange organization and to all Windows domains that contain Exchange recipients. You can assign this role to people that want to look at the Exchange configuration (for example, to see connector settings) but that don't perform changes.

You receive the following permissions when you're part of this role:

- Read permission to the Exchange organization tree in the configuration partition of Active Directory
- Read access to all domains that have been prepared for Exchange

Exchange Server Administrators

The Exchange Server Administrators role was designed to delegate access for one or more servers to either a security group or a user. Exchange Server Administrators can administer one or more particular Exchange server(s), but they cannot change anything of global impact to the Exchange organization. For example, they can manage storage groups or databases on their server(s), but they cannot move mailboxes to a server they don't have permission on.

This is the only administrative role whose scope can be set on one or more Exchange servers. All other roles are organization-wide!

You receive the following permissions when you're part of this role:

- Owner permissions on server object(s) within the configuration partition
- Local Administrator on the Exchange server(s)
- Membership to Exchange View-Only Administrators thus you can view the complete Exchange configuration

You can delegate this role to users and global or universal security groups, but not to domain local groups.

The Split-Permissions Model

Some organizations, especially the more complex and geographically widely dispersed, may face the problem of the standard Exchange administrative roles not fitting in their security system. For example, suppose an administrator of a location in Germany needs to manage his mailboxes. Being part of the Exchange Recipient Administrators group grants him full permissions on all user objects in all domains, whereas he manages only a single OU in one domain of a complex forest. In this case, a more granular split-permissions model needs to be implemented to address this incongruity.

Split permissions are especially useful when you are thinking of separating the following tasks from each other:

- User-related
- Contact-related
- Group or dynamic distribution list–related
- Recipient management for some or all the aforementioned tasks

As details of the split-permissions model go far beyond the scope of this book and the scope of the exam, I will present just the basic concept so you understand what needs to be done.

Basically the split-permissions concept of Exchange Server 2007 is based on the following two tasks:

- You assign the user or group the Exchange View-Only Administrators role.
- You assign the user or group specific Exchange-related permissions on the Active Directory objects (e.g., for all user objects of a specific organizational unit).

I call this concept "just the permissions needed," so permission is granted only on specific attributes. Using the Exchange Management Shell, you can use the `Add-ADPermission` command to delegate just the right permissions.

The split-permissions model goes into more depth than just delegating full control over an organizational unit. It's about managing only the Exchange-related attributes. Thus, an administrator with split permissions can create a mailbox for a user, but is not able to reset the password for that user. That is the key difference!

Server Provisioning

Besides the administrative roles, Exchange Server 2007 also supports *server provisioning*, or delegation of the ability to install servers. Exchange administrators now have the flexibility of a setup command to create the necessary server object within the configuration partition and to delegate the permissions required to install the rest of the server to a user account.

To provision a server you first must create a computer account for the new Exchange server (if it does not yet exist). Then log on to an existing Exchange server in your organization using an account that is a member of the Exchange Organization Administrators group. In your Exchange binary folder you must use the following command:

```
Exsetup /NewProvisionedServer:<FQDN of server name> /
ServerAdmin:<domain\account>
```

Figure 1.2 shows an example of the server provisioning giving the user account ANDY the permission to install the Exchange server EX99. Once the provision is finished, you can see the provisioned server object in the EMC in Server Configuration. It appears with the server role Provisioned.

FIGURE 1.2 Server provisioning

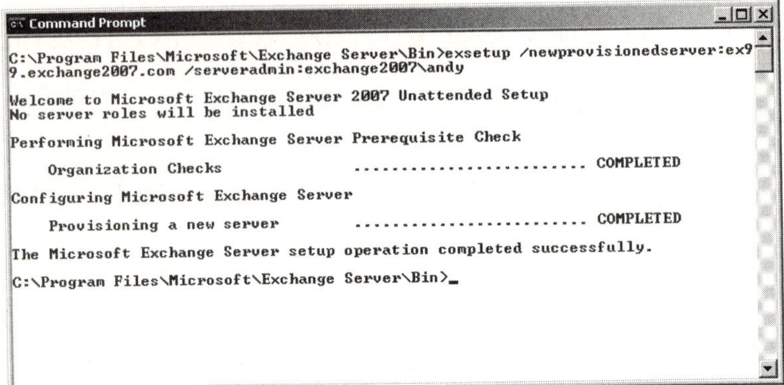

You cannot delegate the first Exchange Server 2007 server installation; this server must be installed by an account that is a member of the Exchange Organization Administrators group.

You can remove a server that has been provisioned or where the provision failed using the following command:

```
Exsetup /RemoveProvisionedServer:<FQDN of server name>
```

Real World Scenario

The Practical Case for Server Provisioning

For smaller Exchange installations, server provisioning might seem like something you'll never need. This is true if you're talking about single-site Exchange installations that are run by a single Exchange administrator. But once you have a multisite Exchange installation where every site wants to manage their Exchange servers on their own, you might have trouble.

In a combined Exchange organization, there must be a single instance that controls the global topics such as connectors or settings. If everybody manages these settings, and if your fellow admin configures something wrong, then your users may not be able to send/receive emails for some time. So, what can you (as the "global" Exchange administrator) do to solve this?

You can install Exchange Server for your fellow administrators or give them Exchange Organization Administrators permission so they can do it on their own. The best solution is to use server provisioning—you can pre-assign the administrators with the correct permissions so they can install their own Exchange server and do not interfere with any global settings as they just have Exchange Server Administrators permission on their server.

Evaluating and Planning Server Deployment Based on Best Practices, Budget, and Other Business Factors

This section will look at what is required to make up a good server deployment plan. Business factors and budget are discussed here, as are best practices. The discussion should provide you with a good understanding of when to place a server at a specific location and when not to.

Planning Exchange Server 2007 Placement

In this section you will learn how to plan the placement of Exchange Server 2007. Deciding where to put a Mailbox server is one of the most critical planning aspects of the Exchange design. Thus it's important to analyze what's available today before stepping down into the different areas that you need to consider in your design.

Analyze What You Have Today!

Understanding what is currently implemented in terms of messaging and Active Directory is an important starting point. You should investigate any area of importance that might have influence in creating your Exchange design.

Active Directory Site Topology

As a first step in planning where to deploy servers, you always should have a solid understanding of your Active Directory site topology. This is especially important in medium-to-large organizations, where the site topology can get geographically or politically dispersed and complicated.

A good practice is to collect all information and to document it so you can review it with your Active Directory team. Consider collecting the following items for your documentation:

- Sites and their subnet associations
- Subnets that have overlapping site associations or do not belong to any site
- IP site links and member sites
- IP site link costs
- Domain controllers in each site (including which domain controllers are global catalog servers)

Assessing this material will give you a solid understanding of you network and where you could place Exchange servers.

Gathering Business Requirements

Besides collecting the technological requirements, remember to include what business requirements you have for the Exchange Server 2007 design. You should consider the following in your plans:

IT strategy: Administrative model, migration strategy, etc.

Budget: How much is available for hardware, how much for software, etc.?

Licensing and maintenance requirements: What licenses are available, what are "end-of-life" products, details about maintenance contracts, etc.?

Acceptable downtime for messaging: Current Service Level Agreement on messaging, the current disaster recovery strategy, etc.

Security policies: Special considerations regarding the companies security policies, such as message encryption, SPAM filtering, or virus protection.

Regulatory requirements: Does your company's market segment have any special requirements for archiving or tracking (SOX, etc.)?

Client access needs: What kind of access do the clients expect (mobile, voice, fax, etc.)?

Messaging information: How is messaging currently used, how many messages are received/sent internally or from the Internet, and what external connections exist?

Consider Domain Controller and Global Catalog Servers

In planning your Exchange Server 2007 placement, always consider domain controller or global catalog servers. These factors are especially important as Exchange Server 2007 does not start without communicating to a global catalog server. Thus it is vital that you consider the following in your planning:

- At least one domain controller of the same domain as the Exchange server must be available in the AD site where you plan to install Exchange Server 2007.
- At least one global catalog must be available in the same AD site where you plan to install Exchange Server 2007.
- For redundancy reasons, it's always good to have at least two global catalog servers available in an AD site where Exchange Server 2007 will be installed.
- If you use 64-bit domain controllers, it increases the directory service performance significantly, even though 32-bit domain controllers are still supported.

Especially in large organizations with more than 20,000 objects in your Active Directory, you should consider upgrading to 64-bit domain controllers.

- As in previous Exchange versions, the recommended 4:1 ratio of Exchange cores to global catalog cores applies for Exchange Server 2007. For example, if you have two

Exchange servers with four cores per servers, you should have at least two cores dedicated for global catalogs.

- If you're planning to host Exchange servers for multiple domains at a single AD site, then you must include domain controllers from each domain for which you host resources.

Exchange Server 2007 System Requirements

You must also understand the system requirements for Exchange Server 2007; that way you can plan your server hardware accordingly. Table 1.2 lists these requirements.

TABLE 1.2 System Requirements for Exchange Server 2007

Component	Minimum Requirement
Processor	x64 architecture–based computer with Intel processor (that supports Intel Extended Memory 64 Technology—EM64T) or AMD processor that supports AMD64. Intel Itanium family IA64 cores are not supported.
Operating system	Microsoft Windows Server 2003 x64 or Windows Server 2003 R2 x64, Standard or Enterprise Edition.
Memory	2 GB of RAM per server.
Available hard-disk space	1.2 GB where you install Exchange Server 2007 200 MB on system drive.
File format	Disk partitions must be in NTFS file format, not the file allocation table (FAT) file system.

Using Exchange Server 2007 on Member Servers or Domain Controllers

You must also consider on what Windows 2003 server role you want to install Exchange Server 2007: member servers or domain controllers. Even though Microsoft supports the installation of Exchange Server 2007 on domain controllers, I strongly advise against it. This is because you need to be a local administrator to manage an Exchange Server 2007 server, and local administrators will automatically receive Admin permissions on all of your domain controllers.

There might be circumstances, such as branch-office situations, in which you do not have a choice, as hardware is spare or budget is limited. I've seen situations where a single piece of hardware held everything: domain controller, Exchange server, file and print services. However, avoid that if possible.

As a protective feature, Dcpromo, which is the command to promote a Windows 2000 or 2003 member server to a domain controller, cannot be run anymore once you have installed Exchange Server 2007 on a Windows 2003 member server. After Exchange Server 2007 is installed, changing the role from a member server to a domain controller or vice versa is not a Microsoft-supported scenario.

Exchange Server 2007 Roles

In order to manage Exchange Server 2007 in a more natural way, server roles were implemented. These roles enable administrators to easily choose which features should be installed on an Exchange server. They provide the following advantages over the model used in previous Exchange versions:

- They reduce attack surface, as only required roles are installed.
- They allow you to install the servers for their intended role only.
- They provide more possibilities for scalability and reliability.
- They lower complexity to reduce system outages.

In Exchange Server 2007 you can choose from five server roles, namely Mailbox server, Hub Transport server, Client Access server (CAS), Unified Messaging server, and Edge Transport server. The following table provides you with an overview as well as the main planning aspects for each role. More details about the Exchange Server 2007 roles are covered in later chapters of this book.

TABLE 1.3 Exchange Server 2007 Roles Overview

Server Role	Description	Planning Aspect
Mailbox server	Hosts your mailboxes as well as public folder databases.	You must plan Exchange servers at the AD sites where most of the users are located or depending on your IT Strategy in key regional datacenters. Detailed planning for this role is covered in Chapters 2 and 9 of this book.

TABLE 1.3 Exchange Server 2007 Roles Overview *(continued)*

Server Role	Description	Planning Aspect
Hub Transport server	Manages all internal message routing within the Exchange organization as well as hosts transport rules that can be applied to messages.	Required in every AD site where a mailbox server is installed. In this AD site a global catalog must be available. A rule of thumb regarding sizing: one Hub Transport processor per three Mailbox server cores. For redundancy reasons you should have at least two Hub Transport servers in larger or critical AD sites.
Client Access server (CAS)	This role hosts the Availability service and Autodiscover needed for Outlook 2007, Exchange ActiveSync, client protocols such as POP3, IMAP4, Outlook Web Access, Outlook Anywhere, and Web services.	Is required in every AD site where a Mailbox server is installed. Recommendation is one CAS processor per four Mailbox cores.
Unified Messaging server	Connects Exchange with your telephone system or private branch exchange (PBX) to have voice access to your mailbox or receive faxes.	Supports approximately 60 concurrent calls per server. Planning aspect should include the number of users as well as how they use Unified Messaging. A single Unified Messaging server can host approximately 3,000 heavy users.
Edge Transport server	Acts as a smart host and SMTP relay in your perimeter network and handles all Internet-facing mail flow. Provides antispam and antivirus functionality. Provides address rewriting and process rules to protect the internal network.	Depending on the size of your organization, you should plan at least two servers to provide redundancy in case of problems. It can handle 100 messages per second, including antivirus software scanning.

Exchange Server 2007 server roles can coexist on a single Exchange machine with a few rules to consider:

- The Mailbox role, Hub Transport role, Client Access role, and Unified Messaging role can coexist on a single server if the Mailbox server is not clustered.
- On clustered Mailbox servers, only the Mailbox role can be installed.
- Edge Transport cannot be shared with any other server role.

Figure 1.3 provides an overview of all the Exchange Server 2007 roles, their functionality, and their connections.

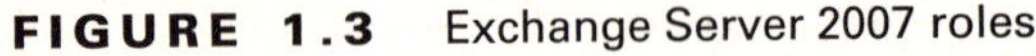

FIGURE 1.3 Exchange Server 2007 roles

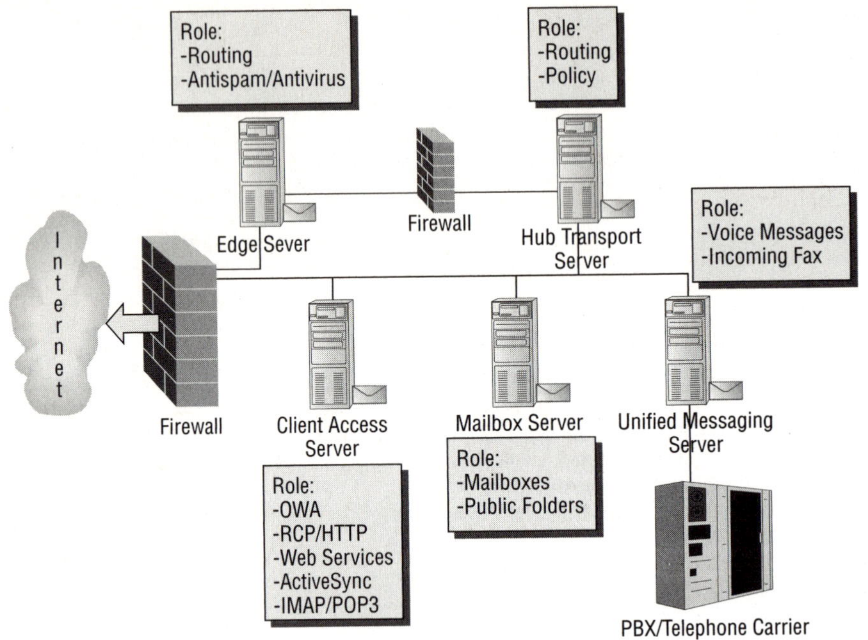

In a smaller organization you will probably end up having a server that hosts multiple roles, mainly the Mailbox, Client Access, and Hub Transport roles. The larger the organization, the more dedicated those server roles will get.

Exchange Server 2007 Editions and Licenses

The next important area to consider when planning your Exchange server deployment is which editions of Exchange Server 2007 you will use and what type of licenses you will buy for your users. This topic is especially important, as it can save you money if you plan thoroughly.

Exchange Server 2007 Editions

As in previous Exchange versions, there are two server editions available: Standard and Enterprise. Whereas the Standard Edition is targeted for small-to-medium companies, it also can be used for specific server roles as well as in small branch offices. The Enterprise Edition supports failover cluster and more storage groups and databases, and thus is targeted to large companies. Table 1.4 provides an overview of each edition's offerings.

TABLE 1.4 Exchange Server 2007 Edition Offerings

Feature	Standard Edition	Enterprise Edition
Storage group support	5 storage groups	50 storage groups
Database support	5 databases	50 databases
Database limit	16TB storage limit	16TB storage limit
Single-copy clusters	Not supported	Supported
Local continuous replication	Supported	Supported
Cluster continuous replication	Not supported	Supported

As a general guideline, you should consider Exchange Server 2007 Enterprise Edition for large Mailbox servers that host 1,000-plus users or that need high availability due to their importance. All other servers, like Hub Transport or Client Access servers, should have Exchange Server 2007 Standard Edition to preserve your budget.

Exchange Server 2007 Client Access Licenses

Exchange Server 2007 comes with two client access license (CAL) editions that are also called Standard and Enterprise. The difference from the server editions is that the CAL is an additive license, so you always need to buy a Standard Edition CAL and then add an Enterprise Edition CAL to gain advanced functionality, such as managed folders.

Both CAL editions can run against either server edition; thus a Standard CAL can run against an Enterprise Edition server and vice versa. Table 1.5 shows an overview of what each CAL edition offers.

TABLE 1.5 Exchange Server 2007 Client Access Licenses

Features	Standard CAL	Enterprise CAL
Email, shared calendaring, contacts, tasks	X	
Outlook Web Access	X	
Exchange ActiveSync	X	

TABLE 1.5 Exchange Server 2007 Client Access Licenses *(continued)*

Features	Standard CAL	Enterprise CAL
Unified Messaging		X
Per-user/per-distribution list journaling		X
Managed email folders		X
Forefront security		X

Making Up a Server-Placement Plan

After considering all these points, you are ready to pull it all together. Build a table that consists of the following columns to plan you server placement:

- Server role (Mailbox, CAS, etc.)
- Number of users to be hosted on this server (special for Mailbox servers)
- AD site location
- Number of global catalog servers in AD site
- Domain
- Windows 2003 server role (e.g., member server)
- Exchange Server 2007 server edition (Standard or Enterprise)

Once again, consider the following general rules regarding Exchange server roles when creating your server-placement plan:

- Hub Transport servers must communicate with global catalog servers. Thus there must be at least one in its AD site.
- Mailbox servers must be located in the same AD site where Hub Transport servers are available. All sending of email is done using the Hub Transport server.
- As the Client Access server provides the connectivity point to the Mailbox servers, a Client Access server must be deployed to the same AD site where Mailbox servers are located. Every user uses the Client Access server to connect directly to the Mailbox server to retrieve messages, but sending messages is done through the Hub Transport server.
- Unified Messaging servers must be located in the same AD site with a Hub Transport server, as they submit messages through this server. The Unified Messaging server should also be located in a hub site or near the IP/Voice over Internet Protocol (VoIP) gateway or IP private branch exchange (IP/PBX).

This list will provide you with an overview and start your planning considerations but you should also consider areas that are covered in the next sections.

Evaluating Network Topology and Providing Technical Recommendations

Evaluating the network topology on which Exchange Server 2007 will communicate is important so that you will not be surprised by problems that have been forgotten in planning. Especially in the network area, changes need time to be implemented, so considering this well will save time later when implementing Exchange Server 2007.

Reviewing Current and Planned Network Topology

The first step is to collect all information about your network, the perimeter network, and its external collections as thoroughly as possible from a variety of sources. They include the following:

- Physical network topology (verify that TCP/IP is used everywhere, and that IPv4 or IPv6 and IP subnets are used according to location)
- Physical network connections or links internally (LAN and WAN links, router, etc.)
- Any external physical network connection (e.g., Internet, partner companies, etc.)
- Interconnection of physical network connections (i.e., hub-and-spoke, ring or star, point-to-point)
- Physical network speed (separate between guaranteed bandwidth and available bandwidth for every network link)
- Any network protection that might interfere (e.g., firewalls that protect physical links or network link encryption devices that reduce the link speed)
- Firewall port availability to external and internal systems
- Server name resolution used in locations or between locations (i.e., DNS/WINS name resolution)
- Defined namespaces in DNS
- Perimeter network servers (any servers that are located in a perimeter network, especially any server that provides SMTP-relay functionality)

Make sure you write down any changes that might occur in the near future so you can include them in the planning from the start.

In large organizations, gathering this information might be quite a time-consuming effort, as you have to sit together with many different network teams to get a thorough understanding of the details of the network! If you want to evaluate a global network including many sites, make sure you talk to at least one network team on every continent and ask them for their opinions. This will provide you with much insight into their current network problems and potential that you can use when planning the messaging design.

Avoiding Pitfalls by Providing Technical Recommendations

The following list provides ways to avoid potential pitfalls on the network topology side. Any problems must be rectified before Exchange Server 2007 can be installed at the location.

- Make sure that the physical network speed of locations that will host Exchange Server 2007 have at least 64 Kb per second of bandwidth available.
- Exchange Server 2007 supports TCP/IP v4 (IPv4) addresses only, not IPv6 addresses. If you already implemented IPv6 addresses anywhere in your company, make sure that the company also supports IPv4 addresses; otherwise the clients will not be able to communicate with Exchange Server 2007.
- IP subnets should map to the locations of the company and should be non-overlapping between locations. However, sometimes single locations have multiple IP subnets, which is fine. If IP subnets are spanned between multiple physical locations, make sure the WAN link between them matches LAN link speed—i.e., 10 megabits per second (Mbps) or more.
- Make sure your Active Directory sites match IP subnets for each location.
- Domain Name System (DNS) must be used for network name resolution.
- DNS is configured correctly in your Active Directory forest, using a single, unified namespace.
- Active Directory uses service (SRV) resource records in DNS to register a list of domain controllers for client use. If you do not use Windows Server 2003 DNS Service for Active Directory, make sure that your DNS server software supports this!
- DNS must be able to resolve Internet DNS URLs to successfully deliver messages to the Internet. The DNS configuration must allow this.
- The company must have its own domain and domain name. Exchange Server 2007 requires an appropriate mail exchanger (MX) resource record in DNS to receive messages from the Internet.
- You cannot use a disjoint DNS namespace! A *disjoint namespace* is the scenario in which the primary DNS suffix of a computer does not match the suffix of the domain name where that computer resides.

Designing and Planning for New Exchange Features

Several new features in Exchange Server 2007 need special consideration in your design. For automation of administrative tasks you can use the Exchange Management Shell, or you can implement voice access to your mailboxes using the Unified Messaging server role. It is also worth considering in your design that the Edge Transport server role can replace existing third-party smart hosts. They are covered in this section.

The Exchange Management Shell

The Exchange Management Shell (Figure 1.4) is a new task-based command-line shell and scripting language that will tremendously ease the way you do administration. Using the EMS you can perform every task that can be done in the Exchange Management Console, and additional tasks that cannot be done there.

FIGURE 1.4 The Exchange Management Shell

```
Machine: ex01 | Scope: exchange2007.com

         Welcome to the Exchange Management Shell!

 Full list of cmdlets:          get-command
 Only Exchange cmdlets:         get-excommand
 Cmdlets for a specific role:   get-help -role *UM* or *Mailbox*
 Get general help:              help
 Get help for a cmdlet:         help <cmdlet-name> or <cmdlet-name> -?
 Show quick reference guide:    quickref
 Exchange team blog:            get-exblog
 Show full output for a cmd:    <cmd> | format-list

Tip of the day #34:

Do you want to see a list of all devices that synchronize with a user's mailbox?
 Type:

 Get-ActiveSyncDeviceStatistics

A variety of information is returned including device name, operating system, an
d last sync time.

[PS] C:\Documents and Settings\exorgadmin>_
```

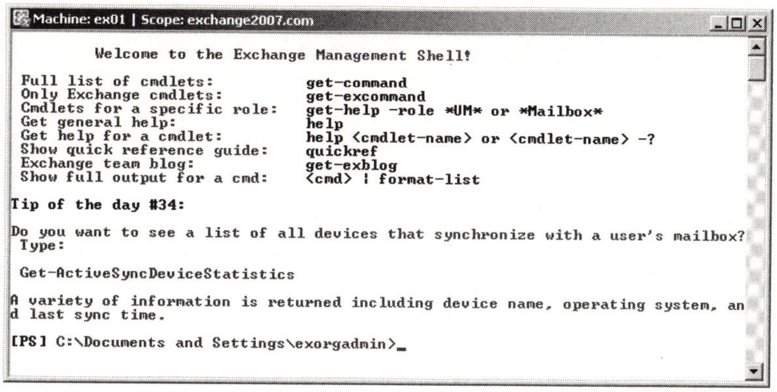

The planning aspect of this new feature is mainly that all Exchange administrators should get training to understand the basics of how to use the EMS and how to create batch processes that ease their daily business lives. By default, the Exchange Management Shell can be used by anybody that has Exchange-related permissions. Thus, Exchange Server Administrators or Exchange Recipient Administrators can use it to modify configuration or object attributes.

Unified Messaging

Unified Messaging is one of the key new features in Exchange Server 2007. Using it you will be able to access your mailbox not only with Microsoft Outlook, but also using a standard telephone line. Unified Messaging provides the following features to the user:

Call answering: Acts like an answering machine.

Fax receiving: You can receive a fax, but not send a fax!

Voice access to your mailbox: Listen to, forward, and reply to email messages and voice mail, listen to calendar entries and accept or reject them, dial contacts, or set voicemail "out of office" messages.

User configuration: Gives you voice access to your Unified Messaging system. You can define a personal greeting or describe how to search in the organization's directory.

The Unified Messaging IP Gateway

The Unified Messaging (UM) IP Gateway connects your telephone system to your Exchange environment. It is used with a legacy PBX to convert the circuit-switched protocols found on a telephony network to IP-based packet-switched protocols. To support Exchange Server

2007 Unified Messaging, one or both of the following can be used to connect the telephony network infrastructure to your data network infrastructure:

- IP/PBX (a single device)
- PBX (legacy) and an IP/VoIP gateway (two separate devices)

Of course, depending on the size of your organization, you might include additional UM IP Gateways depending on the requirements of your telephony network. You should talk to your telephony people in your organization to plan how to best implement this feature for your organization.

A Unified Messaging Deployment Plan

To implement Unified Messaging in your organization, you must follow these common steps:

1. Deploy the Unified Messaging server role: Depending on the size of your organization and number of users you want to connect using Unified Messaging, you should add the role to an Exchange server or set up a dedicated Unified Messaging server in your environment.
2. Receive telephone lines or organize channels: Start talking to your telephone people to receive phone lines that you can organize.
3. Deploy IP/VoIP gateways: Once you receive the information, you can start to deploy IP/VoIP gateways and add the channels or numbers.
4. Make sure you have the correct Client Access License (CAL) for your users! They need an Enterprise CAL for using Unified Messaging.

Edge Transport

Another new feature in Exchange Server 2007 is the implementation of a smart host and SMTP relay version of Exchange Server that is not part of your company's domain and will be placed in the perimeter network or directly on the Internet. A smart host is a designated server through which an email server routes all outgoing messages. Placing previous Exchange Server implementations outside your company's firewall was always dangerous: the Active Directory and Exchange Server needed full access to your company's network, so any security threads could have spread into your company easily.

As a solution, most of the Exchange Server implementations that I know about use dedicated smart-relay software, mainly based on Linux operating system. The Edge Transport server now fills this gap. It uses the Active Directory Application Mode (ADAM) to store configuration and recipient information locally. Thus only information that is needed on the server is stored there. It handles all Internet-facing mail flow as well as provides protection against spam and viruses.

Antivirus and Antispam

The Edge Transport server includes some sophisticated agents that help you to prevent messages that include spam or viruses from entering the organization. They provide different layers of protection, including attachment, connection, content, recipient, and sender filtering, as well as a sender ID agent.

Messaging Policy and Compliance

To satisfy any legal, regulatory, or internal requirements to filter, process, or store messages going inside and outside the organization, the Edge Transport role is equipped with the following agents:

Address Rewrite agent: This agent lets you modify SMTP addresses on messages that go inside or outside of the Exchange organization. This is especially useful in scenarios where the internal email address should not be disclosed or should be standardized after a company merger.

Edge Rules agent: Using rules, you are able to control the flow of messages that are sent or received from the Internet. The rules are based on specific words or text patterns in the message subject, body, header, or From field, the spam confidence level (SCL), or attachment type. Actions include quarantining a message, dropping or rejecting messages, appending additional recipients, or logging an event.

Planning for the Edge Transport Server

To plan the implementation of the Edge Transport server, consider the following issues:

- Edge Transport servers are stand-alone servers. Never plan to integrate them into your Active Directory, as they still will use ADAM and not utilize AD.
- An Edge Transport server can be subscribed to an Active Directory site. This will integrate the Edge Transport into the Exchange organization, starting synchronization of all Exchange organizational configurations (e.g., accepted domains). If you do not integrate the Edge server into your Exchange organization it will act as a stand-alone server and you also will not be able to use the antispam features, recipient lookup, or safe list aggregation features.
- Plan where you want to place Edge Transport servers in your perimeter network. For load-balancing consider installing multiple machines for every Internet connection.
- You can coexist with available smart host servers, but to receive the full benefit you should concentrate on a single implementation only.

Designing Organization Configuration to Meet Routing Requirements

This section will show you how Exchange Server 2007 routing works and what design-related aspects you should include in your Exchange Server 2007 implementation plan. After a discussion of internal message routing, we will look at external message routing.

Real World Scenario

Using Edge Transport Servers to Ease Administration

A great benefit of using Edge Transport servers for smart-host functionality is when you use Edge subscription in your Exchange organization. A subscription basically connects the stand-alone Edge Transport server to your configuration information; thus you will be able to configure your Edge Transport servers using Exchange Management Console or Exchange Management Shell.

I have seen companies that had quite a few smart-host servers out there sitting at the Internet connection points. Whenever there was an SMTP address change or a new address to add, we needed to configure it at every smart host that routed messages. Guess what happened? Occasionally some servers were missed, and so sometimes the message resulted in a non-delivery receipt (NDR) and sometimes not. Figuring out where the problem resides was then an extremely difficult task.

Now, with the Edge Transport role, we plan to homogenize our entire smart-host server farm using Exchange Server 2007. That way we can reduce not only the number of servers installed, but also the administrative effort.

Internal Message Routing

In Exchange 2000 and Exchange 2003 you defined message routing inside an Exchange organization by using routing groups and routing group connectors. Exchange Server 2007 introduces major changes to internal message routing:

- The message-routing topology and routing decisions are based on the Active Directory site topology (AD sites and IP site links).
- Routing is configured automatically, so you do not need to configure any routing group connectors.

Table 1.6 provides an overview of internal message routing in Exchange Server 2007 as it correlates to Exchange 2000/2003.

TABLE 1.6 Internal Message Routing in Exchange Server 2007 Compared to Exchange 2000/2003

Exchange Server 2007	Exchange Server 2000/2003
Hub Transport server	Dedicated bridgehead server
Active Directory site	Routing group

TABLE 1.6 Internal Message Routing in Exchange Server 2007 Compared to Exchange 2000/2003 *(continued)*

Exchange Server 2007	Exchange Server 2000/2003
IP site link	Routing group connector
Cost of IP site link	Cost of routing group connector

Routing between Exchange Server 2007 and Exchange 2000/2003 is explained in Chapter 4, "Designing and Planning Coexistence and Migrations." Here I will focus entirely on the Exchange Server 2007 routing technology.

Before we dig deeper into Exchange Server 2007 internal message routing, two concepts that should be explained—namely the Exchange Server 2007 routing table and the least-cost routing path.

The Exchange Server 2007 Routing Table

Every Exchange Server 2007 Hub Transport server calculates the routing topology based on the Active Directory configuration that includes AD sites, AD site links, Exchange servers and their relation to AD sites, SMTP connectors, third-party connectors, and mailbox and public folder stores; as well as legacy Exchange 2000/2003 routing groups and connectors. This will make up what is called the *routing table*.

The routing table is calculated every time the Hub Transport server is started or when configuration changes (e.g., Active Directory change notifications) occur.

Least-Cost Routing Path

When multiple routing paths exist for a message, the routing path is calculated based on an algorithm to select a single path over which the message will be routed. The following logic is used:

- Calculate the cost to the target AD site by adding all IP site link costs or connector costs between the source and the target site. If there are multiple paths, only the path with the lowest aggregated cost will be used.
- If there are multiple paths with the same lowest aggregated costs, the routing path with the least hops is selected.
- If there are still multiple paths available, the site name with the lowest alphanumeric name is selected. Starting with the site name to the target AD site, the algorithm will go backward along the path until it finds a site name that doesn't match.

Remember: there might be other factors like message size limits or connector scope that can influence the least-cost routing path!

Hub Transport Server Routing Rules

As explained before, Hub Transport server is the only Exchange Server 2007 server role to route messages within an Exchange organization. Of course, the Edge server role can also route messages, but only to and from the Internet.

Another difference between Exchange Server 2007 and previous Exchange versions is that any message must now be sent through a Hub Transport server, even if the recipient is on the same Mailbox server as the sender.

Internal message routing in Exchange Server 2007 uses SMTP as its primary message-transport protocol and is based on the following two basic rules:

If the message target recipient is within the same AD site the Hub Transport server delivers the message directly to the Mailbox server where the recipient mailbox resides.

If the message is targeted to a recipient located in a different AD site the Hub Transport server sends it directly to a Hub Transport server in the target AD site. This means that the message does not relay to each AD site along the least-cost routing path as previous versions of Exchange did! It will choose the target Hub Transport server using round-robin load-balancing mechanisms. Only if the preferred Hub Transport server becomes unavailable will it choose another Hub Transport server.

As most large-scale network environments are complex, some situations require special configurations. What happens when the target AD site is offline due to network problems? Or what about firewall settings where network traffic is forced to flow through specific AD sites? These issues are covered in the following paragraphs.

Queue at Point of Failure

Exchange Server 2007 uses the least-cost routing path information when no Hub Transport server in the destination AD site responds due to network issues or server outages. In this situation the least-cost routing path will be used in reverse order: from the destination AD site to the source AD site. All AD sites will be contacted along this path, and if a Hub Transport server is available, the message will be queued there in a retry state. Thus the message will be delivered to a Hub Transport server that seems to be the closest one to the target Hub Transport server from the IP site link cost perspective. This is called *queue at point of failure.*

For example, say you have Site 1, Site 2, and Site 3 that have a cost of 5 and are connected Site 1 to Site 2, and Site 2 to Site 3. Hub Transport servers exist in all three sites. Let's assume that we have a message being sent from Site 1 to Site 3. Under normal behavior the Hub Transport server in Site 1 would send it directly to the server in Site 3. However, if the server in Site 3 is offline, the message cannot be sent directly. Queue at point of failure would be when the Hub Transport server delivers the message to the server in Site 2 for queuing, as it knows that this site is closer to the target site (Site 3) than its own server is.

Hub Sites

One way to interfere with the least-cost routing path is by defining hub sites through which all message flow must be relayed. You can think of this situation as a former hub-and-spoke design with a messaging backbone.

You might have hub sites if a firewall prevents direct communication between certain AD sites or if a company policy exists where all message traffic must be routed through a special AD site.

A hub site is considered only when it lies on the least-cost routing path calculated by the Hub Transport server. Before you implement hub sites, it is important that you review your Active Directory topology to make sure that the least-cost routing path always includes the AD sites you want to define as hub sites.

You can configure hub sites using the Exchange Management Shell and the `Set-AdSite` command. You have to do this site by site, so keep track of what changes you made!

The following command shows an example where I set the hub site to the AD site Site2. You have to be Exchange Organization Administrator to configure this.

```
Set-AdSite -Identity "Site2" -HubSiteEnabled $true
```

Modifying IP Site Link Costs

The Active Directory site topology might not be optimum for Exchange message routing in specific cases. For that reason there is a way to modify the least-cost routing path by modifying the cost of IP site links. Doing so will add an Exchange-specific cost to the IP site link but will not modify the current setting in Active Directory costs. Of course, if you set an Exchange cost, this overrides the Active Directory cost for message-routing purposes.

After considering your Active Directory site topology and placing your servers in the right sites, you should carefully consider if you need to implement Exchange-related IP site link costs, as they are quite hard to manage.

The following Exchange command-shell command assigns an Exchange-specific cost of 20 to the IP site link called Link3-4:

```
Set-ADSiteLink -Identity "Link3-4" -ExchangeCost 20
```

Delayed Fan-Out

In a message that is addressed to multiple recipients, the routing technology I explained before would mean that a copy is created for every recipient. However, Exchange Server 2007 uses a technique called *delayed fan-out* to preserve bandwidth when routing messages with many recipients.

After each recipient has been resolved by the Hub Transport server, Exchange Server 2007 compares the routing path for each recipient. The splitting of messages into multiple copies does not occur until a Hub Transport server is reached, which splits up the routing path. Microsoft calls such a Hub Transport server a *fork* in the routing path.

For example, we have a message addressed to one recipient in every AD site, Site 1, Site 2, Site 3, and Site 4. From an Active Directory standpoint, they are all connected sequentially, Site 1 to Site 4. The first message will get transferred to Site 2 as a single message where the Hub

Transport will deliver a local copy to the recipient in Site 2 and deliver one message, including recipients in Site 3 and Site 4, to the Hub Transport server in Site 3. As you can see, especially for messages with large numbers of recipients, this feature saves a lot of bandwidth.

External Message Routing

Now you've got a grip on internal message routing, so let's turn to routing of the external variety. In this section I will provide an overview of what features exist for message routing to external systems, like the Internet or foreign systems.

In Exchange Server 2007, external connectors are classified in the following three ways:

- Send connectors
- Receive connectors
- Foreign connectors

These types of connectors can be configured on Hub Transport and Edge Transport servers. Connectors can be configured using the Exchange Management Console, but many more details are available when using the Exchange Management Shell.

Send and Receive connectors always use SMTP as their message protocol, where Foreign connectors might use other message protocols, such as X.400, to transmit messages.

You do not need to configure an Internet connection if you have an Edge Transport server, as it will be installed automatically when you subscribe the Edge Transport server to the Exchange organization.

Send Connectors

Using Send connectors you can configure an outbound SMTP connection. Send connectors allow you to do the following:

- Set one or more source servers that the connector uses to deliver messages.
- Configure a dedicated address space for the connector.
- Decide where to route the messages to (by using a smart host or just using DNS MX resolution).

Here's how Send connectors factor into planning: If you don't use Edge Transport servers as Internet smart-relay hosts, then you should include Send connectors wherever you have a network connection point, such as a direct partner connection, an internal re-route, or an Internet connection.

Receive Connectors

To receive external messages, you need a Receive connector. This connector acts as an inbound connection point that you can configure to accept connections based on IP address ranges and port numbers.

Real World Scenario

Using Direct Connectors to Business Partners

In my company we work very closely with a couple of other companies; we also have a direct network link connecting us all together. This link is used to exchange confidential data as well as access to certain systems.

As these links normally are utilized only during specific times of the day, it's a big benefit to configure Send and Receive connectors using these links. They have their own SMTP address space, and messages use only the direct connection.

Not only does my company save the traffic that would be generated by all the messages first being sent to the Internet and then being received by the target again, but we also improve security as messages are not routed over the Internet.

You can configure a Receive connector on a per-server scope only. Thus, if you want to have many servers receive messages, you need to configure every server.

Receive connectors have configuration limits that you can set, such as number of active connection, maximum message size, or maximum recipients per message. You also can set the type of authentication required to send a message. What does this have to do with planning? Well, you should configure Receive connectors at every Hub Transport server that serves an external inbound connection. Also, you should have dedicated Receive connectors for your applications that want to send messages so that you understand how many applications send messages to your system.

Foreign Connectors

A Foreign connector does not use the SMTP protocol for communication. Third-party Short Message Service (SMS) gateways or fax gateways are examples.

To be able to communicate with these third-party systems, the connector uses a Drop directory on the Hub Transport server to send messages to the foreign gateway servers. Foreign gateway servers can send messages to Exchange Server 2007 by using the Replay directory.

Every foreign connector has an address space assigned to it that includes the following elements:

Connector Scope: What Hub Transport servers can use the connector

AddressSpaceType: For example, fax or SMTP

AddressSpace: An valid address space for the AddressSpaceType

AddressSpaceCost: Routing costs

Table 1.7 shows a list of connectors that are no longer available in Exchange Server 2007, and it describes how to maintain their functionality in Exchange Server 2007.

TABLE 1.7 Discontinued Connectors and What to Do in Exchange Server 2007

Connected System	What to Do
Lotus Notes/Domino 5.x or earlier	Retain a computer with Exchange Server 2000/2003 in your Exchange organization.
Lotus Notes Domino 6.x or later	Implement SMTP as your mail-routing protocol and use Microsoft Transporter Suite for Lotus Domino for directory sync.
Novell Groupwise	Retain a computer with Exchange Server 2000/2003 in your Exchange organization.
X.400 connectivity	Retain a computer with Exchange Server 2000/2003 in your Exchange organization.

Planning for Foreign connectors is a key task when doing an Exchange Server 2007 design. You should consider the following in your plan:

- Consolidate Foreign connectors to save budget.
- Plan for fault tolerance when implementing Foreign connectors; make sure the Drop directory is available.
- Make sure the third-party connector is fully supporting Exchange Server 2007 before you move it over to the Exchange server, especially if you are in an environment where Exchange 2000/2003 still exists.

Remember: if you need Exchange 2003 servers in your environment, you need to install them before installing Exchange Server 2007!

Viewing the Routing Table

Unfortunately the WinRoute tool that was used to view the routing table in Exchange Server 2000/2003 does not work with Exchange Server 2007. Microsoft did not provide any replacement with the release version of Exchange Server 2007, but will provide a new version in Exchange Server 2007 Service Pack 1.

The Routing Log Viewer for Exchange Server 2007 can read the routing topology from your Hub Transport and Edge Transport server roles and will provide a view into the routing table logs. The Routing Log Viewer tool will be part of the Mail flow tools within the Toolbox in Exchange Server 2007 Service Pack 1.

Summary

Planning a message service for a medium-to-large organization is quite a time-intensive and difficult task. You have to consider many factors, and you have to be especially aware of products that might interfere with the message service. Exchange Server 2007, with its tight integration with Active Directory, requires an Exchange messaging IT pro to have an excellent understanding of all Active Directory–related technologies, such as the impact of IP sites and IP site links.

To start off your planning, you should thoroughly investigate what is available within the company itself.

- From a technical perspective, you need to understand the company's network topology, its Active Directory implementation, how messaging is done today, and what other products might interfere with the messaging system.
- It is also crucial to know about the business factors of the company: What is the future IT strategy? Who are the key stakeholders of the IT system and what are their expectations? Are large data centers in their focus, or do they like to build more sites with messaging servers? You should also consider the company's acceptable amount of server downtime, their existing Service Level Agreements, and any security or regulation requirements.

If you can consider all these topics together and if you understand what Exchange Server 2007 can offer, then you have a good way to create a solid plan for a messaging service. And that is exactly what is required to be an excellent Exchange messaging IT professional.

Exam Essentials

Understand how Exchange Server 2007 relies on Active Directory Exchange Server 2007 depends heavily on Active Directory and has certain requirements in terms of Service Packs applied to domain controller or global catalog servers. You need to understand the requirements of Exchange Server 2007 on the Active Directory, and what functional mode your domains and forest must run in. Also, it is important to know which domains need to be prepared for Exchange and how the preparation is done.

Know about the Exchange Server 2007 administrative roles and permissions To design a good Exchange Server 2007 permissions model, you need to have a good understanding of which administrative roles you have available for delegating certain tasks, and of how they apply to your system. You should understand when to use the split-permissions model and when you need to use server provisioning.

Understand the different Exchange Server 2007 roles and their planning aspects Exchange Server 2007 comes with new server roles that all have specific functions and need separate planning. To build a good plan for implementing these roles, you need to understand all requirements as well as their specific features. Additionally, it is important to understand budgetary decisions (e.g., what Exchange Server edition you will use) and other business factors that might impact where you plan to install an Exchange server.

Have a solid understanding of your network topology The network topology is the basis of a good messaging environment and thus it is very important to know exactly what is going on in your organization's network, as well as where its external connections are. Based on this evaluation, you must understand what requirements Exchange Server 2007 has on the network topology to prevent problems. Understanding each technical recommendation in this chapter will help you there.

Get to know the new features of Exchange Server 2007 As Exchange Server 2007 introduces a couple of new features that might improve your user's working experience, you need to have a good understanding of what the benefits of these new features are and of how to plan them into your overall messaging design. In particular, the Unified Messaging and Edge Transport server roles offer quite a bit of potential.

Understand how Exchange Server 2007 improves message routing As the routing topic is key to every messaging system, you must have a thorough understanding of what is improved by Exchange Server 2007. What aspects of internal and external message routing are different from previous versions of Exchange? Be sure you understand exactly when you need to define a hub site and when to define Exchange-specific costs. You should also be able to describe the term *delayed fan-out*.

Review Questions

1. What Active Directory requirements do you have if you want to install Exchange Server 2007 into your forest? (Select all that apply.)

   A. Windows Server 2003 Service Pack 1 or later must be installed on the server that hosts the Schema Master role.

   B. All domains where you want to install Exchange Server 2007 must run in Windows 2003 domain functional mode.

   C. Domains where you install Exchange Server 2007 must run in Windows 2000 native domain functional mode.

   D. Install at least Windows Server 2003 Service Pack 1 on all global catalogs that are located in AD sites where you plan to install Exchange Server 2007.

2. Which groups in the following list will be created in the Microsoft Exchange Security Groups container during Exchange Server 2007 setup? (Select all that apply.)

   A. Exchange Recipient Administrators

   B. Exchange View-Only Administrators

   C. Exchange Servers

   D. ExchangeLegacyInterop

   E. Exchange Organization Administrators

3. What actions in the following list does the setup command `/PrepareAD` perform? (Select all that apply.)

   A. Prepares all domains (`/PrepareDomain`)

   B. Extends the schema if it was not extended yet

   C. Configures global Exchange objects in the configuration partition

   D. Prepares the root domain (`/PrepareDomain`)

4. Which of the following statements regarding Exchange Server 2007 domain preparation (`Setup /PrepareDomain`) is correct? (Choose one.)

   A. All domains must be domain-prepared; otherwise Exchange Server 2007 will not work correctly.

   B. All domains that will include Exchange Server 2007 servers, as well as the root domain, need to be domain-prepared.

   C. The root domain (even if no Exchange Server 2007 is installed in it) and all domains that will include either Exchange Server 2007 servers or Exchange-related objects like mailboxes must be domain-prepared.

   D. All domains that will include Exchange Servers 2007, as well as the root domain (even if no Exchange Server 2007 is installed in it) and domains that include global catalog servers that are part of an Exchange Server 2007 AD site must be domain-prepared.

5. What permission do you need to prepare a child domain for Exchange Server 2007 (i.e., run `Setup /PrepareDomain`)? (Select all that apply.)

   A. Exchange Organization Administrators permission on the Exchange organization.

   B. Administrator permission on the Exchange Server.

   C. Domain Admin permission in that domain (if the domain existed when `/PrepareAD` ran).

   D. If the domain that did not exist when you ran `/PrepareAD`, you need to be member of the Exchange Organization Administrators group as well as Domain Admin.

6. In order to manage all Exchange-related objects in the Active Directory, what Exchange role do you need to perform this task? You do not have any extra Active Directory permissions like Domain Admin assigned to your account! (Select all that apply.)

   A. Exchange Organization Administrators

   B. Exchange Recipient Administrators

   C. Exchange View-Only Administrators

   D. Exchange Server Administrators

7. The user Joel has Exchange Server Administrator permissions on Server A and Server B. What statement is true regarding his permissions? (Choose one.)

   A. Joel is able to move mailboxes between Server A and Server B.

   B. Joel can change the Exchange organization configuration (e.g., adding a new address list) and also any Exchange Server configuration (e.g., dismount a database) on Server A and Server B.

   C. Joel can add and remove mailboxes to Server A and Server B as well as move mailboxes between those servers.

   D. Joel can change any Exchange Server configuration (e.g., dismount a database) on Server A and Server B.

8. The Exchange Server Administrator role can be delegated to the following Active Directory objects. (Select all that apply.)

   A. User object

   B. Universal security group object

   C. Global group object

   D. Local group object

9. In my Exchange organization, I want to delegate the right to install an Exchange Server 2007 server for a user called Andy. As I don't want to give full permissions using the Exchange Organization Administrators group, what can I do instead? (Choose one.)

   A. I can create a server object for Andy's new server and try to delegate using the Exchange Server Administrator role.

   B. I can add Andy to the Exchange Recipient Administrators group and give him local Administrator permission on his new Exchange Server 2007 server. That will be sufficient to install Exchange Server 2007.

   C. I can create a computer object in Active Directory for the Exchange Server 2007 server and use the `/ProvisionServer` command with Exchange setup.

   D. I can create a computer object in Active Directory for the Exchange Server 2007 server and use the `/NewProvisionedServer` command with Exchange setup.

10. Which of the following statements regarding domain controller and global catalog requirements for Exchange Server 2007 is correct? (Select all that apply.)

    A. At least one global catalog must be available in the same AD site where you plan to install Exchange Server 2007.

    B. At least one domain controller of the same domain as the Exchange server must be available in the AD site where you plan to install Exchange Server 2007.

    C. All domain controllers must be upgraded to 64-bit.

    D. All global controllers in the AD site where you plan to install Exchange 2003 must be upgraded to Windows Server 2003 Service Pack 1 or later.

11. You are about to create a server plan for a smaller location (fewer than 250 mailboxes) where, based on business factors, the decision was made to install an Exchange mailbox server. A domain controller that is a global catalog is available in the AD site. The budget is not the biggest one; based on best practices, what should you do? (Choose one.)

    A. To preserve budget you should install the Exchange Mailbox role on the domain controller.

    B. You should buy one new server that will host the Exchange Mailbox role, the Client Access role, and the Hub Transport role for that location. Nothing more needs to be done.

    C. You should buy three new servers, one for each role: Mailbox, Client Access, and Hub Transport.

    D. You should buy one new server where the Exchange Mailbox role is being installed on. Nothing more needs to be done.

12. Andy is working on an Exchange Server placement plan for a larger site (3000-plus mailboxes). The business factors dictate that the Mailbox server must be highly available. Additionally, the company heard about a new Exchange Server 2007 feature to call into their mailboxes and the IT decision-maker wants to use it. Which of the following routes should Andy take? (Choose one.)

    A. He should install a clustered Mailbox server that includes the Hub Transport, the Client Access, and the Unified Messaging roles on a single clustered machine. This will provide sufficient availability for the messaging system.

    B. He should install a clustered Mailbox server and two other servers: one for Client Access and Unified Messaging roles and one for the Hub Transport server.

    C. He should install a clustered Mailbox server and install three other servers: two of those hosting the Client Access and Hub Transport server roles, and one for the Unified Messaging role.

    D. He should install a normal Mailbox server that includes all four server roles required: Mailbox, Hub Transport, Client Access, and Unified Messaging server.

13. Which of the following are network requirements of Exchange Server 2007? (Select all that apply.)

    A. TCP/IP v4 (IPv4).

    B. TCP/IP v6 (IPv6).

    C. Domain Name Service (DNS).

    D. AD sites must be connected by a permanent WAN or LAN link.

14. Which of the following are features included in Exchange Server 2007 Unified Messaging? (Select all that apply.)

    A. Call answering

    B. Fax sending

    C. Voice access to mailbox

    D. Delayed fan-out

15. Your messaging system currently includes five Internet connections where per connection you have two smart hosts each running on the Linux operating system. You are planning to replace them using Exchange Server 2007. You want to manage them centrally in your Exchange organization.

    A. You need to install the Edge Transport server role on 10 servers that are stand-alone and use the Edge subscription to the closest Exchange Hub Transport hosting AD site.

    B. You need to install the Edge Transport server role on 10 servers that will join the Active Directory and use the Edge subscription to the closest Exchange Hub Transport hosting AD site.

    C. You need to install the Hub Transport server role on 10 servers that will join the Active Directory and just configure connectors between each server and the closest Exchange Hub Transport servers.

    D. You need to install the Hub Transport server role on 10 servers as stand-alone and configure connectors between each server and the closest Exchange Hub Transport servers.

16. Which of the following is included in the Exchange Server 2007 routing table? (Select all that apply.)

    A. Active Directory sites

    B. Active Directory site links

    C. Exchange servers and their relation to AD sites

    D. Exchange Client Access servers

    E. Exchange mailbox and public folder stores

17. Joel sends a 5 MB message to 100 recipients located in five AD sites; the local one is Site 1 and there are four distant sites called Site 2, Site 3, and Site 4. These AD sites are all hosting Exchange Server 2007 Hub Transport servers and include IP site links that are configured in the following way: Site 1 – Site 2, Site 2 – Site 3, Site 2 – Site 4, Site 2 – Site 5. Which of the following statements about what will happen with the message is true? (Choose one.)

    A. The Hub Transport server in Site 1 will connect to all other sites and send one message for each recipient.

    B. The Hub Transport server in Site 1 will calculate the routing path for every recipient and connect to all four sites to send one message per site that include the recipients for their respective site. The Hub Transport will deliver the message to all local recipients directly to their mailbox store.

    C. The Hub Transport server in Site 1 will calculate the routing path for every recipient and deliver the mail to all local recipients. For all recipients that are not in the same site, it will create a single message to be sent to the Hub Transport server in Site 2. This server will again calculate the routing path for every recipient and deliver the mail to all distant sites (one message for each site) as well as to the local recipients.

D. The Hub Transport server in Site 1 will deliver the message to all local recipients and send one message to Site 2. There the Hub Transport server will also deliver the message to all local recipients and send one message to Site 3. This will continue until we've reached all recipients.

18. We're in an Active Directory environment that includes four AD sites: Site 1, Site 2, Site 3, and Site 4. They are all linked sequentially, Site 1 – Site 2, Site 2 – Site 3, and Site 3 – Site 4. All AD sites include Hub Transport servers. A message will be sent from Site 1 to Site 4 but all Hub Transport servers are not available using a direct connect. What will happen? (Choose one.)

A. The message will stay on the Hub Transport server in Site 1 until a Hub Transport server in Site 4 is reachable.

B. The message will be transferred from Site 1 to Site 2 and stay there until a Hub Transport server in Site 4 is reachable.

C. The message will be transferred from Site 1 to Site 3 and stay there until a Hub Transport server in Site 4 is reachable.

D. The message will be transferred to another Hub Transport server in Site 1 to try a different connection to Site 4.

19. What external connectors are available on a Hub Transport server? (Select all that apply.)

A. Send connector

B. SMTP connector

C. Foreign connector

D. Lotus Notes Domino connector

E. Receive connector

F. X.400 connector

20. Sigi is an administrator at a global company with 10,000 users that have mailboxes. The company's IT strategy is to consolidate as much as possible but be careful that all users are still able to use the full functionality of their Outlook 2007 client. Their Active Directory consists of 5 domains that include a root domain that is empty. They currently have firewalls between 2 of their 10 AD sites installed. Active Directory and messaging administration is separated. What is important to consider when planning a message system in this environment? (Select all that apply.)

A. The network topology has to be evaluated if data center consolidation is possible.

B. The AD site design must be reviewed.

C. All domains that include Exchange-related objects or Exchange servers have to be prepared; as does the empty root domain.

D. An extra forest for Exchange Server 2007 must be implemented to ease the process of separated administration.

E. As they have firewalls between AD sites, the Exchange routing feature of setting hub sites must be used.

Answers to Review Questions

1. A, C, D. Exchange Server 2007 requires only the Windows 2000 native domain functional mode, even though it is a good practice to use the Windows Server 2003 domain functional mode. From the software side it is required to install Windows Server 2003 Service Pack 1 or later on domain controllers and global catalog servers that communicate with Exchange Server 2007.

2. A, B, C, D, E. Exchange Server 2007 setup creates an organizational unit in root domain called Microsoft Exchange Security Groups, including the following universal security groups (USGs): Exchange Organization Administrators, Exchange Recipient Administrators, Exchange View-Only Administrators, Exchange Servers, ExchangeLegacyInterop.

3. B, C, D. The Prepare Active Directory command `Setup /PrepareAD` extends the schema if it was not already extended, configures global Exchange objects in the configuration partition (e.g., Exchange Administrative Group—FYDIBOHF23SPDLT), creates an organizational unit in the root domain called Microsoft Exchange Security Groups with five groups, and prepares the root domain. The command to prepare all domains is `Setup /PrepareAllDomains`.

4. C. The root domain has to be prepared every time, no matter if Exchange-related objects or servers will be installed to it. Other domains that need to be prepared are those that will include Exchange Server 2007 or Exchange-related objects like mailboxes, groups, or contacts. Domains that include global catalog servers that are contacted by Exchange Server 2007 do not need to be prepared.

5. C, D. To run `/PrepareDomain` in a child domain you must be a Domain Admin if the domain existed during `/PrepareAD`; otherwise you need to be a Domain Admin as well as a member of the Exchange Organization Administrators group. As you can run this command from any server, you do not need to be an Administrator on the Exchange Server.

6. A, B. Only as an Exchange Organization Administrator or an Exchange Recipient Administrator can you manage Exchange-related objects throughout the Active Directory in any domain. The Exchange View-Only Administrator and the Exchange Server Administrator need extra permission on the domain, organizational unit, or object level before being able to manage them in Exchange.

7. D. Joel can only perform any server-related task. He cannot modify any global configuration, such as adding an address List, nor is he able to add or move any mailboxes to his Exchange servers, as he needs extra permissions on these mailboxes to do that.

8. A, B, C. You can delegate the Exchange Server Administrator role to any object that is globally Active Directory–available. Because a domain local group is available only in the domain where it exists, it cannot be used for delegation.

9. D. If you chose A, Andy would be an Exchange Server Administrator for an existing server but would not be able to install a new Exchange server to the organization. Answer B would provide him the permission to manage any recipient object (e.g., assign a mailbox to a user) as well as local Administrator permissions on the new server; he still would not have sufficient permissions to install an Exchange server. Option C does not exist as an Exchange setup syntax; thus will also fail.

10. A, B, D. In the site where you plan to install Exchange Server 2007 you must have a global catalog as well as a domain controller from the same domain where Exchange Server 2007 is installed. Also, all global catalog servers located in the same AD site as Exchange Server 2007 servers need to be upgraded to Windows Server 2003 Service Pack 1 or later. In order to increase performance, you can upgrade your domain controller to 64-bit machines, but this is not a requirement.

11. B. In a smaller location the best practice is to put all three roles (Hub Transport, Client Access, and Mailbox) required for a site on a single machine. This will preserve the budget but provide full functionality. Installing Exchange Server 2007 on a domain controller is generally not recommended, and buying three machines would not be good for the budget. The last option, using a single server and installing only the Exchange Mailbox role on it does not work because a Mailbox server always requires a Hub Transport and a Client Access role to be installed in the same AD site.

12. C. The first option is not correct as you cannot add other roles to a mailbox server that is clustered. The second option is valid, but provides high availability only for the mailbox store. If either the Client Access server or the Hub Transport server goes down, the complete location will not be able to send messages. Thus it is not a preferred option. The third option considers all aspects: the clustered Mailbox server as well as the Hub Transport and Client Access server roles installed on both machines, thus providing failover. Unified Messaging is part of the Client Access server, so that requirement is also satisfied. The last option does not provide sufficient availability for a large site.

13. A, C, D. Exchange Server 2007 requires TCP/IP v4 and does not support TCP/IP v6 yet. The DNS must be installed as the primary name-resolution method. All AD sites that host Exchange Servers must have a permanent WAN or LAN link between them—dial-up is not supported anymore in an Exchange Server 2007 organization.

14. A, C. Only call answering and voice access to mailbox are features of Unified Messaging. Sending faxes is not supported, but receiving faxes is. Delayed fan-out is not a feature of Unified Messaging, but rather a feature of Exchange Server 2007 routing.

15. A. In order to replace the existing smart relay servers, you should install the same number of stand-alone Edge Transport servers (important as they are located in an insecure network), and in order to receive organizational configuration from the Exchange organization, the servers must establish an Edge subscription each. Using the Hub Transport server for these tasks is not correct as this server role is not as secure for Internet-facing traffic as the Edge Transport server is. Joining an Edge server to a domain is also not secure!

16. A, B, C, E. The Exchange routing table consists of AD sites, AD site links, Exchange servers and their relation to AD sites, SMTP connectors, third-party connectors, mailbox and public folder stores, as well as legacy Exchange 2000/2003 routing groups and connectors. Client Access servers do not route any messages, and thus are not part of the routing table.

17. C. This question is about a routing feature called delayed fan-out. Basically, a message with multiple recipients is kept as one message until the routing path divides. In our situation this means that the message is kept as a single message until Site 2. There it will be divided, as Site 3 and 4 are directly connected to Site 2. The great benefit is bandwidth savings, especially considering that the message was 5 MB in size. Option A would be the most bandwidth-consuming one, so it is wrong. Option B would send a single message for each site, not considering the routing path; therefore it is also wrong. Option D considers sending a message from Site 1 to Site 2 and then to Site 3 and then to Site 4, which is not the way delayed fan-out is implemented in Exchange Server 2007.

18. C. This question is about an Exchange Server 2007 routing feature called queue at point of failure. If the Hub Transport server cannot make a direct connection to the target AD site, it will calculate the least-cost routing path for the message and go backwards. Thus the Hub Transport server will first try to connect to the target AD site named Site 4, then try Site 3, and if no Hub Transport is reachable there it would give Site 2 a try. As every Hub Transport server is capable of communicating with other AD sites, there would are no intra-AD site transfer of messages in Exchange Server 2007.

19. A, C, E. Exchange Server 2007 includes only three types of external connectors: a Send connector and a Receive connector that both support SMTP message transfer, and a Foreign connector that uses a Drop directory to send and receive messages from any foreign system, like a fax system. Old connectors like Lotus Notes Domino or X.400 connector are not available in Exchange Server 2007.

20. A, B, C, E. This is quite a complex scenario that includes an awful lot of information. The key here is to ask if the topics make sense during planning. This is true for option A, as it is always key to evaluate the network topology—especially the bandwidth—before considering a data center approach. Option B is obvious: you have to review the AD site design. Option C should test your skills regarding domain preparation in a multidomain environment, and is also true. Option D is wrong. You can also have a split-permissions model within a single forest; thus you do not need to plan for an extra forest implementation. Option E is important and valid, as it will optimize any routing that occurs in the Exchange organization. If you have firewalls between AD sites, you must configure a hub site so Exchange routing knows about it.

Chapter 2

Designing and Planning Server High Availability

MICROSOFT EXAM OBJECTIVES COVERED IN THIS CHAPTER:

- ✓ Evaluate role availability requirements and design solutions.
- ✓ Define a high-availability solutions based on client types and client loads.
- ✓ Plan policies to handle unsolicited e-mail and virus outbreaks.

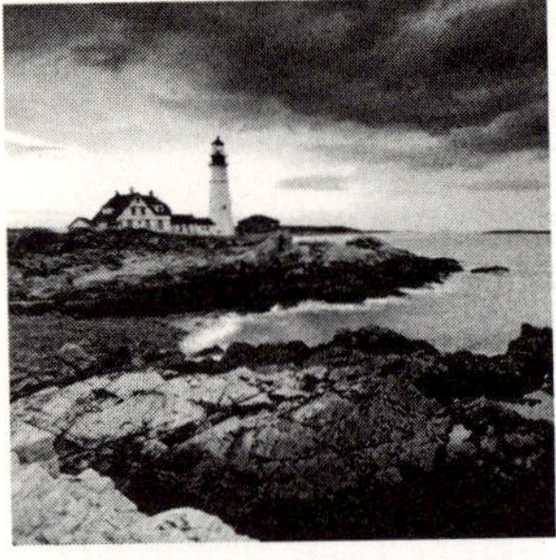

Because messaging has become one of the most mission-critical services that IT provides, designing and planning a highly available Exchange Server system is one of the most important skills that an Exchange Server professional must demonstrate.

The main subjects of this chapter are as follows:

- Determining availability requirements
- Implementing fault tolerance and redundancy within your environment
- Implementing redundancy for Hub Transport servers, Client Access servers, Unified Messaging, Mailbox servers, and Edge Transport servers
- Implementing message hygiene

Evaluate Role Availability Requirements and Design Solutions

The term *high availability* can mean many things. The availability of a system is usually measured in increments of time, and a system is typically considered to be highly available if it is accessible at least 99 percent of the time. However, even a system that is available 99 percent of the time may not be sufficient for some situations. That is why defining availability requirements in a Service Level Agreement (SLA) is so important.

An SLA establishes the required availability of a system and *how* availability will be measured. (For example, would an Exchange server that is available to half of your users considered available or unavailable?) When you design an Exchange Server 2007 system, you must determine your availability requirements from the SLA and base your fault tolerance and redundancy plan upon that information.

Availability is sometimes discussed in terms the number of *9s* offered. If someone says their system offers "five *9s*" of availability, they mean their system is available 99.999 percent of the time. Each *9* adds a significant reduction in the amount of unscheduled downtime expected of the system. For example, a system that promises three *9s* of availability (99.9 percent) can be expected to have less than 8.76 hours of unscheduled downtime in a year, but a system that promises four *9s* of availability (99.99 percent) is expected to have less than 52.56 *minutes* unexpected downtime per year. (We say "unscheduled downtime" because scheduled outages for maintenance are not usually counted against availability measurements.)

Implementing Fault Tolerance and Redundancy within Your Environment

Ensuring that a system is highly available essentially boils down to implementing fault tolerance and redundancy in the appropriate places. Although the terms can be easily confused, *fault tolerance* refers to a system's ability to deal with and recover from errors or failures, and *redundancy* refers to the use of duplicate elements in a system so that the system can tolerate the failure of one of the elements.

Confused?

Try this example. A mirrored disk volume uses two disks to store the exact same data. That way, if one of the disks fails, then the data is still available on the other disk. So, is it an example of fault tolerance or redundancy? Actually, it's both. Because the data itself is stored in duplicate, it's an example of redundancy. However, the mirrored volume itself, when considered as a whole, is deemed to be fault-tolerant because it can survive a failure within the system.

Error-correcting memory is a perfect example of fault tolerance. The servers in a Web-server farm are an example of redundancy.

Why is this important? Because for your Exchange Server 2007 system to be highly available, you've got to build into it both fault tolerance and redundancy.

Using Fault-Tolerant Server Hardware

Fault-tolerant systems begin with fault-tolerant hardware. Today's server hardware can be purchased with built-in redundancy and fault tolerance for several subsystems. Redundant power supplies can keep a server running even if one of them fails. Error-correcting random access memory (RAM) can recover from some of the more common memory errors that would otherwise cause a server to crash. Multiple network interface cards (NICs) can be installed to allow an administrator to quickly reconfigure networking should the primary NIC fail. Some NICs even have multiple ports so that automatic failover can occur in the event that the active port fails.

Understanding RAID

However, the most common, and arguably most important, subsystem into which redundancy is often configured is storage. Redundant arrays of independent disks (RAIDs) can be used to protect a disk subsystem against data loss, even if a physical disk is lost. The most commonly used RAID levels include the following:

- RAID 0: Striping
- RAID 1: Mirroring
- RAID 5: Striping with parity
- RAID 0+1: Mirrored stripe sets

RAID 0 is used to improve write performance by splitting the write operation over multiple drives. However, RAID 0 does not add any redundancy, so data loss will occur if a drive fails.

RAID 1 uses two physical disks to store the exact same data; if one disk fails, you still have a complete copy of everything on the other disk. The big drawback is only half of the storage space you purchased appears "useable."

RAID 5 offers a balance of performance and fault tolerance by implementing a stripe set (improved performance) with a parity check (redundancy). RAID 5, which requires at least three physical disks, splits the write operation across "*n*–1" disks (that is, if you have five disks, the write operation is split across four of the disks) to improve performance. At the same time, the RAID controller calculates parity information and stores it on the remaining disk. The result is that, if a disk is lost, the data on that disk can be re-created by comparing the data on the surviving disks and the parity information. (In RAID 5, the parity information is distributed among the disks, so that the contents of any given disk are 1/*n* parity info and (*n*–1)/*n* actual data.) Using a parity disk means lower cost per storage unit (with RAID 5, you lose only 1/*n* of the storage space you bought, as opposed to half with RAID 1), but the performance gain of striping is partially offset by the calculation of the parity information. Thus, RAID 5 doesn't offer quite the performance increase that RAID 0 does, but it does offer some write improvement along with redundancy not offered by RAID 0.

RAID 0+1, sometimes called *RAID 10*, offers both the performance increase of RAID 0 striping and the redundancy of RAID 1. In RAID 10, you build a RAID 0 stripe set and then implement a RAID 1 mirror of the entire stripe set. Because the RAID controller isn't calculating parity data, the RAID 1 mirror doesn't introduce an offsetting performance decrease in offering the redundancy. However, as with any RAID 1 implementation, RAID 10 uses half the storage space purchased for redundancy, so only half of what you bough appears useable. Also, because a RAID 0 stripe set requires at least two disks, and because a RAID 0 mirror doubles the disk requirements, a RAID 10 set requires a minimum of four physical disks. Thus, RAID 10 is the more expensive than the other RAID levels we've discussed.

Selecting RAID Levels for Exchange Storage

In general, if money is no object, you should go RAID 10 on everything; it's the best performance and offers full fault tolerance. To balance cost, performance, and fault tolerance, you should use RAID 5. If you need the least-expensive implementation of data redundancy, use RAID 1. And when you need speed but don't care about fault tolerance (say, for a volume dedicated to your page file), use RAID 0.

When designing a storage system for Exchange Server 2007, however, you need to consider what data is being stored and why. The extensible storage engine (ESE) database employed by Exchange Server uses database and transaction log files to improve *recoverability*. If the database is ever lost or corrupted, you can recover the database up to the point of the failure by restoring a previous version of the database from backup and replaying the transaction log files that were made after the backup.

The most common mistake people make when deploying Exchange Server is to store the database files and transaction log files on the same storage volume. If you do this and that storage volume later becomes damaged, then the odds that you can recover the database to the point of failure are seriously diminished. Many administrators (and, more frightening, server hardware vendors and consultants) suggest placing the database files and transaction log files on different partitions of the same RAID 1 or RAID 5 volume. This might let you keep it straight in your head, but it does nothing to improve performance or recoverability. Yes, using a RAID 1 or RAID 5 volume protects against the failure of a single physical disk. But what if two disks fail? (It's been known to happen!) Or what if the RAID controller starts writing garbage instead of data? Then you're in trouble.

Database files and transaction log files should be stored on different RAID volumes. And, if possible, those RAID volumes should use different RAID controllers. As already mentioned, you should use RAID 10 volumes for both databases and transaction log volumes, if you have the budget to do so. If not, then RAID 5 offers a good balance for the random-access read/write operations of database files, and RAID 1 is okay for transaction logs. However, for absolutely the best performance for transaction logs, use RAID 10 across as many drives as you can and do not store anything else on the transaction log volume.

Redundancy for Active Directory Services

It's no secret that Exchange Server is highly integrated with Active Directory (AD). All of the redundancy and fault tolerance you add to your Exchange organization design would be pointless if you failed to provide fault tolerance in the domain controllers and global catalog servers that Exchange uses constantly.

In each AD site where you have Exchange Server 2007 computers, have an appropriate number of domain controllers and global catalog servers. Implement redundancy, even if it means having an extra domain controller or global catalog server in an AD site. Deploy your domain controllers and global catalog servers on solid, reliable, fault-tolerant hardware. AD is your foundation; build it right.

Define High Availability Solutions Based on Client Types and Client Loads

Knowing how to build fault tolerance and redundancy into your Exchange Server 2007 computers and supporting services is only the first step in designing a highly available Exchange system. You also need to understand the various Exchange Server 2007 roles, how they operate, and the appropriate method for adding redundancy or fault tolerance to each role.

Implementing Redundancy for Hub Transport Servers

Exchange Server 2007 breaks functionality into separate server roles. All message flow in Exchange Server 2007 requires the Hub Transport server role. Thus, if your Hub Transport server is down, then you cannot send messages to anyone: Not even to users on the same Exchange Server 2007 Mailbox server. Not even to users whose mailboxes are in the same mailbox database. Not even to yourself! Therefore, unless you are deploying Exchange Server 2007 on a single server in an environment that doesn't require high availability, you need redundancy for the Hub Transport server role.

Hub Transport Redundancy within the Site

More. That's all it takes. Nothing fancy, nothing challenging. To provide redundancy for Hub Transport servers within an Active Directory (AD) site, you simply install more of them.

When a message is placed in a Mailbox server's submission queue, the Mailbox server notifies a Hub Transport server in its AD site that the message is ready to be processed. If the Mailbox server doesn't reach the first Hub Transport server it tries to contact, then it just tries another Hub Transport server in the same site, as shown in Figure 2.1.

If the Mailbox server can't reach any Hub Transport servers in the same AD site, then the message just sits in the submission queue until a Hub Transport server in the same AD site is available.

You don't need any clustering or load balancing to implement redundancy for the Hub Transport role. When you install a Hub Transport server, it is listed in AD and registered with Domain Name System (DNS) servers. When the Mailbox server needs to notify a Hub Transport server that a message is ready to process, it finds all of the registered Hub Transport servers in the same AD site. Thus, merely adding additional Hub Transport servers in each AD site increases the availability of the Hub Transport role.

FIGURE 2.1 Hub Transport server redundancy

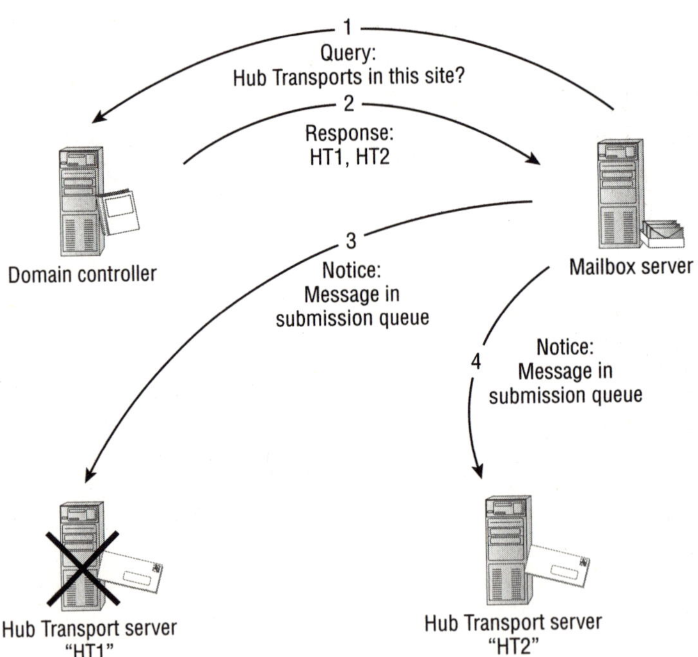

Hub Transport Redundancy between Sites

Likewise, for site-to-site message-routing redundancy, you just need multiple Hub Transport servers in each AD site. If a Hub Transport server in one site needs to route a message to another site, then it retrieves the list of Hub Transport servers in the target site. If the first server on the list is unavailable, then the sending Hub Transport server just tries the next one on the list. If the second one isn't available, it tries the next one and so on.

If none of the Hub Transport servers in the target site are available (if, for example, the WAN link to that site is down), and if another route to that AD site is available for transferring messages, then the sending Hub Transport server will attempt to route the message through an intermediary site. In that case, the sending Hub Transport server in the originating site retrieves the list of Hub Transport servers that exist in the intermediary site and tries to route the message to the first server on the list and, if that server is unavailable, then the sending Hub Transport server tries each listed server until it finds an available Hub Transport server or exhausts the list. If that happens, then the sending Hub Transport just looks for the next-higher-cost route to the original destination site.

The list of Hub Transport servers in an AD site is delivered in round-robin fashion. That is, each time a computer requests the list of Hub Transport servers for an AD site, the order of the list is rotated. For example, assume a site has four Hub Transport servers: Hub-A, Hub-B, Hub-C, and Hub-D. When the first request for Hub Transport servers is made, the list returned is "Hub-A, Hub-B, Hub-C, Hub-D." The second time the list is requested, the response is "Hub-B, Hub-C, Hub-D, Hub-A." For each subsequent request, the server previously listed first is moved to the end of the list. This process provides an elementary form of load distribution without requiring that the Hub Transport servers be configured for true load balancing. This concept is illustrated in Figure 2.2.

Implementing Redundancy for Client Access Servers

As with previous versions, Exchange Server 2007 supports a variety of clients. The preferred client is Microsoft Office Outlook 2007, but all versions of Outlook will work with Exchange Server 2007. Outlook relies upon the messaging application programming interface (MAPI). Other clients include Microsoft Office Outlook Web Access (OWA), which is a web-based client; any Internet client that uses Post Office Protocol 3 (POP 3) or Internet Message Access Protocol 4 (IMAP 4), such as Windows Mail and Outlook Express; and Windows Mobile clients that use Exchange ActiveSync (EAS).

In Exchange Server 2007, Client Access servers are required for any non-MAPI client. Thus, if you're using any client other than Microsoft Office Outlook and the Client Access server fails, the non-Outlook users will be unable to access their mailboxes. Additionally, several Outlook 2007 features, such as Autosiscover and the Availability service, require the Client Access server as well. So, if the Client Access server fails, Outlook 2007 users may have difficulty using their mailboxes or using all features of Outlook.

FIGURE 2.2 Round-robin listing of Hub Transport servers

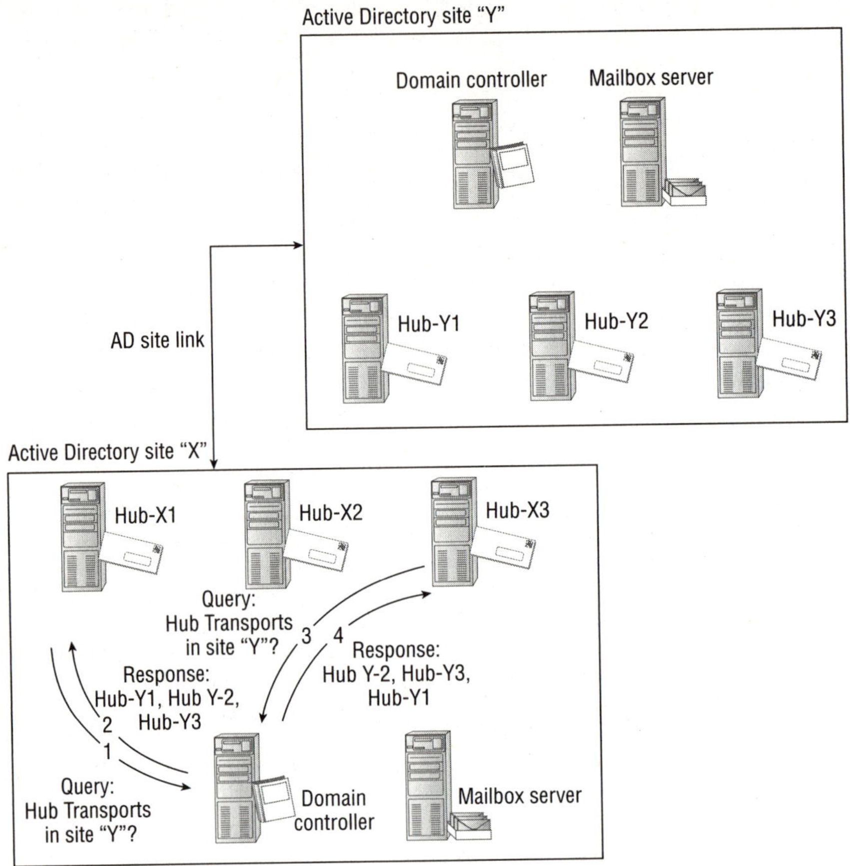

Implementing redundancy for Client Access servers is a little more complicated than for Hub Transport servers, but not much. The first step is the same: install multiple servers in each AD site with a Mailbox server. However, the Client Access servers installed in each site should be load balanced. One option for load-balancing your Client Access servers is to use third-party load-balancing hardware. Another option is to implement Windows Network Load Balancing (NLB). NLB lets an administrator add a shared IP address to the network interface cards (NICs) of all members in the NLB cluster. Because, from the client perspective, all Client Access servers appear to be servers with identical content, NLB can be used for both high availability and scalability.

Watch for the phrase "servers with identical content" whenever you take a Microsoft exam. Whenever you see these words, ask yourself, "Will NLB address this issue?" Most of the time you see that phrase, NLB is at least part of the correct answer.

Regardless of whether you select NLB or third-party load-balancing hardware, the Address (A) records that will be used to point to the Client Access servers should be pointed to the shared IP address. This goes for not just the names that users will type in the address bar of their web browsers for OWA and the server-name fields of other clients for POP3 or IMAP4, but also for the records that Outlook 2007 needs, such as the "autodiscover" record that is required for the Autodiscovery feature.

Implementing Network Load Balancing

NLB is supported on Windows 2000 Advanced Server, Windows 2000 Datacenter Server, and all editions of Window Server 2003. NLB is implemented at the NIC level. To implement NLB, you enable NLB in the properties of the NIC and configure the NLB properties, such as the shared IP address and the fully qualified domain name (FQDN) of the cluster, and the dedicated IP address this cluster member will use when communicating with other cluster members.

All members of an NLB cluster must be a member of the same IP subnet. (The shared IP address must also be one of the IP addresses configured for the NIC in the IP properties.) Additionally, you should attach your NLB cluster members to a hub rather than a switch. Because switches filter packets based on media access control (MAC) address, it is highly possible that attaching your NLB cluster members to a switch would interfere with the proper filtering/forwarding decision for packets addressed to the virtual MAC address assigned to the shared IP address. Because hubs do not filter packets, connecting your NLB cluster members to a hub then connecting that hub to a switch eliminates this problem. An example of Client Access server configuration with NLB is shown in Figure 2.3.

While you could use a virtual LAN (VLAN) to implement an NLB cluster by using cluster members that are in different physical locations, few Exchange deployments would benefit from such a configuration. Further, implementing an NLB cluster on the Internet-facing side of cluster members that reside in different locations and have different Internet connections would not load-balance across the Internet connections. Instead, all traffic would need to be routed through one of the Internet connections and then directed internally to the NLB cluster members in the other locations.

Round-Robin DNS

You could attempt to load-balance across Internet connections by using round-robin Address (A) records in DNS. In fact, some might suggest using round-robin records instead of NLB clustering for Client Access server high availability. While using round-robin for balancing across Internet connections is fine, using round-robin in place of NLB for Client Access servers in the same AD site is not preferred, for two reasons:

- Round robin entries are rotated only by the authoritative DNS server; any DNS server that caches a round-robin response will provide the IP address list in the same order until the time to live (TTL) for the cached entry expires.

FIGURE 2.3 Client access servers and Network Load Balancing

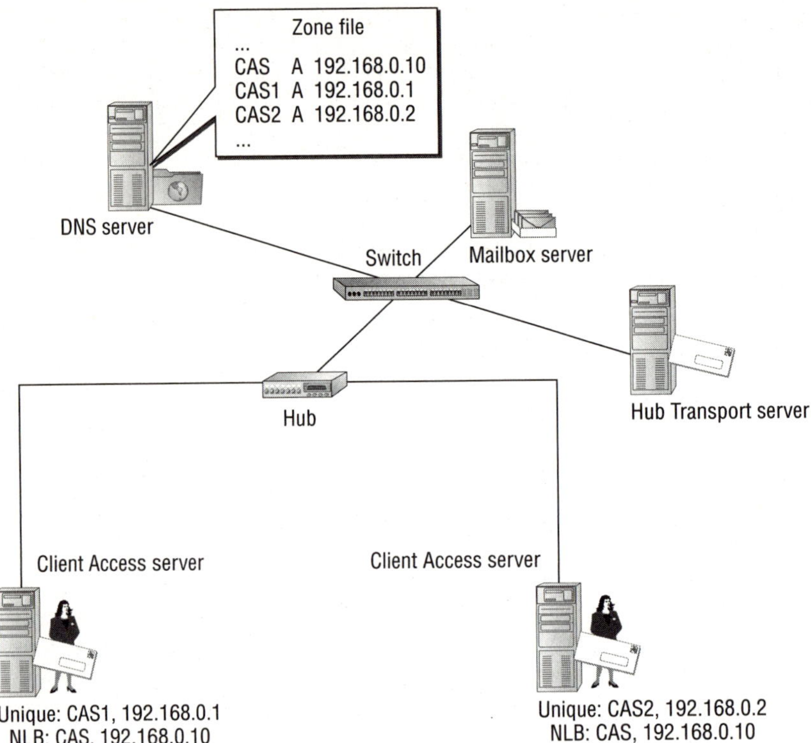

- Round-robin records do not truly balance load; instead, round-robin records, at best, balance the initial contact, and they don't take into account the variety of factors that can disrupt the balance, such as DNS caching and offline servers. NLB, does a somewhat better job of distributing load based on actual requests (as opposed to initial contact) and rebalances whenever cluster membership changes.

Implementing Redundancy for Unified Messaging

If you implement Unified Messaging, then you are using Exchange Server 2007 to manage phone calls, voicemail, and faxes. Thus, if your Unified Messaging server, or any other component, such as a Voice over IP (VoIP) gateway, fails, then your voice and fax services could be unavailable. This scenario is arguably even worse than losing email. So, if you're going to implement Unified Messaging, you must build redundancy into your Unified Messaging components.

Fortunately, implementing redundancy in your Unified Messaging isn't very difficult. First you should have multiple Unified Messaging servers in each site where you deploy Unified Messaging servers. But beyond that, you must have multiple paths for the calls to reach the Unified Messaging servers. This means you must have redundancy in your VoIP gateways.

In corporate phone systems, calls are typically delivered by trunk lines to a private branch exchange (PBX). A PBX is a device that works like a phone-company switching system but it is located in the corporate office and is often owned and managed by the business rather than the phone company. In traditional PBX phone systems, each office extension is directly wired to the PBX, and the PBX routes calls from extension to extension or between an external trunk line and an internal extension.

In VoIP phone systems, extensions are not directly wired to a PBX but are, instead, configured as clients on an IP-based network. A VoIP gateway or hybrid IP-PBX device routes calls to extensions by using IP.

PBX *hunt groups* are used to associate the PBX to a VoIP gateway. If you deploy multiple VoIP gateways, you can create multiple hunt groups to balance call volume between your VoIP gateways. VoIP gateways locate Unified Messaging servers by using *dial plans*. When trying to hand off a call, a VoIP gateway will try each Unified Messaging server in the dial plan until one accepts the call. If you've deployed multiple VoIP gateways, then configure a single dial plan on each VoIP, and configure each dial plan to include all available Unified Messaging servers. That way, your inbound calls will not be affected by the failure of either a Unified Messaging server or a VoIP gateway. This concept is illustrated in Figure 2.4.

FIGURE 2.4 Full redundancy for Unified Messaging servers

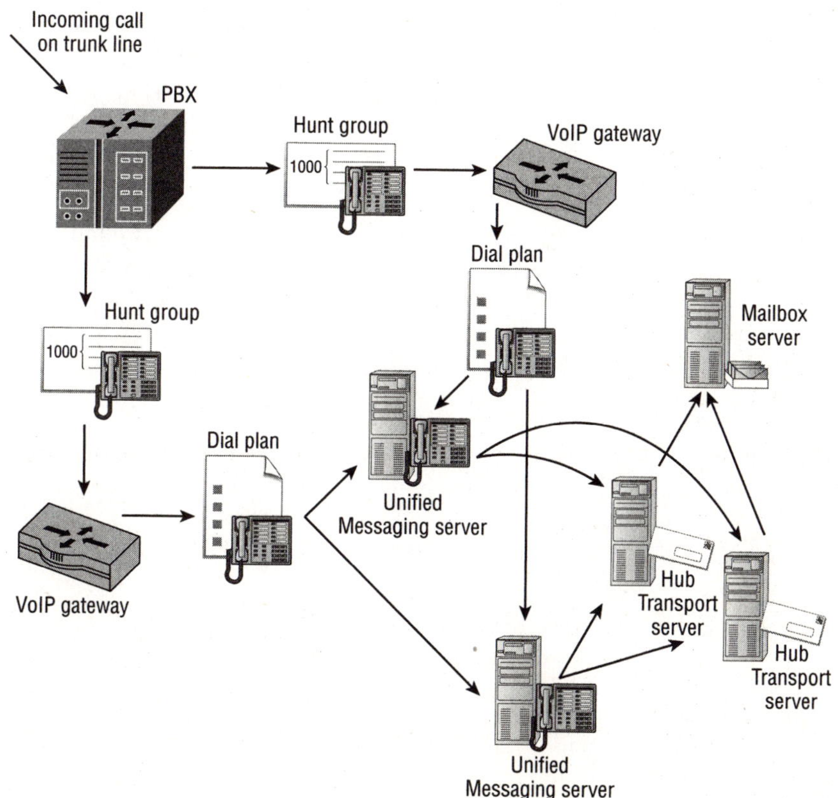

Unified Messaging servers need to have high-speed, reliable connections to the VoIP gateway, which, in turn, require high-speed, reliable connections to the PBX. While Unified Messaging servers require a connection to Mailbox servers, Unified Messaging servers do not necessarily require high-speed, reliable connections to all supported Mailbox servers.

When users create their own custom prompts, such as a personalized voice mailbox greeting, those prompts are stored in the individual user mailboxes. If a Unified Messaging server is processing a call for a user, and the Unified Messaging server cannot access that user's mailbox, then the Unified Messaging server will not have access to that user's custom prompts and will, therefore, be required to use a default prompt instead.

Implementing Redundancy for Mailbox Servers

If all Hub Transport servers go down, no mail flows; but users can still get to the mailbox, so they can still read email that been received, check their calendars, and so forth. If all Client Access servers go down, then access through non-MAPI clients, such as OWA or EAS, is unavailable but users can still access their mailboxes by using Outlook. Failure of all Edge Transport servers affects mail flow only between the Exchange organization and the Internet, and failure of all Unified Messaging servers affects just that the Unified Messaging services.

But when any Mailbox server fails, the users who have mailboxes on that server do not have access to *any* of their email, calendars, contacts, or anything else stored in the mailbox. Thus, the Mailbox server is clearly the most important role to make highly available.

Redundancy Options for Mailbox Servers

With previous versions of Exchange Server, Mailbox servers could be clustered to provide high availability. Clustered Mailbox servers required Windows Clustering, which relies upon a shared disk subsystem and expensive cluster-compatible hardware. This is still supported in Exchange Server 2007, but there are some new options as well. Let's look at all of the options, starting with the traditional clustering.

Single Copy Cluster

Previously, Exchange Server supported both active/active and active/passive clustering. Active/active clusters could contain only two nodes; in the event of a node failure, the remaining active node had to do all of the work of the failed node as well as all of its own work. Active/passive clusters, the preferred option, could contain up to eight nodes, one of which had to be passive and ready to take over if one of the active nodes failed.

Exchange Server 2007 still supports traditional, shared-disk subsystem clustering. However, only active/passive clustering is supported. In Exchange Server 2007, a traditional cluster is known as a *single copy cluster* (SCC). SCC still requires the expensive, specialized server hardware that Windows clustering has always needed, which means that it's not necessarily the easiest option to configure for Mailbox high availability. An example of a three-node SCC clustered mailbox implementation is shown in Figure 2.5.

FIGURE 2.5 Three-node single copy cluster (SCC) clustered Mailbox server

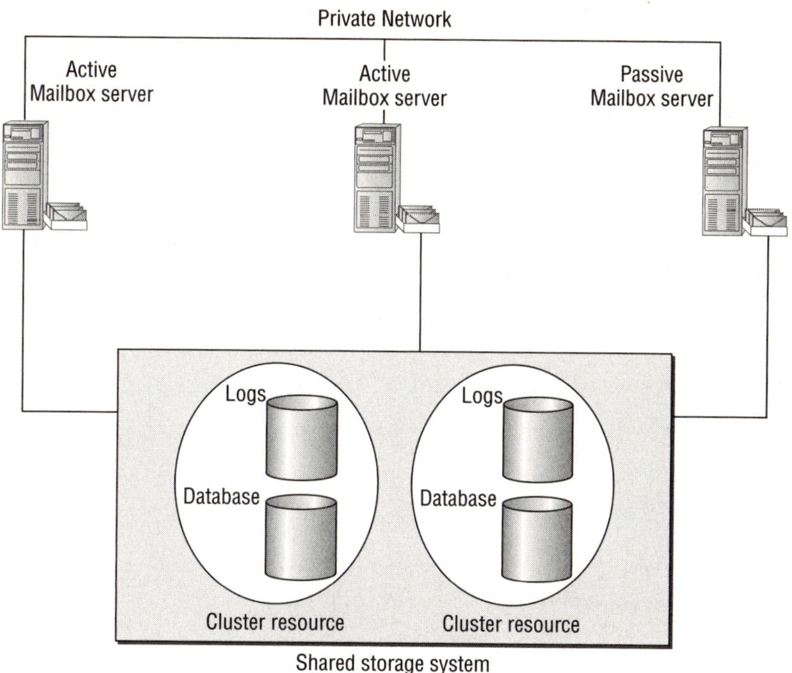

Bear in mind that "single copy" doesn't have to mean that there's really only a single copy. Assuming that your shared storage relies upon a storage area network (SAN), you could employ SAN mirroring to ensure that you have a backup copy of the database in case the SAN is lost.

There's another option if you want clustered servers and redundant data storage. It's called cluster continuous replication, and we'll discuss shortly in the section that bears that name. However, first we'll cover a data-redundancy option that requires only a single server.

Local Continuous Replication

In addition to SCC, Exchange Server 2007 offers two new options for Mailbox high availability: Local continuous replication and cluster continuous replication. *Local continuous replication* (LCR) is a new feature of Exchange Server 2007, available in both Standard Edition and Enterprise Edition, that copies all transactions in a storage group to a backup-copy storage group on another volume on the same Exchange Server 2007 computer. When LCR is used, an administrator can quickly recover from a data-volume failure and nonreplicated database corruption by mounting the backup database in place of the original production database. When such an event occurs, the Exchange administrator must manually make the switch from the production database to the backup copy. Thus, you should expect at least a few minutes of downtime during the manual failover process.

When you implement LCR, you're telling Exchange to keep a second database up-to-date with the log files from the active database. You need to realize that doing so places additional demand on server resources. That is, you should typically have more RAM and a faster processor (or multiple processors) in an LCR server. Also, the second copy of the database needs to be on a different physical disk or RAID volume. (What's the point in keeping a backup copy on the same disk? If you lose the disk, you lose both copies. Not to mention the performance degradation that could occur!) Additionally, you're creating a second copy of the log files for the storage group, so you'll need a separate disk or RAID volume for those files as well.

Thus, when you implement LCR on a server, you're going to need a minimum of four storage volumes or *logical units* (LUNs). These can be individual hard disks or RAID volumes. You need one LUN each for the following:

- The active database
- The active transaction logs
- The passive database
- The passive transaction logs

These LUNs are, preferably, *in addition* to the disks used for the operating system, page file, and Exchange binaries. (However, you could put either the active or passive database on the same LUN as those other files if you're not concerned about the performance degradation doing so introduces.)

An LCR Mailbox configuration is illustrated in Figure 2.6.

FIGURE 2.6 Local continuous replication (LCR) example

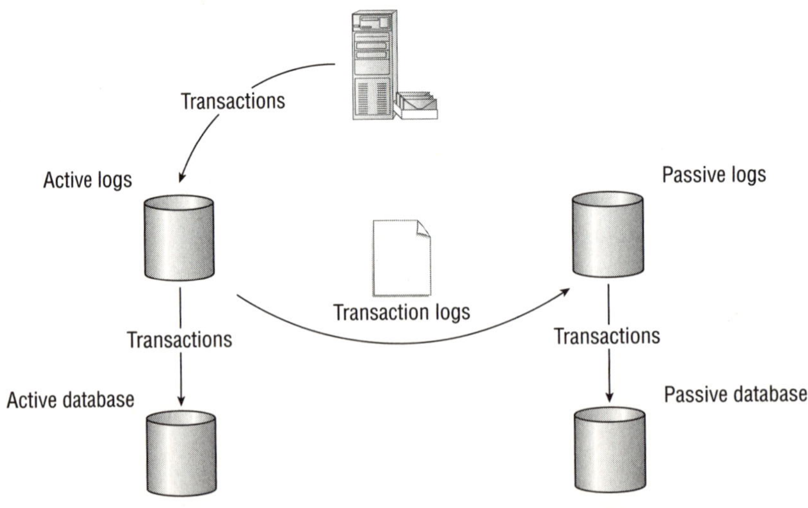

If you have the space for enough hard disks in the computer, then you could use local storage, or *directly attached storage devices* (DASDs), for both your active and passive databases. (External disk arrays that are directly connected to the Exchange Server computer are also considered local storage.) However, in many cases you'll want to use a SAN for at least some of the storage. If you have to split your databases between local storage and SAN, leave the active database on local storage and use the SAN for the passive database.

You should at least consider using NTFS mount points for your LCR databases and logs. For example, you could create four empty folders, such as the following:

- C:\ACTIVE.DB
- C:\ACTIVE.LOG
- C:\PASSIVE.DB
- C:\PASSIVE.LOG

You could mount each of the storage volumes as an NTFS mount point to one of these empty folders, then configure your Exchange Server 2007 Mailbox server to use the mount-point folders for storing the files indicated by the name.

This way, if your active database ever failed or became corrupt, you wouldn't need to reconfigure Exchange. Instead, you could simply dismount the failed database, disable LCR, dismount all four of the NTFS mount points, then mount the passive database storage volume to C:\ACTIVE.DB, mount the passive logs storage volume to C:\ACTIVE.LOG, and finally remount the database in Exchange.

Cluster Continuous Replication

Exchange Server 2007 Enterprise Edition has another high-availability feature for Mailbox servers. *Cluster continuous replication* (CCR), like LCR, makes a backup copy of the storage group. However, instead of storing the backup on another local disk volume, CCR copies the production storage group to another server. Specifically, the copy is sent to the passive node of a two-node active/passive Windows cluster.

The result is that you can implement an Exchange Server 2007 Mailbox server on a Windows cluster without failing over any disk resources. That means that you can avoid the expense of a shared disk subsystem or cluster-compliant hardware! It also means that you can implement *geo-clustered* Mailbox servers (Mailbox server clusters where the nodes are in different physical locations) that can survive the loss of access to the site where the database resource resides. (To be fair, you could do this with SCC and asynchronous SAN mirroring too.)

Figure 2.7 shows a typical cluster continuous replication (CCR) clustered Mailbox server design.

Real World Scenario

Standby Continuous Replication

Although the exams cover the original release, Exchange Server 2007 Service Pack 1 adds one more high-availability option for Mailbox servers: *standby continuous replication* (SCR), which is essentially a cross between LCR and CCR.

Suppose you need to implement high availability for Exchange Server 2007, but your budget is limited and you can purchase only two servers. To implement high availability, you need redundancy for all of the Exchange Server 2007 roles you'll implement. That means one of the things you'll have to do is ensure that the Mailbox server role survives the failure of an entire server. Implementing LCR doesn't suffice because your backup database must reside on a local volume; you cannot place an LCR backup on a network share, even if you map a drive to that share. And, as noted later, in the section "Clustering and Server Roles," clustered Mailbox servers cannot host any other Exchange Server 2007 roles. Using CCR requires a minimum of four servers for full redundancy: two for the clustered Mailbox servers, and two more for redundancy of the other roles.

SCR, on the other hand, is a perfect solution in this situation. With SCR, you can place your backup storage group on a different server. (In fact, you can use SCR to make multiple backup copies on several servers; LCR and CCR offer only a single backup copy of the storage group.) The idea is that you can put the backup on another server, even in another physical location, without the overhead of Windows Clustering. Thus, like LCR, SCR requires a manual failover. However, because SCR does not involve clustering, your SCR Mailbox servers can also host the other server roles; you just need to configure the appropriate redundancy options for those other roles.

FIGURE 2.7 Cluster continuous replication (CCR) example

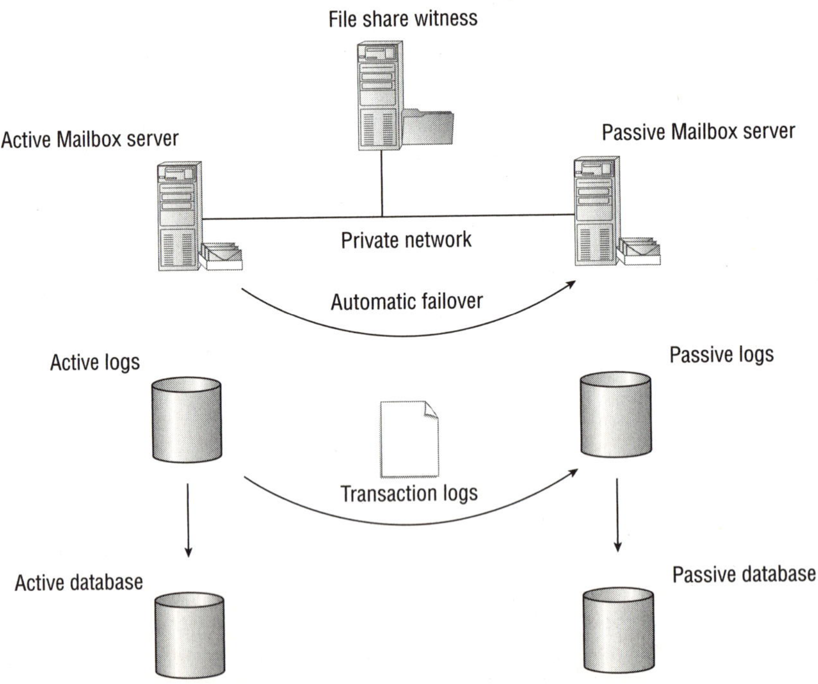

How Continuous Replication Works

Exchange Server 2007, like previous versions, uses the extensible storage engine (ESE) for mailbox and public folder databases. ESE databases consist of a database file and several transaction logs. Before transactions are committed in the database file, those transactions must be recorded in a transaction log file. Both LCR and CCR use a process known as *log shipping*. With log shipping, the backup copy of the database is maintained by simply copying the log files from the production database to the backup location and replaying the transactions in those log files into the backup database. Thus, when you implement LCR or CCR, you must first make a copy of the original database to the backup location, which is known as *seeding the backup database*.

In previous versions of Exchange, each transaction log file was 5 MB. To better facilitate continuous replication, Exchange Server 2007 uses 1 MB log files instead. The smaller size makes replication of the log files both faster and more reliable; it also significantly decreases the potential for data loss should you have to fail over to the backup database.

However, because a log file is not copied from the active database to the passive database until the log file is full and closed, the current log file is never available to the passive database. That means if a failure occurs some data may be lost. Exchange Server 2007 will use a storage location, known as the *transport dumpster*, on the Hub Transport server to recover this data. You should configure the size of the transport dumpster to be 1.5 times the size of your maximum message size.

Clustering and Server Roles

Be aware that clustering nodes have some special requirements not shared by other Mailbox servers. First, even though Exchange Server 2007 supports active/passive clusters, Windows Clustering requires that a minimum of three servers participate in the cluster to avoid a problem known as *split-brain syndrome*, which is really a fancy way of saying that multiple nodes each think that they should own a particular set of cluster resources. An example of where split brain might otherwise occur is when two nodes, one active and one passive, lose the network connections between them. When this happens, the passive node no longer receives heartbeats from the active node, but the active node does not receive communication that the passive node is taking over, so both nodes think they're the active one. Windows clustering avoids this by requiring a *majority node set* to communicate for any node to operate as active. That means that more than 50 percent of the nodes must be communicating and agree on which servers should be active.

With SCC, you can elect to have up to eight nodes in the cluster, so long as at least one of the nodes is passive. However, with CCR, you have just two nodes in the CCR cluster. So, in order to have a majority node set with CCR, you can implement a Windows *file share witness*. The file share witness is a shared folder on a Windows Server computer that is available to the both the active and passive nodes on the private cluster network. The file share witness computer can be running any Windows Server operating system; it does not need to have Windows clustering configured.

Some best practices recommend that the file share witness be installed on a Hub Transport server in the same AD site as the clustered Mailbox server. Presumably, this recommendation is based on the idea that every Mailbox server needs to have access to a Hub Transport server in the same AD site for message routing.

When preparing to configure your CCR clusters, be sure to install either the update described in Microsoft Knowledge Base article Q921181 (http://support.microsoft.com/kb/921181/en-us) or Windows Server 2003 Service Pack 2 on all of the computers that will participate in the cluster. This fix enables the use of the Windows file share witness.

The second major difference between SCC and CCR Mailbox servers and all other Mailbox servers is that when you implement SCC or CCR, you cannot deploy any other role on the clustered Mailbox servers. This means that if you're implementing a high-availability Exchange Server 2007 solution and your Mailbox server uses SCC or CCR as part of its high-availability strategy, then a minimum of four servers is required: the active Mailbox server; the passive Mailbox server; and a pair of redundant servers for the Hub Transport, Client Access, and, if used, the Unified Messaging roles. And if your high-availability Exchange Server 2007 organization design includes redundant Edge Transport servers, then you'll need at least two of those as well, for a minimum of six servers.

Although CCR clustered Mailbox servers can host a public-folder database, they do not support public-folder replication. Thus, CCR clustered Mailbox servers cannot host any replicated public folders, including the system public folders on Exchange Server 2000 and Exchange Server 2003 computers.

Implementing Redundancy for Edge Transport Servers

Edge Transport servers aren't strictly required. You can send messages to and receive messages from the Internet by using just Hub Transport servers. However, Edge Transport servers are recommended for spam and virus filtering of messages outside your Exchange organization and the processing of rules on Internet mail. If you use an Edge Transport server, and if that server fails, then all transfer of messages between your Exchange organization and the Internet will stop.

Implementing redundancy for Exchange Server 2007 Edge Transport servers is fairly simple. First, you install multiple Edge Transport servers, then you ensure that both your internal Exchange Server 2007 Hub Transport servers and simple mail transport protocol (SMTP) servers on the Internet know about them.

Edge Transport servers should be installed in a screened subnet between your internal network and the Internet. To configure your internal Exchange organization to use an Edge Transport server, you create an Edge Transport subscription for the site. To make the outbound Edge Transport function redundant, you just install multiple Edge Transport servers in the screened subnet and create multiple Edge Transport subscriptions.

You can establish high availability for the inbound functions of the Edge Transport server in either of two ways, both of which involve changes to DNS. Inbound messages are routed to your Edge Transport servers by using Mail Exchanger (MX) records in DNS. MX records specify the name of the inbound SMTP sever to which email for a domain should be sent. To establish inbound high availability for Edge Transport servers, you can either create multiple

MX records, each pointing to a different Edge Transport server, or you can create one MX record that points to a hostname for which you have created multiple A records. Figure 2.8 illustrates the use of multiple MX records for Edge Transport server redundancy.

FIGURE 2.8 Using multiple Mail Exchanger (MX) records to establish redundancy for Edge Transport servers

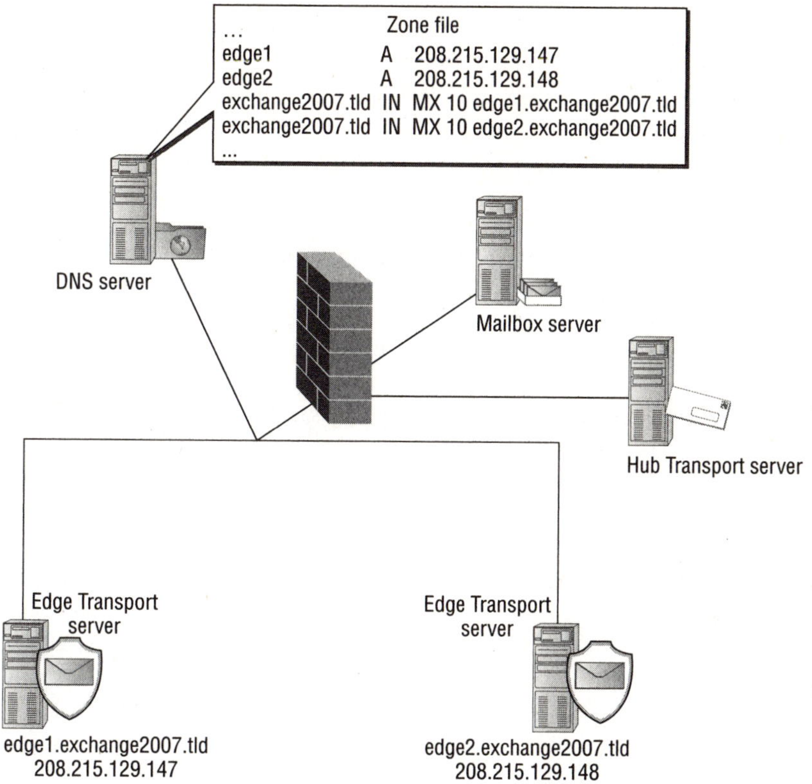

Using multiple MX records is the preferred solution for two reasons:

- MX records contain a weight or preference setting. Thus, if you choose, you can assign different preferences to each of your Edge Transport servers and thereby control the order in which a sending sever attempts to transfer messages to your network.
- In addition the limitations of round-robin A records mentioned previously in the chapter, relying on round-robin for high availability can cause problems with some older SMTP servers. When round-robin is used, an A-record query for the name of the inbound SMTP must be answered with multiple IP addresses. Some older SMTP servers will only try to contact the first IP address listed when an A-record query is answered with multiple IP addresses. Thus, if you have a long-term outage of one of your SMTP servers and rely upon round-robin instead of multiple MX records, it's very likely that some inbound mail will be returned to the sender as undeliverable.

Plan Policies to Handle Unsolicited Email and Virus Outbreaks

You can implement all of the fault tolerance and redundancy in the world, and it's not going to help if your Exchange Server computers are overwhelmed by unsolicited email, become the entry point for virus infection, or even become infected themselves. Therefore, having a set of comprehensive antispam and antivirus policies for your messaging system is an important aspect of designing a highly available Exchange Server 2007 system.

Implementing Message Hygiene

The goal of message hygiene is to block as many junk and virus-infected messages as possible while minimizing the number of *false positives*, legitimate messages that appear to be malicious or spam, that are blocked. One of the best ways to protect your Exchange Server 2007 system is by deploying Edge Transport servers. Edge Transport servers let you perform your antivirus and antispam filtering on inbound messages before those messages reach your internal Exchange Server computers or any other computers in your AD forest. But regardless of whether you use Edge Transport servers, you need to practice good message hygiene.

Defense-in-Depth

The first thing to understand about message hygiene, or any security strategy for that matter, is that you really should take a layered approach by protecting your systems at as many levels as you can. We call that *defense-in-depth*. For messaging systems, it means not only scanning the messages themselves on the messaging server for viruses and spam, but scanning the operating system and files on the server; scanning the messages and files at the client; and scanning the data at security perimeters, such as firewalls and gateways, as that traffic passes through our network.

Antivirus Scanning

It is highly recommended that your defense-in-depth approach also include scanning tools from multiple vendors. Think about it: What is the point of scanning for viruses and spam at all of these different places if your tools all come from the same vendor and, therefore, use the same definition files? If you did that, then anything that was missed at the firewall is going to be missed at the gateway, the server, and the client too. Microsoft Forefront Security for Exchange Server (formerly Microsoft Antigen) is a tool that includes nine different scanning engines in one product, and those different engines (along with the definition files from the respective vendors) can be used to significantly increase the likelihood that you'll intercept whatever the latest virus or spam threat is.

Although Forefront Security for Exchange Server includes nine different scanning engines, you can only configure it to use five or fewer for any individual job. And it's recommended that you use only the default Real-time Scan Job running most of the time. However, if you have multiple Exchange Server 2007 servers, then you can configure Forefront Security for Exchange Server to use different engines on different servers to maximize the likelihood of catching the latest malware.

Forefront Security for Exchange Server includes additional advanced features, such as the stamping of scanned messages and the use of different scanning agents for Mailbox, Hub Transport, and Edge Transport servers.

Real World Scenario

File-Based Virus Scanning on Exchange Server Computers

When you implement virus scanning for your Exchange Server 2007 Mailbox servers, you should install both an Exchange-aware antivirus product to scan the actual messages, and a file-based antivirus product to scan the file system. But as long as people have been installing antivirus software on Exchange Server computers, they have been making the mistake of using the file-based virus scanner to scan the Exchange databases and log files. Doing that is a very easy way to destroy your database.

In fact, it's not terribly uncommon for companies that have recently fired an Exchange Server administrator to find their Exchange databases have become corrupt. It's usually because, on the way out, the disgruntled ex-employee configured the file-based virus scanner to scan the Exchange database and logs.

You do need to install a file-based virus scanner on every server, including your Exchange Server computers, to keep them from getting infected at the file level. However, you should always exclude the Exchange database files (`*.edb`) and transaction log files (`*.log`) from the extensions that the file-based scanner will inspect. This is because the file-based scanner is not aware of the Exchange database and log-file data structure, which results in occasional false positives on identifying viruses and, more frequently, file corruption when the file-based scanner attempts to repair an infected data structure.

Today, many server-compatible file-based virus scanners will automatically exclude the Exchange database and transaction log extensions when they are installed on an Exchange Server computer. However, you should always double-check the file-extension exclusions after installing a file-based antivirus product on any Exchange Server computer.

Attachment Filtering

Another way that Edge Transport servers can protect your network against viruses is through attachment filtering. By default, Edge Transport servers strip from messages the attachment types that are most likely to carry malicious code. You can customize the file types that attachment filtering strips by adding or removing file extensions from the list.

Exchange Server 2007 Antispam Features

If you implement Edge Transport servers, you can configure a new option called *safe sender list aggregation* to reduce the number of false positives for spam filtering. In Outlook, each user can add users to a list of safe senders. Safe senders are assumed to never send spam. The idea behind safe sender aggregation is that if one user says that a particular sender is safe, then that sender is unlikely to be sending spam to anyone. So, when safe sender list aggregation is enabled, the Edge Transport servers, through the EdgeSync process, retrieves every user's safe sender list and combines then into a single list of safe senders who will not have their messages filtered at the Edge Transport server level.

Exchange Server 2007 can be configured to use a number of methods for blocking inbound messages that may be spam. These methods include connection filters, Sender ID filtering, use of real-time block lists, content filtering, and consideration of sender reputation.

Connection filters do just what their name implies: filter inbound messages based on the source of the connection itself. That is, the Exchange Server computer compares the IP address of the SMTP server that is sending the message to IP Block and IP Allow lists configured for Exchange.

Sender ID filtering is based upon Sender Policy Framework (SPF) technology, which uses DNS records to attempt to validate the legitimacy of the message. With Sender ID, Exchange queries the DNS server for the SMTP domain listed for the message sender. For example, you could configure SPF records in DNS to indicate that all servers referenced by your MX records are valid senders, or you could use SPF records to explicitly list the valid outbound mail servers for your domain. If the message is being sent from a valid sending IP address or a valid sending server listed in that domain's SPF records, then the message is accepted. However, if the message is coming from an address that isn't listed as valid for the SMTP domain, then you can configure Exchange to drop the message, bounce it back to the sender, or accept the message but flag it as suspicious.

Real-time block lists (RBLs) are third-party services that attempt to provide continuously updated information on domains or IP addresses that are actively sending spam. IP-based RBLs are considered to be more reliable than domain-based RBLs because anyone sending spam is likely using a falsified email address anyway. Be aware that, even if you use IP-based RBLs, using an RBL can cause the rejection of legitimate email from parties with whom you do business. This could be the result of a spammer exploiting an open relay or simply obtaining email services from the same hosting provider as the valid sender.

Content filtering uses the words and other information within the message itself to determine if a message is spam. When a message arrives, Exchange compares the contents of the message to known spam patterns, such as well-known phrases and message composition, to assign a numerical *spam confidence level* (SCL). The higher the SCL, the more likely it is that the message is spam. Exchange can be configured to place messages that exceed a specified SCL rating in the recipient's Junk Email folder and to completely drop messages that exceed a higher specified SCL rating. Content filtering also uses administrator-configured word lists to flag messages as spam.

Be particularly careful with content filter word lists. The word "mortgage," for example, might seem a perfect word for a content filter list. But wait until you have to explain to the CEO why messages from his or her lender aren't getting through!

Sender reputation is an analysis of the recent behavior of the message sender. When a message arrives, Exchange assigns a numerical sender reputation level (SRL) to the sender of that message. As with SCL, the higher the SRL, the more likely the sender is a spammer. The SRL is affected by factors such as whether that sender has performed an open relay test; whether the HELO IP or domain name matches the actual IP or reverse DNS lookup, and the SCL of messages recently sent by the same sender.

Table 2.1 summarizes the various antispam strategies:

TABLE 2.1 Methods for Blocking Inbound Messages in Exchange Server 2007

Method	Description
Connection filtering	Messages are blocked or allowed based on the source IP address.
Sender ID filtering	Messages are blocked or flagged because the sender doesn't match policy specified by the DNS records.
Real-time block lists	Messages are blocked because a third-party RBL provider says that domain or IP address is sending spam.
Content filtering	Messages are blocked based on keywords and patterns within the message.
Sender reputation	Messages are blocked based on recent behavior of the sender.

Hosted Services

In addition to the antivirus features of Forefront Security for Exchange Server and the antispam features built into Exchange Server 2007, you may want to consider *Exchange Hosted Filtering*. Exchange Hosted Filtering is one of several fee-based service products known collectively as Exchange Hosted Services, which allow Exchange administrators to transfer responsibility for some of the more difficult-to-manage aspects of maintaining an Exchange Server organization to Microsoft or third-party Microsoft Partners.

With Exchange Hosted Filtering, you redirect your MX records to the hosted filtering servers. Those servers block unwanted messages and scan all email for viruses before forwarding the remaining messages to your Exchange system. This process is illustrated in Figure 2.9.

FIGURE 2.9 Exchange Hosted Filtering example

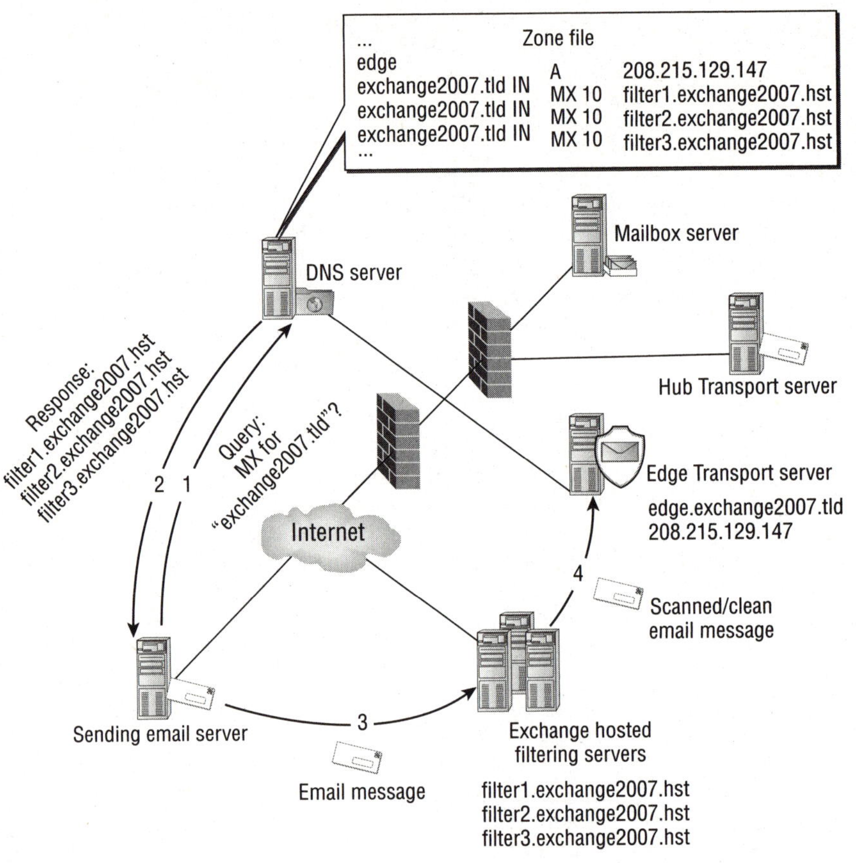

Several third parties also offer similar hosted filtering services.

Anti-Malware Product Considerations

Although Exchange Server 2007 includes some very comprehensive antispam and antivirus features, you might elect to use third-party products along with or instead of the Microsoft offerings. Some of the things you should consider when selecting third-party products for antivirus and antispam include the following:

- Frequency and timeliness of engine and definition updates
- Ease of and automation for obtaining and deploying engine and definition updates
- Administration features
- User notification and "quarantine release" options
- Vendor reputation and technical support
- Exchange Server 2007 integration and support

Updates for Exchange Server 2007 and Forefront Security products are delivered through Microsoft Updates. You can ensure your Exchange Server 2007 computers get these updates by configuring Automatic Updates, implementing Windows Server Update Services (WSUS), or using the Inventory Tool for Microsoft Updates (ITMU) with the Distribute Software Updates Wizard in Microsoft Systems Management Server (SMS) 2003.

If you decide to use a third-party antivirus solution for Exchange, be sure to select a product that is fully Exchange Server 2007–compatible. Exchange Server 2007 includes two features that your antivirus solution should support: antivirus stamping and transport agents. With antivirus stamping, when a message is scanned, the product and version of the scanning engine is attached to the message. When that message is sent to other Exchange Servers, the stamp tells the server that it's unnecessary to rescan the message with the same tool. Transport agents are tools that can be used to scan messages, for any number of criteria, not just for virus infection, at Hub Transport and Edge Transport servers. It is highly recommended that your selection of antivirus products includes transport agents for Exchange Server 2007 Hub and Edge Transport servers as well as a Microsoft Virus Scanning API (VSAPI)–compliant engine for your Mailbox servers.

Real World Scenario

When Hygiene Measures Fail

Although cleaning any discovered viruses has typically been the recommended course of action in days past, the evolving methods and severity of attack vectors are leading to the recommendation that any messages be deleted if they are suspected of containing viruses.

Nevertheless, it is highly likely that, at some point, your anti-malware measures will not be enough, and you will be faced with a serious spam, phishing, or virus outbreak. Being prepared with a plan of action for such an event is another critical aspect of maintaining a highly available Exchange Server 2007 system.

Your organization is going to get spam. There is no perfect filtering solution because spammers are always adjusting their tactics to beat the latest filtering techniques. But if you encounter a significant increase in the number of spam messages that get through your filtering processes, try to find a key word or phrase common to most of those messages and add that to your content-filtering keyword list. You may want to do that on a temporary basis, until your antispam product definitions are updated to deal with the new technique. If the spam outbreak contains phishing messages, be sure to also educate your users about the scam.

If you have a virus outbreak, then practice good virus containment and cleaning techniques:

1. Disconnect from the Internet.
2. Isolate the known infected systems from everything else. If possible, also isolate the known clean systems from the systems you're not sure about.
3. Use a stand-alone computer to connect to the Internet and download the latest virus fixes, antivirus engines, antivirus definition, and other applicable software updates.
4. Clean and/or protect all of your systems with the newly obtained software.
5. Verify the integrity of your operating systems, programs, and data before reconnecting any of the isolated computers.
6. Reconnect to the Internet and resume email transfer.

Summary

Availability requirements are defined by SLAs. The SLA will tell you which Exchange Server 2007 roles need redundancy. Start with fault-tolerant hardware. Each Exchange Server 2007 role can be made highly available through redundancy, but the redundancy options are unique for each role. Mailbox servers have the most complex and interesting redundancy options: LCR, CCR, and SCC. Message hygiene is just as critical as fault tolerance and redundancy for maintaining a highly available Exchange Server 2007 system. Use defense-in-depth techniques and comprehensive antispam and antivirus policies to maintain message hygiene.

Exam Essentials

Understand how to interpret SLA requirements Be able to identify and interpret SLA requirements in exam scenarios. Understand how to translate SLA requirements into feature configurations. For example, if an exam scenario says that OW must remain available even if two servers fail, know that you'll need at least three Client Access servers configured as an NLB cluster.

Understand how to implement high availability for each Exchange Server 2007 role For the Hub Transport role, simply add additional Hub Transport servers in each AD site that needs high availability. For the Client Access server role, implement NLB clusters for high availability. For Mailbox servers, use LCR where some unexpected downtime is acceptable and use CCR where automatic failover is required to minimize downtime. SCC can be used for traditional, shared-disk clustering of Mailbox servers. High availability can be implemented for Edge Transport servers by using either NLB or round-robin DNS records, although the latter has some limitations. High availability for Unified Messaging can be achieved by installing multiple Unified Messaging servers in each dial plan and implementing round-robin DNS entries.

Understand how to configure Network Load Balancing NLB requires a unique IP address for each node and a shared IP address for the cluster. A shared hostname should also be assigned to the NLB cluster. NLB cluster members should be connected to a hub, not a switch. You need to exclude any non-NLB services, such as SMTP on a Hub Transport server, if you are going to implement multiple highly available roles on a single server.

Understand how to configure DNS for redundancy options Hub transport servers do not require any special DNS configuration for redundancy. One address (A) record should point to an NLB cluster; you should not use round-robin for the hostname of an NLB cluster. All Client Access server functions, including Autodiscovery and the Availability service, should be published under the shared hostname and IP address for the NLB cluster. You can configure round-robin A records that point to multiple NLB clusters in order to rotate requests between them. You can also use round-robin A records to rotate your inbound mail between multiple Edge Transport servers; however, multiple Mail Exchanger (MX) records, which can be prioritized, is preferable.

Understand the requirements of Mailbox server redundancy options LCR and CCR require four storage volumes, or logical units (LUNs), for each storage group protected. You can use directly attached storage devices (DASDs) or storage area networks (SANs) for LCR, but you cannot use shares on other computers for either the active or passive databases. Both CCR and SCC require Windows clustering; however, because CCR does not use shared storage, only SCC requires hardware that is on the Windows Server Catalog as supported for clustering. Only the Mailbox server role can be deployed on a CCR or SCC clustered Mailbox server. Both LCR and CCR require exactly one database per storage group.

Understand message hygiene Know how to design and implement antispam and antivirus policies. Understand Microsoft's antivirus offerings. Understand the antispam features built into Exchange Server 2007. Know how to evaluate Hosted Services and third-party product offerings. Know what to do when measures fail.

Review Questions

1. You are designing an Exchange Server 2007 solution for your company. Your company has 900 employees who use email. The hardware design of your Mailbox servers will support up to 300 mailbox users, but the hardware does not support shared-disk clustering. Your network consists of a single Active Directory site. Your users will use Microsoft Office Outlook 2007 and Microsoft Office Outlook Web Access to access their mailboxes. Neither the Edge Transport nor Unified Messaging roles will be deployed. You need to design a highly available Exchange solution. Users must not be affected by the failure of a single server. Your design must use the fewest number of servers possible. How many Exchange Server 2007 computers should you deploy?

   A. 3

   B. 4

   C. 6

   D. 8

   E. 10

2. You are implementing a highly available Exchange Server 2007 solution for your company. Your Mailbox servers are deployed as CCR clustered Mailbox servers. One Client Access server and one Hub Transport server have been deployed in each Active Directory (AD) site. You need to implement high availability for the Hub Transport and Client Access server roles. Which of the following actions should you perform? (Select two.)

   A. Install additional Hub Transport servers in each AD site.

   B. Install additional Hub Transport servers in each AD site and configure network load balancing (NLB).

   C. Install additional Client Access servers in any AD site.

   D. Install additional Client Access servers in each AD site and configure NLB.

3. You are implementing high availability for your company's Exchange Server 2007 Standard Edition Mailbox servers. Your company has established the following requirements: (1) in the event of a mailbox failure, disruptions should be minimized, (2) Mailbox failover must be automatic, and (3) cost should be minimized as much as possible without violating the other requirements. Which of the following actions should you perform?

   A. Implement local continuous replication (LCR). Seed the backup databases on unused volumes on each server.

   B. Implement LCR. Seed the backup databases on alternate servers.

   C. Purchase an additional Exchange Server 2007–compatible computer for each existing Mailbox server. Purchase Exchange Server 2007 Enterprise Edition licenses for all existing and newly acquired Mailbox servers. Install each new computer as the active node of a cluster continuous replication (CCR) cluster. Move all mailboxes to the active CCR nodes. Reinstall all of the original Exchange Server 2007 Mailbox servers as Exchange Server 2007 Enterprise Edition passive nodes in the appropriate CCR cluster.

   D. Purchase an additional Exchange Server 2007–compatible computer for each existing Mailbox server. Purchase Exchange Server 2007 Standard Edition licenses for newly acquired Mailbox servers. Install each new computer as the active node of a single copy cluster (SCC) cluster. Move all mailboxes to the active SCC nodes. Reinstall all of the original Exchange Server 2007 Mailbox servers as passive nodes in the appropriate SCC cluster.

4. You are implementing high availability for your Edge Transport servers. Which of the following technologies should you use?

   A. NLB

   B. Round-robin A records

   C. Round-robin MX records

   D. CCR

5. You are deploying a high-availability solution for your Exchange Server 2007 organization. You have Mailbox servers deployed in three Active Directory (AD) sites. A Client Access server has been deployed in each AD site. Your users access their mailboxes by using Office Outlook 2007 and Office Outlook Web Access (OWA). Your company's Internet connection and screened subnet are located in the corporate headquarters. You need to establish high availability for your Client Access servers. Which of the following actions should you perform? (Select two.)

   A. Install additional Client Access servers only on the internal network in the corporate headquarters.

   B. Install additional Client Access servers only in the screened subnet at the corporate headquarters.

   C. Install additional Client Access servers in each AD site.

   D. Configure round-robin A records for the Client Access servers.

   E. Implement NLB for the Client Access servers.

6. You are implementing high availability for your Exchange Server 2007 organization. You have seven Mailbox servers in three Active Directory (AD) sites. Each site also has an Exchange Server 2007 computer that hosts the Hub Transport and Client Access server roles. You need to implement high availability for the Mailbox servers. Your company has established the following requirements: (1) mailbox data must be easily recoverable in the event of a data volume failure, and (2) additional servers must not be required. Which of the following technologies should you configure for your Mailbox servers?

   A. LCR

   B. CCR

   C. SCC

   D. NLB

   E. RAID 0

7. You are upgrading from Exchange Server 2003 to Exchange Server 2007. You currently have an active/active cluster of Exchange Server 2003 computers; the cluster servers are named Mbx1 and Mbx2. Each of the clustered Mailbox servers hosts 300 mailboxes. The server hardware is x64-compatible. Local disk space on the cluster computers is limited. You need to host the 600 mailboxes on Exchange Server 2007. Your budget will not permit the purchase of additional server computers or disk space. Which of the following steps should you perform? (Select three.)

   A. Upgrade the operating system on Mbx1 and Mbx2

   B. Remove Exchange Server 2003 from Mbx1 and Mbx2.

   C. Perform an in-place upgrade to Exchange Server 2007 on Mbx1 and Mbx2.

   D. Install Exchange Server 2007 on two additional servers.

   E. Configure Mbx1 and Mbx2 as an active/passive SCC cluster.

   F. Configure Mbx1 and Mbx2 as an active/passive LCR cluster.

8. You are responsible for designing the storage group layout for your Exchange Server 2007 Mailbox server. Your email users are split into two categories: executives and associates. All mailboxes must be backed up on a daily basis. However, executive mailboxes must be recovered within one hour of a failure; associate mailboxes must be recovered within six. Recovering all mailboxes simultaneously would require four hours. You decide to implement local continuous replication (LCR) for all mailboxes. You add sufficient storage space to the Mailbox server. You need to ensure your storage group layout will support LCR as well as your backup and restore requirements. Which of the following should you do?

   A. Create a single storage group. Create one database for both executive and associate mailboxes.

   B. Create a single storage group. Create one database for executive mailboxes and create another database for associate mailboxes.

   C. Create one storage group with one database for executive mailboxes. Create another storage group with one database for associate mailboxes.

   D. Create one storage group for executive mailboxes and another storage group for associate mailboxes. Store all mailbox data in a single database.

9. You are implementing high availability for your Client Access servers. Your company's SMTP domain name is exchange2007.local. Your Client Access servers have the following addresses:

192.168.10.10	shared
192.168.10.11	CAS1
192.168.10.12	CAS2
192.168.10.13	CAS3

   Which of the following DNS records should you create? (Select all that apply.)

   A. `autodiscover    IN  A  192.168.10.10`

   B. `cas1        IN  A  192.168.10.10`

   C. `exchange2007.local IN  MX  10  cas2. exchange2007.local`

   D. `exchange2007.local IN  MX  10  cas3. exchange2007.local`

10. You are implementing high availability for your Exchange Server 2007 organization. Employees of your company access their mailboxes over the Internet by using Microsoft Office Outlook Web Access (OWA). Your network includes a single Active Directory site. Your company requires that all OWA traffic that crosses the Internet be encrypted. You need to ensure that OWA access is not affected by the failure of a single Client Access server. Which of the following actions should you perform? (Select two.)

    A. Implement round-robin A records for the Client Access servers.

    B. Implement NLB for the Client Access servers.

    C. Request a web server certificate for each Client Access server and install the certificates on the respective servers.

    D. Request one web server certificate for all Client Access servers and install that certificate on all Client Access servers.

11. You are implementing high availability for your Exchange Server 2007 organization. Employees of you company access their mailboxes over the Internet by using Microsoft Office Outlook Web Access (OWA). Your network includes three physical locations. Each location has a full T1 connection to the other two locations. Each location has its own Internet connection. An Active Directory (AD) site has been configured for each location. Your company requires the following: (1) OWA access to mailboxes must not be disrupted by the failure of a single Client Access server at a location and (2) OWA access to mailboxes must remain available even if one or two locations lose their Internet connections. Which of the following actions should you perform?

    A. Deploy one Client Access server at each location. Implement NLB for these Client Access servers.

    B. Deploy one Client Access server at each location. Configure round-robin A records for the Client Access servers.

    C. Deploy multiple Client Access servers at each location. Implement one NLB cluster for all Client Access servers at all locations.

    D. Deploy multiple Client Access servers at each location. Implement an NLB cluster for the Client Access servers at each location. Configure round-robin A records for the NLB clusters at all locations.

12. You have assumed the management of an existing Exchange Server 2007 organization. The organization consists of a single server. The server has two storage volumes: one RAID 5 volume and one RAID 1 volume. The previous administrator configured the server with the operating system, Exchange program files, and Exchange database files on the RAID 5 volume and the transaction log files on the RAID 1 volume. The server has a single storage group, which contains only one database. Your management wants you to implement an additional layer of fault tolerance for the mailbox database. However, budget constraints require that you minimize the cost of the change. You decide to implement Local Continuous Replication. Which of the following actions should you perform? (Select all that apply.)

    A. Purchase an additional server to host the passive database and logs.

    B. Purchase an additional server to host the non-Mailbox server roles.

    C. Purchase additional storage to host the passive database and logs.

    D. Move the transaction logs to the RAID 5 volume; place the passive database and logs on the RAID 1 volume.

13. You are planning to implement Unified Messaging for your existing Exchange Server 2007 organization. Your deployment currently includes two Active Directory (AD) sites, each of which contains a cluster continuous replication (CCR) clustered Mailbox server and a pair of servers running the Hub Transport and Client Access server roles. You need to ensure that failure of a single Unified Messaging server does not disrupt Unified Messaging for the users of that server. Your company does not want to use any existing computers for Unified Messaging. Which of the following actions should you perform?

    A. Purchase two new servers for Unified Messaging. Install one Unified Messaging server in each AD site. Implement multiple dial plans.

    B. Purchase two new servers for Unified Messaging. Install both Unified Messaging servers in one AD site. Implement a single dial plan.

    C. In each site, move the Hub Transport and Client Access server roles to the clustered Mailbox servers. In each site, reuse the former Hub Transport/Client Access servers as Unified Messaging servers. Implement multiple dial plans.

    D. In each site, install an active Unified Messaging server on the passive node of the clustered Mailbox server. In each site, install a passive Unified Messaging server on the active node of the clustered Mailbox server. Implement a single dial plan.

14. You are a messaging professional. You are responsible for the implementation of your Voice over IP (VoIP) gateways and Unified Messaging servers for your company's Exchange Server 2007 organization. Your Exchange organization includes a clustered continuous replication (CCR) clustered Mailbox server, a pair of network load balanced (NLB) Client Access servers, and a pair of redundant Hub Transport servers. Your Active Directory forest includes a single domain and a single site. You need to deploy a highly available Unified Messaging solution. You need to provide the highest level of redundancy possible. Which of the following actions should you perform? (Select two.)

    A. Install multiple Unified Messaging servers and a single dial plan.

    B. Install a single Unified Messaging server and multiple dial plans.

    C. Install a single VoIP gateway and a single hunt group.

    D. Install multiple VoIP gateways and multiple hunt groups.

15. You are implementing redundancy for elements of your Exchange Server 2007 organization. Your current Exchange deployment includes a single server that hosts the Mailbox, Hub Transport, Client Access, and Unified Messaging server roles. You are responsible for ensuring that Unified Messaging elements are highly available. Your organization has established the following requirements: (1) the handling of new voice and inbound fax calls should not be disrupted by the failure of a single server or VoIP gateway, (2) custom voice prompts should not be disrupted by the failure of a single server, and (3) the lowest possible number of new servers should be used without violating the other requirements. You have implemented the appropriate redundancy for Unified Messaging servers and VoIP gateways. Which additional action should you perform?

    A. Implement LCR for the Mailbox server role.

    B. Move the Mailbox server role to a CCR clustered Mailbox server.

    C. Install additional Client Access servers and implement round-robin A records in DNS.

    D. Move the Hub Transport server role to an NLB cluster.

16. You are responsible for designing your company's antispam measures for Exchange Server 2007. Currently, you use Edge Transport servers and some of the antispam features of your Edge Transport server to limit the amount of junk mail that users receive in their inboxes. Lately, the number of false positives in your spam filtering has increased. Your company wants to reduce the number of legitimate messages incorrectly blocked as spam without significantly increasing the number of junk messages delivered to your users' Inboxes. Your company does not want to incur any additional expenses in achieving the goal. Which of the following actions should you perform?

    A. Decrease the SCL for rejecting messages.

    B. Decrease the SRL for rejecting messages.

    C. Subscribe to Exchange Hosted Filtering.

    D. Implement safe sender list aggregation.

17. You are responsible for designing your antivirus strategy for your Exchange Server 2007 organization. Your company has decided to include Microsoft Forefront Security for Exchange Server as part of the antivirus strategy. On which servers should you install Forefront Security for Exchange Server? (Select all that apply.)

    A. Client Access servers

    B. Edge Transport servers

    C. Hub Transport servers

    D. Mailbox servers

    E. Unified Messaging servers

18. You are responsible for security in your Exchange Server 2007 organization. You have installed Microsoft Forefront Security for Exchange Server and a third-party file-level antivirus product. In order to strengthen your defense-in-depth approach, you want to use another antivirus product to scan messages on the Exchange Server computer. You also need to minimize the cost of the additional protection as much as possible without compromising the plan to enhance messaging security. Which of the following actions should you perform? (Select two.)

    A. Install a VSAPI-compliant product on your edge and Hub Transport servers.

    B. Install a VSAPI-compliant product on your Mailbox servers.

    C. Install a transport agent–based product on your Edge Transport and Hub Transport servers.

    D. Install a transport agent–based product on your Mailbox servers.

    E. Configure the file-level antivirus product to also scan Exchange `*.edb` and `*.log` files.

19. You are a messaging consultant. Several months ago, you assisted a client in deploying Exchange Server 2007 for their company. You followed antivirus and antispam best practices for both outgoing and incoming email. The client contacts you about a problem. The client states that for the past two weeks certain SMTP domains have been rejecting email sent from the client's Edge Transport servers. You investigate. You find that neither the client's SMTP domain nor their Edge Transport server IP addresses appear on any common real-time block lists (RBLs). You also find that the only change to the configuration in the past month was that the client added Exchange Hosted Filtering to their anti-malware measures. The problems sending email began soon after the client added Exchange Hosted Filtering. What should you recommend that the client do to resolve the issue?

    A. Subscribe to Exchange Hosted Continuity.

    B. Modify their SPF records.

    C. Add MX records for their Edge Transport servers and assign a lower priority than the existing MX records.

    D. Add MX records for their Edge Transport servers and assign the same priority as the existing MX records.

    E. Disable RBL filtering on the Edge Transport server.

20. You are responsible for message hygiene for your Exchange Server 2007 organization. When Exchange Server 2007 was deployed, several of the antispam features of Exchange Server 2007 were configured, and Microsoft Forefront Security for Exchange Server was installed on the appropriate servers. Additionally, appropriate antivirus software was deployed on all client and server computers. Reports of virus-infected and unwanted junk mail have been steadily increasing over time. You confirm that no configuration changes have been made in the antivirus and antispam features since deployment. Which of the following actions should you perform? (Select two. Each correct answer represents a complete solution.)

    A. Subscribe to Exchange Hosted Filtering.

    B. Increase the SCL for rejecting messages.

    C. Increase the SCL for placing messages in the Junk Email folder.

    D. Implement WSUS.

Answers to Review Questions

1. D. The company has 900 email users; at 300 users per server, you need three active Mailbox servers. Without a shared disk system, you'll also need cluster continuous replication (CCR) to ensure that users are not affected by the failure of a single Mailbox server. That means three passive Mailbox servers, for a total of six so far. No other roles can be deployed on a clustered Mailbox server, so the Hub Transport and Client Access server roles need to go on another server; that makes seven. Those non-Mailbox roles need redundancy too, so that's one more server, for a total of eight.

2. A, D. You should install additional Hub Transport servers in each AD site. You should also install additional Client Access servers in each AD site and implement NLB. You should not implement NLB for Hub Transport servers. Installing some additional Client Access servers in just one of the sites would be insufficient alone.

3. C. LCR can be implemented on Standard Edition, but LCR requires manual failover. For minimal disruption, you need to get additional hardware and install Exchange Server 2007 Enterprise Edition by using the clustered Mailbox server option. SCC requires Enterprise Edition as well as a shared disk subsystem.

4. B. Given the choices, you should implement round-robin A records in DNS to establish high availability for Edge Transport. You could use multiple MX for your Edge Transport servers, but MX records are ordered, not round-robin. Network Load Balancing (NLB) should be used for Client Access servers. Cluster continuous replication (CCR) is for Mailbox servers.

5. C, E. You should deploy additional Client Access servers in each AD site and implement network load balancing (NLB). Specifically, you should implement one Client Access server NLB cluster in each AD site. If you limit the additional Client Access servers to the headquarters, then your Client Access servers will not be highly available in your other AD sites. Client access servers should not be deployed in a screened subnet.

6. A. You should implement local continuous replication (LCR) for your Mailbox servers. Cluster continuous replication (CCR) and single copy clustering (SCC) require additional servers. Network Load Balancing (NLB) is used to make multiple Client Access servers highly available. RAID 0 is data striping only; RAID 0 is used for improved performance, not for high availability.

7. A, B, E. You need to upgrade Windows Server 2003 Enterprise Edition to the x64 version, remove Exchange Server 2003 so that Exchange Server 2007 can be installed as an active/passive single copy cluster (SCC) cluster. Exchange Server 2007 does not support direct, in-place upgrade from any previous version. Your budget does not permit the purchase of additional servers. Implementing cluster continuous replication (CCR) requires a local copy of the databases on each node of the cluster. In this scenario, local disk space is limited, and your budget does not support purchase of additional disk space. Of course, you will have to take additional steps to ensure messaging continuity, such as temporarily moving all mailboxes to one of the new servers while upgrading the old ones.

8. C. You should create one storage group and database for executive mailboxes and another storage group and database for executive mailboxes. Both LCR and CCR storage groups are limited to a single database. Putting the executive and associate mailboxes in a single database would prevent restoring executive mailboxes within the one-hour time limit. Databases cannot span storage groups.

9. A. Address (A) records for Client Access server services should be pointed at the network load balancing (NLB) shared IP address. The A records for individual server names, such as CAS1, should not be pointed at the shared IP address. Mail Exchanger (MX) records are for inbound SMTP mail only, and thus should be pointed to either Edge Transport servers or Hub Transport servers.

10. B, D. You should implement network load balancing (NLB) for the Client Access server, request one web server certificate for all Client Access servers, and install that certificate on all Client Access servers. Round-robin Address (A) records do provide high availability for Client Access servers. Using a different certificate for each Client Access server would not allow encrypted access to the NLB cluster by using a single hostname, so that would not facilitate high availability for the Client Access servers.

11. D. You should deploy multiple Client Access servers in a Network Load Balancing (NLB) cluster at each location. To implement redundancy *between* the Client Access server NLB clusters, and thus ensure that OWA remains available even if one or two of the Internet connections is lost, you should implement round-robin A records for the NLB clusters in all locations. Using round-robin A records for all Client Access servers without NLB within the location does not establish high availability within the locations. You cannot implement a single NLB cluster for Client Access servers in multiple locations because all cluster members must be on the same IP subnet. (Using a Virtual LAN would not work because the Client Access servers must be accessible from the Internet.)

12. C. You need additional storage space to create additional logical unit numbers (LUNs) for the passive database and passive storage logs. You can't put the passive database or logs on another server with LCR. The LCR server can host non-Mailbox roles.

13. B. You should purchase two new servers, install them as Unified Messaging servers in one of the AD sites, and implement a single dial plan. You don't necessarily need to have Unified Messaging servers in every AD site that has mailbox and Hub Transport servers. However, for high availability you need multiple Unified Messaging servers in the same site. Those servers must be in the same dial plan for redundancy. No other Exchange Server 2007 roles can be installed on the clustered Mailbox servers.

14. A, D. You should implement multiple VoIP gateways and multiple hunt groups as well as multiple Unified Messaging servers and a single dial plan to provide the greatest level of redundancy. (Technically, you would have one dial plan for each VoIP gateway. However, from the perspective of the Unified Messaging servers, it's a single dial plan.)

15. B. You should move the Mailbox server role to a cluster continuous replication (CCR) clustered Mailbox server to ensure that custom voice prompts are not be disrupted by a single server failure. All other requirements in the scenario have been satisfied by the actions already taken. Implementing local continuous replication (LCR) does not ensure that custom voice prompts are not disrupted by a single server failure because LCR requires manual intervention after a failure.

16. D. Implementing safe sender list aggregation on the Edge Transport server configures the combining of all individual safe sender lists into a single safe sender list for the entire Exchange organization. This will likely reduce the number of false positives in your spam filtering. Because few users will add spammers to their safe senders list, using safe sender aggregation will not significantly increase the number of junk messages that are delivered to users' Inboxes. Subscribing to Exchange Hosted Filtering would violate the company's requirement that no additional fees be incurred and would probably increase the number of false positives in the short term. Decreasing the spam confidence level (SCL) or the sender reputation level (SRL) would increase the number of false positives, not decrease it.

17. B, C, D. You should install Forefront Security for Exchange Server only on your Edge Transport, Hub Transport, and Mailbox servers. Forefront Security for Exchange Server includes antivirus agents for Mailbox servers, Hub Transport servers, and Edge Transport servers. Forefront Security for Exchange Server does not include antivirus agents for Client Access and Unified Messaging servers.

18. B, C. The Mailbox server role does not support transport agent–based antivirus tools, so you should install a traditional VSAPI-based product to scan messages on Mailbox servers. You should install a transport agent–based antivirus product, not a VSAPI-compliant product, on Edge and Hub Transport servers. You should never allow a file-based antivirus product to scan Exchange `*.edb` and `*.log` files; doing so would quickly lead to database corruption.

19. B. Given the scenario, the most likely reason that messages are being rejected is a problem with Sender ID. Specifically, the almost certain cause of the message rejection by only certain domains is that the client's Sender ID policy no longer permits messages sent by the client's Edge Transport server because the MX records have changed. (If your Sender ID policy specifies that only the servers specified by you MX records can send mail, then changing the MX records changes your Sender ID policy.) The reason that only certain domains are rejecting messages is that not all companies have implemented Sender ID filtering. To correct the problem, modify the SPF records to indicate that your client's Edge Transport servers are legitimate sending SMTP servers for the domain.

20. A, D. You can resolve the problem by either subscribing to Exchange Hosted Filtering or implementing Windows Server Update Services (WSUS). With antivirus and antispam features, you must update the antivirus and antispam definitions and engines. Implementing WSUS gives you an easy-to-manage method of doing this. Another option is to offload responsibility for antivirus and antispam filtering to the Exchange Hosted Filtering services. With Exchange Hosted Filtering, the antispam and antivirus technologies are kept current by the service provider.

Designing Recovery and Messaging Services to Meet Business Demands

MICROSOFT EXAM OBJECTIVES COVERED IN THIS CHAPTER:

- ✓ Designing disaster recovery, backup, and restore solutions
- ✓ Evaluating existing business requirements to define supporting infrastructure
- ✓ Designing and recommending strategies for dependent services that impact high availability

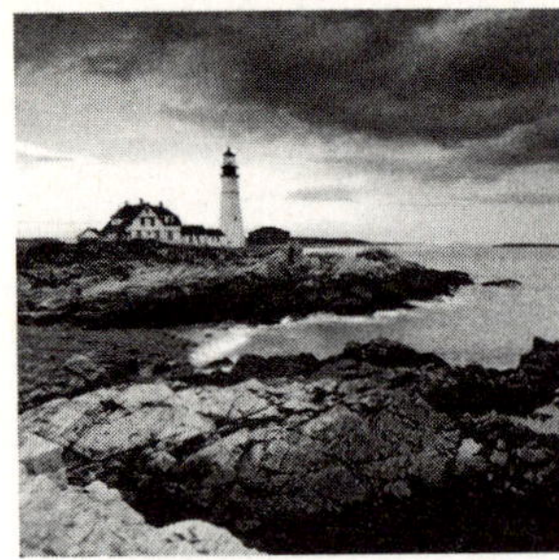

As you saw in Chapter 2, "Designing and Planning Server High Availability," Exchange 2007 offers a lot of possibilities to establish high availability. But all these new features, like LCR and CCR, do not take away the need to create a disaster-recovery plan. In this chapter we will dive into the backup and restore solutions available for use with Exchange 2007. We will also evaluate the existing business requirements to define supporting infrastructure, and we will dive into the strategies you can use to design and recommend strategies for Exchange-dependent services that impact high availability.

The main subjects of this chapter are as follows:

- Exchange-aware backup solutions
- Backup and restore requirements for every Exchange Server 2007 role
- Business requirements that influence the supporting infrastructure
- Overview of possible dependent services that impact high availability

Designing Disaster Recovery, Backup, and Restore Solutions

If disaster strikes, you should be able to recover your data as soon as you want it to be recovered, shouldn't you? In this part of the chapter, we will see what data needs to be backed up for every Exchange 2007 server role, and how this backup can be made and restored. After going through all possible backup procedures, we will highlight the different recovery possibilities you can use.

Exchange-Aware Backup Application

Every article or book you read dealing with disaster recovery and Exchange confirms that you have to use an Exchange-aware backup application. But why? The reason is quite simple. An Exchange-aware backup tool will tell Exchange that it is going to make a backup of its database files and log files, it will check every page of the database file for corruption, and after finishing the backup, the backup tool will make sure that the database files are marked as being successfully backed up and all log files that are redundant will be purged automatically!

In previous versions of Exchange (until Exchange 2000 SP2 was released), patch information was kept in a separate file, the so-called `<database_name>.pat` file. This patch file was designed to hold database changes that affected both parts of the database that were already backed up, and parts of the database that weren't yet backed up.

Table 3.1 lists the four possible backup and restore types, with a description and an explanation of how Exchange implements them.

TABLE 3.1 Exchange Backup and Restore Types

Backup/Restore Type	Description	Exchange Usage
Normal	Makes of backup of all files and marks the files as being backed up.	Makes a backup of the database files and the log files that have uncommitted entries in them at the time of backup. After backup has finished, all log files prior to the checkpoint at the time the backup started are purged. The database file's headers are updated to reflect the time of last normal backup.
Copy	Makes a backup of all files, but doesn't mark the files as having been backed up.	Makes a backup like the normal backup does, but doesn't purge log files and doesn't edit the database header.
Incremental	Makes a backup of all files that have changed since the last time they were marked as being backed up, and marks the files as being backed up.	Backs up log files that have been created since the last backup occurred, and purges the ones that are committed to the database files at the time of backup
Differential	Makes a backup of all files that have changed since the last time they were marked as being backed up, but doesn't mark the files as having been backed up.	Backs up logs files that have been created since the last backup, but doesn't delete any log file from the disk.

Each backup type has pros and cons that need to be considered when designing your disaster-recovery plan.

A *normal backup* (Figure 3.1), aka a *full backup*, is the easiest one to manage, both for backup and restore. A *copy backup* is also easy to manage, but since it does not purge the log files you need to make sure that the log files are removed to prevent your Exchange databases from going down due to lack of disk space. *Incremental and differential backups* will result in smaller backup files, but they rely on an existing normal or copy backup to be usable.

FIGURE 3.1 Overview of Exchange-aware normal backup

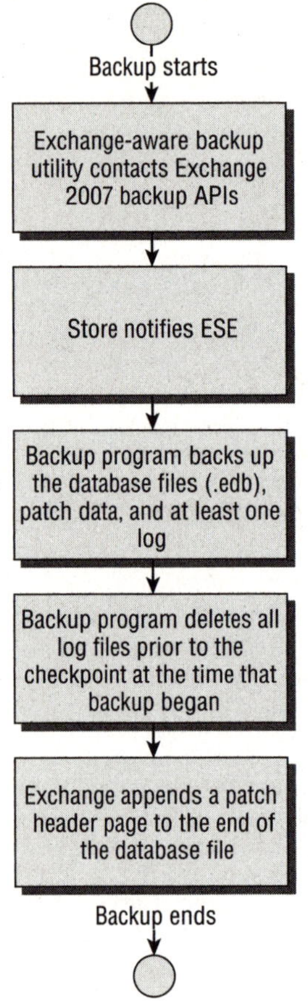

Using incremental and/or differential backups is not an option for a storage group that has circular logging enabled.

Supported Exchange-Aware Backup Methods

Exchange 2007 supports two different backup methods, namely *streaming backup* and the *Volume Shadow Copy Service backup*. These can be used to make a normal, copy, incremental, or differential type of backup.

Legacy Streaming Backup

As you will see in Chapter 4, "Designing and Planning Coexistence and Migrations," when we talk about transitioning an existing Exchange 2000 or Exchange 2003 messaging environment to Exchange 2007, Microsoft is de-emphasizing some features that were recommend for usage in the previous versions of Exchange. One of the features that is de-emphasized but still supported is the use of a streaming backup to make a backup of your Exchange database files. If you decide to back up your Exchange database files by using the Exchange streaming backup API, this implies that every page in your database is read in turn, and that the checksum integrity of each page is verified during the backup process, just like the checksum integrity of transaction log files is checked before they are backed up.

Volume Shadow Copy Service Backup (VSS)

The Volume Shadow Copy Service (aka Volume Snapshot Service, or *VSS*) was introduced in Exchange 2003, and is more powerful in Exchange 2007. In short, VSS is responsible for the coordination of the communication between the requestors (backup applications), writers (applications like Exchange 2007), and providers (components that create the shadow copies, be they software, hardware, or system components). It is important to note that even though Exchange 2007 is a valid writer, the built-in backup tool for Windows 2003 (`Ntbackup.exe`) provides Volume Shadow Copy Service backup support for Exchange databases, it does so only if you make a file-level-based backup of the database files! It does not provide a requestor, so if you want to use VSS for Exchange 2007, you will need to turn to third-party applications.

There are three requirements that any third-party VSS application must meet if you want to use it as a supported VSS backup solution:

- Database and transaction log file integrity must be verified by the backup application. This is because during a VSS backup there is no opportunity for Exchange to read each database file in its entirety and to verify its checksum integrity.
- Exchange Server 2007 database, transaction log, and checkpoint files must be backed up exclusively through the Microsoft Exchange Server 2007 writers for the Windows Server 2003 Volume Shadow Copy Service.
- Restores onto an Exchange server must be performed exclusively using the Exchange Store Writer.

In Exchange 2003 this last requirement was more restricted, since your VSS backup solution had to restore exclusively onto the original location using the Exchange Store Writer. This limitation of original location implied that you were able to restore a VSS backup only to an Exchange computer where the server name and the file path matched the ones from the Exchange computer where the VSS backup was taken. In Exchange 2007, VSS backups can be restored to the same storage group, to an alternate storage group on the same or a different server, or to a non-Exchange location as supported by the Exchange 2007 Store Writer.

VSS backups cannot be restored to the replica location using Exchange VSS components, but they can be restored as a file-level restore from VSS backups.

Deciding between Legacy Streaming and VSS

You cannot combine streaming and VSS backup technologies—not during backups and not during restores. It is impossible to make a legacy incremental backup after a VSS full backup, as it is impossible to combine a VSS differential backup with a legacy full backup at restore time. So you will have to choose a method. Table 3.2 lists a couple of important features to keep in mind when selecting your Exchange-aware backup method.

TABLE 3.2 Comparison of Streaming and VSS Exchange-Aware Backup

Feature	Exchange-aware Legacy Streaming Backup	Exchange-aware VSS
Can use Ntbackup	Yes	No
Can make normal backup of production database	Yes	Yes
Can make copy backup of production database	Yes	Yes
Can make differential backup of production database	Yes	Yes
Can make incremental backup of production database	Yes	Yes
Can make normal backup of passive database copy	No	Yes
Can make copy backup of passive database copy	No	Yes
Can make differential backup of passive database copy	No	Yes
Can make incremental backup of passive database copy	No	Yes
Backups can be selected at database level	Yes	Yes
Backups can be selected at storage-group level	Yes	Yes
Maximum one backup job running against a specific storage group	Yes	Yes

TABLE 3.2 Comparison of Streaming and VSS Exchange-Aware Backup *(continued)*

Feature	Exchange-aware Legacy Streaming Backup	Exchange-aware VSS
Separate storage groups can be backed up at the same time	Yes	Yes
Backup can be restored to an alternate location	No	Yes

Other Options

When talking about backup and restore methods for Exchange Server 2007, some other features have to be considered, like backing up an Exchange Mailbox server deployed with local continuous replication (LCR) or an Exchange Mailbox server deployed using cluster continuous replication (CCR). In addition, you should know that as an alternative to making an online backup of Exchange, it is still possible (though not recommended) to make an offline backup of your Exchange database files. This part of the chapter will go through the considerations concerning LCR, CCR, and offline backups.

Using LCR and CCR

As you saw in Chapter 2, enabling LCR for a storage group or CCR for a Mailbox server results in the creation of a passive database copy. The main goal of this passive copy is to replace the active database in case it's unavailable. But these passive copies can also serve as a source database file for making backups. Be careful; you can make VSS backups from only the copy location!

If you want to make a backup of the passive copy of the database files for which you have LCR or CCR enabled, you need to use a third-party solution or Microsoft's Data Protection Manager version 2 (which is expected to be released by the end of 2007).

Using Offline Backups

You can also dismount all your stores, and then make an offline backup of your Exchange database files. The biggest advantage of making an offline backup is that you don't need to use an Exchange-aware backup tool; any file-system backup tool can make a backup of a dismounted database file. But even though it is possible, Microsoft does not recommend using offline backups. That's because your store will not be checked for database corruption, and your database files will not be accessible for the end users!

Using CCR

You are the Exchange administrator, and you currently have a server in your environment with Exchange Server 2007 deployed. You are currently using Ntbackup to schedule a normal backup daily. After examining the backup log, you notice that your normal backups are not finished by the time users log into their mailbox in the morning. You want to decrease the number of normal backups, and you would like to be able to recover mail service and access to mailboxes as soon as possible in case of a hardware failure or database failure of one of your Exchange databases.

To meet those requirements, you can deploy two new Exchange servers configured as CCR, and two additional Exchange servers that hold the Client Access server role and the Hub Transport server role. By deploying the CCR Exchange server, you can recover in no time from a database failure, hardware failure, and even system failure of your Exchange Mailbox server. You can also decrease the number of normal backups. By having two Client Access servers and Hub Transport servers, you also have high availability for mail services.

Be careful; there is one situation where Microsoft urges you to make an offline backup, and that is when an online backup fails. In this scenario it is best practice to make a copy of your database prior to troubleshooting your database files.

Designing Disaster Recovery

There are several aspects to designing disaster recovery. In this section, you will first learn about the various Exchange Server 2007 roles. We'll then turn to Active Directory. Finally, you'll learn about how to handle client-side data.

Exchange Server 2007 Roles

Let's take a look at the Exchange Server 2007 roles: Mailbox server, Hub Transport server, Unified Messaging server. Then we will dig into the data that needs to be backed up for the Edge Transport server role.

Mailbox Server Role

The primary task of Exchange Server 2007 deployed with the Mailbox server role is hosting user mailboxes. Therefore, the mailbox database files are the most important ones to back up, so you will be able to restore the end-user data as soon and as easily as possible. If your Exchange organization hosts public folders, it is also necessary to keep your public-folder database files in mind when creating your backup schedules.

Table 3.3 lists the critical data specific to the Mailbox server role, and its available backup methods.

TABLE 3.3 Critical Data Specific to the Exchange 2007 Mailbox Server Role

Critical Data	Backup Method
Exchange database files (public and private)	Exchange-aware backup application
Exchange transaction log files	Exchange-aware backup application
Exchange full-text index catalog	None
Offline address book (OAB)	File-system backup
Configuration data	Active Directory backup
Windows registry	System-state backup or registry export

As you can see in Table 3.3, you will need an Exchange-aware backup application if you want to be able to make a backup of your Exchange database files and Exchange transaction log files. There is no need to panic when you see that there is no backup method available for backing up the Exchange full-text index catalog, because this catalog can be easily rebuilt. Exchange database files, on the other hand, cannot be rebuilt—that's why it is important to have a backup available. The Mailbox server role stores all its configuration data in Active Directory.

Exchange Server 2007 mailbox stores are fully indexed by default, allowing users to quickly search for information from Outlook Web Access or Outlook. This indexing data is stored by default in a directory in the same location as the database files. If there is a problem with the indexing database, or if you have to recover your database files, the search index might be unsynchronized. You will need to rebuild the search index catalog. To do that, you only have to stop the Microsoft Exchange Search service, delete the old catalog, and start the Microsoft Exchange Search Service again.

Hub Transport Server Role

The Hub Transport server is responsible for sending and receiving mail inside the Exchange organization. You can also configure your Hub Transport server to provide messaging services to the Internet.

The Hub Transport server communicates with the following clients:

- POP and Internet Message Access Protocol (IMAP) clients. Since POP and IMAP are retrieve-only protocols, they connect to a Hub Transport server to send mails.
- Other Hub Transport servers in same Exchange organization.
- Edge Transport server. When an Edge Transport server is deployed, a Hub Transport server can be configured to send all outbound mails to the Edge Transport server. The

Edge Transport server can be configured as an SMTP relay for both inbound and outbound mail. If EdgeSync is enabled, the Hub Transport server will also synchronize new, modified, and deleted recipient and configuration information from Active Directory to the Edge Transport server.

Table 3.4 lists the critical data specific to the Hub Transport server role, and its available backup methods.

TABLE 3.4 Critical Data Specific to the Exchange 2007 Hub Transport Server Role

Critical Data	Backup Method
Message queues	None
Message tracking and protocol log files	File-level backup
Configuration data	Active Directory backup
Windows registry	System-state backup or registry export

It is not necessary to make a backup of the message-tracking log files and/or protocol log files to be able to restore the functionality of the Hub Transport server, but it might be needed for compliance reasons. Message-tracking logs allow you to trace the path a message took, and protocol logs allow you to maintain a history of every message flow that passed a connector on your Exchange servers.

The Hub Transport server role stores all its configuration data in Active Directory. Message queues are not backed up, but they can be mounted on another Hub Transport server if they need to be recovered from a failed Hub Transport server. You can move a queue database (and its associated transaction log files) to any Hub Transport server in the same Exchange organization or in a different Active Directory forest, as long as the target Hub Transport server is installed with the same Exchange 2007 service packs and security updates as the source Exchange server.

Client Access Server Role

The name of the Client Access server role accurately reflects its main function: it provides clients access to their mailboxes using an Internet access protocols like POP3, IMAP4, HTTP, Outlook Anywhere, or Exchange ActiveSync. But the Client Access server role also provides functions for MAPI clients version 2007 and later, as it is responsible for providing Autodiscover services, offering the Offline Address Book for download, and providing the Availability web service for Outlook 2007 and later clients.

Here's a list of clients from which the Client Access server accepts connections:

- Outlook 2003 and later, using Outlook Anywhere
- Outlook 2007 and later, using HTTPs (Autodiscover, Availability web service)

- Internet browsers (like Internet Explorer, Eudora, Netscape) using Outlook Web Access (OWA)
- Mobile devices (PDA) using Exchange ActiveSync
- POP3 and IMAP4 clients

Table 3.5 lists the critical data specific to the Client Access server role, and its available backup methods.

TABLE 3.5 Critical Data Specific to the Exchange 2007 Client Access Server Role

Critical Data	Backup Method
Configuration data	Active Directory backup, Internet Information Services (IIS) metabase backup, and file-system backup
Windows registry	System-state backup or registry export

The Client Access server does not store all of its configuration data in Active Directory like the Mailbox server and Hub Transport server do. You can find configuration data of the Client Access server in Active Directory, in the Internet Information Services (IIS) metabase, and in local configuration files.

The following data is stored locally on the Client Access server:

- Microsoft Office Outlook Web Access site and `Web.config` file
- IMAP4 and POP3 protocol settings

These files should be backed up using a file-level backup.

`Web.config` is an XML file that contains configuration settings for your ASP.NET web applications. Some Outlook Web Access settings need to be configured by making changes to this `web.config` file, such as the number of connections that can be held open.

The following configuration data is stored partly locally on the Client Access server, and partly in the Active Directory configuration partition. The following configuration information should be backed up using an Active Directory backup and a file-level backup:

- Availability web service
- Outlook Web Access virtual directories

The following configuration information is stored in the IIS metabase, and should be backed up using a system-state backup or metabase export of websites:

- Autodiscover
- Web services configuration

Some of the configuration regarding Exchange ActiveSync is stored locally, some is stored in Active Directory, and some is retained in the IIS metabase. Therefore you will need to make a backup of the ActiveSync configuration data by using an Active Directory backup tool, a file-level backup tool, and a system-state backup or metabase export of websites.

If the IIS metabase and Active Directory are not in sync, your Client Access server might start showing errors. Therefore Microsoft recommends keeping a detailed log of all customizations you do after deploying the Client Access server to make sure you can reapply all these changes in case of a recovery.

Unified Messaging Server Role

In short, if you deploy the Unified Messaging server role, you allow your Unified Messaging–enabled users to retrieve voicemail, email, and fax messages in their mailboxes. You can also have your users enabled to call their mailboxes, and have their mail and appointments read to them, or let your users manage their mailboxes using their phone (such as for postponing meetings and sending an email). For more information about Unified Messaging, please refer to Chapter 1, "Designing and Planning Messaging Services," and Chapter 12 "Planning the Exchange Server 2007 Server Role Deployment."

Table 3.6 lists the critical data specific to the Unified Messaging server role, and its available backup methods.

TABLE 3.6 Critical Data Specific to the Exchange 2007 Unified Messaging Server Role

Critical Data	Backup Method
Custom audio prompts	File-level backup
Incoming calls	None
Configuration data	Active Directory backup
Windows registry	System-state backup or registry export

Whenever the Unified Messaging server receives an incoming call, it will be stored in two files. The `.eml` email message file contains the message-routing information, and the `.wav` audio file is the recording of the voice message that was left by the caller. These files are stored locally on the Unified Messaging server until they are delivered to the intended recipient(s). In case of a failure of the Unified Messaging server, these files can be dropped in the Pickup folder on a Hub Transport server and will still be delivered.

Edge Transport Server Role

The Edge Transport server role in Exchange 2007 is responsible for allowing mail flow between your Exchange organization and the Internet, and controlling this mail flow by providing antivirus and antispam protection and the ability to enable transport rules.

Table 3.7 lists the critical data specific to the Edge Transport server role, and its available backup methods.

TABLE 3.7 Critical Data Specific to the Exchange 2007 Edge Transport Server Role

Critical Data	Backup Method
Message queues	None
Message tracking and protocol logs	File-level backup
Configuration data	Active Directory Application Mode (ADAM)
Windows registry	System-state backup or registry export

The Edge Transport server role is deployed as a stand-alone box, and cannot store any of its configuration information in Active Directory. To store its configuration and any replicated recipient and configuration information in Active Directory, the Edge Transport server roles uses ADAM. Whenever you have enabled EdgeSync, you can restore most of the configuration by running the synchronization again. Any customizations can be backed up by exporting the configuration to an XML file using a script (`ExportEdgeConfig.ps1`). The Edge Transport server roles contains queues that cannot be backed up like with the Hub Transport server. In case of a failure, the SMTP queues can be recovered on any other Edge Transport server available, just like with the Hub Transport server role.

Active Directory

As you have already seen in this chapter, Exchange stores most of its configuration data in Active Directory. Therefore it is absolutely necessary to include Active Directory in you Exchange disaster-recovery design.

Microsoft does not prohibit running Exchange 2007 on computers that also function as Windows domain controllers. However, for security and performance reasons Microsoft does not consider this a best practice. Once you have deployed Exchange 2007 on a member server you cannot promote it to a domain controller anymore, nor can you demote a domain controller once Exchange 2007 is installed on a domain controller.

An Active Directory database has three containers: the domain container, the configuration container, and the schema container. As shown in Figures 3.2 through 3.4, Exchange configuration data is stored in all three containers.

FIGURE 3.2 Exchange Information stored in the Active Directory domain partition

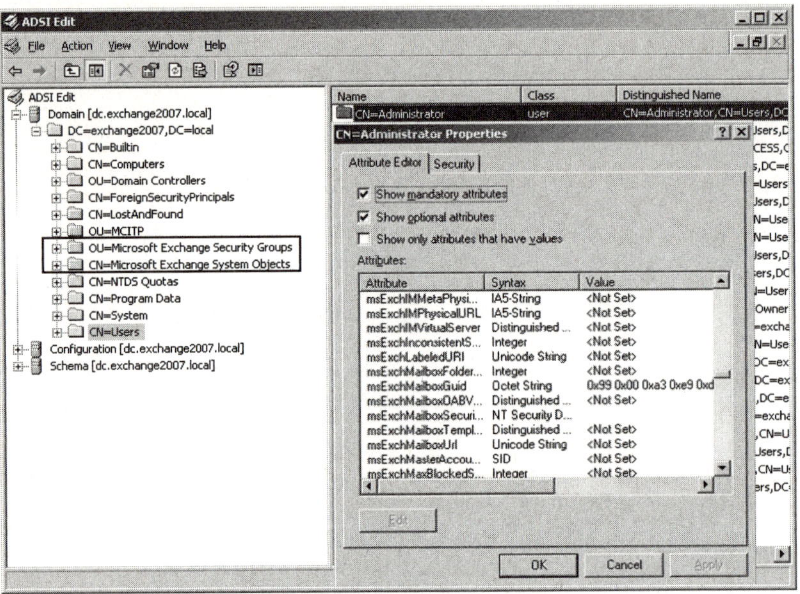

FIGURE 3.3 Exchange Information stored in the Active Directory configuration partition

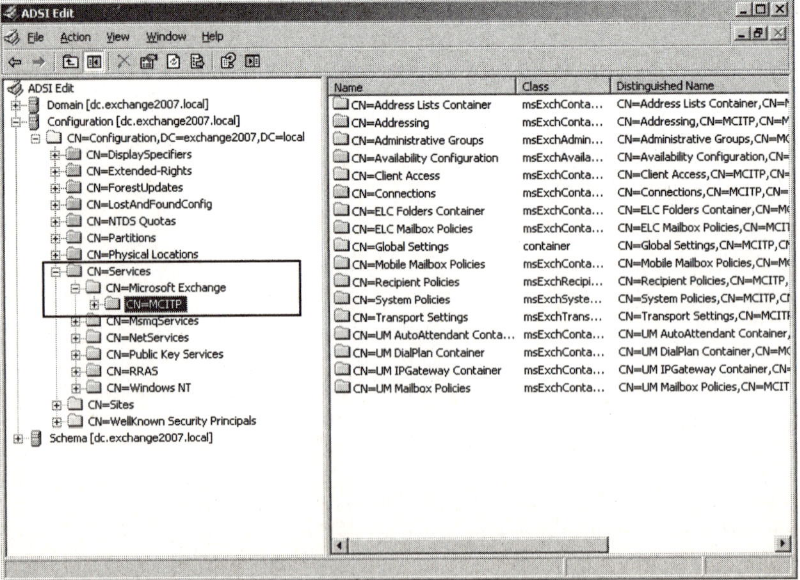

FIGURE 3.4 Exchange Information stored in the Active Directory schema partition

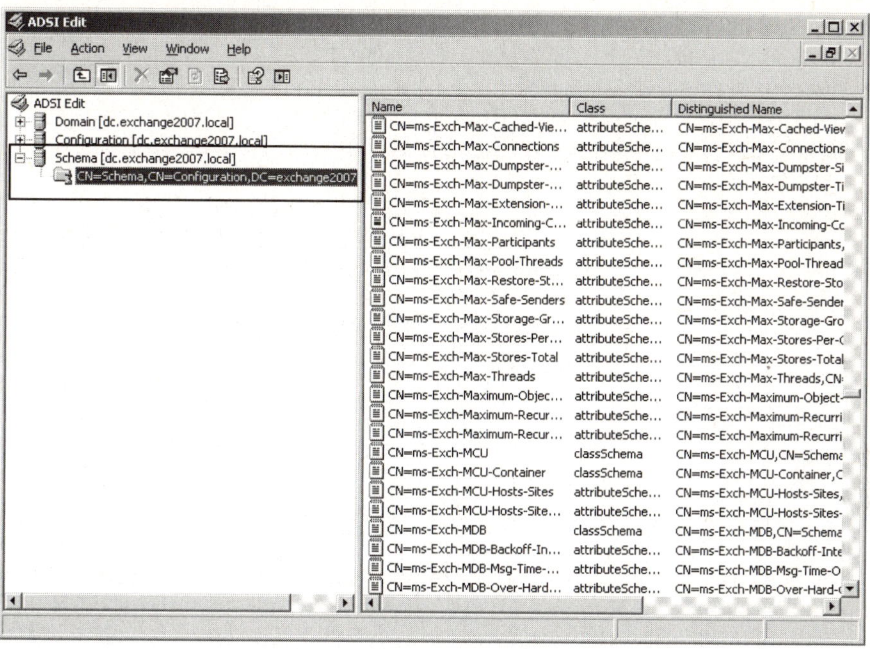

The best way to protect Active Directory is to make it as redundant as possible. You can deploy multiple domain controllers and global catalogs in multiple locations to prevent single points of failures. But deploying multiple domain controllers and global catalogs is not enough; you will need to plan regular backups of your Active Directory database—the so-called *system state*.

Client-Side Data

When it comes to Exchange, it is important to think about disaster-recovery strategies for any data that is stored locally on the client. Table 3.8 lists the most common end-user data types, and the possible backup methods available.

TABLE 3.8 Critical Client-Side Data

Critical Data	Backup Method
Personal-folder files (`.pst` files)	File-level backup
Offline-folder files (`.ost` files)	File-level backup
Outlook customization files	File-level backup
Outlook profile	Registry backup

An .ost file is used to store an offline copy of all the end-user data that exists in a user's mailbox on an Exchange server. The .ost file is created automatically when you run Outlook 2003 or later in Cached Exchange Mode. Since the .ost file is a synchronized copy of the user's mailbox, it can be easily re-created in case of a failure by again synchronizing all the data on the server that is running Exchange.

A personal-folder file is not a copy of a user's mailbox; losing a .pst file frequently means losing data because in most cases the .pst file is the only file that contained a copy of that data.

Microsoft did not enable personal-folder files to be used as a long-term, continuous method of storing messages in an enterprise environment. You should consider other real archiving solutions for achieving this. It is unsupported to use .pst files over a local area network (LAN) or a wide area network (WAN) link.

The maximum size of a .pst file depends of the version of Outlook you are using: Microsoft Office Outlook 2003 and 2007 can support .pst files up to 20 GB, whereas previous versions were limited to 2 GB. The reason for this limit of 2 GB is the format of the PST file being ANSI-code, in Outlook 2003/2007 you have the option to create a PST in UNIcode file format, thereby increasing the limit up to 20 GB.

Be aware that not all .pst files have the limit up to 20 GB; in earlier versions of Outlook, IMAP4 accounts and HTTP accounts use .pst files that do not use the Unicode format. Therefore, the .pst files for IMAP accounts or for HTTP accounts are limited to 2 GB, even when configured in Outlook 2003 or 2007.

Losing a MAPI profile is not a major issue. Your users can easily re-create their MAPI profiles by using the Exchange 2007 Autodiscover service, as long as you have Outlook 2007 (or later) deployed.

Check the documentation of your POP3 and IMAP4 clients to make sure you fully understand how to protect their data.

Restoring Exchange 2007 Storage Groups and Stores

In this part of the chapter you will see Exchange 2007's options for recovering the following:

- A single item
- A single mailbox
- A single database
- A complete server

Recovering a Single Item

In Exchange 2007 the deleted item retention time for mailbox database is by default set to 14 days, as shown in Figure 3.5. This means that if a user deletes an item from his or her mailbox, that item will be available for recovery using Outlook or Outlook Web Access for at least 14 days. If you have checked the box next to Do Not Permanently Delete Items Until The Database Has Been Backed Up, any deleted item will be permanently deleted only if the item has been in the dumpster for 14 days and the item has been backed up by using an Exchange-aware backup program.

FIGURE 3.5 Deleted item retention time

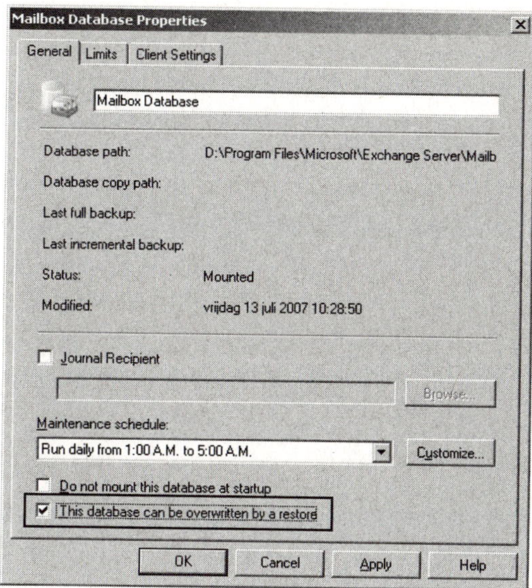

When writing your disaster-recovery plan, keep in mind the following features linked to deleted item retention time:

- Activating deleted item retention time will increase the disk-capacity requirements for your Exchange Mailbox servers.
- As an administrator, you can recover items in the dumpster using the Exchange Management Shell cmdlet `Export-Mailbox`.
- Users can recover their own items in the dumpster by using Outlook or Outlook Web Access.
- If you move a mailbox between stores, items in the dumpster will not be moved.
- Items in the dumpster do not count toward the total size of the mailbox.

Recovering Deleted Items from the Dumpster

Until Outlook 2007, you are not allowed by default to look at the dumpster attached to any folder other than the Deleted Items folder, even though Exchange keeps the deleted items in the dumpster. To enable the Recover Deleted Items command on all your folders, simply close Outlook, open the registry, and add one `DWORD Value`:

```
Location=HKEY_LOCAL_MACHINE/Software/Microsoft/Exchange/Client/Options
DWORD Value= DumpsterAlwaysOn
Value = 1
```

Restart Outlook and you will be able to use Recover Deleted Items on every folder. Depending on the version of Outlook, you may be able to recover more. In Outlook 2007 the option to recover deleted items is enabled by default for all folders and items.

- If you need to recover an item for which the deleted item retention time has passed, you need to use another recovery strategy, such as the recovery storage group or a recovery server (as described later in this chapter).
- Deleted item retention time can be configured per database and can be set per user, as in Figure 3.6. If a user does not follow the database defaults, the user's setting takes precedence!

FIGURE 3.6 Deleted item retention time user settings

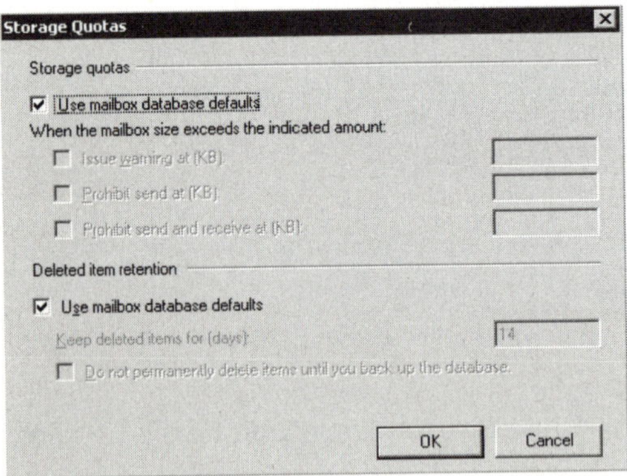

Recovering a Single Mailbox

In Exchange 2007 the deleted item retention time for a mailbox database is by default set to 30 days, as shown in Figure 3.7. This means that if a mailbox is deleted, or if a mailbox-enabled user is deleted, that the mailbox is not purged from the Exchange database but instead it will be marked for deletion and will be deleted from the database only when the deleted mailbox retention time has passed. If you have checked the box next to Do Not Permanently Delete Items Until The Database Has Been Backed Up, any deleted mailbox will be permanently deleted only if the deleted mailbox has been backed up by using an Exchange-aware backup program.

FIGURE 3.7 Deleted mailbox retention time

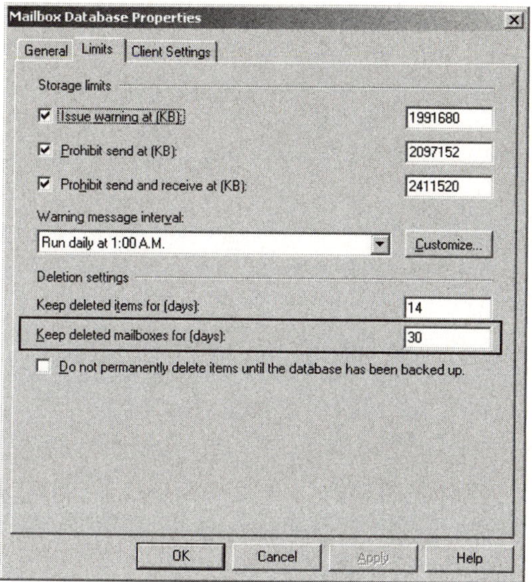

Restoring a Single Database

If your production database is corrupt and you don't have LCR or CCR enabled, you will need to restore a backup to get your database back online. A few requirements have to be met to make sure that your restore will be successful:

- The information store service needs to be running.
- The database that you are recovering needs to be dismounted.
- The database you are recovering needs to be marked as available for restore, as can be seen in Figure 3.8.

If you are restoring an offline backup, you just need to restore the `.edb` database file. If you are restoring an online backup, you will have to restore both the `.edb` database file and the log files that contain uncommitted entries at the time of backup. When the exchange-aware backup program restores the online backup of Exchange, the current database file will be overwritten by the backed-up `.edb` database file. During the restore, Exchange will also restore the required log files to a temporary location, including a file called `restore.env`. This `restore.env` contains a list of log files that are required to successfully perform a hard recovery against your database. When the restore has finished, Exchange will process the uncommitted entries in the restored log files against the restored database file, and bring the database back in a consistent state. When the database is mounted at that stage, all logs created after the backup will be replayed against the database, thereby bringing the database to the last consistent state prior to failure.

FIGURE 3.8 Allowing database restore

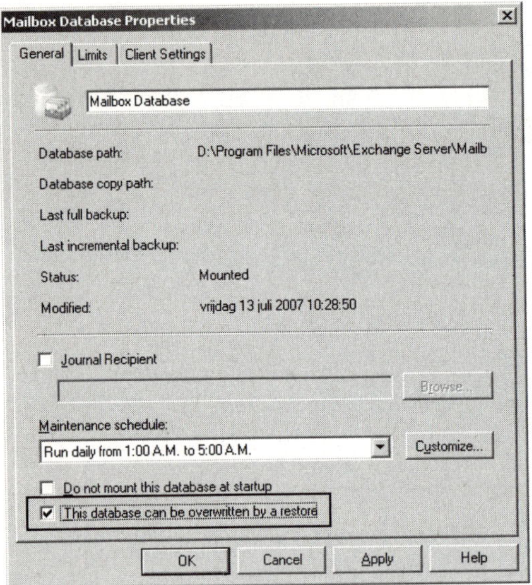

If circular logging is enabled for the storage group to which the database file belongs, the database will be restored to the state of the last full backup.

Recovering a Mailbox Database via Database Portability

Exchange 2007 introduces a new feature called *database portability*. It enables you as an administrator to restore an online or offline backup of an Exchange database to a database created on any Exchange server in the Exchange organization.

Database portability is offered only on mailbox databases. Public-folder databases are not portable.

If truth be told, database portability is not really a new feature in Exchange 2007—both Exchange 2000 and 2003 allowed you to restore a backup to a database created on another exchange server in the same Exchange organization and administrative group, but it was quite an administrative strain to get this up and running. In Exchange 2000/2003, users in your Active Directory would still refer to the old Exchange server name if you restored this way; you would have to change those references manually or use a script to reflect the new server name. In addition, your users would have to update their Outlook profiles to connect to the new server.

In Exchange 2007 it is much easier due to the introduction of the `move-mailbox -configurationonly` Exchange Management Shell cmdlet, which will change the information for the users in the Active Directory domain partition so that the account points to the mailbox on the new Mailbox server. After Active Directory replication has completed, all users will have access to their mailboxes on the new Exchange server. Users will need to make changes to their Outlook profile, though, unless you have Outlook 2007 and later clients that can take advantage of the Autodiscover service.

Exercise 3.1 outlines the steps for using database portability.

EXERCISE 3.1

A Detailed Overview of Database Portability

Imagine user Ilse, who has a mailbox on server EX2007 in database Mailbox Database, storage group First Storage Group. This situation is shown in the Exchange Management console and Exchange Management Shell images here.

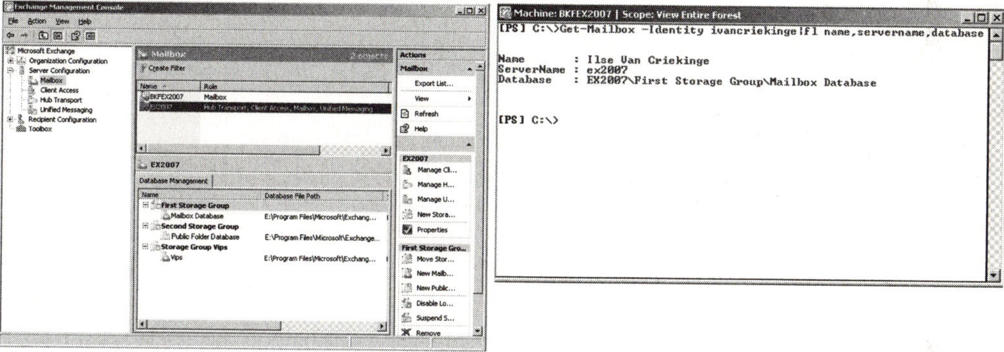

Disaster strikes! Exchange server EX2007 fails, and you decide to recover the database Mailbox Database on another server in your organization, called BKFEX2007. Here's how.

1. As shown here, you restore an Exchange-aware online backup you took previously from the production database, and mount the database.

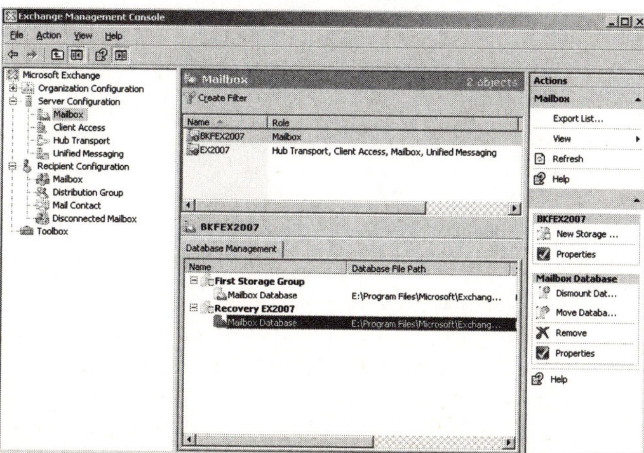

EXERCISE 3.1

2. You still need to modify the user account(s) settings so that the account points to the mailbox on the new Mailbox server. You can make this modification by using an Exchange Management Shell cmdlet, as shown in the following images.

   Here's what the Settings mailbox looks like before you move its configuration.

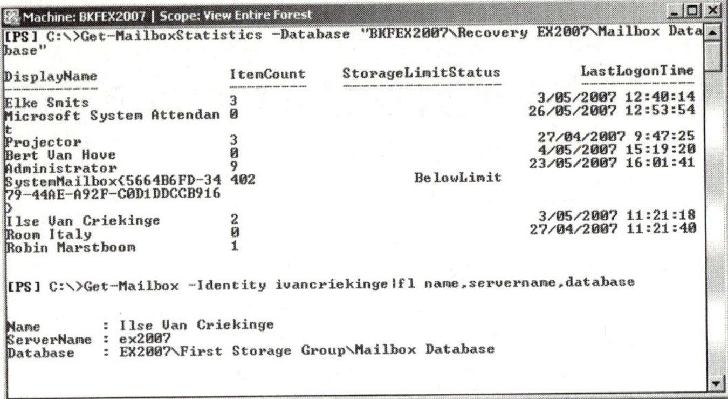

```
Machine: BKFEX2007 | Scope: View Entire Forest
[PS] C:\>Get-MailboxStatistics -Database "BKFEX2007\Recovery EX2007\Mailbox Data
base"

DisplayName                 ItemCount    StorageLimitStatus        LastLogonTime
-----------                 ---------    ------------------        -------------
Elke Smits                  3                                   3/05/2007 12:40:14
Microsoft System Attendan   0                                  26/05/2007 12:53:54
t
Projector                   3                                  27/04/2007 9:47:25
Bert Van Hove               0                                   4/05/2007 15:19:20
Administrator               9                                  23/05/2007 16:01:41
SystemMailbox{5664B6FD-34   402                BelowLimit
79-44AE-A92F-C0D1DDCCB916
}
Ilse Van Criekinge          2                                   3/05/2007 11:21:18
Room Italy                  0                                  27/04/2007 11:21:40
Robin Marstboom             1

[PS] C:\>Get-Mailbox -Identity ivancriekinge|fl name,servername,database

Name       : Ilse Van Criekinge
ServerName : ex2007
Database   : EX2007\First Storage Group\Mailbox Database
```

   Here is the Usage Management Shell to move only the mailbox configuration.

```
Machine: BKFEX2007 | Scope: View Entire Forest
[PS] C:\>Get-Mailbox -Identity ivancriekinge|fl name,servername,database

Name       : Ilse Van Criekinge
ServerName : ex2007
Database   : EX2007\First Storage Group\Mailbox Database

[PS] C:\>Move-Mailbox -ConfigurationOnly -TargetDatabase "BKFEX2007\Recovery EX2
007\Mailbox Database" -Identity ivancriekinge

Confirm
Are you sure you want to perform this action?
Moving mailbox: Ilse Van Criekinge (ivancriekinge@proexchange.local) to
database: BKFEX2007\Recovery EX2007\Mailbox Database. This operation will only
modify the mailbox's Active Directory configuration. Mailbox content can be
potentially lost, and this mailbox will be inaccessible until the changes are
completed.
[Y] Yes  [A] Yes to All  [N] No  [L] No to All  [S] Suspend  [?] Help
(default is "Y"):y
```

   Finally, the settings mailbox after you've moved its configuration.

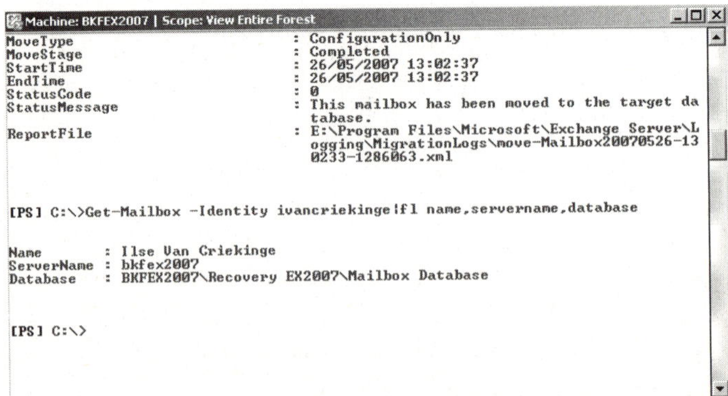

```
Machine: BKFEX2007 | Scope: View Entire Forest
MoveType                          : ConfigurationOnly
MoveStage                         : Completed
StartTime                         : 26/05/2007 13:02:37
EndTime                           : 26/05/2007 13:02:37
StatusCode                        : 0
StatusMessage                     : This mailbox has been moved to the target da
                                    tabase.
ReportFile                        : E:\Program Files\Microsoft\Exchange Server\L
                                    ogging\MigrationLogs\move-Mailbox20070526-13
                                    0233-1286063.xml

[PS] C:\>Get-Mailbox -Identity ivancriekinge|fl name,servername,database

Name       : Ilse Van Criekinge
ServerName : bkfex2007
Database   : BKFEX2007\Recovery EX2007\Mailbox Database

[PS] C:\>
```

EXERCISE 3.1

3. Once active directory replication has completed, Ilse will be able to access her mailbox on the new Exchange server. Moving her mailbox will be transparent to Office Outlook 2007 clients if you have enabled Autodiscover. But for older clients, the reconfiguration of the clients has to be done manually.

Recovering Items via the Recovery Storage Group

Introduced in Exchange 2003, the Recovery Storage Group feature has been enhanced in Exchange 2007. The recovery storage group is a storage group that allows you as an administrator to mount a second copy of an Exchange mailbox database to recover deleted items and mailboxes. The recovery storage group is most commonly used when you need to recover an item when the item isn't stored in the dumpster anymore.

To restore one item or one mailbox, you can also use a brick-level recovery. Microsoft does not provide brick-level backup tools for Exchange Server 2007, so you will need to use third-party tools to enable brick-level backup. Brick-level backups are not designed to protect an Exchange server, but rather to protect one mailbox at a time. It is therefore not an alternative to an Exchange-aware database backup/restore.

Differences between a Recovery Storage Group and a Normal Storage Group

A *recovery storage group* is a special kind of storage group, and there are a few important differences between it and a normal storage group:

- You can create only one recovery storage group per Exchange server, as opposed to 50 normal storage groups on an Exchange Enterprise Edition server or 5 normal storage groups when using an Exchange Standard Edition server.
- You can restore a database to a recovery storage group, but you cannot make an Exchange-aware backup of an Exchange database that belongs to a recovery storage group.
- You cannot change any database path or log-file path for a recovery storage group.
- You cannot set the databases in a recovery storage group to mount when the information store starts. You will have to mount them manually every time the information store service starts.
- Even though MAPI is the only supported protocol to gain access to mailboxes in the recovery storage group, you cannot gain access to a mailbox in the recovery storage group by using Outlook or Outlook Web Access.
- You cannot connect a mailbox in a recovery storage group to a user.
- Online maintenance is not run against a database file in the recovery storage group.
- System- and mailbox-management policies are not applied to a database file in the recovery storage group.

Limitations and of the Recovery Storage Group

You cannot use the recovery storage group to recover the following:

- Public folders
- Entire servers

Additionally, you cannot use the recovery storage group to recover multiple databases at the same time if they don't belong to the same storage group in production.

However, a recovery storage group allows you to restore a database, and then you can extract the data from the deleted mailbox and copy it to a target folder or mailbox in the original production database. You can copy the mail to any mailbox in the Exchange organization! It is possible to restore a VSS backup to a recovery storage group, which wasn't possible in Exchange 2003!

Administering the Recovery Storage Group

To manage the recovery storage group you can use the Exchange Management Shell, as shown in Figure 3.9, or you can use the Database Recovery Management tool.

The recovery storage group is not visible in the Exchange Management Console.

FIGURE 3.9 The recovery storage group is manageable only by using the Exchange Management Shell

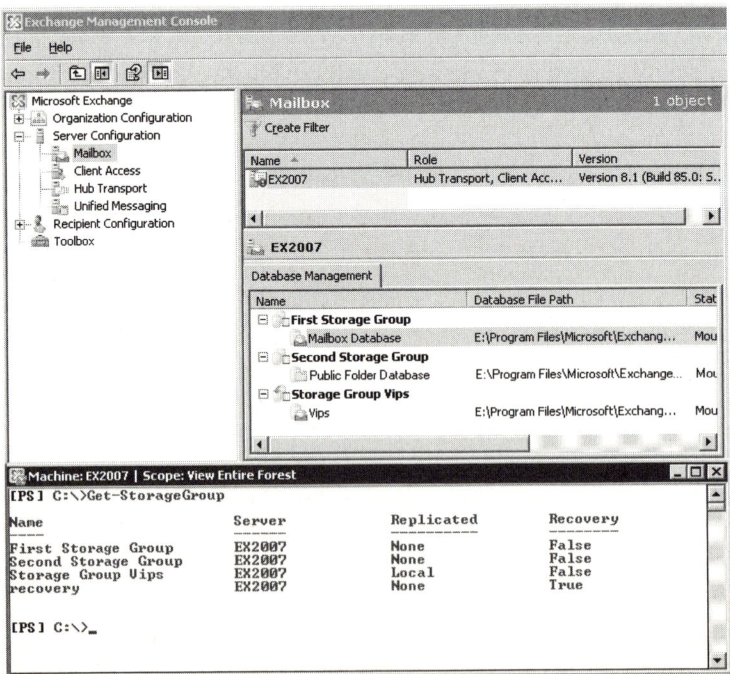

The Database Recovery Management tool provides best practices and a wizard to manage the recovery using a recovery storage group. Together with the Database Troubleshooter tools you will be able to reduce recovery time and streamline the recovery process after database problems happen on production servers that are running Microsoft Exchange. You can find them in the Exchange Management Console in the Toolbox section, as shown in Figures 3.10 and 3.11.

FIGURE 3.10 The Database Recovery Management tool

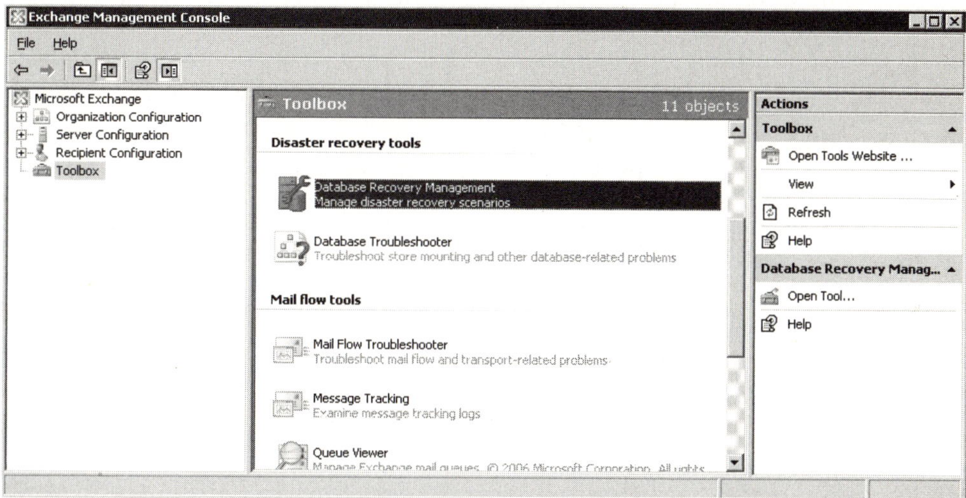

If you have created a recovery storage group, every Exchange-aware backup program will restore to the recovery storage group. It is therefore best practice to remove the recovery storage group and all its files as soon as the recovery has completed successfully.

Restoring Mail Service via Dial-Tone Recovery

Introduced in Exchange 2003, *dial-tone recovery* (also referred to as *messaging dial-tone recovery*) has been enhanced in Exchange 2007. A dial-tone recovery is the process of restoring mail service immediately by giving users access to a brand-new mailbox. If you need to enable users to send and receive email as soon as possible after the failure of a database or a server, you should include dial-tone recovery in your disaster-recovery plan! After enabling dial-tone access for the user mailboxes, you will restore the failed database to the same server or to an alternate server. After restoring the database, you just need to merge the data from the production database with the data in the dial-tone database. Table 3.9 lists the possible dial-tone setups you can use.

FIGURE 3.11 The Microsoft Exchange Troubleshooting Assistant

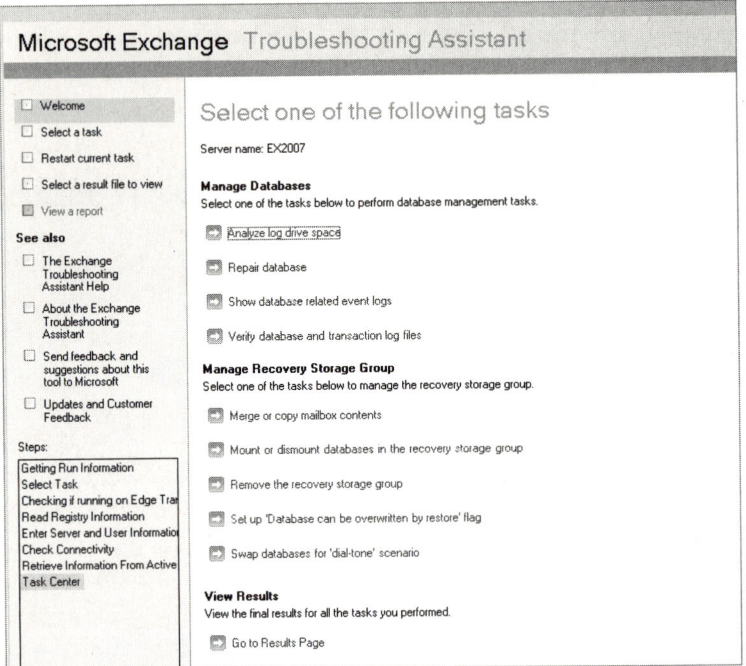

TABLE 3.9 Possible Dial-Tone Setups

Location Dial-Tone Database	Restore Production Database To	User Profile Needs Reconfiguration?
Original database	Recovery storage group	No
Original database	Alternate server	No
Alternate server	Original database	Yes
Alternate server	Recovery storage group	Yes
Alternate server	Alternate server	Yes

The Exchange Server Database Recovery Management tool includes a wizard that will help you merge the dial-tone database with the production database after the production database has been restored and put back into production. For every other dial-tone strategy you will need to use the Exchange Management Shell.

Exercise 3.2 outlines the steps for using dial-tone recovery.

EXERCISE 3.2

Detailed Overview of Dial-Tone Recovery

Let's have a closer look at the dial-tone procedure that the Exchange Server Database Recovery Management tool allows you to do using wizards.

Imagine that you have an Exchange 2007 server, EX2007, with a few storage groups, as shown here. You have a user named Ilse, with a mailbox in the mailbox database (first storage group).

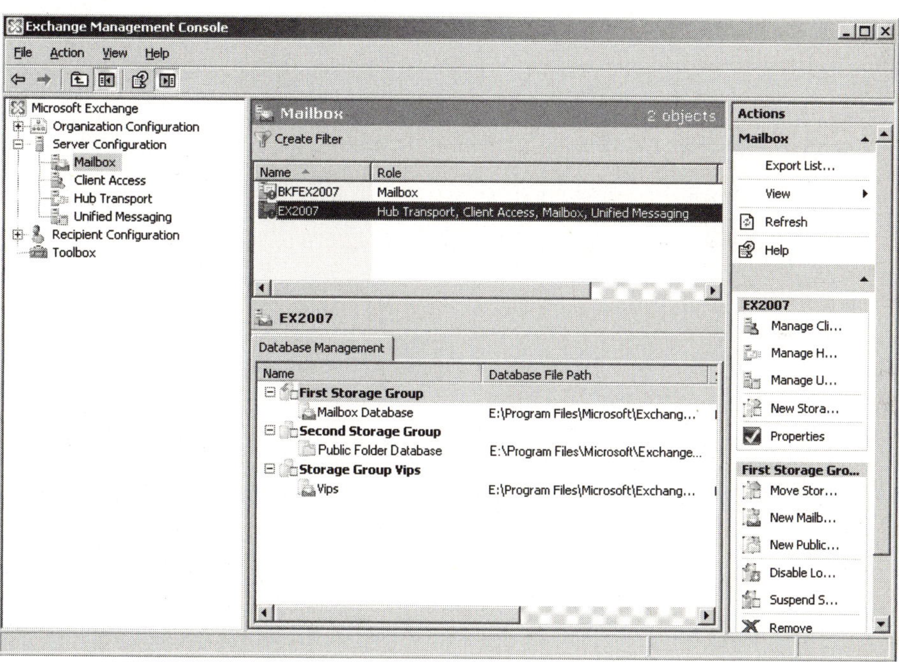

EXERCISE 3.2 ***(continued)***

Disaster strikes! One moment, the Exchange Server mailbox database doesn't mount anymore, as shown here.

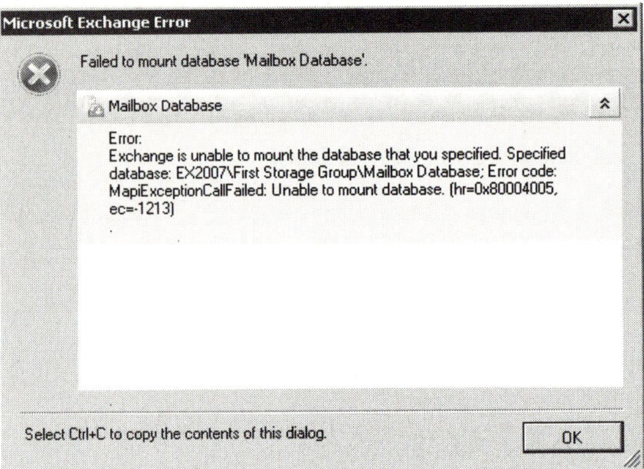

If you move the faulty database file to a new location and you mount the database, Exchange will ask you if you want to create a new (dial tone) database, as shown here.

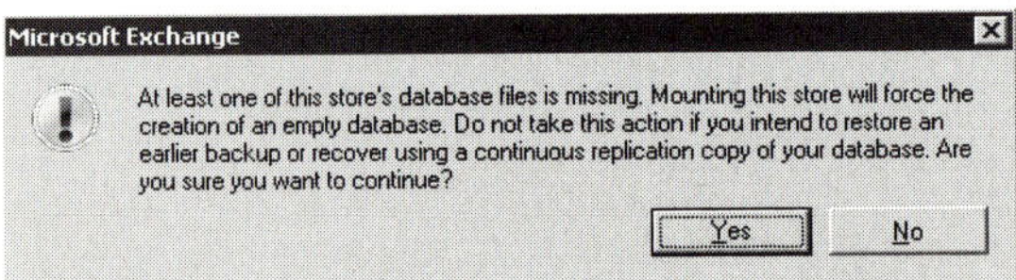

If your users use Outlook 2003 or later in cached mode, they will get a warning message when they launch Outlook, as you can see here.

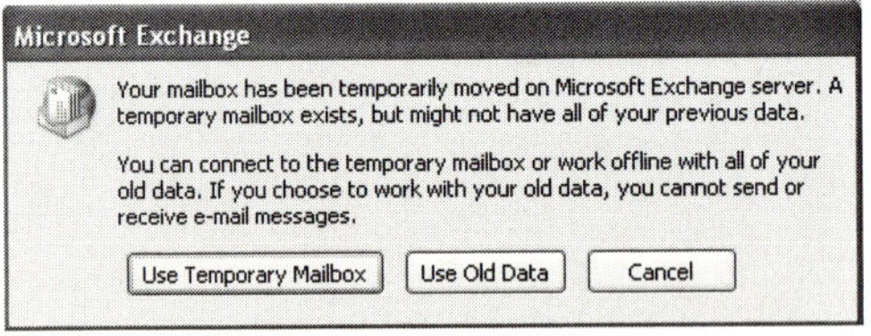

EXERCISE 3.2 *(continued)*

If a user chooses to connect to their temporary mailbox, they will open their mailbox in the dial-tone database. The user will be able to send and receive mail! If a user chooses to use Old Data, the user will connect to their `.ost` file and will be able to browse all items in their mailbox. Outlook needs to be restarted to switch between the temporary mailbox and old data.

Now your users can work; you can continue to restore the production database to the recovery storage group:

1. Restore the database.

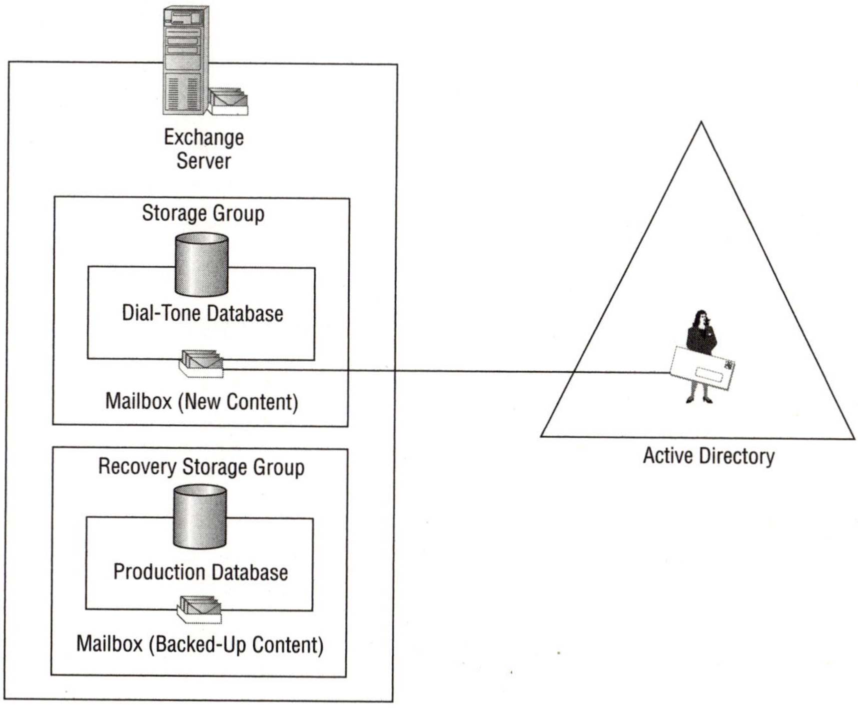

EXERCISE 3.2 *(continued)*

2. Swap the dial-tone database with the restored database.

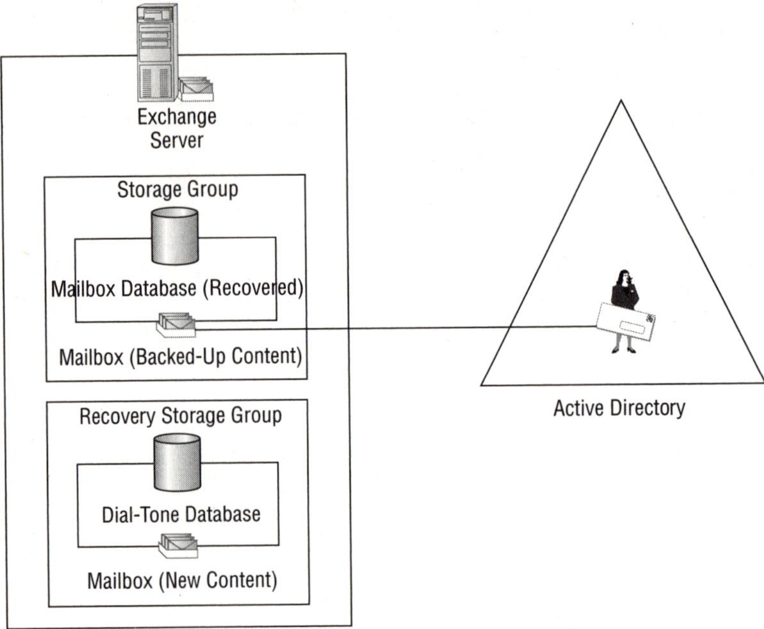

3. Merge the few messages between the dial tone database and the production database.

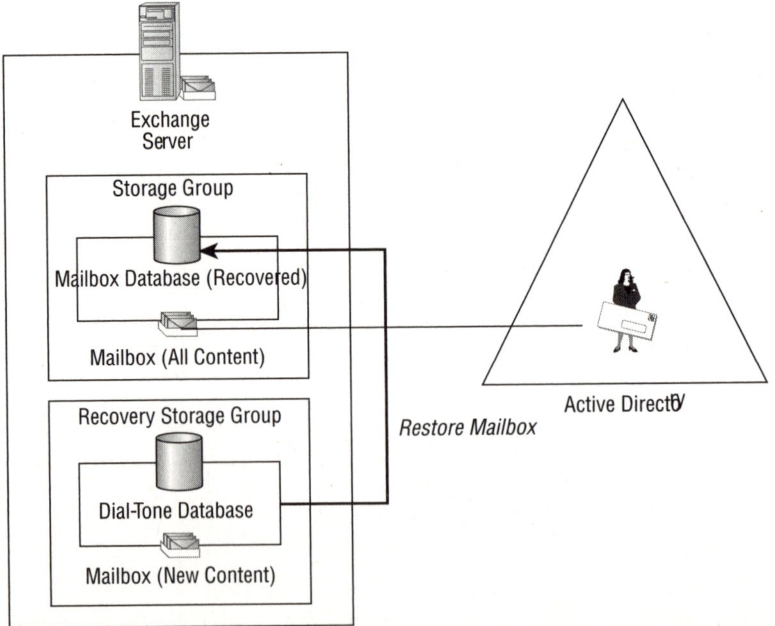

Recovering a Complete Server

Sometimes it will be necessary to restore an entire Exchange server—for example, when faulty hardware causes you server to crash. The procedures to restore your Exchange servers will depend on the server's configuration. You have three options for server recovery:

- Restore the server
- Rebuild the server
- Recover the server functionality on another server

Let's have a look at all three options and what they require and offer in return.

Restore the Server

When you choose to restore your server from backup, you can be sure that everything will match the Exchange server as it was prior to the failure. But in order to take this route, you need the following:

- A full server backup.
- A system-state backup.
- Replacement hardware that is very similar to the failed server. Even though Windows 2003 is pretty nifty when it comes to detecting plug-and-play devices, you will not be able to restore a server to a new server that requires a different hardware abstraction layer.

In addition to these requirements, you have to make sure that the Exchange Server computer account still exists in Active Directory!

Rebuild the Server

This option implies that you will install a new machine with the same name, but hardware may differ. And then you will install Exchange Server 2007 in the so-called Recover Server Mode. During installation Exchange will have a look at Active Directory to get a grip on its required configuration. The biggest requirement to have a successful installation of exchange in Recover Server Mode is, therefore, that the server information be available in Active Directory.

If you are able to complete the Recover Server Mode installation, you will still need to do the following:

- For the Mailbox server role, restore all storage groups and databases.
- For the Client Access server role, reapply all customizations.
- For the Unified Messaging server role, restore any customizations (if the Unified Messaging server is the prompt publishing point server you will need to restore the custom audio prompts).

You could also use the Recover Server Mode installation to migrate a Client Access server, Hub Transport server, Unified Messaging server, or a nonclustered Mailbox server to new hardware.

You cannot use the Recover Server Mode installation in the following situations:

- To rebuild the Edge Transport server
- To repair a failed installation
- To modify the Exchange Server roles installed on a computer
- To restore clustered Mailbox servers

As with all previous versions of Exchange, you cannot use the Recover Server Mode installation to restore a clustered Mailbox server to a stand-alone exchange Mailbox server, or vice versa.

To restore clustered Mailbox servers, you have to use the `ExSetup /RecoverCMS` command after you have installed Exchange Server 2007 on the cluster's passive node.

Recover the Server Functionality on Another Server

As already stated in this chapter, the best way to prevent loss of functionality for the non-Mailbox server roles is to deploy multiple servers with the Client Access server role, Hub Transport server role, Unified Messaging server role, and Edge Transport server role. In case of a server failure, you can deploy a new Exchange server and make the necessary changes to use the new server rather than the failed server.

To recover the Mailbox server role on another server, you will need to deploy a new Exchange 2007 Mailbox server in your organization and restore the storage groups and stores to that server. You will also need to make some changes in Active Directory to make sure users know they need to connect to the new server. (Refer to the "Recovering a Mailbox Database via Database Portability" section earlier in this chapter for detailed information.)

Repairing Messaging Databases

You should repair a database only when it is not feasible to restore it from backup or when you do not have a passive-copy or replica of the database. Exchange Server 2007 provides you with two tools for repairing an Exchange database: `ESEUTIL.EXE` and `ISINTEG.EXE`.

If you have to use `ESEUTIL.EXE` and `ISINTEG.EXE` to fix database corruption, you should contact Microsoft Product Support Services for assistance.

`ESEUTIL` is a command-line tool that can be used to inspect, defragment, and repair a private- or public-folder database in Exchange Server 2003. `ISINTEG` is another command-line tool that can check and repair information and relationships between mailboxes, folders, items, and attachments in an Exchange database (private or public).

Figure 3.12 shows the options available for using `ESEUTIL.EXE`, and Figure 3.13 shows those for `ISINTEG.EXE`.

FIGURE 3.12 Modes of operation for ESEUTIL.EXE

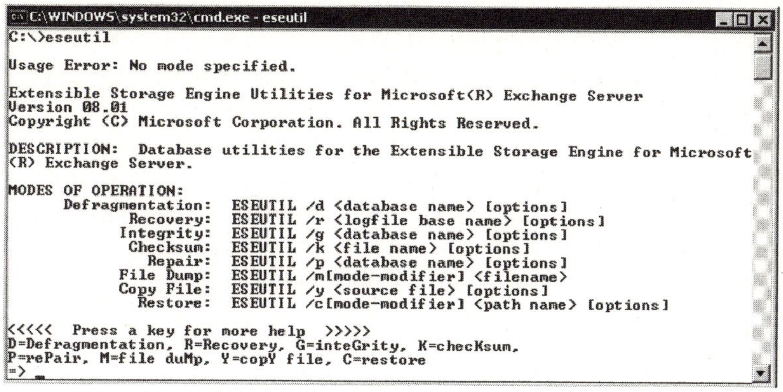

```
C:\WINDOWS\system32\cmd.exe - eseutil
C:\>eseutil

Usage Error: No mode specified.

Extensible Storage Engine Utilities for Microsoft(R) Exchange Server
Version 08.01
Copyright (C) Microsoft Corporation. All Rights Reserved.

DESCRIPTION:  Database utilities for the Extensible Storage Engine for Microsoft
(R) Exchange Server.

MODES OF OPERATION:
      Defragmentation:  ESEUTIL /d <database name> [options]
             Recovery:  ESEUTIL /r <logfile base name> [options]
            Integrity:  ESEUTIL /g <database name> [options]
             Checksum:  ESEUTIL /k <file name> [options]
               Repair:  ESEUTIL /p <database name> [options]
            File Dump:  ESEUTIL /m[mode-modifier] <filename>
            Copy File:  ESEUTIL /y <source file> [options]
              Restore:  ESEUTIL /c[mode-modifier] <path name> [options]

<<<<<  Press a key for more help  >>>>>
D=Defragmentation, R=Recovery, G=inteGrity, K=checKsum,
P=rePair, M=file duMp, Y=copY file, C=restore
=> _
```

FIGURE 3.13 Modes of operation for ISINTEG.EXE

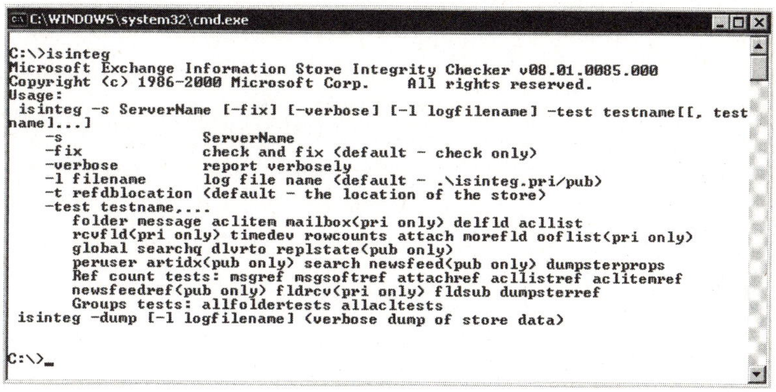

```
C:\WINDOWS\system32\cmd.exe

C:\>isinteg
Microsoft Exchange Information Store Integrity Checker v08.01.0085.000
Copyright (c) 1986-2000 Microsoft Corp.    All rights reserved.
Usage:
 isinteg -s ServerName [-fix] [-verbose] [-l logfilename] -test testname[[, test
name]...]
    -s                ServerName
    -fix              check and fix (default - check only)
    -verbose          report verbosely
    -l filename       log file name (default - .\isinteg.pri/pub)
    -t refdblocation  (default - the location of the store)
    -test testname,...
       folder message aclitem mailbox(pri only) delfld acllist
       rcvfld(pri only) timedev rowcounts attach morefld ooflist(pri only)
       global searchq dlvrto replstate(pub only)
       peruser artidx(pub only) search newsfeed(pub only) dumpsterprops
       Ref count tests: msgref msgsoftref attachref acllistref aclitemref
       newsfeedref(pub only) fldrcv(pri only) fldsub dumpsterref
       Groups tests: allfoldertests allacltests
 isinteg -dump [-l logfilename] (verbose dump of store data)

C:\>_
```

High Availability Public Folders

Public folders are de-emphasized in Exchange 2007, but you can still create them in a pure Exchange 2007 environment! As in previous versions of Exchange, the best way to provide redundancy for your public folders is to replicate them to another public-folder store in your Exchange 2007 environment.

But remember—it is not possible to use LCR or CCR against a public-folder store if there are more Mailbox servers in your Exchange environment that home the public folder hierarchy!

To recover a deleted public folder or deleted public-folder content, you can use the following options:

- Deleted item retention time
- LCR or CCR
- Recovery server

Exchange 2007 does not support the following:

- Using LCR or CCR against a public-folder store if there are more Mailbox servers in your exchange environment that home the public folder hierarchy.
- Recovering public folders by using the recovery storage group.
- Using database portability; public-folder databases are not portable.

Using a recovery server is the next best thing to using deleted item retention time which is the best option to recover a Public Folder or a Public Folder item. Replication doesn't really help in case of deletion, because if you restore a public folder from backup, the deletion will occur again due to replication!

Figure 3.14 shows the process for recovering public-folder databases using a recovery server.

FIGURE 3.14 Recovering public folders

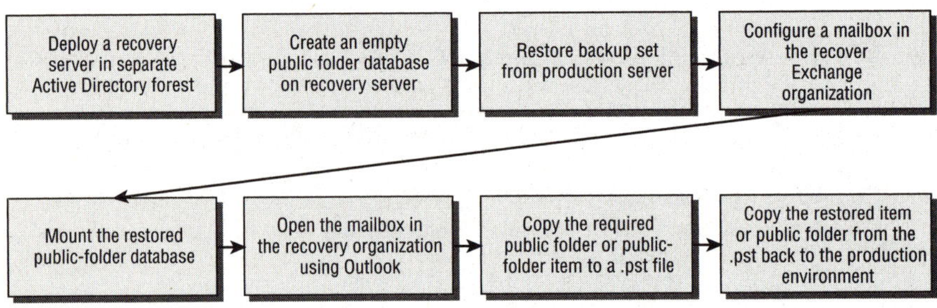

Evaluating Existing Business Requirements to Define Supporting Infrastructure

When creating a disaster-recovery plan, you need to outline the business requirements that your messaging environment must meet. In other words, you have to design your infrastructure to be able to guarantee the promised level of availability as specified in your Service Level Agreement.

Table 3.10 lists the most common business requirements and the options for meeting them.

TABLE 3.10 Common Business Requirements and Options for Meeting Them

Business Requirement	Option
If one Exchange server fails, users still have to be able to access their mailbox and be able to send and receive mail.	Deploy CCR. Deploy single-copy clustering (SCC). Deploy multiple Client Access and Hub Exchange servers in the same site.
If an Exchange mailbox database is lost due to corruption, users should still be able to access their mailboxes.	Deploy CCR. Deploy LCR.
If an Exchange mailbox database is lost due to corruption, you should be able to recover the database as it was at the time of the last full backup.	Deploy circular logging for the storage group to which the database belongs.
If a geographical location is hit by disaster, you should be able to recover all mail services without restoring backup files.	Deploy geographically dispersed clustering with CCR.
If an Exchange mailbox database is lost due to corruption, users should still be able to access their mailboxes without administrator intervention.	Deploy CCR. Deploy SCC.
If an Exchange mailbox database is lost due to corruption, you should be able to restore the database and allow recovery until the point of failure.	Schedule backups. Do not enable circular logging for the storage to which the database belongs.
You want to make a normal backup once a week, and all other days you just want to back up the changes. If you need to restore, you just want to restore your normal backup and one additional backup to get back online.	Schedule a normal backup once a week. Schedule a differential backup on all other days.

Do not forget to test your backups, and do not forget to test your disaster-recovery plan!

Designing and Recommending Strategies for Dependent Services that Impact High Availability

Creating a disaster-recovery plan for your messaging environment involves more than just your Exchange servers themselves. You have to include a disaster-recovery plan for all dependent services that have to be up and running to provide a fully functional messaging environment.

If you use the following dependent services in Exchange Server 2007, be sure to include them in your disaster-recovery plan:

- Active Directory directory service
- Certificates
- Domain Name Service (DNS)
- Exchange Server hardware
- Firewall
- Data center infrastructure
- Network topology
- Supporting software (antispam, antivirus, fax, etc.)

Designing high availability and disaster recovery of these dependent services is beyond the scope of this book, but remember that you have to include them when you are writing your disaster-recovery plan for Exchange.

Summary

This chapter covered disaster recovery, backup, and restore. Let's have a look at all the potential risks we discussed in this chapter, along with the options we talked about to mitigate those risks. Table 3.11 lists potential risks and mitigation options.

TABLE 3.11 Risk-Mitigation Options in Exchange Server 2007

Risk	Risk Mitigation Strategy
Loss of a single message	Deleted item retention time. Recovery storage group.
Loss of a single mailbox	Deleted mailbox retention time. Recovery storage group.

TABLE 3.11 Risk-Mitigation Options in Exchange Server 2007 *(continued)*

Risk	Risk Mitigation Strategy
Loss of a mailbox database	Implement LCR or CCR. Exchange-aware backup/restore. Recovery storage group and database portability.
Loss of a public-folder database	Replication. Implement LCR or CCR if possible. Recovery server.
Loss of a storage group	Implement LCR or CCR. Exchange-aware backup/restore.
Loss of an Exchange Mailbox server	Implement CCR or SCC. Exchange-aware backup/restore. Exchange Recovery mode setup.
Loss of an Exchange Hub Transport server	Implement redundancy by deploying multiple Hub Transport servers. Backup/restore. Exchange Recovery Mode setup.
Loss of an Exchange Client Access server	Implement redundancy by deploying multiple Client Access servers. Backup/restore. Exchange Recovery Mode setup.
Loss of an Exchange Unified Messaging server	Implement redundancy by deploying multiple Unified Messaging servers. Backup/restore. Exchange Recovery Mode setup.
Loss of an Exchange Edge Transport server	Implement redundancy by deploying multiple Edge Transport servers. Backup/restore. Use `ExportEdgeConfig` to back up Edge configuration.
Loss of a supporting service (DNS, Active Directory)	Implement redundancy by deploying multiple DNS servers, domain controllers, and global catalogs. Create an Active Directory disaster-recovery plan.

It is important that you have a clear understanding of all business requirements that are set for your messaging environment so you can implement the necessary backup and restore procedures to meet those requirements. We have gone through the most common business requirements and what you can do to satisfy them. Last but not least, we have covered the importance of including all the dependent services in your disaster-recovery setup guide.

Exam Essentials

Understand the difference between recovering a Mailbox server role and the other Exchange server roles. Know that for the Exchange Server 2007 Mailbox server role, Hub Transport server role, Client Access server role, and Unified Messaging server role the configuration is almost completely stored in Active Directory. For the Edge Transport server role, know that you can only make a backup using the built-in scripts. In addition, you will get questions on the Exchange-aware backup methods that exist for Exchange Server 2007 database files. Make sure you know the different types that exist to make a backup, and that there are different methods to restore database functionality.

Evaluate existing business requirements to define supporting infrastructure. Make sure you know the pros and cons for every recovery strategy that is possible with Exchange 2007. If your organization requires you only to be able to recover until the point of the last full backup, you can enable circular logging for every storage group. If, on the other hand, your business requires that the failure of any Exchange server in your organization should not impact any user, you have to think about deploying CCR or SCC.

Design and recommend a strategy for dependent services that impact high availability. Many times on the exam you will get questions about Active Directory! Make sure you know that your exchange server is useless if there are no Global Catalogs available! Make sure that you know that you also need to keep track of the disaster-recovery requirements for any supporting software for Exchange (like anti-spam, anti-virus, etc.)

Review Questions

1. You are an Exchange administrator responsible for 750 mailboxes. Your Exchange organization contains three Exchange Server 2007 boxes: the first one holds the CCR Mailbox server role (EX1), the second one holds the Hub Transport server role (EX2), and the third one has the Client Access server role installed (EX3). Your users complain that they are unable to send and receive mail when EX2 is down. You need to make changes to your current messaging environment so that the failure of one Exchange server does not mean your users won't be able to send and receive mail. You are not allowed to buy additional hardware. What option can you choose?

   A. Deploy the Hub Transport server role on the Client Access server.

   B. Deploy the Hub Transport server role on the Mailbox server.

   C. Deploy a new Hub Transport server in the organization.

   D. Deploy the Client Access server role on the Hub Transport server.

2. You are an Exchange administrator responsible for an Exchange 2007 organization, Bubbels. The organization has five exchange servers deployed, the following table shows. Users can use Outlook Anywhere and Outlook Web Access to gain access to their mailboxes from outside the organization. Users complain that Outlook Web Access and Outlook Anywhere are unreachable. Further investigation reveals that EX3 is down. What should you do to make sure the crash of one Exchange server doesn't interrupt Outlook Anywhere and Outlook Web Access?

Server Name	Role
EX1	Mailbox server
EX2	Client Access server
EX3	Client Access server
EX4	Hub Transport server
EX5	Hub Transport server

   A. Configure round-robin for EX2 and EX3.

   B. Configure round-robin for EX4 and EX5.

   C. Configure network load balancing for EX2 and EX3.

   D. Configure network load balancing for EX4 and EX5.

3. Your Exchange Mailbox server is down, and you need to recover mail service as soon as possible for your users. Your users currently use Outlook 2003. You do not have the time to reconfigure all client workstations. You are allowed to recover mail previously backed up during the maintenance window after working hours. What can you do? (Select two options; each of which presents part of the solution.)

   A. Deploy a new Mailbox server.

   B. Use `movemailbox -configurationonly` to reflect the new Mailbox server in Active Directory.

   C. Instruct your clients to use the new server if they want to send/receive mails.

   D. Remove the failed database file and create a new dial-tone database.

   E. Use the Exchange Server Database Recovery Management tool to complete the dial-tone recovery procedure.

4. You are an Exchange administrator responsible for an Exchange 2007 organization. Your Exchange Mailbox server is configured with one storage group, and contains two mailbox databases—one for management and one for other employees of your organization. You need to configure your Mailbox server to allow immediate recovery in case of a database corruption for your managers. You are not allowed to buy additional hardware. What should you do? (Select two options; each option presents part of the solution.)

   A. Enable LCR for the storage group.

   B. Create a new LCR-enabled storage group and Mailbox store for management.

   C. Move the mailboxes of the managers to the new store.

   D. Deploy a second Mailbox server.

   E. Enable CCR for the storage group.

5. You are an Exchange administrator responsible for an Exchange 2007 organization where all clients gain access to their mailboxes by using Outlook 2007 or Outlook Web Access. You have deployed policies to prevent other clients from gaining access to their mailboxes. One day the hardware of one of your Exchange Mailbox servers breaks down. You are allowed to restore a backup of your Exchange databases, but you need to start restoring immediately. How would you start recovering?

   A. Wait for the hardware vendor to replace faulty hardware.

   B. Restore the backup to another Mailbox server in your organization, and use `movemailbox -configurationonly` only to reflect the new Mailbox server in Active Directory.

   C. Restore the backup to a recovery server and recover old mails by exporting them to a `.pst` file.

   D. Reinstall your Exchange server on another box by using the recover server mode.

6. You are an Exchange administrator and you just migrated your three Exchange 2003 servers to Exchange 2007. You have bought new 64-bit hardware and you deployed one stand-alone Mailbox server and two Hub Transport/Client Access server roles. You make a daily online backup of your Active Directory system state, and you use an Exchange-aware backup agent to back up your storage groups and stores. One day your Exchange Mailbox server goes down due to a hardware failure and you realize that you do not have a hardware-maintenance contract. You do have a spare server in your closet. What are your options to restore access to old mail ASAP?

   A. Use the spare server to perform an Exchange Recovery Mode installation.

   B. Use the spare server to install another Mailbox server in the same organization, and restore the last backup on the new server.

   C. Deploy the Mailbox server role on one of the Client Access/Hub Transport servers, and restore the last backup on that server.

   D. Deploy a new Mailbox server on the spare server, point your clients to the new server, and recover the old mail using a recovery server.

7. You are an Exchange administrator responsible for three Exchange servers: one Mailbox server, one Client Access server, and one Hub Transport server. You use Ntbackup to make twice-a-day a normal backups of your Exchange storage groups and stores. You notice that the performance of your mail server goes down while you are making this normal backup. You should be able to ensure recoverability if an Exchange database file turns corrupt, decrease the number of normal backups, and not need to buy additional hardware. Which two actions could you take? (Each action presents part of the solution.)

   A. Deploy two new Exchange Mailbox servers and deploy CCR.

   B. Deploy two new Exchange Mailbox servers and deploy windows clustering.

   C. Enable LCR for the storage groups.

   D. Schedule one full backup every week, and a differential backup every day.

8. You are an Exchange administrator responsible for one Exchange 2007 server installed with Mailbox, Hub Transport, and Client Access server roles. One morning your Exchange database file does not mount anymore, and you notice that your backups are not usable. You need to recover as much data as possible and provide your users with mail service as quickly as possible; what are your options? (Choose all that apply.)

   A. Delete the corrupt database file and let Exchange create a new database file.

   B. Move the corrupt database file to a recovery server and let Exchange create a new database file.

   C. Move the corrupt database file to a recovery storage group and let Exchange create a new database file.

   D. Use `ESEUtil.exe` and `ISINTEG.exe` to recover as much data as possible from the database file on the recovery server, while creating a new database file on the production server.

   E. Use `ESEUtil.exe` and `ISINTEG.exe` to recover as much data as possible on the failed production database files.

9. You are an Exchange administrator responsible for an Exchange 2007 organization that contains one CCR-enabled Exchange 2007 Mailbox server and two Exchange servers with both a Client Access server and the Hub Transport server role installed. You have also deployed an Edge Transport server in the DMZ, a network accessible from the outside, but separated from your internal network, and you have configured EdgeSync. One day your Edge Transport server goes down and you notice that it is due to faulty hardware. You have a spare machine you can use to deploy an Edge Transport server. What steps can you take to recover the Edge Transport server's functionality with the fewest administrative actions? (Choose three actions; each action forms part of the solution.)

   A. Install the Edge Transport server role on the new server, which has been given the same name as the crashed Edge Transport server.

   B. Install the Edge Transport server role on the new server, which has been given a different name than the crashed Edge Transport server.

   C. Run `setup /m:recoverserver` to install the Edge Transport server on the spare server that has been installed using the same name as the crashed Edge Transport server.

   D. Rerun EdgeSync.

   E. Run `ImportEdgeConfig.ps1` to validate and restore the configuration of the Edge Transport server you have backed up previously using `ExportEdgeConfig.ps1`.

10. You are an Exchange Administrator responsible for an Exchange 2007 organization that contains one Exchange 2007 server, deployed with the Mailbox server role, Hub Transport server role, and Client Access server role. Your Active Directory forest contains two domains, as seen in the following image.

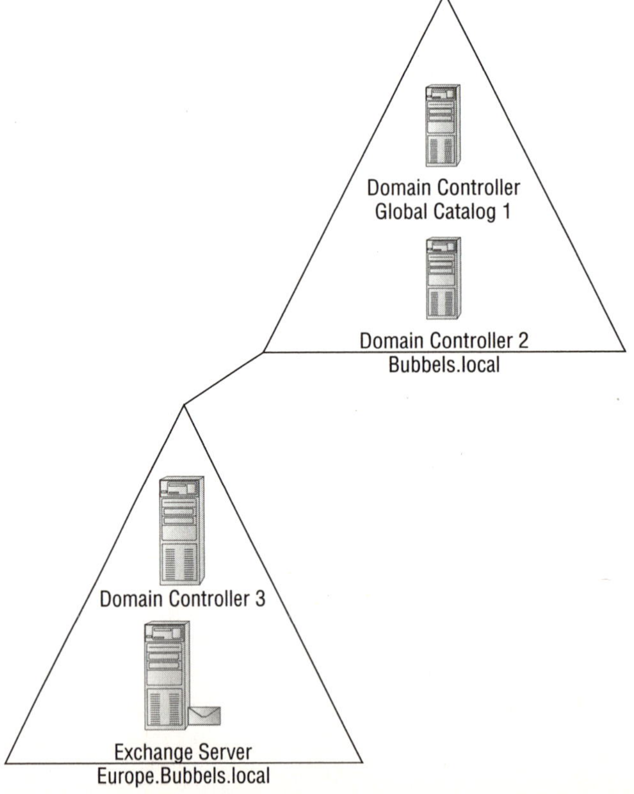

You come into the office one day and notice that your Exchange server is down and that everything is up and running except for Domain Controller 1 in the Root Domain Bubbels.Local. What can you do to prevent Exchange Server failure when Domain Controller 1 goes down?

A. Move the Exchange server to the root domain.

B. Configure Domain Controller 2 and Domain Controller 3 as global catalog.

C. Install an additional Exchange server in the Root Domain and move all resources to the new server.

D. Run `ExportEdgeConfig.ps1` on the Exchange server.

11. You are an Exchange Administrator responsible for an Exchange 2007 organization that has recently been transitioned from an Exchange 2003 organization. You currently have two Exchange Mailbox servers that each house a public-folder store. You are in the process of replacing public folders with Windows SharePoint Services, but this is not yet completed. A user asks you to recover a deleted public folder. You notice that the public folder is not in the dumpster anymore. What can you do to restore the public folder?

A. Recover the deleted public folder using the recovery storage group.

B. Recover the deleted public folder using the recovery server principle.

C. Recover the deleted public folder by restoring a backup of the public store to one of the two Mailbox servers.

D. You cannot recover the public folder anymore.

12. You are an Exchange Administrator responsible for one Exchange Mailbox server that contains both a mailbox store and a public store. You want to be able to recover access to both mailboxes and public folders in case of a database failure. You do not want to buy additional hardware. What can you do?

A. Configure LCR

B. Configure CCR

C. Configure SCC

D. Nothing; schedule backups

13. You are an Exchange Administrator responsible for an Exchange 2007 organization that consists of one Exchange 2007 Mailbox server, one Client Access server, and one Hub Transport server. You have followed all guidelines available to back up your environment, and now you are faced with a Client Access server failure. You have a spare box (different hardware than for the original server) ready to take over the functionalities of the failed server. What three actions should you take to successfully recover your Client Access server?

A. Restore file-level backup and system-state backup of the Client Access server.

B. Install a Client Access server using `Setup /m:RecoverServer`.

C. Restore file-level backup to restore the Availability web service and Outlook Web Access virtual directories settings.

D. Reapply any customizations that you have logged after deploying the Client Access server.

14. You are an Exchange Administrator responsible for an Exchange 2007 organization that consists of one Exchange 2007 Mailbox server, one Client Access server, and one Hub Transport server. You need to be able to trace the path a message took for six months, and you need to be able to provide an overview of the messages that have passed a connector on your Exchange servers. What critical data should be backed up? (Choose all that apply.)

    A. Message-tracking log files

    B. Protocol log files

    C. Message queues

    D. Local configuration data

15. You are an Exchange Administrator responsible for an Exchange 2007 organization that consists of one Exchange 2007 Mailbox server, one Client Access server, one Hub Transport server, and one Unified Messaging server. You have created several custom audio prompts. What should be included in your backup plan for your Unified Messaging server?

    A. Back up your Active Directory.

    B. Back up your custom audio prompts using a file-level backup.

    C. Back up your SMTP queues.

    D. Back up your IIS metabase.

16. You are an Exchange administrator responsible for a single Exchange Server 2007 deployment that houses 500 mailboxes. You need to provide high availability and your management does not want to buy additional hardware, but you are allowed to make changes to the current hardware. What could you do to achieve those goals? (Select three.)

    A. Implement LCR

    B. Add additional disk storage to your current server

    C. Add additional memory to your current server

    D. Add an additional network card to your current server

    E. Deploy two new Exchange Mailbox servers configured with CCR

17. You are an Exchange administrator and your company wants to deploy a new application on your Exchange Client Access server. You need to test the application. How should you configure your test environment?

    A. Build a lab environment that is the same as your production environment.

    B. Test the application in your production environment.

    C. Use a single Exchange server to test the application.

    D. Deploy the application after making a backup of your production environment.

18. You are an Exchange administrator responsible for two Exchange servers that both have the Mailbox server role, Client Access server, and Hub Transport server role installed. One day, one of the two Exchange servers crashes and you need to restore mail service as soon as possible for your clients. What recovery strategy should you choose?

    A. Use the recovery storage group.

    B. Use dial-tone recovery using database portability.

    C. Wait for hardware replacement and recover the original server.

    D. Deploy a new server using `setup /m:RecoverServer`.

19. You are an Exchange administrator and you recently deployed Exchange Server 2007. You need to implement a backup solution. You do not have the budget to buy a third-party backup solution. Which solution should you implement?

    A. Use Ntbackup to schedule an Exchange-aware online backup of your storage groups.

    B. Use Ntbackup to schedule a file-level backup of your Exchange database files.

    C. Do not implement a backup program yet—wait for budget.

    D. Use Ntbackup to schedule a file-level backup of your dismounted database files.

20. You are an Exchange administrator and you are planning a migration from Exchange 2000 Server to Exchange Server 2007. You need to design your organization in that way that it will provide the highest availability for mailboxes, client access, and routing. What messaging topology would you consider implementing?

    A. Deploy a single Exchange Server 2007server, as Mailbox server, Client Access server, and Hub Transport server.

    B. Deploy an Exchange Server 2007 Mailbox server with LCR, and an additional Hub and Client Access server.

    C. Deploy two Exchange Server 2007 Mailbox servers configured with CCR, and two additional Exchange servers with both Client Access server and Hub Transport server roles installed.

    D. Deploy two Exchange Server 2007 Mailbox servers configured with simple cluster solution, and two additional Exchange servers with both Client Access server and Hub Transport server roles installed.

Answers to Review Questions

1. A. The Hub Transport server is the role that provides mail flow inbound to and outbound from your Exchange organization. You will need to deploy an additional Hub Transport server to provide failover if the current Hub Transport server fails. Since you are not allowed to buy additional hardware, you will have to deploy the Hub Transport server on an existing Exchange server in your organization. You cannot deploy the Hub Transport server role on a clustered Mailbox server, so you can only deploy it server on the existing Client Access server.

2. C. Outlook Web Access and Outlook Anywhere require access to a Client Access server. The choice between round-robin and network load balancing is clear: network load balancing will never guide your user to a server that is unavailable. For more information about Round Robin, please refer to Chapter 2.

3. D and E. Since your clients are still using Outlook 2003, you cannot use the database portability feature as specified in options A, B, and C because this would require you to reconfigure all client workstations. You can, however, create a new dial-tone database and use the Exchange Server Database Recovery Management tool to guide you through the process of restoring a previous backup set in a recovery storage group and merging old and new data in the production database.

4. B and C. You cannot enable LCR for a storage group that has more than one store. You cannot enable CCR since it is not allowed to buy additional hardware. You need to create a new storage group and enable LCR for the new storage group. Then you need to create a new mailbox database and move all the mailboxes of the managers to the new mailbox store.

5. B. Because you have to start restoring immediately, you cannot wait for the faulty hardware to be replaced. You can restore the backup on another server in your Exchange organization, and then issue the `movemailbox -configuration only` cmdlet to make sure that your users can connect to their new Mailbox server. Since all your clients use Outlook 2007, your clients can take advantage of the Autodiscover service to connect automatically to the new Mailbox server.

6. A. Because your Active directory is still up and running, you can use the spare server to install Exchange in Exchange Recovery Mode.

7. C and D. Because you do not want to buy additional hardware, options A and B can be excluded. Enabling LCR for your storage group will provide you with a copy of your database files that can be used in case of a failure of the production database. Enabling LCR enables you to decrease the number of normal backups! (It does not eliminate the need to make full backups, though.)

8. B and C. You cannot use a backup to restore a previous version of the database file, so you can only try to recover as much data as possible. By moving the corrupt database file to a recovery server, you can run the `ESEUtil.exe` and `ISINTEG.exe` recovery tools against the database file. You cannot run those tools against a database in a recovery storage group. Exchange will create a new database file, so users can start sending and receiving mails again while you recover as much data as possible.

9. A, D, and E. You can use the cloned configuration process for recovering an Edge Transport server to a new box. You will need to perform a clean installation of an Edge Transport server, and you need to use the same server name as the crashed Edge Transport server's. After installing the Edge Transport server, you can use the built-in script `ImportEdgeConfig.ps1` to validate the previously made backup and to import the configuration of the crashed Edge Transport server to the new Edge Transport server. To import the recipient and configuration again from Active Directory you will finish the recovery process by running EdgeSync again.

10. B. Exchange stores almost all its configuration data in Active Directory. A global catalog is a special kind of domain controller that knows something about every object in the Active Directory forest. Exchange will query a global catalog to find out more about its users or its configuration. If no global catalog is available, Exchange will not be able to query Active Directory.

11. B. You can only use the recovery server to recover a deleted public folder that is not available in the dumpster anymore. You cannot use the recovery storage group to recover public folders, and you cannot restore a backup to one of the Mailbox servers since replication would delete the public folder again.

12. A. Configuring CCR and SCC means that you have to buy additional hardware, which wasn't planned. You can configure local continuous replication (LCR) however, since you have only one Exchange server in your environment that homes public folders.

13. B, C, and D. The Client Access server does not store all its configuration information in Active Directory. Some is also stored locally on the file system, and some is stored in the IIS metabase. To recover successfully from a failure, you will need to reinstall the Client Access server using the recover server mode installation. You also need to restore a file-level backup to restore customizations concerning the Availability web service and the Outlook Web Access virtual directors. Since you cannot restore the IIS metabase (they won't be in sync anymore), you will need to reapply all customizations that you have done after deploying the crashed Client Access server.

14. A and B. It is necessary to make a backup of the message-tracking log files and protocol log files for compliance reasons. You cannot back up your message queues, but you could mount them on another Hub Transport server in the same organization any time. Configuration information is not stored locally, but in Active Directory.

15. A and B. The Unified Messaging server stores its configuration in Active Directory. Whenever you create custom audio prompts, these are stored locally, so you will have to include them in your backup schedule using a file-level backup. There is no reason to back up the IIS metabase or the SMTP queue database.

16. A, B and C. Enabling LCR provides high availability but requires additional hard-disk space and additional memory.

17. A. You have to test an application before you deploy it in production. It is best practice to test an application in a lab environment that matches the production environment as closely a possible.

18. B. Since you need to restore mail service as soon as possible, you cannot wait for replacement hardware or use the `RecoverServer` setup mode. You need to use database portability to allow users to open their mailboxes on the second server. You can recover old mail by using the dial-tone procedure.

19. A. You have to make a backup with an Exchange-aware backup tool, and Ntbackup is Exchange-aware. Making an online backup is preferred since Exchange checks its database files during backup.

20. C. Implementing CCR provides the best protection for database failure, operating-system failure, and network failure. By deploying two Client Access servers and a Hub Transport server, there is high availability for those services as well.

Chapter 4

Designing and Planning Coexistence and Migrations

MICROSOFT EXAM OBJECTIVES COVERED IN THIS CHAPTER:

- ✓ Designing and planning migration of legacy Exchange features
- ✓ Designing migration strategies
- ✓ Planning coexistence for Exchange Server 2003 and Exchange Server 2007

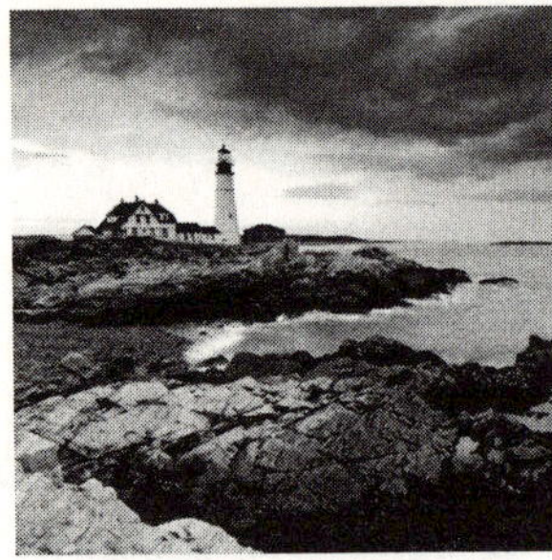

It is extremely unlikely that Exchange Server 2007 would be implemented in an environment where no messaging had existed before. Therefore, in most cases you will be responsible for a migration from an existing platform, as well as a period of coexistence between the old and the new. To offer an example of this process, this chapter will deal with migration from and coexistence with Exchange Server 2003.

The main subjects of this chapter are as follows:

- Designing and planning migration of free/busy functionality
- Designing and planning migration of public folders
- Designing and planning migration of offline address books
- Designing and planning migration of the Recipient Update Service (RUS) functionality
- Designing an inter-forest migration strategy
- Designing an intra-forest migration strategy
- Coexistence with Exchange Server 2003

Designing and Planning Migration of Legacy Exchange Features

You will need to migrate legacy Exchange features from Exchange Server 2003 to Exchange Server 2007 to preserve data and functionality for end users, to provide support for clients older than Outlook 2007, and to ensure interoperability during your migration to Exchange Server 2007. The primary legacy features you need to be concerned with are Exchange Server 2003 system folders, public folders, offline address books, and the Exchange Server 2003 Recipient Update Service.

Free/Busy Functionality

System folders in Exchange Server 2003 provide two of the legacy 2003 features that you will need to migrate to Exchange Server 2007. These 2003 system folders provide free/busy information, which Exchange Server 2003 uses to determine users' availability when scheduling meetings. In Exchange Server 2007, the Availability service supplements or replaces these 2003 system folders. System folders also host the offline address books for Exchange Server 2003, which Microsoft Outlook uses to provide access to Exchange recipients in the organization when they are disconnected from the Exchange server. To learn more about offline address books, see the "Offline Address Books" section later in this chapter.

Exchange Server 2003 Free/Busy Folders

The functionality provided by free/busy folders in Exchange Server 2003 has been replaced by the Availability service in Exchange Server 2007. You can view the free/busy folder for an Exchange Server 2003 administrative group as follows:

1. On an Exchange Server 2003 computer, open Exchange System Manager from Start ➤ All Programs ➤ Microsoft Exchange ➤ System Manager.
2. In Exchange System Manager, expand Administrative Groups, then expand the administrative group in question.
3. Under the administrator group, expand the Folders object, then right-click the Public Folders object and select View System Folders, as shown in Figure 4.1.

Figure 4.2 shows the free/busy folder for an Exchange Server 2003 administrative group; the actual folder name is SCHEDULE+ FREE BUSY, and contains separate subfolders for each Exchange administrative group. To optimize performance, Outlook by default publishes a user's free/busy information every 15 minutes as well as when Outlook is shut down. Each message published contains the user's complete free/busy information for the next two months. The amount of free/busy information published is configurable through Outlook's Options dialog, as is the update interval (15 minutes by default).

FIGURE 4.1 Viewing system folders in Exchange System Manager

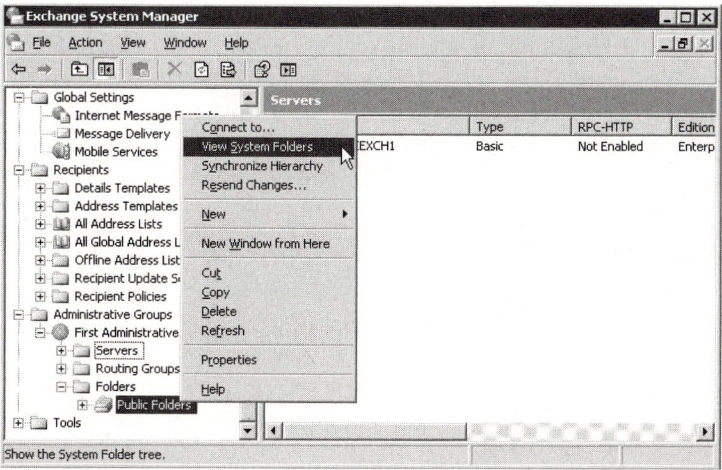

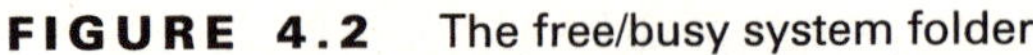

FIGURE 4.2 The free/busy system folder

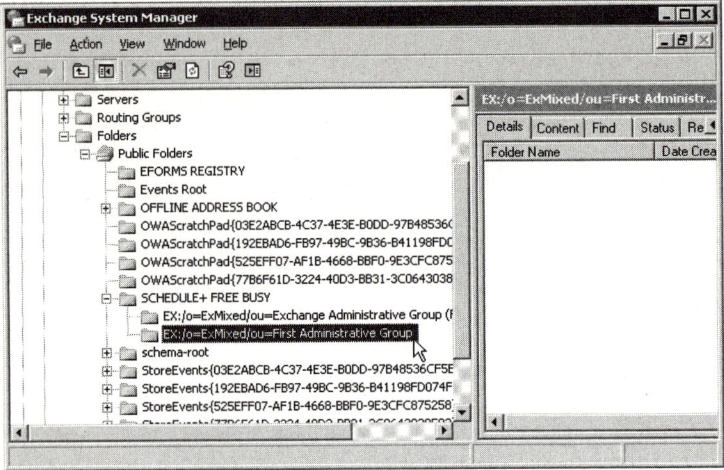

The migration of free/busy folders and other system folders from Exchange Server 2003 to Exchange Server 2007 is covered in the "Migrating Public Folders" section later in this chapter.

Exchange Server 2007 Availability Service

In Exchange Server 2007, the free/busy functionality previously provided by system folders has been replaced by the Availability service. Rather than storing free/busy information in public folders, the target mailbox's free/busy data is accessed directly from the calendar (via the Availability service), eliminating the 15-minute publishing latency inherent in the approach of Exchange Server 2003 and earlier. The result of this is more secure, consistent, and up-to-date availability data as well as providing access to the new Scheduling Assistant functionality.

The Availability service is deployed as a web service on the Client Access Server role, and is discovered by Outlook 2007 clients through Autodiscover. The Outlook 2007 Scheduling Assistant (as well as Outlook Web Access) uses the Availability service to do the following:

- Obtain free/busy information for Exchange 2007 mailboxes
- Retrieve live free/busy from other Exchange 2007 forests
- Retrieve published free/busy from Public Folders (for legacy mailboxes or for mailboxes using legacy Outlook clients)
- View working hours of attendees
- Display meeting-time suggestions

The Availability service is used only by Outlook 2007 clients whose mailboxes reside on Exchange Server 2007. Previous versions of Outlook, as well as Outlook 2007 clients whose mailboxes are on Exchange Server 2003 or earlier, rely on the free/busy system folders. Therefore, if clients use Outlook 2003 or earlier, or mailboxes are stored on Exchange Server 2003 or earlier, system folders have to be maintained in the environment.

Free/Busy Retrieval in Various Single-Forest Topologies

Table 4.1 illustrates the different methods of free/busy information retrieval in various single-forest topologies.

TABLE 4.1 Free/Busy Retrieval in Various Topologies

Client	Logged-on Mailbox	Target Mailbox	Free/Busy Retrieval Method
Outlook 2007	Exchange 2007	Exchange 2007	The Availability service reads free/busy information from the target mailbox.
Outlook 2007	Exchange 2007	Exchange 2003	The Availability service makes HTTP connections to the `/public` virtual directory of the Exchange 2003 mailbox.
Outlook 2003	Exchange 2007	Exchange 2007	Free/busy information is published in local public folders.
Outlook 2003	Exchange 2007	Exchange 2003	Free/busy information is published in local public folders.
Outlook Web Access 2007	Exchange 2007	Exchange 2007	Outlook Web Access 2007 calls the Availability service API, which reads the free/busy information from the target mailbox.
Outlook Web Access 2007	Exchange 2007	Exchange 2003	Outlook Web Access 2007 calls the Availability service API, which makes an HTTP connection to the `/public` virtual directory of the Exchange 2003 mailbox.
Any	Exchange 2003	Exchange 2007	Free/busy information is published in local public folders.

Accessing the Availability Service

Outlook 2007 clients locate the Availability service through the Autodiscover service, so it is crucial that the Autodiscover service be configured for Outlook 2007 clients to perform calendaring functions.

Most Autodiscover service configuration is performed automatically in a single-forest environment with no external Outlook access configured. Circumstances where Autodiscover requires additional configuration include the following:

- Gaining external access to Exchange Web Services (Outlook Anywhere, known as RPC over HTTP in Exchange Server 2003)
- Accessing free/busy data in cross-forest topologies
- Accessing the Availability service with NLB (Network Load Balancing) arrays of CAS (Client Access Server) computers

Exercise 4.1 outlines how to configure the external URL for the Availability service.

EXERCISE 4.1

Configuring the External URL for the Availability Service

1. Click Start ➤ Programs ➤ Microsoft Exchange Server 2007, and then select Exchange Management Shell.
2. In the Exchange Management Shell, modify the external URL parameter for the availability services using the `Set-WebServicesVirtualDirectory` cmdlet as follows, where ***CAS_Server*** is the hostname of the CAS computer and ***fully_qualified_domain_name*** is the externally accessible DNS hostname of the CAS computer—for example, **mail.exchange2007.com**.

```
Set-WebServicesVirtualDirectory -Identity " CAS_server\EWS (Default Web Site) "
-ExternalUrl "Https://fully_qualified_domain_name/EWS/Exchange.asmx"
```

3. If the command is successful, there will be no output from PowerShell, as shown in the image here.

EXERCISE 4.1 *(continued)*

The result of the `Set-WebServicesVirtualDirectory` cmdlet can be verified using the `Get-WebServicesVirtualDirectory` cmdlet as follows:

```
Get-WebServicesVirtualDirectory -Identity "CAS_server\EWS (Default Web Site)"
```

The output of the cmdlet will be as shown in this image:

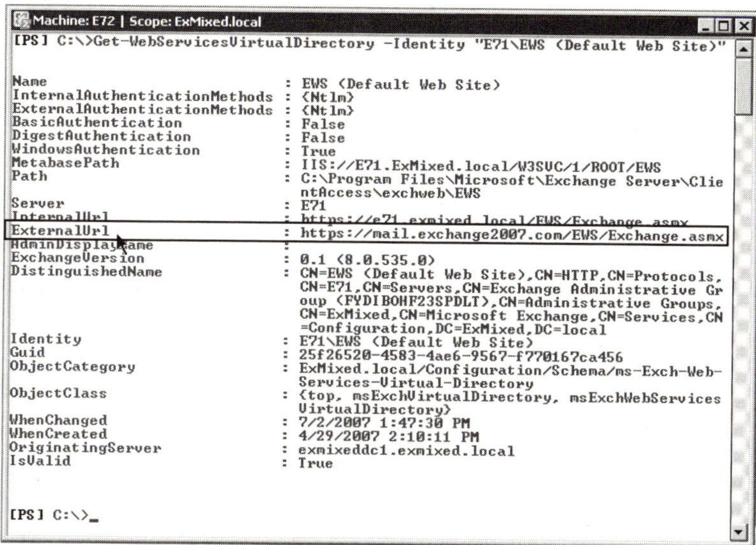

Note that the `Set-WebServicesVirtualDirectory` cmdlet is also used to set the `-InternalURL` parameter for NLB clusters of CAS computers. For example, to set the Availability service to use an internal NLB cluster named `nlb.wiley.com` instead of `cas1.wiley.com`, you would run the following cmdlet:

```
Set-WebServicesVirtualDirectory -Identity "CAS_server" -InternalUrl "Https://
nlb.wiley.com/EWS/Exchange.asmx"
```

Migrating Public Folders

Microsoft has de-emphasized public folders in Exchange Server 2007—for example, free/busy calendaring functionality is provided by the Availability service, and offline address books are now distributed using HTTP or HTTPS and BITS (Background Intelligent Transfer Service). Additionally, Microsoft is encouraging the use of SharePoint for collaboration, and is providing guidance for migrating public folders to SharePoint. However, public folders are still fully supported, and system folders in particular are actually *required* in certain topologies. Furthermore, for many enterprises that have developed custom applications or forms using public folders, transitioning the data held in public folders to SharePoint is simply not feasible, so this data must be migrated to Exchange Server 2007.

In the rest of this section, references to public folders also apply to system folders unless otherwise stated.

The following are the public folder features that have been removed or de-emphasized. The strategy for dealing with these features is to retain a computer running Exchange 2000 or Exchange Server 2003 in the organization. This applies to the following public folder features:

- Public folder graphical user interface (GUI) management
- Non-MAPI top-level hierarchies in a public folder store
- Public folder access using Network News Transfer Protocol (NNTP)
- Public folder access using IMAP4
- Public folder access via Outlook Web Access (OWA)

In the RTM (Release to Manufacturing) version of Exchange Server 2007, public folders were configurable only through the Exchange Management Shell and were not accessible via OWA. However, in Exchange Server 2007 Service Pack 1, public-folder configuration was added to the Exchange Management Console (EMC) GUI, as was public-folder access via OWA, as shown in Figures 4.3 and 4.4.

FIGURE 4.3 Public-folder management through SP1 EMC

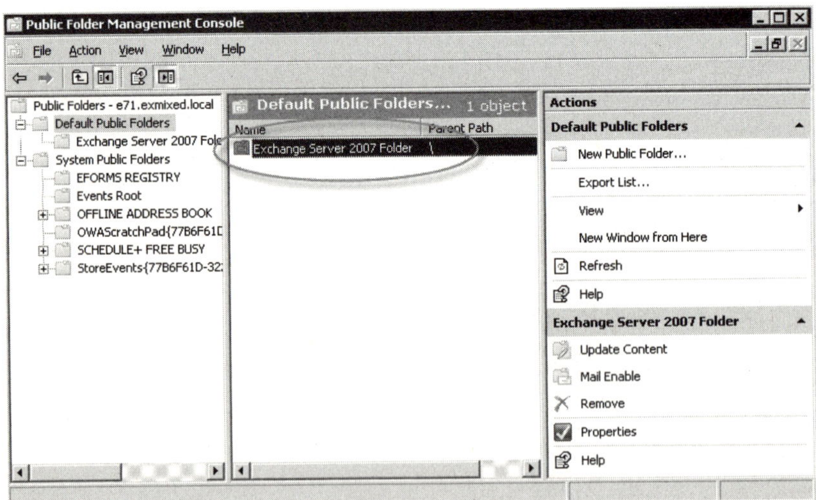

FIGURE 4.4 Public folder access through SP1 OWA

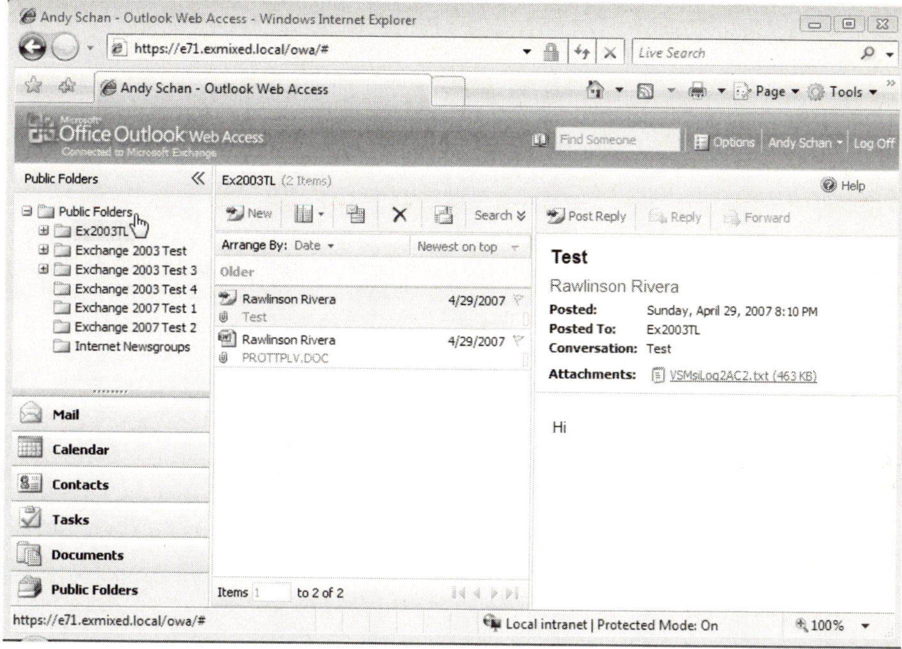

Public Folder Hierarchy

The public folder hierarchy is contained in the public-folder database, and is replicated to all public-folder databases in the Exchange organization, regardless of whether that database contains replicas of public folders. This replication is independent of the public-folder content replication, and is message-based.

The hierarchy contains information on the following:

- Client public-folder permissions
- A public folder's description
- Public folder priority settings
- The public folder replication schedule
- A public folder's position within the public-folder hierarchy
- The replica list for each public folder (which public folder databases host copies of the public folder)

The hierarchy is referred to by clients accessing public folders, and provides the folder listing displayed within Outlook as well as referrals to the appropriate public-folder replica so that clients can access the data contained within the public folders.

Public Folder Content

Public folder content is also contained within the public-folder database. Unlike with the public folder hierarchy, public folder data is replicated selectively to databases hosting replicas of the particular public folder, dictated by the replica lists configured by the administrator and stored in the public folder hierarchy. Like with the public folder hierarchy, public folder content replication is message-based.

For various reasons, you may elect to deploy dedicated public folder servers in your environment. A common error in planning and deploying multiple dedicated public folder servers for redundancy is to configure all the mailbox databases to use one of the dedicated servers as their client's default public folders database. Unfortunately, the default public folder database is the location from which clients access the hierarchy, which provides them with information on public-folder replicas and which databases contain that content. This means that if the configured default public folder database is inaccessible, clients have no way to locate other public folder replicas. In this case, it is better to create public folder databases on each mailbox server to provide the hierarchy to the clients, and host all the public-folder data on the dedicated servers. This way, if one of the dedicated public-folder servers becomes unavailable, clients can be referred to other replicas.

Creating a Public Folder Database

When you install the first Exchange Server 2007 computer hosting the Mailbox server role into an existing Exchange Server 2003 environment, a public folder database is created on that computer by default, and as with Exchange Server 2003 there can be only one public folder database per Exchange Server 2007 computer. However, in an environment with a large number of public folders, you may want to deploy a dedicated Exchange Server 2007 public folder server.

Exercise 4.2 outlines the steps to create a public folder database on an Exchange Server 2007 Mailbox server.

Although it is technically possible to create a public-folder database in an existing storage group, Microsoft recommends in Exchange Server 2007 that you create a separate storage group for each database—whether they are mailbox or public folder databases.

EXERCISE 4.2

Public Folder Database Creation

To create a public-folder database, you first create a new storage group, and then you create the database itself. Let's walk through the steps for each.

Creating a New Storage Group

There are six steps to create a new storage group.

1. Click Start ➢ Programs ➢ Microsoft Exchange Server 2007, and then select Exchange Management Console (EMC).
2. Under the Microsoft Exchange root object, expand the Server Configuration work center and then select the Mailbox node.
3. Within the Mailbox result pane, select the server on which you want to add a storage group.
4. In the right-hand Actions pane for that Mailbox server, click the New Storage Group link as seen here.

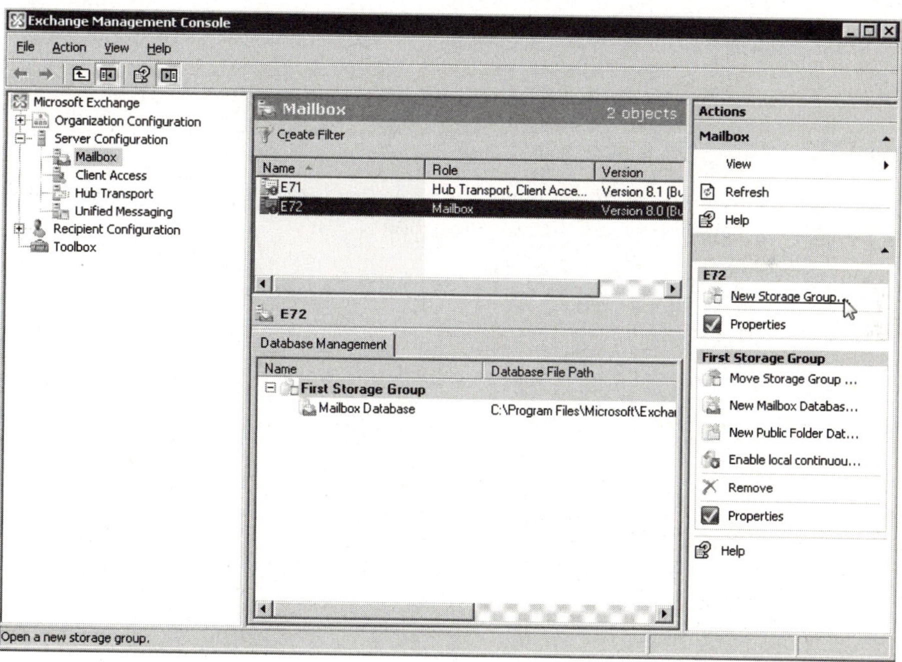

EXERCISE 4.2 *(continued)*

5. In the New Storage Group wizard shown in the next image, provide a name for the storage group, specify the log files path and the system files path as necessary, and then select New.

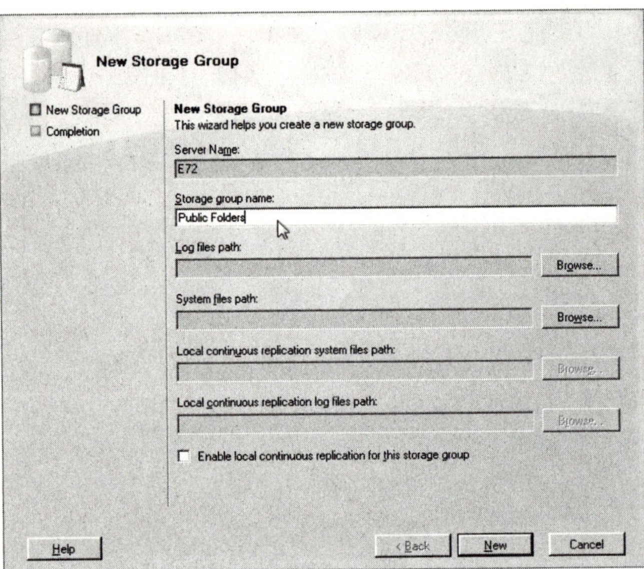

6. Click Finish on the Completion screen of the New Storage Group wizard shown here to complete the wizard and create the storage group.

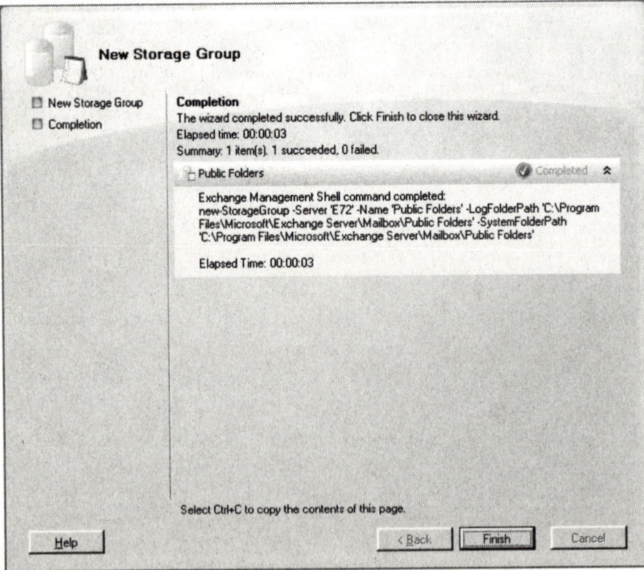

EXERCISE 4.2 *(continued)*

Creating the Database

Now you are ready to create the database. Just follow these steps.

1. In the Exchange Management Console, highlight the storage group created previously and select New Public Folder Database from the Action pane as seen here.

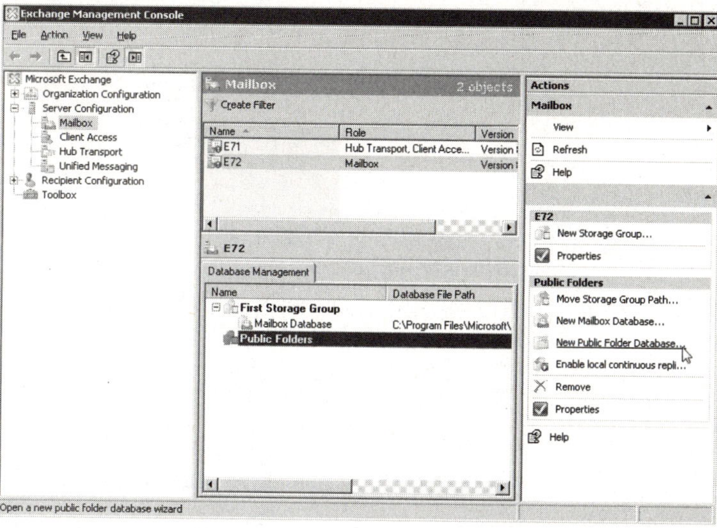

2. In the New Public Folder Database wizard shown next, enter a name for the database and specify a database path to place the database on a separate disk from the storage group's transaction logs. Click New to create and mount the database.

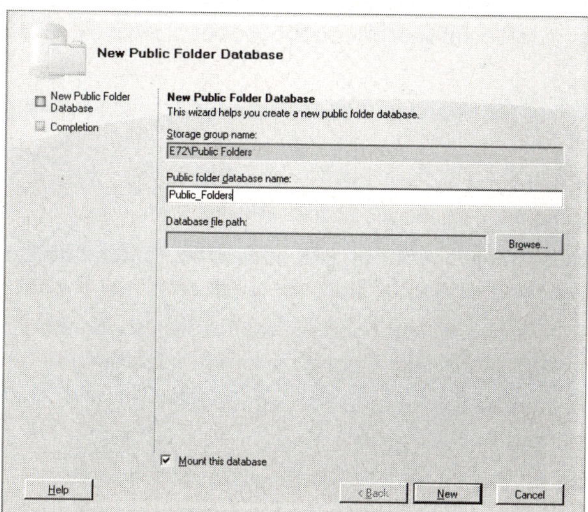

EXERCISE 4.2 *(continued)*

3. Click Finish on the Completion screen to close the New Public Folder Database wizard.

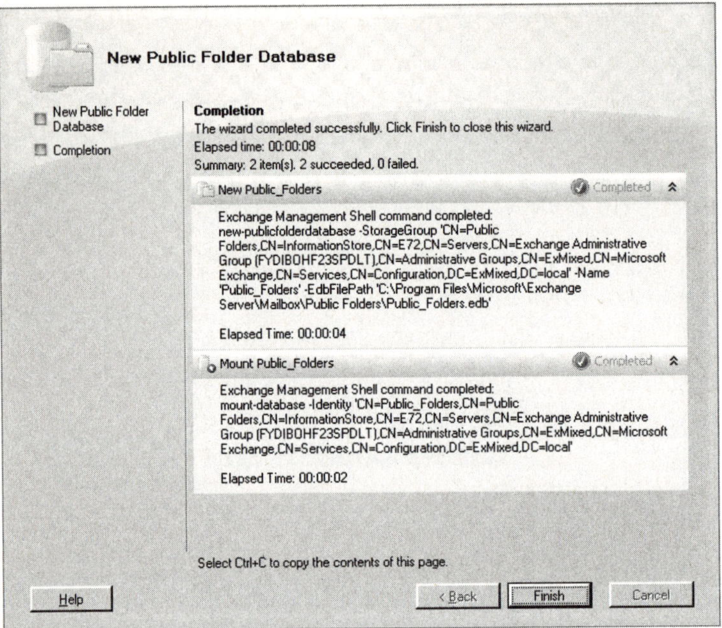

Migrating Public Folder Content

You can migrate public folders from Exchange Server 2003 to Exchange Server 2007 in several ways. All public folder migration methods accomplish the same basic sequence of events, however:

1. You create replicas of the source public folders on the target server (Exchange Server 2007).
2. The public folder hierarchy is then replicated by Exchange, reflecting the changes you have made in the replica lists for the public folders.
3. Based on the replica changes made by you, the public folder data is replicated from the source server (Exchange Server 2003) to the target server by Exchange.
4. The source server is then removed from the replica lists of the public folders, either manually by you or automatically through a script or Exchange utility.
5. The updated public folder hierarchy reflecting the removal of the source server from the replica lists is replicated by Exchange.
6. Exchange removes the public folder data from the source server.

Public Folder Replication

When you are planning your public folder implementation, it is important to note that there are two types of replication involved (and in some cases, three). Here are the two most common:

- The public folder hierarchy, which contains the replica lists and client permissions, among other data, and is replicated separately from the public folder data
- The public folder data, which, as mentioned earlier, replicates separately from the hierarchy

Neither of those replications are accomplished by Active Directory replication. Public-folder hierarchy and data replication are message-based and the data is not stored in Active Directory. These system messages can be tracked using the same mechanisms as user messages; as a consequence, email connectivity, routing, and addressing play a large role in the successful replication of public folders.

The third type of replication that is used is Active Directory replication, but only if mail-enabled public folders exist in the environment. These *are* represented in Active Directory, so they can be assigned addresses and be listed in the address books. This is the only time when Active Directory replication plays a direct role in public-folder replication.

Migrating Public Folders Using Exchange System Manager

You can move public folders from Exchange Server 2003 to Exchange Server 2007 using the Exchange System Manager GUI. Exercise 4.3 walks you through the necessary steps to do so.

Although using Exchange System Manager to migrate public folders is possible, this method may not be very practical in an enterprise environment with a large number of public folders. You would probably employ scripts, the Exchange Server 2007 Exchange Management Shell, third-party tools, or some combination of those elements to achieve the economies of scale required in a large public-folder migration.

EXERCISE 4.3

Migrating Public Folders with Exchange System Manager

In lieu of using the Exchange Server 2007 Exchange Management Shell (built on PowerShell) you can migrate public folders using the Exchange Server 2003 Exchange System Manager GUI. Let's walk through the steps required to accomplish this.

1. On the Exchange Server 2003 computer or management station, click Start ➢ All Programs ➢ Microsoft Exchange ➢ System Manager.

EXERCISE 4.3 *(continued)*

2. Within Exchange System Manager, expand Administrative Groups, expand the administrative group containing the Exchange Server 2003 public folders, expand Folders, and expand Public Folders.

3. If you will be migrating system folders, right-click Public Folders and select View System Folders from the context menu, as shown here.

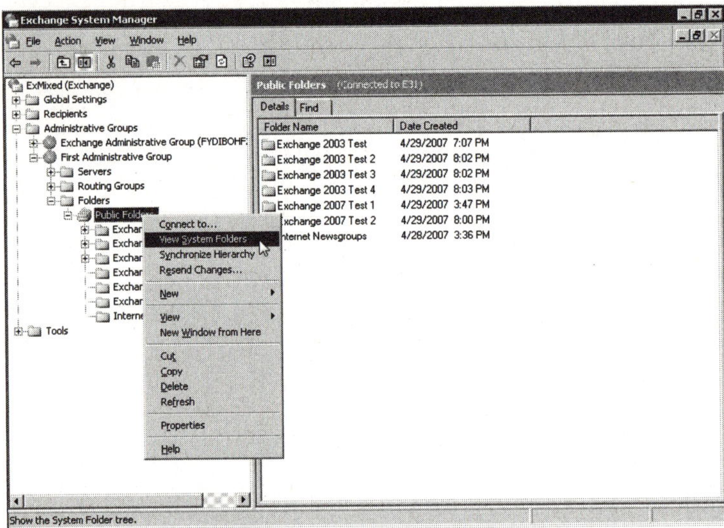

4. Under Public Folders, right-click the public folder to move to Exchange Server 2007 and select All Tasks ➢ Manage Settings from the context menu as shown here.

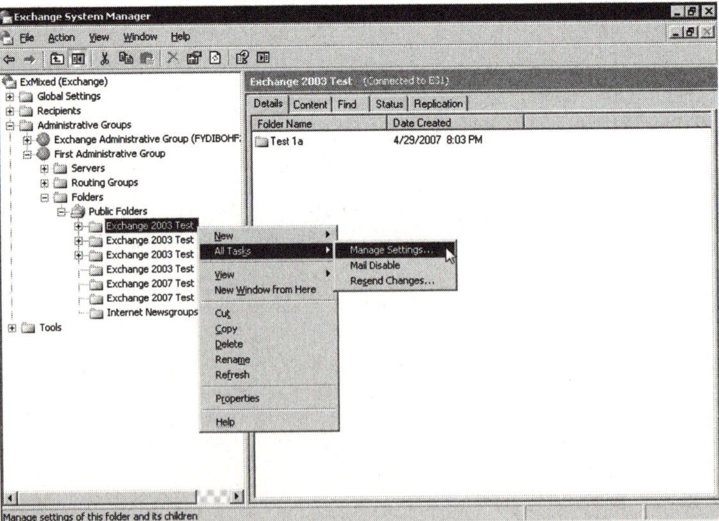

EXERCISE 4.3 *(continued)*

5. On the Welcome screen of the Manage Public Folder Settings Wizard, click Next.

6. On the Specify Action screen, select Modify Lists of Replica Servers and click Next.

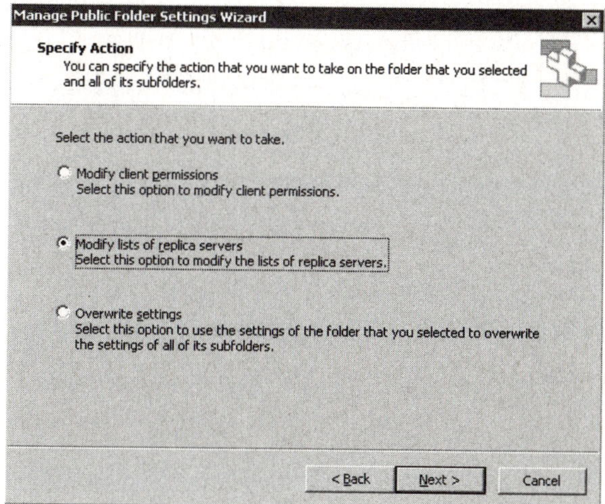

EXERCISE 4.3 *(continued)*

7. On the next Specify Action screen, select Replace a Server and click Next.

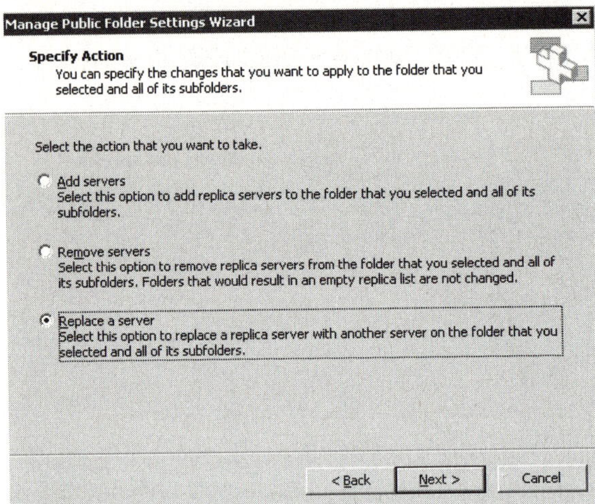

8. On the Replace a Replica Server screen, confirm that Replica Server to Replace has the source Exchange Server 2003 computer listed. Select the target Exchange Server 2007 computer from the Replacement drop-down list and click Next.

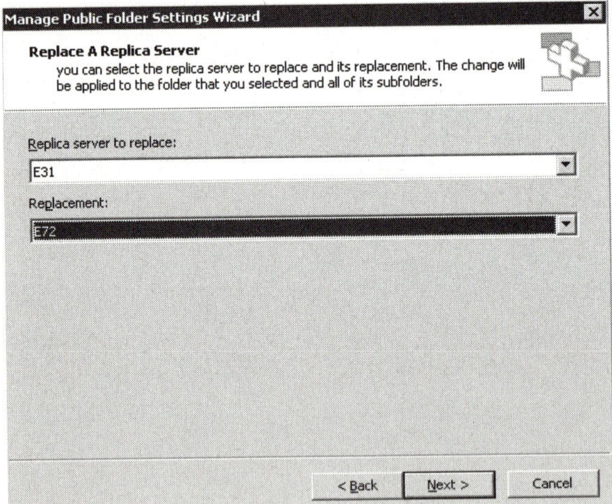

EXERCISE 4.3 *(continued)*

9. On the Completing the Manage Public Folders Settings Wizard screen, confirm your selections and click Finish.

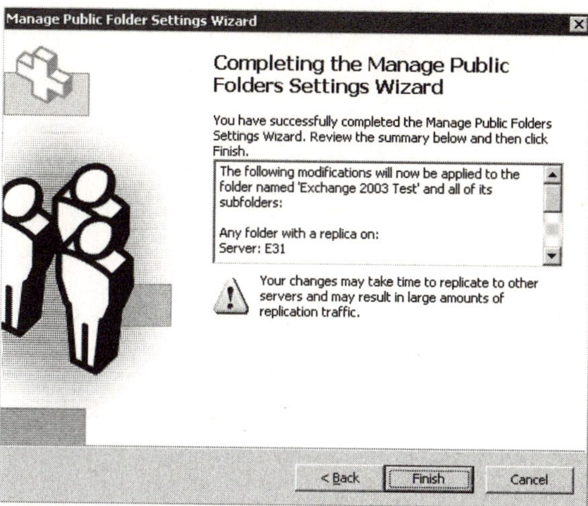

Migrating Public Folders Using Scripts

A more practical method of migrating public folders from Exchange Server 2003 to Exchange Server 2007 is to use scripts via the Exchange Management Shell. Exchange Server 2007 comes with several PowerShell scripts for managing public folders, including the `MoveAllReplicas.ps1` and `AddReplicaToPFRecursive.ps1` scripts, which can be used to move public folder replicas. These scripts can be found in the `c:\Program Files\Microsoft\Exchange Server\Scripts` directory, where *`c:`* is the drive where Exchange Server 2007 was installed.

Exercise 4.4 outlines the steps for migrating public folders using the `MoveAllReplicas.ps1` and `AddReplicaToPFRecursive.ps1`scripts.

EXERCISE 4.4

Migrating Public Folders with Scripts

In most larger environments, you will find it more practical to use the PowerShell scripts provided with Exchange Server 2007 to migrate your public folders. This exercise will walk you through the steps necessary to accomplish this.

1. Start the Exchange Management Shell by selecting Start ➢ All Programs ➢ Microsoft Exchange Server 2007 ➢ Exchange Management Shell.

2. Within the Exchange Management Shell, enter **`cd "c:\Program Files\Microsoft\Exchange Server\Scripts"`** and press Enter.

EXERCISE 4.4 *(continued)*

3. To move a public folder called Ex2003TL and all of its subfolders within that hierarchy from Exchange Server 2003 to Exchange Server 2007, run the following command:

```
ReplaceReplicaOnPFRecursive.ps1 -TopPublicFolder "\Ex2003TL" -ServerToAdd
Targetserver -ServerToRemove Sourceserver
```

In that command, the following is true:

Targetserver is the Exchange Server 2007 server folders are being moved to.

Sourceserver is the Exchange Server 2003 server public folders are being removed from.

4. To replicate all public folders from Server01 to Server02, run the following command:

```
MoveAllReplicas.ps1 -Server Sourceserver -NewServer Targetserver
```

In that command, the following is true:

Sourceserver is the source Exchange Server 2003 computer.

Targetserver is the target Exchange Server 2007 computer.

Offline Address Books

In Exchange Server 2003 and earlier, offline address books (OABs) were stored in and distributed from public folders—system folders in particular. However, Exchange Server 2007 has introduced a new method of distributing offline address books called Web-based distribution that uses HTTP (or HTTPS) and BITS. This new distribution mechanism has the potential to provide greater control over distribution points, support more concurrent clients, and reduce bandwidth consumption.

In a new Exchange Server 2007 environment, Web-based distribution is configured by default, and for internal use no further configuration is generally required. If you did not specify that you have clients running Entourage or Outlook 2003 or earlier during setup, then no public folder databases are created and offline address book distribution will be exclusively web-based.

As in Exchange Server 2003, the offline address book can be generated in three versions to support various clients, as Table 4.2 outlines:

TABLE 4.2 Offline Address Book Versions

OAB Version	Clients Supported
Version 2	Outlook 98 SP1 or earlier
Version 3	Outlook 98 SP2 or later
Version 4	Outlook 2003 SP2 or later

If you require OAB versions prior to version 4 in your environment to support older Outlook clients, then you will also need to retain public folder distribution.

When introducing Exchange Server 2007 into an existing Exchange 2000 Server or Exchange Server 2003 organization (a much more common scenario), however, you will need to configure web-based distribution if you will be supporting Outlook 2007 clients. When you introduce the first Exchange Server 2007 server into your organization, the offline address book remains hosted on Exchange 2000 Server or Exchange Server 2003, and web-based distribution is unavailable, as shown in Figure 4.5. After all clients have been upgraded to Outlook 2007 and all mailboxes have been moved to Exchange Server 2007, public folder distribution can be disabled.

FIGURE 4.5 Exchange Server 2003 offline address book

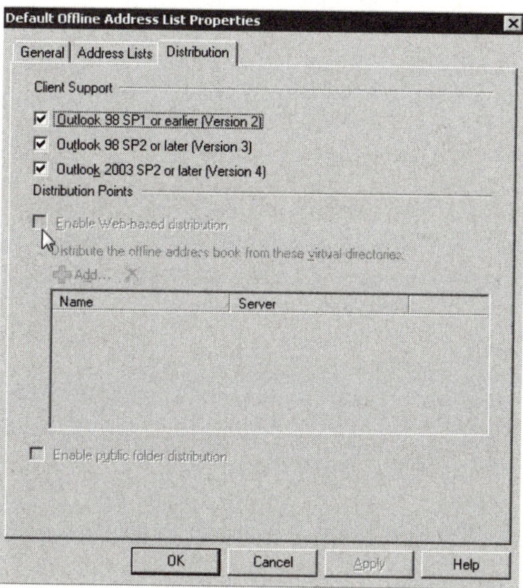

To enable web-based distribution, the offline address book needs to be moved to an Exchange Server 2007 computer, as Exchange 2000 Server and Exchange Server 2003 do not support this feature.

If you have users with Outlook 2007, then during the migration phase to Exchange Server 2007 from Exchange 2000 Server or Exchange Server 2003, you will need to support both web-based and public-folder distribution for offline address books until all users are migrated. Additionally, if any users will be remaining on Outlook 2003 or earlier after the migration is completed, you will need to continue supporting public-folder distribution for your offline address books.

Migrating Offline Address Books Using Exchange Management Console

Exercise 4.5 outlines the steps to move an offline address book from Exchange Server 2003 to Exchange Server 2007 and enable web-based distribution.

EXERCISE 4.5

Migrating an Offline Address Book with Exchange Management Console

As with many Exchange Server 2007 tasks, you can migrate offline address books through the Exchange Management Console GUI or with PowerShell via the Exchange Management Console. In this exercise, you will walk through the offline address book migration using the GUI.

Moving the Offline Address Book

1. Click Start ➢ Programs ➢ Microsoft Exchange Server 2007, and then select Exchange Management Console.
2. Under the Microsoft Exchange root object, expand the Organization Configuration work center and then select the Mailbox node.
3. Within the Mailbox result pane, select the Offline Address Book tab.
4. In the right-hand Actions pane, select the Move link in the Default Offline Address List section, as shown here.

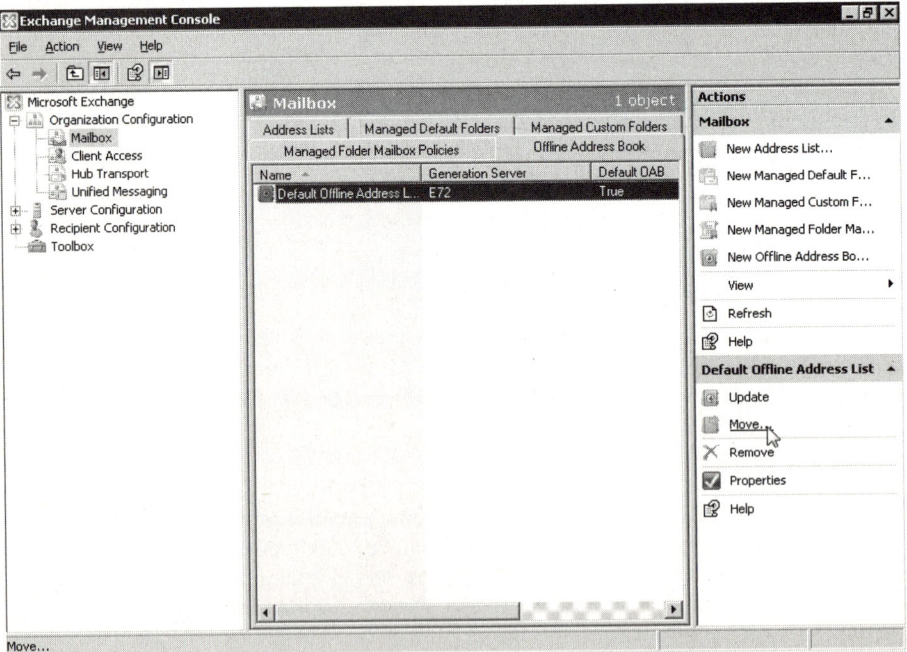

EXERCISE 4.5 *(continued)*

5. In the Move Offline Address Book wizard shown next, click Browse and select the Exchange Server 2007 computer to move the offline address book to. Select Move to begin the move operation.

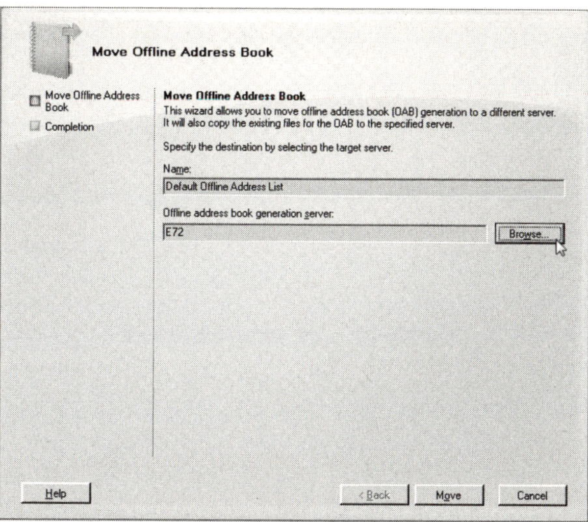

6. On the Completion screen of the Move Offline Address Book wizard, read the warning advising you not to turn off public-folder publishing before the offline address book is generated on the target folder, and then click Finish.

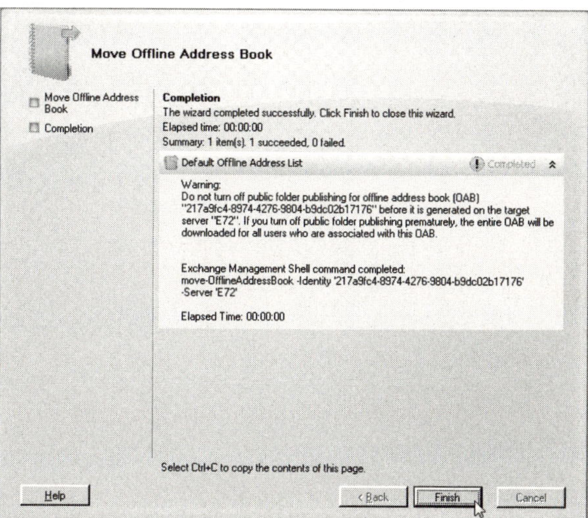

EXERCISE 4.5 *(continued)*

Enabling Web-Based Distribution

Once you have moved the offline address book to Exchange Server 2007, you can enable web-based distribution for Outlook 2007 clients as outlined here.

1. Back in the Mailbox node of the Organization Configuration work center, select the Offline Address Book tab.

2. In the right-hand Actions pane, select the Properties link in the Default Offline Address List section, as shown here.

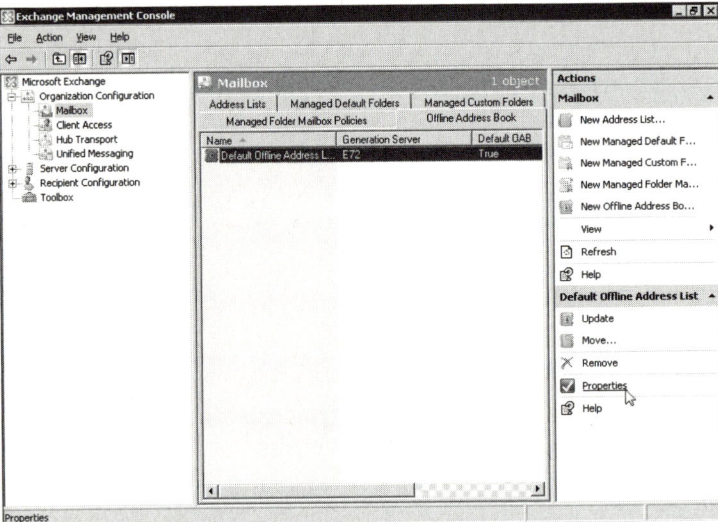

3. In the Default Offline Address List Properties dialog, select the Distribution tab, then select the Enable Web-Based Distribution check box. Click Add to access the Select OAB Virtual Directory dialog.

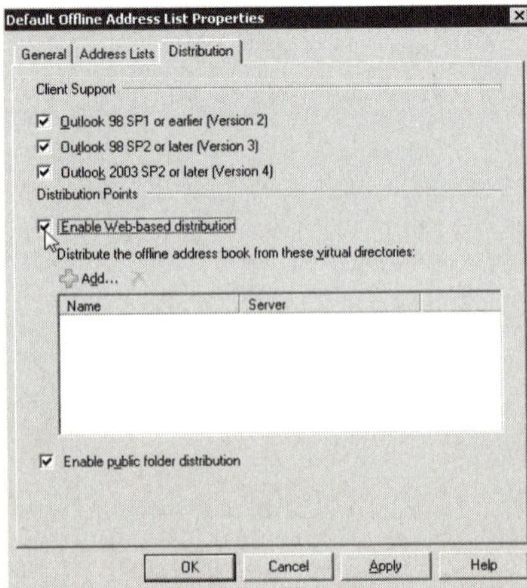

EXERCISE 4.5 *(continued)*

4. In the Select OAB Virtual Directory dialog, select the virtual directory to host the OAB and click OK to return to the Default Offline Address List Properties dialog.

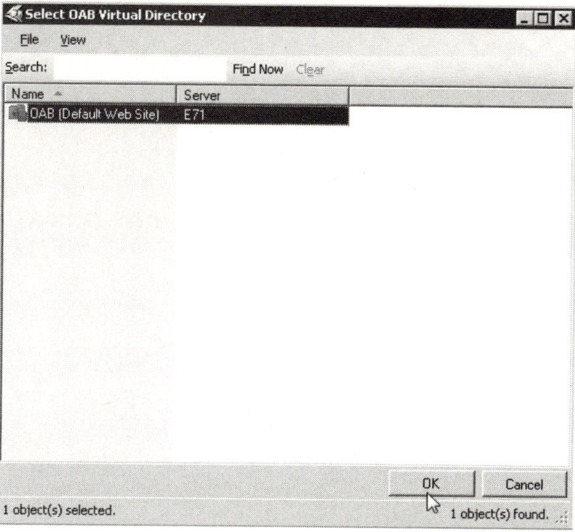

5. Click OK to apply the changes and close the Default Offline Address List Properties dialog.

6. Back in the Exchange Management Console, select Update in the right-hand Actions pane in the Default Offline Address List section, as shown here. Select Yes in the confirmation dialog to regenerate the address book.

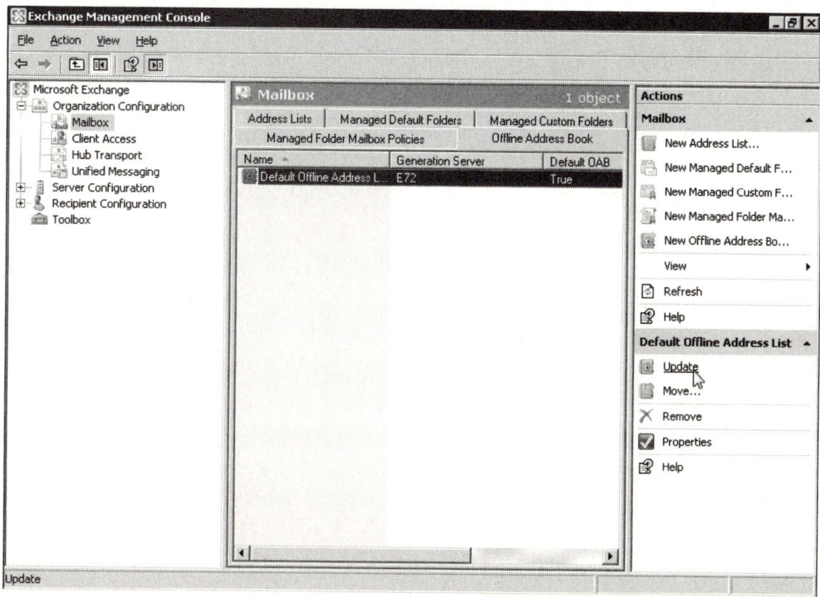

Migrating Offline Address Books Using Exchange Management Shell

Alternatively, migrating the offline address book can be accomplished using Exchange Management Shell cmdlets.

For an Exchange organization with a single offline address book, the cmdlet to move the Default Offline Address List from an Exchange Server 2003 computer called E31 to an Exchange Server 2007 computer called E72 would be as follows:

```
Get-OfflineAddressBook -Server E31 | Move-OfflineAddressBook -Server E72
```

The `Move-OfflineAddressBook` cmdlet requires the GUID of the offline address book to be moved. The `Get-OfflineAddressBook` cmdlet retrieves the Default Offline Address List from the source server, and this output is then piped to the `Move-OfflineAddressBook` cmdlet to provide the GUID of the offline address book to be moved.

The Default Offline Address List on Exchange Server 2007 computer E72 can be updated as follows:

```
Get-OfflineAddressBook -Server E72 | Update-OfflineAddressBook
```

Enabling web-based distribution for this address book requires either determining the virtual directory to be used for a distribution point or creating a new one for the purpose. In an environment with a single Exchange Server 2007 Client Access Server (CAS) named E71, the following cmdlets will determine the OAB virtual directory on E71, then configure web-based distribution for the Default Offline Address List using the OAB virtual directory on E71 as the distribution point:

```
$a=Get-OabVirtualDirectory -Server E71
```

and

```
Set-OfflineAddressBook "Default Offline Address List" -VirtualDirectories $a
```

Recipient Update Service Migration

The Recipient Update Service (RUS) component first introduced in Exchange 2000 Server and carried over to Exchange Server 2003 has been removed from Exchange Server 2007. This is because recipients in Exchange Server 2007 are fully provisioned as they are created, making the RUS unnecessary. However, you need to provide RUS functionality in a mixed environment for the duration of your migration. You also need to know how to update recipients in your Exchange Server 2007 organization when your migration is completed.

An Overview of RUS

Introduced in Exchange 2000 Server and used in Exchange Server 2003 as well, the job of the RUS is to locate newly created recipient objects in Active Directory and provision them by creating Exchange-specific attribute values in Active Directory. The RUS is also responsible for updating existing objects by modifying the appropriate attributes in Active Directory. There are two types of the RUS in an Exchange organization: One is called the Enterprise Configuration Recipient Update Service, and there is only one instance of this type per organization. The second type is the domain Recipient Update Service; as its name implies, there is one instance of the domain RUS for each domain that contains mailbox-enabled users.

When a mail or mailbox-enabled recipient object (such as a user or group) is created in Exchange 2000 Server or Exchange Server 2003 using the Active Directory Users and Computers (ADUC) console, a few key attributes are set immediately by the console. This allows the RUS to discover the new object and backfill the remaining Exchange-specific attributes in an asynchronous process.

In Exchange Server 2007, the primary changes in this process are that recipient objects are fully provisioned as they are created in the Exchange Management Console GUI or the Exchange Management Shell command shell, and that the background process to discover and update objects has been removed. In essence, the "service" part of Recipient Update Service no longer exists. This means that mailboxes can be used immediately after being created in Exchange Server 2007; in Exchange 2000 Server or Exchange Server 2003 the RUS had to stamp the user object before the mailbox was accessible. When the RUS worked, it was great, but when problems arose it could be complicated to troubleshoot—because it was an asynchronous process it was difficult to determine if it wasn't working, or if was just working slowly.

Another role of the RUS was to apply recipient policies in Exchange 2000 Server and Exchange Server 2003, and to update recipients when recipient policies were modified. Because the RUS is not present in Exchange Server 2007, you need to implement various processes to update recipients due to changes in policies; this will be covered in the next section.

RUS Migration Considerations

There are implications of the asynchronous recipient update process being removed from Exchange Server 2007 in a mixed environment. One implication is that setting an Exchange Server 2007 computer as the "Exchange server" for an existing RUS instance through the Exchange System Manager GUI will cause that instance to stop working. Until all recipients have been moved to Exchange Server 2007, you must retain the RUS functionality on an Exchange 2000 Server or Exchange Server 2003 computer, including for domains containing only Exchange Server 2007 computers.

Even after all recipients have been moved to Exchange Server 2007, some user-provisioning tools or processes may partially provision users expecting the RUS to complete the provisioning process, and changes to E-mail Address Policies in Exchange Server 2007 may have to be applied to existing users. This procedure can be accomplished easily with the `Update-EmailAddressPolicy` and `Update-AddressList` cmdlets. The `Update-EmailAddressPolicy` cmdlet updates recipients based on the defined E-mail Address Policies, and the `Update-AddressList` cmdlet updates your address lists with recipients changes, so these cmdlets should be run together and in that order.

Running these cmdlets is easier if you combine them with their corresponding `get` cmdlets as follows:

```
Get-EmailAddressPolicy | Update-EmailAddressPolicy
Get-AddressList | Update-AddressList
```

In addition, to update the Global Address List you can run the following:

```
Get-GlobalAddressList | Update-GlobalAddressList
```

Designing Migration Strategies

The most common Exchange Server 2007 scenario you will encounter is a migration from Exchange 2000 Server or Exchange Server 2003 to Exchange Server 2007. In this section, we will cover the primary factors to consider when planning your migration strategy.

Message Routing

One of the most important factors to consider when designing your Exchange Server 2007 migration strategy, whether it's an inter-forest or intra-forest migration, is your Active Directory site design. In Exchange 2000 Server and Exchange Server 2003, mail routing between servers in different locations was controlled by routing groups and the routing group connectors created between them using link-state routing. A routing group was defined as a collection of Exchange servers that have full-time, high-bandwidth connectivity between all members. This was done to separate Exchange message routing from Active Directory replication.

In Exchange Server 2007, the concept of routing groups has been dropped and message routing between servers in different locations is implemented by leveraging the existing Active Directory site topology and least-cost routing. This means that before implementing Exchange Server 2007, your Active Directory site structure should be reviewed for configuration errors and optimized as necessary to accommodate Exchange Server 2007's requirements. In a mixed environment with Exchange 2000 Server or Exchange Server 2003, all Exchange 2007 computers are associated with a single routing group to allow for message routing to those earlier versions of Exchange.

In a mixed environment all Exchange Server 2007 computers are placed in a single routing group named Exchange Routing Group (DWBGZMFD01QNBJR). The DWBGZMFD01QNBJR is a simple shift replacement cipher; if you change each letter and number to the next letter in the alphabet or number in sequence, you get EXCHANGE12ROCKS.

Exchange Server 2007 and Exchange 2000 Server or Exchange Server 2003 computers can't be in the same routing group, and you can't create additional routing groups to hold Exchange Server 2007 computers. Exchange Server 2007 computers must reside in Exchange Routing Group (DWBGZMFD01QNBJR), and this routing group can't be renamed.

Exchange Server 2007 and Administrative Groups

Exchange 2000 Server and Exchange Server 2003 used the concept of administrative groups to allow for delegation of subsets of the Exchange organization to different administrators. While delegation of administration is a good thing, this model was not as flexible as it could have been.

For example, an Exchange Server 2003 or Exchange 2000 Server computer could not be moved from one administrative group to another; once a computer was deployed into an administrative group it was stuck there unless it was removed and re-installed.

In Exchange Server 2007, administrative groups have been replaced with a much more flexible delegation model that allows for delegation from the organization level down to the server level, as well as by roles (for example, Exchange Recipient Administrators). For coexistence purposes, when Exchange Server 2007 is introduced into an Exchange 2000 Server or Exchange Server 2003 organization, all Exchange Server 2007 computers are installed in an administrative group called Exchange Administrative Group (FYDIBOHF23SPDLT).

Similar to the Exchange Server 2007 routing group, the FYDIBOHF23SPDLT portion of the Exchange Server 2007 administrative group's name is a simple shift replacement cipher; in this case if you change each letter and number to the *previous* letter in the alphabet or to the previous number in sequence, you again arrive at EXCHANGE12ROCKS.

Managing Mailboxes in a Coexistence Environment

In a coexistence environment, Exchange Server 2003 mailboxes are managed using the Active Directory Users and Computers (ADUC) snap-in extension for Exchange, while Exchange Server 2007 mailboxes are managed with the Exchange Server 2007 Exchange Management Console (GUI) or Exchange Management Shell (command line).

Exchange Server 2007 mailboxes must not be managed by using the Exchange Server 2003 tools. This is not blocked from happening, but Exchange Server 2007 mailboxes modified with the ADUC Exchange Server 2003 snap-in will not be fully functional.

All mailbox moves between Exchange Server 2003 and Exchange Server 2007 (in either direction) can be performed with the Exchange Server 2007 tools, but the Exchange Server 2003 move mailbox functionality can't be used for any mailbox moves involving Exchange Server 2007 as either source or destination. In addition, you can modify and remove Exchange 2000 Server and Exchange Server 2003 mailboxes with the Exchange Server 2007 tools, but you can't create mailboxes on Exchange 2000 Server or Exchange Server 2003 with the Exchange Server 2007 tools. To create Exchange 2000 Server or Exchange Server 2003 mailboxes, you must use the ADUC Exchange snap-in.

Discontinued Features

Table 4.3 details the Exchange 2000 Server features that are not supported in Exchange Server 2007. If any of these features need to be retained, Exchange 2000 Server computers must be maintained in the environment or the service must be migrated to an Exchange Server 2007–supported equivalent.

TABLE 4.3 Exchange 2000 Server Features Not Supported in Exchange Server 2007

Exchange 2000 Server Feature	Replacement Product or Service
Key Management Service (KMS)	Microsoft PKI
Mobile Information Service	Exchange ActiveSync
Instant Messaging Service	Office Communications Server
Chat Service	Office Communications Server
Conferencing Service	Office Communications Server
MS Mail Connector	None
cc:Mail Connector	None

The following list shows the Exchange Server 2003 features not supported in Exchange Server 2007. Organizations using the GroupWise Connector need to either maintain an Exchange Server 2003 computer to run this service or migrate from GroupWise to Exchange Server 2007.

- Novell GroupWise Connector
- Network News Transfer Protocol (NNTP)

Inter-Forest Migration

One consideration when migrating to Exchange Server 2007 is whether to introduce Exchange Server 2007 into your existing Exchange 2000 Server or Exchange Server 2003 organization, or to deploy Exchange Server 2007 into a separate organization. As the rule of one Exchange organization per Active Directory forest still applies, this means deploying a separate AD forest as well. An inter-forest migration is considerably more complex than an intra-forest one, but you may have to undertake it for reasons such as the following:

- Company divestiture—a division of your organization is splitting off due to business or technical reasons.
- Company merger, acquisition, or consolidation—you are consolidating from multiple forests down to fewer forests or one forest.
- Separating Active Directory and Exchange administration.

In many ways, the implications of and requirements for migrating to a new forest are the same as migrating to and from any two disparate messaging systems; for example, the following requirements hold true for any migration between different messaging systems or forests:

- Planning name resolution
- Configuring Message routing (cross-forest connectors)

- Directory synchronization
- Calendaring (free/busy data sharing)
- Migration
- Decommissioning or reprovisioning of old systems

As the deployment of Exchange Server 2007 in a separate forest is similar to that of deployment in an existing Exchange Server 2003 forest, this section will focus on the mechanics of a cross-forest migration. The deployment of Exchange Server 2007 in an existing Exchange Server 2007 forest, including the order to deploy Exchange Server 2007 server roles, will be covered in the "Intra-Organization Migration" section of this chapter.

Due to the complexity, the reasons for an inter-forest migration should be completely understood. If the goals of the project can be met by cleaning up or reconfiguring the existing environment and then performing an intra-forest migration, that would be the preferred method.

Planning Name Resolution

Although we won't go into detail here, the cornerstone to communication between the two forests is name resolution, particularly DNS. Any issues can be avoided by carefully planning your Active Directory and DNS namespaces to ensure that computers in both forests can locate resources in the opposing forest.

A best practice when designing Active Directory and DNS for multiple forests is to avoid using a contiguous namespace across forests—for example, `companya.com` in forest A and `exchange2007.companya.com` in forest B. A contiguous namespace is generally assumed to be part of the same forest, and going against this convention can lead to confusion, and support and technical challenges. A multiple-forest topology is already complex, so it's best to avoid this scenario entirely.

Configuring Cross-Forest Connectors

The next step in an inter-forest migration is establishing message routing by creating SMTP Send and Receive connectors between the Exchange Server 2007 Edge Transport server and the Exchange Server 2003 bridgehead server or the Exchange Server 2007 Hub Transport server and the Exchange Server 2003 bridgehead server. The steps to establish the connectors are as follows:

1. Create a user account in the Exchange 2003 forest to use for authentication to the receiving server in the Exchange 2007 forest.
2. Create a Send connector and select Internal as the usage for this connector on either the Exchange 2007 Edge Transport server or Hub Transport server.

3. Create an SMTP connector on Exchange 2003.
4. Modify the registry on the Exchange 2003 server to allow the Exchange 2003 server to send and receive XExch50 properties anonymously as follows:
    1. Open Registry Editor on the Exchange Server 2003 computer.
    2. Locate the HKEY_LOCAL_MACHINE\SYSTEM\CurrentControlSet\Services\SMTPSVC\XEXCH50 key.
    3. Right-click the XEXCH50 key and select New ➤ DWORD Value. Enter **SuppressExternal** for the value name. By default, the value data is 0. This dictates that the XEXCH50 properties are transmitted anonymously to the Exchange Server 2007 computer.
    4. Right-click the XEXCH50 key and select New ➤ Key. Enter the number of the SMTP virtual-server instance as the key value. The default virtual server instance is 1; if a second SMTP virtual server has been created, it will be instance 2.
    5. Right-click the key that you just created for the SMTP virtual server instance and select New ➤ DWORD Value from the context menu.
    6. In the details pane, enter **Exch50AuthCheckEnabled** for the value name. By default, the value data is 0. This indicates that when email is sent anonymously, the XEXCH50 properties are transmitted as well.

Directory Synchronization

The next step in an inter-forest migration is to establish directory synchronization between the two forests to provide a common address book, and to lay the groundwork for sharing calendaring (free/busy) information across the forests. The directory synchronization process creates Active Directory contact objects in each forest representing users and groups from the other forest. Directory synchronization is most commonly implemented using Microsoft Identity Integration Server (MIIS) 2003 or the Identity Integration Feature Pack 1a for Microsoft Windows Server Active Directory.

As part of the directory synchronization process in the Exchange Server 2007 forest, it is necessary to update the Exchange Server 2007 email address policies and address lists. This can be done by creating an Exchange Management Shell script and scheduling it to run as necessary. A sample script is as follows:

```
Get-EmailAddressPolicy | Update-EmailAddressPolicy
Get-AddressList | Update-AddressList
Get-GlobalAddressList | Update-GlobalAddressList
```

Creating this script is necessary because, as covered earlier in this chapter, there is no equivalent to the Recipient Update Service asynchronous process in Exchange Server 2007; all users are completely provisioned as they are created using the Exchange Server 2007 tools.

Free/Busy Data across Forests

To share free/busy data across forests, directory synchronization must first be established as outlined in the previous section. The Exchange Server 2007 Availability service in a single-forest topology was covered earlier in this chapter in the "Free/Busy Functionality" section. To provide for sharing free/busy data across Exchange Server 2003 and Exchange Server 2007 forests, the Inter-Organization Replication tool can be used. This tool can be downloaded from `http://www.microsoft.com/downloads/details.aspx?familyid=e7a951d7-1559-4f8f-b400-488b0c52430e&displaylang=en`.

The Inter-Organization Replication tool is a Microsoft-supplied utility for replicating public folders, including system folders, between Exchange organizations. It can be used to replicate the free/busy system folders between forests; the obvious requirement for this is that free/busy folders must be implemented in both forests, including the Exchange Server 2007 target forest.

Another caveat with the Inter-Organization Replication tool is that it is not supported with Exchange Server 2007 public folders as either the source or target. This means that an Exchange Server 2003 public-folder store must exist in the target forest; for a new forest this means deploying Exchange Server 2003 into the forest before introducing Exchange Server 2007, as Exchange Server 2003 computers can't be added to a native Exchange Server 2007 forest.

As the Inter-Organization Replication tool needs to read and write to both organizations, a service account with Publishing Editor permission for each top-level folder and subfolder to be replicated needs to be created in both forests.

Mailbox Migration between Forests

Once coexistence in the form of message routing, directory synchronization, and free/busy sharing have been established, migration of mailboxes can begin.

When mailboxes are moved between forests, any clients with Outlook configured in cached mode will have a complete rebuild of their offline cache initiated. This can take a considerable amount of time for remote users and/or those with large mailboxes. In addition, clients running Outlook 2003 or earlier will need their Outlook profiles reconfigured to point to the target server when the mailbox move is completed. Finally, in the case of a significantly different organizational structure in the target environment, calendar meetings and appointments can be disconnected from the originators.

In earlier versions of Exchange, the Exmerge utility was the primary tool for moving mailboxes between forests. In Exchange Server 2007, however, inter-forest mailbox moves are accomplished with the `Move-Mailbox` cmdlet in the Exchange Management Shell. Scripts can be built around this cmdlet to provide extremely powerful, scalable, and flexible mailbox-migration functionality.

The `Move-Mailbox` cmdlet can interoperate only with Windows Server 2003 domain controllers; to use `Move-Mailbox` for cross-forest migrations, you must have at least one Windows Server 2003 domain controller on both the source and destination Active Directory forests.

Exercise 4.6 outlines the steps for moving a mailbox from an Exchange Server 2003 forest (source) to an Exchange Server 2007 forest (destination).

EXERCISE 4.6

Cross-Forest Mailbox Moves

1. On the Exchange Server 2007 computer where the `Move-Mailbox` cmdlet will be run, in the Exchange Management Shell, run the following to create a credential object for the source forest:

   ```
   $SourceCredential = Get-Credential
   ```

   You will be prompted for credentials for the source forest; this account needs to have move mailbox permissions in that forest.

2. Also on the Exchange Server 2007 computer where the `Move-Mailbox` cmdlet will be run, run the following in the Exchange Management Shell to create a credential object for the target forest:

   ```
   $TargetCredential = Get-Credential
   ```

   You will be prompted for credentials for the target forest; this account needs to have move mailbox permissions in that forest.

3. Run the `Move-Mailbox` cmdlet as shown here to move the mailbox:

   ```
   Move-Mailbox -TargetDatabase "target_mailbox_database" -Identity john
   -GlobalCatalog global_catalog_FQDN -SourceForestGlobalCatalog source_global_
   catalog_FQDN -NTAccountOU "Target_OU" -SourceForestCredential $SourceCredential
   -TargetForestCredential $TargetCredential
   ```

   Here's an example of a complete `Move-Mailbox` cmdlet:

   ```
   Move-Mailbox -TargetDatabase "Target Server\First Storage Group\Mailbox
   Database" -Identity john -GlobalCatalog GC01.exchange2007.com
   -SourceForestGlobalCatalog GC02.exchange2003.com -NTAccountOU
   "OU=OrgUnit01,DC=exchange2007,DC=com" -SourceForestCredential
   $SourceCredential -TargetForestCredential $TargetCredential
   ```

4. Check the output of the cmdlet to confirm that the mailbox move was successful.

5. For clients running Outlook 2003 or earlier, the Outlook profile must be modified to point to the target server.

In a resource-forest scenario, using this procedure alone will result in the source forest containing an enabled user account, and the target forest containing a disabled user account and the mailbox for that user account. If you want to move the user account to the target forest as well, you can use tools such as the Active Directory Migration Tool version 3.0 (ADMT v3) before or after the mailboxes are moved.

Decommissioning

Once the mailbox migration is complete and all other Exchange services have been migrated to the new forest, the old forest may be decommissioned. Primarily, this will depend on whether user accounts are being migrated to the target forest, or if the source forest is being retained as an account forest, with the new forest as a resource forest. User-account migration can be performed with the Active Directory Migration Tool or third-party utilities.

Intra-Organization Migration

By far the simpler method of migrating to Exchange Server 2007 is to implement it in the existing Exchange 2000 Server or Exchange Server 2003 organization. In an intra-organization migration, the sequence of events is as follows:

1. Install Windows Server 2003 on the Exchange Server 2007 computer.
2. Prepare Exchange 2000 Server or Exchange Server 2003 permissions.
3. Extend the Active Directory Schema.
4. Prepare Active Directory.
5. Install Exchange Server 2007 on the first computer.
6. Deploy other Exchange Server 2007 server roles.
7. Move mailboxes to Exchange Server 2007.
8. Remove legacy Exchange computers.

Installing Windows Server 2003

The computer that will be running Exchange Server 2007 requires 64-bit Windows Server 2003 SP1 or higher. The 32-bit version is supported for evaluation and training purposes only.

Although Windows Server 2003 R2 is not required, it does contain components that are prerequisites for Exchange Server 2007, such as the .NET Framework Version 2.0 and Microsoft Management Console (MMC) 3.0. If previous versions of Windows Server 2003 are used, these components will need to be installed separately before Exchange Server 2007 can be installed on the computer.

The following prerequisite software must be present on Windows Server 2003 in order to install Exchange Server 2007:

- .NET Framework Version 2.0
- Microsoft Management Console (MMC) 3.0
- Microsoft Windows PowerShell

Preparing Legacy Exchange Permissions

The first step in preparing the legacy Exchange environment for Exchange Server 2007 is to grant specific Exchange permissions in each domain containing Exchange 2000 Server or Exchange Server 2003 computers. The reason for this is to allow the Exchange 2000 Server or Exchange Server 2003 Recipient Update Service to function correctly after the Active Directory schema is updated for Exchange 2007.

To prepare the legacy Exchange permissions, run the following from a command prompt from the Exchange Server 2007 setup directory:

```
Setup /PrepareLegacyExchangePermissions
```

You must be a member of the Enterprise Admins group to run this command to prepare every domain in the forest. To run this command for a specific domain, or if the forest has only one domain, you must be delegated the Exchange Full Administrator role and you must be a member of the Domain Admins group in the domain to be prepared.

Extending the Active Directory Schema

The next step in migrating to Exchange Server 2007 is to extend the Active Directory schema. Exchange Server 2007 adds many new attributes and classes to the schema and modifies existing classes and attributes.

To extend the Active Directory schema for Exchange Server 2007, run the following from a command prompt from the Exchange Server 2007 setup directory:

```
Setup /PrepareSchema
```

You must be a member of the Schema Admins group and the Enterprise Admins group to run this command.

Among the other schema changes noted, Exchange Server 2007 also adds numerous attributes to the global catalog, which can impact your AD replication and the size of the AD database on your global catalog servers.

If the legacy Exchange permissions have not been prepared previously, this step will automatically perform the PrepareLegacyExchangePermissions step as well as extend the AD schema.

Preparing Active Directory

The final step in readying your Active Directory environment for Exchange Server 2007 is to prepare AD by running the `setup /PrepareAD` command. This command verifies that the schema has been updated, configures global Exchange objects in Active Directory, creates the Exchange universal security groups (USGs) in the root domain, sets permissions on the Exchange configuration objects, and prepares the current domain. This command also creates the Exchange 2007 administrative group called Exchange Administrative Group (FYDIBOHF23SPDLT) and the Exchange 2007 routing group called Exchange Routing Group (DWBGZMFD01QNBJR).

To prepare Active Directory for Exchange Server 2007, run the following from a command prompt from the Exchange Server 2007 setup directory:

```
Setup /PrepareAD
```

To run this command, you must be a member of the Enterprise Admins group, the computer where you run this command must be able to contact all domains in the forest on port 389, and you must be an Exchange Full Administrator if you have Exchange Server 2003 servers in your organization. In addition, this command must be run on a computer in the same domain and Active Directory site as the schema master.

If the legacy Exchange permissions have not been prepared and the schema has not been extended, running the `setup /PrepareAD` command will perform all three steps, assuming the prerequisite permissions are held by the account running the command, and the computer the command is run from is in the same domain and Active Directory site as the schema master.

Installing Exchange Server 2007 on the First Computer

The details of how to install Exchange Server 2007 are outside the scope of the book, but there are a few points to keep in mind when designing your migration:

- Your Exchange 2000 Server or Exchange Server 2003 organization must be set to Native Mode (no pre-Exchange 2000 servers).
- In addition to the prerequisite software listed earlier in this chapter, the following Windows components are required for the Mailbox server role:
  - Network COM+ access
  - Internet Information Services
  - World Wide Web service
- The following components are required by the Client Access server role:
  - World Wide Web service
  - Remote Procedure Call (RPC) over Hypertext Transfer Protocol (HTTP) Proxy Windows networking component
  - ASP.NET v2.0
- The features available depend on the version of Exchange Server 2007 installed, as outlined in Table 4.4.

TABLE 4.4 Exchange Server 2007 Offerings by Edition

Feature	Standard Edition	Enterprise Edition
Storage group support	5 storage groups	50 storage groups
Database support	5 databases	50 databases
Database storage limit	No software storage limit; storage limit is hardware-dependent	No software storage limit; storage limit is hardware-dependent
Single-copy clusters	Not supported	Supported
Local continuous replication	Supported	Supported
Cluster continuous replication	Not supported	Supported

Deploying Other Exchange Server 2007 Server Roles

Unless the Mailbox, Client Access, and Hub Transport roles are all installed on the first Exchange Server 2007 computer, the Exchange Server 2007 server roles should be implemented in the following order:

1. Client Access server role
2. Hub Transport server role

The Edge Transport server role, if it is deployed, should be implemented after the Hub Transport server role.

3. Mailbox server role

The Client Access Server Role

The Client Access server role should be implemented before all other server roles. Exchange 2000 Server or Exchange Server 2003 front-end servers can't access Exchange Server 2007 mailboxes, but the Exchange Server 2007 Client Access server role can provide access to both Exchange Server 2007 and Exchange Server 2003 mailboxes.

Users with mailboxes on Exchange 2000 Server or Exchange Server 2003 will receive the Exchange 2000 Server or Exchange Server 2003 OWA experience until their mailboxes are moved to Exchange Server 2007.

Combining all of the discussed roles (with the exception of the Edge Transport server role) in various combinations on the same Exchange Server 2007 computer is possible. However, in the case of OWA access to Exchange 2000 Server or Exchange Server 2003 mailboxes, if the Client Access role is on a computer also holding Exchange Server 2007 mailboxes, then Exchange 2000 Server or Exchange Server 2003 users will be redirected to the Exchange 2000 Server or Exchange Server 2003 mailbox server and be prompted for logon credentials twice. If the Client Access server role is on a dedicated computer, Exchange 2000 Server or Exchange Server 2003 users will be proxied transparently to their mailbox server by the Client Access server with no additional authentication prompts.

The Hub Transport Server Role

In Exchange 2000 Server and Exchange Server 2003, messages between servers were delivered using SMTP, but messages between users in the same mailbox database were delivered directly to the mailbox. Exchange Server 2007 introduces the Hub Transport server role, and all messages in the organization are processed by the Hub Transport role, without exception. This provides a mechanism for applying messaging policy and compliance, antispam, and antivirus features to all messages (including between recipients on the same database) that is much easier than with the direct delivery model used in Exchange 2000 Server and Exchange Server 2003.

A Hub Transport server role must be deployed in every Active Directory site that contains a Mailbox server role, although both roles can be deployed on the same Exchange Server 2007 computer.

The Edge Transport Server Role

The Edge Transport server role can be deployed at any time during the migration, but it will not be fully functional until the Hub Transport server role is deployed and the Edge Transport server is subscribed. The Edge Transport server role must be implemented on a separate server, and should not be a member of the Active Directory forest.

The Exchange Server 2007 setup process prevents you from installing the Edge Transport server role with any other server roles. However, there is nothing preventing installation of the Edge Transport server role on an Active Directory domain member server, although it is highly recommended that the Edge Transport server role be installed on a stand-alone computer.

The Mailbox Server Role

The Mailbox server role hosts the mailbox and public-folder databases, assuming public folders are implemented on Exchange Server 2007. As no message routing or Internet-protocol access is provided by the Mailbox server role (unlike in earlier versions of Exchange), the Client Access and Hub Transport server roles should be implemented before the Mailbox server role.

In an environment where OWA and other Internet protocols (IMAP4, POP3) are not used, it is possible to deploy Exchange Server 2007 without the Client Access role and have clients access their mailboxes exclusively with Outlook using MAPI. This is not very practical, however, as the Client Access role also provides other important services, such as OAB distribution, the Autodiscover service, the Availability service, and Outlook Anywhere (formerly known as RPC over HTTP).

Moving Mailboxes to Exchange Server 2007

Moving mailboxes to Exchange Server 2007 within a single forest is similar to moving mailboxes between forests (outlined earlier in this chapter in the "Mailbox Migration between Forests" section), with a few differences:

- When using the Exchange Management Shell, you do not need to specify the `-SourceForestCredential` and `-TargetForestCredential` parameters, as these are required only for cross-forest mailbox moves.
- For mailbox moves within the same forest, the Exchange Management Console GUI can be used.
- The following permissions are required:
  - Exchange Server Administrator role
  - Local Administrators privileges for both the source and target servers
- Only one instance of the Move Mailbox wizard can be run from the Exchange Management Console at a time, although you can open multiple Exchange Management Consoles and run one instance of the Move Mailbox wizard from each console.

Items in the dumpster (Deleted Items Recovery) will not be moved when mailboxes are moved, although items in the Deleted Items folder will be retained.

Removing Legacy Exchange Computers

The last legacy Exchange servers are removed from the organization as follows:

1. Confirm that you have the required permissions to remove the last Exchange 2000 Server or Exchange Server 2003 computer from the organization. The account you use must have the following permissions:
   - Exchange Organization Administrator role in Exchange Server 2007
   - Exchange Full Administrator role in Exchange 2000 Server or Exchange Server 2003
2. Confirm legacy Exchange features are decommissioned.

Before removing Exchange 2000 Server or Exchange Server 2003 servers, confirm that none of the services listed in the "Discontinued Features" section of this chapter are in use.

3. Confirm all mailboxes are moved to Exchange Server 2007 as outlined in the "Inter-Forest Migration" and "Intra-Organization Migration" sections of this chapter.
4. Migrate or remove all public folders as outlined in the "Migrating Public Folders" section of this chapter.
5. Move the public-folder hierarchy from the legacy Exchange administrative group to the Exchange Server 2007 administrative group as follows:
    1. Open the Exchange System Manager console on the Exchange 2000 Server or Exchange Server 2003 computer.
    2. Within Exchange System Manager, expand Administrative Groups, right-click Exchange Administrative Group (FYDIBOHF23SPDLT), select New, and then select Public Folders Container.
    3. Expand the legacy Exchange administrative group that contains the public-folder tree, expand Folders, and then drag Public Folders to Folders under the Exchange 2007 administrative group.
6. Move OAB generation to Exchange Server 2007; all offline address books need to have their generation process moved to Exchange Server 2007 prior to your removing the last legacy Exchange server.
7. Create Send connectors on Exchange Server 2007 Hub Transport or Edge Transport server roles to replace the outbound SMTP connectors on your legacy Exchange servers.
8. Remove legacy public-folder stores using the Exchange 2000 Server or Exchange Server 2003 Exchange System Manager console. Exchange System Manager in Exchange 2003 Service Pack 2 (SP2) prevents you from removing a public-folder store until all the public-folder replicas have completed their background move process. In versions of Exchange earlier than Exchange Server 2003 SP2, you should confirm that the public-folder replicas have moved before removing the public-folder store.
9. Verify inbound mail is routing to Exchange Server 2007 Hub Transport or Edge Transport computers by doing the following:
    - Check your DNS Mail Exchange (MX) records and confirm that they resolve to Exchange Server 2007 Hub Transport or Edge Transport computers.
    - In the Exchange Server 2007 Exchange Management Console, under Organization Configuration, verify that no Exchange Server 2003 or Exchange 2000 Server computers are listed as the smart host for any Send connectors.
10. Verify inbound protocol services such as the following have their DNS records and IP addresses pointing to Exchange Server 2007 Client Access server role computers. Also

confirm that all clients are correctly configured to point to Exchange Server 2007 computers for these services:

- ActiveSync
- Outlook Web Access
- Outlook Anywhere
- POP3
- IMAP4
- Autodiscover service
- Other Exchange Web services

11. Delete all routing-group connectors connecting the Exchange 2000 Server or Exchange Server 2003 routing groups to the Exchange Server 2007 routing group. These connectors can be deleted via the legacy Exchange System Manager console, or by using the `Remove-RoutingGroupConnector` cmdlet in the Exchange Management Shell.
12. Remove any legacy Exchange recipient policies that contain only Mailbox Manager policies and don't contain E-mail Address policies. These can be deleted using the legacy Exchange System Manager console. For any legacy Exchange recipient policies that contain both Mailbox Manager policies and E-mail Address policies, remove the mailbox manager portion of the policy as follows:
    1. In Exchange System Manager, expand Recipients, and then select Recipient Policies.
    2. Right-click the policy, and then select Change Property Pages.
    3. Clear the Mailbox Manager Settings check box, and then click OK.

Do not delete any recipient policies that have email address definitions that you still want defined in your organization. Exchange Server 2007 will use these policies when new recipients are provisioned.

13. For each domain, delete the Recipient Update Services domain instance using the legacy Exchange System Manager console by right-clicking it and selecting Delete.
14. Uninstall Legacy Exchange.

Exchange 2000 Server or Exchange Server 2003 can now be uninstalled by using Add or Remove Programs from Control Panel.

Exchange Server 2003 or Exchange 2000 Server administrative groups that at any time contained mailboxes should not be deleted, as the LegacyExchangeDN property on mailboxes moved from Exchange 2000 Server or Exchange Server 2003 to Exchange Server 2007 still references the legacy administrative group. Outlook 2003 and earlier reference the LegacyExchangeDN property to retrieve free/busy information; if the administrative group is deleted, free/busy lookups will fail. All versions of Outlook also use the LegacyExchangeDN property for delegate access; if the legacy Exchange administrative group is deleted, Outlook can't find the delegated user.

15. Delete the Recipient Update Services (Enterprise Configuration) instance. The RUS instance can't be deleted using Exchange System Manager, but is deleted by using ADSI Edit (`AdsiEdit.msc`) as follows:
    1. Open ADSI Edit, then expand Configuration ➢ CN=Configuration ➢ CN=<domain> ➢ CN=Services ➢ CN=Microsoft Exchange ➢ CN=<Exchange organization name> ➢ CN=Address Lists Container, and then select CN=Recipient Update Services.
    2. In the result pane, right-click Recipient Update Service (Enterprise Configuration), click Delete, and then click Yes to confirm the deletion.

Planning Coexistence for Exchange Server 2003 and Exchange Server 2007

The term *coexistence* refers to the interoperability of Exchange 2000 Server or Exchange Server 2003 with Exchange Server 2007 during the period of migration while the organization is transitioning to Exchange Server 2007. Coexistence encompasses message-routing differences between Exchange 2000 Server or Exchange Server 2003 and Exchange Server 2007 (including Send and Receive connectors), administrative differences, and coexistence with server roles.

Message Routing Differences

There are significant differences in message routing between Exchange Server 2003 and Exchange Server 2007. In this section we will walk through these changes and outline the actions necessary to ensure successful coexistence.

Link-State Routing in a Coexistence Environment

In a coexistence environment with a single routing-group connector between Exchange Server 2003 and Exchange Server 2007, no changes to link-state routing in Exchange Server 2003 are necessary.

If additional routing-group connectors are configured between Exchange Server 2007 and Exchange Server 2003, though, minor link-state updates must be disabled in Exchange Server 2003 to avoid the potential of routing loops. When Exchange Server 2003 detects that a connector is down, it communicates minor link-state updates throughout the organization and determines another route based on link-state routing. As Exchange Server 2007 uses least-cost routing and does not use link state, the potential exists to direct a message back through a path that Exchange Server 2003 is trying to route around, resulting in a possible routing loop. Suppressing minor link-state updates causes Exchange Server 2003 to use least-cost routing and eliminates the potential for routing loops. Link-state updates should be suppressed on all Exchange Server 2003 computers in the organization to ensure consistent routing behavior.

You may want to create additional routing-group connectors in a legacy Exchange environment composed of multiple routing groups to optimize message routing between the legacy Exchange routing groups and the Exchange Server 2007 routing group. These connectors must be created using the `New-RoutingGroupConnector` cmdlet in the Exchange Management Shell. This automatically updates the membership of the ExchangeLegacyInterop universal security group with the specified legacy Exchange servers so the legacy Exchange servers have the necessary permissions to send and receive mail from the Exchange Server 2007 Hub Transport server.

Send and Receive Connectors

SMTP transport for an Exchange Server 2007 organization is provided by the Hub Transport server role. Unlike in Exchange 2000 Server and Exchange Server 2003, where routing-group connectors provided messaging connectivity between locations, the Hub Transport uses an implicit connector called the *intra-organization Send connector* to route messages between Active Directory sites. During installation of the Hub Transport server role, two explicit Receive connectors are created. The first Receive connector receives SMTP traffic from all sources on port 25. The second Receive connector receives SMTP traffic from non-MAPI clients, listening on port 587.

Both of the Receive connectors configured on Exchange Server 2007 Hub Transport servers require authentication by default; in an environment where Edge Transport computers are not deployed and Internet mail is received directly on the Hub Transport server, the default Receive connector receiving SMTP traffic from the Internet must have anonymous access enabled to accept SMTP messages from the Internet.

A Send connector must be configured to route messages to the Internet. The preferred method to connect Exchange Server 2007 to the Internet is to deploy the Edge Transport server role in a perimeter network and to route messages to remote domains through the Edge Transport computer. When you subscribe the Edge Transport server to the Exchange organization, the necessary connectors are created automatically.

X-EXCH50 Data

A proprietary ESMTP verb named X-EXCH50 is used in Exchange Server 2003 to transmit information about messages and recipients that can't be included in the messages themselves. Because this is a proprietary verb, EXCH50 data can't be propagated to a non-Exchange server. Exchange Server 2007 supports a mapping between Multipurpose Internet Mail Extensions (MIME) and MAPI that accommodates the data transmitted by EXCH50 in Exchange Server 2003, but Exchange Server 2007 can also propagate the EXCH50 data to Exchange Server 2003 computers for compatibility purposes.

Within a single forest, the routing-group connectors between Exchange Server 2003 and Exchange Server 2007 automatically support sending and receiving EXCH50 data, but if Exchange Server 2003 and Exchange Server 2007 are in separate forests without a trust relationship, the Exchange Server 2003 bridgeheads may need to be modified to allow for sending and receiving EXCH50 properties anonymously.

Real World Scenario

Implementing Additional Send Connectors

As part of your Exchange Server 2007 deployment, you have implemented the Edge Transport server role and subscribed it to your Exchange organization. This configuration has served you well up to now, but now your company has entered into a partnership arrangement with another company. You need to implement and enforce secure message routing between your environment and the partners without affecting other message flow.

Subscribing the Edge Transport server to the Exchange organization automatically creates a single Send connector to the Internet, and the tasks for creating and modifying Send connectors are disabled on the Edge Transport server. In this case, to implement an additional Send connector in your environment, you must create the additional Send connector on a Hub Transport server and specify the Edge Transport server as the source server for the connector. This new configuration is then routed to the Edge Transport server through the EdgeSync process.

Message Tracking

The message-tracking schemas are significantly different between Exchange Server 2003 and Exchange Server 2007; this means that messages sent and received by Exchange Server 2007 can be tracked only by Exchange Server 2007 computers. Additionally, Exchange Server 2007 has no Windows Management Instrumentation (WMI) support, so Exchange Server 2007 can't track messages traversing Exchange Server 2003. The result of this is that a message traversing both Exchange Server 2003 and Exchange Server 2007 can't be tracked with the same tools, but must be tracked with a combination of the Exchange Server 2003 and Exchange Server 2007 utilities.

Administration Differences

Exchange 2000 Server and Exchange Server 2003 use Administrative Groups to delegate administrative permissions for management purposes. While Exchange Server 2007 has dropped this model, it is still supported in a mixed environment for coexistence purposes. This was covered in greater detail earlier in this chapter in the "Exchange Server 2007 and Administrative Groups" section, but some points bear calling out here:

- After Exchange Server 2007 has been introduced into the Exchange organization, all organizational-level settings must be managed with the Exchange Server 2007 administration tools.
- The legacy (Exchange 2000 Server and Exchange Server 2003) Exchange System Manager and Active Directory Users and Computers Exchange snap-in must be used to manage legacy Exchange servers and mailboxes respectively.
- Exchange Server 2007 computers and mailboxes must be managed by using the Exchange Server 2007 Exchange Management Console or Exchange Management Shell.

Real World Scenario

Managing a Mixed Environment

As we've seen in this section, managing a mixed Exchange Server 2003 and Exchange Server 2007 environment presents challenges in several areas. This is why the ultimate goal of your Exchange Server 2007 implementation should always be a native Exchange Server 2007 environment, with all legacy Exchange servers decommissioned.

In many cases, the primary goals of the Exchange Server 2007 implementation are to consolidate the environment and simplify its management to lower the total cost of ownership (TCO). Maintaining a mixed environment with all the coexistence challenges that accompany it means that rather than simplifying your environment, you now have two systems to manage (Exchange Server 2003 and Exchange Server 2007) instead of a single one. Coexistence with Exchange Server 2003 should be a step in your journey to Exchange Server 2007, not your final destination.

Additionally, a mixed environment presents many opportunities for human error, by inadvertently administering Exchange Server 2003 servers using Exchange Server 2007 tools or vice versa. This can result in messaging service degradation or even outages, causing your end users to be unable to do their jobs. It can take a long time to build up the reputation your Exchange environment has with your user community, but it takes only a single outage to destroy that reputation.

Server Role Coexistence

The server roles introduced in Exchange Server 2007 present some coexistence issues and considerations that you should take into account when planning your Exchange Server 2007 implementation. We will cover these items in the following sections.

The Edge Transport Server Role

The Edge Transport server role is typically deployed in an environment where Exchange Server 2007 has been deployed into the Exchange organization. However, it is possible to deploy the Edge Transport server for an existing Exchange Server 2003 organization without requiring any Active Directory preparation or configuration changes to the organization. This can provide an added layer of antivirus and antispam protection for the organization.

In an environment where Exchange Server 2007 has not been deployed, though, the feature set provided by the Edge Transport server is limited; for example, an Edge Subscription can't be created, so Recipient Lookup and safe-list aggregation are not available.

The Mailbox Server Role

The Exchange Server 2007 Mailbox server role can coexist with Exchange 2000 Server and Exchange Server 2003 servers; to provide message flow between the servers, the Exchange Server 2007 Hub Transport role is required in each Active Directory site containing an Exchange Server 2007 Mailbox server role.

Public folders and mailboxes can be moved across Exchange 2000 Server, Exchange Server 2003, and Exchange Server 2007; public-folder migration was covered in the "Migrating Public Folders" section of this chapter, while mailbox migrations were covered in detail in the "Inter-Forest Migration" and "Intra-Organization Migration" sections.

The Client Access Server Role

The functionality provided by the Client Access server role is generally equivalent to the functionality provided by front-end servers in Exchange 2000 Server and Exchange Server 2003. The Client Access server role can coexist with Exchange 2000 Server and Exchange Server 2003 Mailbox servers as outlined in the following list:

- Users will receive the OWA experience of the server their mailboxes reside on. That is, users with mailboxes on Exchange Server 2003 will see the Exchange Server 2003 OWA client, while users with mailboxes on Exchange Server 2007 will see the Exchange Server 2007 OWA client.
- Similar to the OWA experienced outlined in the previous bullet point, users see the version of Exchange ActiveSync based on where their mailboxes reside.

User mailboxes must be on Exchange Server 2003 SP2 or Exchange Server 2007 to have Direct Push, Exchange search, and Global Address List lookup.

- Users with mailboxes on Exchange Server 2003 connect to the Client Access server role using the URL `http://<servername>/exchange`.
- Users with mailboxes on Exchange Server 2007 connect to the Client Access server role using the URL `http://<servername>/exchange` or `http://<servername>/owa`.

Summary

Many people equate the difficulty of the transition from Exchange 2000 Server or Exchange Server 2003 to Exchange Server 2007 to the transition from Exchange Server 5.5 to Exchange 2000 Server or Exchange Server 2003. There is no doubt that there are significant challenges to migrating and coexisting with Exchange Server 2007 and Exchange 2000 Server or Exchange Server 2003. However, these challenges are easily overcome with proper planning.

Legacy Exchange features whose functionality has changed significantly or is being provided differently include free/busy functionality, public folders, offline address books, and the Recipient Update Service. You must take these into account when planning your migration to Exchange Server 2007. In addition, services that have been discontinued, such as the Exchange 2000 Server Key Management Services and the Exchange Server 2003 GroupWise Connector, require you to retain those legacy Exchange servers, discontinue those services, or migrate those services to Exchange Server 2007–compatible equivalents.

A crucial factor in any Exchange Server 2007 migration's success is planning your migration strategy properly. This includes considering cross-forest migration versus an intra-forest implementation, deploying the Exchange Server 2007 server roles in the appropriate order, and planning for the changes in functionality, such as the removal of the Recipient Update Service.

Finally, coexistence is a part of any Exchange Server 2007 migration; there will always be a period of time in which interoperability must be maintained for end users to continue to do their jobs, which is really what it's all about in the end.

Exam Essentials

Understand how the functionalities previously provided by system folders are provided by Exchange Server 2007, and when system folders may need to be retained. In Exchange Server 2007, functionalities previously provided by system folders in Exchange 2000 Server and Exchange Server 2003 have been replaced by web-based services. You should understand how these new services work, how to migrate them, and when the legacy system folders may need to be retained.

Understand the role of public folders in Exchange Server 2007, how and why to migrate them, and when Exchange Server 2003 public-folder databases may need to be maintained. Although public folders have been de-emphasized in Exchange Server 2007, you should know the various reasons they may need to be migrated to Exchange Server 2007. In addition, you should understand the circumstances in which Exchange 2000 Server or Exchange Server 2003 public folder databases may need to be maintained in the environment. Finally, you should also know the various means of migrating public folders and their pros and cons.

Know how the Recipient Update Service functionality has been replaced. The Recipient Update Service in Exchange 2000 Server and Exchange Server 2003 has been supplanted in Exchange Server 2007 by having recipient objects fully provisioned as they are created rather than by a background process. You should understand the implications of this for both migrations and coexistence. You should also know the various PowerShell commands relating to updating recipients, and when to use and/or script these to coexist with previous versions of Exchange or legacy processes, such as user provisioning or directory synchronization solutions.

Understand the differences between inter-forest and intra-forest migrations, and when to perform each. You should understand the reasons for choosing either an inter-forest or an intra-forest migration. Know the requirements for each type of migration, and understand the implications and the prerequisites. You should also understand the impacts on end users, including on Outlook configurations, and when (and if) migrating Active Directory accounts should be performed.

Know the various components and functional differences involved in coexistence. As the vast majority of Exchange Server 2007 deployments are into existing Exchange 2000 Server or Exchange Server 2003 environments, you should have a solid understanding of the interaction and coexistence between the systems. This includes message routing, administrative differences (especially which versions of Exchange management tools to use, and when), and the interaction between Exchange Server 2007 server roles and the equivalent functionality in previous Exchange versions.

Review Questions

1. You have completed the migration of all your users from Exchange Server 2003 to Exchange Server 2007, and you want to ensure that all clients running Outlook 2003 can access free/busy information when the Exchange Server 2003 servers are decommissioned. What should you do?

   A. Configure the `-InternalURL` parameter for the Availability service using the `Set-WebServicesVirtualDirectory` cmdlet.

   B. Run the `Set-AutoDiscoverVirtualDirectory` cmdlet on the Exchange Server 2007 Client Access server role to specify the internal URL for Outlook clients.

   C. Create an Exchange Server 2007 public folder database and migrate the SCHEDULE+ FREE BUSY folders from Exchange Server 2003 to Exchange Server 2007.

   D. Do nothing; the Availability and Autodiscover services are configured automatically in Exchange Server 2007.

2. You are migrating from Exchange Server 2003 to Exchange Server 2007. What services provided with system folders in Exchange Server 2003 are provided through different mechanisms in Exchange Server 2007? Choose all that apply.

   A. Free/busy

   B. Autodiscover service

   C. Offline address books

   D. Network News Transfer Protocol (NNTP)

3. You are migrating your organization from Exchange Server 2003 to Exchange Server 2007. Your organization uses public folders extensively, and you have a large number of users who access public folders from Outlook Web Access. How can you ensure that these users will continue to have access to public folders after the migration?

   A. Implement Exchange Server 2007 Client Access Servers. Migrate all public folders to Exchange Server 2007 before moving mailboxes. Migrate the users' mailboxes to Exchange Server 2007.

   B. Migrate all public folders to Exchange Server 2007. Implement Exchange Server 2007 Client Access servers. Migrate user mailboxes from Exchange Server 2003 to Exchange Server 2007.

   C. Retain Exchange Server 2003 front-end servers for OWA clients. Migrate all user mailboxes from Exchange Server 2003 to Exchange Server 2007, and migrate all public folders from Exchange Server 2003 to Exchange Server 2007.

   D. Implement Exchange Server 2007 Client Access servers. Migrate all user mailboxes from Exchange Server 2003 to Exchange Server 2007. Retain public folders on an Exchange Server 2003 public-folder database.

4. You are planning the migration of your organization's public folders from Exchange Server 2003 to Exchange Server 2007. What Exchange Management Shell commands or scripts can you use to migrate public-folder data from Exchange Server 2003 to Exchange Server 2007? Choose all that apply.

   A. The `MoveAllReplicas.ps1` script

   B. The `ReplaceUserPermissionOnPFRecursive.ps1` script

   C. The `New-PublicFolderDatabase` cmdlet

   D. The `Remove-PublicFolderDatabase` cmdlet

   E. The `ReplaceReplicaOnPFRecursive.ps1` script

5. You have completed the migration of mailboxes, public folders, and system folders from Exchange Server 2003 to Exchange Server 2007. You have begun upgrading clients from Outlook 2003 to Outlook 2007 and all new users are being provided with Outlook 2007. New users are reporting that they are unable to access the offline address book. What is the most likely cause?

   A. The permissions on the offline address book system folders have not been configured for Exchange Server 2007 mailboxes.

   B. The offline address book has not been configured for web-based distribution.

   C. The offline address book has not been configured to generate Version 3 client support.

   D. Public-folder distribution has been disabled for the offline address book.

6. You are planning your organization's migration from Exchange Server 2003 to Exchange Server 2007. All clients are currently running Outlook 2007. What steps need to be taken to ensure that clients will be able to access the offline address book when the migration is completed? Choose all that apply.

   A. Configure the offline address book to include the default Global Address List.

   B. Implement the Exchange Server 2007 Client Access server role.

   C. Move the offline address book from Exchange Server 2003 to Exchange Server 2007.

   D. Enable web-based distribution.

   E. Enable public-folder distribution.

7. Your organization is migrating from Exchange Server 2003 to Exchange Server 2007. Some mailboxes have been migrated to Exchange Server 2007 and new mailboxes are being created on Exchange Server 2007 using the same automated process that was used in your Exchange Server 2003 environment. You have discovered that new users are not able to access their mailboxes in Exchange Server 2007, and existing users do not see the new users in the Global Address List. What do you need to do to correct this?

   A. Modify the domain Recipient Update Service to use an Exchange Server 2007 computer.

   B. Retain an Exchange Server 2003 computer to host the offline address book until all mailboxes have been migrated to Exchange Server 2007.

   C. Disable cached mode in Outlook 2003 and Outlook 2007 until the migration has completed.

   D. Configure the `Update-EmailAddressPolicy`, `Update-AddressList` and `Update-GlobalAddressList` cmdlets to run on a daily schedule.

8. You are planning your organization's migration from Exchange Server 2003 to Exchange Server 2007. While testing the migration process in the lab, after implementing Exchange Server 2007 you discover that changes to Exchange Server 2003 recipient policies are not being reflected in the Global Address List. What is the most likely cause of this?

    A. The domain Recipient Update Service has been modified to point to an Exchange Server 2007 server.

    B. Exchange Server 2007 mailboxes were added to the organization before the Exchange Server 2007 Client Access server role was introduced.

    C. The offline address book is not generating Version 4 files.

    D. Exchange Server 2003 system folders have not yet been migrated to Exchange Server 2007.

9. Your organization is planning a migration from Exchange Server 2003 to Exchange Server 2007. Your current Exchange Server 2003 environment consists of four routing groups connected by low-bandwidth connections. Your Active Directory infrastructure is defined as a single Active Directory site. You will be deploying Exchange Server 2007 computers in every location that presently contains Exchange Server 2003 computers. What should you include in your migration planning?

    A. Move all Exchange Server 2003 computers to the same routing group before implementing the first Exchange Server 2007 computer.

    B. Modify your Active Directory topology to define Active Directory sites corresponding to each location that contains Exchange Server 2003 computers.

    C. Leave the existing Active Directory site unchanged. Define a separate Active Directory site to contain all Exchange Server 2007 computers.

    D. As Exchange Server 2007 computers are deployed, move them to the routing group that contains the Exchange Server 2003 computers they are co-located with.

10. You are planning a migration from Exchange Server 2003 to Exchange Server 2007. The current Exchange Server 2003 organization consists of multiple routing groups connected across a WAN (Wide Area Network) with very low bandwidth. You plan to deploy Exchange Server 2007 in each location, migrate all users to Exchange Server 2007 in that location, then start on the next location. The Active Directory site topology mirrors the Exchange Server 2003 routing-group topology. You need to ensure optimal message routing during the migration. What should you include in your migration planning?

    A. As Exchange Server 2007 is implemented in each location, move the Exchange Server 2003 computers in that location to the same routing group as the Exchange Server 2007 computers.

    B. As Exchange Server 2007 is implemented in each location, move the Exchange Server 2007 computers in that location to the same routing group as the existing Exchange Server 2003 computers in that location.

    C. Create new routing groups corresponding to each location. As Exchange Server 2007 is deployed, move the Exchange Server 2007 computers to the new routing group defined for that location and define a routing-group connector to the existing Exchange Server 2003 routing group.

    D. Create additional routing-group connectors between Exchange Routing Group (DWBGZMFD01QNBJR) and each of the Exchange Server 2003 routing groups.

11. Your existing Exchange Server 2003 organization has been designed with multiple administrative groups corresponding to different user communities and the support groups responsible for managing those servers. You are designing the Exchange Server 2007 migration for your company, including the delegation of server administration. What can you include in your planning? (Choose all that apply.)

    A. As Exchange Server 2007 computers are deployed, add them to the administrative group that corresponds to the Exchange Server 2003 computer they are replacing.

    B. In the Exchange Management Shell, delegate permissions as necessary using the `Add-ExchangeAdministrator` cmdlet.

    C. In the Exchange Management Console, delegate permissions as necessary under the Organization Configuration work center.

    D. As Exchange Server 2007 is deployed, modify the existing Exchange Server 2003 computers using ADSIEdit to move them to the Exchange Administrative Group (FYDIBOHF23SPDLT) administrative group.

    E. Until all mailboxes are migrated to Exchange Server 2007, instruct the support groups to manage Exchange Server 2007 mailboxes using Active Directory Users and Computers with the Exchange Server 2003 extensions.

12. As part of your migration from Exchange Server 2003 to Exchange Server 2007, you are designing the administration strategy for the support team. You need to keep to a minimum the number of tools they must use. What instructions should you give the support team until the migration is completed?

    A. Instruct them to manage all Exchange Server 2003 and Exchange Server 2007 users, servers, and organization settings with the Exchange Server 2007 management tools.

    B. Instruct them to manage Exchange Server 2003 recipients with Active Directory Users and Computers with the Exchange Server 2003 extensions. Manage Exchange Server 2003 computers with the Exchange Server 2003 Exchange System Manager. For Exchange Server 2007, manage recipients and servers with the Exchange Server 2007 Exchange Management Console and Exchange Management Shell. Manage all organization settings using the Exchange Server 2007 management tools.

    C. Instruct them to manage all Exchange Server 2003 and Exchange Server 2007 users, servers, and organization settings with the Exchange Server 2003 management tools.

    D. Instruct them to manage all recipients and servers with the Exchange Server 2003 management tools, and to manage all organization settings with the Exchange Server 2007 management tools.

13. When designing an inter-forest migration, in what order should the following steps be taken or established?

    A. Migration of users

    B. Message routing

    C. Directory synchronization

    D. Name resolution

    E. Decommissioning of old servers

    F. Calendaring

14. You are planning an inter-forest migration from a forest running Exchange Server 2003 to a forest running Exchange Server 2007. All clients run Outlook 2003, and will continue to run Outlook 2003 after the migration. During the pilot phase of the migration, you discover that users whose mailboxes are moved to the Exchange Server 2007 forest with the `Move-Mailbox` cmdlet can't receive mail from existing users in the Exchange Server 2007 forest. What should be added to the migration plan?

    A. Use the Exmerge utility for all inter-forest mailbox migrations.

    B. Modify the Autodiscover service in the Exchange Server 2007 forest to include an external URL.

    C. Modify the Outlook 2003 profiles of the users moved to Exchange Server 2007 to point to the Exchange Server 2007 computer.

    D. Delete the Outlook 2003 cache file from the client computers.

15. You are designing your company's migration from Exchange Server 2003 to Exchange Server 2007, and are planning for the preparation of Active Directory. Which of the following steps require Enterprise Admin, Schema Admin, or Domain Admin privileges? Choose all that apply.

    A. Installing Exchange Server 2007 on the first computer

    B. Preparing Active Directory

    C. Extending the Active Directory schema

    D. Preparing legacy Exchange permissions

    E. Deploying the first Hub Transport server role

16. What Exchange Server 2007 server role should be implemented before all other roles?

    A. Hub Transport role

    B. Client Access role

    C. Edge Transport role

    D. Mailbox role

17. You are designing your organization's migration from Exchange Server 2003 to Exchange Server 2007, and you are planning server role placements to determine the number of Exchange Server 2007 computers required. Which server role must be deployed on its own and cannot coexist with any other server role?

    A. Edge Transport role

    B. Mailbox role

    C. Client Access role

    D. Hub Transport role

18. You are migrating from Exchange Server 2003 to Exchange Server 2007. Some users who have been migrated report that they need access to items they deleted yesterday just before logging off. All clients are Outlook 2007, and all Outlook profiles are configured to empty the Deleted Items folder when the user logs off. You need to implement procedures to provide clients access to deleted mail during the migration. What two recommendations can you make? (Each answer is a complete solution.)

    A. Advise clients to use the Recover Deleted Items functionality of Outlook 2007 after the mailbox move to recover items as necessary.

    B. Advise clients to use the Recover Deleted Items functionality of Outlook 2007 to recover all deleted items before their mailbox is moved to Exchange Server 2007.

    C. Modify the deleted item retention time on the Exchange Server 2003 source mailbox database to match the setting on the Exchange Server 2007 target database.

    D. Restore the source mailbox database to a recovery server. Access the restored mailboxes, recover the required deleted items, and import these to the client's Exchange Server 2007 mailbox.

19. You are planning your organization's migration from Exchange Server 2003 to Exchange Server 2007. Your Exchange Server 2003 organization consists of multiple routing groups with one as the central routing point and all other routing groups connecting through it. You implement the first Exchange Server 2007 computers, and configure routing-group connectors between the Exchange Server 2007 routing group and the existing Exchange Server 2003 routing groups and verify messaging connectivity. After you have started migrating mailboxes, one of your WAN links goes down and mail between Exchange Server 2003 and Exchange Server 2007 started looping. Normal mail routing was restored when the WAN link was repaired, but you need to ensure that these symptoms don't occur in the future before the migration is completed. What should you do to avoid these symptoms in the future?

    A. Using the `Set-AdSiteLink` cmdlet, configure Exchange-specific costs on your Active Directory site links.

    B. Using Exchange System Manager, increase the cost on the routing-group connector that the messages were looping over.

    C. Disable minor link-state updates on all Exchange Server 2003 computers in the organization.

    D. Add the Exchange Server 2003 servers to the ExchangeLegacyInterop group in Active Directory.

20. You are defining your company's support and troubleshooting procedure for your migration from Exchange Server 2003 to Exchange Server 2007. Your Exchange support team frequently uses message tracking to troubleshoot issues and provide delivery information on request to clients. You need to provide guidance to the support team on how to track messages during the migration and afterwards. What should you recommend?

    A. Advise the support team to use the Exchange Server 2003 message tracking tools to track messages across Exchange Server 2003 computers, and to use the Exchange Server 2007 Exchange Troubleshooting Assistant to track messages across Exchange Server 2007 computers.

    B. Advise the support team to use the Exchange Server 2003 Message Tracking Center to track all messages.

    C. Advise the support team to use the Exchange Server 2007 Exchange Troubleshooting Assistant to track all messages.

    D. Advise the support team to use the `Get-MessageTrackingLog` cmdlet in the Exchange Management Shell to track all messages.

Answers to Review Questions

1. C. As Outlook 2003 clients can't use the Availability service, the SCHEDULE+ FREE BUSY system folders must be migrated to Exchange Server 2007 to provide free/busy information to Outlook 2003 users after the Exchange Server 2003 computers have been removed.

2. A, C. Free/busy functionality and offline address books are provided in system folders in Exchange Server 2003, but are provided through web-based distribution in Exchange Server 2007. The Autodiscover service provides automatic Outlook configuration for Outlook 2007 clients in Exchange Server 2007, and locates the Availability service for Outlook 2007 clients, but this service did not exist in Exchange Server 2003.

3. D. To allow users access to public folders via Exchange Server 2007 OWA, you must retain public folders on an Exchange Server 2003 public-folder database. Another alternative is to deploy Exchange Server 2007 SP1, which provides public-folder access via OWA.

4. A, E. The `MoveAllReplicas.ps1` and `ReplaceReplicaOnPFRecursive.ps1` scripts provide the ability to replicate public-folder data from an Exchange Server 2003 database to an Exchange Server 2007 database. The `ReplaceUserPermissionOnPFRecursive.ps1` script will modify public-folder permission, but will not move data. The `New-PublicFolderDatabase` and `Remove-PublicFolderDatabase` cmdlets will create or delete public-folder databases, but will not replicate the public-folder data; using these without migrating the folders would result in the loss of all data in public folders.

5. B. The offline address book is not accessible to Outlook 2007 users because web-based distribution has not been configured; this is not configured by default when migrating from Exchange Server 2003 to Exchange Server 2007. There are no permissions to configure for Exchange Server 2007 mailboxes versus Exchange Server 2003 mailboxes. Version 3 OABs are for Outlook 98 SP2 or later clients (not Outlook 2007 clients), while disabling public-folder distribution would affect Outlook 2003 or earlier clients; Outlook 2007 clients access the OAB using web-based distribution.

6. B, C, D. Client Access servers are required in order to host the OAB distribution points, as well as to host the Autodiscover service to provide the OAB URL to clients. The OAB must be moved to Exchange Server 2007 to allow web-based distribution, which is required for Outlook 2007 clients. The OAB already includes the default Global Address List by default, and public-folder distribution is not required for (and not used by) Outlook 2007.

7. D. As Exchange Server 2007 does not have a Recipient Update Services that runs in the background to provision Exchange recipients, the Exchange Management Shell cmdlets must be run on a regular basis to provision new recipients and add them to the address lists. Pointing the domain Recipient Update Service to an Exchange Server 2007 computer will cause it to quit working entirely for both Exchange Server 2003 and Exchange Server 2007 recipients. Retaining the offline address book on an Exchange Server 2003 computer or disabling cached mode will have no effect on the issue, as it is caused by users being created by a legacy process that relied on the RUS functionality.

8. A. If an Exchange Server 2003 domain Recipient Update Service is modified to use an Exchange Server 2007 server, the RUS will stop working as Exchange Server 2007 doesn't support the asynchronous update process. Adding Exchange Server 2007 Mailbox servers before introducing the Client Access server role may cause OWA and free/busy issues, but won't prevent Exchange Server 2003 users from appearing in the GAL. The offline address book and Exchange Server 2003 system folders have no bearing on the provisioning of Exchange Server 2003 recipients.

9. B. As Exchange Server 2007 doesn't use the concept of routing groups, you must define Active Directory sites corresponding to the message-routing topology desired. Moving all Exchange Server 2003 computers to the same routing group will adversely affect the existing message routing, while defining a single site for all Exchange Server 2007 computers will cause messages between servers in the same location to be routed across low-bandwidth connections. Exchange Server 2007 computers are placed in a single routing group named Exchange Routing Group (DWBGZMFD01QNBJR) as they are installed; they cannot be moved from this routing group, and Exchange Server 2003 computers cannot be added to this routing group.

10. D. For backwards compatibility, all Exchange Server 2007 servers are placed in a single routing group named Exchange Routing Group (DWBGZMFD01QNBJR). Exchange Server 2007 computers can't be moved from this routing group, and Exchange Server 2003 computers can't be added to it. A default routing-group connector is created between the Exchange Server 2007 routing group and an existing Exchange Server 2003 routing group to provide messaging connectivity. To accommodate an existing Exchange Server 2003 routing topology, additional routing-group connectors to the existing Exchange Server 2003 routing groups can be created.

11. B, C. As Exchange Server 2007 has dropped the concept of administrative groups, server administration can be delegated using the `Add-ExchangeAdministrator` cmdlet or by using the Add Exchange Administrator wizard through the Organization Configuration work center's action pane. Exchange Server 2007 computers must always be in the Exchange Administrative Group (FYDIBOHF23SPDLT), and Exchange Server 2003 computers can't be added to this administrative group or moved from the administrative group they were installed in.

12. B. All Exchange recipients and computers should be managed using the tools corresponding to the versions of the recipients and computers, while organization settings should be managed with the Exchange Server 2007 tools once Exchange Server 2007 has been introduced. Exchange Server 2007 recipients can be modified using the Exchange Server 2003 tools, but they will not be fully functional afterwards. Exchange Server 2003 recipients can be managed using the Exchange Server 2007 tools, but it is recommended to use the Exchange Server 2003 tools. Exchange Server 2003 recipients cannot be created using the Exchange Server 2007 management tools.

13. D, B, C, F, A, E. When planning an inter-forest migration, name resolution must be established between the forests before message routing can be configured. After message routing is working, directory synchronization can be established. Free/busy information cannot be shared between forests without directory synchronization, and only after all the above are established can users be migrated without impact. The last step in any migration is the decommissioning or re-provisioning of the old system.

14. C. When Outlook 2003 client mailboxes are moved across forests, the Outlook 2003 profile must be modified to point to the target server; otherwise the clients will continue to access the Exchange Server 2003 mailbox as the `Move-Mailbox` cmdlet does not disable the source Active Directory account. The Exmerge utility in Exchange Server 2003 has been removed from Exchange Server 2007, and inter-forest mailbox moves can be accomplished with the `Move-Mailbox` cmdlet in the Exchange Management Shell. The Autodiscover service allows Outlook 2007 clients to configure their profiles automatically, but is not used by Outlook 2003. Under the circumstances described, deleting the Outlook 2003 offline cache would just cause another cache to be built against the Exchange Server 2003 mailbox.

15. B, C, D. While preparing Active Directory and extending the Active Directory schema obviously require AD permissions, preparing legacy Exchange permissions involves modifying the permissions for the Recipient Update Service in each domain, which also requires Enterprise Admin privileges or Domain Admin and Exchange Full Administrator privileges, depending on the forest topology. Installing the first Exchange Server 2007 computer or the first Client Access server role does not require Active Directory administrative permissions.

16. B. The Exchange Server 2007 Client Access role should be implemented before all other Exchange Server 2007 server roles, to provide for OWA, Availability, Autodiscover, and other functionality for end users. The Hub Transport role should be implemented before the Mailbox role, but is not the first role to be deployed. The Edge Transport role can be deployed at any time, but is not fully functionally until the Hub Transport role is present. The Mailbox role is the last role to be deployed, with the possible exception of the Hub Transport role.

17. A. The Edge Transport server role cannot be installed on an Exchange Server 2007 server containing any other server roles. In addition, it is recommended to install the Edge Transport server role on a stand-alone system, and not on a domain-member server.

18. B, D. Items in the Deleted Items Recovery dumpster are not retained when mailboxes are moved, so clients must recover all deleted items to their Deleted Items folder before their mailbox is moved, or else the Exchange Server 2003 mailbox database must be restored and items recovered from it and imported into the user's mailbox after the move.

19. C. Exchange Server 2003 uses link-state routing, while Exchange Server 2007 uses least-cost routing. While this is not an issue in a default migration, where there is a single routing-group connector between Exchange Server 2003 and Exchange Server 2007, where multiple routing-group connectors have been configured between the systems it is recommended to disable minor link-state updates on all Exchange Server 2003 computers, which causes Exchange Server 2003 to use least-cost routing the same as Exchange Server 2007 and avoids the potential of mail loops.

20. A. Messages sent and received by Exchange Server 2003 can be tracked only by Exchange Server 2003 message-tracking tools. Similarly, messages sent and received by Exchange Server 2007 can be tracked by Exchange Server 2007 tools only. This is due to significant differences in the message-tracking schemas between the Exchange versions, as well as Exchange Server 2007 not having Windows Management Instrumentation (WMI) support.

Defining Policies and Security Procedures

MICROSOFT EXAM OBJECTIVES COVERED IN THIS CHAPTER:

- ✓ Plan the antivirus and anti-spam implementation
- ✓ Plan the network layer security implementation
- ✓ Plan the transport rules implementation
- ✓ Plan the messaging compliance implementation

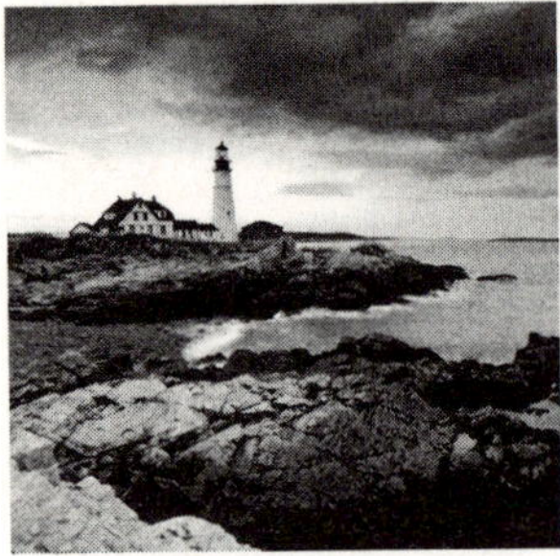

In this chapter we will look at how Exchange Server 2007 can help you manage message security. We will dive into the various alternatives available to help you meet regulatory and legal requirements when designing your Exchange deployment. In addition we will highlight procedures you can enable for content filtering and options that are available for ensuring secure messaging is deployed.

The main subjects in this chapter are as follows:

- Designing a solution to address regulatory and legal requirements
- Designing procedures for message content filtering
- Designing secure messaging

Designing a Solution to Address Regulatory and Legal Requirements

Email is a means of communication that is very easy to use. It's also very easy to *abuse,* by exchanging business and private information that ought to be kept confidential. It is therefore very important that you as an Exchange administrator can control the message flow inside your organization, and the message flow between your Exchange organization and the outbound messaging environments to prevent confidential information from being exposed. In this part of the chapter, we will first look at the various legal and company requirements that might encourage you to set up email policies, and we will then look at the policies that are available in Exchange Server 2007.

Legal-Compliance Requirements

Every country has its own legal system. In this chapter we will not be able to cover all legal-compliance requirements that exist in every country in the world, but we will cover the most commonly encountered laws and regulations.

United States

The United States has several laws and regulations that specify compliance requirements. This part of the chapter gives an overview of the most important ones.

Sarbanes-Oxley Act of 2002 (SOX)

The Sarbanes-Oxley Act of 2002 is a United States federal law, also known as the Public Company Accounting Reform and Investor Protection Act of 2002, and commonly abbreviated as SOX. It was put in place to prevent new accounting and corporate scandals from popping up without control. SOX describes and enforces several rules to improve the accuracy and reliability of information that is disclosed to the general public. The following types of companies must comply with this Sarbanes-Oxley Act of 2002:

- U.S. public companies
- Foreign tax filers in U.S. markets
- Privately held companies with public debt

Since a lot of information is transferred using email, it is mandatory for a company to implement a mail environment that enables them to be SOX-compliant. Section 404 of the Sarbanes-Oxley Act of 2002 covers the management assessment of internal controls, forcing management to be able to prove that they control the information flow. Companies can comply with the Sarbanes-Oxley Act of 2002 only by introducing a mail environment like Exchange 2007 that allow companies to control email by allowing transport rules, journaling rules, and messaging records management (MRM) rules to be created and enforced in the organization. (We'll talk more about this in the "Messaging Policies" section of this chapter.)

Gramm-Leach-Bliley Act (Financial Modernization Act of 1999)

The Gramm-Leach-Bliley Act is a 1999 act of the U.S. Congress. In short, it allows commercial and investment banks to consolidate. There are, however, two important rules in the Gramm-Leach-Bliley Act that require companies to enforce compliance rules in their organization:

The Financial Privacy Rule regulates the collection and disclosure of customers' personal financial information by financial institutions. This rule also applies to companies that receive such information, even if they are not financial institutions.

The Safeguards Rule specifies that all financial institutions are required to design, implement, and maintain safeguards to protect customer information. This rule also applies to financial institutions that receive customer information for other financial institutions, like credit-reporting agencies.

Health Insurance Portability and Accountability Act of 1996 (HIPAA)

The Health Insurance Portability and Accountability Act of 1996 not only requires the Department of Health and Human Services to establish national standards for electronic health care transactions and national identifiers for providers, health plans, and employers, but it also addresses the security and privacy of health data. HIPAA has led to a major improvement in the use of electronic data interchange for more industries as they also adopt the standards set by this act.

USA PATRIOT Act of 2001

The USA PATRIOT Act (officially called the Uniting and Strengthening America by Providing Appropriate Tools Required to Intercept and Obstruct Terrorism Act of 2001), was signed into law by George W. Bush in 2001. This act expands the means that U.S. law-enforcement agencies are allowed to use to fight against terrorism in the United States and abroad. Among other things, the act states that U.S. law-enforcement agencies can be granted permission to monitor email communications.

Canada: The Personal Information Protection and Electronic Documents Act

The first version of the Personal Information Protection and Electronic Documents Act was released in 2000 and was updated in April 2006. The act was created to support and promote electronic commerce by protecting personal information.

Australia: The Federal Privacy Act

The Federal Privacy Act contains the legislation, regulations, codes, determinations, and guidelines that affect private-sector business, health-service providers, and Commonwealth and Australian Capital Territory government agencies.

Europe: The European Union Data Protection Directive (EUDPD)

The European Union Data Protection Directive (EUDPD) standardizes the protection of data privacy for citizens of the European Union by providing baseline requirements that all member states must achieve through national regulations. These regulations apply not only to European Union member countries, but also to foreign countries that are doing business with European Union companies or that handle personal information about European Union citizens.

Japan: The Personal Information Protection Act

The Personal Information Protection Act of April 2005, specifies strict regulations for Japanese companies, and also affects companies that are doing business with Japanese companies by setting rules to protect data privacy for citizens of Japan.

Company-Compliance Requirements

A lot of companies configure their mail environment to comply with one or more of the previously listed legal requirements. In addition to the legal requirements, additional policies may be specified to meet company-specific compliance requirements. The most common example of such a company-compliance requirement is the need to configure a disclaimer.

A disclaimer is text that provides you as a company with a form of protection against liability for damages that might result from mail sent from your messaging environment. Disclaimers are not only added to mail messages, but are also often available on websites.

Messaging Policies

Exchange Server 2007 includes messaging polices that can be used to address most of the legal and corporate requirements for managing information. Exchange Server 2007 provides three different types of messaging policies:

- Transport policies
- Journaling policies
- Messaging records management policies

Transport Policies

Transport policies enable you to control the message flow for your Exchange organization. Transport policies can be deployed to control both inbound and outbound message flow, and you can create and enable transport rules on both the Hub Transport server and the Edge Transport server. You can create a transport rule by using either the Exchange Management Console or the Exchange Management Shell. To create a transport rule, you need to specify the following:

- To whom or to what messages the transport rules applies
- Actions that needs to be performed when the conditions are true for a message
- Any exception that would cause the transport rule not to be processed against the message

Table 5.1 lists the possible actions for Transport Rules you can configure on the Hub Transport server and on the Edge Transport server.

TABLE 5.1 Hub Transport Server and Edge Transport Server Transport Rules

Action	HUB	EDGE
Log an event with message	YES	YES
Prepend the subject with string	YES	YES
Apply message classification	YES	NO
Append disclaimer	YES	NO
Set the spam confidence level to value	YES	YES
Set header with value	YES	YES
Remove header	YES	YES
Add a recipient in the To field addresses	YES	YES

TABLE 5.1 Hub Transport Server and Edge Transport Server Transport Rules *(continued)*

Action	HUB	EDGE
Copy the message to addresses	YES	YES
Blind carbon copy (bcc) the message to addresses	YES	YES
Drop connection	NO	YES
Redirect the message to addresses	YES	YES
Put message in spam quarantine mailbox	NO	YES
Reject the message with status code and response	NO	YES
Send bounce message to sender with enhanced status code	YES	NO
Silently drop message	YES	YES

Transport rules are often used to add a disclaimer to email messages. As mentioned previously, disclaimers are typically used to provide legal text or other text to messages that are sent outside the organization. Sometimes disclaimers are also used to add text to messages that enter the organization.

For more-detailed information on how to deploy Edge and Hub Transport server rules, please refer to Chapters 12 and 15.

Journaling Policies

Journaling policies allow you as an Exchange administrator to keep track of email messages that are sent and received by users in your Exchange organization. In Exchange Server 2007 you can enable journaling for a mailbox database (Figure 5.1).

Journaling was possible in previous versions of Exchange, but Exchange Server 2007 also includes the possibility to create journaling policies that enable you as an administrator to enable journaling for just one user or for multiple users, or for one or multiple distribution groups. Enabling per-user or per-distribution-group journaling requires an Exchange Enterprise Client Access License, as shown in Figure 5.2.

FIGURE 5.1 Enabling journaling for a mailbox database in Exchange Server 2007

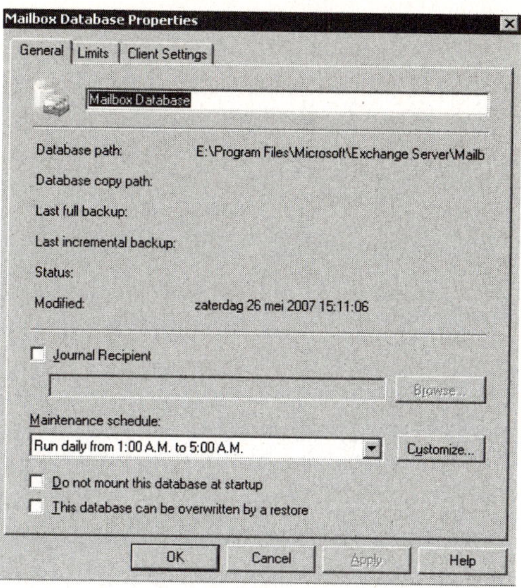

FIGURE 5.2 Premium journaling in Exchange Server 2007

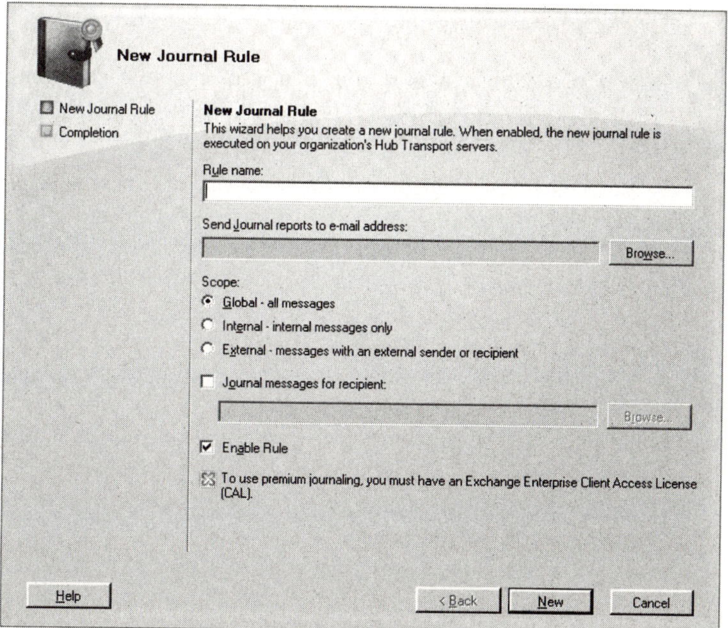

Another difference from previous versions of Exchange is the way that messages are journaled. The journaling agent on the Hub Transport server will journal a message and will capture as much detail as possible about the original message in a journal report. That report will be then be sent to the journal mailbox (Figure 5.3).

FIGURE 5.3 A journal report

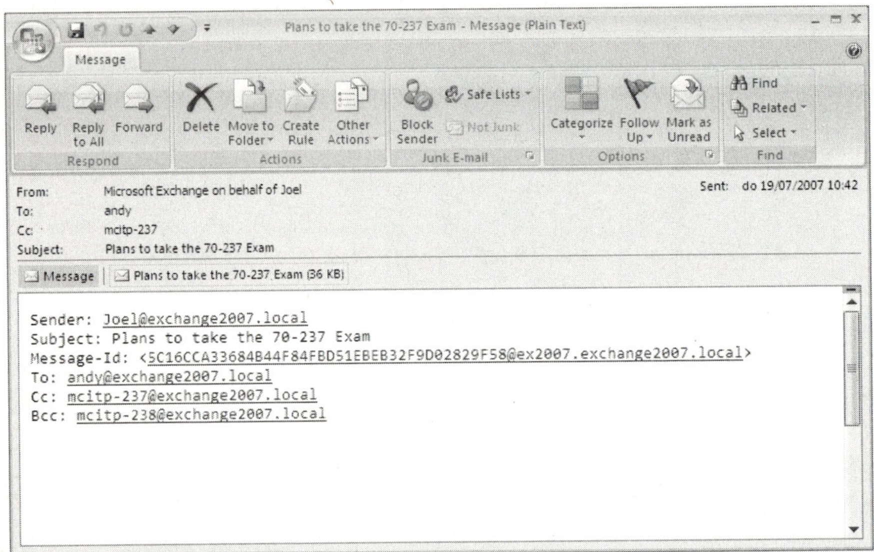

For more detailed information on how to deploy journaling policies, please refer to Chapter 15.

Messaging Records Management Policies

With messaging records management policies, you can control the way messages are stored inside mailboxes in your mail organization. As an administrator, you can create policies that apply to the default mail folders, or you can create custom managed folders and define managed content settings for them. Messaging records management policies can help you as an Exchange administrator to achieve compliance requirements, because you can control what happens to items stored in a user's mailbox.

Managed Default Folder

In Exchange Server 2007 you can set messaging records management policies for any or all of the existing default mail folders, like Inbox or Sent Items. It is also possible to create a new default managed folder. Figure 5.4 shows the default managed folders; a custom created folder, called MCITP, appears at the end of the list.

You can then set managed content settings for that new default managed folder, and use a managed folder policy to distribute the folder to a user. A user will only have one default managed folder for a given type of folder. For example, when you create a new Inbox, a user will still have only one Inbox.

FIGURE 5.4 Default and custom-created default managed folders in Exchange Server 2007

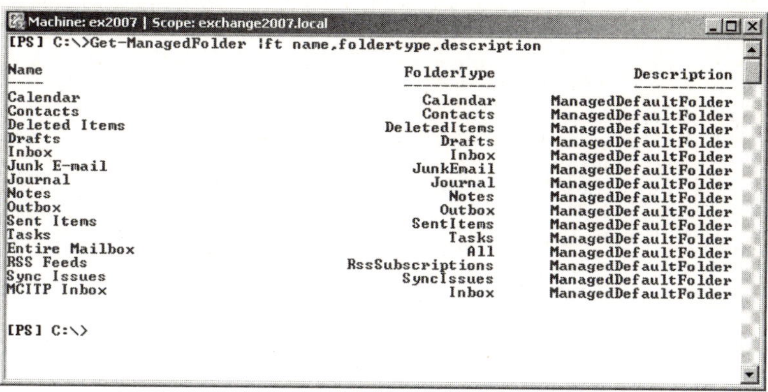

Managed Custom Folder

In Exchange Server 2007 you can also create custom managed folders that will appear to the users as a folder like Inbox, Sent Items, or any other folder, as shown in Figure 5.5. By using custom default folders, you can give your users an additional folder that they can use to archive items for legal requirements. If your company is required, for example, to keep track of all email communication concerning a particular project, you can create a dedicated custom folder for that project and specify different retention settings for that folder compared to the other folders in a user's mailbox.

FIGURE 5.5 Managed custom folders in Outlook 2007

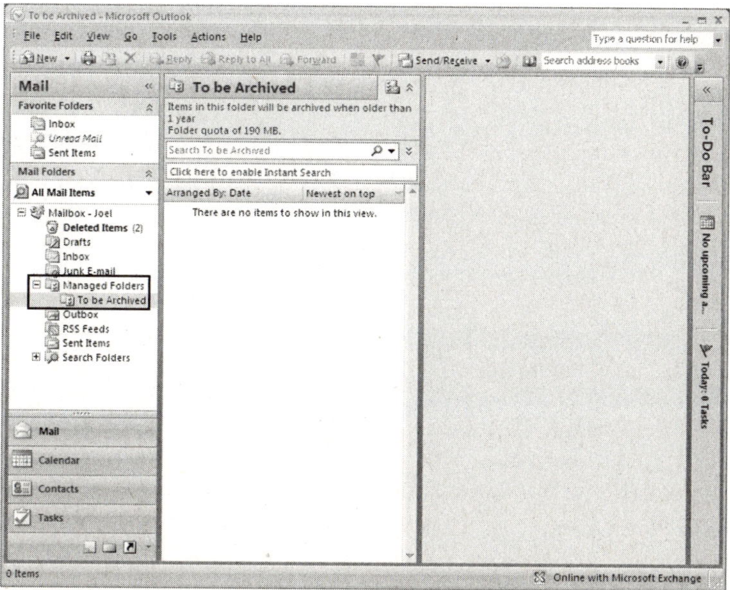

Managed Content Settings

For both default and custom managed folders, you can specify managed content settings to control retention for items in the folder, as shown in Figure 5.6. You can even configure a kind of journaling that will allow a copy of the item to be sent to a specified mailbox, mail-enabled user, mail-enabled contact, or mail-enabled group, as in Figure 5.7.

FIGURE 5.6 Managed content settings managed folders

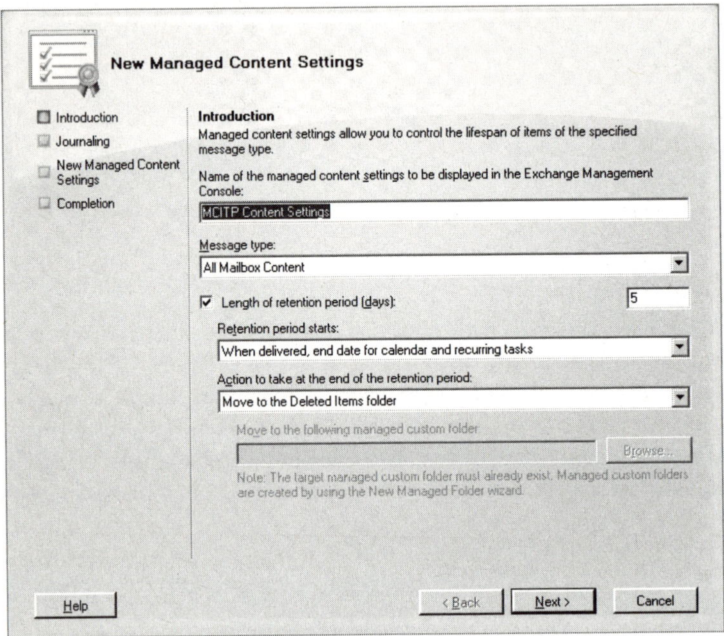

Outlook Version

To be able to use all functionalities provided with managed folders, your clients should use Outlook 2007 or later. When you apply a message records management policy to a user, you will receive the warning message shown in Figure 5.8.

FIGURE 5.7 Outlook version warning for managed folders

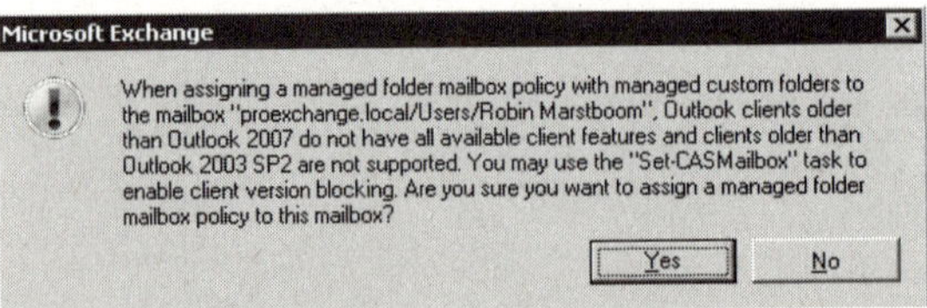

FIGURE 5.8 Journaling in managed content settings

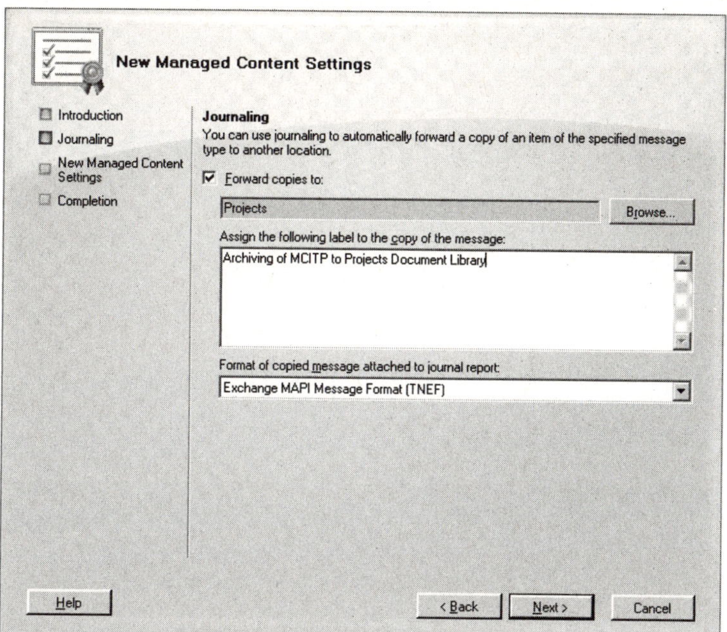

Exchange CAL Required

When you apply a managed folder policy to a user, you will see the notification that messaging records management is a premium feature that requires an Exchange Enterprise Client Access License. At the time of writing however, Microsoft has decided to allow messaging records management to be used against a client with a Standard Client Access License. For more-detailed information on how to deploy messaging records management policies, please refer to Chapter 13.

Message Classifications

Message classifications are new to Exchange Server 2007. After installing Exchange Server 2007, you can use the built-in message classifications outlined in Table 5.2. An Exchange administrator can change these descriptions using the Exchange Management Shell.

Outlook supports message classifications between users who run Exchange Server 2003 or earlier, but Exchange Server 2003 or earlier do not recognize these message classifications.

When a user sends an email and grants it a message classification, the message will be marked, and both sender and recipient will receive a description to notify them of this classification, as seen in Figures 5.9 and 5.10.

FIGURE 5.9 Message classification sender description

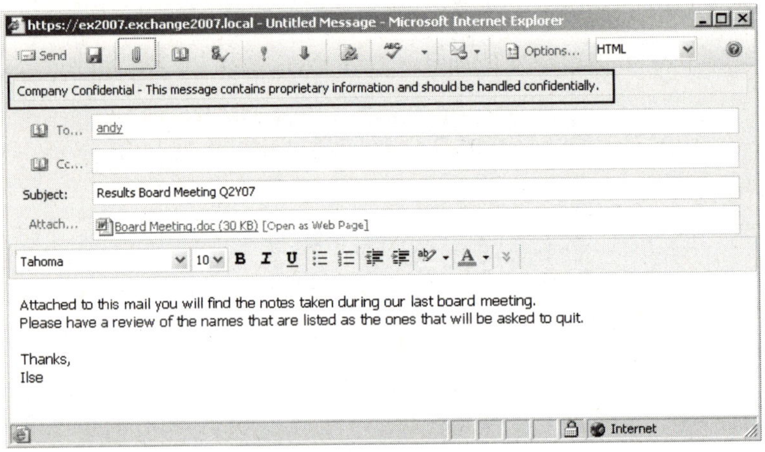

FIGURE 5.10 Message classification recipient description

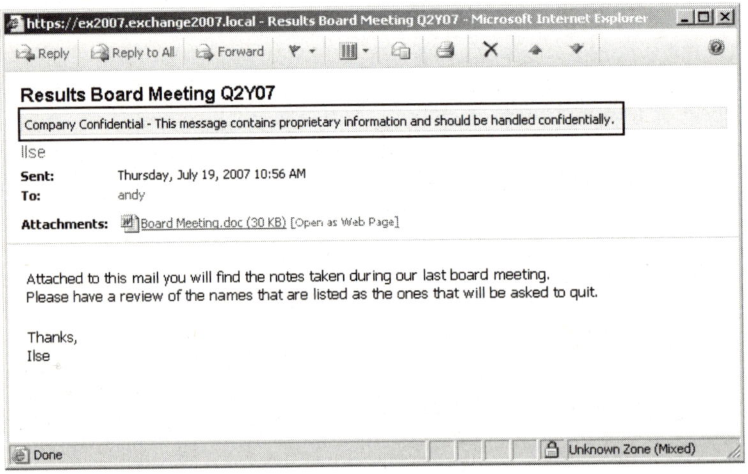

TABLE 5.2 Message Classifications, Sender and Recipient Description

Name	Recipient Description	Sender Description
A/C Privileged	This message is either a request for legal advice from an attorney or a response by an attorney to a request for legal advice. It should be treated confidentially, should only be sent to people with a need to know, and should only be forwarded by an attorney.	This message is either a request for legal advice from an attorney or a response by an attorney to a request for legal advice. It should be treated confidentially, should only be sent to people with a need to know, and should only be forwarded by an attorney.
Attachment Removed	An attachment was removed from this email message because the attachment was determined to pose a possible security risk.	A system-generated classification to inform users that an attachment was removed from this message.
Company Confidential	This message contains proprietary information and should be handled confidentially.	This message contains proprietary information and should be handled confidentially.
Company Internal	This message contains sensitive information that should only be delivered to internal recipients.	This message contains sensitive information that should only be delivered to internal recipients.
Originator Requested Alternate Recipient Mail	This message is an originator requested alternate recipient message.	This message is an originator requested alternate recipient message.
Partner Mail	~BC	~BC

Using message classifications is possible when using Outlook Web Access. If you want to enable the use of message classifications in Outlook you will need to deploy on the client computer a local file (`Classifications.xml`) that contains the definitions of the message classifications. You will also need to create and deploy a registry key that will enable the use of message classification by referencing the `Classifications.xml` file on the client computer.

For more-detailed information on how to deploy message classifications, please refer to Chapter 16.

Designing Procedures for Message Content Filtering

When we talk about designing procedures for message content filtering, what we really mean is using the tools that are available to keep spam and viruses away from your Exchange organization. Before we dig into the myriad of antispam settings you can configure as an Exchange administrator when working with an Exchange Server 2007 organization, we will look at the possible antivirus and antispam approaches you as an administrator can take. After that we will investigate the options available for protecting your Exchange environment against viruses.

Managing antivirus and antispam solutions for your environment, including your messaging organization, requires more than just protecting your Exchange servers. You have to provide security measures to defend every location and every level in your network. Coming back to your messaging environment, you should design and deploy a so-called *defense-in-depth model* in your messaging organization. Table 5.3 lists the solutions that you can include in your antivirus and antispam design.

TABLE 5.3 Defense-in-Depth Model in a Messaging Organization

Security Challenge	Security Measures
Network	Deploy a firewall at the network edge.
	Deploy host-based firewalls.
	Implement network segments.
	Physically secure servers and computers.
Client	Install and maintain client-side antivirus software.
	Enable antispam and antiphishing features available in messaging clients.
	Educate your users.
Exchange server	Install and configure server-side antivirus software on Mailbox and Hub Transport servers.
	Install and configure antispam solutions on Hub Transport server, if needed.
Internet edge	Install and configure antivirus and antispam software on an SMTP server that is directly accessible from the Internet.

Exchange Hosted Services

If you want to add an additional layer of security to your messaging environment, you can use the services provided by Exchange Hosted Services. With Exchange Hosted Services you have all Internet mail destined for you mail environment screened (with antispam and antivirus) and then delivered to your Exchange organization. Using Exchange Hosted Services will make sure that most spam and viruses are stopped before they reach your SMTP gateway servers. You only need to change your Mail Exchanger (MX) record in DNS to point to the network of data centers located at numerous sites along the Internet backbone. There is no need to buy and configure additional hardware.

Exchange Hosted Services is a rebranding of Frontbridge Technologies, bought by Microsoft in August 2005.

Exchange Hosted Services is more than just antispam and antivirus. It is suite of products designed to make your life as an administrator easier. Table 5.4 lists the different solutions that are included with Exchange Hosted Services. You can choose which parts of the solution you want to take on for your messaging environment.

TABLE 5.4 Exchange Hosted Services Solutions Overview

Solution	Explanation
Exchange Hosted Archive	Messages that meet criteria defined by you as administrator can be archived at the Exchange Hosted Services data centers. Both internal and external mail can be archived.
Exchange Hosted Continuity	Using this part of the Exchange Hosted Services allows your organization to have continuous access to messaging services in case of a failure of your Exchange organization.
Exchange Hosted Filtering	Provides complete filtering services to block all unwanted email messages from entering your Exchange organization.
Exchange Hosted Encryption	Provides the ability to send secured email messages to recipients outside your own Exchange organization. The Identity-Based Encryption (IBE) technology is used.

Antispam

Out of the box, Exchange Server 2007 provides quite a few interesting features that allow you as an administrator to protect your messaging environment against spam. In this part of the chapter we will define spam, and then we will look at the antispam features that you can configure within Exchange Server 2007.

What Is Spam?

Spam is a phenomenon that has become more and more of a problem the last couple of years. A message can be classified as spam when it is clear that the recipient is not important to the content of the mail, and even more, the recipient hasn't done anything to make public that he/she wanted to receive the message. The biggest problem with spam is the number of messages that users receive every day, and the amount of time they lose while going through those messages. Besides that, your Exchange servers might be under pressure because they need to handle the workload as well.

What's in a word? It is said that the word *spam* finds its origin in a *Monty Python* sketch called "Spam." In the sketch, one table in a café is occupied by a group of Vikings wearing horned helmets. It develops into a semi-argument between the waitress who has a menu limited to having Spam in just about everything ("Spam, Spam, Spam, Spam, sausage, eggs and Spam"), and Mrs. Bun, who is the only one in the room who does not want it. Whenever the word *Spam* is repeated, the group of Vikings begin singing and/or chanting.

Requirements of Antispam Features

When you start implementing one or multiple spam-filtering solutions, you should know the requirements that you as administrator have and that your clients have. As an administrator you have to investigate if the antispam features allow you to have the following:

- Integration with existing administrative tools
- Easy detection and recoverability of false positives
- Reporting possibilities to enable tracking of spam senders, spam recipients, and the amount of spam

Your clients might require the opportunity to define their own list of safe senders, and might request the ability to access the quarantined messages to decide themselves if a message is indeed spam. The Exchange Server 2007 antispam features meet the requirements in the preceding list, both for the administrator and the client.

Enabling Antispam Features

To prevent productivity loss for your users and to make sure that your Exchange servers are not damaged, it is important to stop spam before it enters your Exchange organization. The Exchange Server 2007 Antispam features can be enabled and configured on the Edge Transport server or on a Hub Transport Server inside your Exchange organization. It is, however, advised to configure them on the Edge Transport server, given the general rule that it is better to stop spam and viruses before they enter the Exchange organization.

Antispam Features in Exchange Server 2007

The following Antispam features can be enabled and configured on both the Hub Transport server and the Edge Transport server:

- Connection filtering
- Sender filtering
- Recipient filtering
- Sender ID filtering
- Content filtering
- Sender reputation filtering

Connection Filtering

You can enable and configure connection filtering by specifying IP addresses on the IP Allow list or IP Block list, or by entering an IP Block list provider. Whenever an SMTP session is initiated against your Edge or Hub Transport server, your server will first check to see if the connecting IP address is listed on the IP Allow list. If it is, the mail will be accepted and no other filtering will be applied to his message. If it isn't listed on the IP Allow list, the local IP Block list will be examined. If the IP address is found, the message will be rejected. If it is not found, your Exchange server will check the Real-Time Block (RBL) lists of any IP Block list provider you have specified. Depending on the reply, the mail will be accepted or rejected. Figure 5.11 shows the configuration options for connection filtering.

FIGURE 5.11 Connection filtering configuration options

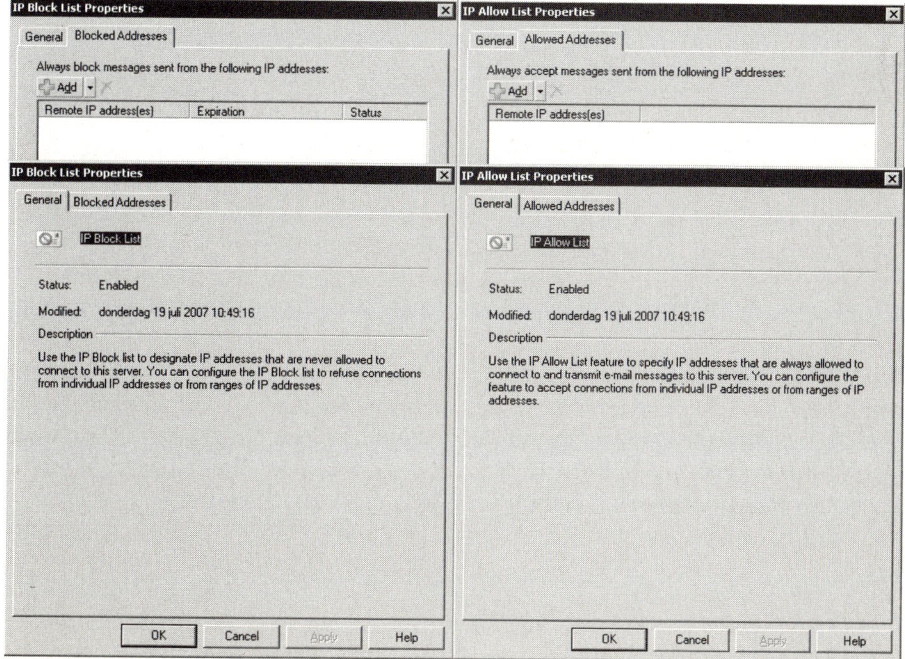

Sender Filtering

Enabling and configuring sender filtering allows you to list email addresses from which your organization does not want to accept mail. If the sender's email address is blocked or its domain is blocked, your server can reject the connection, or your server can be configured to accept the message with the blocked sender information. The message will be processed but the blocked sender information will be included as one of the criteria when content filtering processes the email message. Figure 5.12 shows the configuration options for sender filtering.

FIGURE 5.12 Sender Filtering

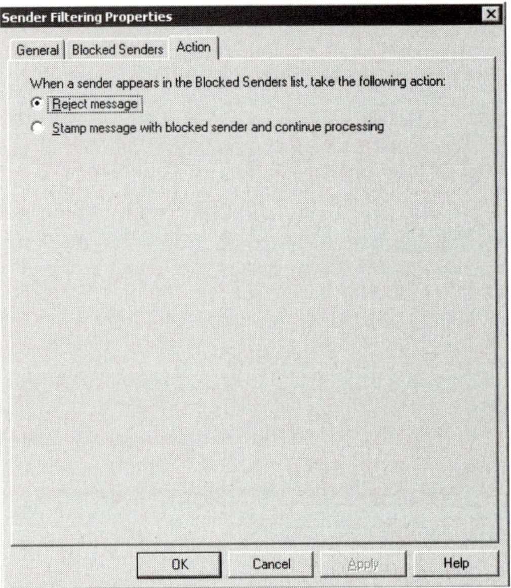

Recipient Filtering

Enabling and configuring recipient filtering, allows you to specify a list of email addresses your organization does not want to accept mail for. You can even filter mail that is sent to recipients that are not in the directory but are enabled on the Edge Transport server role; this requires EdgeSync to be configured. Figure 5.13 shows the configuration options for recipient filtering.

Sender ID Filtering

Sender ID Filtering can be configured to accept, reject, or delete a message when the sender ID validation fails. When you choose to accept the message, the message will be processed but the sender ID status will be included as one of the criteria when content filtering processes the email message. Figure 5.14 shows the configuration options for sender ID filtering.

FIGURE 5.13 Recipient Filtering

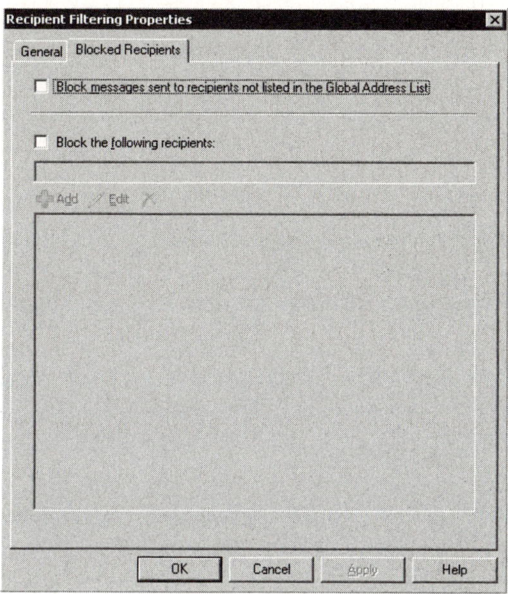

FIGURE 5.14 Sender ID filtering

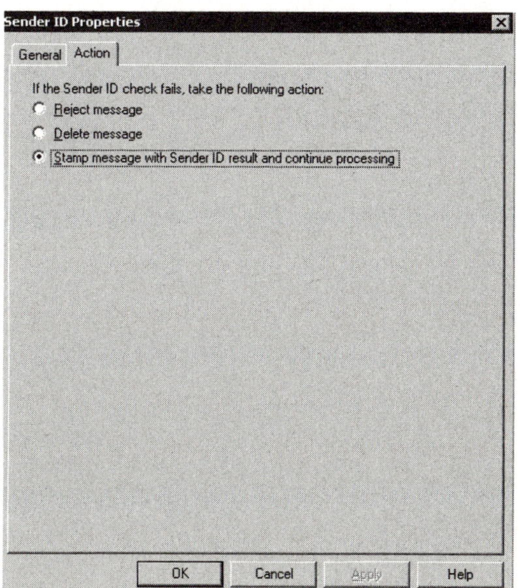

Sender ID filtering was introduced with Exchange Server 2003 Service Pack 2 an antispam feature. Sender ID filtering will check if the sender (or most probable sender) is sending the mail using the SMTP services of a server that is authorized to send mail from that sender's domain. Sender ID filtering can provide you with a valid result only if the sender's domain has a Sender Policy Framework (SPF) record registered in DNS. The registration of an SPF record is not mandatory. For more information about the usage and purpose of the SPF record, please refer to RFC 4408.

Content Filtering

Unless the sender is known as a safe sender for the intended recipient, content filtering will process the message and assign it a spam confidence level (SCL). Depending on the value of the SCL, the message can be deleted, rejected, quarantined, or put in the recipient's Junk E-Mail folder. Figure 5.15 shows the configuration options for Content Filtering.

FIGURE 5.15 Content filtering

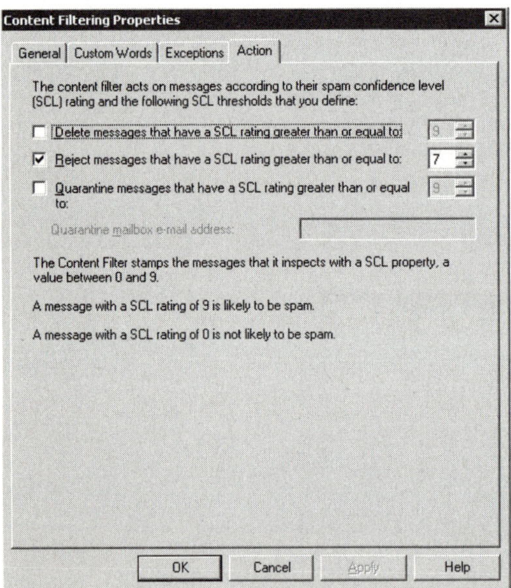

Sender Reputation Filtering

Sender reputation filtering can cause an IP address to be listed on the IP Block list that is checked during connection filtering. Sender reputation filtering will filter messages based on information about recent email messages received from particular senders. A sender will be assigned a sender reputation level (SRL), and if the sender appears to be a known spammer, the sender's IP address will be added for a configurable time to the IP Block list.

Figures 5.16 and 5.17 show the configuration options for sender reputation filtering.

FIGURE 5.16 Sender reputation properties: Sender Confidence tab

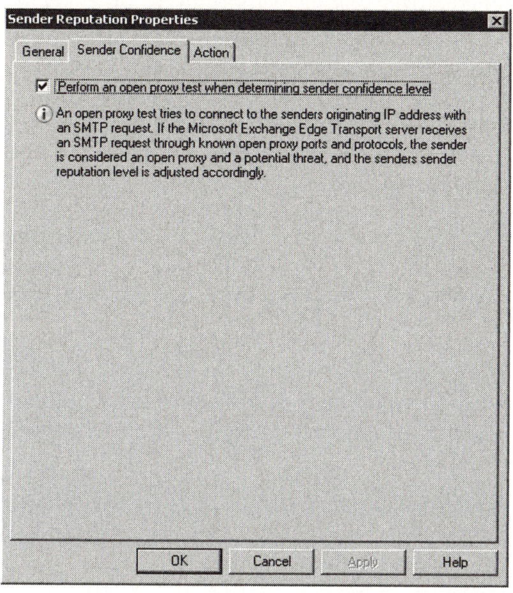

FIGURE 5.17 Sender reputation properties: Action tab

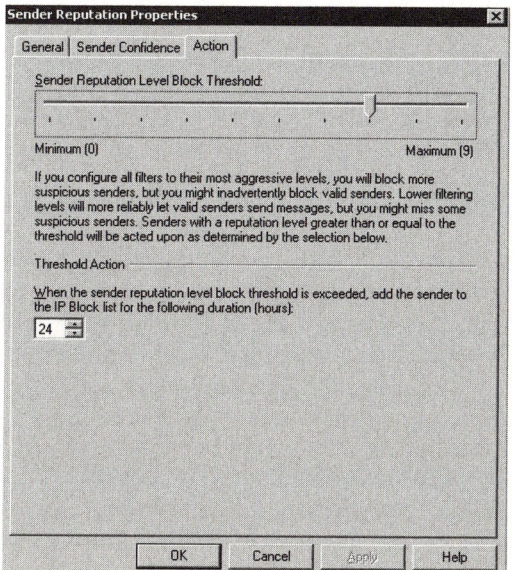

Bypassing Spam-Filtering Rules

It is possible to bypass all spam-filtering features you have configured for a specific recipient by changing the value of the AntiSpamBypassEnabled property from False to True using the Exchange Management Shell, as can be seen in Figure 5.18.

FIGURE 5.18 Bypassing all spam-filtering features

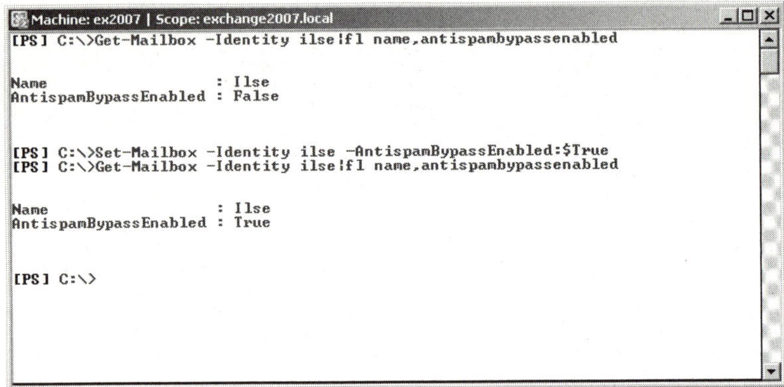

For more information about enabling and configuring the Exchange Server 2007 antispam features, please refer to Chapter 14.

Antivirus

Exchange Server 2007 does not provide a complete antivirus solution out of the box, but it does offer you several possibilities to protect your messaging organization against disruptions caused by malware or viruses. In this part of the chapter we will provide an overview of the antivirus options Exchange Server 2007 has in store for you as an Exchange administrator.

Antivirus API

The first antivirus API was released by Microsoft for Exchange Server 5.5 Service Pack 3. The introduction of this API meant that antivirus software vendors no longer needed to use MAPI to scan and protect mailboxes and public folders against viruses. With this antivirus API they received the ability to gain access to the information store without jeopardizing the data integrity of the database files. Exchange Server 2007 has the Exchange Virus Scanning API, also called VSAPI, that a lot of third-party vendors integrate closely with to provide seamless protection.

Microsoft Forefront Security for Exchange Server

In 2005 Microsoft acquired Sybari and its Antigen products. Microsoft has rebranded and extended the functionalities of the Antigen product line into Forefront. Microsoft Forefront Security for Exchange Server uses the Exchange Virus Scanning API, and is, according to Microsoft, uniquely suited for Exchange Server 2007 environments.

Microsoft Forefront Security for Exchange Server not only provides advanced protection by providing multiple scan engines at multiple layers, but it also provides a very simple and cost-effectively manageable security interface for your messaging environment. Thanks to its tight integration with Exchange 2007, implementing Microsoft Forefront Security for Exchange will, in addition, improve availability and performance of your messaging organization.

Transport Rules

As you have already covered in this chapter, transport rules are rules that enable you to control the message flow for your Exchange organization. Transport rules can be deployed to control both inbound and outbound message flow. You can create and enable transport rules both on the Hub Transport server and on the Edge Transport server. You can create a transport rule by using the Exchange Management Console or the Exchange Management Shell. To create a transport rule, you need to specify the following:

- To whom or what messages the transport rules apply
- Action that needs to be performed when the conditions are true for a message
- Any exception that would cause the transport rule to not be processed against the message

Transport rules can be used to help you protect your organization from viruses. Once you have determined the characteristics that allow you to uniquely identify a virus, you can define actions on it. You can choose to drop the SMTP connection, delete the message, or reject the message. If you want to have a copy of the message to investigate it further, you can choose to deliver the message to a quarantine mailbox.

Attachment Filtering

Attachment filtering allows you to block attachments from entering your Exchange organization, by attachment content type or by attachment file name. By configuring attachment filtering you can block viruses from entering your production environment.

Attachment filters can be managed by using the Exchange Management Shell. After installing the Edge Transport server role, the Attachment Filtering Agent will by default be enabled, as seen in Figure 5.19.

FIGURE 5.19 Default attachment-filtering configuration

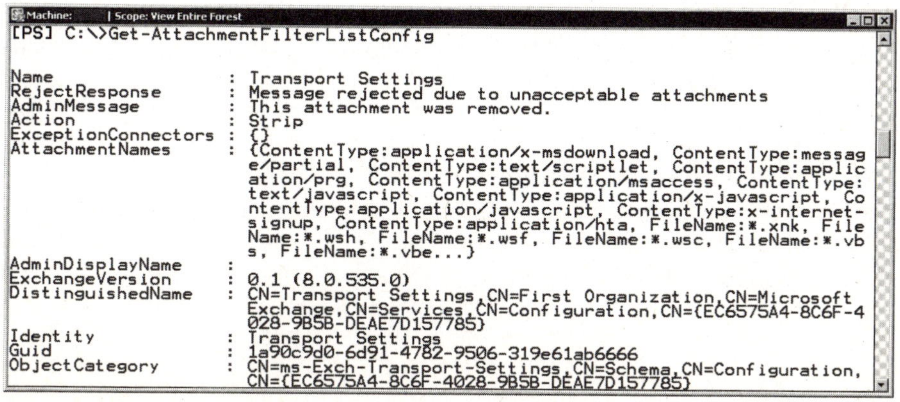

```
Machine:      | Scope: View Entire Forest
[PS] C:\>Get-AttachmentFilterListConfig


Name                 : Transport Settings
RejectResponse       : Message rejected due to unacceptable attachments
AdminMessage         : This attachment was removed.
Action               : Strip
ExceptionConnectors  : {}
AttachmentNames      : {ContentType:application/x-msdownload, ContentType:messag
                       e/partial, ContentType:text/scriptlet, ContentType:applic
                       ation/prg, ContentType:application/msaccess, ContentType:
                       text/javascript, ContentType:application/x-javascript, Co
                       ntentType:application/javascript, ContentType:x-internet-
                       signup, ContentType:application/hta, FileName:*.xnk, File
                       Name:*.wsh, FileName:*.wsf, FileName:*.wsc, FileName:*.vb
                       s, FileName:*.vbe...}
AdminDisplayName     :
ExchangeVersion      : 0.1 (8.0.535.0)
DistinguishedName    : CN=Transport Settings,CN=First Organization,CN=Microsoft
                       Exchange,CN=Services,CN=Configuration,CN={EC6575A4-8C6F-4
                       028-9B5B-DEAE7D157785}
Identity             : Transport Settings
Guid                 : 1a90c9d0-6d91-4782-9506-319e61ab6666
ObjectCategory       : CN=ms-Exch-Transport-Settings,CN=Schema,CN=Configuration,
                       CN={EC6575A4-8C6F-4028-9B5B-DEAE7D157785}
```

Exercise 5.1 outlines the steps for configuring the attachment-filtering agent to block attachments by MIME type and file name.

EXERCISE 5.1

Configuring Attachment Filtering to Block Attachments by MIME Type and File Name

Attachment filtering by content type or file name can be configured only on the Exchange Server 2007 Edge Transport server role.

1. Log on the Edge Transport server with an account that is a member of the local Administrators group.

2. Start the Exchange Management Shell.

3. Check if the attachment-filtering agent is enabled on the Edge Transport server role by entering the cmdlet `Get-TransportAgent`. You will get an output like the one shown here.

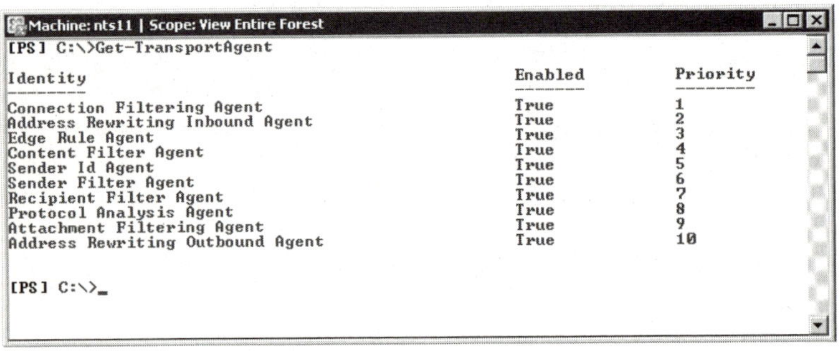

```
Machine: nts11 | Scope: View Entire Forest
[PS] C:\>Get-TransportAgent

Identity                              Enabled          Priority
--------                              -------          --------
Connection Filtering Agent            True             1
Address Rewriting Inbound Agent       True             2
Edge Rule Agent                       True             3
Content Filter Agent                  True             4
Sender Id Agent                       True             5
Sender Filter Agent                   True             6
Recipient Filter Agent                True             7
Protocol Analysis Agent               True             8
Attachment Filtering Agent            True             9
Address Rewriting Outbound Agent      True             10

[PS] C:\>_
```

If the attachment-filtering agent were not enabled, you would need to issue the command `Enable-TransportAgent -Identity "Attachment Filtering Agent"`.

To add a new attachment filter that filters email attachments that have the specific MIME content type of JPEG, you need to enter the following cmdlet: `Add-AttachmentFilterEntry -Name image/jpeg -Type ContentType`.

To add a new attachment filter that filters email attachments based on a file name or file name extension, like `.XYZ`, run the following command: `Add-AttachmentFilterEntry -Name *.XYZ -Type FileName`.

You can configure on the Edge Server a RejectResponse that will be mailed to the sender when their message has been rejected by the Edge Transport server attachment-filtering agent. In addition to rejecting the message, you can also configure the Edge Transport server attachment-filtering agent to strip the attachment and to deliver the mail to the intended recipient without the blocked attachment. The recipient will see a note in the email message that a particular attachment has been blocked. The attachment itself is not available for recovery. Next to stripping and rejecting the email message, you can also configure the email message to be silently deleted whenever it meets any of the predefined criteria. Neither the sender nor the recipient will get a message to warn them about the nondelivery.

As an administrator, you can also configure exceptions for particular connectors. Attachment filters are not applied to email messages that are received through these connections. All these settings can be configured using the Exchange Management Shell by making changes to the AttachmentFilterListConfig (Figure 5.20).

FIGURE 5.20 AttachmentFilterListConfig

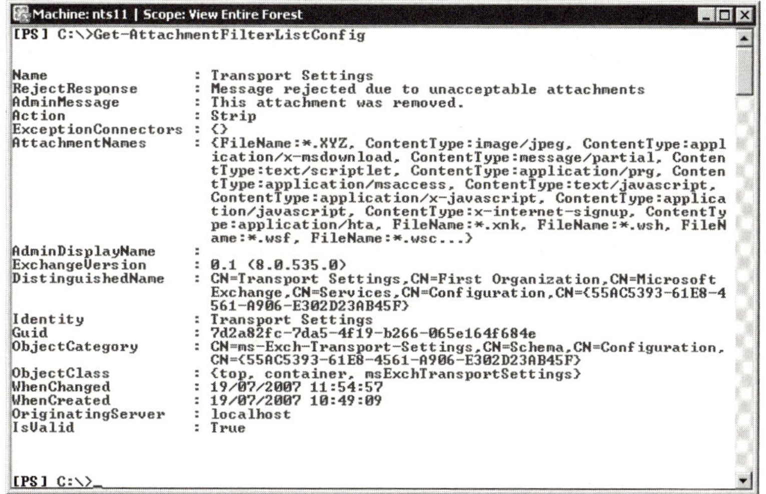

```
Machine: nts11 | Scope: View Entire Forest
[PS] C:\>Get-AttachmentFilterListConfig


Name                 : Transport Settings
RejectResponse       : Message rejected due to unacceptable attachments
AdminMessage         : This attachment was removed.
Action               : Strip
ExceptionConnectors  : {}
AttachmentNames      : {FileName:*.XYZ, ContentType:image/jpeg, ContentType:appl
                       ication/x-msdownload, ContentType:message/partial, Conten
                       tType:text/scriptlet, ContentType:application/prg, Conten
                       tType:application/msaccess, ContentType:text/javascript,
                       ContentType:application/x-javascript, ContentType:applica
                       tion/javascript, ContentType:x-internet-signup, ContentTy
                       pe:application/hta, FileName:*.xnk, FileName:*.wsh, FileN
                       ame:*.wsf, FileName:*.wsc...}
AdminDisplayName     :
ExchangeVersion      : 0.1 (8.0.535.0)
DistinguishedName    : CN=Transport Settings,CN=First Organization,CN=Microsoft
                       Exchange,CN=Services,CN=Configuration,CN={55AC5393-61E8-4
                       561-A906-E302D23AB45F}
Identity             : Transport Settings
Guid                 : 7d2a82fc-7da5-4f19-b266-065e164f684e
ObjectCategory       : CN=ms-Exch-Transport-Settings,CN=Schema,CN=Configuration,
                       CN={55AC5393-61E8-4561-A906-E302D23AB45F}
ObjectClass          : {top, container, msExchTransportSettings}
WhenChanged          : 19/07/2007 11:54:57
WhenCreated          : 19/07/2007 10:49:09
OriginatingServer    : localhost
IsValid              : True


[PS] C:\>_
```

Forefront Security for Exchange Server extends the attachment-filtering agent's capabilities. Using Forefront allows you as administrator to scan and block more file types, like RAR archives, and it also allows you to check if files have been renamed that are compressed as Zip or LZH files. Without Forefront, the attachment filtering checks if a file has been renamed, but is not able to perform this test against files that are compressed as Zip or LZH files. Furthermore, Forefront Security for Exchange Server enables you to quarantine blocked attachments and to customize the warning message that is sent to the sender and/or the recipient.

Designing Secure Messaging

When you are designing your messaging environment, you will have to include security in your design. In this chapter we have already covered what policies you have available in Exchange Server 2007 to help you comply with any legal requirement that is set for your country of origin. We have also seen what antispam and antivirus features are configurable within Exchange Server 2007 to make sure that your mail environment is protected as soon as it is in production. In this part of the chapter, we will have a closer look at how you can make your mail environment even more secure by taking into account administrative security, options to secure SMTP email, using Information Rights Management, and implementing procedures to enable signing and sealing of messages.

Administrative Security

When designing and deploying your Exchange organization it is important to make sure that all of your administrators have the rights they need to do what they are supposed to do. You should also make sure that people are not allowed to perform any administrative tasks against your Exchange organization that they shouldn't be able to execute; you always want to avoid creating overprivileged users. Second to physically securing your Exchange servers is making sure that you delegate adequate administrative permissions.

Delegating administrative permissions can be done using the Exchange Management Console or the Exchange Management Shell. Using the delegation wizards in the Exchange Management Console will make sure that a user is granted the necessary permission within Active Directory to perform the required tasks. You can delegate Exchange permissions by giving a user a predefined Exchange Administrator role. Exchange Server 2007 offers four built-in Exchange Administrator roles you can delegate, as outlined in Table 5.5.

TABLE 5.5 Exchange Administrator Roles

Exchange Administrator Role	Associated Rights
Exchange Organization Administrator	Full control over every property and every object in the Exchange organization
Exchange Recipient Administrator	The ability to modify properties and objects associated with Exchange recipients, including users, contacts, groups, dynamic distribution groups, and public-folder objects
Exchange View-Only Administrator	The ability to view configuration of Exchange, but not the permission to make changes
Exchange Server Administrator	Full control over the specified server or multiple servers' configuration data

Exercise 5.2 outlines the steps for delegating the Exchange Server Administrator role to a new administrator, Andy, using the Exchange Management Console.

EXERCISE 5.2

Delegating the Exchange Server Administrator Role to a New Administrator Using the Exchange Management Console

1. Open the Exchange Management Console.
2. In the console tree, click Organization Configuration.
3. Right-click Organization Configuration and select Add Exchange Administrator.
4. On the Add Exchange Administrator page, click Browse to select Andy, the new user to whom you want to delegate an Exchange Administrator role.
5. Under Select the Role and Scope of this Exchange Administrator, select the Exchange Server Administrator role, and select the Exchange server, Exchange2007, to which Andy will have access, as shown here. Click Add.

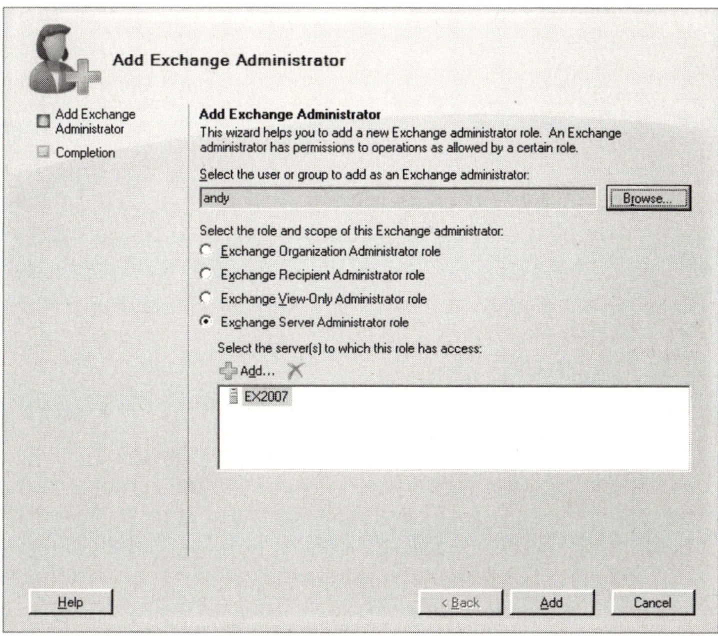

6. On the Completion page, click Finish to complete the task.

EXERCISE 5.2 *(continued)*

After finishing, you will notice that Andy has been granted the Exchange Server Administrator role and the Exchange View-Only Administrator role as can be seen in the Exchange Management Console.

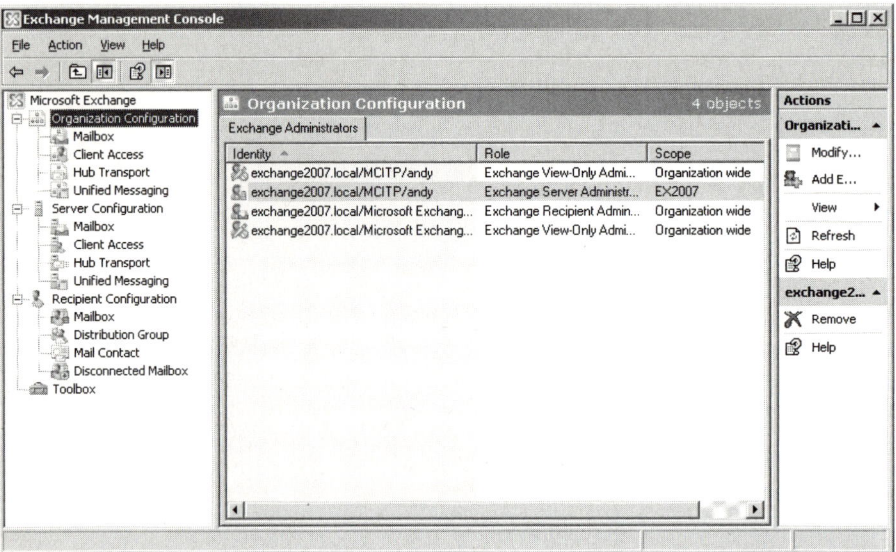

By granting Andy the Exchange Server Administrator role, you have added Andy to the universal security group Exchange View-Only Administrators, and you have explicitly granted Andy full control on the Exchange Server configuration of the Exchange server named Exchange2007.

Securing SMTP Email

Almost every email message that is sent on the Internet is sent using SMTP. SMTP is an acronym for Simple Mail Transfer Protocol, and it is not secure. SMTP messages can be captured and read by using a network sniffer, protocol analyzer, or network analyzer. Because of the inherent lack of security with SMTP email, you should implement technologies that will provide additional security. The following options are available to implement the required level of security:

- Authentication
- Transport Layer Security
- IPSec
- S/MIME

In this part of the chapter, we will provide an overview of different technologies that are available to increase SMTP security.

Authentication

Requiring authentication on your SMTP Send and/or Receive connectors will enable you to configure who is allowed to send mail to and from your Exchange organization.

If you require authentication on your default SMTP Receive connector, you will block almost all email from the Internet since almost all SMTP servers use anonymous connections when sending email. It is best practice to only enable authentication to provide additional security for email sent from organizations you're associated with.

Table 5.6 lists the different authentication options that are available for both Send connectors and Receive connectors.

TABLE 5.6 Receive and Send Connector Authentication Options

Connector Type	Authentication Options
Receive Connector	Transport Layer Security (TLS)
	Domain security (mutual authenticated TLS)
	Basic authentication
	Basic authentication over TLS
	Exchange Server authentication
	Integrated Windows authentication
	Externally secured (for example, with IPSec) authentication
Send Connector	None
	Basic authentication
	Basic authentication over TLS
	Exchange Server authentication
	Externally secured authentication

You can specify who is authorized to send SMTP email messages to your Exchange Hub Transport server by configuring which permission groups your Hub Transport Server is allowed to receive email messages from, as can be seen in Figure 5.21.

FIGURE 5.21 Permission groups configured with a Receive connector

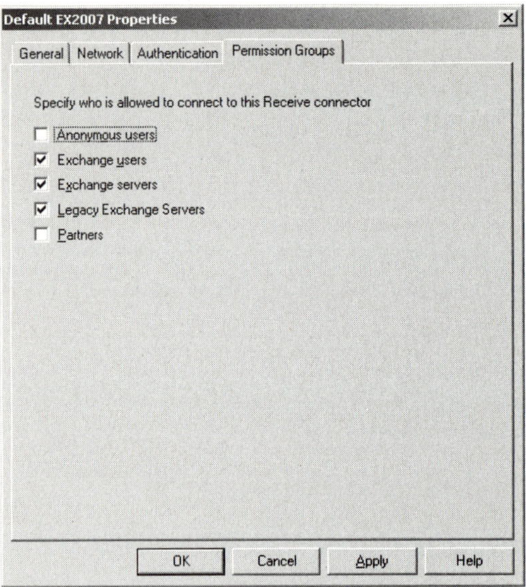

Transport Layer Security

Transport Layer Security, as defined by RFC 2246, is a protocol that establishes a secure connection between a client and a server. TLS requires both client and server to have a valid certificate. TLS uses the certificates to authenticate client and server, and to encrypt all data that is exchanged between client and server. Configuring and enabling TLS will ensure that in your Exchange organization every SMTP connection that is initiated will be authenticated and encrypted.

IPSec

Internet Protocol Security, IPSec, is a method to secure application traffic between a client and a server. IPSec can use certificates, Kerberos authentication, or a preshared key to authenticate client and server, and create the necessary encryption keys.

S/MIME

Secure/Multipurpose Internet Mail Extensions (S/MIME) enables digital signing and sealing for email messages. Using digital certificates enables users to allow recipients to validate them as a sender, and it also allows them to make sure that the email-message content can be read only by the intended recipient(s).

Signing

By digitally signing an email message, you will allow for the recipient to validate the message sender, and you will allow for the recipient to be ensured that the message hasn't been modified in transit. If you want to allow your users to digitally sign their email messages, you need to provide them with a digital certificate.

Sealing

Sealing an email message will allow you to make sure that only the sender and the intended recipient of the email message can decrypt the content of the email message. If you want to allow your users to send encrypted email messages, you need to provide your users with a digital certificate, and you need to ensure that your users can access the certificate and the public key of the intended recipients of the sealed email message.

Sealing your email messages means that those email messages cannot be scanned for policy compliance, viruses, or spam.

Exchange Server 2007 does not yet support S/MIME for Outlook Web Access, nor does it support S/MIME for Windows Mobile 6.0 devices. This functionality should be included, however, with Exchange Server 2007 Service Pack 1.

PKI Requirements to Implement SMTP Security

To enable signing, sealing, Transport Layer Security, and IPSec, you need to have digital certificates. You can use a public key infrastructure (PKI) to create, deploy, and manage digital certificates. When you implement a PKI, you can choose to implement your own private certificate authority (CA), or you can choose to obtain certificates from a commercial CA. Obtaining a certificate from a commercial CA has one major advantage against using your own private CA: the certificate issuer will be trusted by external clients by default. Deploying your own CA has other advantages, since it will allow you to automate certificate distribution via group policies, but external clients will not trust your CA by default.

It is possible to integrate your private CA with a commercial CA by purchasing a certificate from the commercial CA and using that certificate when creating the private CA. This way you will be able to create, deploy, and manage your own certificates that will be trusted by external clients.

Information Rights Management

Both Microsoft Office 2003 and Microsoft Office 2007 provide users with the ability to safeguard their digital information from unauthorized use by restricting permissions to content in documents, workbooks, and presentations by using Information Rights Management (IRM).

Requirements IRM

Before your clients can use Information Rights Management to restrict permissions, you are required to have Microsoft Windows Rights Management Services (RMS) for Windows Server 2003 within the organization or via a Microsoft service.

Microsoft also hosts a limited-time trial IRM service for customers who do not host their own RMS server. This service enables users to share protected documents and email messages using Microsoft Passport instead of Active Directory as the authentication mechanism. You will not be able to create custom rights templates when using this Microsoft service.

In addition, your clients also need to deploy the Windows Rights Management client. At the time of writing, you have to make sure all your clients that are working with a computer running Windows XP have the Windows Rights Management Services (RMS) client Service Pack 2 (SP2) installed. Computers running Windows Vista already have Windows Rights Management Services installed.

Real World Scenario

Securing Email Content with IRM

Imagine that you are an Exchange administrator responsible for an Exchange Server 2007 organization that houses mailboxes for 120 users. You have received from the legal department the request to increase mail security for mail that is sent between your company and a particular customer, since it seems that confidential email messages have been forwarded by them to your competitors.

Your options to eliminate this security breach are limited: you could disallow mail traffic between your company and the customers, or you could implement a system that sets permissions on mail sent by your company to the customer.

Accordingly, you decide to implement your own Windows Rights Management Services server, and you create a custom template that users can use to mark an email message as confidential, thereby disabling the ability to forward and/or print the email message. Since you know that the customer also uses an RMS solution, you make sure that the customer receives the necessary rights to be able to read email messages that are sent by your sales department.

The disadvantage of your solution is that users need to mark messages themselves as confidential. However, you have agreed with the legal department that this problem is outweighed by the fact that the messages cannot be forwarded to your competitors.

Outlook and IRM

Deploying RMS for Windows Server 2003 within your organization or via a Microsoft service allows you to protect confidential email messages, enforce document rights, protect sensitive intranet content, and it configure protection for content stored at the server level. To provide these abilities, you need to use RMS-aware applications like Microsoft Office 2003 or Microsoft Office 2007.

IRM can be used in Microsoft Office Outlook 2003 and Microsoft Office Outlook 2007 to prevent email forwarding, copying, editing, or printing. To deploy IRM in Outlook you just need to follow a few steps, as can be seen in Figure 5.22.

FIGURE 5.22 Steps to enable IRM in Microsoft Office Outlook

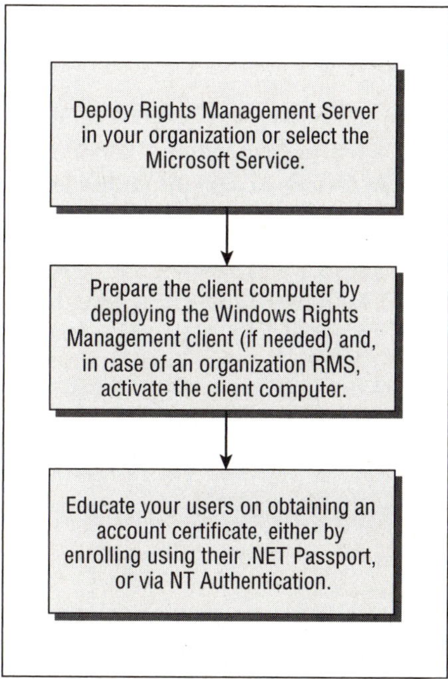

Exercise 5.3 outlines the steps to use IRM in Microsoft Office Outlook 2007.

EXERCISE 5.3

Steps to Restrict Permissions in Microsoft Office Outlook 2007 Using IRM

To restrict permissions, follow these steps:

1. Compose a new email message using Microsoft Office Outlook 2007.

EXERCISE 5.3 *(continued)*

2. To restrict permissions for the email message, click the Office button and select Permission ➢ Manage Credentials.

3. If your computer does not have the Windows Rights (RM) Management client installed, you will be prompted to deploy this client, as shown here.

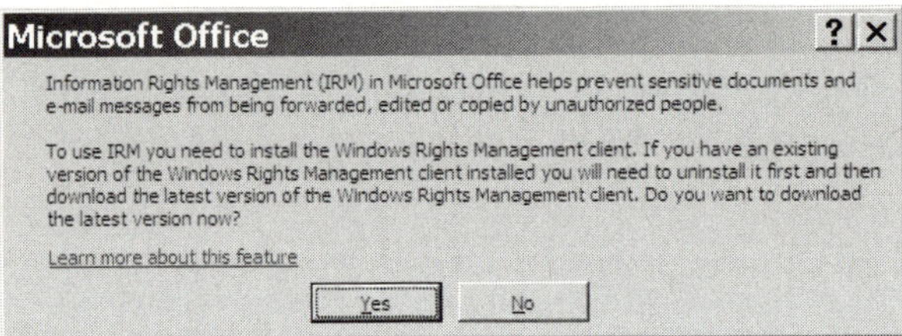

4. When the Windows Rights Management client is installed, you will be prompted to sign up for the service. You can choose to log in to a Rights Management server deployed in your organization, or if it is unavailable you can choose to sign up for the free trial IRM service offered by Microsoft (we've done the latter in this exercise).

5. Sign in to .NET Passport by typing your email address and password for your Microsoft .NET Passport, MSN email account, or Hotmail email account. If you don't have a .NET Passport, create one.

6. Type the email address that you used to sign in to the Microsoft .NET Passport; this will be used to create the Rights Management account certificate. Click Next. You can then select whether you want to create a standard, or temporary certificate, as shown here.

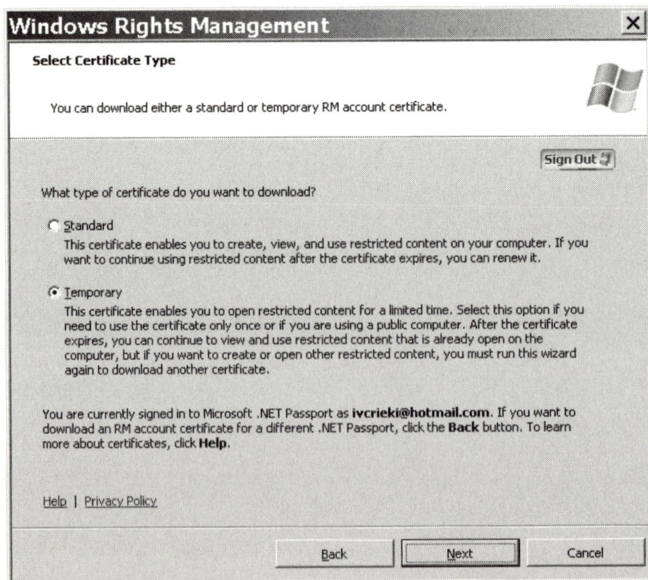

EXERCISE 5.3 *(continued)*

7. Close the Windows RM Account Certification wizard.

8. Click the Office button again, and select Permission ➤ Manage Credentials. You will be requested to select a user account that you want to use to create content with restricted permission, as shown here. Select the account that you just enabled, and click OK.

9. You will see that your email message is now secured. Your email message can be read only by recipients that successfully authenticate against the Microsoft RMS server, and recipients will not be able to forward, print, or copy content.

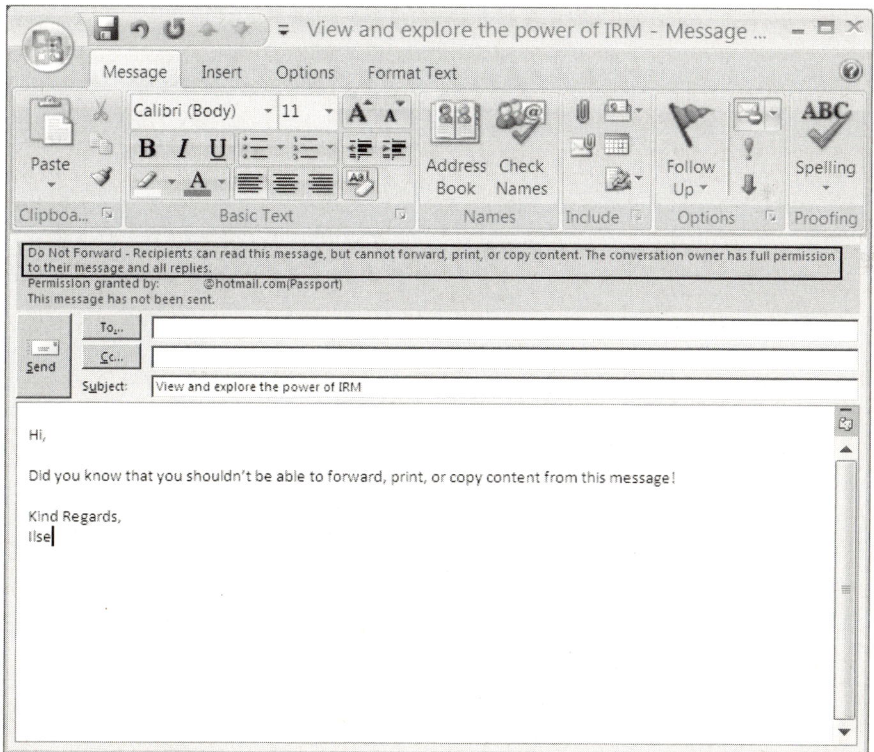

EXERCISE 5.3 *(continued)*

In Outlook 2007, a recipient would do the following to read an email message with restricted permissions:

10. When receiving an email message that has restricted permissions, the user won't see the content of the message immediately, and will have to authenticate himself or herself against the RMS server. (In the example shown in the following graphic, it's the Microsoft RMS server.)

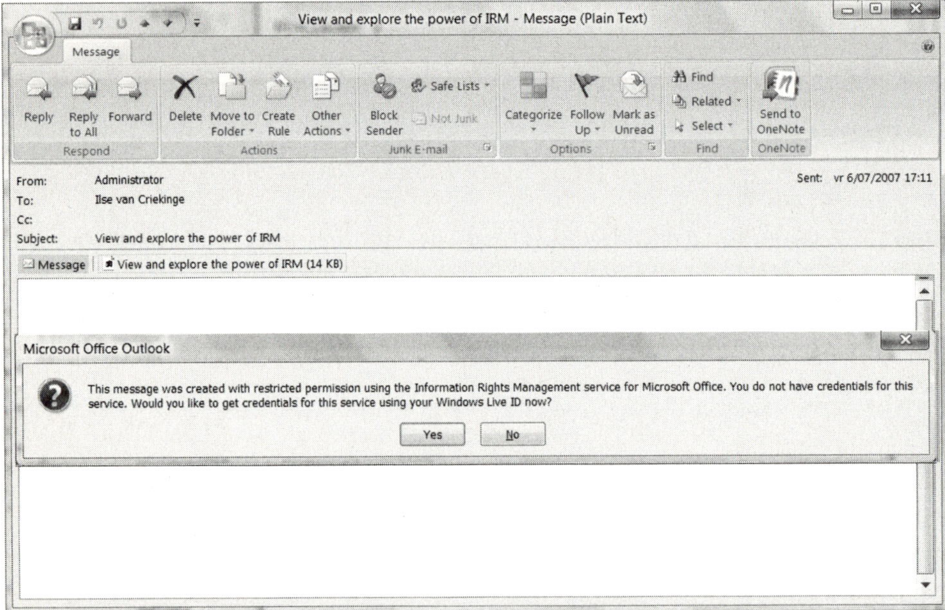

11. If the user doesn't have a RM account certificate, they will be offered the chance to get one.

12. Once the user has an RM account certificate, they will be validated against the Microsoft RMS server, as seen here.

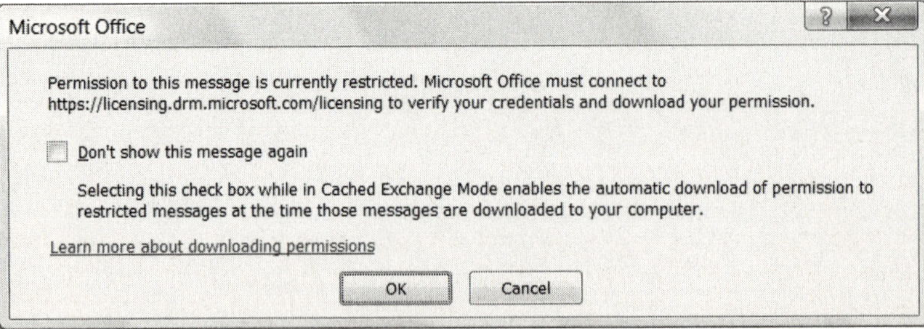

EXERCISE 5.3 *(continued)*

13. The email message will made readable, but the user won't be able to overcome the restricted permissions. Here's what happens when the user tries to employ the Windows Vista Snipping Tool to grab the email message:

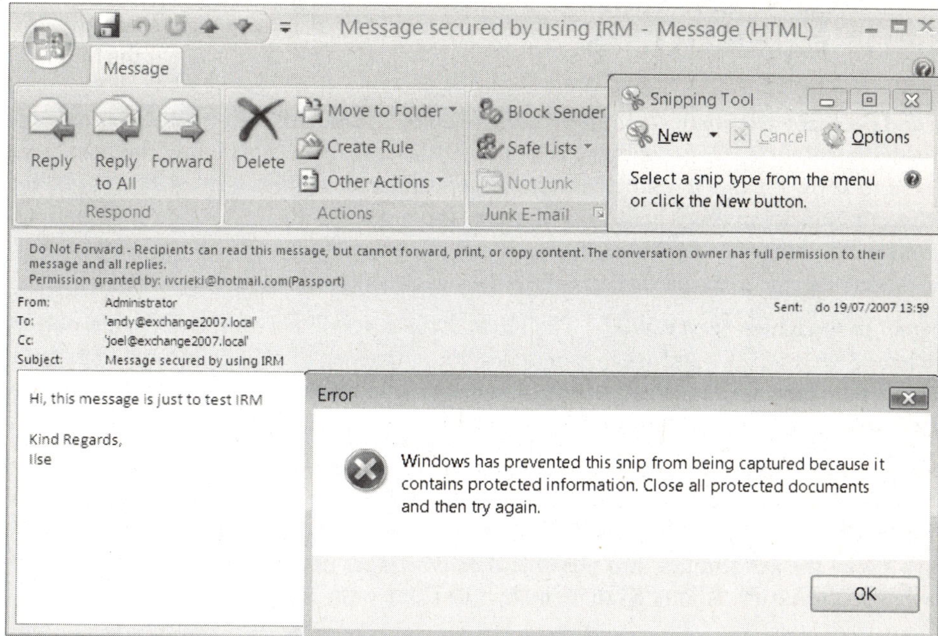

Summary

In this chapter we have looked at all features that Exchange Server provides to you as an Exchange administrator to secure your messaging environment to comply with your company's requirements and with those required by law.

First we looked at some legal-compliance requirements that are widely known, including requirements in the United States, Canada, Australia, Europe, and Japan. Then we went over the three types of messaging policies that Exchange Server 2007 provides to comply with any legal or corporate requirement: transport policies, journaling policies, and messaging records management policies.

If you want to design a secure messaging environment, you need to include procedures for message content filtering, and we covered that in the second part of the chapter. We investigated the antispam and antivirus abilities that Exchange Server 2007 offers. We also mentioned two new parts of the Microsoft family that can help you provide more security: Exchange Hosted Services and Microsoft Forefront for Exchange Server.

Finally, we covered some additional tweaking you should do to make your Exchange organization as secure as possible. We investigated how you can secure your environment by delegating Exchange Administrator roles and by securing SMTP email. To finish we covered Information Rights Management.

Exam Essentials

Legal and company requirements for messaging policies There are both legal and company requirements that force you to configure messaging policies to control mail flow and mail storage. You need to know the difference between transport rules and journaling rules. You might also receive a question about client licensing requirements, and about the archiving possibilities transport rules offer. A lot of questions on the exam ask you about the possible configuration options for messaging records management and about message classifications.

Antispam in Exchange Server 2007 The exam focuses very hard on the antispam options in Exchange Server 2007, and what is added if you introduce Exchange Hosted Services and Microsoft Forefront for Exchange to your Exchange environment. Make sure that you know what the different antispam filtering options entail.

Exchange Administrative Permissions The exam will check if you know about the new Exchange Administrator roles; make sure that you can list them and that you know what rights users will get when they are delegated an Exchange Administrator role. You have to know the advantages and possible disadvantages of securing SMTP email traffic, and what Information Rights Management can offer your Exchange organization.

Review Questions

1. You are an Exchange administrator, and you have a single Exchange Server 2007 server with 250 mailboxes. Your management wants you to implement what is needed to make sure that messages they send cannot be read by anyone other than the intended recipient. What should you implement?

   A. Sender filtering

   B. Recipient filtering

   C. Content filtering

   D. Message encryption

   E. Digital signatures

2. You are an Exchange administrator, and you have an Exchange Server 2007 organization with one Client Access server/Hub Transport server Exchange Server 2007 instance, and one Exchange Server 2007 Mailbox server with 250 mailboxes. Your Exchange server receives more spam messages than legitimate emails, and you want to reduce the number of spam messages that reach your messaging environment, but you do not want to invest in new hardware or software. What are your options?

   A. Deploy antispam agents on the Mailbox server.

   B. Deploy antispam agents on the Hub Transport server.

   C. Deploy the Edge Transport server role in your environment.

   D. Use Exchange Hosted Services.

3. You are an Exchange administrator, and you have an Exchange Server 2007 organization with one Client Access server/Hub Transport server Exchange Server 2007 instance and one Exchange Server 2007 Mailbox server with 250 mailboxes. Your Exchange server receives more spam messages than legitimate mails, and you want to reduce the number of spam messages that reach your users' mailboxes, but you do not want to invest in new hardware or software. What are your options?

   A. Deploy antispam agents on the Mailbox server.

   B. Deploy antispam agents on the Hub Transport server.

   C. Deploy the Edge Transport server role in your environment.

   D. Use Exchange Hosted Services.

4. You are an Exchange administrator, and you have a single Exchange Server 2007 server that houses 300 mailboxes. You would like to keep track of the emails that are sent and received by the legal department in your organization. You are using a Standard Edition license of Exchange Server 2007, and you currently have five stores in use. What should you do? Choose two answers; each part presents part of the solution.

   A. Create a mail-enabled universal distribution group, U_Legal_Department, and make every user of the legal department a member of that group.

   B. Create a journaling rule that will journal every email sent and received by members of the mail-enabled universal group U_Legal_Department.

   C. Move all mailboxes of users in the legal department to a new mailbox store, Store_Legal.

   D. Enable journaling on the new store, Store_Legal.

5. You are an Exchange administrator responsible for an Exchange 2007 organization that contains two Exchange 2007 Mailbox servers, one Client Access server, and one Hub Transport server. Your company recently acquired an Exchange 2007 organization. You do not intend to merge the two companies, but it is important that you secure all mail flow between the two organizations that have a dedicated T1 Line to link them together. What should you do?

   A. Create a dedicated SMTP Send connector and require authentication.

   B. Create a dedicated SMTP Send connector.

   C. Install and configure MIIS.

   D. Install and configure the Exchange organization's connector.

6. You are an Exchange administrator responsible for a single Exchange Server 2007 organization. You've received a request that when other SMTP servers perform Sender ID filtering your domain name cannot be spoofed by nonauthorized users. What should you create?

   A. Register an SPF record in DNS.

   B. Create an SPF record in the registry of your Exchange server.

   C. Register an MX record in DNS.

   D. Register an MX record in the registry of your Exchange server record in DNS.

7. You are an Exchange administrator responsible for an Exchange 2007 organization that contains two Exchange 2007 Mailbox servers, one Client Access server, and one Hub Transport server. Your legal department requests that you include a disclaimer with all messages that are sent out from your Exchange organization. How can you accomplish this with the least amount of administrative effort?

   A. Create and register a transport event sink on your Exchange Hub Transport server.

   B. Create a transport rule that adds a disclaimer to all messages that are sent outside the organization.

   C. Create a transport rule that adds a disclaimer to all messages that are sent inside the organization.

   D. Educate your users to add a signature to all messages they send outside.

8. You are an Exchange administrator responsible for an Exchange 2007 organization that contains two Exchange 2007 Mailbox servers, one Client Access server, and one Hub Transport server. Your management would like you to investigate if it is possible to prepend the word *SPAM* to every message that is delivered to a user's Junk E-Mail folder. How can you accomplish this with the least amount of administrative effort?

A. Configure a transport rule to prepend the subject of an email with *SPAM* when a message reaches a predefined SCL.

B. Configure a journaling rule to prepend the subject of an email with *SPAM* when a message reaches a predefined SCL.

C. Create and register a transport event sink to prepend the subject of a mail with *SPAM* when a message reaches a predefined SCL.

D. Create and deploy a group policy to prepend the subject of an email with *SPAM* when a message reaches a predefined SCL.

9. You are an Exchange administrator responsible for an Exchange 2007 organization that contains two Exchange 2007 Mailbox servers, one Client Access server, and one Hub Transport server. Your management requests that you keep the size of your database files under control. You have reached an agreement with your management to control the size of the mailboxes by managing the amount of time messages are retained in the Deleted Items folder. You are required to create two kinds of policies; the first one enables a user to keep items in the Deleted Items folder for 7 days, the second one for 60 days. What should you do to successfully configure these requirements? Select three; each answer is a part of the solution.

A. Create two mailbox stores.

B. Create two new managed default folders, type Deleted Items.

C. Move users to the mailbox store that is configured with the required deleted item retention time.

D. Create two new managed folder policies, each one responsible for a different managed default folder, both called Deleted Items, and attach it to the users needed.

E. Create managed content settings that reflect the specified criteria for each new managed default folder, type Deleted Items.

F. Configure the required deleted item retention time for the mailbox stores.

10. You are an Exchange administrator, and you have a single Exchange Server 2007 that houses 300 mailboxes. You have recently deployed an Exchange Server 2007 Edge Transport server, and you need to configure a way to reject any mail that is coming from any known relayers. What should you configure?

A. Sender filtering

B. Recipient filtering

C. Content filtering

D. Connection filtering

11. You are an Exchange administrator, and you have a single Exchange Server 2007 server that houses 300 mailboxes. You have recently deployed an Exchange Server 2007 Edge Transport server, and you need to configure a way to reject as much mail as possible from domain spoofers. What should you configure?

    A. Sender filtering

    B. Recipient filtering

    C. Sender ID filtering

    D. Connection filtering

12. You are an Exchange administrator responsible for an Exchange 2007 organization that contains two Exchange 2007 Mailbox servers, one Client Access server, and one Hub Transport server. You would like to grant your network administrator the permission to give existing users a mailbox on your Exchange servers. What role should you delegate to your network administrator?

    A. Exchange Organization Administrator

    B. Exchange Recipient Administrator

    C. Exchange View-Only Administrator

    D. Exchange Server Administrator

13. You are an Exchange administrator responsible for an Exchange 2007 organization that contains two Exchange 2007 Mailbox servers, one Client Access server, and one Hub Transport server. You recently hired a new Exchange administrator and added her to the Domain Admins group, but you need to grant her all permissions to the entire Exchange organization. What role should you delegate to your new colleague?

    A. Exchange Organization Administrator

    B. Exchange Recipient Administrator

    C. Exchange View-Only Administrator

    D. Exchange Server Administrator

14. You are an Exchange administrator responsible for an Exchange 2007 organization that contains two Exchange 2007 Mailbox servers, one Client Access server, and one Hub Transport server. All your users use Microsoft Office Outlook 2007. Your management has decided that it has to be possible for users to mark every email they send to a customer as A/C Confidential. What should you do? Select two; each option is part of the solution.

    A. Deploy a local file (`Classifications.xml`) on the client computers.

    B. Create and deploy a registry key on the client computers that enables the use of message classifications.

    C. Deploy a local file (`Classifications.xml`) on the Exchange Mailbox servers.

    D. Create and deploy a registry key on the Exchange Mailbox servers that enables the use of message classifications.

15. You are an Exchange administrator, and you have a single Exchange Server 2007 server that houses 300 mailboxes. A single user in your organization asks you if there is a way to restrict permissions on an email message he's sending to a customer. He wants to prevent the customer from forwarding or copying the contents of the email message. The user in question uses Microsoft Office Outlook 2007. What can you offer him?

    A. Digital signatures

    B. Message encryption

    C. Information Rights Management

    D. A secure SMTP connection to that customer's mail organization

16. You are an Exchange administrator responsible for an Exchange 2007 organization that contains two Exchange 2007 Mailbox servers, one Client Access server, and one Hub Transport server. Your users use either Microsoft Office Outlook 2000 or Microsoft Office Outlook XP to open their mailboxes. All your clients are running Windows XP Professional SP2. Your management wants you to deploy and configure a Rights Management server. What should you do first so that your clients can use the abilities offered by IRM? Select two; each answer is a complete solution.

    A. Upgrade to Windows Vista

    B. Upgrade Microsoft Office Outlook to Microsoft Office 2003

    C. Upgrade Microsoft Office Outlook to Microsoft Office 2007

    D. Deploy Windows Rights Management server

17. You are an Exchange administrator, and you have a single Exchange Server 2007 server that houses 300 mailboxes. Your management wants customers to be sure that messages they receive from your organization are sent by your organization. In addition, your management wants to make sure that in case someone outside your organization altered the message, the recipient knows about this. What should you implement?

    A. Sender filtering

    B. Recipient filtering

    C. Content filtering

    D. Message encryption

    E. Digital signatures

18. You are an Exchange administrator responsible for an Exchange 2007 organization that contains two Exchange 2007 Mailbox servers, one Client Access server, and one Hub Transport server. You recently hired a new Exchange administrator who will be responsible for your Hub Transport server and your Client Access server. What role should you delegate to your new colleague?

    A. Exchange Organization Administrator

    B. Exchange Recipient Administrator

    C. Exchange View-Only Administrator

    D. Exchange Server Administrator

19. You are an Exchange administrator, and you have a single Exchange Server 2007 server that houses 300 mailboxes. You recently deployed an Edge Transport server role. You would like to configure your Edge Transport server to block all messages that contain attachments with an extension .XYZ. What should you do?

A. Enable and configure attachment filtering on your Exchange Server 2007 server.

B. Enable and configure attachment filtering on your Edge Transport server.

C. Enable and configure content filtering on your Hub Transport server.

D. Enable and configure content filtering on your Edge Transport server.

20. You are an Exchange administrator responsible for an Exchange 2007 organization that contains two Exchange 2007 Mailbox servers, one Client Access server, and one Hub Transport server. You would like to enable attachment filtering, and you choose to deploy an Edge Transport server. You would like to have blocked attachments sent to a quarantine mailbox; what should you do?

A. Enable and configure attachment filtering.

B. Enable and configure content filtering.

C. Enable and configure recipient filtering.

D. Enable and configure Microsoft Forefront Security for Exchange Server.

Answers to Review Questions

1. D. Encrypting messages will make sure that only the intended recipient can view the contents. Sender filtering, recipient filtering, and content filtering are used to prevent spam from entering the exchange organization. Digital signatures will allow the recipient of the message to be sure the sender actually sent the message but the message itself will not be encrypted when sent.

2. D. You don't want to invest in new hardware and software, so you cannot go for the Edge Transport server role. You want to stop spam before it reaches your messaging environment, thereby eliminating the possibility of deploying the antispam agents on the Hub Transport server. It is not possible to deploy antispam agents on the Mailbox server. You can only choose to use Exchange Hosted Services.

3. B. You don't want to invest in new hardware and software, so you cannot go for the Edge Transport server role. Since you want to reduce the amount of spam that reaches your users' mailboxes, you should enable the antispam transport agents on your Hub Transport server. You don't want to stop spam from entering your organization, you just want to stop spam from reaching the user's mailboxes, thereby there is no requirement to go for Exchange Hosted Services.

4. A and B. Because you are using the Standard Edition version of Exchange Server 2007, you are not able to create an additional store since you already have the maximum number of stores in use. The Standard Edition version of Exchange only supports the creation of five stores. You can, however, create a new universal distribution group and use a new feature available in Exchange Server 2007: per-distribution-group journaling.

5. A. It is best practice to enable authentication to provide additional security for email sent from associated organizations. Creating a dedicated SMTP Send Connector does not provide secure mail flow if you don't require authentication. Installing and configuring MIIS would enable directory synchronization which is not asked for in this scenario. The Exchange organization's connector does not exist.

6. A. Sender ID filtering can provide you with a valid result only if the sender's domain has a Sender Policy Framework (SPF) record registered in DNS.

7. B. You can use the Exchange Management Console or Exchange Management Shell to configure disclaimers on computers that have the Hub Transport server role installed. Creating and registering a transport event sink is not recommended. Educating your users will require more effort than creating a transport rule. You shouldn't apply a transport rule to messages that are sent inside your organization, because you only want messages that go outside the organization to receive a disclaimer.

8. A. You can configure a transport rule to prepend a subject with a string, and you can specify the value of the SCL as a condition. A journaling rule is used to journal messages, and therefore not valid for changing a message subject. Creating a transport event sink would require administrative effort to create and deploy it. Group policies cannot be used to change the subject of a mail.

9. B, C, and E. Deleted item retention time is the amount of time that messages that are deleted from the mailbox are available for recovery. We are covering the messages that are still in the mailbox, in the Deleted Items folder, so deleted item retention time doesn't matter here. Instead, it is feasible to create two new Deleted Items managed folders and specify for each one different managed content settings, and use managed folder policy to hand them out to the users that need those settings.

10. D. You can configure connection filtering to check with real-time Block lists if the connecting SMTP server is a known relaying server.

11. C. Sender ID filtering will check if the sender (or most probable sender) is sending the mail using the SMTP services of a server that is authorized to send mail from that sender's domain. If there is an SPF record configured for the SMTP mail domain, you can check if domain spoofing is done. Sender filtering only provides the ability to block mail from specific domains, without checking if it's spoofed or not. Recipient filtering is used to filter mail sent to specified recipients, and Connection filtering is used to check if the connection was initiated from a valid IP address.

12. B. A user needs to have the Exchange Recipient Administrator role in order to be able to give users a mailbox.

13. A. To be able to fully manage an Exchange organization, a user needs to be delegated the Exchange Organization Administrator role.

14. A and B. If you want to enable the use of message classifications in Outlook, you need to deploy on the client computer a local file (`Classifications.xml`) that contains the definitions of the message classifications. And you also need to create and deploy a registry key that will enable the use of message classification by referencing the `Classifications.xml` file on the client computer. You don't need to add a registry key on the Exchange Mailbox servers, and you don't need to deploy a local file on the Exchange Mailbox servers.

15. C. Information Rights Management can be used in Microsoft Office Outlook 2003 and Microsoft Office Outlook 2007 to prevent email forwarding, copying, editing, or printing. Implementing signing and sealing will not prevent a user from forwarding or copying the contents of an email message. A secure SMTP connection only secures the SMTP mail flow, but does not imply that the email message is not able to be forwarded or copied.

16. B and C. You need at least Microsoft Office Outlook 2003 to be able to use the services provided by IRM. You can use the abilities offered by IRM by running Office Outlook 2003 (or later) on XP Professional. You don't need to have Windows Rights Management server, since you can use the limited-trial version offered by Microsoft.

17. E. Digital signatures provide authentication, nonrepudiation, and data integrity. By digitally signing your email messages, you enable recipients to verify if the email message has been sent by the person or organization that claims to have sent the message, and you enable recipients to verify if the message has been altered.

18. D. You need to delegate the role of Exchange Server Administrator since you want your new colleague to have full control over the specified servers' configuration data.

19. B. Attachment filtering allows you to block attachments from entering your Exchange organization, by attachment content type, or by attachment file name. You can enable and configure attachment filtering only on the edge Transport server. Content filtering is set as an SCL value for messages so you can configure your Edge or Hub Transport server to block them, quarantine them, or deliver them to a user's junk mail folder.

20. D. Forefront Security for Exchange Server enables you to quarantine blocked attachments. Attachment filtering, content filtering, and recipient filtering do not allow you as an administrator to have blocked attachments sent to a quarantine mailbox.

70-238: Pro: Deploying Messaging Solutions with Microsoft Exchange Server 2007

Planning an Upgrade to Exchange Server 2007

MICROSOFT EXAM OBJECTIVES COVERED IN THIS CHAPTER:

- ✓ Plan the Exchange Server 2007 migration implementation
- ✓ Plan the Exchange Server 2007 upgrade implementation

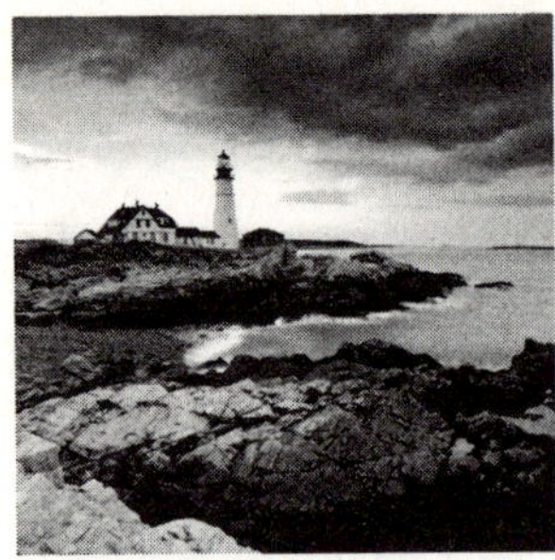

Before we start talking about upgrading to Exchange Server 2007, it is important to make the distinction between two types of upgrades: transitioning and migrating. When you decide to upgrade your existing Exchange 2000 Server or Exchange Server 2003 to Exchange Server 2007, you will be *transitioning* your Exchange organization to 2007. However, when you decide to upgrade your existing Exchange 2000 Server or Exchange Server 2003 to a new Exchange Server 2007 organization you will be *migrating* to Exchange Server 2007. Upgrading from Exchange 5.5 or any other third-party messaging system to Exchange Server 2007 is also referred to as migrating to Exchange 2007. In this chapter we will cover everything that has to be considered when planning a transition to Exchange 2007. In Chapter 7, "Plan a Migration to Exchange Server 2007," you will get detailed information about all possible migration scenarios that exist for Exchange Server 2007.

It is true that the transition process itself is the same for an Exchange Server 2003 or an Exchange 2000 Server organization. But there are features from Exchange 2000 Server and Exchange Server 2003 that are not supported anymore in Exchange Server 2007. If you decide to transition to Exchange Server 2007, you will need to plan a solution for all features that do not exist anymore in Exchange Server 2007. In this chapter we will dig into all those features, and we will have a look at the best way to transition your Exchange 2000 Server or Exchange Server 2003 organization to Exchange Server 2007.

The main subjects in this chapter are as follows:

- Exchange 2000 Server features not supported in Exchange Server 2007
- Exchange Server 2003 features not supported in Exchange Server 2007
- Features that are gone in Exchange Server 2007
- De-emphasized features in Exchange Server 2007
- Planning the upgrade process from Exchange 2000 Server and Exchange Server 2003

Planning for Migration of Legacy Exchange Features

In this part of the chapter we will have a look at all features that were available in Exchange 2000 Server and Exchange Server 2003, but are not supported anymore in Exchange Server 2007. We will also highlight the features that are de-emphasized in Exchange Server 2007.

Exchange 2000 Server Features Not Supported in Exchange Server 2007

In this part of the chapter, we will have a look at all discontinued features that were available in Exchange 2000 Server:

- cc:Mail connector
- MS Mail connector
- Exchange 2000 Conferencing Server
- Exchange Chat Service
- Exchange Instant Messaging
- Key Management Service
- Microsoft Mobile Information Server

cc:Mail Connector

The Lotus cc:Mail connector is one of the four connectors included with Exchange 2000 Server. The Lotus cc:Mail connector provides the possibility to connect your Exchange 2000 Server organization to any DB8-type cc:Mail post office. Users that are using cc:Mail are created in Active Directory as mail-enabled contacts or as mail-enabled users. Mail flow and directory synchronization are controlled by configuring this connector.

Cc:Mail was discontinued in 2001. The latest version of cc:Mail was released in 2000, version 8.5. Originally developed by Microsoft in the '80s, Lotus Development took over the technology in 1992.

If you want to continue to use a cc:Mail connector, plan to keep at least one Exchange 2000 Server in your organization.

MS Mail Connector

The MS Mail connector can be used to connect an MS Mail server to your Exchange 2000 Server organization.

The last version of MS Mail that was released is version 3.5. There was no new version planned due to the release of a new mail system, called Microsoft Exchange Server. To position this new product as the successor of MS Mail, Microsoft decided to release the first version of Microsoft Exchange Server as version 4.0.

If you want to continue to use an MS Mail connector, plan to keep at least one Exchange 2000 Server in your organization.

Exchange 2000 Conferencing Server

Exchange 2000 Conferencing Server was a separate component that you could install once you had an Exchange 2000 Server organization deployed. Exchange 2000 Conferencing Server allowed you to do the following:

- Share applications
- Share desktops
- Share whiteboards
- Transfer files
- Host text-based chat sessions
- Exchange audio and video signals

Everything was based on four core components/technologies:

- Conference Management Service
- IP multicast
- T.120
- H.323

If you want to continue to use Exchange 2000 Conferencing Server, plan to keep at least one instance of Exchange 2000 Server in your organization.

Exchange Chat Service

You could deploy the Exchange Chat Service in addition to an Exchange 2000 Server or on any Windows 2000 box in an Active Directory environment where Exchange 2000 Server was deployed. Following protocol standards set for Internet Relay Chat (IRC (RFC 1459), and the Internet Relay Chat Extension (IRCX). Implementing Exchange Chat Service allowed you to do the following:

- Use IRC clients such as Microsoft Chat Service
- Create channels for one-to-many and many-to-many text conversation
- Enable administrators to moderate the use of and access to chat communities with bans and classes
- Allow users to host or moderate a chat channel's content

If you want to continue to use Exchange Chat Service, plan to keep at least one instance of Exchange 2000 Server in your organization.

Instant Messaging

Exchange Instant Messaging provided real-time collaboration services in Exchange 2000 Server. All Instant Messaging communication used the protocol RVP. Installing Instant Messaging enabled users to do the following:

- Exchange small messages without the overhead of composing and sending email
- Exchange small messages when email transfer is interrupted

- Propagate and view presence information of other users
- Control who can and who cannot contact you

Instant Messaging could be installed as part of an Exchange 2000 Server deployment, or you could deploy Instant Messaging on a non-Exchange server in an Exchange 2000 Server environment.

If you need to be able to support Exchange Instant Messaging, plan to keep at least one instance of Exchange 2000 Server in your organization.

Microsoft has developed a new product to provide both instant messaging and collaboration functionality to the enterprise. Originally launched in 2003 as Live Communications Server 2003, a new version, Live Communications Server 2005, was released in 2005. In August 2007 the latest version, named Office Communications Server 2007, was presented by Microsoft.

Key Management Service

The Key Management Service was one of the least implemented features in an Exchange 2000 Server organization. Installing the Key Management Service enabled you as an Exchange administrator to provide users with the option to sign and/or seal their messages.

Exchange 2003 and Exchange 2007 leverage the Windows Server 2003 public key infrastructure (PKI) architecture to provide Exchange users the possibility to sign and seal their messages.

If you need to be able to provide the Exchange Key Management Service, plan to keep at least one instance of Exchange 2000 Server in your organization. It is, however, best practice to migrate the Exchange Key Management Service to the Windows Server 2003 PKI architecture. Figure 6.1 shows an overview of the process of this migration.

Microsoft Mobile Information Server

Microsoft Mobile Information Server provided users with the ability to gain access to their Exchange 2000 mailboxes by using a mobile device. Using Outlook Mobile Access enabled users to browse through their mail and calendars using a cell phone. In addition, users were able to reply to mail and perform real-time searches. Using Microsoft Server ActiveSync made it possible for users to sync their mailboxes with their PDAs.

Exchange Server 2003 provided Outlook Mobile Access and Microsoft Server ActiveSync out of the box, without requiring Microsoft Mobile Information Server. Outlook Mobile Access which isn't supported anymore in Exchange Server 2007, as we will cover later in this chapter.

If you need to be able to provide the Microsoft Mobile Information Server services to some users, plan to keep at least one instance of Exchange 2000 Server in your organization.

FIGURE 6.1 Migrating Exchange Key Management Service to the Windows Server 2003 PKI architecture

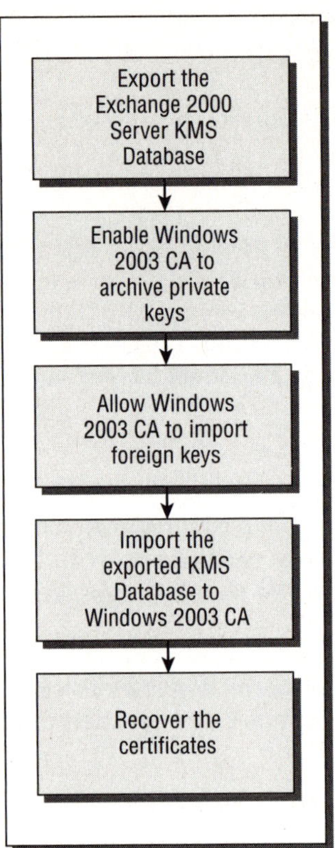

Exchange 2003 Server Features Not Supported in Exchange Server 2007

In this part of the chapter, we will look at all discontinued features that were available in Exchange 2003 Server:

- Connector for Lotus Notes
- Connector for Novell GroupWise
- NNTP
- Outlook Mobile Access
- X.400 connector
- Administrative groups
- Routing groups

- Active/Active clustering
- Coexistence with Exchange Server 5.5
- Public-folder access using Outlook Web Access (OWA)

Connector for Lotus Notes

Out of the box, Exchange Server 2003 provided tools to enable coexistence with a Lotus Notes messaging environment. When you ran the installation of Exchange Server 2003 you would have the choice to install the following components:

- Microsoft Exchange Lotus Notes connector
- Microsoft Exchange Calendar connector

The Microsoft Exchange Lotus Notes connector enabled both directory synchronization and mail flow between a Lotus Notes environment and an Exchange organization. The Microsoft Exchange Calendar connector allowed users to gain access to free/busy information from users housed on Lotus Notes.

In March 2007 Microsoft released an updated version of the Microsoft Exchange Lotus Notes connector, which replaces the built-in connector that ships with Exchange Server 2003 (including SP2). This new Lotus Notes connector includes support for iNotes and Domino Web Access clients, improved Unicode support, and enhanced message routing between Exchange and Domino.

The Microsoft Exchange Lotus Notes connector has been cut from Exchange Server 2007. In its place, Microsoft has chosen to include a brand-new Microsoft Transporter Suite for Lotus Domino. This new suite is an easy-to-use shared management console, and a command-line environment, that offers you planning resources, coexistence tools, and migration tools to move from Lotus Domino to Exchange Server 2007. (For more information about this suite, consult Chapter 7.) It is possible to enable SMTP mail connectivity from Exchange Server 2007 to a foreign Lotus Notes environment. You could also deploy Microsoft Identity Integration Server 2003 to perform directory synchronization between Exchange and Lotus Notes.

Be careful about versions! If you want to use the Microsoft Transporter Suite for Lotus Domino you need to have at least version 6 to enable coexistence (Lotus Domino 5 is not supported for SMTP mail routing because it does not support native MIME or iCal; therefore, to enable mail flow, you will need to implement the Lotus Notes connector for Exchange Server 2003 on an Exchange Server 2003 server!). If you just want to move mailboxes from Lotus Domino, you can use the Microsoft Transporter Suite to migrate from Lotus Domino versions 5.x, 6.x, and 7.x.

Connector for Novell GroupWise

Installing and configuring the connector for Novell GroupWise allowed an Exchange organization to establish connectivity with a Novell GroupWise mail environment. If you were to install just the connector for Novell GroupWise you would be able to establish mail connectivity and directory synchronization between your Exchange organization and your Novell GroupWise environment. By adding the Calendar connector you would also enable users to gain access to free/busy information of users housed in your Novell GroupWise environment.

Exchange Server 2007 does not support the connector for Novell GroupWise anymore. If you need to provide connectivity to a Novell GroupWise environment, plan to keep at least one Exchange Server 2003 in your organization.

If your Exchange organization requires mail connectivity only to a foreign Novell GroupWise environment, you could use SMTP send connectors to set up mail flow. If you want your Exchange users to see Novell GroupWise users as mail-enabled contacts, you could implement Microsoft Identity Integration Server (MIIS) 2003. But remember: you will not be able to exchange free/busy information using MIIS 2003. If you need this ability, you will have to install and configure the connector for Novell GroupWise and the Calendar connector on an Exchange 2000 Server or Exchange Server 2003 server in your Exchange organization.

NNTP

When you wanted to install Exchange 2000 Server or Exchange Server 2003, you had to have the Network News Transfer Protocol (NNTP) installed. This protocol was necessary for exchange to be able to create its public folders. But after installation you were able to disable this Internet protocol, or you could configure NNTP services for your Exchange organization. You were able to set up news groups, and you were able to configure news feeds. Users could use an NNTP client like Outlook Express to gain access to those news groups and news feeds.

Exchange Server 2007 does not require you to use NNTP! Exchange Server 2007 does not support NNTP anymore as an Internet protocol, either. If your Exchange organization needs to be able to provide NNTP services, plan to keep at least one Exchange Server 2003 server in your organization.

Outlook Mobile Access

Exchange Server 2003 offered two built-in mobile services: Microsoft Exchange ActiveSync, and Outlook Mobile Access. Outlook Mobile Access enabled users to access their Exchange Server mailboxes by using a browser-enabled mobile device, using Extensible Hypertext Markup Language (XHTML), compact HTML (cHTML), or standard HTML browsers.

If you have users that require Outlook Mobile Access, plan to keep at least one Exchange Server 2003 server in your organization.

X.400 Connector

Ever since the release of Exchange 2000 Server, Exchange has used SMTP as its default routing protocol. But you were always able to create and configure an X.400 connector to connect your Exchange organization to a foreign X.400 mail environment, to connect to another Exchange organization, or to connect two routing groups in the same Exchange organization. If you created a mailbox-enabled user in an Exchange 2000 or Exchange 2003 organization, that user would receive by default an SMTP address and an X.400 address. In Exchange Server 2007, the X.400 connector is not supported anymore. When you create a mailbox-enabled user in Exchange Server 2007, the user will not get an X.400 address, as can be seen in Figure 6.2.

FIGURE 6.2 Mailbox-enabled users in Exchange Server 2007 do not receive an X.400 address.

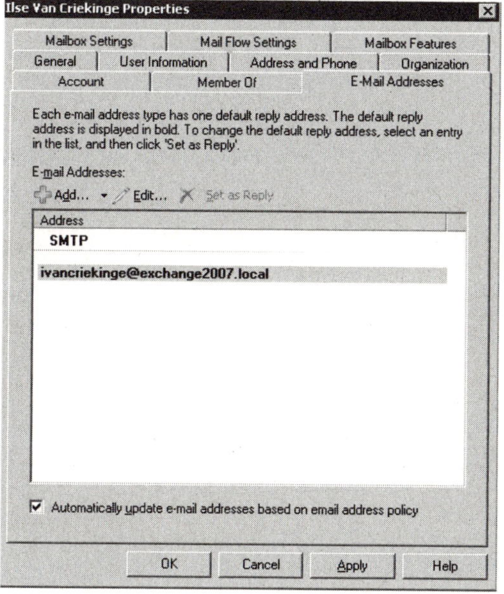

When you are transitioning an Exchange 2000 or 2003 organization to Exchange 2007, all users will still receive an X.400 address in addition to a SMTP address, even if the users are already housed on an Exchange Server 2007 server. After the transition is complete, you can change the recipient policies to remove the X.400 address.

If your Exchange organization needs to provide connectivity to a foreign X.400 mail environment, plan to keep at least one Exchange 2000 Server or Exchange Server 2003 server in your organization.

Administrative Groups

Administrative groups were introduced with the release of Exchange 2000 Server. Every Exchange 2000 Server or Exchange Server 2003 server that you would install would be made a member of an administrative group. An Exchange organization could consist of one or more administrative groups. The main purpose of administrative groups was to delegate control on an organization level or on an administrative group level. As an Exchange administrator, you were able to delegate three such levels of control:

- Exchange Full Administrator
- Exchange Administrator
- Exchange View Only Administrator

In Exchange Server 2007, Microsoft has removed administrative groups. For compatibility reasons, every Exchange Server 2007 server that is installed in an existing Exchange 2000 or Exchange 2003 organization will be made a member of a fixed single administrative group, called Exchange Administrative Group (FYDIBOHF23SPDLT). To delegate permissions in an Exchange 2007 organization, Microsoft introduced four new roles, as can be seen in Figure 6.3:

- Exchange Organization Administrator
- Exchange Recipient Administrator
- Exchange View-Only Administrator
- Exchange Server Administrator

FIGURE 6.3 Exchange 2007 administrator roles

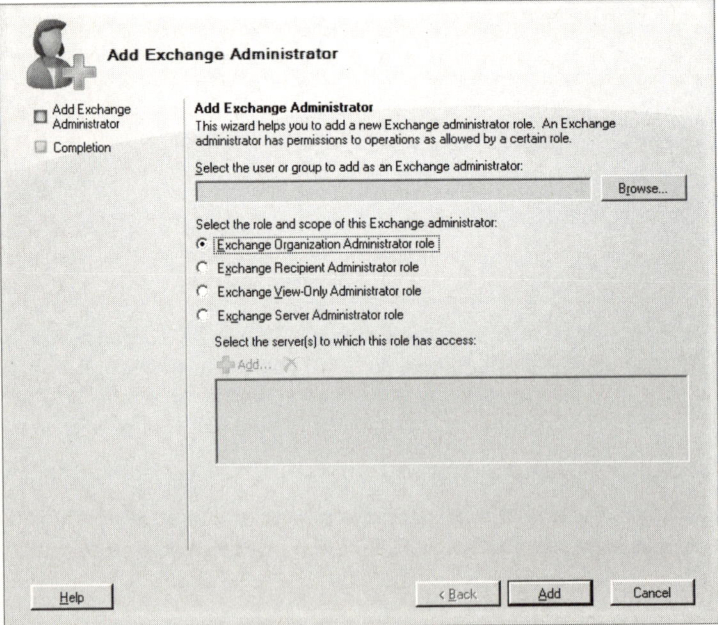

These new roles allow for more granularity when delegating permissions in your Exchange organization.

It is not supported to move an Exchange Server 2007 to an administrative group other than the default Exchange Administrative Group (FYDIBOHF23SPDLT). Furthermore, it is prohibited to move an Exchange 2000 Server or an Exchange Server 2003 server to this special Exchange 2007 administrative group!

Routing Groups

Routing groups were introduced with the release of Exchange 2000 Server. Every Exchange 2000 Server or Exchange Server 2003 that you would install would be made a member of a routing group. Exchange servers that belonged to the same routing group in an Exchange 2000 or Exchange 2003 environment were expected to have a reliable connection to one another. You couldn't control mail flow between servers in the same routing group, but you could configure mail flow between routing groups by specifying limits, schedules, or permissions. To connect routing groups in Exchange 2000 or Exchange 2003 organizations, you could use X.400 connectors, SMTP connectors, or routing group connectors.

In Exchange 2007, the routing of messages between servers is based on Active Directory sites. To maintain backward compatibility with Exchange 2000 and Exchange 2003, all Exchange 2007 servers will be made members of a predefined routing group, called Exchange Routing Group (DWBGZMFD01QNBJR). It is not supported to move an Exchange Server 2007 server to a routing group other than the default Exchange Routing Group (DWBGZMFD01QNBJR). Additionally, it is prohibited to move an Exchange 2000 Server or an Exchange Server 2003 server to this special Exchange 2007 routing group!

Active/Active Clustering

You could deploy Exchange 2000 Server and Exchange Server 2003 as an Active/Active cluster. Doing so meant that both nodes in the two-node cluster would be active at the same time, and were accessible for clients. Even though it was supported in previous versions of Exchange, it was not recommended to deploy an Active/Active cluster, since you had to bear the four-storage-group limit in mind and you had to be sure that both your nodes would be able to support the extra workload of the other active node in case of a failover. It is not supported to deploy an Exchange Server 2007 as an Active/Active cluster.

Coexistence with Exchange Server 5.5

Exchange Server 2007 does not support coexistence with Exchange Server 5.5. If your Exchange organization still uses Exchange Server 5.5, you will need to transition first to Exchange 2000 Server or Exchange Server 2003, followed by transitioning to Exchange Server 2007.

Exchange Server 5.5 can still exist next to an Exchange 2007 environment, but direct interoperability is not possible.

Public-Folder Access Using OWA

As you will see in the following section, Microsoft has decided to include public folders in Exchange Server 2007, but as a de-emphasized feature. In Exchange Server 2007 it is not possible to gain access to public folders using Outlook Web Access.

Microsoft has announced that public-folder access using Outlook Web Access will be possible with the release of Service Pack 1, scheduled to be released in late 2007, as seen in Figure 6.4.

FIGURE 6.4 Public-folder access using OWA Exchange 2007 SP1 Beta

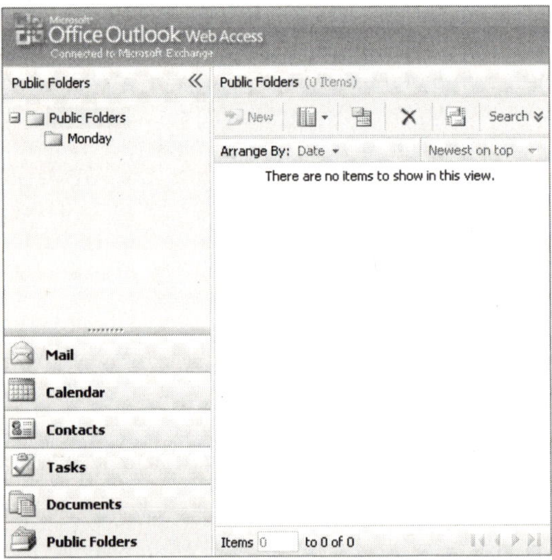

De-Emphasized Features in Exchange Server 2007

In this part of the chapter we will look at some features that are still available in Exchange Server 2007 but that are de-emphasized. In short, it means that the following features might not be supported in a next version of Exchange:

- Public folders
- CDOEx (CDO 3.0), WebDAV, and ExOLEDB

- Store events
- Streaming backups

Public Folders

When Microsoft released Exchange Server 2007, they listed public folders among the features that are still available. However, they suggested that companies should start investigating how public folders could be replaced by using, for example, Windows SharePoint document libraries.

In Exchange Server 2007 RTM, public folders can be managed only by using the Exchange Management Shell, since they are not shown in the Exchange Management Console. You cannot gain access to your public folders using Outlook Web Access, as you saw earlier in this chapter. Microsoft has, however, decided to include two important features with regards to public folders in Exchange Server 2007 Service Pack 1:

- Public Folder Management Console, which is a new configuration-management tool to manage public folders, as seen in Figure 6.5
- Public-folder access using OWA

FIGURE 6.5 Public Folder Management Console in Exchange Server 2007 Service Pack 1 Beta

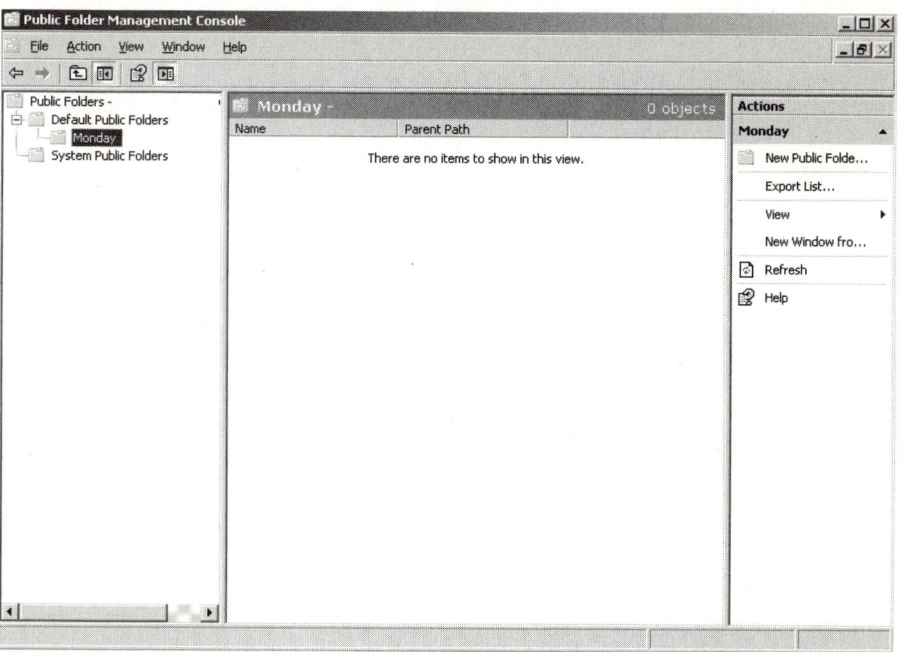

CDOEx (CDO 3.0), WebDAV, and ExOLEDB

Collaboration Data Objects for Exchange (CDOEx) are used to write applications based on Exchange Server. Web Distributed Authoring and Versioning (WebDAV), and Exchange Object Linking and Embedding Databases (ExOLEDBs) are just like the CDOEx APIs that were initially shipped with Exchange 2000 Server to provide capabilities for accessing Exchange Server mailbox data from an application. To develop Exchange applications, you should look at the new API released with Exchange Server 2007: Exchange Web Services (EWS). This new API provides a lot of advantages, including these two:

- EWS provides better Outlook interoperability for standalone line-of-business and portal applications than in previous versions.
- EWS APIs work from servers other than the Exchange Servers themselves.

Microsoft urges you to migrate any existing Exchange application to EWS.

Store Events

Exchange store events are used in Exchange 2000 Server and Exchange Server 2003 to control what happens when a certain event (like an email message that enters or leaves your Exchange store) occurs. Even though you can still create and run Exchange store events against an Exchange Server 2007 store, it is highly recommend to replace this de-emphasized feature by using either transport rules or Exchange Web Services.

For more information about transport rules, please refer to Chapter 5, "Defining Policies and Security Procedures."

Streaming Backup

As you saw in Chapter 3, "Designing Recovery and Messaging Services to Meet Business Demands," using the Exchange streaming backup API implies that every page in your database is read in turn, and that the checksum integrity of each page is verified during the backup process, just like the checksum integrity of transaction log files is checked before they are backed up. Microsoft recommends that you implement the Volume Shadow Copy backup since it is faster and more reliable. For more information about streaming backup methods and Volume Shadow Copy backup, please refer to Chapter 3.

Planning the Exchange Server 2007 Upgrade Implementation

Planning the upgrade process is the same no matter if you are planning a transition from Exchange 2000 Server, Exchange Server 2003, or a mixed Exchange 2000 Server and Exchange Server 2003 organization. In this part of the chapter, we will cover all the steps that you have to plan once you have decided to transition your current Exchange organization to Exchange Server 2007. The steps involved are shown in Figure 6.6.

FIGURE 6.6 The process for upgrading to Exchange Server 2007

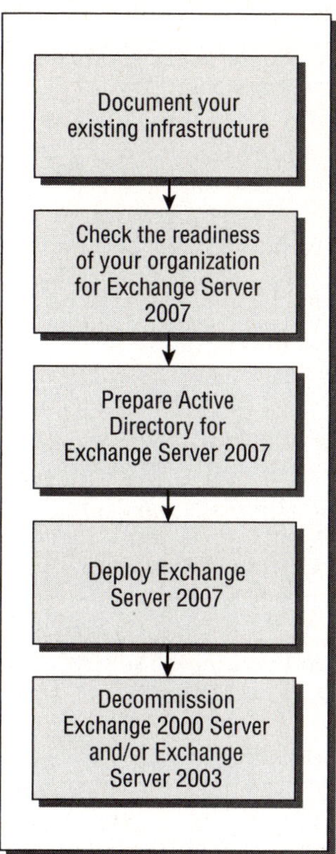
Document your existing infrastructure
Check the readiness of your organization for Exchange Server 2007
Prepare Active Directory for Exchange Server 2007
Deploy Exchange Server 2007
Decommission Exchange 2000 Server and/or Exchange Server 2003

Documenting Your Existing Infrastructure

Once you have decided to move to Exchange Server 2007, the first step is to assess and document your existing infrastructure. You should not only document your existing Exchange environment, but you should also make sure that you have information about your deployed Active Directory and your existing physical network.

Exchange Organization Settings

Table 6.1 shows you the information you need to know from your existing Exchange organization.

TABLE 6.1 Gathering Information about Your Exchange Organization Settings

Exchange Organization Setting	What You Need to Know About It
Exchange organization mode	Is it mixed or native?
Exchange Server hardware	What is your processor (size and type), memory, disk storage, and network speed?
Exchange Server version	What version server are you using, and what is the latest service pack deployed?
Exchange Server designated role	Is it a front-end server, back-end server, Bridgehead server, Mailbox server, and/or a public-folder server?
Administrative groups	How many administrative groups do you have in your organization, and why?
Exchange administrators	Who is delegated what permissions?
Storage groups and stores	How many storage groups and stores do you have?
Routing groups	How many routing groups does your organization have, and how are they connected?
Mail connectivity inbound and outbound	How is inbound and outbound mail flow configured for your Exchange organization?
Policies	What are your recipient policies, mailbox store policies, public-folder store policies, and server policies?
Protocol configuration	What are your enabled protocols and server settings?
Antispam and Antivirus software and settings	Does your current Exchange organization have antispam and antivirus software running, and what kind of filtering rules are defined?
SMTP namespaces	For which namespaces is Exchange responsible for mail delivery?
Exchange-aware products	What Exchange-aware products are installed? (Examples include backup/restore software, fax software, antispam solutions, and antivirus solutions.)

Active Directory Settings

As you have already seen in Chapter 3, Exchange Server 2007 stores most of its configuration information in Active Directory just like Exchange 2000 Server and Exchange Server 2003 did, with the exception of the Exchange Server 2007 Edge Transport server role that stores its configuration data in Active Directory Application Mode (ADAM). When you decide to transition to Exchange Server 2007 you need to keep track of the following:

- Active Directory topology (how many domains are deployed)
- Active Directory forest functional level
- Active Directory domain functional levels
- Active Directory domain controller and global catalog deployed
- Active Directory domain controller and global catalog operating system and service pack level

Exchange 2007 uses Active Directory sites for routing; therefore it is also important to gather the following information:

- Active Directory sites
- Active Directory site links
- Active Directory site-link costs

Network Settings

Microsoft recommends that you document your network settings to make sure you are prepared to start deploying Exchange Server 2007. The following network settings are worth documenting:

- Firewall deployment
- Demilitarized zone (DMZ) deployment
- Physical network (bandwidth, network backbone)

Checking Your Organization's Readiness for Exchange Server 2007

After documenting your current infrastructure, you need to schedule a check to see if your organization is ready for Exchange Server 2007. You can run the check yourself by keeping in mind all features that are not supported in Exchange Server 2007 and by making sure that you know all the prerequisites that have to be met before installing Exchange Server 2007. But you can also use the Exchange 2007 Readiness Check included with the Exchange Best Practices Analyzer v2.7 and later, as seen in Figure 6.7.

FIGURE 6.7 Exchange Readiness Check Exchange Best Practices Analyzer v2.7

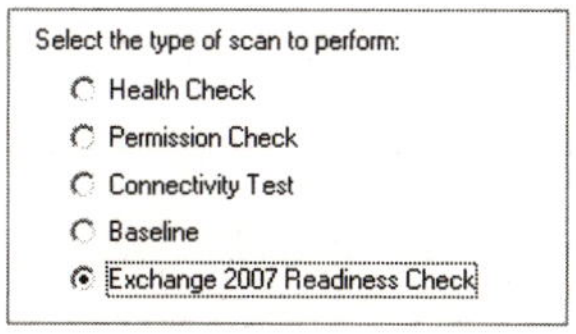

The Exchange Best Practices Analyzer (ExBPA) tool was first released in September 2004. Since the start, it has been a free tool available for download from the Internet. In Exchange Server 2007 it is a built configuration-management tool inside the Exchange Management Console. The main goals of ExBPA are to analyze an existing Exchange environment and to give you a report on what can and should be changed to make it run more smoothly. All recommendations are based on Microsoft's best practices.

In ExBPA version 2.7 the Exchange 2007 Readiness Check appeared for the first time. When you run the Readiness Check, the tool will perform checks to validate if your overall topology is ready for Exchange Server 2007, and it will also check in more depth whether all your deployed Exchange 2000 Server and Exchange Server 2003 servers have received the necessary updates and configuration settings to be able to coexist with Exchange Server 2007. The list of checks that are performed when running the Exchange 2007 Readiness Check is contained in a file called `ExBPA.Readiness.xml`, as seen in Figure 6.8.

After running the Exchange Readiness Check, you will get a report that shows you all critical issues and warning issues, as seen in Figure 6.9.

It is important to remember that the ExBPA tool does not make any changes to your Exchange environment! It will only help you highlight potential problems if you were to proceed with the Exchange Server 2007 deployment.

FIGURE 6.8 Checks included in ExBPA.Readiness.xml (ExBPA v.2.8)

XML Notepad - C:\ExBPA.Readiness.xml

File Edit View Insert Window Help

C:\ExBPA.Readiness.xml

Tree View | XSL Output

XSLT Location: ... Transform

```
  transition to Exchange 2007 is possible  -->
<!-- // EXTERNAL DEPENDENCIES:  -->
<!-- //      None  -->
<Object Type="Group" Name="Exchange Server 2007 Readiness Check" Task="Ex2007Readiness" SecurityContext="ADLOGON">
  <!-- // Statistics  -->
  <Object Type="Group" Name="Readiness Summary">
     <Setting Key1="Processed"/>
    <!-- // Categorization of deployment for transition documentation  -->
     <Setting Key1="Documentation"/>
   </Object>
  <!-- // Get basic directory naming context information  -->
  <Object Type="Directory" Name="cn" Class="Forest" GroupingClass="True">
     <Setting Key1="rootDomainNamingContext" Substitution="ROOTDN"/>
     <Setting Key1="configurationNamingContext" Substitution="CONFIGDN"/>
     <Setting Key1="schemaNamingContext" Substitution="SCHEMADN"/>
    <!-- // Find out if the Active Directory schema has already been upgraded  -->
    <Object Type="Group" Name="Active Directory Schema">
      <Object Type="Directory" Key2="cn=ms-Exch-Schema-Version-Pt,%SCHEMADN%">
         <Setting Key1="rangeUpper"/>
       </Object>
      <!-- // Find out more about this forest and what is installed  -->
      <!-- // The following object will exist in the schema if Identity Integration Server is installed
        -->
      <Object Type="Directory" Key2="cn=MS-MIIS-PCNS-Target,%SCHEMADN%">
         <Setting Key1="cn"/>
       </Object>
      <!-- // The following object will exist in the root domain if High Volume Exchange is installed  -
        ->
```

Error List | Dynamic Help

FIGURE 6.9 ExBPA transition documentation

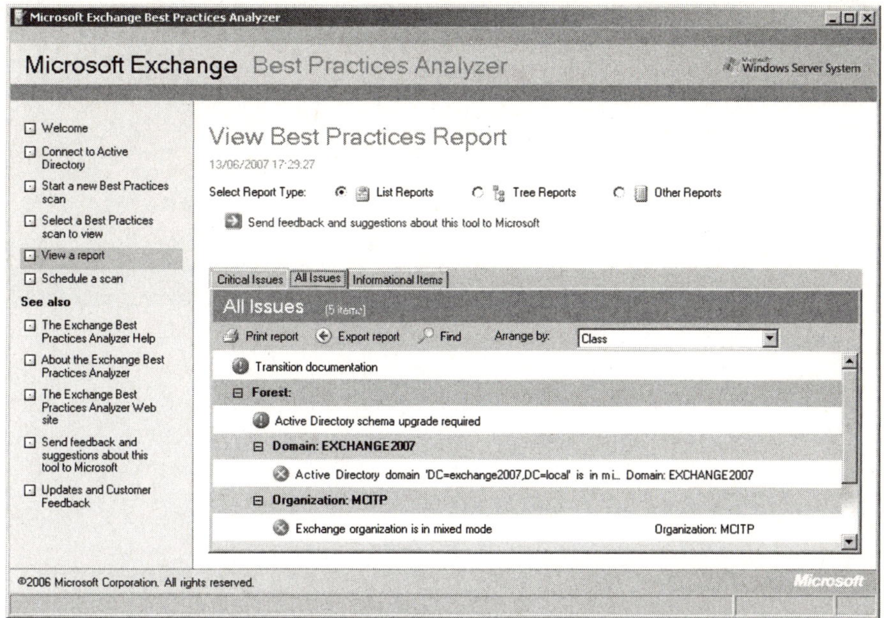

When you run the Exchange Readiness Check, you may come across either critical issues or warning issues. *Critical issues* are issues that you need to resolve before you can deploy your first Exchange Server 2007. *Warning issues* are just warnings and will not prevent you from deploying your first Exchange Server 2007, but they are issues that you should investigate since they can prevent users from having the best possible experience with the Exchange Server 2007 deployment. A typical example of a critical issue is that your Exchange Organization is running in Mixed Mode.

Installation of ExBPA

You do not need to install the ExBPA on an Exchange Server; it is even not recommended to do so. You can deploy and run the ExBPA on any computer that is a member of an Active Directory domain and meets the following requirements:

- Operating system: Windows 2000 Professional, Windows XP Professional, Windows Vista, Windows 2000 Server, or Windows 2003 Server
- Software requirements: .NET Framework 1.1, IIS common files, common HTTP features (if using Vista)

The Exchange Best Practices Analyzer can be run to analyze a mixed-mode or native-mode Exchange Server 2003, Exchange 2000 Server, and Exchange Server 5.5 system. Pure Exchange Server 5.5 topologies are not supported.

Running the Exchange 2007 Readiness Check

Exercise 6.1 outlines the steps to run the Exchange 2007 Readiness Check.

EXERCISE 6.1

Running the Exchange 2007 Readiness Check

To run the Readiness Check, follow these steps:

1. Click Start.
2. Click Programs.
3. Click Microsoft Exchange Best Practices Analyzer.
4. Click Go to Welcome Screen.
5. Connect to Active Directory.
6. Specify the scope for this scan, and select the type of scan to be performed: Exchange 2007 Readiness Check, as seen below.

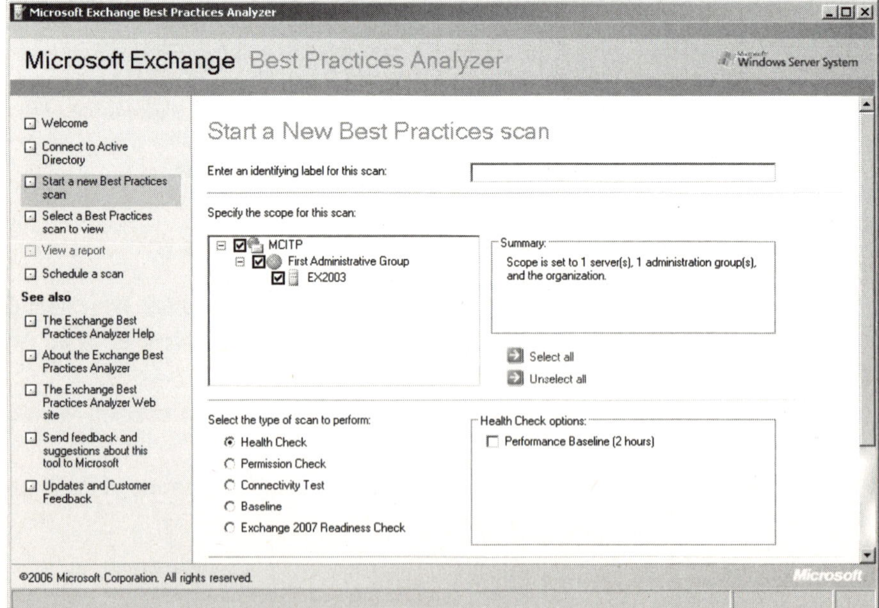

EXERCISE 6.1 *(continued)*

7. When the scanning is complete, you can select View a Report to get a report of the performed Best Practices scan.

The Best Practices Report will show all critical issues and warning issues, as seen below.

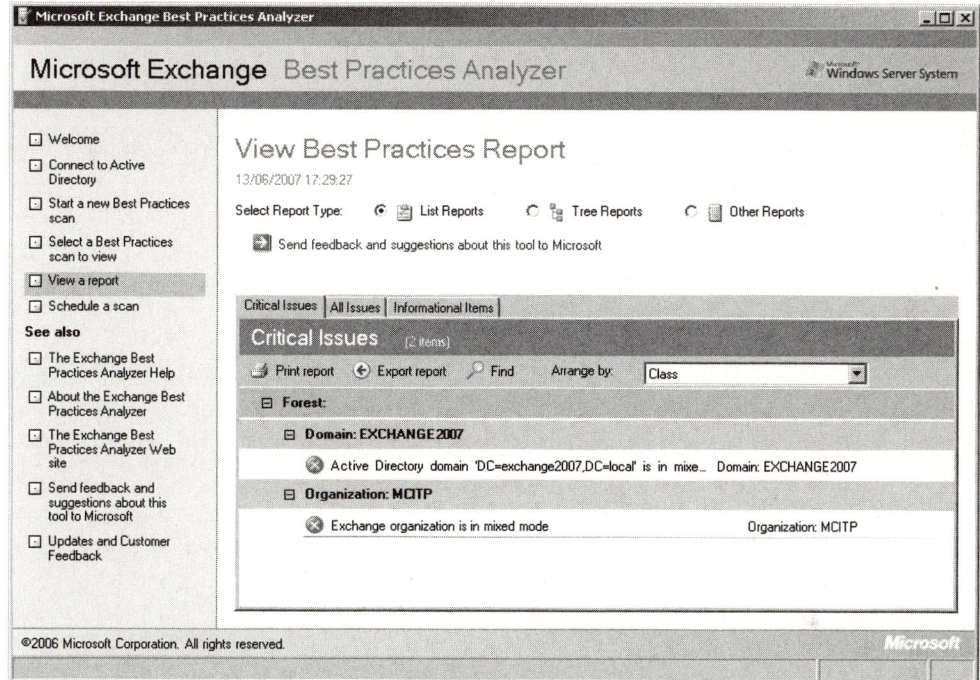

Preparing Active Directory for Exchange Server 2007

After you have confirmed that your infrastructure is ready for Exchange Server 2007, you can plan to prepare Active Directory for Exchange Server 2007. If you want to prepare Active Directory for Exchange Server 2007, you need to make sure of the following:

- You have the required permissions.
- You perform this procedure on a computer on which you have deployed .NET Framework 2.0 and Windows PowerShell.

You can prepare your Active Directory and your domains using the 32-bit version of Exchange Server 2007.

To prepare Active Directory and your domains, run the following:

1. `Setup /PrepareLegacyExchangePermissions`
2. `Setup /PrepareSchema`
3. `Setup /PrepareAD`
4. `Setup /PrepareDomain` or `Setup /PrepareAllDomains`

If you want to use command-line parameters to install or set up Exchange Server 2007, you will need to use `Setup.Com`. If you use `Setup.Exe` you will get the error message shown in Figure 6.10.

FIGURE 6.10 Setup.exe cannot accept command-line parameters

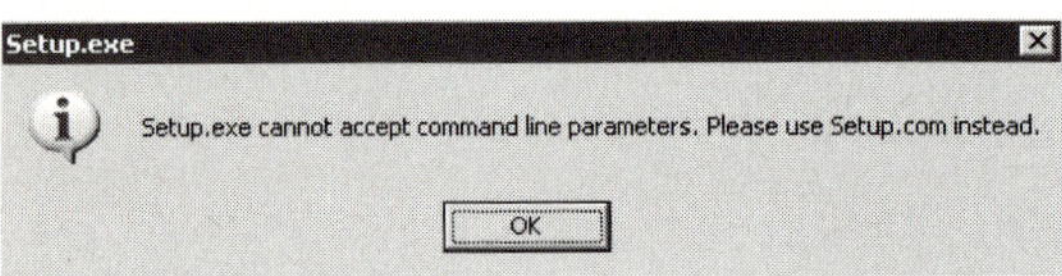

In this part of the chapter we will look at the reasons why you need to run those steps to prepare your Active Directory and your domains. We will also cover the permissions you require to successfully complete the steps, and we will investigate where you need to run the commands.

Setup /PrepareLegacyExchangePermissions

To run `Setup /PrepareLegacyExchangePermissions`, you need to be a member of the Enterprise Admins group. You need to run this command from a domain that is able to contact all other domains in the forest.

Here's what `Setup /PrepareLegacyExchangePermissions` does: In Exchange 2000 and Exchange 2003, the Recipient Update Service is responsible for updating several attributes once you choose to mail-enable a user or group. The Recipient Update Service is capable of doing this, since the Exchange Enterprise group was given the necessary permissions to modify the required property sets when the domain was prepped for Exchange. In Exchange 2007, the way permissions are set has been completely rewritten, as you have seen before in this chapter. To provide the ability of giving administrators just the permission to manage Exchange-related attributes, Exchange Server 2007 delegates to the Exchange Recipient Administrators the necessary permissions on a new property set called Exchange-Information. Running `Setup /PrepareLegacyExchangePermissions` will also give the legacy Recipient Update Service the necessary permissions to modify this new property set. Every domain that has been prepped for Exchange 2000 or Exchange 2003 has to be modified in this step.

If you add a new domain after deploying Exchange Server 2007, and you prep that domain for Exchange 2000 or Exchange 2003, make sure that you rerun `Setup /PrepareLegacyExchangePermissions`. If you don't, then the Exchange 2000 or Exchange 2003 Recipient Update Service will not be able to function correctly.

It's not mandatory to run `Setup /PrepareLegacyExchangePermissions`. If you choose not to run it, then it will be run automatically when running `Setup /PrepareSchema` or `Setup /PrepareAD`.

Exercise 6.2 outlines the steps to run `Setup /PrepareLegacyExchangePermissions`.

EXERCISE 6.2

Running Setup /PrepareLegacyExchangePermissions

Here's how to run `Setup /PrepareLegacyExchangePermissions`:

1. Click Start.
2. Open a command prompt.
3. Change the directory to your Exchange Server 2007 installation source and enter the command `Setup /PrepareLegacyExchangePermissions`.
4. When setup completes successfully, close the command prompt, as shown here.

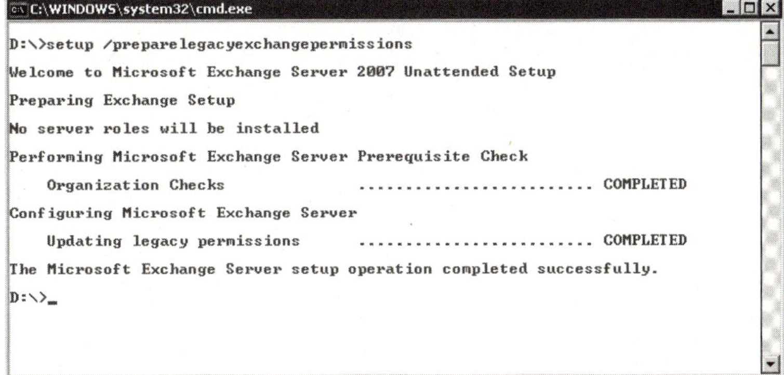

After running the `Setup /PrepareLegacyExchangePermissions` command, you need to wait for the changes to be replicated to all domain controllers in your Active Directory forest before you can continue with the next step.

Setup /PrepareSchema

To run `Setup /PrepareSchema`, you need to be a member of both the Enterprise Admins group and the Schema Admins group. You'll need to run this command on a computer that is in the same domain and the same Active Directory site as the Schema Master.

By running `Setup /PrepareSchema`, you will extend your Active Directory schema with Exchange 2007–specific attributes.

It is not supported and not possible to install an Exchange 2000 Server or Exchange Server 2003 server in an Active Directory forest that has been prepped for Exchange Server 2007 without an Exchange 2000 Server or Exchange Servers 2003 server available.

It's not mandatory to run `Setup /PrepareSchema`. If you choose not to run it, then it will be run automatically when running `Setup /PrepareAD`. If you did not run `Setup /PrepareLegacyExchangePermissions` before running `Setup /PrepareSchema`, setup will first run `Setup /PrepareLegacyExchangePermissions`, and then continue with `Setup /PrepareSchema`.

Exercise 6.3 outlines the steps to run `Setup /PrepareSchema`.

EXERCISE 6.3

Running Setup /PrepareSchema

There are four steps to run `Setup /PrepareSchema`.

1. Click Start.
2. Open a command prompt.
3. Change the directory to your Exchange Server 2007 installation source and enter the command `Setup /PrepareSchema`.
4. When setup completes successfully, close the command prompt, as seen here.

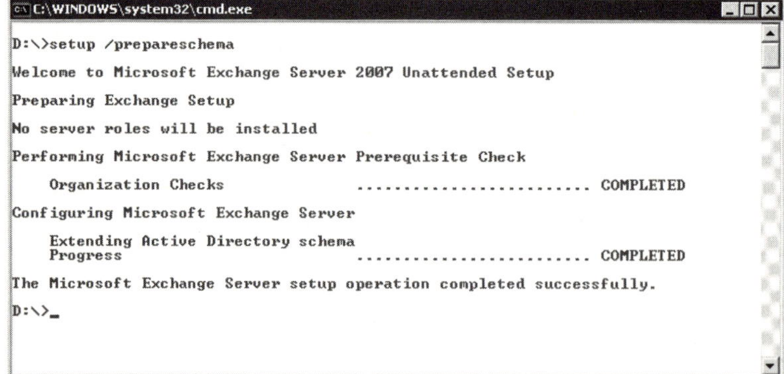

After running the Setup /PrepareSchema command, you need to wait for the changes to be replicated to all domain controllers in your Active Directory forest before you can continue with the next step.

Setup /PrepareAD

To run `Setup /PrepareAD`, you need to be a member of the Enterprise Admins group and you need to be delegated Exchange Full Administrator permission on the Exchange 2000 or Exchange 2003 organization. You need to run this command on a computer that is in the same domain and the same Active Directory site as the Schema Master.

Running `Setup /PrepareAD` will do the following:

- Configure global Exchange objects in Active Directory
- Create the universal security groups in the root domain, as seen in Figure 6.11.
- Prepare the domain it is run in.

Exercise 6.4 outlines the steps to run `Setup /PrepareAD`.

FIGURE 6.11 Universal security groups created after running `Setup /PrepareAD`

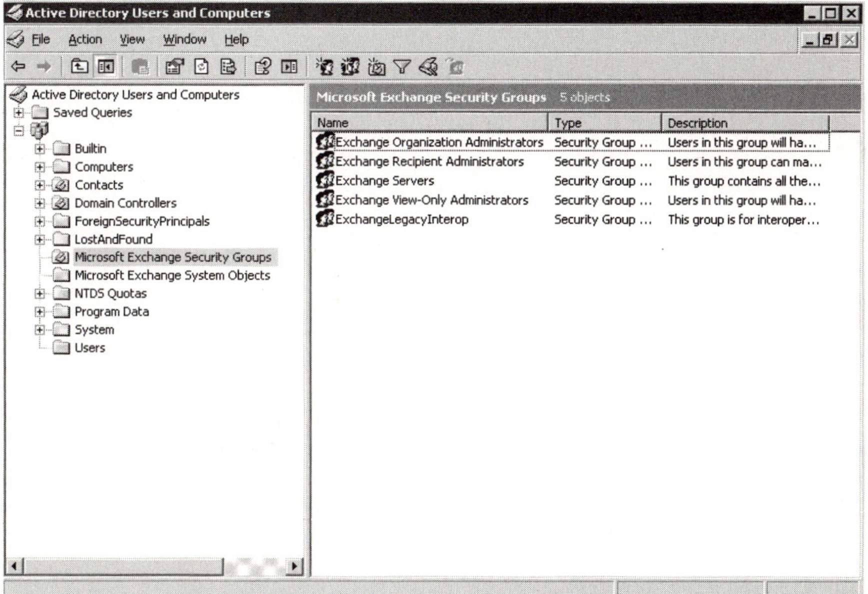

EXERCISE 6.4

Running Setup /PrepareAD

Again, there are just four steps to follow.

1. Click Start.
2. Open a command prompt.
3. Change the directory to your Exchange Server 2007 installation source and enter the command `Setup /PrepareAD`.
4. When setup completes, successfully close the command prompt.

After running the `Setup /PrepareAD` command, you need to wait for the changes to be replicated to all domain controllers in your Active Directory forest before you can continue with the next step.

Setup /PrepareDomain or Setup /PrepareAllDomains

To run `Setup /PrepareDomain` or `Setup /PrepareAllDomains` you need to be a member of the Enterprise Admins group or the Domain Admins group in the domains that you are prepping. You'll need to run this command on a computer that is in the domain you are prepping and that is able to contact all domains you are prepping.

Running `Setup /PrepareDomain` will prepare the domain it is run in. You can also run `Setup /PrepareDomain:<FQDN of domain>` if you want to prepare another domain than the one you're logged on to. It will do the following:

- Create a new global group in the Microsoft Exchange System Objects container in Active Directory Users and Computers, called Exchange Install Domain Servers, as shown in Figure 6.12
- Create a new domain local group called Exchange 12 Domain Servers and make it a member of the Exchange Servers universal security group in the root domain
- Grant the permission to manage auditing and security logs to the Exchange Server universal security group, as shown in Figure 6.13

`Setup /PrepareAllDomains` does exactly the same thing as `Setup /PrepareDomain`, but running `Setup /PrepareAllDomains` will prepare all domains in your Active Directory forest.

FIGURE 6.12 Exchange Install Domain Servers

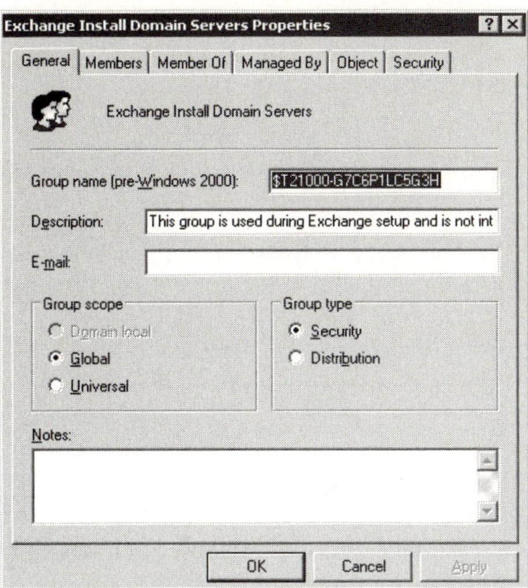

FIGURE 6.13 Choosing to manage auditing and security logs

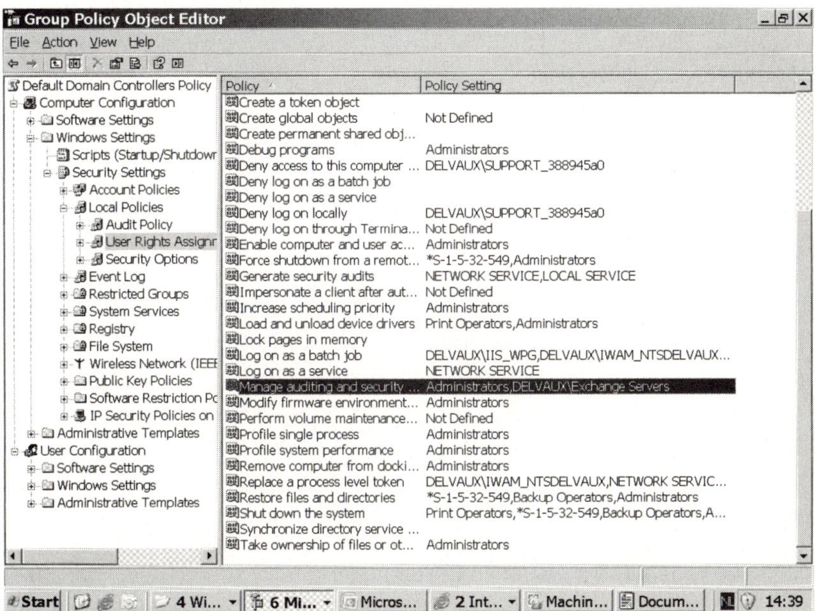

Exercise 6.5 outlines the steps to run `Setup /PrepareDomain` (the steps to prepare `Setup /PrepareAllDomains` are similar).

EXERCISE 6.5

Running Setup /PrepareDomain

Here are the steps for running `Setup /PrepareDomain`.

1. Click Start.
2. Open a command prompt.
3. Change the directory to your Exchange Server 2007 installation source and enter the command `Setup /PrepareAD`.
4. When setup completes successfully, close the command prompt.

After running the `Setup /PrepareDomain` command, you need to wait for the changes to be replicated to all domain controllers in your domain before you can start deploying Exchange Server 2007.

Deploying Exchange Server 2007

When you are ready to deploy Exchange Server 2007, it is recommended to deploy Exchange Server 2007 roles in a predefined order, as seen in Figure 6.14.

Deploying and Configuring Client Access Servers

You should introduce the Client Access server role as the first Exchange Server 2007 role in your Exchange organization. You will need to transition the functionality of your Exchange 2000 or Exchange 2003 front-end servers to the Exchange 2007 Client Access server role. This does not mean that you need to deploy a Client Access server in every site that will contain Exchange 2007 Mailbox servers before you can continue with the transitioning process. But it *does* mean that in every site where you plan to implement a Mailbox server role, you first need to deploy a Client Access server. Table 6.2 shows the interaction between Exchange 2007 and Exchange 2003.

TABLE 6.2 Exchange 2007 and Exchange 2003 Outlook Web Access

URL Entered	Connect To	Mailbox Housed On	Result
`http://ex2007/owa`	Ex2007 CAS	Exchange 2003 Back-End	Not Possible
`http://ex2007/exchange`	Ex2007 CAS	Exchange 2003 Back-End	Exchange 2003 OWA

TABLE 6.2 Exchange 2007 and Exchange 2003 Outlook Web Access *(continued)*

URL Entered	Connect To	Mailbox Housed On	Result
`http://ex2007/exchange`	Ex2007 CAS	Exchange 2007 Mailbox server	Exchange 2007 OWA
`http://ex2007/owa`	Ex2007 CAS	Exchange 2007 Mailbox server	Exchange 2007 OWA
`http://ex2003/exchange`	Ex2003 Front-End	Exchange 2007 Mailbox server	Not possible
`http://ex2003/exchange`	Ex2003 Back-End	Exchange 2007 Mailbox server	Exchange 2007 OWA

FIGURE 6.14 Exchange Server 2007 deployment process

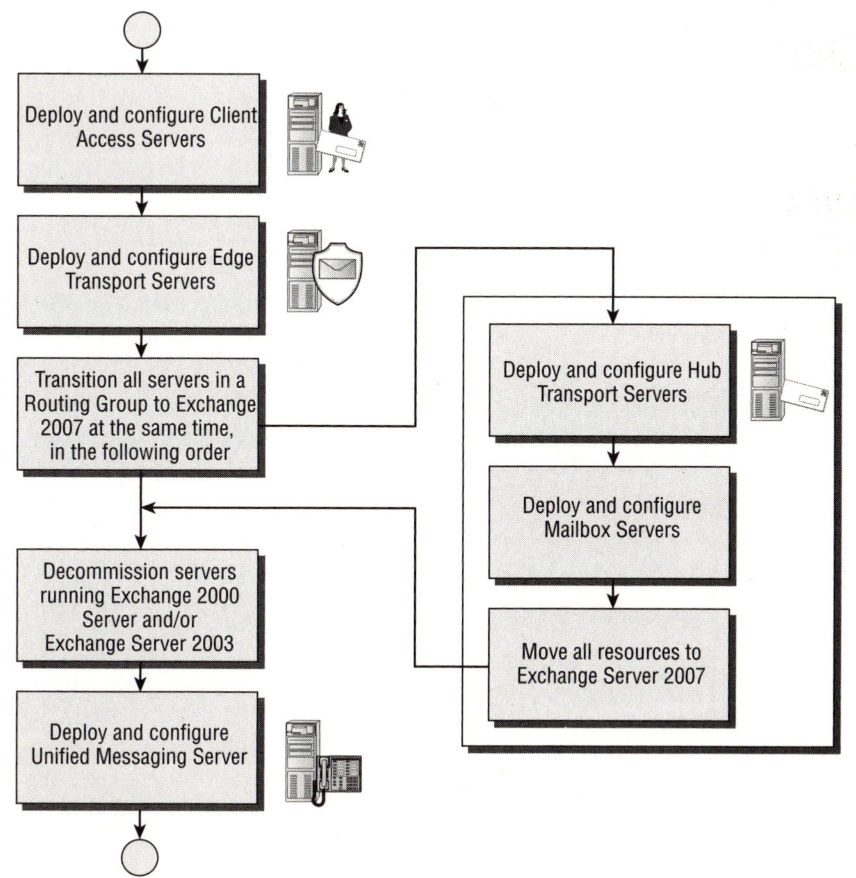

After deploying the first Exchange 2007 server role in your existing Exchange organization you might wonder how this will show up in your existing Exchange organization. When you look at the Exchange System Manager, you will see a new administrative group, as shown in Figure 6.15.

If you look at the Exchange Management Console, you will not see any Exchange Server 2003 or Exchange 2000 servers listed there. You can, however, see all the Exchange servers deployed in your Exchange organization by issuing the Exchange Management Shell cmdlet `Get-ExchangeServer`, as seen in Figure 6.16.

FIGURE 6.15 Exchange System Manager after deploying the first Exchange 2007 server role

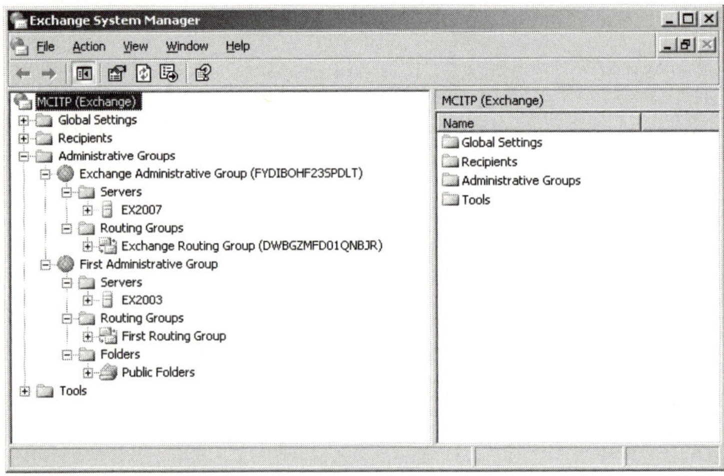

FIGURE 6.16 Deployed Exchange servers using the Exchange Management Shell cmdlet Get-ExchangeServer

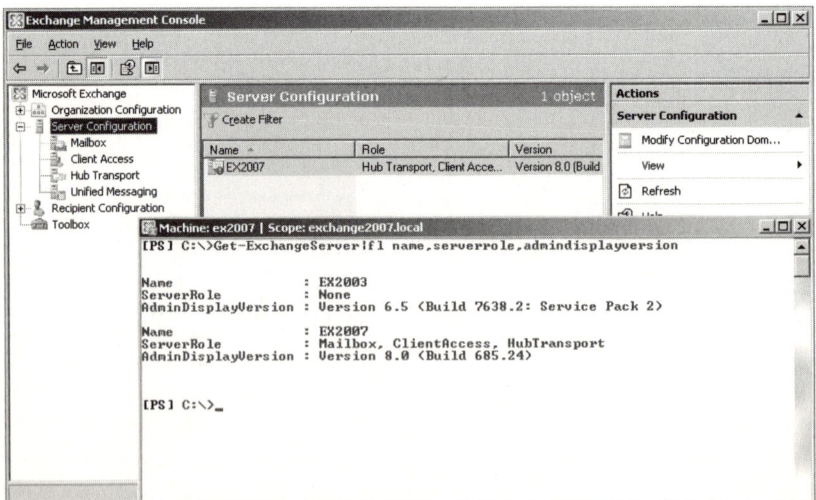

Deploying and Configuring Edge Transport Servers

Edge Transport servers are new to Exchange Server 2007, and they can be deployed in any phase of the transitioning process. You can even add an Edge Transport server to an Exchange 2000 or Exchange 2003 organization without transitioning the organization to Exchange 2007.

Deploying the Hub Transport Server and Mailbox Server Roles

Due to the changes in routing, Microsoft strongly recommends that you transition all Exchange servers in a routing group to Exchange 2007 at the same time.

First you will deploy the Hub Transport server, because an Exchange 2007 Mailbox server is unable to route messages inbound or outbound if no Hub Transport server can be found in the same site. When you install the first Exchange 2007 Hub Transport server in an existing Exchange 2000 or Exchange 2003 organization, you will be prompted to specify an existing Exchange server that will be used as a Bridgehead server for the routing-group connector that will be created between the Exchange 2007 routing group and the existing Exchange organization, as seen in Figure 6.17.

Changes to this routing-group connector can be made only using the Exchange Management Shell when the first Hub Transport server is deployed in the Exchange organization.

FIGURE 6.17 Exchange Server 2007 mail-flow setup

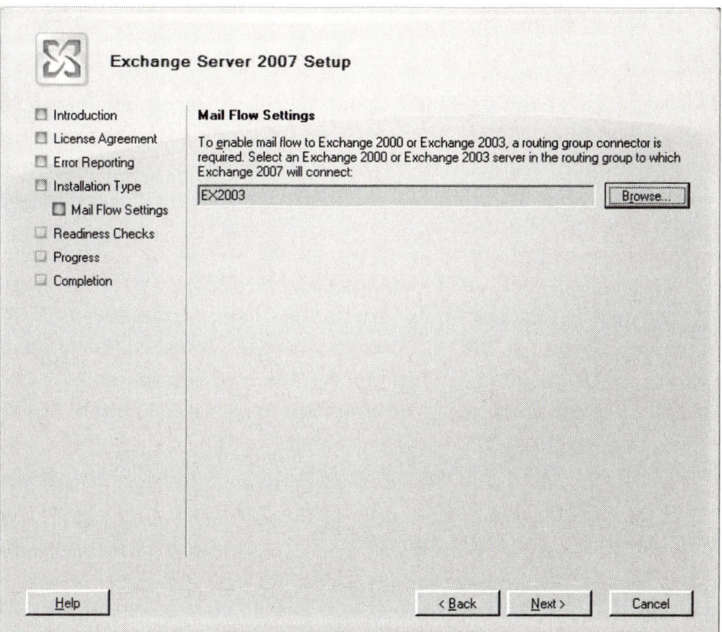

You can use the Exchange Management Shell to create additional routing-group connectors between the Exchange 2007 routing group and any routing group that contains Exchange 2000 or Exchange 2003 servers. Before you create additional routing-group connectors, you must remember to suppress minor link-state updates, which Exchange 2000 and Exchange 2003 use to be able to mark connectors as down. You need to suppress minor link-state updates to force Exchange 2000 and Exchange 2003 servers to always use the least-cost route to make sure that routing loops cannot occur.

Transitioning and Outlook Web Access

Imagine that you are an Exchange administrator and you are planning the transition process to Exchange 2007. Your current Exchange organization contains three Exchange 2003 back-end servers and one Exchange 2003 front-end server; all Exchange Server 2003 servers have been upgraded to Service Pack 2.

All your users are accustomed to gaining access to their mailboxes using Outlook Web Access, and some have the ability to use Outlook 2003 configured for RPC over HTTP access to their mailbox. When they connect to Exchange, they enter the URL `https://webmail.exchange2003.local/exchange`.

You are planning to introduce an Exchange 2007 Client Access server, an Exchange 2007 Hub Transport server, and an Exchange 2007 Mailbox server configured as cluster continuous replication (CCR) in the organization. You want to move the mailboxes of the IT department first so they can test the new Exchange Server functionalities prior to transitioning your entire Exchange organization.

Here's what to do: After installing the three Exchange servers, deploy a new certificate to the Client Access server and enable Outlook Anywhere on the Client Access server. Before you move mailboxes to the new Exchange 2007 CCR Mailbox server, you should change the DNS registration for `webmail.exchange2007.local` to point to the new Exchange 2007 Client Access server. Your users can continue using Outlook Web Access and Outlook Anywhere by entering `https://webmail.exchange2007.local/exchange`.

After deploying the Hub Transport server role, you can continue with the Mailbox server role deployment. Once the Mailbox server role is deployed, you can start moving mailboxes and public folders to Exchange Server 2007.

Moving All Resources to Exchange 2007

The next step will be to move all resources from Exchange 2000 and/or Exchange 2003 to Exchange 2007, including the following:

- Mailboxes (using the Exchange Management Console as seen in Figure 6.18 or Exchange Management Shell)

FIGURE 6.18 Moving mailboxes using the Exchange Management Console

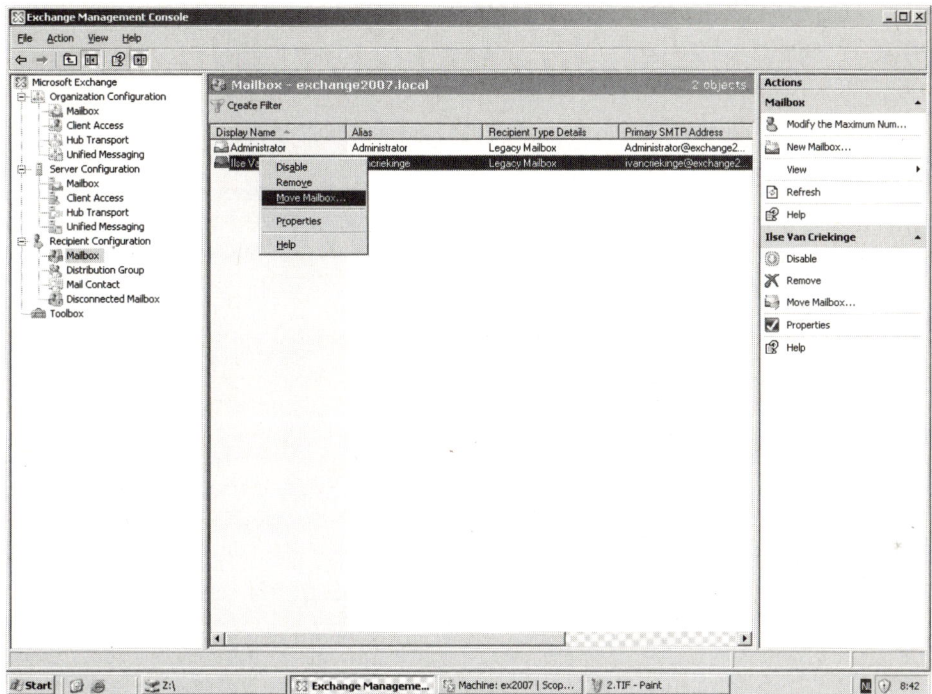

- Public folders (using the Exchange Management Shell or Exchange System Manager)
- Connectors (using the Exchange Management Console or Exchange Management Shell)
- System public folders (using the Exchange Management Shell or Exchange System Manager)

Table 6.3 lists the tools you can use to perform these tasks (ESM for Exchange System Manger, ADUC for Active Directory Users and Computers, EMC for Exchange Management Console, or EMS for Exchange Management Shell).

TABLE 6.3 Tools to Perform Exchange Tasks During Transitioning

Task	ESM	ADUC	EMC	EMS
Move mailboxes			x	x
Move public folders	x			x
Move connectors			x	x
Move system public folders	x			x

Do not forget to plan the phase of coexistence between Exchange 2000 Server, Exchange Server 2003, and Exchange Server 2007. Please refer to Chapter 4, "Designing and Planning Coexistence and Migrations," for more information about planning coexistence.

Decommissioning Exchange 2000 and Exchange Server 2003 servers

To decommission the Exchange 2000 and/or Exchange Server 2003 servers, you need to uninstall the servers so they will be removed from the Exchange organization. Before you remove the last Exchange 2000 or Exchange 2003 server from the Exchange 2007 organization, make sure that you check the following items:

- All mailboxes are moved to Exchange 2007 (use Exchange Management Shell or Exchange Management Console to check).
- All pubic folder replicas (including system public folders) are moved to Exchange 2007 (use Exchange Management Shell).
- The generating server for offline address books has changed to an Exchange Server 2007.
- Outbound and inbound mail flow has been verified.
- Inbound protocol services has been verified (OWA, Outlook Anywhere, etc.).

Once you have checked those points, you are ready to take following actions to decommission your last Exchange 2000 or Exchange Server 2003 server. Follow these steps:

1. Remove all public folders and mailbox databases from Exchange 2000/2003.
2. Delete any existing Mailbox manager policies.
3. Move the public-folder hierarchy from the Exchange 2000 or 2003 administrative group to the Exchange 2007 Administrative Group (use Exchange System Manager).
4. Delete the domain Recipient Update Services (use Exchange System Manager).
5. Delete the Enterprise Recipient Update Service (use ADSI Edit).

ADSI Edit is one of the support utilities included with the Windows Server Support Tools. ADSI Edit allows you to connect to your Active Directory partitions, using LDAP.

6. Uninstall Exchange 2000 or 2003 by using Add/Remove Programs.

Deploying and Configuring the Unified Messaging Server

The Unified Messaging server should be deployed as the last Exchange 2007 server role since it can work only against an Exchange 2007 Mailbox server and it needs an Exchange 2007 Client Access server and Exchange 2007 Hub Transport server for full functionality. For more information about Unified Messaging, please refer to Chapter 12, "Planning the Exchange Server 2007 Server Role Deployment."

Summary

In this chapter, we looked at how to plan an upgrade from Exchange 2000 Server or Exchange Server 2003 to Exchange Server 2007. We started with going through possible migration steps for legacy Exchange features. Then, we covered all features that were available in Exchange 2000 Server, but are no longer available in Exchange Server 2007, like instant messaging, and video conferencing. Then, we covered all features that were available in Exchange Server 2003 but are not present anymore in Exchange Server 2007, like the X.400 connector.

Next, we discussed some features that are de-emphasized but still present in Exchange Server 2007, like Public Folders, Store Events, and Streaming Backups.

In the second part of this chapter, we went through the steps of planning for a successful migration to Exchange Server 2007. We covered how you can check the readiness of your Exchange organization for Exchange Server 2007, followed by the steps to prepare your Active Directory environment. We finished the chapter by going over the installation sequence of the different Exchange 2007 Server roles, and the process for removing the last Exchange 2000 Server or Exchange Server 2003.

Exam Essentials

Plan the Exchange Server 2007 upgrade implementation. You need to know that you first need to prep your Active Directory for Exchange Server 2007, and that you need to install the different Exchange server roles in a specific order. First you will need to deploy a Client Access server, followed by an Edge Transport server (if required), and then a Hub Transport server and a Mailbox server in every site you want to transition to Exchange Server 2007. It is also important that you know what you should do to decommission your Exchange 2000 and

Exchange 2003 servers. You have to make sure that all resources are moved to Exchange Server 2007, including mailboxes, public folders, system public folders, and connectors.

Plan for migration of legacy Exchange features. It is important that you plan in advance what you are going to do with features that are either not supported or are de-emphasized in Exchange Server 2007. You have to know that you need to keep at least one Exchange 2000 Server or Exchange Server 2003 server if you want to continue using any of the features that are no longer supported in Exchange Server 2007. These features include the Lotus Notes connector, Novell GroupWise connector, X.400 connector, Exchange Key Management Server, Mobile Information Server, Exchange Instant Messaging, cc:Mail connector, MS Mail connector, Microsoft Exchange Chat Server, Exchange 2000 Conferencing Server, Outlook Mobile Access, NNTP, and Outlook Web Access to public folders.

Review Questions

1. You are an Exchange administrator and you are preparing your Active Directory forest for Exchange 2007. You currently have a single-domain environment, with two Exchange 2003 servers. One Exchange Server 2003 server is configured as a front-end server and the other is configured as a back-end server. You decide to log on to the Schema Master and to run `Setup /PrepareLegacyExchangePermissions`, but you receive an error that setup requires .NET Framework version 2.0. What should you do on the Schema Master before you can successfully run `Setup /PrepareLegacyExchangePermissions`? Select two options; each option is part of the solution.

   A. Install .NET Framework 2.0

   B. Install Internet Information Services

   C. Install Windows PowerShell

   D. Install Exchange management tools

2. You are an Exchange administrator and you are currently planning a transition from your Exchange 2000 organization to Exchange Server 2007. Your users require access to public folders using Outlook Web Access. Currently your organization uses public folders for sharing contacts and documents. What should you do to make sure users can gain access to public folders using Outlook Web Access?

   A. Move all public folders to a new Exchange 2007 Client Access server.

   B. Keep one Exchange 2000 back-end server in your organization to house public folders.

   C. Migrate public folders to Windows SharePoint Services v3.0 and publish WSS via Outlook Web Access.

   D. Move all public folders to a new Exchange 2007 Client Access server.

3. You are an Exchange administrator and you are responsible for an Exchange organization that contains four Exchange 2003 servers. Your company has recently merged with a company that uses Novell GroupWise. You are planning to migrate your Exchange mail environment to Exchange 2007; there are no immediate plans to migrate Novell GroupWise to another mail environment. Management has stated that mail flow, directory synchronization, and free/busy information from Novell GroupWise users should be available for your Exchange users. Which two actions should you include in your transition plan to Exchange 2007?

   A. Implement Novell GroupWise and Calendar connector on any of the existing Exchange 2003 servers.

   B. Plan to implement Novell GroupWise and Calendar connector on a new Exchange 2007 Mailbox server.

   C. Plan to keep at least one Exchange Server 2003 server in your Exchange organization to host the implemented Novell GroupWise and Calendar connectors.

   D. Migrate the Novell GroupWise environment to Exchange 2003.

4. You are an Exchange administrator and you have two Exchange 2003 servers deployed. One is configured as a front-end server, and the other one as a back-end server. Some users use Outlook Mobile Access to gain access to their mailboxes. You are planning to transition to Exchange 2007; what two options do you have to make sure your users won't loose functionality due to the transition?

   A. Keep an Exchange Server 2003 for your Outlook Mobile Access users.

   B. Educate your Outlook Mobile Access users to use ActiveSync, and transition to Exchange Server 2007.

   C. Implement Microsoft Mobile Information Server to provide Outlook Mobile Access for mailboxes on Exchange Server 2007.

   D. Configure Outlook Anywhere to provide Outlook Mobile Access to your users after moving them to Exchange 2007.

5. You are an Exchange administrator and your Exchange organization contains both Exchange 2007 and Exchange 2000 servers. You add a new child domain to your Active Directory forest, and you install a new Exchange 2000 server in that child domain to provide mail services to users in the child domain. When you create a new user in the child domain, you can give that user a mailbox on the new Exchange 2000 server, but the mailbox is never stamped with an email address. What should you do to make sure that the user gets an email address?

   A. Move the Exchange 2000 server to your root domain.

   B. Run `setup /domainprep` in the child domain.

   C. Run `setup /preparelegacyexchangepermissions` in the child domain.

   D. Create a new Recipient Update Service for the child domain.

6. You are an Exchange administrator and you are planning to transition your current Exchange organization from Exchange 2003 to Exchange 2007. Your Active Directory forest contains three domains, as can be seen here.

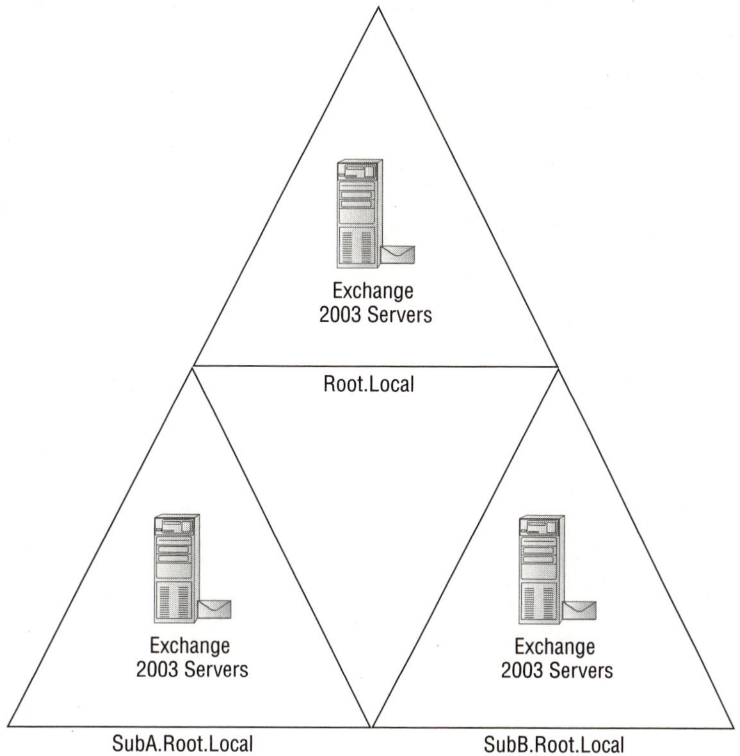

Every domain currently houses multiple Exchange 2003 servers. You want to prepare all your domains for Exchange Server 2007 by running `Setup /PrepareAllDomains`. You want to run this command logged onto the computer in the root domain with an account that has the necessary permissions. The account you log on with has to be a member of which groups? (Select two answers; each answer is a complete solution.)

A. Schema Admins

B. Enterprise Admins

C. Administrators group of all three domains

D. Exchange Domain Servers

7. You are an Exchange administrator and you are planning to transition your current Exchange organization from Exchange 2003 to Exchange 2007. You currently have two Exchange 2003 servers: one front-end server and one back-end server. Which Exchange 2007 server role should you deploy first?

   A. Client Access server role

   B. Mailbox server role

   C. Hub Transport server role

   D. Unified Messaging server role

8. You are an Exchange administrator and your IT manager has asked you to provide him with a report to verify if your Exchange 2003 organization is ready to be transitioned to Exchange 2007. What tool can you use to get the required report?

   A. Exchange Migration Wizard

   B. Exchange Best Practices Analyzer Tool v2.7 or later

   C. Exchange Management Pack for Microsoft Operations Manager 2005

   D. Log Parser

9. You are an Exchange administrator and your Exchange organization contains both Exchange 5.5 servers and Exchange 2003 servers. You are planning a transitioning to Exchange 2007. What three actions should you take before you can deploy your first Exchange Server 2007?

   A. Remove Active Directory connector(s)

   B. Decommission all Exchange 5.5 servers

   C. Turn your Exchange organization into Native Mode

   D. Deploy Exchange 2000 Server

10. You are an Exchange administrator and you are responsible for an Exchange 2003 organization. You are currently using a streaming Exchange-aware backup tool to back up all your Exchange servers. You are planning to deploy a new backup solution, and you want this backup solution to be ready for your planned Exchange 2007 transition later. What kind of backup solution for Exchange should you implement?

    A. File-level backup

    B. Open-file backup

    C. Streaming backup

    D. Volume Shadow Copy Service backup

11. You are an Exchange administrator and you are responsible for a native Exchange 2003 organization that contains one administrative group and five routing groups, one per region (as can be seen here). The routing groups (abbreviated RG) are connected by routing group connectors (abbreviated RGC), as can be seen here.

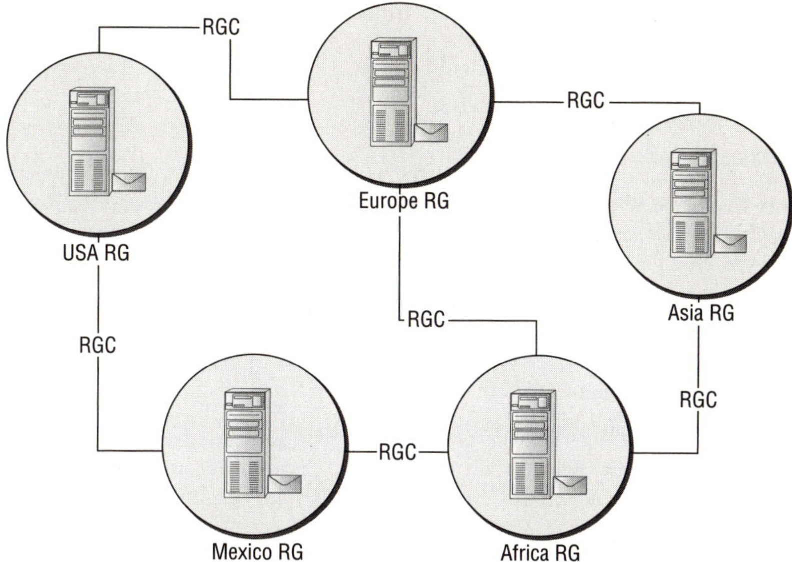

What should you do before you deploy your first Exchange 2007 Hub Transport server?

A. Disable major link-state updates

B. Disable minor link-state updates

C. Move all Exchange 2003 servers to one routing group

D. Remove all connectors between all routing groups

12. You are an Exchange administrator and you are currently in the process of transitioning your Exchange 2003 organization to Exchange 2007. You have just installed your first Exchange 2007 Mailbox server role, and you want to start moving all mailboxes. What tools can you use to move mailboxes from Exchange 2003 to Exchange 2007? (Select two; each option is a complete solution.)

A. Active Directory Users and Computers

B. Exchange System Manager

C. Exchange Management Console

D. Exchange Management Shell

13. You are an Exchange administrator and you are currently in the process of transitioning your Exchange 2003 organization to Exchange 2007. You have just installed your first Exchange 2007 Mailbox server role, and you want to start replicating all public folders. What tools can you use to replicate public folders from Exchange 2003 to Exchange 2007? (Select two; each option is a complete solution.)

    A. Active Directory Users and Computers

    B. Exchange System Manager

    C. Exchange Management Console

    D. Exchange Management Shell

14. You are an Exchange administrator and you are currently in the process of transitioning your Exchange 2003 organization to Exchange 2007. When you deployed your first Hub Transport server you specified Exchange Server 2003 MAILS01 as the Bridgehead server for the routing-group connector between the Exchange 2003 routing group and the Exchange 2007 routing group. Now you want to change the Exchange 2003 Bridgehead server to MAILS02. How can you change the Bridgehead server?

    A. Via Exchange Management Shell

    B. Via Exchange Management Console

    C. Via Exchange System Manager

    D. Via Registry

15. You are an Exchange administrator and you are in the process of transitioning your Exchange 2003 organization to Exchange 2007. You have mailboxes both on Exchange 2003 and on Exchange 2007. Your users use Outlook 2003 or Outlook 2007 to open their mailboxes. Your users complain that they don't see free/busy information for all users. It seems that free/busy information is available only for users housed on the same server. You need to make sure that everybody has access to free/busy information of everybody in the Exchange organization. What should you do? (Select two; each option is part of the solution.)

    A. Replicate the free/busy system public folder from Exchange 2003 to Exchange 2007.

    B. Replicate the free/busy system public folder from Exchange 2007 to Exchange 2003.

    C. Instruct all your users to use Outlook 2007.

    D. Instruct all your users to use Outlook 2003.

16. You are an Exchange administrator and you are in the process of transitioning your Exchange 2000 organization to Exchange 2007. You still have one cc:Mail post office that you need to keep for some legacy applications. What should you do to maintain this cc:Mail post office when designing your new Exchange 2007 organization?

    A. Install the cc:Mail connector on the Exchange 2007 Mailbox server.

    B. Install the cc:Mail connector on the Exchange 2007 Hub Transport server.

    C. Install the cc:Mail connector on the Exchange 2007 Client Access server.

    D. Keep one Exchange 2000 back-end server to house the cc:Mail connector.

17. You are an Exchange administrator and you are in the process of transitioning your Exchange 2003 organization to Exchange 2007. Some users use an NNTP client to gain access to public folders. What should you include in your design to provide the same service to your clients after completing the transition to Exchange 2007?

    A. Keep an Exchange 2003 back-end server to provide NNTP services to public folders.

    B. Enable NNTP on the Exchange 2007 Client Access server.

    C. Enable NNTP on the Exchange 2007 Mailbox server.

    D. Enable NNTP on the Exchange 2007 Hub Transport server.

18. You are an Exchange administrator and you recently migrated from a Lotus Notes environment to a new Exchange 2007 organization. Your manager would like to use Outlook Mobile Access, and wants you to investigate what you should do to implement Outlook Mobile Access. What should you do?

    A. Install Exchange Server 2003 and configure Outlook Mobile Access.

    B. Enable Outlook Mobile Access on the Exchange 2007 Client Access server.

    C. Enable Outlook Mobile Access on the Exchange 2007 Mailbox server.

    D. It is not possible to enable Outlook Mobile Access in the current Exchange 2007 environment.

19. You are an Exchange administrator and you are in the process of transitioning your existing Exchange 2000 organization to Exchange 2007. You would like to rename the Exchange Administrative Group (FYDIBOHF23SPDLT) to Exchange Administrative Group (Vips). How should do this?

    A. Using the Exchange Management Console.

    B. Using the Exchange Management Shell.

    C. Using the Exchange System Manager.

    D. Using ADSI Edit.

    E. Renaming this administrative group is not supported.

20. You are an Exchange administrator and you are in the process of transitioning your existing Exchange 2000 organization to Exchange 2007. You would like to keep just one routing group that you had before you deployed your first Exchange 2007 Hub Transport server. What options do you have?

    A. Move all Exchange servers to the new Exchange 2007 routing group, Exchange Routing Group (DWBGZMFD01QNBJR).

    B. Move all Exchange servers to your existing Exchange 2003 routing group.

    C. You cannot move all Exchange servers in the same routing group; Exchange Server 2007 Hub Transport servers have to remain in their own special routing group.

    D. Create a new routing group in Exchange 2007 and move all Exchange servers in that new routing group.

Answers to Review Questions

1. A, C. You can only prep Active Directory for Exchange Server 2007 on a computer if you have the required permissions and if you have deployed .NET Framework 2.0 and Windows PowerShell. You can install Windows PowerShell only once you have deployed .NET Framework. Since you get an error stating that .NET Framework isn't yet installed, you will also need to deploy Windows PowerShell before you can successfully complete `setup /preparelegacyexchangepermissions`. Exchange management tools and Internet Information Server are not required.

2. B. Public folders are not accessible using Outlook Web Access in Exchange Server 2007 RTM; you will have to keep one Exchange 2000 server in the organization to be able to gain access to public folders using Outlook Web Access. Microsoft recommends migrating public folders to SharePoint, but in Exchange Server 2007 RTM it is not possible to publish Windows SharePoint Services contact lists via Outlook Web Access (publishing document libraries is possible, however).

3. A, C. To provide mail connectivity, directory synchronization, and free/busy data synchronization you will have to implement the Novell GroupWise connector in addition to the Calendar connector. Since this connector is cut from Exchange 2007, you will need to keep at least one Exchange 2003 server in your mail environment. It is not possible to implement the Novell GroupWise and Calendar connector on Exchange 2007. Since there are no immediate plans to migrate from Novell to Exchange, you can not include this migration in your transition plan to Exchange 2007.

4. A, B. You have only two options: keep one Exchange 2003 server or educate your users to use ActiveSync. Outlook Mobile Access is not available in Exchange 2007, and Microsoft Mobile Information Server does not function against an Exchange 2007 server.

5. C. If you add a new domain after deploying Exchange Server 2007 and you prep that domain for Exchange 2000 or Exchange 2003, make sure that you rerun `setup /PrepareLegacyExchangePermissions`. If you don't, the Exchange 2000 or Exchange 2003 Recipient Update Service will not be able to function correctly. Moving Exchange servers between domains is not supported. You do not need to prep the domain, since it is already prepped, and you do not need to create a new Recipient Update Service for the child domain, since it already exists.

6. B, C. To run `Setup /PrepareDomain` or `Setup /PrepareAllDomains` you need to be a member of the Enterprise Admins group or the Domain Admins group in the domains that you are prepping.

7. A. You should introduce the Client Access server role as the first Exchange Server 2007 role in your Exchange organization. You will need to transition the functionality of your Exchange 2000 or Exchange 2003 front-end servers to the Exchange 2007 Client Access server role.

8. B. Starting with version 2.7, the ExBPA contains the Exchange 2007 Readiness Check. When you run the Readiness Check, the tool will perform checks to validate if your overall topology is ready for Exchange Server 2007, and it will also check in more depth if all your deployed Exchange 2000 servers and Exchange Server 2003 servers have received the necessary updates and configuration settings to be able to coexist with Exchange Server 2007. All information will be stored in the transition documentation. Exchange Migration Wizard does not exist in Exchange 2007. Log Parser allows you to read message tracking log files and other log files, but it does not provide you with the required information, and neither does the Exchange Management Pack for Microsoft Operations Manager 2005.

9. A, B, C. It is not supported, nor is it possible to transition an Exchange 5.5/2003 organization to Exchange 2007. You first need to remove any Active Directory connectors, decommission any Exchange 5.5 servers, and turn your exchange organization into native mode. There is no need to deploy Exchange 2000 Server to be ready to deploy Exchange 2007.

10. D. You always need to take a backup of Exchange with an Exchange-aware backup solution, so you cannot use A or B! Microsoft recommends that you implement the Volume Shadow Copy Service backup since it is faster and more reliable than streaming backup.

11. B. Minor link-state updates must be suppressed to prevent message looping when a route is recalculated. Minor link-state updates are the updates to mark a link as up or down. Major link-state updates concern the configuration of Exchange.

    You cannot move all servers to the same routing group since it is impossible to move a server that is designated as a bridgehead server for a connector, like the routing group connector. By removing all connectors between all routing groups, you would disable all mail flow between those routing groups, which is not desired, and not needed.

12. C, D. You can move mailboxes from Exchange 2003 to Exchange 2007 using only the Exchange Management Shell or the Exchange Management Console.

13. B, D. You can replicate public folders from Exchange 2003 to Exchange 2007 only using the Exchange Management Shell or the Exchange System Manager. You cannot initiate replication of public folders using Active Directory Users and Computers. Public Folders cannot be managed using the Exchange Management Console up until Exchange 2007 Sp1.

14. A. You can change the destination Bridgehead server on the routing group connector for Exchange 2007 only using the Management Shell. Additionally, you can change the local Bridgehead server on Exchange 2003 only using the Shell.

15. A, B. Exchange 2003 uses the system free/busy public folder to provide free/busy information to all users. Exchange 2007 provides free/busy information via Exchange Web Services for Outlook Web Access users, and for Outlook 2007 or later users. For earlier clients, Exchange 2007 still uses the system free/busy public folder. Since you have users that use Outlook 2003 and Outlook 2007, and you have mailboxes housed on Exchange 2003 and Exchange 2007, you need to replicate the content both from Exchange 2003 to Exchange 2007 and the other way around, from Exchange 2007 to Exchange 2003. Upgrading all your users to Outlook 2007 would not resolve the problem, since Outlook 2007 still requires access to the system public folder for users located on Exchange 2003. Upgrading all your users to Outlook 2003 would not resolve the problem, since Outlook 2003 requires access to the system public folder for users located on Exchange 2007 and Exchange 2003.

16. D. Exchange 2007 does not support the cc:Mail connector provided with Exchange 2000 Server. If you want to continue using a cc:Mail connector you have to keep at least one Exchange 2000 server in your organization.

17. A. Exchange 2007 does not support NNTP anymore. If your exchange organization needs to be able to provide NNTP services, you have to plan to keep at least one Exchange Server 2003 server in your organization.

18. D. Outlook Mobile Access is not supported in Exchange Server 2007. You need an Exchange Server 2003 server to provide Outlook Mobile Access, but it is not possible to install an Exchange Server 2003 in a new Exchange 2007 organization.

19. E. It is not supported to rename the default Exchange Administrative Group (FYDIBOHF23SPDLT).

20. C. It is not allowed to move Exchange 2003 servers in the default Exchange 2007 routing group. Additionally, it is not allowed to move Exchange 2007 servers to any other routing group. It is not possible to create a new routing group in Exchange 2007.

Planning a Migration to Exchange Server 2007

MICROSOFT EXAM OBJECTIVES COVERED IN THIS CHAPTER:

- ✓ **Plan the Exchange Server 2007 migration implementation.**
- ✓ **Plan interoperability with third-party messaging systems.**

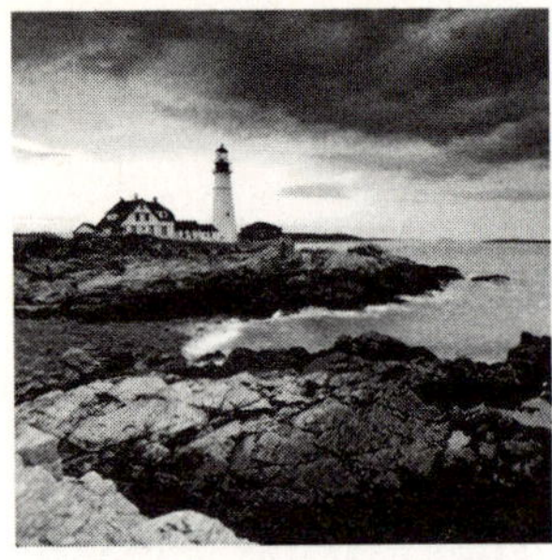

Over the last few years, messaging systems have evolved into an important aspect of our lives. Businesses depend on messaging systems, and your users probably rely on messaging systems for all of their contacts, communications, appointments, addresses, meeting schedules, notes, and many other reasons. In most business environments, messaging systems have a high availability requirement because business revenue is seriously affected if the messaging system is down. Therefore, the upgrade process should be taken seriously. As an architect, consultant, system engineer, or system administrator, you must understand the ins and outs of the migration, transition, and upgrade before you start upgrading the messaging environment.

Whether you have a single Exchange server in your organization or thousands of servers across different geographical locations, the first step before you upgrade or migrate to Exchange 2007 is to perform an organization-wide assessment. In my own experience, for a medium to large organization, this assessment process usually takes anywhere from two to six weeks as you gather and analyze the information about your current network, Active Directory sites, Active Directory topology, user data, mailbox restrictions, mailbox policies, routing groups, administrative groups, SMTP connectors, foreign connectors, backup strategy, security information, Outlook Web Access, and more. All planning steps should be taken carefully before migrating from a legacy Exchange environment to Exchange 2007. Business author Brian Tracy estimates that one minute on planning and organizing your deployment will save you five minutes during execution and implementation, which means you get a full 500 percent return on your planning during the implementation phase.

Like Exchange 2000 and Exchange Server 2003, Exchange Server 2007 also depends on Active Directory to store configuration information, recipient information, distribution lists, custom recipients, Exchange organization data, and information about other resources. You must communicate with the Active Directory team to not only gather information, but also to ensure that your Active Directory is healthy and there are no replication or authentication issues.

This chapter is about planning, but it also offers step-by-step exercises to migrate, upgrade, and implement Exchange 2007 in coexistence mode. This chapter covers most of the aspects of migration.

The main subjects of this chapter are as follows:

- Migrating from Exchange 5.5 servers
- Migrating from Exchange 2000 and 2003 servers
- Migrating from third-party messaging systems
- Decommissioning the old infrastructure

Key Vocabulary for This Chapter

Before we delve into the main topics covered in this chapter, you should be familiar with the following terminology:

Legacy Exchange server. I'll use this phrase to refer to Exchange 5.5 servers.

Legacy Exchange environment. I'll use this phrase to refer to the Exchange 5.5 environment.

Previous version of Exchange. I'll use this phrase to refer to Exchange 2000 and Exchange 2003 servers. For any specific Exchange product, I'll use the specific name of the individual product (for example, Exchange Server 2003 Standard Edition or Exchange Server 2003 Enterprise Edition).

Exchange system or **messaging system.** When I use either of these phrases, I'll be referring to the whole Exchange world, including Exchange 5.5, Exchange 2000 Server, Exchange Server 2003, and Exchange Server 2007.

Messaging infrastructure. I'll use this phrase to refer to all the components in your messaging environment, including Bridgehead servers, Mailbox servers, Client Access servers, Unified Messaging servers, Hub Transport server, Edge Transport servers, Outlook Web Access, and more.

Third-party messaging system. I'll use this phrase to refer to Lotus Notes (or "Notes") and Novell GroupWise messaging environments. For any specific third-party messaging product, I'll use the specific name along with the version information (for example, Lotus Notes 6.0). From time to time, I'll also use "non-Exchange messaging" products to refer to third-party messaging systems.

Windows Server 2003 or **Windows 2003.** I'll use Windows Server 2003 or Windows 2003 to refer to the entire line of Windows Server 2003 products. For any specific Windows 2003 product, I'll use the specific name of the individual product (for example, Windows Server 2003 Standard Edition).

But wait; there's more: Before getting into technical details, tools, processes, steps, strategies, and other aspects of migration, it is also important to clarify the terms *migration, transition,* and *coexistence.*

Migration. The term *migration* is often used to refer to the migration process and methodologies to migrate from one messaging system to another messaging environment without retaining configuration data of the old messaging system. Here's an example: Suppose you are running Exchange in your organization and there is a company acquisition and merger. As a result, you are now merging two Exchange organizations into one organization, and you migrate user data from one Exchange organization to another *without retaining configuration data from the old organization.* (When I use the term *configuration data*, I mean for policies, mailbox restrictions, organization names, filter rules, connector information, routing rules, etc.) Another example would be migrating mailboxes and data from a Lotus Notes or GroupWise system to Exchange 2007 without retaining their configuration information.

Transition. The term *transition* is another term that refers to moving data from legacy Exchange systems to Exchange 2007 and then decommissioning the old Exchange systems. A good example of this approach would be introducing Exchange 2007 into an existing Exchange 2000 or Exchange 2003 organization and then moving mailboxes, data, and public-folder information from a previous version of Exchange to Exchange 2007. Generally, the transition process is not a single-step process, and it is not going to happen over a weekend. In my own experience, these migrations and transitions require a phased approach lasting weeks or months, during which the source messaging systems and the target Exchange 2007 messaging system will coexist. In fact, transition happens in several phases. During each phase, we introduce only one component of Exchange 2007 into our environment and then move certain features and services from the legacy Exchange system to the new Exchange Server 2007 server.

Coexistence. During the migrating and transition from old Exchange environment to Exchange 2007, the Exchange organization will have *coexistence* of multiple versions of Exchange. The coexistence mode refers to a mixed environment of Exchange 2000 or Exchange 2003 with Exchange 2007. The coexistence mode is designed to have messaging stability throughout the transition process without affecting your business, users, and organization.

Migrating from Exchange Server 5.5

Exchange 2007 is a radically different animal from Exchange 5.5. Exchange 5.5 was a self-contained messaging system and had its own configuration partition and directory services to hold recipient information. Exchange 2000 and later versions (including Exchange 2003 and Exchange 2007) depend on Active Directory to store recipient information, configuration information, distribution lists, mailboxes, mailbox policies, connector information, custom recipients, and other messaging organization–related information. Every article or book that deals with migrating and upgrading Exchange 5.5 organizations to Exchange 2007 will confirm that Exchange 2007 does not support an upgrade of Microsoft Exchange Server 5.5 to Exchange Server 2007. You have to go through a *transit* migration, which means that you have to upgrade Exchange 5.5 to an Exchange 2000 or 2003 server before moving to Exchange Server 2007. Why? Because, your Exchange organization must be running in the native mode before you start introducing and implementing Exchange Server 2007. To perform this kind of upgrade, you must perform a transition upgrade, which means that you have to spread the migration process into two different phases:

Phase 1. Migrate your Exchange 5.5 organization to an Exchange 2000 or Exchange 2003 organization

Phase 2. After migrating from the Exchange Server 5.5 to an Exchange 2000 or 2003 server, you can then upgrade the Exchange 2000/2003 organization to an Exchange 2007 organization.

Figure 7.1 gives you a basic overview of an Exchange 5.5 upgrade process.

FIGURE 7.1 Transition path to upgrade from Exchange 5.5

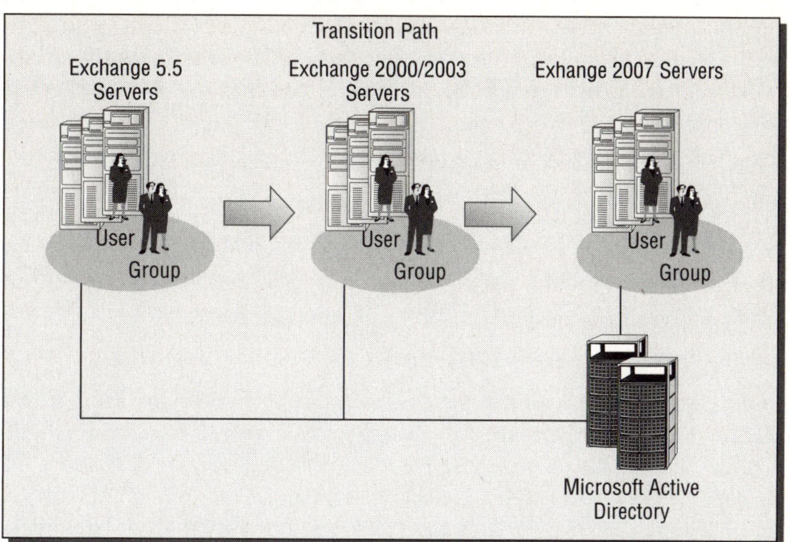

This route may seem long; however, it is supported by Microsoft and ensures a stable, secure, and manageable email platform. There are many vendors out there who have developed tools and utilities to migrate from Exchange 5.5 to Exchange Server 2007 without any transit migration. One of them is Quest, which enables organizations to directly migrate from Exchange 5.5 to Exchange Server 2007 with true coexistence without any transit migration. Do your homework before you begin migrating from Exchange 5.5 to Exchange 2007.

Migrating from Exchange 2000 Server or Exchange Server 2003

In this chapter, my examples will focus on performing a migration from Exchange Server 2003. However, there is no procedural difference between installing Exchange Server 2007 in an Exchange 2000 or Exchange 2003 organization. The steps, methodologies, concepts, and procedures mentioned here for Exchange Server 2003 are also applicable for Exchange 2000 Server.

There are different scenarios of migration and transition; however, it is impossible to cover all the scenarios in one chapter. Some scenarios are simpler than others because they involve only moving data from legacy systems to the Exchange environment without doing any restructuring of Exchange organization and merging with another Exchange organization. Businesses are frequently subjected to forces of mergers, acquisitions, de-mergers, restructuring, reorganizing, hiring, and firing. If your organization is seeking to consolidate its messaging operation to meet demands for messaging and collaboration services, you may have to do some restructuring. As part of these ongoing changes, you may restructure your Exchange organization to not only reduce the total cost of ownership, but also because the old messaging infrastructure does not meet current business and technical needs.

If you are lucky enough to have a working Exchange 2003 environment with no restructuring, then the migration process might be relatively simple for you. In a nutshell, the process involves the following:

1. Replace Exchange 2003 front-end servers with Client Access servers.
2. Replace Bridgehead servers with the Hub Transport servers.
3. Install new Exchange 2007 Mailbox servers into an existing Exchange 2003 organization, and then move mailboxes from Exchange 2003 to the Exchange Server 2007 server.
4. Move public folders from Exchange 2003 to Exchange 2007.
5. Decommission Exchange Server 2003 servers.

Seems simple, right? Yes, it is simple because it does not involve any kind of restructuring and consolidation. However, there are still complexities involved because Exchange 2007 is an x64-bit product and works only on x64-bit hardware and operating systems. The process also involves several preparation steps, including assessing your Active Directory, updating Active Directory schema, raising the domain and forest functional level, backing up the old Exchange Server 2003 servers, and migrating and decommissioning foreign connectors.

Because you cannot perform an in-place upgrade, you must install the new Exchange Server 2007 in your existing Exchange 2003 organization and then move mailboxes and public folders to the Exchange Server 2007 server.

On the other hand, if your organization has undergone mergers, de-mergers, or acquisitions since the installation of Exchange 2003, or if you are one of those unlucky people who inherited an Exchange environment that does not have the proper architecture for your current needs, then you have to go through the process of restructuring your environment. Restructuring may occur during any part of migration. Depending on your business and technical requirements, you may choose to restructure Exchange before introducing Exchange 2007 in your environment, or you can restructure after Exchange 2007 has been put in place.

Many organizations are consolidating several back-end Exchange Server 2003 servers to fewer Exchange 2007 Mailbox servers (or just a single one) because Exchange 2007 supports more-powerful hardware and software. The consolidation process is not simple. It involves intensive testing in a lab and making sure that users don't experience a decline in performance. Restructuring an Exchange organization also is complicated because it involves consolidation; however, it is out of the scope of the exam and therefore not covered in this book.

Exchange Server 2007 and Windows Server Operating Systems: Upgrading to x64-bit

The major change to Exchange 2007 is that it now runs only on an x64-bit platform. Exchange 2007 is solely a 64-bit application, and it is designed for 64-bit Windows and 64-bit technologies to provide server scalability and management.

Compared to Exchange 2003, Exchange Server 2007 can support a large pool of memory. Because earlier versions of Exchange were designed to run on 32-bit platforms, they were limited to using only 4 GB of memory. Now, with x64-bit hardware, 64-bit Windows, and its support for 8 TB of RAM memory, an Exchange Server 2007 can support up to 32 GB of RAM without any problem. Thus, Exchange 2007 easily supports databases that are hundreds of gigabytes in size.

Because Exchange 2007 is available only in an x64-bit version for production, it is not possible to do an in-place upgrade because previous versions of Exchange exist only in an x32-bit version. (There is a 32-bit version of Exchange 2007 that is available for testing and evaluation purposes only; it cannot be used in a production environment.)

Exchange 2007 is designed and tested for x64-bit hardware and operating systems; therefore, it requires an x64-bit version of Windows Server 2003. When it comes to operating system and hardware bus speed, the servers you have been using for Exchange 2003 (and previous versions) probably will not be suitable for Exchange 2007. Because most organizations are still using 32-bit server hardware, the migration path from Exchange 2000 or 2003 to Exchange 2007 typically requires an upgrade of hardware and operating system.

Exchange 2007 can be installed on a server running either Windows Server 2003 R2 or Windows Server 2003 SP1 or higher.

Choosing between Exchange 2007 Standard Edition and Enterprise Edition

Before installing Exchange 2007, you have to decide which version of Exchange 2007 is suitable for your organization. Exchange 2007 Standard Edition has been designed to meet the messaging requirements of small to medium organizations. (Standard Edition is a good candidate for all Exchange 2007 roles in which a server with a limited database storage capacity is sufficient. Edge Transport, Hub Transport server, and Client Access server are good examples.) Exchange 2007 Enterprise Edition is designed to meet the messaging requirements of a large corporate environment in which the server requires more messaging databases and clustering for high availability and redundancy.

Table 7.1 describes the differences between the Standard and Enterprise editions, including which features they support.

TABLE 7.1 Differences Between Standard and Enterprise Editions

Feature	Standard Edition	Enterprise Edition
Storage groups	5 storage groups	50 storage groups
Database support	5 databases	50 databases

TABLE 7.1 Differences Between Standard and Enterprise Editions *(continued)*

Feature	Standard Edition	Enterprise Edition
Database storage limits	16 TB	16 TB
Single-copy cluster	Not supported	Supported
Local continuous replication	Supported	Supported
Cluster continuous replication	Not supported	Supported

Choosing between Exchange 2007 Standard CAL and Enterprise CAL

Before purchasing Exchange 2007 for your environment, you have to decide which version of client access license (CAL) is suitable for your organization. Exchange 2007 introduces Standard client access license (Standard CAL) and Enterprise client access license (Enterprise CAL). Standard CAL provides access to email, Outlook Web Access, ActiveSync, and so on. Enterprise CAL provides additional features like Unified Messaging, per-user journaling for archiving and compliance support, message filtering, and enhanced antivirus and antispam functionality. You can mix and match the server editions with the CAL editions. For example, you can use Standard CALs against the Enterprise server edition or vice versa.

You will notice that the Enterprise CAL is basically an additive CAL, which means that you must buy the Standard CAL before you buy an Enterprise CAL.

Table 7.2 provides a quick comparison to illustrate what features are included with the Exchange Server Standard CAL and Exchange Server Enterprise CAL.

TABLE 7.2 Differences Between Standard and Enterprise CAL

Feature	Standard CAL	Enterprise CAL
Email	Yes	No
Calendar sharing, contacts, tasks	Yes	No
ActiveSync	Yes	No

TABLE 7.2 Differences Between Standard and Enterprise CAL *(continued)*

Feature	Standard CAL	Enterprise CAL
Unified Messaging	No	Yes
Journaling for archiving and compliance	No	Yes
Exchange hosted filtering	No	Yes
Forefront Security	No	Yes

Real World Scenario

Moving from Exchange 2003 to Exchange 2007 Using Transition Instead of Migration

At publication time, there is no in-place upgrade option available to move from 2003 to 2007. However, even if there *were* such an option, I would never recommend it to my clients, as my experience tells me that in-place upgrades are riskier and that there are more possibilities of failure during these kinds of upgrades. To keep it simple, why not just build a new box and move mailboxes from one system to the other?

Instead of an in-place upgrade, I prefer to do transit migration by moving mailboxes and data from a legacy system to Exchange 2007. This approach is simple and straightforward as compared to doing a migration from Exchange 5.5 to Exchange 2003.

Yes, I remember—It was just like a "hell" to migrate from Exchange 5.5 to Exchange 2000/2003. Directory synchronization and replication between the two systems were complicated processes. On the other hand, the steps for moving, transiting, and upgrading from Exchange 2003 to Exchange 2007 are relatively easy, quick, and painless. You just have to install Exchange 2007 in an existing Exchange 2003 organization and then use the Move Mailbox Wizard or the `Move-mailbox` PowerShell command to move mailboxes on to the new platform. Decommission your legacy Exchange systems, and you are done.

Introducing new Exchange Server 2007 servers into an existing Exchange 2003 organization is known as a *transition* approach. Transition is different from migration. Used here, *transition* means moving data from legacy Exchange systems to Exchange 2007 and then decommissioning the old Exchange systems. On the other hand, migration is used to represent moving from one messaging system (for example, Lotus Notes or GroupWise) to an Exchange environment.

I prefer the transition approach for Exchange 2007. Why? Because I believe it offers more granular control. You can move individual users or a few mailboxes at a time to the new platform. If there are any problems, you can just move the mailboxes back to the original environment. In terms of availability, you can build parallel environments and move a few users at a time without doing any "cutover" migration.

Whatever you do, don't forget to make a full backup of your Exchange servers! Make sure you have offline and online backup and tapes available onsite before you start migration. (For more information about backup strategies and Exchange backup, please see Chapter 9.)

Readiness Checklist: Nine Steps to Getting Your Organization Ready for Exchange Server 2007

This section details the various steps involved in a transition. You will need to gather and analyze information about your Active Directory forest and existing Exchange organization and then test your design, processes, and procedures in a lab environment before you proceed. Designing an Exchange system is not a linear process, but an iterative one. You may have to keep reading and improving the process to adapt to the complexities involved with the migration and upgrade. Generally, the more iterations and discussions you go through, the better and smoother your design and implementation process will be.

To gather information about your Active Directory and Exchange organization, you can use Microsoft Exchange Server Best Practices Analyzer Tool (ExBPA) 2.7 or later. This tool includes the Exchange 2007 Readiness Check scan, which allows you to send the results to an XML output file. I recommend running this scan during the early stages of your planning to ensure that your Exchange 2000/2003 environment is ready for the big change.

Table 7.3 lists the critical information you should collect from your existing Active Directory, Exchange organization, and infrastructure.

TABLE 7.3 Critical Information to Collect before Migration

Component	Settings and Information To Document
Active Directory	Active Directory sites and subnet associated with each site Location of Global Catalog AD Site links and cost associated with each link Forest functional level Domain functional level Geographical location of domain controllers and other infrastructure servers Exchange administrators and security groups Group policies

TABLE 7.3 Critical Information to Collect before Migration *(continued)*

Component	Settings and Information To Document
MS Exchange	Organization name Functional level of organization: Mixed or native Server hardware—i.e., processor, memory, disk space, etc. Antivirus and antispam software settings Server roles, such as front-end and back-end servers and Bridgehead servers. Exchange administrators and security groups Backup and disaster-recovery plan and practices Exchange routing policies, SMTP settings, and permissions Routing groups and foreign connectors Address filter and message-size restrictions Storage groups and databases Private and public database size Exchange CAL, external contacts, and distribution groups Location of log files and transaction files External and internal Domain Name Service (DNS) settings and information Mail Exchanger record information Front-end/OWA customization settings and information Firewall settings, including ports open SMTP relay settings Location of servers in Active Directory OU Group policy settings related to Exchange Server Exchange Server security settings and OS hardening settings Certificate information installed on your front-end server
Infrastructure	DNS servers, forwarders, and zone information WINS servers, replication schedule, and push/pull partner configuration Physical and logical network structure Network connections and bandwidth Trust relationship between forests IP address settings

You also should use the following checklist to ensure that your infrastructure (i.e., your network, software, domain controllers (DCs), global catalogs (GCs), DNS, hardware, clients, and other important elements of your Exchange organization) meets the requirements for Exchange 2007. If you meet all of the following requirements, then your infrastructure is ready for Exchange 2007. If not, you may want to go back and upgrade certain elements to prepare your infrastructure for Exchange 2007.

The following steps are presented by Microsoft in its online documentation, but they are reworded here for clarity.

1. Perform an Active Directory Health Check to ensure that there are no Active Directory and DNS issues.

2. Check the service-pack level on the domain controller that is performing the Schema Master role to ensure that it has Microsoft Windows 2003 SP1 or later installed.
3. Ensure that you have at least one DC and GC in each Active Directory site that is running Windows 2003 SP1 or later.
4. Ensure that the Active Directory domain functional level is set to Windows 2000 Server native or higher for all Active Directory domains, where you will be installing Exchange 2007 or hosting the Exchange 2007 recipients.
5. Set the forest functional level to Windows Server 2000 native or higher.
6. Ensure that there are no Exchange 5.5 servers in your Exchange organization, and then convert your Exchange organization from mixed mode to native mode.
7. Verify that you are running the correct service pack version on Exchange 2000 and 2003 Servers.
8. Ensure that the Exchange 2007 hardware meets the minimum hardware requirements.
9. Run an Exchange 2007 Readiness Check using the Exchange Best Practices Analyzer.

The following sections describe these nine preparation steps in detail. Before implementing Exchange 2007 in your environment, you should go through all of these steps to ensure that your environment is ready for transition.

Step 1: Performing an Active Directory Health Check

As Exchange 2000 and later depends on your Active Directory to store recipient, connection, and configuration information, it is important to perform an Active Directory health check on your Active Directory forest. You can use the DCDIAG, NETDIAG, REPLMON, and REPLADMIN utilities available on the Windows 2003 Server CD in the support tools. These are great utilities, and you can run them in verbose mode to check almost all aspects of your Active Directory to discover any anomalies you may encounter during the installation of Exchange 2007. Review the output of these utilities to ensure that there are no Active Directory issues, that your Domain Name System is configured correctly, and that there are no DNS issues in your forest, domain, or in any site.

During installation of Exchange 2007, Exchange 2007 Setup quickly conducts a minor health check to check service-pack level, inconsistency in organization name, DNS communication, and more. However, to perform an extensive health check, use the Readiness Check tool and support tools utilities available with the Windows 2003 Server CD.

Step 2: Checking Windows Server 2003 and FSMO roles

The second step in preparing the Active Directory forest is to make sure that the domain controller with the Schema Master role is running on a system that has at least 2003 SP1 or higher installed. This does not mean that you have to upgrade your entire domain to Windows 2003; it simply means that your Schema Master domain controller must be at least Windows Server 2003 SP1. You can verify this by checking the properties of your system.

Step 3: Checking the Domain Controller and the Global Catalog

The third step is to ensure that you have GC servers in each site that has 2003 SP1 or higher installed. Exchange 2007 gets its recipient information and directory information only from GC servers installed on systems with SP1 or higher. You do not have to upgrade all GC servers in your entire domain. You just need at least one GC server with SP1 in each site where you plan to install Exchange 2007. This requirement cannot be ignored because it supports features such as browsing address books from Outlook Web Access, Exchange 2007 service notifications, and much more.

Step 4: Changing the Domain Functional Level for Exchange Server 2007

The fourth step is to ensure that your domain functional level is set to Windows 2000 Server native or higher, as described in Exercise 7.1. This simply means that you can no longer have Windows NT 4.0 domain controllers in your domain. You can still have Windows NT 4.0 workstations or servers, but the domain controllers must be upgraded to either Windows 2000 Server or Windows Server 2003.

EXERCISE 7.1

Changing the Domain Functional Level to Native or Higher

To change the domain functional level:

1. Click Start ➢ All Programs ➢ Administrative Tools, and then click on Active Directory Users and Computers.
2. Right-click on your Active Directory domain and choose Raise Domain Functional Level in the context menu.
3. Change the domain functional level to Windows 2000 native or Windows Server 2003, as shown here.

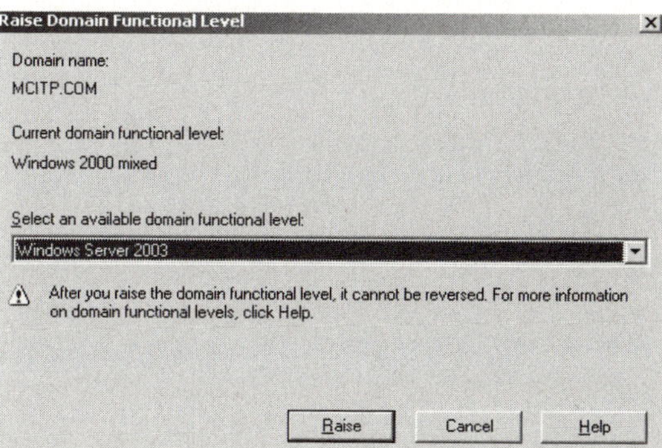

EXERCISE 7.1 *(continued)*

4. You will see a warning box that reads, "This change affects the entire domain. After you raise the domain functional level, it cannot be reversed." Click OK to continue.

5. The information message shown here will appear, indicating that the domain functional level has been raised. Click OK.

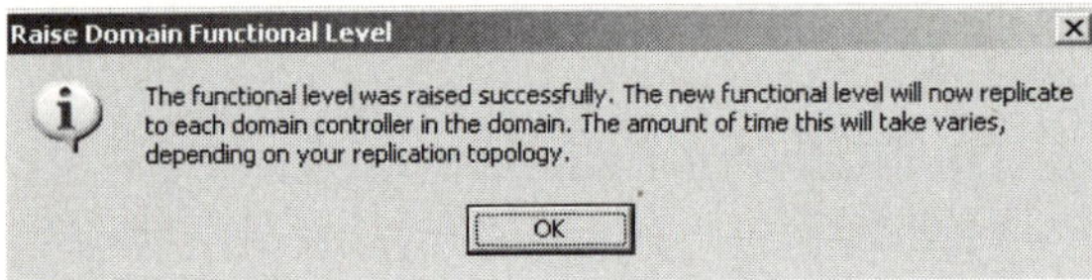

Step 5: Changing the Forest Functional Level for Exchange Server 2007

Next you need to ensure that your forest functional level is set to Windows 2000 Server native or higher, as outlined in Exercise 7.2. All DCs in the forest should be running Windows Server 2003.

EXERCISE 7.2

Changing the Forest Functional Level to Windows 2000 Server Native or Higher

To change the forest functional level, do the following:

1. Click Start ➤ All Programs ➤ Administrative Tools, and then click on Active Directory Domains and Trusts.

2. Right-click on your Active Directory Domains and Trusts, and then click on Raise Forest Functional Level in the context menu.

3. In the Select an Available Forest Functional Level box, click Windows Server 2003 and then select Raise, as shown here.

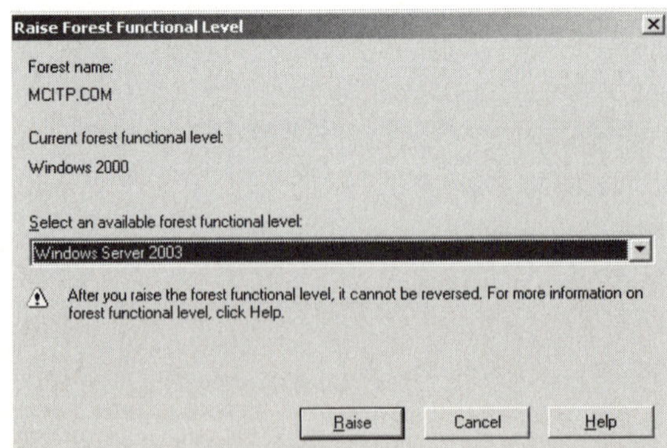

EXERCISE 7.2 *(continued)*

4. You will see a warning box that reads, "This change affects the entire forest. After you raise the forest functional level, it cannot be reversed." Click OK to continue.

5. The information message shown below will appear, indicating that the forest functional level has been raised successfully. Click OK.

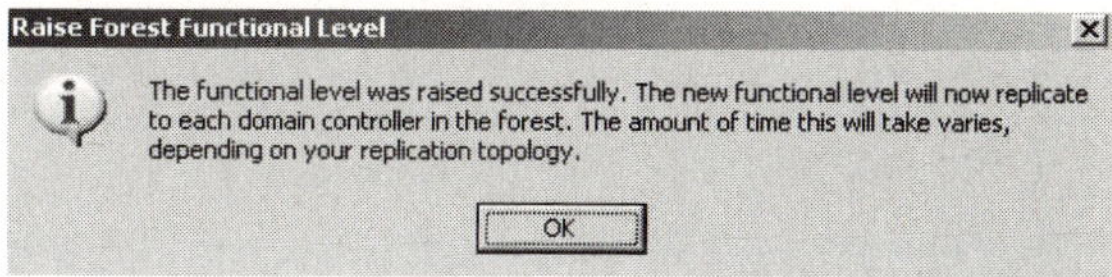

Step 6: Changing the Exchange 2003 Operation Mode from Mixed to Native

Initially, when you install Exchange 2000/2003, your Exchange organization operates in mixed mode to accommodate pre-Exchange 2000 servers. In mixed mode, you may still have few Exchange 5.5 servers running in your organization. Mixed mode operates in the interest of preserving backward compatibility with older versions of Exchange.

One of the requirements of Exchange 2007 is to have your Exchange organization in native mode instead of mixed mode. What would happen if you still have pre-Exchange 2000 in your environment? Well, you don't have lot of choices. You have to get rid of the Exchange 5.5 servers or transfer the functionality to Exchange 2000 and later servers and decommission the Exchange 5.5 servers. Once you have no Exchange 5.5 servers and no plans to use any of the services and connectors installed on Exchange 5.5 servers, you can switch from mixed mode to native mode to take advantage of the benefits of native mode. An organization running in native mode cannot accommodate Exchange 5.0 or 5.5 servers. You can have only Exchange 2003 or Exchange 2000 computers in your organization.

Some of the benefits of running your Exchange 2003 organization in native mode are as follows:

- You can rename your Exchange organization.
- You can move mailboxes in the same administrative groups.
- When Exchange Server 2003 is running in mixed mode, your Exchange Server 2003 will treat any Exchange 5.5 sites as if they are the administrative groups. Likewise, your Exchange 5.5 server will treat any Exchange 2003 administrative groups as sites.
- Creating Query-Based Distribution Groups (QBDG), which are distribution groups that use LDAP filters to dynamically choose group members.
- SMTP becomes the default routing protocol between the Exchange servers, whereas in mixed mode your servers will continue using X.400 for backward compatibility.
- You can consolidate administrative groups and define administrative groups and routing groups with greater flexibility.

- There are some performance improvements in the native mode. For example, native mode routing groups use faster 8BITMIME data transfer between the Exchange Bridgehead servers, whereas Exchange 5.5 servers use 7BITMIME. This change means a substantial improvement in performance in terms of the amount of data that you can send across a routing group connector.
- Native mode supports multiple routing groups within the same administrative group.
- Servers can be moved between routing groups.
- Routing groups can consist of servers from different administrative groups.
- The InetOrgPerson object class can be mailbox-enabled or mail-enabled.

Your Exchange organization must be running in the native mode before you install your first Exchange Server 2007 in the organization. Exercise 7.3 outlines the instructions to set the Exchange 2003 operation mode to native.

EXERCISE 7.3

Changing the Exchange 2003 Operation Mode from Mixed to Native

To change the Exchange 2003 operation mode, do the following:

1. Log on to the Exchange server on which you want to perform the operation.
2. Click Start ➤ All Programs ➤ Microsoft Exchange, and then click on System Manager.
3. Right-click on your Exchange 2003 organization, and then click on Properties in the context menu.
4. Click on Change Mode, as shown here.

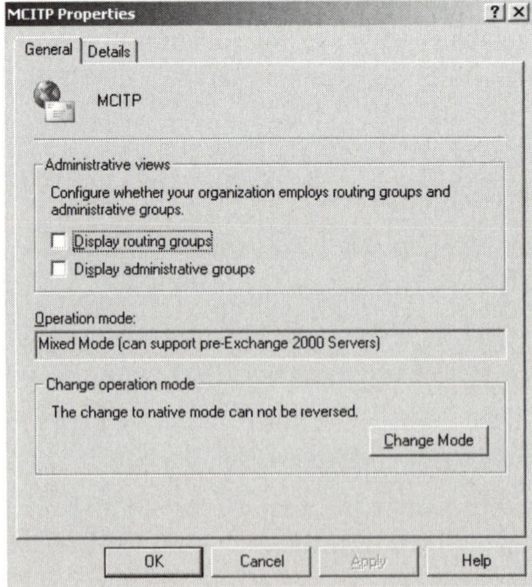

EXERCISE 7.3 *(continued)*

5. You will see a warning box that says, "Once this operation is complete, the mode of this organization cannot be set back to Mixed Mode. Are you sure you want to change the mode of this organization to Native Mode?" Click Yes to continue as shown here.

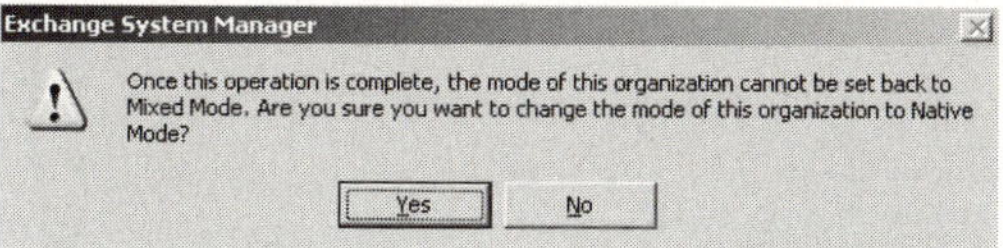

6. The information screen shown here will appear, indicating that the Exchange operation mode has been changed successfully. Click OK.

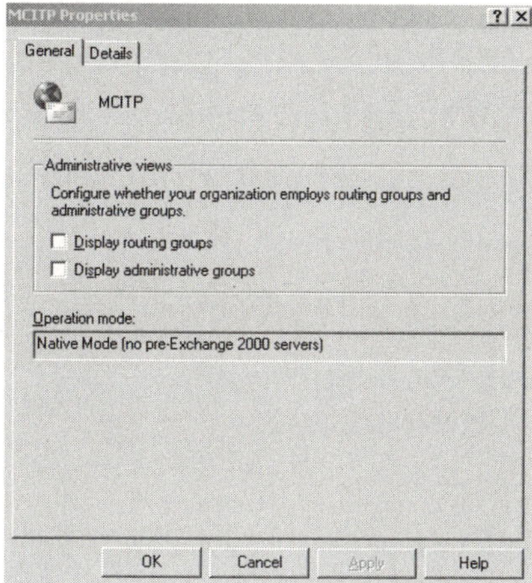

Step 7: Verifying the Service Pack Version on Exchange Server

Next, ensure that you are running the correct service pack version on your Exchange servers. You should have Service Pack 3 installed on Exchange 2000 servers and Service Pack 2 installed on Exchange 2003 servers. To verify the service pack version, open Exchange System Manager and click on the help menu.

Step 8: Ensuring that the Exchange 2007 Hardware Meets the Minimum Requirements

The next step in the process is to make sure that you meet the minimum hardware requirements. You must be running a 64-bit Windows Server 2003 SP1 or later, on 64-bit hardware.

Step 9: Running an Exchange 2007 Readiness Check Using Exchange Best Practices Analyzer

To ensure that you have completed all the requirements for Exchange 2007 deployment and your Active Directory forest is ready to accommodate Exchange 2007, you should run ExBPA 2.7 or above from Microsoft. ExBPA, as noted earlier, is a tool that is used to check the health of your Exchange organization. It is built into Exchange 2007, but you can download the latest version from Microsoft. If Internet connectivity is available, ExBPA will attempt to automatically update itself from the Internet each time you run it.

Besides checking configuration errors in your Exchange deployment, ExBPA allows you to run a Readiness Check on your existing Exchange deployment and provides you with a to-do list of changes and decisions that need to be made before Exchange 2007 can be deployed in your organization. The Exchange Readiness Check analyzes each Exchange 2003/2000 server in your organization to verify that it has the necessary updates, service packs, and configuration in place to support Exchange 2007.

Exercise 7.4 outlines the instructions to run the Exchange 2007 Readiness Check on your Exchange organization.

EXERCISE 7.4

Running an Exchange 2007 Readiness Check

To run an Exchange 2007 Readiness Check, complete the following steps:

1. Log on to the Exchange server on which you want to perform the operation.
2. Click Start ➢ All Programs ➢ Microsoft Exchange, and then click on Best Practices Analyzer Tool.
3. Click on Do Not Check for Updates on Startup.
4. Click on Go to Welcome Screen.
5. Click on Select Options for a New Scan as shown here.

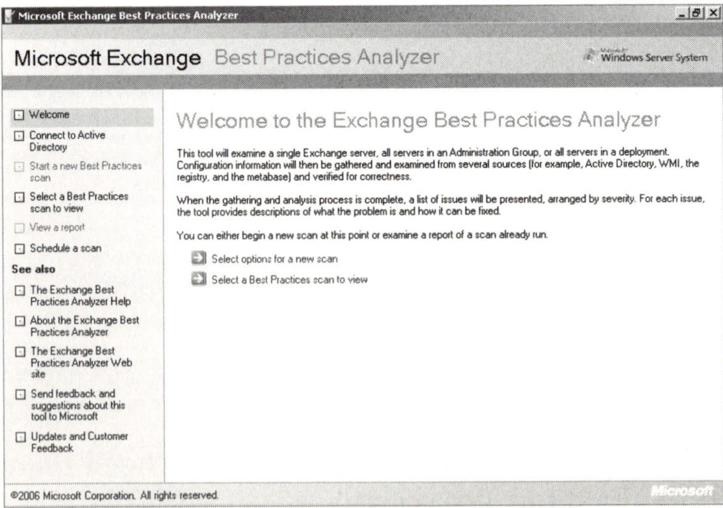

EXERCISE 7.4 (continued)

6. Type in your Active Directory server name, and then click on Connect to the Active Directory Server, as shown below.

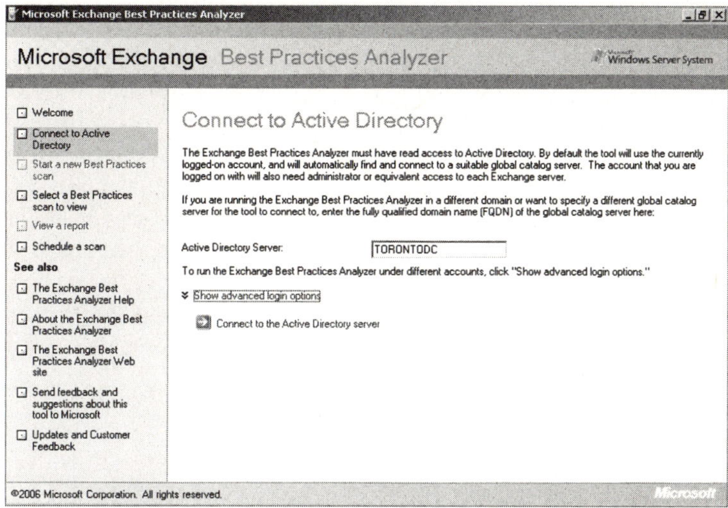

7. Type in the label name for this scan.

8. Click on Exchange 2007 Readiness Check.

9. Click on Start Scanning.

10. You will receive a report, as shown below, which can be exported in XML format.

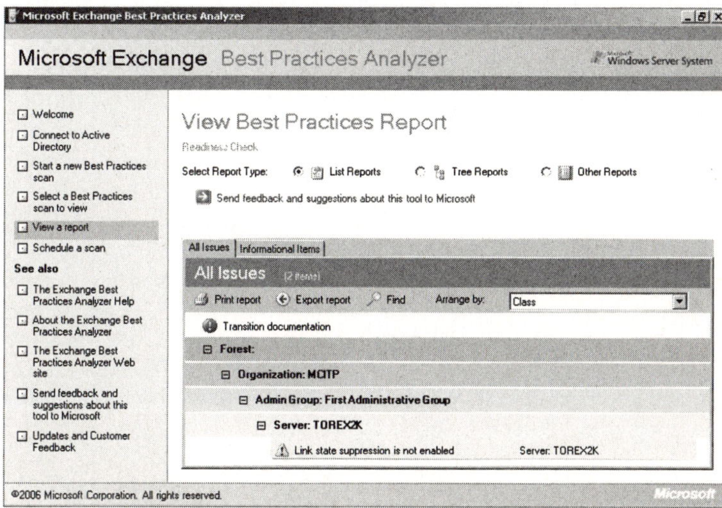

As shown in the graphics in Exercise 7.4, the link-state session settings are not suppressed. Before starting the migration from an Exchange 2003 server to an Exchange 2007 server, you may want to suppress the link-state updates on Exchange 2000 or 2003 servers. By suppressing link-state updates, you minimize the network traffic. The link-state updates in previous versions of Exchange related network link status information to other servers in the Exchange organization if the network link status changed. The link-state functionality was helpful because each routing group master updated its link-state tables using this setting.

Suppressing link states on Exchange 2000 or 2003 servers marks the connectors as being down, which forces Exchange servers to use another available least-cost routing option for messages. In some environments, it is advantageous to turn off link-state routing or suppress it on certain servers instead of all servers in the legacy Exchange organization. Exchange 2007 does not require link-state updates because it uses Active Directory sites to route the information. Because routing is determined from Active Directory sites, the Exchange link-state update functionality has been discontinued.

To suppress link-state updates, follow these steps:

1. Log on to the server on which you want to run this command.
2. Click Start ➢ Run, and type **cmd.exe.** Then press Enter or click OK.
3. Type **Regedit.**
4. Navigate to `HKEY_LOCAL_MACHINE\System\CurrentControlSet\Services\RESvc\Parameters.` Right-click on Parameters, then select New ➢ DWORD.
5. Double-click on SuppressStateChanges and enable it by entering **1** in the data value field.
6. Restart the Exchange server.

Preparing Active Directory for Exchange 2007

Once you have raised the functionality level of the forest and domain, you are ready to prepare Active Directory schema for Exchange 2007. You may recall that `/forestprep` and `/domainprep` switches were used to prepare the Active Directory forest and domain for Exchange 2000/2003. With Exchange 2007, things have been slightly improved and modified. During the installation of Exchange 2007, Setup will automatically execute `PrepareAD` to populate your Active Directory schema with Exchange 2007 classes, objects, and attributes. Alternatively, you can prepare your forest and domain by manually running the switches available with `Setup.com`.

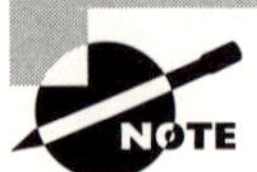

After you run each of these switches, you must wait for replication to occur before you proceed with the next switch. Why? Because you want to make sure that your Active Directory infrastructure is stable and all DCs have the same set of information. Use REPLMON, REPLADMIN, ADSI Edit, and other tools to ensure that your changes have been successfully replicated across your Active Directory forest.

To prepare the Active Directory schema, forest, and domain for Exchange 2007 installation, you need to understand the switches available with the `Setup.com` command and how they will affect your Active Directory forest and Exchange Server environment.

Preparing for Coexistence

The first command you need to run is `Setup.com /pl` or `/PrepareLegacyExchangePermissions`. This command is required if you have previous versions of Exchange servers in your environment. This command creates the ExchangeLegacyInterop universal security group in your Active Directory forest, which is required in the coexistence mode because it allows the previous versions of Exchange Server to send email to the Exchange 2007 Mailbox servers through the Hub Transport servers. This command also modifies the permissions of the Enterprise Exchange Servers group to allow the Recipient Update Service to run; otherwise Recipient Update Service won't function correctly after the Active Directory schema has been updated with Exchange 2007 specific attributes. You must be a member of the Enterprise Admins Active Directory group to run this command.

Exercise 7.5 outlines the instructions to run the `Setup.com /PrepareLegacyExchangePermissions` command.

EXERCISE 7.5

Running Setup.com /PrepareLegacyExchangePermissions

To run the `Setup.com/PrepareLegacyExchangePermissions` command, follow these steps:

1. Log on to the server on which you want to run this command.
2. Insert the Exchange Server 2007 DVD (Standard or Enterprise version).
3. Click Start ➢ Run, then type **cmd.exe**. Press Enter or click OK.
4. In the command-prompt windows, navigate to the DVD-ROM drive where you have Exchange Server 2007 media (for example, go to the E: drive if that is the one assigned to the DVD-ROM).
5. Change the folder by typing **CD i386**, then press Enter.
6. Type `Setup.com/PrepareLegacyExchangePermissions` as shown below, and press Enter to run the `/PrepareLegacyExchangePermissions` command.

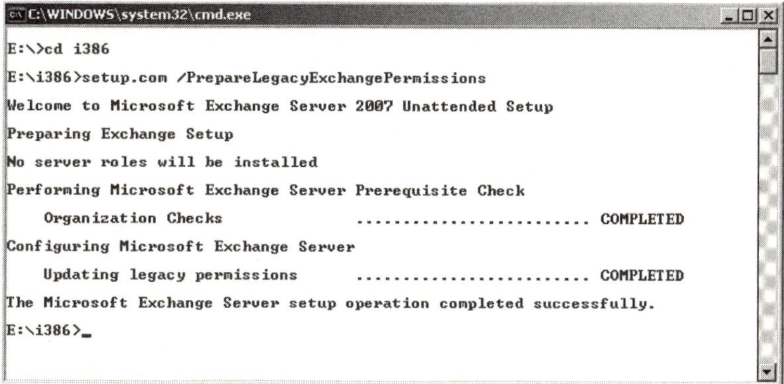

Preparing the Active Directory Schema

Next, you will run the `Setup.com /PrepareSchema` command. This command prepares the schema for the Exchange Server 2007 installation. It updates the schema with Exchange 2007 specific objects, classes, and attributes by importing LDAP Data Interchange Format (LDIF) files. It also enhances and modifies existing classes, objects, and attributes. You can run the `Setup.com/PrepareSchema` command before running `Setup.com/PrepareLegacyExchangePermissions`. Doing so will automatically run the `/PrepareLegacyExchangePermissions` command for you. You must be a member of the Schema Admins and Enterprise Admins groups to run this command.

Exercise 7.6 outlines the instructions to run the `/PrepareSchema` command.

EXERCISE 7.6

Running /PrepareSchema

Here's how to run the `/PrepareSchema` command:

1. Log on to the server on which you want to run this command.
2. Insert the Exchange Server 2007 DVD (Standard or Enterprise version).
3. Click Start ➢ Run, then type **cmd.exe**. Press Enter or click OK.
4. In the command-prompt windows, navigate to the DVD-ROM drive where you have Exchange Server 2007 media.
5. Change the folder by typing **CD i386**. Press Enter.
6. Type `Setup.com/PrepareSchema` as shown below, and press Enter to run the `/PrepareSchema` command.

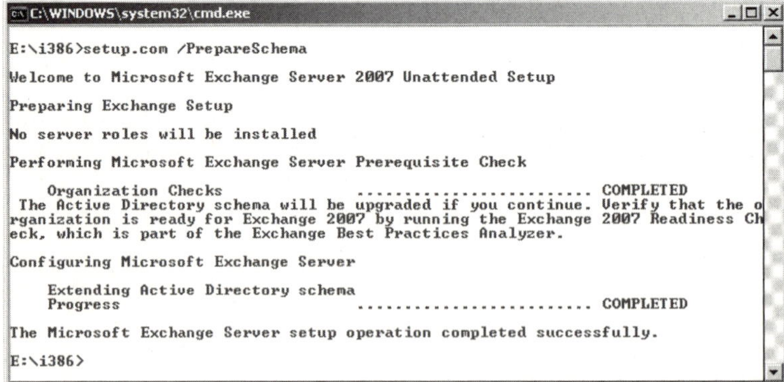

```
C:\WINDOWS\system32\cmd.exe

E:\i386>setup.com /PrepareSchema

Welcome to Microsoft Exchange Server 2007 Unattended Setup

Preparing Exchange Setup

No server roles will be installed

Performing Microsoft Exchange Server Prerequisite Check

    Organization Checks          ......................... COMPLETED
 The Active Directory schema will be upgraded if you continue. Verify that the o
rganization is ready for Exchange 2007 by running the Exchange 2007 Readiness Ch
eck, which is part of the Exchange Best Practices Analyzer.

Configuring Microsoft Exchange Server

    Extending Active Directory schema
    Progress                     ......................... COMPLETED

The Microsoft Exchange Server setup operation completed successfully.

E:\i386>
```

Preparing the Active Directory

The next step is to run the `Setup.com/PrepareAD` command on the domain controller that is the Schema Master in your root domain. You can run the `Setup.com /PrepareAD` command before running `Setup.com /PrepareLegacyExchangePermissions` and `Setup.com / PrepareSchema`. Doing so will automatically run the `/PrepareLegacyExchangePermissions` and `/PrepareSchema` commands for you.

`/PrepareAD` performs the following activities:

- Extends the Active Directory schema by creating new classes, objects, and attributes or modifying the existing ones.
- Creates the Exchange organization in AD.
- Creates the Microsoft Exchange System Objects container in the root domain partition to store Exchange configuration data and information.
- Verifies that the schema in your AD forest has been updated by checking the `ObjectVersion` property in the Active Directory.
- Creates the Exchange Routing Group (DWBGZMFD01QNBJR) and Exchange Administrative Group (FYDIBOHF23SPDLT). Exchange 2007 uses these groups to store configuration data and to communicate with earlier versions of Exchange. Exchange 2007 doesn't use administrative groups and routing groups like previous versions of Exchange, but it must create these groups to coexist with Exchange 2000 and 2003.
- Creates the universal security group OU for Exchange 2007 and populates it with Exchange Organization Administrators, Exchange Recipient Administrators, Exchange Servers, Exchange View-Only Administrators, and ExchangeLegacyInterop group.

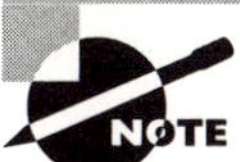

You must be a member of Enterprise Admins group to run the `/PrepareAD` command.

Exercise 7.7 outlines the instructions to run the `/PrepareAD` command.

EXERCISE 7.7

Running /PrepareAD

Follow these steps to run the `/PrepareAD` command:

1. Log on to the server on which you want to run this command.
2. Insert the Exchange Server 2007 DVD (Standard or Enterprise version).
3. Click Start ➢ Run, then type **cmd.exe**. Press Enter or click OK.
4. In the command-prompt windows, navigate to the DVD-ROM drive where you have Exchange Server 2007 media.

EXERCISE 7.7 *(continued)*

5. Change the folder by typing **CD i386**. Press Enter.
6. Type `Setup.com /PrepareAD` as shown below, and press Enter to run the `/PrepareAD` command.

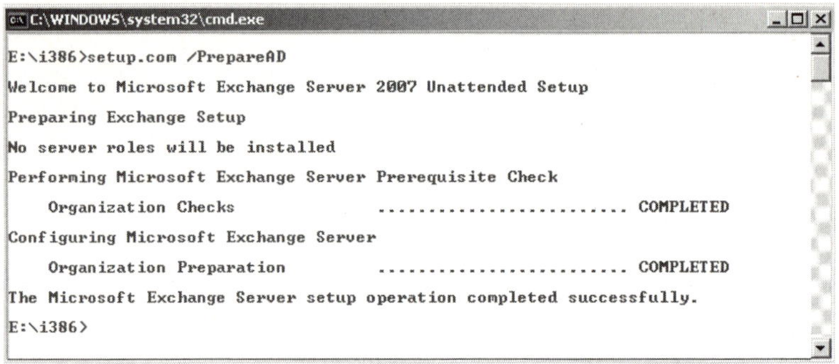

```
E:\i386>setup.com /PrepareAD
Welcome to Microsoft Exchange Server 2007 Unattended Setup
Preparing Exchange Setup
No server roles will be installed
Performing Microsoft Exchange Server Prerequisite Check
    Organization Checks          ......................... COMPLETED
Configuring Microsoft Exchange Server
    Organization Preparation     ......................... COMPLETED
The Microsoft Exchange Server setup operation completed successfully.
E:\i386>
```

Preparing the Active Directory Domains

Finally, you need to run the `Setup.com /PrepareDomain` command or `/PrepareDomain <domainname>` or `/PrepareAllDomains`. This command does the following:

- Prepares your domain/all domains for Exchange Server 2007 by creating a new domain global group called Exchange Install Domain Servers in the root domain.
- Sets permissions on the domain container for the Exchange Servers, Exchange Organization Administrators, Exchange Mailbox Administrators, and Authenticated Users.
- Creates the Microsoft Exchange System Objects container and sets permissions on this container for the Exchange Servers, Exchange Organization Administrators, Exchange Mailbox Administrators, and Authenticated Users.
- Creates a new domain global group in the current domain called Exchange Install Domain Servers and adds the Exchange Install Domain Servers group to the Exchange Servers universal security group in the root domain.

You must run this command in every domain/child domain in your forest in which you want to install Exchange 2007. You must be a member of the Enterprise Admins and Domain Admin groups to run this command.

Exercise 7.8 outlines the instructions to run the `/PrepareAllDomains` command.

EXERCISE 7.8

Running /PrepareAllDomains

Use these steps to run the `/PrepareAllDomains` command:

1. Log on to the server on which you want to run this command.

EXERCISE 7.8 *(continued)*

2. Insert the Exchange Server 2007 DVD (Standard or Enterprise version).
3. Click Start ➤ Run, then type **cmd.exe**. Press Enter or click OK.
4. In the command-prompt windows, navigate to the DVD-ROM drive where you have Exchange Server 2007 media.
5. Change the folder by typing **CD i386**. Press Enter.
6. Type `Setup.com /PrepareAllDomains` as shown below, and press Enter to run the `/PrepareAllDomains` command.

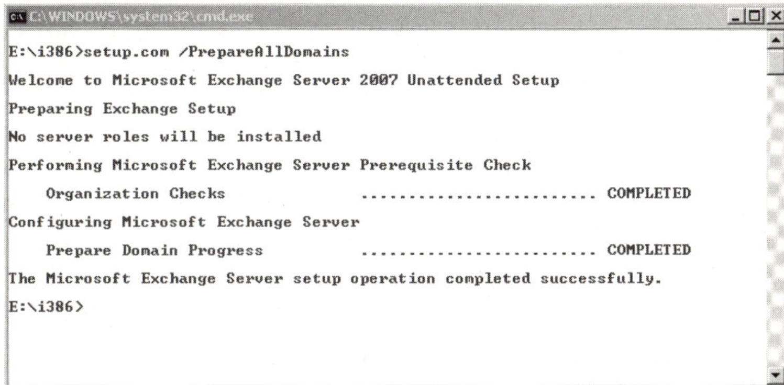

```
E:\i386>setup.com /PrepareAllDomains
Welcome to Microsoft Exchange Server 2007 Unattended Setup
Preparing Exchange Setup
No server roles will be installed
Performing Microsoft Exchange Server Prerequisite Check
    Organization Checks          ........................ COMPLETED
Configuring Microsoft Exchange Server
    Prepare Domain Progress      ........................ COMPLETED
The Microsoft Exchange Server setup operation completed successfully.
E:\i386>
```

Installing Exchange 2007 in an Exchange 2003 Organization

Once you have gone through the planning list, your Active Directory forest and Exchange 2003 organization are ready to migrate to the Exchange Server 2007 environment. As discussed earlier, you cannot perform an in-place upgrade from Exchange 2000/2003 to Exchange 2007; however, you can install Exchange Server 2007 in an existing Exchange 2003 organization and then move your Exchange mailboxes and other resources from Exchange 2003 to Exchange Server 2007. Generally, this multi-Exchange environment is referred to as *coexistence mode*.

Coexistence mode occurs when you have multiple versions of Exchange servers in your organization. Exchange 2007 supports coexistence with Exchange 2003 and Exchange 2000 Server, but not with Exchange 5.5. If you are using Exchange 5.5, you must upgrade to Exchange 2000 Server or Exchange Server 2003 before you introduce Exchange Server 2007.

Checking for Required Software and Windows Components

Now that you've got a basic understanding about coexistence mode, it's time to begin installing and configuring Exchange 2007 in your Exchange 2003 organization. Before installing

Exchange 2007, you must make sure that the required software and Windows components are installed on the server prior to launching Exchange 2007 Setup.

The required software for any of the Exchange Server 2007 roles includes the following:

- Microsoft .NET Framework Version 2.0
- Microsoft .NET Framework hotfix (`NDP20-KB926776-x86.exe`)
- Microsoft Management Console (MMC) 3.0
- Windows PowerShell V1.0
- Hotfix for Windows x64 (KB904639)

If you have not installed any of this software, when you launch the Exchange Server 2007 Setup, you will be provided with links to install each one separately.

Depending on the Exchange Server 2007 role you are planning to install, different Windows components are required. Table 7.4 lists each role and the required Windows components.

TABLE 7.4 Windows Components Required for Each Role

Role	Windows Components Required
Mailbox server	Enable network COM+ (Component Object Model+) access Internet Information Services World Wide Web Service Hotfixes mentioned in MS Knowledge Base articles 904639 and 918980
Client Access server	World Wide Web Service RPC over HTTP Proxy Windows networking component ASP.NET v2.0 Ensure that POP3 service from Windows has not been installed.
Hub Transport server	No additional Windows components are required by the Hub Transport server; however you must ensure that the SMTP and NNTP services are *not* installed on the Hub Transport server.
Edge Transport server	Must have a DNS suffix configured Active Directory Application Mode (ADAM) SP1 Ensure that the SMTP and NNTP services are *not* installed on the Edge server.
Unified Messaging Server	Microsoft Speech service Microsoft Windows Media Encoder Microsoft Windows Media Audio Voice Codec Microsoft Core XML Services (MSXML) 6.0

Preparing Exchange Server 2007

Exercise 7.9 outlines the steps for installing Exchange Server 2007 prerequisites on an Exchange Server 2007 machine. These prerequisites are as follows:

- Microsoft Management Console 3.0
- Microsoft .NET Framework 2.0
- Microsoft Windows PowerShell

In the lab environment, the E: drive is assigned to the DVD-ROM.

EXERCISE 7.9

Installing Exchange Server 2007 Prerequisites

To install the Microsoft Management Console 3.0, do the following:

1. Click Start ➤ Run, type **E:\MMC3.0\WindowsServer2003-kb907265-x86-enu.exe**, and then click OK.
2. Click Next to begin the installation.
3. Click I Agree, and then click Next to continue.
4. Click Finish.

Complete the following steps to install the Microsoft .NET Framework 2.0:

5. Click Start ➤ Run, type **E:\dotnet2.0\dotnetfx.exe**, and then click OK.
6. Click Next to begin the installation.
7. Check I Accept the Terms of the License Agreement, and then click Install.
8. Click Finish to continue.

To install the Microsoft .NET Framework 2.0 hotfix, do the following:

9. Click Start ➤ Run, type **E:\Dotnet2Hotfix\NDP20-KB926776-X86.exe**, and then click OK.
10. Click OK to install the Dotnet 2.0 hotfix.
11. Click I Accept to accept the licensing agreement.
12. Click OK to continue.

EXERCISE 7.9 *(continued)*

Do the following to install Microsoft Windows PowerShell:

13. Click Start ➢ Run, type **E:\Windows PowerShell\WindowsServer2003-kb926139-x86-enu.exe**, and then click OK.
14. Click Next to begin the installation.
15. Click I Agree and click Next.
16. Click Next to begin the installation by accepting the default installation location.
17. Click Install to install the Windows PowerShell.
18. Click Finish.

Finally! The Exchange Server 2007 Installation

After installing the prerequisites, the next step is to determine how many Exchange Server 2007 servers you require in your Exchange 2003 organization. Exchange 2007 uses role-based deployment, which means that you have to decide in advance what kind of functionalities you need in your messaging environment. As discussed in previous sections, the server role is nothing more than the logical grouping of features, services, and functionalities to perform specific tasks in your environment. To determine the best way to meet the needs of your organization, you have several questions to consider. Which role(s) should you install on your first Exchange Server 2007? Should you combine multiple roles on one server or install them separately on each individual server? How much cost is involved? How much downtime is involved? How can you deploy Exchange Server 2007 roles without affecting your end users?

We recommend that the first Exchange 2007 role you introduce in your Exchange 2003 environment be the Client Access server (CAS).

After that, you should implement the Hub Transport server. The Hub Transport server is very important in your messaging infrastructure because it routes email inside and outside of your organization. The Mailbox server and Unified Messaging server both require a Hub Transport server to route messages. You also must have a Hub Transport server to route emails in coexistence mode. Also in the coexistence mode, the Hub Transport server can work with the Exchange 2003/Exchange 2000 Bridgehead server, which means that you just have to configure connectors between Exchange 2003/Exchange 2000 Bridgehead servers and Exchange Server 2007 servers to start mailflow in your mixed environment.

After introducing the CAS and Hub Transport servers, you can install the Exchange 2007 Mailbox server in your organization. Mailbox servers hold mailboxes only. Once you have the Mailbox server, you are ready to move mailboxes from your Exchange 2003/Exchange 2000 servers to the Exchange 2007 environment.

It is important to understand that these roles can be combined. For example, you can combine the CAS, Hub Transport server, and Mailbox server on one machine; however, combining these roles is not recommended for medium or large messaging infrastructures.

Remember, if you select the Typical installation, it automatically installs the Client Access server, Hub Transport server, and Mailbox server on one machine, and you will be unable to install the Edge Transport server role, Unified Messaging server role, and cluster Mailbox servers during this installation. To install the CAS, Hub Transport, Mailbox, and Unified Messaging roles on the same machine, select the Custom install.

Exercise 7.10 outlines the steps to install Exchange Server 2007. The following exercise uses the Typical installation rather than Custom.

EXERCISE 7.10

Installing Exchange Server 2007

Do the following to install the Exchange Server 2007:

1. Log on to the server on which you want to install Exchange 2007.
2. Install Exchange Server 2007 prerequisites.
3. Insert the Exchange 2007 installation media into the DVD drive.
4. As soon as you insert the Exchange 2007 media into the DVD drive, `Setup.exe` will start automatically. If it does not, explore your DVD drive and then double-click on `E:\i386\Setup.exe`. The Exchange 2007 splash screen will appear. If you have already installed the required software of .NET Framework 2.0, .NET Framework 2.0 patch, Microsoft Management Console (MMC) 3.0, and Windows PowerShell 1.0, each link will be grayed out as shown below.

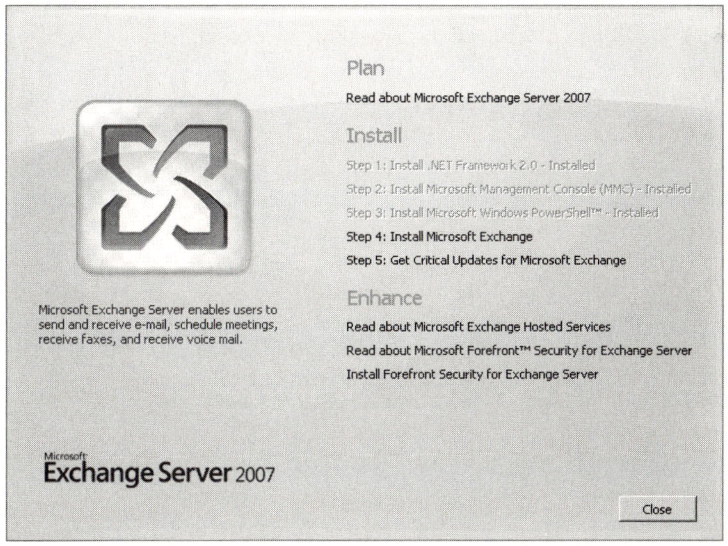

EXERCISE 7.10 *(continued)*

5. Click on Install Microsoft Exchange to begin with the Installation. Setup will copy the necessary files and begin initializing. You will see the Exchange Server 2007 Introduction page as shown below. Click Next.

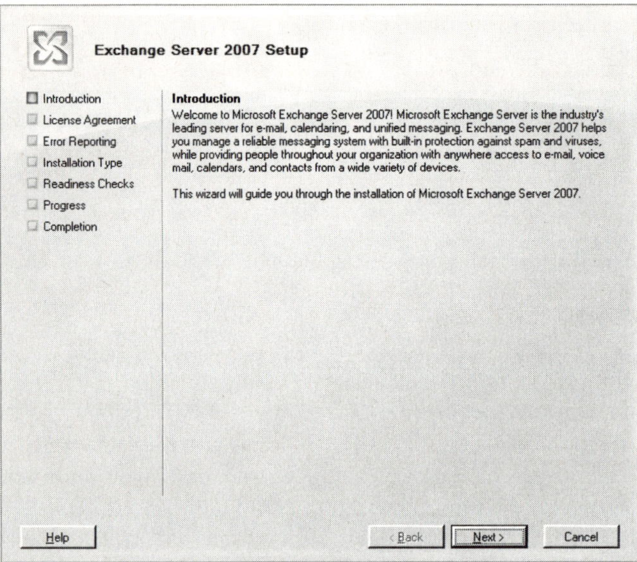

6. Read the license agreement. Click I accept the terms in the license agreement on the License Agreement page as show here, and then click Next.

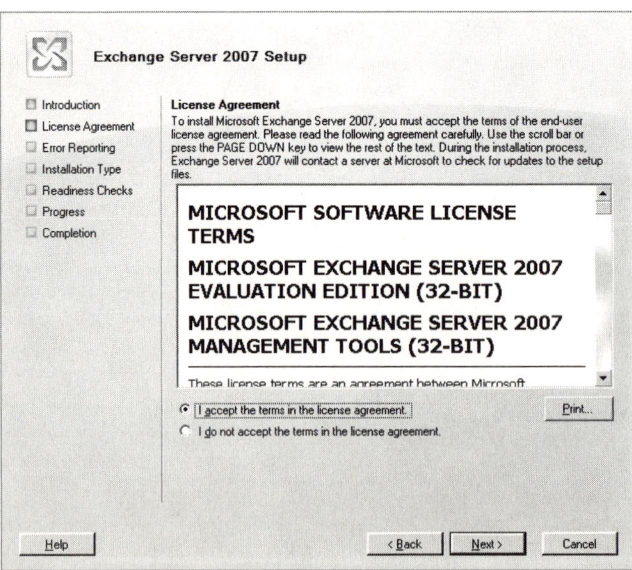

7. Choose the appropriate selection on the reporting page, then click Next.

EXERCISE 7.10 *(continued)*

8. Next, choose the type of installation. This exercise covers the Typical installation, which installs the Hub Transport, Client Access, and Mailbox server roles. (If you plan to deploy cluster Mailbox server, Unified Messaging server, or Edge Transport server roles, or perhaps one or two server roles, you should choose Custom installation instead of Typical.) On the Installation Type page, click Typical Exchange Server Installation as shown below. If you want to change the installation path, click on Browse, locate the appropriate path, and then click OK. Click Next.

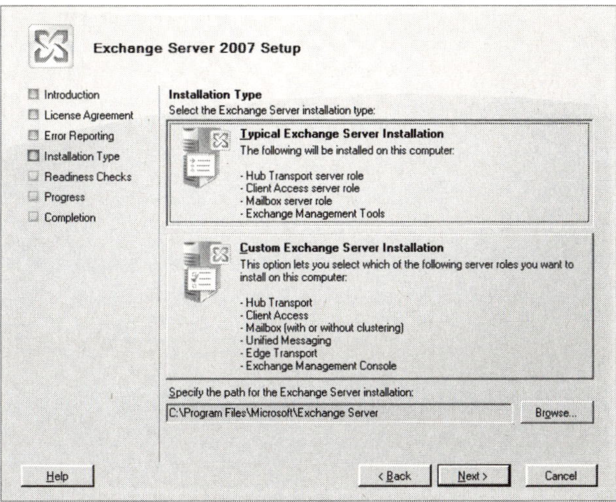

9. To establish mailflow between the Exchange 2000/2003 and the Exchange 2007 routing groups, you need to create a routing-group connector. On the Mail Flow Settings page, click Browse to locate an Exchange 2003 Bridgehead server. (In my lab environment, this is TOREX2K server.) Select an Exchange 2003 Bridgehead server to which you will create the initial routing group connector, as shown below, and then click OK. Click Next to continue.

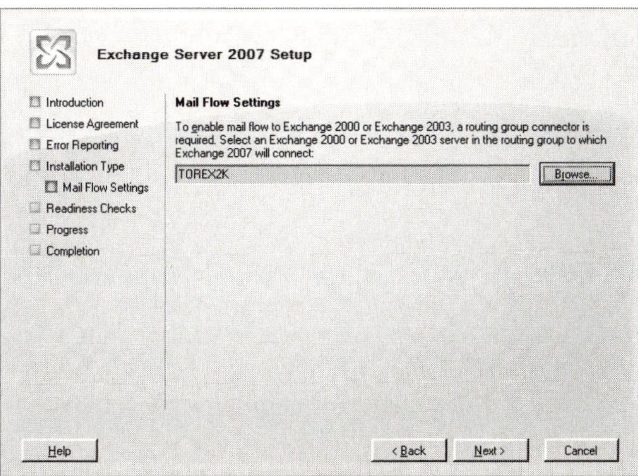

EXERCISE 7.10 *(continued)*

10. After you click Next on the Mail Flow Settings page, the Exchange 2007 Setup wizard will go through a set of prerequisite checks to ensure that you have all the necessary software, Windows components, and hotfixes installed. Click Install to begin the installation, as shown below.

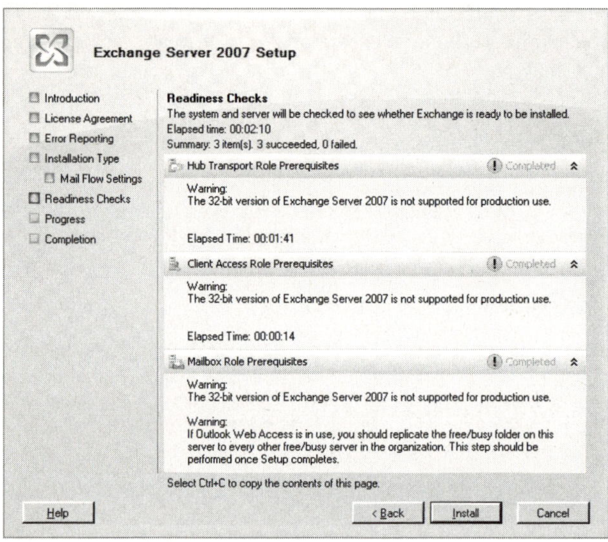

11. Setup will then prepare your organization, copy Exchange files from the source (DVD ROM) to the destination path on your hard drive, and install the server roles automatically. Click Finish, as shown below.

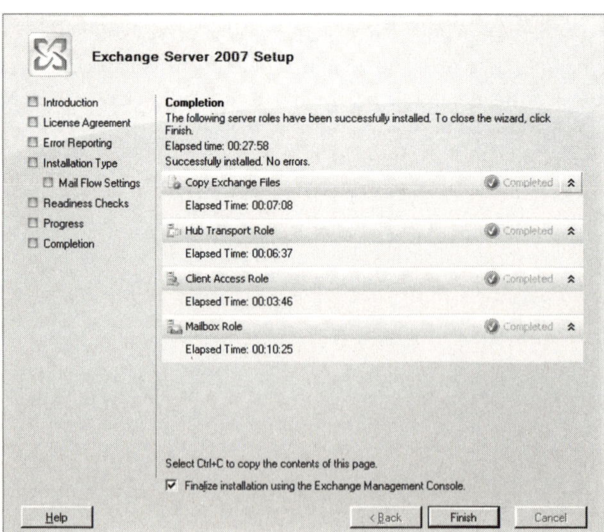

To perform an unattended installation, you can use something similar to the following syntax:

```
Setup/mode:install /roles:ClientAccess,HubTransport,Mailbox
/LegacyRoutingServer:Exch2000.yourcompany.com
```

Finalizing Your Exchange 2007 Installation

Now that you've installed Exchange 2007 let's move on to the post-installation tasks. Some of these post-installation tasks will validate the installation by verifying that it completed without any serious warnings or errors, while others will ensure that your server is operational and configured properly for your environment. If you didn't get any warnings or errors during the installation, there is a good chance that everything is in perfect shape, and then you just have to go through finalizing your deployment, which is explained in the next section.

The post-installation tasks include the following:

Exchange 2007 Services. Verify that you have Exchange 2007 services installed and started automatically.

Review the Exchange Setup log files. This involves reviewing the ExchangeSetup.log and ExchangeSetup.msilog log files located under the %systemdrive%\ExchangeSetupLogs folder to ensure that there are no errors related to Exchange 2007 installation. The ExchangeSetup.log contains all the information about the status of prerequisite and system Readiness Checks. It also contains information about every task that is performed during the Exchange Server setup and is the most important log available for troubleshooting pre- and post-installation warning and errors.

Verify Exchange folder structure. Verify the Exchange folder structure created during installation. The default folder is located at C:\Program Files\Microsoft\Exchange Server. Table 7.5 shows the default folder structure.

TABLE 7.5 Table 7.5. The Default Exchange Folder Structure

Folder	Contents
Bin	Executables that are used for management of the Exchange server
ClientAccess	Client Access Server configuration files
Logging	Log files
Mailbox	Schema files, `.dll` files, database files, and database log files for the Mailbox databases and public-folder databases

TABLE 7.5 Table 7.5. The Default Exchange Folder Structure *(continued)*

Folder	Contents
Scripts	Exchange Management Shell scripts
Setup	XML configuration files and data
TransportRoles\agents	Binary files for agents
TransportRoles\data	Data files used by the mail queue and ADAM
TransportRoles\Logs	Log files for message tracking and routing
TransportRoles\Pickup:	Message awaiting delivery to submission queues
TransportRoles\Shared	Configuration files for agents
UnifiedMessaging	Configuration and setup files for Unified Messaging and speech recognition

Review event logs. This involves examining the Windows application logs and the system logs for any warnings, information, and errors related to the Exchange Server 2007 setup and services.

Verify server roles are installed. Ensure that you can open Exchange Management Console and can see your Exchange Server 2007 servers, including the one you just installed.

Obtain the latest Exchange critical updates. Exchange Server 2007 is constantly evolving. To avoid threats, problems, and security issues, it is essential to patch your Exchange Server 2007 with the latest service packs and security patches. We recommend installing the latest patches and service pack after testing them in a lab.

Run Microsoft Exchange Best Practice Analyzer. It is a good idea to run the Exchange Best Practices Analyzer tool to configure Exchange Server 2007 according to Microsoft Exchange best practices.

Finalizing Deployment of the Exchange Server 2007 Server

Now that you've installed Exchange 2007, let's finalize the deployment. The first time you launch the Exchange Management Console, the Exchange node will be selected, and you'll find two new tabs under this node: Finalize Deployment and End-to-End Scenario. You must examine the recommended deployment tasks listed in both tabs and perform the ones that are relevant to your environment. The tasks listed in Finalize Deployment tab are important because they apply to default features that need additional configuration. Figure 7.2 shows you the Finalize Deployment tab.

The End-to-End Scenario tab provides a list of optional tasks that are relevant for your environment. Although they are optional, it's a good idea to review and complete them. Figure 7.3 shows you the End-to-End Scenario tab.

FIGURE 7.2 The Finalize Deployment tab

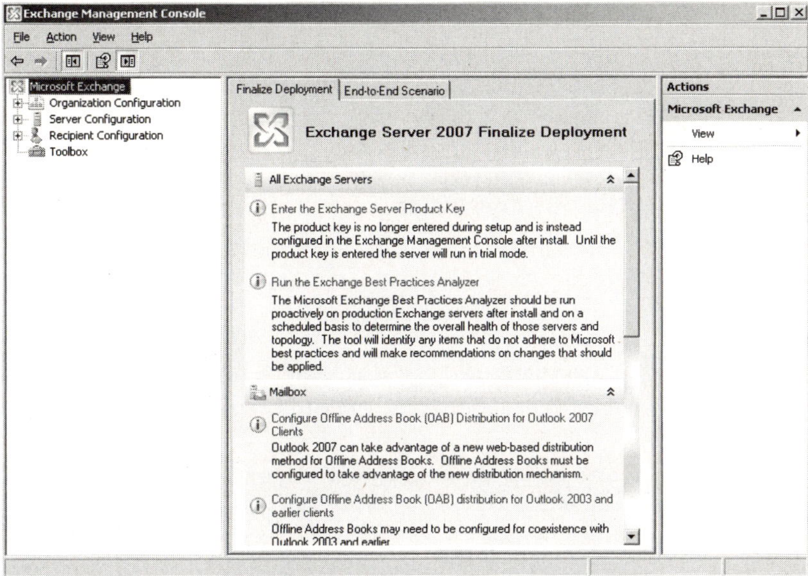

FIGURE 7.3 End-to-End Scenario tab

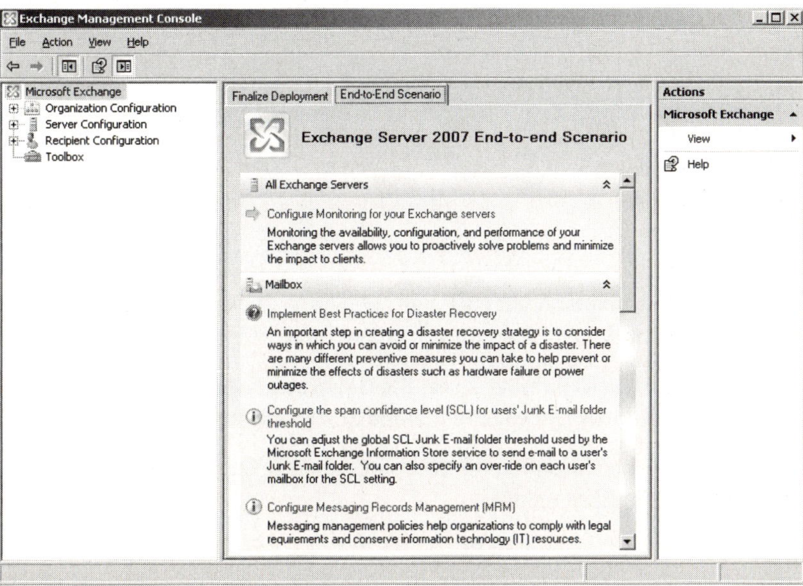

Licensing Exchange Server 2007

Exchange 2007 has a built-in grace period of 120 days, which means that you have to license your product within that grace period. The first time you launch the Exchange Management Console, you will see the warning message shown in Figure 7.4.

FIGURE 7.4 Licensing grace period warning

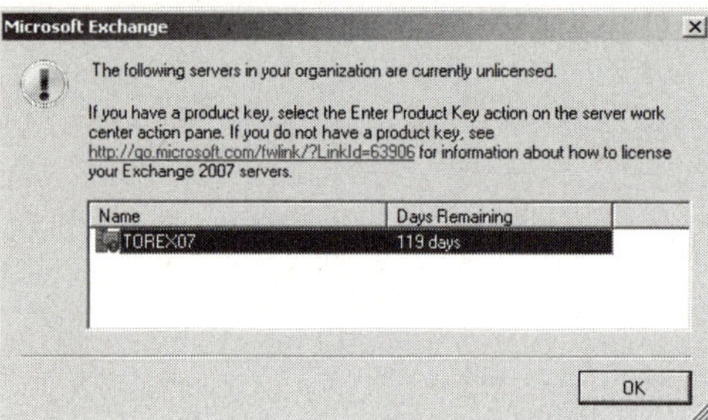

If you have a Standard or Enterprise product key ready, it is a good time to license your Exchange Server 2007. Exercise 7.11 outlines the steps to license Exchange Server 2007.

EXERCISE 7.11

Licensing Exchange Server 2007

To license the Exchange Server 2007, follow these steps:

1. Log on to Exchange Server 2007.
2. Open the Exchange Management Console, and then select the Server Configuration work center node.
3. Select the server that requires the product key.
4. In the action pane, click the Enter Product Key link.
5. In the Enter Product Key wizard, enter your Exchange 2007 product key and click Enter.
6. Click Finish.
7. To verify that your Exchange Server 2007 has been properly licensed, open the Properties page for your server by right-clicking on your server and then clicking on Properties.
8. You should see a product ID number under the General tab. If your Exchange Server 2007 is not licensed, it will show Unlicensed instead of a product ID number.

If you have licensed your Exchange Server 2007 with an Enterprise key, you cannot downgrade or convert it to a Standard edition.

To license from Exchange Management Shell, use the `Set-ExchangeServer` command: `Set-ExchangeServer -Identity Servername -ProductKey`.

Coexistence: Life After Installation

You've successfully installed and licensed Exchange 2007. Now, with Exchange Server 2007 running in an Exchange 2003 organization, you are in coexistence mode. What's next? The following sections describe the tasks you will need to perform to complete your migration, including moving mailboxes, configuring user profiles, and replicating public folders.

In the Mean Time: Administration Tips for Exchange 2003 and Exchange 2007 Coexistence

In coexistence mode, there are several considerations for performing day-to-day administration tasks. Some features are not available in Exchange 2007, which means you will need to use the Active Directory Users and Computers (ADUC) MMC snap-in and Exchange System Manager. On the other hand, there are certain features available only in Exchange 2007, which will require you to use Exchange 2007 tools. Although the transition can be confusing, you'll get the hang of it over time.

Some of the administrative tasks that you need to consider in coexistence mode are as follows:

- Do not use the Active Directory Users and Computers (ADUC) MMC snap-in to manage your Exchange 2007 recipient objects.
- Exchange Server 2007 server will inherit most of the Exchange 2003 global settings automatically because these settings (for example, Internet message formats, SMTP connectors, recipient policies, and Exchange delegation permissions) are stored in Active Directory. All users' mailboxes on the Exchange Server 2007 servers will inherit these settings.
- All organization-level settings should be managed using Exchange Management Console (EMC) or Exchange Management Shell (EMS) instead of using Exchange 2003 System Manager.
- Perform all recipient management tasks by using EMC or EMS instead of the Active Directory Users and Computers (ADUC) MMC snap-in.
- To create, manage, remove, and move Exchange 2007 mailbox-enabled users, use EMC or EMS. You also can use Exchange 2007 management tools to manage an Exchange 2003 mailbox as long as the mailbox has been created with the Exchange System Manager tool.
- To create, manage, remove, and move Exchange 2003 mailbox-enabled users, use the ADUC MMC snap-in and Exchange System Manager.
- To manage any Exchange 2003 and Exchange 2007 mail-enabled objects in a coexistence environment, you can use the ADUC MMC snap-in, EMC, or EMS. There is no restriction on managing mail-enabled objects, except for dynamic distribution groups. The dynamic distribution group uses the new Exchange 2007 OPATH format for its recipient filter and cannot be managed by using the older Exchange tools. Use EMC or EMS to maintain dynamic distribution groups.
- To manage Exchange 2003 Recipient Update Service (RUS), you have to use Exchange System Manager. This service is no longer part of the Exchange 2007 product, and therefore cannot be managed with EMC or EMS.
- To move mailboxes to Exchange Server 2007, use EMC or EMS instead of the Exchange System Manager.

Moving Mailboxes: Using the Exchange 2007 Move Mailbox Wizard and the Move-Mailbox cmdlet

The preferred method to migrate from Exchange 2000 or 2003 environments is the Move Mailbox wizard or the `Move-Mailbox` cmdlet. The Move Mailbox wizard has been around for a while, and it has been improved over the years. In Exchange 2000, the Move Mailbox wizard did not have a scheduling option and had a lot of performance issues. Exchange 2003 and later versions have excellent performance and a scheduling option that allows you to execute mailbox moves after office hours. The Move Mailbox wizard supports multithreading operations to move multiple mailboxes simultaneously and has the ability to deal with corrupt mailbox entries. If it encounters any problems, the wizard automatically attempts to move the mailbox item by item instead of all at once.

Active Directory Users and Computers cannot be used to move mailboxes from Exchange 2003 to Exchange 2007.

The Move Mailbox wizard and the `Move-Mailbox` cmdlet have many different uses, including upgrades, database moves, realignments, physical location changes, mailbox merges, load balancing, troubleshooting, forest merging, and much more. The Move Mailbox method is ideal for organizations that require new hardware and operating systems or that want to reconstruct their Exchange organization.

Using Move Mailbox is also an effective way to minimize the risk associated with a migration from an Exchange Server 2003 server to an Exchange Server 2007 server. The greatest advantage of this approach is in having the ability to build a new system with all the software, settings, third-party utilities, applications, patches, and tools before you even move mailboxes to your Exchange server.

However, there are few disadvantages and limitations associated with Move Mailbox wizard and the `Move-Mailbox` cmdlet. You cannot use the Move Mailbox wizard to move mailboxes across forests. In a multi-forest scenario, you must use the `Move-Mailbox` cmdlet instead of the wizard. Also, the Move Mailbox wizard is an *intra*-organizational migration tool that cannot be used as an *inter*-organizational migration tool. This means that you are limited to using the wizard within the same Exchange organization. You can move mailboxes between Exchange 2000, Exchange 2003, and Exchange 2007 servers by using the Move Mailbox wizard and the `Move-Mailbox` cmdlet.

The `Move-Mailbox` cmdlet can communicate only with Windows 2003 domain controllers. In a cross-forest mailbox move, if you have only a Windows 2000 domain controller, then you cannot use the `Move-Mailbox` cmdlet to move mailboxes to an Exchange 2007 forest.

Here's how the Move Mailbox process works. The Move Mailbox wizard has a built-in multithread functionality. This feature dramatically reduces the time required to move multiple mailboxes without stressing your Exchange server. The wizard can make multiple MAPI connections to the source server, read contents, and write those contents from the source mailbox to the target mailbox on the target server. As soon as it finishes the move operation, it updates the user's attributes in the Active Directory with the location of the new housed server rather than the old mailbox server.

This tool provides you with more granular control. You can either move an individual user or multiple users simultaneously. Check out the following features:

Schedule. In Exchange 2003 and later, you can schedule mailbox moves. Of course, you don't ever want to perform mailbox moves during normal working hours because of the interruptions and lost productivity. Scheduling allows you to define not only a start time but also an end time for the mailbox move. If you are moving many mailboxes and you want to define an end time because of a scheduled reboot or other jobs, you can simply define an end time and it will terminate the outstanding move operations. You can then reschedule to move the remaining mailboxes that were not moved in time.

Error control. The Move Mailbox wizard has built-in functionality to handle corrupted items during the mailbox move. If the wizard encounters corrupted items in a user's mailbox, it can do one of two things: it can be set to create a failure report without moving the mailbox, or it can skip the corrupted items, move the other items, and create a failure report at the end. The beauty of this option is that you can define the number of corrupted items to skip and set the value.

Now that you are familiar with the Move Mailbox wizard and the `Move-Mailbox` cmdlet, it's time to move mailboxes from the existing Exchange servers to the Exchange 2007 environment. In fact, the migration is as simple as selecting the mailbox or mailboxes, and then selecting the new destination server and database. Exercise 7.12 outlines the steps for moving mailboxes with the Move Mailbox wizard.

EXERCISE 7.12

Moving Mailboxes Using the Move Mailbox Wizard

To move mailboxes to the Exchange Server 2007, do the following:

1. Log on to your Exchange Server 2007.
2. Open the Exchange Management Console, and then select the Recipient Configuration.
3. Click on Mailbox container. You will see a list of mailboxes. In the details column, you will see mailboxes flagged as either Legacy Mailbox or as Mailbox User. Mailboxes flagged as Legacy are still on Exchange Server 2003 and need to be migrated to Exchange Server 2007. Mailboxes already on Exchange Server 2007 are shown as Mailbox User.
4. To select the specific mailboxes that you want to move, you can click on a mailbox, hold down the Shift key and select a group of mailboxes, or hold down the Control key and click on the specific mailboxes that you want to migrate.
5. Click on Move Mailbox action in the right column.

EXERCISE 7.12 *(continued)*

6. Choose the server, storage group, and the Mailbox database to which you want to move the mailbox(es), as show below. Click Next to continue.

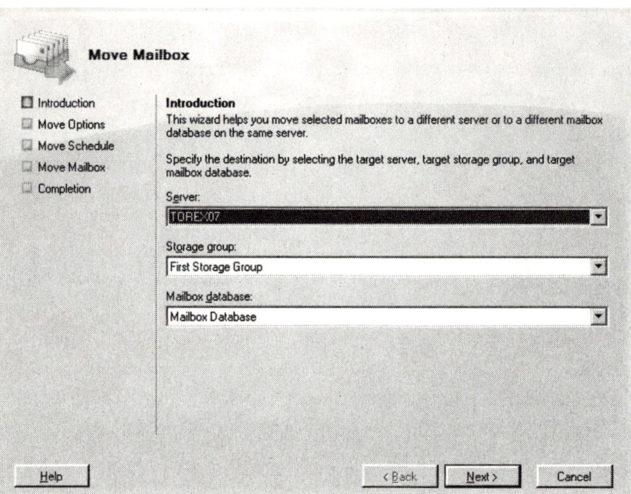

7. At the Move Options screen, shown below, you can adjust the settings to specify how you want to manage corrupted messages in a mailbox during the move. You can choose Skip the Mailbox or Skip the Corrupted Messages if corrupted messages are found during the move process. Usually, we choose to skip the corrupt messages if we want to complete the migration. However, in some scenarios you may want to further troubleshoot the problem and, therefore, you may want to choose Skip the Mailbox. If you decide to skip the corrupted messages, you can also define the number of corrupted items to skip and set the value. Click Next to continue.

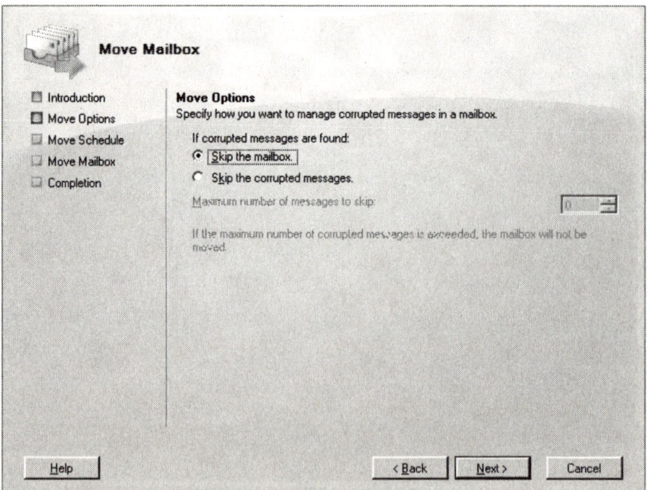

EXERCISE 7.12 *(continued)*

8. At the next screen, Move Schedule, you can choose to move the mailboxes immediately or choose a different time when the users are not on the network. Click Next to continue.

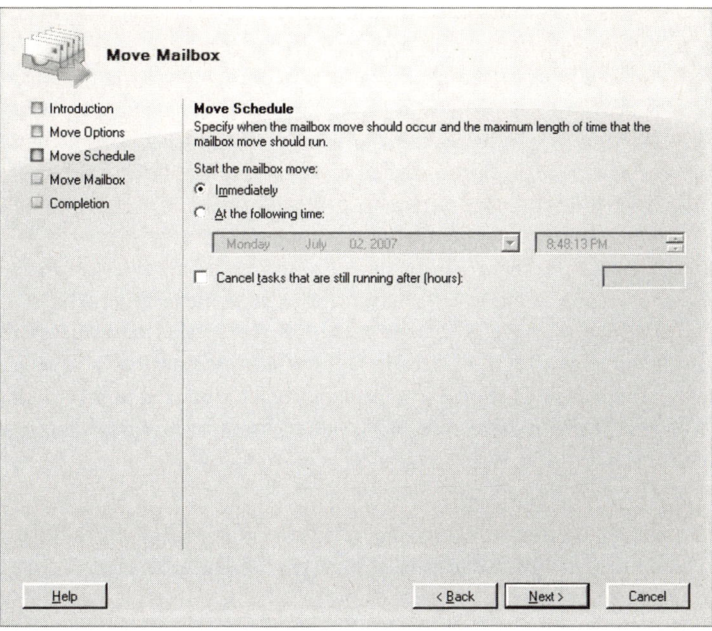

9. At the Summary screen, review the choices you have made. To make any changes, you can click Back. Otherwise, click Move to begin moving the mailboxes.

10. Once you click Move, the actual move time depends on several factors, including bandwidth and speed of your network, amount of data to be moved, location of Exchange servers, and LAN card duplex mode. This is something that should be thoroughly tested in the lab. After the Move Mailbox wizard opens the source, opens the destination, and successfully moves the selected mailboxes, a summary screen of the completed actions appears. Click Finish.

You can perform the same operation using the `Move-Mailbox` cmdlet with the following syntax: `move-mailbox -Identity mcitp-user1 -TargetDatabase 'CN=Mailbox Database,CN=First StorageGroup,CN=InformationStore,CN=TOREX07,CN=Servers,CN=Exchange Administrative Group (FYDIBOHF23SPDLT),CN=Administrative Groups,CN=MCITP,CN=Microsoft Exchange,CN=Services,CN=Configuration,DC=MCITP,DC=COM'`

Configuring User Profiles

After you successfully move mailboxes from Exchange Server 2003 to Exchange Server 2007, the next step is to update the Outlook profile for each user so that users can log on to the relocated mailboxes. There are different ways to update Outlook profiles. You can do it either manually (which requires lot of resources and administrative efforts) or by using third-party utilities (which requires additional software components, software, and licenses). Depending on your environment, keep running your Exchange 2003 servers for few weeks, if possible. This will help your Outlook clients update their profiles automatically without using any utilities.

In Outlook 97, 2000, 2003, and XP, the Outlook profile on each user's system is pointed to the old Exchange Server 2003. If you decide to keep running your Exchange 2003 servers for few weeks, the next time the user opens his Outlook client, the Exchange Server 2003 server will automatically update the profile with the new Exchange Server 2007 information. If you immediately remove the server or decommission the old server, you have to update the profile manually or by using some third-party utilities to achieve this task.

Continuing to run the Exchange 2003 server for few weeks will allow users an opportunity to open the Outlook client so that their profile will update automatically. If some users are out of the office or vacation, their Outlook profile will not be updated and will still point to the Exchange 2003 server. In those cases, you will need to update their profile manually or using third-party utilities.

Here is a general explanation of this process:

1. The user accesses the mailbox by opening his Outlook client. Because the profile contains the information for the old Exchange 2003 server, the Outlook client connects the user to that server.
2. The Exchange Server 2003 server updates the client that the mailbox is now located on the Exchange Server 2007 server.
3. The client updates the Exchange Server 2007 entry in the client's registry. Once this update occurs, it does not need to be repeated.
4. The client sends requests to the Exchange Server 2007.
5. Subsequent logons from that client go directly to the Exchange Server 2007 as the client has new server information.

To update the default Outlook profile to reflect the new server information, you must run `Exprofre.exe` on each client computer. Please keep in mind that this tool is not a manual update. It is just another method to update the Outlook Profile by using the Exchange utilities. This tool collects the information from both the Active Directory and the existing default Outlook profile to determine the name of the server where the user's mailbox is being hosted. It then backs up the existing Outlook profile, modifies it with the new Exchange Server 2007 information, and updates the client registry settings to reflect the changes. If there are any problems, users can simply restore the old profile. To help you troubleshoot problems during the profile update process, the tool generates log file, which can be used to trace any particular step.

`Exprofre.exe` is a command line tool used to update Outlook profiles after you move mailboxes from Exchange Server 2003 to Exchange Server 2007 or across your Exchange organizations.

`Exprofre.exe` is compatible only with Windows Server 2003, Windows Server 2000, and Windows XP. It does not run on Windows NT 4.0 or any 9X operating systems.

We recommend running this tool via login script before the user opens his mailbox. If the user is already running Outlook, the program will warn you that Outlook needs to be closed before you execute this tool.

Replicating Public Folders from Exchange 2003 to Exchange 2007

This section focuses on migrating public folders, which need to be replicated before decommissioning the old Exchange 2003 or 2000 servers.

Microsoft has introduced many different utilities and tools to migrate from Exchange 2003 or 2000 environments to the Exchange 2007 environment. In this section, we will use the PFMigrate utility to create public and system folder replicas on Exchange 2007, and then remove them from an Exchange 2003 or Exchange 2000 server.

Exercise 7.13 outlines the steps to move public folders using the PFMigrate utility.

EXERCISE 7.13

Moving Public Folders Using the PFMigrate Utility

Use the following steps to move public folders to Exchange 2007:

1. Log on to the server on which you want to run this command.
2. Insert the Exchange Server 2003 CD into the CD-ROM drive.
3. Click Start ➢ Run, then type **cmd.exe.** Press Enter or click OK.
4. Type **cd `E:\support\Exdeploy`** and then press Enter.
5. Type **pfmigrate.wsf /S:Exchange2003server /T:Exchange2007server /R /F:c:\pflog.log** to create a report of public-folder replication between the Exchange 2003 and Exchange 2007 servers.
6. Type **pfmigrate.wsf /S:Exchange2003server /T:Exchange2007server /SF /A /F:c:\pflog.log** to replicate system folders from Exchange 2003 to Exchange 2007.
7. Type **pfmigrate.wsf /S:Exchange2003server /T:Exchange2007server /A /F:c:\pflog.log** to replicate public folders from Exchange 2003 to Exchange 2007.
8. After all public folders have replicated, type **pfmigrate.wsf /S:Exchange2003server /T:Exchange2007server /D** to remove the old replicas from the Exchange Server 2003 server.
9. Open the `pflog.log` file to ensure that replication has occurred successfully and that a copy of each public folder exists on the new server.

Migrating from Third-Party Messaging Systems

In previous sections we discussed migration strategies and procedures to migrate from a legacy environment to Exchange 2007. This section focuses on migration from third-party messaging systems (or simply "non-Exchange environments") to the Exchange 2007 environment. These migrations generally require some transition system, a third-party product, and connector to migrate user emails, calendar information, address book, contacts, and other data to the Exchange 2007 environment. These types of migrations can be challenging. In nearly every migration, you may need to run both environments in parallel for a long time. The process to migrate from a non-Exchange environment to Exchange 2007 involves installing Exchange 2007 and then migrating mailboxes, user data, and other information to Exchange 2007.

Migration from SendMail, Qmail, and GroupWise to Exchange 2007 is outside the scope of the exam and the scope of this book. This section provides an overview of the process of analyzing, planning, and migrating from Lotus Notes to Exchange 2007. We will discuss tools, utilities, scenarios, methodologies, procedures, and processes related to Lotus Notes migration.

As you know, many companies are making the decision to migrate to Microsoft platforms. Many Lotus Notes/Domino customers have wanted to migrate to Microsoft Exchange, but delayed the change because of the lack of tools, support, documentation, and experience. Recently, Microsoft has introduced Microsoft Transporter Suite for Lotus Domino to help customers transition from Notes to Microsoft's unified communications and collaboration platforms that are part of Microsoft Exchange Server 2007, Microsoft Office 2007 system, and Microsoft Office SharePoint Server 2007 technologies. When planning a migration from Notes, you will need to consider several factors, including the Domino Directory, messaging, and applications, as shown in Figure 7.5.

FIGURE 7.5 Notes and Microsoft coexistence and migration

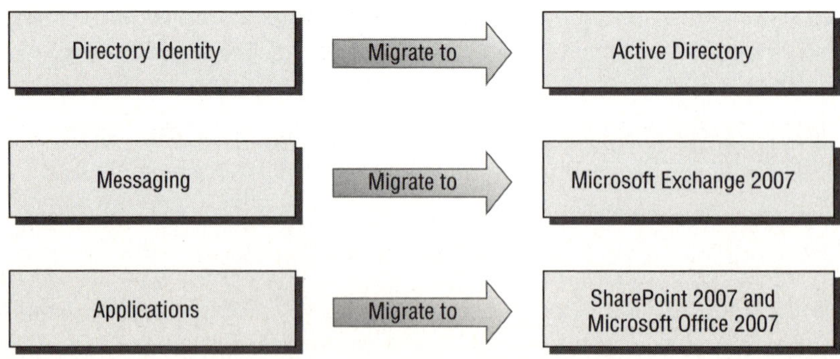

The Transporter Suite for Lotus Domino 2007 is designed for interoperability, coexistence, directory synchronization, and migration from Notes to Active Directory and Exchange Server 2007. There are many new features in this tool as compared to Transporter Suite for Lotus Domino 2007 as compared to previous versions of Transporter Suite for Lotus Domino, which include the PowerShell foundation, ACL migrations, user migrations, scripting, multi-threading, and more. These features are intended to help you when you're migrating accounts, mailboxes, and applications and doing analysis. The Transporter Suite consists of the following components:

Directory Connector. This component synchronizes objects between the Domino Directory and Active Directory. It is similar to Microsoft Connector for Lotus Notes used for in Exchange 2003, which was used to transfer messages between the two messaging systems and to provide directory synchronization in both directions.

Free/Busy Connector. Like its name suggests, this allows users to see calendar free/busy information across the two messaging environments.

Directory Migration. This component performs the directory migration between the two systems, and it creates user accounts in Active Directory for the Domino Directory users.

Mailbox Migration. This component performs the migration of user data from Domino mail databases to Exchange 2007 mailboxes.

Application Migration. The component allows for the migration of Domino applications to Microsoft SharePoint.

To provide a familiar interface for Exchange system administrators, Transporter Suite is equipped with the Transporter Management Console, which is very similar to Exchange Management Console. It also comes with Transporter Command Shell, which is similar to Exchange Management Shell, so that administrators can take an advantage of scripting. Additionally, the Transporter Suite allows you to do the following:

- Analyze the Domino application infrastructure
- Plan, prepare, and synchronize the messaging system (i.e., Domino 6.x/7.x Domino Directory) with Active Directory and Microsoft Exchange
- Coordinate directory coexistence by using Directory Connector for Lotus Domino.
- Coordinate messaging coexistence between Domino 6.x/7.x and Microsoft Exchange 2007 by using native SMTP mail routing (SMTP provides scalability and no additional tools to install, monitor, manage, and troubleshoot. Exchange 2007 no longer needs a "Notes Connector" because it uses SMTP to transfer mail to/from Domino.)
- Synchronize address books
- Migrate mailboxes to Exchange 2007
- Move applications to SharePoint 2007

If you have Domino 6.x/7.x, you can use the Transporter Suite for Lotus Domino to migrate to Exchange 2007; however, if you have Domino 5.x, your options are limited to the following:

Option 1: Upgrade your Domino 5.x environment to Domino 6.x /7.x and then use the Transporter Suite to migrate to Exchange 2007.

Option 2: Use third-party tools such as Quest Notes Migrator for Exchange. Quest Migrator allows you to do the following:

- Convert users' mail, calendars, tasks, and personal address books and stores them in users' new mailboxes on the Exchange Server 2007.
- Utilize its reporting system, which gives you up-to-the-minute status on migration progress.
- Schedule activities to minimize impacts on your organization and to avoid down time.
- Migrate multiple users from multiple servers simultaneously to speed up the entire migration process

Option 3: Install Exchange 2003 in a single-server organization, and then install Microsoft Exchange 2007 in the same organization. While in the mixed mode, you can install the Microsoft Connector for Lotus Notes on Exchange Server 2003 to allow coexistence between Lotus Notes and Microsoft Exchange, and then you can use the Mailbox Move wizard to move the mailboxes from Lotus Notes to Exchange 2007 instead of Exchange 2003. Once you finish moving the mailboxes, you can then decommission the Exchange Server 2003 and the Domino server.

Migration from Notes involves detailed planning, testing, and proof of concept. It is common to find that many businesses have applications data in their Notes environment. In addition to migrating the mailboxes, you must migrate the application data to SharePoint 2007.

Migrating application data to SharePoint is out of the scope of the exam, and is not covered this book.

To migrate from Lotus Notes/Domino to Microsoft Exchange 2007, Microsoft recommends that you plan your project in four phases:

Directory integration. This phase synchronizes user name and email address information between Active Directory and the Domino Directory.

Free/busy lookups. This phase configures free/busy services between Active Directory and the Domino Directory.

Mail migration. This phase involves moving users' mail database data from Lotus Domino to the Exchange server.

Application migration. This phase involves moving applications from Lotus Domino to Microsoft SharePoint.

Email migration projects pose lot of challenges and, if not done properly, can result in numerous pre- and post-migration issues. Preparation is essential for email migration. Make sure that you read the online documentation about Transporter Suite for Lotus Domino 2007 (found at `http://technet.microsoft.com/en-us/interopmigration/bb403105.aspx`) and understand the ins and outs of this tool because it has some built-in limitations, such as version support. As stated before, this tool can support only Lotus Domino 6.x and 7.x for interoperability. If you are using Lotus Domino 5.x, you may have to use third-party tools or use an intermediary Exchange 2003 messaging system to migrate from Domino to Exchange 2007. At the time of writing, this tool is not supported on Windows Vista.

A common migration path would include the following steps:

1. Installing the Notes client and Transporter Suite for Lotus Domino 2007.
2. Establishing messaging connectivity between the two messaging systems.
3. Establishing directory synchronization to share the address books between the users in both messaging systems.
4. Configuring free/busy lookups so that users in both messaging environments will be able to see users' availability on the other system.
5. Migrating users and data from Notes to Active Directory, so that the Domino users' email addresses are represented in the Exchange Global Address List (GAL). Once you migrate users from Notes, you can then move the users' mailbox items from Notes to Exchange 2007.
6. Using Microsoft Application Analyzer for Lotus Domino to start the process of analyzing Domino applications and then migrating applications. After initial assessment and testing, you can then migrate to existing Microsoft SharePoint or off-the-shelf applications.
7. Decommissioning Domino servers.

The next section covers the initial seven phases of migration. Migrating application data to SharePoint is out of the scope of the exam and is not covered in this book. The steps that are included here provide high-level steps that are involved in a migration. The migration process that follows here is not a single way to migrate, but merely demonstrates several steps to migrate to an Exchange environment. Before migrating to Exchange 2007 in your environment, you should go through all of these steps to make sure that you fully understand the migration process and are ready for transition.

Step 1: Installing the Notes Client and Transporter Suite for Lotus Domino 2007

The first step in the process is to install the Notes Client and Transporter Suite onto the Exchange 2007. The following section gives step-by-step instructions to perform the installation. Make sure that you have Microsoft Management Console 3.0 and Windows PowerShell 1.0 installed before you install and configure a workstation with Lotus Notes 6.x or 7.x client to access the Domino domain. Also, Exchange Management Console 2007 is required for user and/or mail migrations.

Exercise 7.14 outlines the instructions to install the Notes 7.x client.

EXERCISE 7.14

Installing the Lotus Notes 7.x Client

Use the following steps to install the Notes 7.x client:

1. Log on to the server on which you want to run this command.

EXERCISE 7.14 *(continued)*

2. Insert the Lotus Notes 7.x client CD, and the installer should automatically load the Installation wizard. If it doesn't automatically load, navigate to the My Computer icon, double-click the Notes CD icon, and run the Setup program to begin the installation. At the Welcome screen, click Next to continue.
3. On the License Agreement screen, read the license agreement, and then click on I accept the terms in the license agreement. Click Next to continue.
4. Type your name and organization name. Click Next to continue.
5. Select the default destination folders as per your organization's best practices. This is an important screen, because you'll want to choose not only where the program is installed, but also where all your Notes data will go. The default location is acceptable for most of the organizations; however, you may have practices defined in your organization to install program software on separate partitions. Once you choose the destination folder, click Next to continue.
6. Accept the default features, and click Next to continue.
7. You have the option of making Notes your default email program. Make sure that the box Make Notes My Default Email Program is unchecked if you use multiple programs on your system. Click Install to begin the installation.
8. When the installation is complete, click Finish.

Once you install the Notes client, you have to configure it to connect with the Domino server. The steps may vary according to your configuration. Please check the Domino documentation to configure the Notes client. Once you configure the Notes client, the next step is to install the Transporter Suite for Lotus Domino 2007—Exercise 7.15 outlines the instructions.

EXERCISE 7.15

Installing the Transporter Suite for Lotus Domino 2007

Follow these steps to install the Transporter Suite:

1. Download the Transporter Suite from the Microsoft website. Note that there are two versions of the file, namely `transporter.msi` for 64-bit systems and `transporter32.msi` for 32-bit systems.
2. Log on to the server where you want to install the Transporter Suite for Lotus Domino. On Exchange 2007, run the relevant MSI installer to begin the installation. At the Welcome screen, click Next to continue.

EXERCISE 7.15 *(continued)*

3. On the License Agreement screen, read the license agreement, and then click on I accept the terms in the license agreement. Click Next to continue.

4. At the Select Components and Install Location screen, ensure that the Microsoft Transporter Tools option is selected, but that the Free/Busy Connector Add-In Task for Lotus Domino is not selected. Click Next to continue. (Note: If required, change the default installation location. The default location is C:\Program Files\Microsoft Transporter Tools.)

5. Click Install to begin installation.

6. When installation is complete, click Finish.

Step 2: Establishing Messaging Connectivity

The second step in the process is to establish messaging connectivity between the two messaging systems. In Exchange 2007, you can use SMTP to establish the messaging connectivity and route emails between the two messaging systems rather than the traditional method of routing messages across the Microsoft Connector for Lotus Notes. SMTP is a great message transporter in a heterogeneous environment. Major software and service vendors support SMTP.

Exercise 7.16 outlines the instructions to establish message connectivity between the two environments.

EXERCISE 7.16

Establishing Messaging Connectivity

Follow these steps to define the remote domain:

1. Log on to Exchange Server 2007.

2. Open the Exchange Management Console and then select the Organization Configuration work center node.

3. Expand the Organization node in the left-hand pane.

4. Click on Hub Transport server.

5. In the Action pane, select New Remote Domain.

6. Type in the remote domain information in the Name field (for example, **Domino_Mail**) and Domain Name field (for example, **mcitp.com**). To include all subdomains, click on Include all subdomains, and then click New to create New Remote Domain.

7. Click Finish to close the New Remote Domain wizard.

EXERCISE 7.16 *(continued)*

8. Right-click on Domino_Mail, and then click on properties.
9. Click on the Message Format tab, and then change the settings of Exchange rich-text format from Determined by Individual User Settings to Never Use.
10. Click Apply, and then click OK to continue.

To create send and receive connectors, do the following:

11. Open the Exchange Management Console, and then select the Organization Configuration work center node.
12. Expand the Organization node in the left-hand pane.
13. Click on the Hub Transport server.
14. Click on the Send Connectors tab to create a send connector between the two messaging systems.
15. In the Action pane, select New Send Connector.
16. Type in the name (for example, **Domino_Outbound**) in the name field for New STMP Send Connector. Click Next to continue.
17. Click Add to add the address space.
18. Type in the domain name in the Domain field (for example, **domino.mcitp.com**), and then click OK. Click Next to continue.
19. Under Network Settings, select Use Domain Name System (DNS) MX Records to route mail automatically. Click Next to continue.
20. Under Source Server, ensure that the appropriate Hub Transport server is selected or click Add to add an appropriate Hub Transport server. Click Next to continue.
21. Click New to create the connector, and then click Finish to complete and close the wizard.
22. Expand the Server Configuration node in the left-hand pane.
23. Click on the Hub Transport server.
24. In the Action pane, select New Receive Connector.
25. Type in the name (for example, **Domino_Inbound**) in the name field for New STMP Receive Connector. Click Next to continue.
26. To add an IP address for the Domino Server, click on Add in the Local Network Settings. Click on Specify an IP address, and type in the IP address of the Domino Server. Click OK to continue. To ensure that the SMTP receive connector will not receive any email from other IP addresses, click on All Available under the Local IP address(es), and then click Remove to remove other IP addresses.

EXERCISE 7.16 *(continued)*

27. Type in the FQDN of the Exchange Server in Specify the FQDN This Connector Will Provide in Response to HELO or EHLO. Click Next to continue.
28. Leave the default settings as they are in Remote Network settings. Click Next.
29. Click New to create the receive connector.
30. Click Finish to close the wizard.

Do the following to assign permissions on the receive connector:

31. Under the Server Configuration node in the left-hand pane, click on the Hub Transport server.
32. Right-click on Domino_Inbound connector, and then click on Properties.
33. Click on the Permission Groups tab.
34. Click on Anonymous users and Exchange Servers.
35. Click on Apply, and then click OK to continue.

Step 3: Establishing Directory Synchronization

The third step in the process is to establish directory synchronization. This step ensures that both organizations have consistent Global Address Lists (GALs), which means that users in both organizations can see every other user from within the Exchange organization and Domino messaging environment. It is important to understand that users will be synchronized into Active Directory as mail-enabled contacts, not as the mail-enabled users. During synchronization, you can create a specific organizational unit (OU) to keep the Domino contacts. You also can choose to use a built-in OU, such as Domino Users. Similarly, your Exchange recipients will be synchronized into the Domino system in the default NAMES.NSF directory. Depending on your environment, you also can configure whether or not your Exchange recipients are synchronized into Domino.

Exercise 7.17 outlines the instructions to create the Directory Connector to establish directory synchronization between the two messaging environments.

EXERCISE 7.17

Creating the Directory Connector

1. Log on to the server on which you want to run this command.
2. Click Start ➢ All Programs ➢ Microsoft Transporter Suite for Domino, and then click on Transporter Management Console.
3. Click the Connect option from the console tree.

EXERCISE 7.17 *(continued)*

4. Right-click on the Connect option and choose Create Directory Connector from the context menu, or choose the same-named option from the Action pane.
5. Click Next on the introduction screen.
6. Click Create to create the connector.
7. Click Finish to exit the wizard.

Once you create the Directory Connector, you are ready to configure the connector for directory synchronization. Exercise 7.18 demonstrates the process to configure the directory synchronization between the two messaging systems.

EXERCISE 7.18

Establishing Directory Synchronization

1. Log on to the server on which you want to run this command.
2. Click Start ➤ All Programs ➤ Microsoft Transporter Suite for Domino, and then click on Transporter Management Console.
3. Right-click on the Directory Connector, and choose Properties from the context menu.
4. Click on the General tab to define the synchronization schedule, global catalog server, and the Domino server. The settings in the General tab are as follows:

   Sync Schedule: Sync Schedule has predefined options ranging from 15 minutes to 24 hours. The drop-down selection box allows you to choose the Never option in addition to other options.

   Global Catalog: Global catalog server settings allow you to choose the global catalog server that will be used to perform the directory synchronization. Click the Browse button and choose the relevant global catalog server.

   Domino Server: Domino server settings allow you to choose the Domino server that you wish to connect to for directory synchronization purposes.

5. Click on the Sync to Active Directory tab, which controls the Domino directories that are synchronized into Exchange. The settings in the Sync to Active Directory tab are as follows:

   Source Domino Directory: This field allows you to define the source Domino Directory. To configure Source Domino Directory, you need to define Domino Directory, domain name field, and SMTP domain name.

EXERCISE 7.18 *(continued)*

Target Active Directory: This field allows you to choose the target OU in Active Directory that will be used to store Domino users as the mail-enabled contacts. Either choose the built-in OU or choose the OU specifically created for Domino users.

6. Click on the Sync to Domino tab, which controls the Active Directory OUs that will be synchronized with Domino. The settings in the Sync to Domino tab are as follows:

   Source Organizational Units: This field allows you to choose the Active Directory OUs that contain the recipients that you wish to synchronize with Domino. You can add multiple OUs by clicking the Add button and then browsing to the relevant OU.

   Target Domino Directory File Name: This field allows you to select the name of the Domino Directory that will receive the Exchange recipient information.

   Routable Exchange Domains: This field allows you to configure the SMTP domain name of Exchange organization as a routable Exchange domain. If your Exchange organization has additional domains, you can add them by clicking the Add button and entering the relevant SMTP domain name into the field in the Add Routable Exchange Domain Entry window.

7. Click on the Advanced tab, which allows you to synchronize groups and contacts. You also can define exceptions to specify groups that you do not want to synchronize into Active Directory.

8. Exit the wizard.

Once you finish the Directory Connector configuration, you must start the service before any synchronization can take place. By default, the Microsoft Exchange Directory Connector Service for Lotus Domino service parameter is set to Manual. Change it to Automatic; otherwise synchronization between the two directories won't work. Once you start the service, you can either wait for the synchronization process to run according to your configured schedule or you can begin the synchronization process immediately by right-clicking the Directory Connector and selecting the Synchronize Now option from the context menu.

Once the synchronization is finished, check the Active Directory OUs and Domino Directory to ensure the contacts and recipients have been replicated successfully between the two directories.

Step 4: Configuring the Free/Busy Connector

The fourth step in the process is configuring the free/busy connector. This is very important as the Directory Connector is limited to synchronizing the recipient and contact information, and it doesn't allow sharing the calendar information across the two messaging environments. The free/busy connector allows users to query free/busy information across both messaging environments.

Key things to remember about the free/busy connector are as follows:

- You must run `Excalcon.exe`, a separate process of Transporter Suite for Lotus Domino 2007, to make free/busy requests work on Domino server.
- Create a foreign domain document in Domino for free/busy information.
- Start the Domino server as a service instead of an application.

Exercise 7.19 outlines the instructions to accomplish all of these tasks.

EXERCISE 7.19

Configuring the Free/Busy Connector

Use the following steps to install `Excalcon.exe`:

1. Log on to the server on which you want to install this component of Transporter Suite.
2. Run the relevant MSI installer to begin the installation. At the Welcome screen, click Next to continue.
3. On the License Agreement screen, read the license agreement, and then click on I Accept the Terms in the License Agreement. Click Next to continue.
4. At the Select Components and Install Location screen, ensure that the Free/Busy Connector Add-In Task for Lotus Domino is selected, but that the Microsoft Transporter Tools option is not selected. Click Next to continue.
5. Click Install.
6. Once the installation is complete, click Finish.
7. Click Start ➢ Run, and then type **notepad.exe**. Press Enter or click OK.
8. Navigate to the C:\Program Files\Lotus\Domino folder, and then open the `notes.ini` file, and modify the `ServerTasks=` line to include the `Excalcon.exe` process. The additional text required to make to the `notes.ini` file is in the following format: `Excalcon <Exchange server FQDN> <Foreign Domain Name>`.
9. Click on the File menu, save, and exit.
10. Once `notes.ini` has been modified and saved, you can restart the Domino server application to invoke the `Excalcon.exe` process. You also can invoke the `Excalcon.exe` process by entering the following command at the Domino server console: **`load excalcon <Exchange server FQDN> <Foreign Domain Name>`**

Complete the following steps to create a foreign domain document:

11. Log on to the server where you want to create the foreign domain document.

EXERCISE 7.19 *(continued)*

12. Open the Domino Administrator program.
13. Click on the Configuration tab.
14. Expand the Messaging node in the left-hand pane.
15. From the list of options presented under Messaging node, select Domains.
16. Click the Add Domain button. The New Domain window will appear.
17. The Basics tab should now be selected by default. Make sure that the basic information is set as follows:

    Domain type: Foreign Domain

    Foreign domain name: Exchange (Note: If you set the foreign domain name to something else, then you have to alter the Directory Connector configuration by running the `Set-DominoDirectoryConnector` cmdlet.)

    Description: Exchange Server 2007

18. Click the Mail Information tab. Make sure that the basic information is set as follows:

    Gateway server name: Type in the name of the Domino server running `Excalcon.exe`.

    Gateway mail file name: Enter **mail.box**.

19. Click the Calendar Information tab. Make sure that the calendar information is set as follows:

    Calendar server name: Type in the name of the Domino server running `Excalcon.exe`.

    Calendar system: Type in the name of the Exchange calendar system. We recommend using **ExchFreeBusy**.

20. Click the Save & Close button to complete the foreign domain creation process, and to save changes and close the window.

To start Domino Server as a service (it must be started as a service and not as an application for free/busy connector and lookups to work), make sure you set Start Domino as a Windows Service and set the option to Always Start Domino as a Service at system startup.

Step 5: Establishing Directory Synchronization

The fifth step in the process is to migrate mailboxes and data from Notes to Exchange 2007. Exercise 7.20 outlines steps to complete this task.

EXERCISE 7.20

Migrating Domino Users

To migrate users from Domino to Exchange Server 2007, complete these steps:

1. Log on to Exchange Server 2007.
2. Open the Transporter Management Console.
3. Expand the Migrate node in the left-hand pane, and then select Directory.
4. In the Action pane, click on Enter Domino Credential. Type in the password, and then click OK.
5. Select multiple users, and then select Migrate Selected Users in the Action pane.
6. In the Domino User Migration wizard, you will see the Welcome screen. Click Next to continue.
7. Choose an appropriate Active Directory container for new accounts. Type in the initial password, and make sure Reset Password on Next Logon is not selected. Click Next to continue.
8. Click on the Create Mailbox check box, and then select the target database.
9. Click Next to continue. Review the configuration summary and then click Migrate.
10. Click Finish.

To migrate mailboxes from Domino to Exchange Server 2007, do the following:

11. Log on to your Exchange Server 2007 server.
12. Open the Transporter Management Console.
13. Expand the Migrate node in the left-hand pane, and then select Mailboxes.
14. Select User, and then select Migrate Selected Mailbox in the Action pane.
15. In the Domino Mailbox Migration wizard, you will see the Introduction screen. Click Next to continue.
16. Choose an appropriate Target Exchange Mailbox database. Click Next to continue.
17. Review the configuration summary and then click Migrate.
18. Click Finish.

Step 6: Application Migration

The sixth step in the process is to analyze application on the Notes environment and then migrate them to Microsoft SharePoint. Further details about assessing those applications and testing and migrating them to SharePoint are out of the scope of the exam and therefore not covered in this book.

Step 7: Decommissioning Domino Servers

The seventh step in the process is to decommission Domino mail servers. Make sure that you have migrated applications from the Domino server to Microsoft technologies. The general guidelines to achieve this are as follows:

1. Verify messaging functionality by sending test messages to migrated users.
2. Send test messages to and from the Internet to migrated users.
3. Migrate all the applications to Microsoft technologies.
4. Verify that all outbound and inbound messages are routed properly between all sites by sending test messages to users.
5. Back up Domino servers.
6. Turn off Domino servers and do testing. Make sure you don't receive any complaints, and there are no issues. Leave the server off for a while before taking more steps to clean up the environment.
7. Uninstall the Domino server.

Decommissioning the Old Infrastructure

This section focuses on removing the last Exchange Server 2003 server from your Exchange organization. Once the last migration phase is complete, the source messaging system may be decommissioned. Decommissioning the Exchange Server 2003 server is not just turning off your system, removing it from Active Directory, and disconnecting it from your network. It is a lengthy process, and it should be taken seriously. Decommissioning the source systems requires detailed planning to ensure that there are no further dependencies among these systems and that no problems are inadvertently created.

Real World Scenario

A Common Decommissioning Mistake

In the real world, it is common to forget to move one particular component from the previous version of Exchange to Exchange 2007. Later on, you notice that the required component is still running on the previous version of Exchange. To resolve these kinds of problems, you may have no choice but to bring the Exchange Server 2003 server back into the production environment or use low-level Active Directory tools to remove references to the Exchange Server 2003 server. If your Exchange legacy system won't decommission properly, it may still be present in the configuration partition and will remain in the Exchange organization configuration tables.

As an example, just imagine that you have an Exchange Server 2003 server in your environment that is still hosting public folders to keep Schedule+ free/busy information to support Outlook 2003 or the previous version of Outlook. As a part of decommissioning, if you just unplugged this server from the network without moving the Schedule+ free/busy information to Exchange Server 2007, your Outlook calendar would stop working immediately. To avoid this problem, you must ensure that either you have migrated public folders into the Exchange 2007 environment or you have only Outlook 2007 clients running in your environment. Why? You don't need the presence of public folders with Outlook 2007 because Availability services provide Schedule+ free/busy information to Outlook 2007 clients via the Web.

Exchange 2003 Bridgehead servers can provide another example. If you simply unplug this server without properly decommissioning it from the Exchange organization, email routing may stop immediately because Bridgehead servers are responsible for routing email messages. Removing Exchange 2003 Bridgehead servers without replacing them with the Hub Transport server may cause serious problems in your email routing and eventually stop messaging functionality. To avoid these problems, you must plan your decommissioning in advance and then implement your plan.

If you are removing the last Exchange Server 2003 server from your organization, you must ensure that you are not using any of the following features that are no longer supported in Exchange 2007:

- Microsoft Mobile Information Server
- Instant Messaging Service
- Exchange 2000 Conferencing Server
- cc:Mail connector
- MS Mail connector
- Key Management Service
- Exchange Chat Service

Similarly, two Exchange 2003 features are no longer supported in Exchange 2007:

- NNTP (Network News Transport Protocol)
- GroupWise Connector

Removing a previous version of Exchange server from your organization also requires that the account delegated to the removal process must have the Exchange Organization Administrator role on Exchange Server 2007 servers and the Exchange Full Administrator role on the Exchange Server 2003 server.

Once your organization no longer needs Exchange Server 2003 servers, it's time to upgrade to the Exchange 2007 organization by removing/decommissioning the older versions of Exchange. The following general steps for decommissioning your Exchange 2000/2003 server from your Exchange 2007 environment are adapted from by Microsoft's online documentation.

1. Move all the mailboxes to an Exchange Server 2007 server.
2. Verify messaging functionality by sending test messages to users.
3. Send test messages to and from the Internet.
4. Move all the public-folder replicas from Exchange 2003 to Exchange 2007.
5. Move the generation process of each offline address book (OAB) to an Exchange Server 2007 server.
6. Replace all SMTP connectors on your Exchange Server 2003 server by creating send connectors on an Exchange 2007 Hub Transport server or the Edge Transport server.
7. Send test messages to users to verify that all outbound and inbound messages are routed properly between all sites.
8. Verify that all inbound messages are routed to your Exchange 2007 Hub Transport server. Check your Mail Exchanger records and make sure that they resolve to Exchange 2007 Hub Transport or Edge Transport servers. Further, you can use the `NSLOOKUP` command to verify the existence of Exchange Server 2007 servers.
9. Make sure all inbound protocol services (ActiveSync, Microsoft Office Outlook Web Access, Outlook Anywhere, POP3, IMAP4, the Autodiscover service, and any other Exchange Web service) are pointing to an Exchange 2007 Client Access server.
10. Turn off your Exchange 2003 servers and do testing. Make sure you don't receive any complaints, and there are no routing issues. We recommend leaving that server off for a while before you start taking more steps to clean up the Active Directory and Exchange Organization.
11. Delete the routing-group connector between previous versions of Exchange and Exchange 2007.
12. Delete all routing-group connectors to the Exchange Server 2003 server.
13. Delete Exchange 2000/2003 recipient policies.
14. Delete the domain Recipient Update Services on Exchange Server 2003 servers.
15. Use ADSI Edit to delete the Recipient Update Service (Enterprise configuration).
16. Uninstall the last Exchange 2000/2003 server from the Add/Remove Programs applet of the Control Panel, and be sure to select Remove as the mode rather than Change.
17. Remove routing groups.

Summary

We've covered a lot of ground in this chapter, all of it focused on migrating from Exchange 2003 to Exchange 2007. We covered migrating from legacy and non-Exchange environments to Exchange 2007. We examined different migration strategies and migration concerns in mixed and coexistence modes. We spent a great amount of time preparing our Active Directory forest for an Exchange Server 2007 deployment, and then we took a step-by-step walk through installing Exchange 2007 prerequisites, which eventually led us to Exchange 2007 installation. We then discussed how to move mailboxes from Exchange 2003 to Exchange Server 2007 by using the Move Mailbox GUI wizard and the `Move-Mailbox` cmdlet. Finally, we covered decommissioning the Exchange 2003 environment.

Exam Essentials

Understand the difference between migration and transition. The term *migration* is often used to refer the migration process and methodologies to migrate from one messaging system to an Exchange organization without retaining configuration data of the old messaging system (as in the case of merging two Exchange organizations). This term also applies to migrating data from other messaging environments like Lotus Notes, GroupWise, and Sendmail to Exchange 2007. The term *transition* refers to moving data from legacy Exchange systems to Exchange 2007 and then decommissioning the old Exchange systems.

Understand what is involved in preparing an Active Directory environment for a transition to Exchange Server 2007. There are several steps involved in preparing your Active Directory forest. Before implementing Exchange 2007 in your environment, you should use tools and utilities like DCDIAG, NETDIAG, REPLMON, and REPLADMIN to ensure that your Active Directory forest is healthy. After checking the health of your Active Directory forest, the next step in the process is to change the domain functional level to Windows 2000 Server native or higher and then change your forest functional level to Windows 2003 Server native. Once we convert the forest and domain mode, the process also requires changing the Exchange mode to native mode. The next step is to prepare Active Directory schema by using switches available with `Setup.com`. You must understand the usage of these switches for the exam.

Understand the Move Mailbox wizard and the Move-Mailbox cmdlet. The preferred method to migrate from the Exchange 2000/2003 environment is to use the Move Mailbox wizard or the `Move-Mailbox` cmdlet. You should understand that Exchange 2007 you are no longer allowed to use Active Directory Users and Computers to move mailboxes. The Move Mailbox wizard supports multithreading operations to move multiple mailboxes simultaneously, along with scheduling to schedule the move after office hours. To automate the move process, you also can use the `Move-Mailbox` cmdlet and one of the several switches available with the `Move-Mailbox` cmdlet.

Know your way around the Exchange Management Console. Many questions on the exam are likely to ask you what configuration is needed to produce a required result. The Exchange Management Console has been completely redesigned to make it easier to navigate and get to tasks, but that doesn't mean it won't be difficult to remember later. Take your time as you review the material in this book to think about what types of configuration and management tasks you find yourself performing in each major node of the Exchange Management Console.

Review Questions

1. You have just received the Exchange Server 2007 installation DVD-ROM and would like to perform an in-place upgrade of your existing Exchange servers. Which of the following can be upgraded to Exchange 2007 by using an in-place upgrade methodology?

   A. Exchange 5.5

   B. Exchange 2000

   C. Exchange 2003

   D. Exchange 2000 and Exchange 2003

   E. None of the above

2. You are planning to re-harvest your Exchange Server 2003 for Exchange 2007 deployment. However, you just noticed that all of the Exchange Server 2003 servers are installed on x32-bit hardware. What will happen if you use the same hardware for your Exchange 2007 deployment?

   A. Exchange 2007 supports only x32-bit hardware and operating systems, so you would be able to re-harvest your existing hardware without any problem.

   B. Exchange 2007 supports x32-bit and x64-bit hardware and operating system, so you would be able to re-harvest your existing hardware without any problem.

   C. Exchange 2007 supports only x64-bit hardware and operating system in the production environment, so you would have to buy additional hardware and x64-bit Windows 2003 operating system for your new deployment.

   D. Exchange 2007 is also available for x32-bit hardware platform; however, you need to get permission from Microsoft to use Exchange 2003 x32-bit in the production environment.

3. The Exchange 2007 Enterprise edition can support up to ______ databases.

   A. 5

   B. 25

   C. 50

   D. 100

4. The Exchange 2007 Enterprise edition is designed to meet the messaging requirements of large corporate environments where servers require more availability and redundancy. The Enterprise edition has support for all of the following except:

   A. 50 storage groups

   B. 50 databases

   C. Local continuous replication (LCR)

   D. No database storage limit

   E. Built-in limited version of McAfee Virus Scan software to scan emails and attachments

   F. Exchange 2007 clustering

5. Exchange organization Native mode supports all of the following benefits except:
   - **A.** Move mailboxes in the same administrative groups
   - **B.** Built-in virus scanning
   - **C.** 8BITMIME data transfers instead of 7BITMIME data transfer
   - **D.** Rename your organization
   - **E.** Consolidate your routing groups as servers can be moved between the routing groups

6. You have completed all the requirements for Exchange 2007 deployment, and your Active Directory forest is ready to accommodate Exchange 2007. Now you must check the health of your Exchange organization. Which tool can you use in Exchange Server 2007 to perform this check?
   - **A.** Exchange Best Practices Analyzer (ExBPA) 2.6
   - **B.** EXBPA 2.7 or above
   - **C.** NETDIAG
   - **D.** DCDIAG
   - **E.** REPLMON (Replication Monitor)

7. After you have raised the functionality level of your forest and domain, it is time to prepare Active Directory schema for Exchange 2007. To operate in coexistence mode, you need to create the ExchangeLegacyInterop universal security group in your Active Directory forest, which allows previous versions of Exchange servers to send email to the Exchange 2007 Mailbox servers through the Hub Transport servers. Which of the following `Setup.com` switches will help you to perform this task?
   - **A.** `PrepareLegacyExchangePermissions`
   - **B.** `PrepareSchema`
   - **C.** `PrepareAD`
   - **D.** `PrepareDomains`
   - **E.** `PrepareAllDomains`

8. After you have prepared the Active Directory schema for coexistence between Exchange 2003 and Exchange 2007, it is time to update the schema with Exchange 2007 specific objects, classes, and attributes by importing LDAP Data Interchange Format (LDIF) files and making modifications to existing classes, objects, and attributes. Which of the following `Setup.com` switches will help you to perform this task?
   - **A.** `PrepareLegacyExchangePermissions`
   - **B.** `PrepareSchema`
   - **C.** `PrepareAD`
   - **D.** `PrepareDomains`
   - **E.** `PrepareAllDomains`

9. Which of the following `Setup.com` switches will automatically run the `/PrepareLegacyExchangePermissions` and `/PrepareSchema` commands for you?

   A. `PrepareLegacyExchangePermissions`

   B. `PrepareSchema`

   C. `PrepareAD`

   D. `PrepareDomains`

   E. `PrepareAllDomains`

10. You want to create a new domain global group called Exchange Install Domain Servers; set permissions on the domain container for the Exchange servers, Exchange Organization Administrators, Exchange Mailbox Administrators, and Authenticated Users; create the Microsoft Exchange system objects container; create a new domain global group in the current domain called Exchange Install Domain Servers; and add the Exchange Install Domain Servers group to the Exchange Servers universal security group in the root domain. Which of the following must be run in every domain/child domain?

    A. `PrepareLegacyExchangePermissions`

    B. `PrepareSchema`

    C. `PrepareAD`

    D. `PrepareDomains`

    E. `PrepareAllDomains`

11. `Setup.com /PrepareAD` perform many activities. Which of the following relate to `/PrepareAD`? (Choose all that apply.)

    A. Extend the Active Directory schema by creating new classes, objects, and attributes or modifying the existing ones.

    B. Create the Exchange organization in AD.

    C. Create the Microsoft Exchange system objects container in the root domain partition to store Exchange configuration data and information.

    D. Add local and remote domains.

    E. Modify SMTP parameters for all Exchange Server 2003 servers to communicate with Exchange Server 2007 servers.

    F. Create an Exchange routing group and Exchange administrative group. Also, create the universal security groups OU for Exchange 2007 and populate it with the Exchange universal security groups.

12. You are planning to install Exchange Server 2007 in your Exchange 2003 organization. Which of the following are prerequisites for Exchange Server 2007? (Choose all that apply.)

    A. Microsoft .NET Framework Version 2.0

    B. Microsoft .NET Framework hotfix (`NDP20-KB926776-x86.exe`)

    C. Microsoft Transaction Services

    D. Microsoft Management Console (MMC) 3.0

    E. Windows PowerShell V1.0

13. You are planning to install an Exchange 2007 Mailbox server in your Exchange 2003 organization. Which of the following are prerequisites? (Choose all that apply.)

    A. Enable network Component Object Model+ (COM+) access

    B. Microsoft Internet Information Services

    C. Microsoft Transaction Services

    D. World Wide Web Service

14. You are planning to install the Exchange 2007 Unified Messaging server in your Exchange 2003 organization. Which of the following are prerequisites for Exchange 2007 Unified Message server? (Choose all that apply.)

    A. Enable network Component Object Model+ (COM+) access

    B. Microsoft Speech Service

    C. Microsoft Windows Media Encoder

    D. Microsoft Transaction Services

    E. Microsoft Windows Media Audio Voice Codec

    F. Microsoft Core XML Services (MSXML) 6.0

15. You are planning to upgrade your Exchange 2000 organization to Exchange 2007. Which of the following Exchange 2000 features are not supported in the Exchange 2007 environment? (Choose all that apply.)

    A. Microsoft Mobile Information Server

    B. Exchange 2000 Conferencing Server

    C. Instant Messaging Service

    D. NNTP (Network News Transport Protocol) and web services

    E. MS Mail connector

16. You are planning to upgrade an Exchange 2003 organization to Exchange 2007. Which of the following Exchange 2003 features are not supported in the Exchange 2007 environment? (Choose all that apply.)

    A. Microsoft Mobile Information Server

    B. NNTP

    C. Instant Messaging Service

    D. GroupWise connector

    E. Exchange Chat Service

17. You've recently completed the installation of a new Exchange 2007 Mailbox server. It is time to activate Exchange Server 2007. Which of the following PowerShell commands must you use to perform the activation for a server named SERVERA?

    A. `Set-LicenseServer SERVERA -ProductKey`

    B. `Set-ExchangeLicenseServer SERVERA -ProductKey`

    C. `Set-ExchangeServer SERVERA -ProductKey`

    D. `Set-ExchangeServer -Identity SERVERA -ProductKey`

18. After you successfully move mailboxes from Exchange Server 2003 to Exchange Server 2007, you are ready to decommission the old Exchange Server 2003; however, the Outlook profile is not updated for each user. Moreover, you are planning to immediately retire your Exchange Server 2003 servers. There are different ways to update an Outlook profile, but the most common is:

    A. Leave your Exchange Server 2003 servers running for few weeks until all users have logged on to the new server.

    B. Use `Profile.exe` to create a new profile on each client machine.

    C. Use `OutlookProfile.exe` to create a new profile on each client machine.

    D. Use `Exprofre.exe` in logon script to back up an existing Outlook profile and create a new profile on each client machine pointing to Exchange Server 2007.

19. Which of the following Exchange 2003 utilities can help you create public- and system-folder replicas on Exchange Server 2007 servers, and then remove them from Exchange 2000/2003 servers?

    A. PF Tools

    B. Exchange System Manager

    C. Exchange Management Console (EMC)

    D. Exchange Management Shell (EMS)

    E. PFMigrate

20. Your organization is planning to migrate from Lotus Notes to Microsoft Exchange 2007. You are responsible for identifying tools, utilities, and implementation strategies to migrate from Domino 6.x/7.x to Exchange 2007. Which of the following can help you to migrate emails from Domino 6.x /7.x to Exchange 2007? (Choose two.)

    A. Connector for Lotus Domino

    B. Transporter Suite for Lotus Domino

    C. Built-in migration connector for Notes in Exchange 2007

    D. Quest Notes Migrator for Exchange

Answers to Review Questions

1. E. It is not possible to do an in-place upgrade from Exchange 5.5, Exchange 2000, or Exchange 2003 to Exchange 2007 as Exchange 2007 is an x64-bit application, and it requires an x64-bit version of Windows Server 2003 to run on. Exchange 2007 is designed and tested for x64-bit hardware and operating systems; therefore, it requires an x64-bit version of Windows Server 2003. Likely, the servers you have been using for previous versions may not be suitable for Exchange 2007 when it comes to OS and hardware bus speed. Therefore, the migration path from Exchange 5.5, Exchange 2000, and Exchange 2003 to Exchange 2007 typically requires an upgrade of hardware and operating system.

2. C. It is not possible to re-harvest your Exchange Server 2003 servers for Exchange 2007 deployment unless you have x64-bit hardware and operating system for your Exchange 2003 environment. Exchange 2007 is designed and tested for x64-bit hardware and operating systems; therefore, it requires an x64-bit version of Windows Server 2003. It is likely that the servers you have been using for previous versions are not suitable for Exchange 2007 when it comes to OS and hardware bus speed. Therefore, you may have to upgrade the operating system and hardware. Exchange 2007 is available for x32-bit hardware platform, but only for testing purposes. You are not allowed to use x32-bit version in the production environment.

3. C. The Exchange 2007 Enterprise edition is designed to meet the messaging requirements of large corporate environments where servers require more availability and redundancy. The Enterprise edition can support 50 storage groups and 50 databases, whereas the Standard edition can support only 5 storage groups and 5 databases. The Enterprise edition also can support local continuous replication (LCR) and Exchange 2007 clustering.

4. E. The Enterprise edition can support 50 storage groups and 50 databases, no database storage limit, local continuous replication (LCR), and Exchange 2007 clustering.

5. B. Virus scanning is not the native mode or mixed mode feature. You have to buy an additional virus scanning software for your organization.

6. B. NETDIAG, DCDIAG, and REPLMON are Windows 2000 and Windows 2003 support tools used to check the health of DNS, Active Directory, domain controllers, operation masters, GC, sites, site links, and more. These tools are useful, but to ensure your existing Exchange organization is ready to accommodate Exchange 2007, you should run ExBPA 2.7 or above. Besides checking for configuration errors in your Exchange deployment, ExBPA allows you to run a Readiness Check against your existing Exchange deployment and provides you with a to-do list of changes and decisions that need to be made before Exchange 2007 can be deployed. The Exchange Readiness Check performs a deep analysis of all Exchange 2000/2003 servers in your organization to verify that they have necessary updates, service packs, and configuration in place to support Exchange 2007.

7. A. The `PrepareLegacyExchangePermissions` switch will create the ExchangeLegacyInterop universal security group in your Active Directory forest. It allows previous versions of Exchange servers to send email to the Exchange 2007 Mailbox servers through the Hub Transport servers.

8. B. The `PrepareSchema` switch will prepare the Active Directory schema for coexistence between Exchange 2003 and Exchange 2007. It will update the schema with Exchange 2007–specific objects, classes, and attributes by importing LDAP Data Interchange Format (LDIF) files and making modifications to existing classes, objects, and attributes.

9. C. `PrepareAD` will automatically run the `/PrepareLegacyExchangePermissions` and `/PrepareSchema` commands for you.

10. D. `PrepareDomain` must be run in every domain. Instead of running `PrepareDomain` command in each domain, you can run `PrepareAllDomains` in the root domain to achieve the same results.

11. A, B, C, E, and F. `Setup.com /PrepareAD` won't add any local and remote domain. Answer A, B, C, E, and F are the activities perform by `Setup.com /PrepareAD`.

12. A, B, D, and E. You don't need Microsoft Transaction Services to install Exchange 2007. Answers A, B, D, and E are prerequisites.

13. A, B, and D. Exchange 2007 Mailbox Server requires all of the above except for Microsoft Transaction Services.

14. B, C, E, and F. Exchange 2007 Unified Messaging server requires Microsoft Speech service, Microsoft Windows Media Encoder, Microsoft Windows Media Audio Voice Codec, and Microsoft Core XML Services (MSXML) 6.0.

15. A, B, C, and E. Several Exchange 2000 features are no longer supported in Exchange 2007, including Microsoft Mobile Information Server, Instant Messaging Service, Exchange 2000 Conferencing Server, cc:Mail connector, MS Mail connector, Key Management Service, and Exchange Chat Service.

16. B and C. There are two Exchange 2003 features that are no longer supported in Exchange 2007 environment: NNTP and GroupWise connector.

17. D. `Set-ExchangeServer -Identity SERVERA -ProductKey` is the right answer. You must use the `-Identity` switch before typing in the Server name.

18. D. `Exprofre.exe` is a utility to update the Outlook profile for each user. You can use this in the login script before the user opens Outlook to back up an existing Outlook profile and create a new profile on each client machine pointing to Exchange Server 2007.

19. E. PFMigrate can create public- and system-folder replicas on Exchange Server 2007 servers, and then remove them from Exchange 2000/2003 servers. It is available on the Exchange 2003 CD.

20. B, D. To migrate from Lotus Notes to Microsoft Exchange 2007, you can use Transporter Suite for Lotus Domino or Quest Notes Migrator for Exchange.

Planning Exchange Server 2007 Interoperability

MICROSOFT EXAM OBJECTIVES COVERED IN THIS CHAPTER:

- ✓ Plan interoperability with Exchange in separate organizations
- ✓ Plan coexistence with Exchange 2000 Server and Exchange 2003 Server in a single organization
- ✓ Plan interoperability with third-party messaging systems

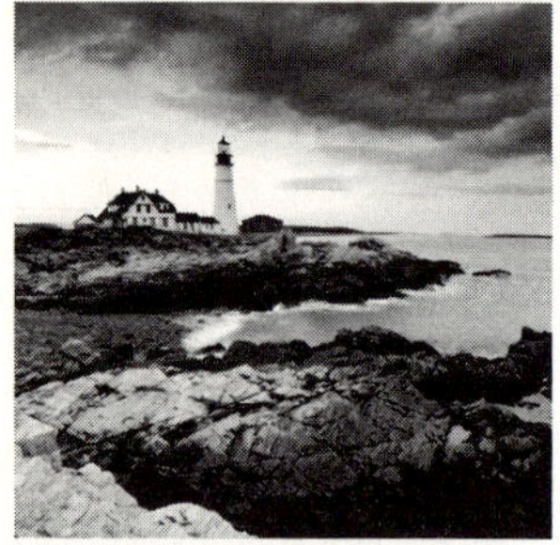

As you plan an Exchange Server 2007 deployment, you must consider numerous factors that depend on the systems that are currently in place and that Exchange is working with. Exchange 2007 supports connectivity and coexistence with Exchange Server 2003, Exchange 2000 Server, federated partners, and Lotus Notes with native tools. This chapter walks through some of the interoperability and coexistence scenarios that Exchange 2007 supports.

The test and this chapter are slanted toward planning more than operations. Therefore, this chapter does not focus on step-by-step procedures. For additional information on step-by-step procedures, refer to the Exchange 2007 documentation from Microsoft.

Any messaging organization, including one with Exchange 2003 or older versions, will have a period of coexistence and will require careful planning for interoperability. If you do not plan for interoperability, message flow or supporting messaging services may not work between the various versions of Exchange or other messaging systems.

Planning Coexistence with Exchange 2000 Server and Exchange Server 2003 in a Single Organization

This section covers one of the most common coexistence situations: coexistence with a legacy Exchange organization, including 2000, 2003, or a combination of both. If you are still running or working with Exchange Server 5.5, all traces of Exchange Server 5.5 computers must be removed from the organization before Exchange 2007 can be installed and supported. Table 8.1 outlines which versions of Exchange can coexist with Exchange 2007.

TABLE 8.1 Supported Coexistence Scenarios with Exchange 2007

Legacy Version	Coexistence with Exchange 2007
Exchange Server 5.5	Not supported
Mixed 5.5, 2000, and 2003	Not supported

TABLE 8.1 Supported Coexistence Scenarios with Exchange 2007 *(continued)*

Legacy Version	Coexistence with Exchange 2007
Exchange 2000 Server	Supported
Exchange Server 2003	Supported
Mixed 2000 and 2003	Supported

Coexistence applies the same to Exchange 2000 and Exchange 2003, which means that the steps to support Exchange 2003 are the same steps that are needed to support Exchange 2000. Although this section focuses on Exchange 2003 support, if you support Exchange 2000, the same steps to provide coexistence hold true.

Why Isn't Exchange 5.5 Supported?

I am sure that you thinking, "Why are Exchange 2000 and Exchange 2003 supported in a coexistence configuration, while Exchange 5.5 is not supported?" When Microsoft says that something is "not a supported configuration," what's most likely being said is that they have not tested this scenario, they don't know if or how to make that work, so they will not support you if you do it. I say "most likely" because there are occasions when "not supported" means "you better have good backups, because that will break things."

There were several factors that led to Exchange 5.5 not being supported in an Exchange 2007 environment, including the following:

Development resources. Like any organization, a software-development team is limited to a given amount of resources and time to dedicate to a project. The Exchange team is no exception. During the development cycle of Exchange 2007, the Exchange team was made up of about 1,000 people. Of those, there is a limited number of testers and developers. The testers and developers have a finite number of hours to invest into testing new features, old features, compatibility, user scenarios, and other issues. With limited resources, the development team did not to include testing and support for Exchange 5.5.

Planned support. Part of the planning process that takes place before coding even begins is mapping out the supported scenarios and creating test plans for them. Once the scenarios are determined, the features that need to be in the product to support these scenarios are set to be tested.

Exchange 5.5 support. Support for Exchange 5.5 originally ended on December 31, 2005. The uproar that resulted made Microsoft reconsider its position. Support for Exchange 5.5 was then extended to January 10, 2006. Microsoft's current position on product support is that it now offers a minimum of 10 years of support for any given product (five years of mainstream support, plus five years of extended support). By the time that Exchange 2007 was in Beta 1, mainstream and extended support for Exchange 5.5 had concluded. Exchange 2007 is a major architecture and feature upgrade, which already had several items that had to be removed from the features list. Spending the extra time to build and test all of the possible Exchange 5.5 scenarios had to be weighed against all of the features that were going into Exchange 2007.

In summary, "not supported" often means "not tested." Other times, it means "doesn't work." Given that knowledge, we don't recommend that you implement actions that are not supported.

Planning for Coexistence of Messaging Services

Deploying Exchange Server 2007 in a legacy Exchange organization requires a bit of planning and design. There are a few rules that will make planning a lot easier. The following is a list of concepts to consider when planning a coexistence environment:

New administrative and routing groups. The Exchange 2007 setup process automatically creates a new Exchange administrative group called FYDIBOHF23SPDLT and an Exchange routing group called DWBGZMFD01QNBJR. The Exchange 2007 Servers are placed in these groups. These groups are solely for backward compatibility with legacy Exchange servers. Although these folders are not needed in a native Exchange 2007 environment, they are needed for coexistence.

Do not modify the Exchange 2007 administrative and routing groups. Do not rename them, do not delete them, do not delete any objects from them, and do not add anything to them, especially legacy Exchange servers. Touching these groups is not supported and is ill-advised.

New security group. When you install the first Hub Transport role into the existing legacy Exchange organization, Exchange 2007 creates a new security group. During set up, you specified a legacy routing server—an existing legacy Exchange Bridgehead that the Exchange 2007 will use as a Bridgehead to the rest of the organization. Exchange 2007 places this legacy server's machine account into this new group, allowing it to authenticate SMTP connections with Hub Transport servers.

New routing-group connector. Exchange 2007 creates a two-way legacy routing-group connector to facilitate mail flow between the legacy routing groups and the new Exchange 2007 servers.

Because all Exchange 2007 servers are in a single, specialized routing group, you may have some routing inefficiencies. If you need to create multiple routing-group connectors to the

Exchange 2007 routing group, you must take some additional steps to prevent routing loops from happening.

If you don't have an existing SMTP connector for the default address space and don't want your first Exchange 2007 Hub Transport server to become a Bridgehead for outbound mail, you'll need to create an SMTP connector in the legacy organization first.

Missed functionality for old mailboxes. Users with mailboxes on legacy Exchange servers are going to miss some the new Exchange 2007 functionality such as Exchange 2007 ActiveSync, Unified Messaging, and messaging records management. Don't feel too bad for these users—there is hope for them. The move process from a legacy Exchange server to an Exchange 2007 Mailbox server will upgrade their mailboxes and allow them to utilize all of the new 2007 functionality.

When moving mailboxes to Exchange 2007, you must use the Exchange 2007 Move Mailbox wizard or the `Move-Mailbox` cmdlet. Otherwise, your mailboxes will not be properly upgraded.

Don't mix the management tools. You can use Exchange 2007 tools only to manage recipient and mailboxes on Exchange 2007 servers. This means that you use the Active Directory Users and Computers (ADUC) extensions to create, delete, or modify mailboxes on 2007 servers.

Don't add Exchange Server 2003 or Exchange 2000 Server computers. Make sure that you will not need any additional Exchange 2000 or 2003 servers before starting the upgrade process; once you install Exchange 2007 into a legacy Exchange organization, you can no longer add any new legacy Exchange servers.

No Exchange Server 5.5, no site replication service, and no Active Directory connector. Before you can start installing Exchange Server 2007 into an existing Exchange organization, the organization must be in Exchange native mode. This means that you cannot have Exchange 5.5 server or Site Replication Service servers, and you need to remove all traces of the Active Directory (AD) connectors that you might have. After these items have been removed, you must manually convert the Exchange organization to native mode.

Legacy services are not supported. There are several legacy Exchange features that are no longer supported in Exchange 2007. To continue using the unsupported features, you need to leave a legacy server in the organization. See Table 8.2 for a complete list of deprecated features, and their replacements.

TABLE 8.2 Deprecated Features in Exchange 2007

Old functionality	Replacement feature
Microsoft Mobile Information Server	Exchange ActiveSync
Instant Messaging service	Office Communications Server 2007

TABLE 8.2 Deprecated Features in Exchange 2007 *(continued)*

Old functionality	Replacement feature
Exchange Chat Service	No replacement
Exchange 2000 Conferencing Server	No replacement
Key Management Service	Windows certificate management functionality
cc:Mail connector	No replacement
MS Mail connector	No replacement
GroupWise connector	No replacement
X.400 connector	No replacement
Connector for Lotus Notes	Lotus Notes Transporter

What Do DWBGZMFD01QNBJR and FYDIBOHF23SPDLT Mean, Anyway?

If you are running Exchange 2000 Server or Exchange Server 2003 and you install Exchange Server 2007, you will have an administrative group named FYDIBOHF23SPDLT and a routing group named DWBGZMFD01QNBJR.

When developing the removal of administrative and routing groups for Exchange Server 2007, the product team had to come up with a unique administrative and routing group names that would not be in use in any of the Exchange organizations in which Exchange Server 2007 would be installed. This means they could not use common names such as "Administrative Group 2" or "RG2." So, why did the product team choose FYDIBOHF23SPDLT and DWBGZMFD01QNBJR? Is there some special meaning or just a random selection of letters and numbers? You've probably played games that involve decoding a phrase using a "secret code" created by assigning a number to each letter in the alphabet. This is sort of like that.

Let's look at FYDIBOHF23SPDLT and do a little letter substitution. If you replace the first letter, F, with the letter prior to it in the alphabet, you get E. If you replace the Y with the letter prior to it in the alphabet, you get X. If you continue through the string, replacing each number or letter with the number or letter that comes before it, you get EXCHANGE12ROCKS. Exchange 12 was the code name for Exchange Server 2007; so, FYDIBOHF23SPDLT is code for "Exchange 2007 is awesome."

What about DWBGZMFD01QNBJR? Rather than using the previous number or letter, you use the number or letter after. This means that the letter after D is E and the letter after W is X. If you continue substituting letters and numbers, you again end up with EXCHANGE12ROCKS.

Preparing for Coexistence with Legacy Exchange servers

Before you install Exchange Server 2007, it's a good idea to perform a readiness check of some kind. The Exchange Server Best Practices Analyzer Tool (ExBPA) is the best free tool available to perform an assessment. ExBPA will scour AD, Exchange servers, registry hives, drivers installed, and other settings. It takes all of the collected data and parses it based on the best practices of the Exchange product team, Product Support Services, and the Exchange communities. The latest version of ExBPA (version 2.7 and later) includes an Exchange 2007 Readiness Check scanning option, which will assess an organization's readiness for Exchange 2007.

For successful coexistence, you must take several steps to prepare to install the first Exchange Server 2007 computer in an organization with supported legacy Exchange versions.

Preparing Active Directory

When preparing Active Directory for the new server, you need to run setup with the `/PrepareLegacyPermissions` switch. This switch will ensure that the legacy Recipient Update Service (RUS) continues to function after the upgrade. As you are probably aware, Exchange 2007 no longer uses the RUS for updating recipients; however, during an upgrade or during a period of coexistence, the RUS functionality is required. When Active Directory is prepared for Exchange 2007, the new permissions policy is also applied. This new permission model removes permissions for modifying specific recipient properties from the Enterprise Exchange Servers group and assigns permissions to the new Exchange Recipient Administrators.

The good news is that if you forget to run `/PrepareLegacyPermissions` first, running `/PrepareAD` will also detect that a previous version of Exchange has been installed and that the legacy permissions should be preserved. Running `/PrepareLegacyPermissions` separately from `/PrepareAD` allows an administrator to be able run each step in a controlled manner.

Real World Scenario

Testing Upgrades and Coexistence

Some of the most harrowing experiences in a messaging administrator's career are performing upgrades and configuring coexistence during the upgrade. There are many reasons for this but typically messaging upgrades are high profile because of the importance that messaging plays in an organization.

If you find yourself planning a upgrade it is best not only to have read the documentation (and fine publications like this) but is also very important to have tested the configuration and upgrade in a lab that closely mimics your production environment. This is important because no matter how well versed you are in how things are *supposed* to work, things do not always work out that way. If you test your plan you will most likely find a number of adjustments that you can make to improve your plan for when you execute it in production. Also, by testing your plan you can be confident that the number of unexpected problems that you will encounter in your plan will be minimized.

In the past it was difficult to acquire enough hardware to properly create a test environment. Today free virtualization products like Microsoft Virtual Server and VMWare Server allow administrators to re-create a production configuration with a minimal amount of hardware, many times one or two desktop machines can be used to get a basic configuration to work with setup.

Not only is the hardware needed but a solid test plan is also needed. A test plan will consist of a list of tasks that would need to be completed to validate that the messaging system is working. Tasks could include: sending and receiving email internally, sending and receiving email externally, checking availability information for users on both messaging systems and so on. These tasks should be completed after every step in your upgrade and coexistence testing so that the step that caused the problem can be pinpointed. Often, companies will create an automated script to perform the tests and gather the results in order to reduce the amount of manual testing that needs to be done.

Be sure to test your plan before executing it on production, this will reduce potential problems, reduce anxiety for the messaging administrators and overall provide a better upgrade and coexistence period.

Preparing Message Routing

The second action that should be taken before the first Exchange Server 2007 computer is installed is to determine how routing will be handled between the legacy Exchange routing group and the new Exchange 2007 routing group. The setup process will automatically create a routing-group connector between the new Exchange 2007 routing group and a selected legacy Exchange routing group. To allow the legacy Exchange servers to send email messages to Exchange 2007 servers, a group named ExchangeLegacyInterop is created during setup. This group contains the legacy Exchange servers that need access to send email to Exchange 2007 servers.

If your Exchange organization has more than one routing group, we recommend that minor link-state changes be suppressed on each of the legacy Exchange servers to prevent message looping. Exchange 2007 will always use the shortest path to deliver a message, whereas legacy Exchange servers will use link-state detection to route around a failure. Because Exchange 2007 does not understand or forward link-state updates, it could try to send email down a path that Exchange 2003 is trying to route around because of a down connector.

To suppress minor link-state changes on each of the legacy Exchange servers, you need to make a registry change; see Exercise 8.1.

EXERCISE 8.1

Making a Registry Change

To make the registry change, complete the following steps:

1. Log on to the legacy Exchange server and open the Registry Editor.

EXERCISE 8.1 *(continued)*

2. Navigate to HKEY_LOCAL_MACHINE\System\CurrentControlSet\Services\RESvc\Parameters.
3. Create a new DWORD value named SuppressStateChanges in the Parameters key.
4. Assign the value to SuppressStateChanges as 1.
5. Close Registry Editor.
6. To have the changes take effect, restart the following services:

    Simple Mail Transfer Protocol (SMTP) service

    Microsoft Exchange Routing Engine service

    Microsoft Exchange MTA Stacks service

The first Exchange server installed in a legacy Exchange organization should be a server with the Client Access server role. Next, install the Hub Transport role and, finally, the Mailbox server role. If you do not follow this "recommended" order, things will not fall apart and the sky will not fall. However, things might not work correctly until you have all three of these server roles installed. Of course, if it works for your environment, you can install all three roles on a single server.

To summarize, installing Exchange 2007 into a legacy Exchange organization performs the following steps:

- Creates the Active Directory universal security group named ExchangeLegacyInterop, which allows legacy Exchange servers to send email to the Exchange 2007 servers.
- Creates the Exchange 2007 administrative group named Exchange Administrative Group (FYDIBOHF23SPDLT).
- Creates the Exchange 2007 routing group named Exchange Routing Group (DWBGZMFD01QNBJR).
- Creates a two-way routing-group connector between Exchange 2007 and a selected Exchange 2003 Bridgehead server.

Preparing for Public Folder Coexistence

Public folders can be replicated between Exchange 2007 and Exchange 2000 and Exchange 2003 servers just by adding a public-folder database on Exchange 2007 and by adding replicas to the public folders. Exchange 2007 added no new public folder features, so there are no coexistence surprises. To allow Exchange 2007 clients to access public folders that do not have replicas on an Exchange 2007 server, you will need to enable public-folder referrals on the routing-group connector between the special Exchange 2007 routing group and the legacy Exchange routing group that contains the public-folder replica to which you need to provide access.

Although the initial release of Exchange 2007 did not have any graphical tools to manage public folders, simple management tools were added in service pack 1.

Preparing for Client Access Server Coexistence

As you now know, the legacy front-end server functionality has primarily been replaced with the Client Access server role. To provide clients with access to Office Outlook Web Access (OWA), IMAP4, POP3, Office Outlook Anywhere, or mobile devices with Active Sync, you must deploy a Client Access server role. The Client Access server role can coexist with the legacy front-end servers; however, there are several requirements to provide coexistence. The following list describes these boundaries:

- A client can use an Exchange 2007 Client Access server for accessing OWA with a mailbox on either Exchange 2007 or Exchange 2003; however, the user will always see the version of Outlook Web Access that their mailbox is hosted on.
- A Client Access server that also has the Mailbox role installed will not proxy to Exchange 2003 servers for OWA access.
- The version of Exchange ActiveSync also depends on the server version that is hosting the user's mailbox. To be able to use direct push, the user's mailbox must be located on a server that is running Exchange Server 2003 Service Pack 2 or Exchange 2007. This also applies to features such as Global Address List lookup and Exchange Search.
- Exchange Server 2003 front-end servers cannot be used to provide OWA service to Exchange Server 2007 mailboxes. Therefore, we recommend deploying a Client Access server before deploying any other role.
- The URL used to access OWA depends on whether the user's mailbox is located on an Exchange Server 2003 server or on an Exchange 2007 server. Use one of the following URLs to reach OWA:
  - If the mailbox is located on an Exchange Server 2003 server, use `http://<servername>/Exchange`.
  - If the mailbox is located on an Exchange 2007 Server, use either `http://<servername>/owa` or `http://<servername>/Exchange`; the users will be redirected to the appropriate URL. During a period of coexistence when mailboxes can be located on either server version, it is safest to instruct users to use `http://<servername>/Exchange`.

Preparing for Unified Messaging Coexistence

The Exchange Unified Messaging role is a new feature in Exchange 2007 and does not support any interoperation between legacy versions of Exchange. Table 8.3 summarizes the coexistence support for each of the roles.

TABLE 8.3 Coexistence Support for the Various Roles in Exchange 2007

Exchange Server 2007 server role	Supported configuration
Client Access server role	No other Exchange 2007 roles are required. A Client Access server role must be installed in each Active Directory site that contains the Mailbox server role. Clients will see the Microsoft Office OWA version that is on their mailbox store.
Hub Transport server role	No other Exchange 2007 server roles are required. Routing-group connectors must exist between the Exchange 2007 Routing Group and each Exchange 2003 Server routing group that should communicate directly with Exchange 2007. Minor link-state updates should be suppressed on every Exchange 2003 computer before you create a second routing-group connector.
Unified Messaging server role	An Exchange 2007 Hub Transport server must be deployed in the same Active Directory site as the Unified Messaging server role. The Unified Messaging server role cannot interoperate with the Exchange Server 2003 computers.
Mailbox server role	An Exchange 2007 Hub Transport server role must be installed in the same Active Directory site as the Mailbox server role.

Planning for Management Tools Coexistence with Legacy Versions of Exchange

Unlike Exchange 2000 and Exchange 2003, Exchange Server 2007 does not use Active Directory Users and Computers for user management. This is a big change from the two previous versions of Exchange, where all mailbox management was done in Active Directory Users and Computers and all server management was done in the Exchange Management tool. With Exchange 2007, server and mailbox management happens from the Exchange Management Shell.

All of the other tools are built on top of the Exchange Management Shell, such as the Exchange Management Console that runs shell commands based on GUI choices to accomplish tasks. This change was made primarily to separate user management from mailbox management. In this way, messaging administrators can manage mailbox settings within the Exchange management tools and the user administrators can manage passwords, groups, and other basic settings from within Active Directory Users and Computers. Before Exchange 2007, in many large organizations the messaging administrators either did not have access to create user accounts or had the user accounts created by another group before creating the mailbox. These management changes allow for a split permissions model, which allows for separating the user and messaging administration roles. Although this seems to be a step back to the Exchange 5.5 administration model, it was a request from many customers. It makes sense for very large organizations; for smaller organizations, it simply means using a different management tool (discussed later in this section).

Now let's cover why you need a few other tools to manage everything in the coexistence world. All of the tools needed to manage the Exchange 2007 features set are fully baked and included in the Exchange Management Shell. The console, however, is a different story. The Exchange team had a limited amount of resources and time to dedicate to getting Exchange 2007 out the door. One of the areas in which they were able to ease the development load was the Exchange Management Console. Therefore, there are several things that you cannot manage from the console in Exchange 2007.

Some of these things are included with Service Pack 1 (SP1); however, there is no plan to add some others. For example, SP1 adds support for public-folder management in the Exchange Management Console that was not there in the RTM version of Exchange 2007. At the time of writing, the recommended tools to support public folders are as follows:

- Use the Exchange Management Shell.
- Leave a legacy Exchange server in the organization to manage the public folders using legacy management tools.
- Manage your folders from an Outlook client logged in as a user who can create, delete, and work with public folders.
- Use some of the public-folder utilities available for previous versions of Exchange, such as PFDAVadmin and PFview.

There are several different scenarios, and tools that you use to support those scenarios. The general rule is that you should use the administrative tools that are specific to the Exchange Server version you are managing. The following is a more in-depth list of the management tools:

- Exchange Server 2007 objects (servers and recipients) should be managed from the Exchange Management Console or the Exchange Management Shell.
- Exchange organization settings should be managed from the Exchange Management Console or the Exchange Management Shell.
- Mailbox properties on legacy mailboxes should be managed from the Exchange System Manager.
- Legacy Exchange servers (2000 and 2003) need to be managed using the legacy Exchange System Manager.
- If you are using any legacy features (Intelligent Message Filter, Internet Mail Wizard, administrative delegation, etc.) not supported in Exchange Server 2007, you must use the appropriate legacy Exchange System Manager.
- To manage legacy recipients, use ADUC on a computer with the legacy Exchange administrative tools installed.
- As noted earlier in this chapter, when you move a mailbox from a legacy server to an Exchange 2007 server you must use the `Move-mailbox` cmdlet in the Exchange Management Shell or move the user from the Exchange 2007 Exchange Management Console. If you do not do this, the mailbox will not be properly upgraded to Exchange 2007 and will miss out on several Exchange 2007 features.

Table 8.4 is the list of global features and where they should be managed:

TABLE 8.4 Managing Global Features in Exchange 2003 and Exchange 2007

Exchange 2003 Feature	Can Be Administered from Exchange 2007	Can Be Administered from Exchange 2003
Intelligent Mail Filter (IMF)—gateway blocking	No	Yes
IMF—Store Junk Email configuration	Yes	Yes
Sender ID filtering	No	Yes
Mobile services	No	Yes
Internet message format	Yes	Yes
Sender filtering and recipient filtering	No	Yes
Connection filtering	Yes	No

The recipient management tools have changed significantly from the legacy Exchange tools. Table 8.5 is a list of Exchange 2003 recipient management tasks and how those should be changed in a coexistence environment.

TABLE 8.5 Managing Recipient Tasks in a Coexistence Environment

Exchange 2003 Feature	Can Be Administered from Exchange 2007	Can Be Administered from Exchange 2003
Details templates and address templates	No	Yes
Address lists	Yes	Yes
Offline address book	Yes	Yes
Recipient Update Service	No	Yes
Mailbox Manager policy	Yes	Yes

If you follow the simple rule of managing the server and the recipient with the same version of the software that the server running the function is, or that the mailbox is hosted on, and you remember the rules outlined in this section, you should have no problems when it comes to managing Exchange in a coexistence environment.

Planning Interoperability with Exchange in Separate Organizations

Business mergers are common occurrences. However, because of regulatory compliance, internal politics, or other issues, the merged companies frequently maintain separate email systems in separate Active Directory forests. Often each business unit needs to share calendar and address-book information to be able to communicate easily. This configuration is known as a cross-forest configuration. How can Exchange 2007 be configured to work in these cross-forest scenarios?

First, the directories need to be synchronized to provide the ability for users to view the remote users in the Global Address List. Next, the availability service must be configured to allow sharing of calendar information among users in each forest.

Planning Directory Synchronization

The first step to providing coexistence between two Exchange 2007 organizations is to synchronize the directories. Synchronizing the directories consists of extracting the data from the source directory and creating entries in the remote directory, enabling the remote users to reference the user information.

At the time of this writing, there were no Microsoft-supported solutions for cross-forest directory synchronization that are supported in an Exchange 2007 native environment. The tools for directory synchronization (Microsoft Identity Integration Server, Microsoft Identity Lifecycle Manager, or Identity Integration Feature Pack for Windows Server 2003) were originally designed for use with Exchange 2000 Server or Exchange Server 2003. Because they were written for these legacy versions, the synchronization service expects that the Recipient Update Service (RUS) for those older versions is present to stamp the synchronized accounts with the missing Exchange attributes. Exchange Server 2007 no longer relies on the RUS and does not provide a similar feature because all of the Exchange 2007 management tools ensure that the created mailboxes have the appropriate attributes.

To use the replication tools written for previous versions of Exchange, a legacy Exchange server must be present to provide RUS services. If you are doing manual directory synchronization between forests, you could use Exchange 2007 cmdlets to export user information to a file and then use that to create contacts or user accounts in the other Exchange organization.

As of this writing, Microsoft is planning to release updated versions of these tools to take advantage of native Exchange 2007 tools and to remove the legacy Exchange 2003 RUS dependencies. Until these tools are released, you will need to keep an Exchange 2003 Server to provide compatibility with cross-forest directory synchronization tools.

Microsoft Identity Lifecycle Management 2007 Service Pack 1 will provide Exchange 2007 organizations directory synchronization support without requiring a legacy RUS server to be maintained in the organization.

Planning Free/Busy Calendaring Interoperability for Exchange Server 2007 Organizations

One of the main reasons to interoperate with a separate Exchange organization is to be able to view availability information for users in both organizations. After directory synchronization is in place, the Availability service needs to be configured.

The Availability service is a web service that retrieves free/busy information from mailboxes and returns the information directly to the client. This is a significant improvement over previous versions of Exchange, where the free/busy data relied solely on the mail client to publish updated free/busy information to a public folder. To use the Availability service to retrieve free/busy information, the user must be using Office Outlook 2007 or Outlook Web Access with a mailbox stored on an Exchange 2007 Mailbox server. Outlook 2003 clients still rely on public folders for distribution of free/busy information.

The Availability service provides two options for cross-forest free/busy information for Outlook 2007 users. The first level is organization-wide free/busy. Organization-wide free/busy returns the default organization level of detail for each remote user. This setting is good where a cross-forest trust is not in place, as a service account in the remote domain is specified for the Availability service to use. To assign a service account the appropriate permission in the remote Exchange 2007 organization, run this command:

```
Set-AvailabilityConfig -OrgWideAccount "RemoteForestEmail.com\<Service Account""
```

Then run the following command in the local domain to add the Availability address space:

```
$a = get-credential
Add-AvailabilityAddressspace -Forestname RemoteForestEmail.com -Accessmethod
OrgWideFB -Credential:$a
```

This command will prompt you to enter the user and password for the service account that will be used to connect to the remote forest.

When adding address spaces, the remote forest name always refers to the default remote email domain for the forest, which doesn't always match the name of the remote forest. As an example the remote forest name might be company.local, however the remote email domain might be company .com, you would use company.com not company.local when specifying the remote forest name.

The second option that the Availability service can provide for a remote Exchange 2007 organization is per-user free/busy. When per-user free/busy is used, the level of free/busy detail can be set by the calendar owner. To use per-user free/busy, a cross-forest trust must be in place. If the remote Exchange organization is running Exchange 2007 and you are required to configure the Availability service for per-user free/busy information, you need to assign service account permissions to retrieve the availability information in the remote forest. To assign these permissions to the Exchange Servers group, you would run the following command in the remote domain:

```
Get-ClientAccessServer | Add-ADPermission -Accessrights Extendedright -
Extendedrights "ms-Exch-
EPI-Token-Serialization" -User "<Remote Domain>\Exchange Servers"
```

On a Client Access server in your local forest, you need to configure the Availability service to be able to retrieve the remote free/busy information. To do this, you must add an Availability address space by running the following command.

```
Add-AvailabilityAddressSpace -Forestname RemoteForestEmail.com -AccessMethod
PerUserFB -UseServiceAccount:$true
```

After the directories are synchronized and the address space is added, Outlook 2007 users can select the remote mailbox from the Global Address List. Then the Availability service will connect to the remote Exchange organization and retrieve the appropriate availability information.

Planning Free/Busy Availability Interoperability for Exchange Server 2007 and Exchange 2003 Organizations

As mentioned earlier, previous versions of Exchange and Outlook used public folders to provide free/busy information. The Exchange Availability service automatically knows how to deal with Exchange 2003 mailboxes by retrieving legacy free/busy information from the public folder of the target server. When setting interoperability with an Exchange 2003 organization, the free/busy public folder must be replicated to the Exchange 2007 organization for reference.

Replicating the free/busy folder should be done using the Microsoft Exchange Inter-Organization (InterOrg) Replication tool. This tool was written for replicating public folders between legacy Exchange organizations. The utility is only officially supported for Exchange 2000 and Exchange 2003 servers; therefore, an Exchange 2003 public-folder server needs to exist in your Exchange 2007 organization to be the target for the free/busy public folder replication. The InterOrg Replication tool requires that the directories be synchronized before you attempt to replicate the free/busy data.

The Microsoft Exchange Inter-Organization Replication tool can be downloaded from the Microsoft website at `http://www.microsoft.com/downloads/details.aspx?FamilyId=E7A951D7-1559-4F8F-B400-488B0C52430E`.

Once the free/busy public folder has been replicated, an address space needs to be added to the Exchange 2007 organization by using the following command:

```
Add-AvailabilityAddressSpace -ForestName RemoteEMailDomain.com -AccessMethod
PublicFolder
```

Planning Interoperability with Third-Party Messaging Systems

In previous versions of Exchange, the foreign directory connectors were part of the base Exchange install and included on the Exchange installation CD. These connectors are not included in Exchange 2007. To provide connectivity to these foreign mail systems, you can keep either an Exchange 2000 or Exchange 2003 server in place. If the system that you need to interoperate with is Lotus Domino, you can use the Microsoft Transporter Suite to facilitate interoperability.

The Transporter Suite is a three-part tool:

Extractor. The extractor collects data from some data source, such as Lotus Notes Domino. The transporter extracts the data and places it in an XML format that the Transporter engine can understand.

Injector. The injectors take XML data generated by the transporter engine and place it in an application such as Exchange 2007, SharePoint Services, or Lotus Domino.

Engine. The engine converts the data from the source extractor, massages the data if needed, and then formats for the injector.

These three components are all wrapped up in a nice MMC 3.0–based console bundled with some PowerShell commands that allow for migrations and coexistence with foreign email and application systems. One of the design concepts that makes the Transporter tool brilliant is that it's an open architecture that allows third-party developers to write custom extractors and injectors. If you wanted to migrate from an email system that had no email extractor available, you could write your own extractor and then use the Transporter engine and injector to migrate from that mail system to Exchange 2007. There are currently extractors to extract email and applications from Notes and place them in Exchange 2007 and SharePoint. Because the groundwork has been laid with the Transport Suite for Lotus Domino, you can imagine that other messaging systems will be supported in the future. Lotus Domino 5.x, 6.x, and 7.x are supported for migrations; however, only 6.x and 7.x are supported for coexistence with the Transporter Suite.

To provide coexistence with third-party messaging systems, there are always at least two major steps:

1. Implement directory synchronization.
2. Implement messaging interoperation.

In the case of Lotus Domino 6.x and 7.x, you also have the option of deploying a feature to allow sharing of free/busy information between the systems. In the next three sections, we will cover the process of using the Transporter Suite to set up coexistence between Exchange 2007 and Lotus Domino.

Planning Directory Synchronization with Third-Party Messaging Systems

The basis for any sort of coexistence is directory synchronization. Directory synchronization adds objects into each messaging system's directory so that users in either system can send email messages to users in either system.

The Directory Connector service for the Domino and Exchange directories must be run on a server with Exchange 2007 running either the Hub Transport or Mailbox role. The server also must have the Notes client 6.x or 7.x installed with Editor or higher access. This account must be in the [UserCreator] and [UserModifier] roles and must have permission to delete documents to allow creation of new documents during synchronization.

Exercise 8.2 outlines the steps for installing and configuring the Directory Connector service.

EXERCISE 8.2

Installing and Configuring the Directory Connector Service

To install and configure the Directory Connector service, perform the following tasks:

1. Run the installation of the latest Microsoft Transporter Suite by running `transporter.msi`.
2. After completing the installation, launch the Transporter Management Console and click on the Create Directory Connector option.
3. Create an organizational unit (OU) in Active Directory to provide a single destination for the user objects that the connector will create.
4. Configure the connector's Sync to Active Directory options, such as the source Domino Servers, the notes service account name and password, the Domino SMTP domain, and target Active Directory OU.
5. Configure the connector's Sync to Domino options, such as the source Active Directory organization units, the routable Exchange SMTP domains, and the target Domino directory.
6. Configure any advanced settings, such as groups that should be excluded from the synchronization.
7. Start the Directory Connector service.

With a little planning, directory synchronization can be set up in a short time. To allow sending email between organizations, more planning is needed.

Planning Messaging Coexistence with Third-Party Messaging Systems

Although there is a tool for extracting and importing email, you may have noticed that there isn't an option for delivering email in the Transporter tool. To provide messaging coexistence,

SMTP is used to deliver email between systems. This means that two domains are needed to deliver email from one system to another. One recommended scenario would be to create a subdomain for each of the systems.

If your company were using `sybex.com` and were planning on implementing coexistence with a new Exchange 2007 organization, the `domino.domain.com` subdomain could be created for the Lotus Domino organization and the `exchange.domain.com` subdomain could be created for the Exchange organization. This way, email from the Internet could be funneled into an Exchange Edge Transport server and then routed to the appropriate destination, as shown in Figure 8.1.

FIGURE 8.1 Single-domain-name routing through Edge servers

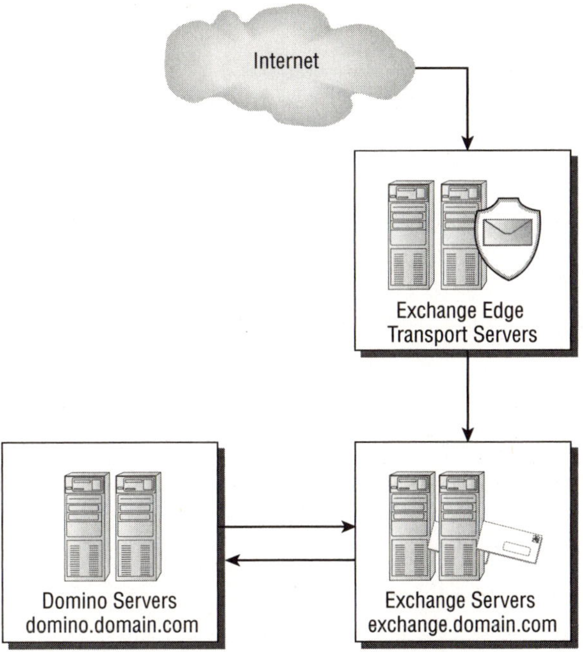

For email to be sent appropriately between the organizations, an email address would need to be added to each user with an email address in the subdomain. For example, even if all outgoing mail from both systems is from `domain.com`, mailboxes hosted on the Exchange 2007 servers would need to have the `exchange.domain.com` assigned. Likewise, Domino accounts would need to have `domino.domain.com` addresses assigned. This way, each messaging system would be able to use DNS to locate the server responsible for receiving mail for users in the opposite mail system.

Alternatively, the inbound mail can be sent to either email system with load-balanced Mail Exchanger (MX) records for the top domain; the email would still be able to route to the appropriate mailbox, as shown in Figure 8.2.

FIGURE 8.2 Single-domain-name routing through either email system

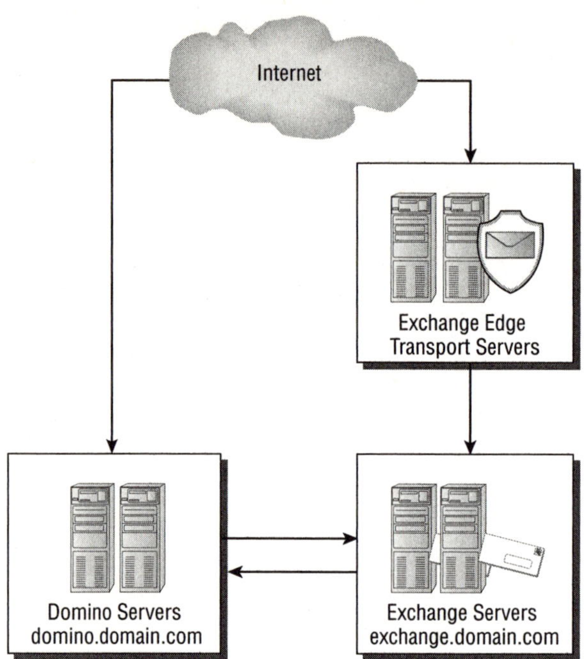

Several variations on the same solution can be used to facilitate SMTP-based message routing. These solutions would include using two separate domains configured like in the previous example except that the domains would be `domain1.com` and `domain2.com` rather than using subdomains.

In each of these scenarios, MX records need to be created so that both organizations know how to deliver email to both email systems.

Planning Free/Busy Availability Interoperability with Third-Party Messaging Systems

The Microsoft Transporter Suite also can provide free/busy information for Domino accounts for Exchange 2007 users. The free/busy interoperability functionality consists of three main components:

- Free/Busy Connector add-in (`excalcon.exe`)
- Free/Busy Connector service
- Exchange Server 2007 Availability service

The Free/Busy Connector add-in runs on a Lotus Domino server and provides connectivity to the Exchange Availability service for availability lookups. It also provides connectivity to the Free/Busy Connector service running on the Exchange server to replicate the Domino user's free/busy information to a public folder that the Availability service can reference when providing information to Exchange 2007 users for Domino users.

After directory synchronization is configured and working, a foreign domain document must be created in Domino, as shown in Exercise 8.3. This can be done from the Lotus Notes 6.x or 7.x client with Editor permissions to the Domino directory.

EXERCISE 8.3

Creating a Foreign Domain Document

Follows these steps to create a foreign domain document:

1. From within Lotus Notes, open the Domino server that will be running `excalcon.exe`.
2. In the Messaging configuration list, navigate to the Domains configuration and add a foreign domain named Exchange.
3. For the Gateway server name, type in the hierarchical name of the server that will be running the Free/Busy add-in and type **mail.box** in the Gateway mail file name.
4. For the Calendar server name, type in the hierarchical name of the server that will be running the Free/Busy add-in.
5. For the Calendar system field, type in something like **FreeBusy**. This will be used when you configure `excalcon.exe`.

Once the foreign domain connector is installed, the Free/Busy Connector add-in task for Lotus Domino can be configured on the Domino server. . The connector executable file is named `excalcon.exe`. This connector must be installed on a Lotus Domino server. Once the installation is complete for the connector, the `NOTES.INI` file must be customized with the Domino and Exchange configuration so that the connector is configured to connect to the correct servers. Once the connector is configured, it must be loaded.

Next, the Free/Busy Connector service must be installed on a server running Exchange 2007 so that it can receive information from the Free/Busy Connector add-in on the Domino server. This is done by running `transporter.msi`.

Last, the public folder and address space need to be set. To set the address space, use the following command:

```
Add-AvailabilityAddressSpace -ForestName domino.domain.com -AccessMethod
PublicFolder
```

Although two-way availability information is available with this solution, there are several caveats to its functionality:

- The Lotus Domino server running the Free/Busy Connector add-in must be running as a service and not an application.
- Recurring meeting requests between Exchange 2007 and Domino cannot updated; they must be deleted and re-created to work properly between systems.
- Exchange resources cannot be scheduled by Notes users for meetings.
- If Transporter is installed on an Exchange Server 2007 computer with both the Mailbox and Client Access server roles, the public folder virtual directory must not require Secure Sockets Layer (SSL) for connectivity.

Planning Messaging Connectivity: SSL and TLS

By default, security is not built into email transmissions. All data streams to and from the server transmitted over POP3, IMAP3, and SMTP are in clear, unencrypted text that anyone with access to your data stream can capture and read. Exchange 2007 has made great leaps forward in helping to improve security. At the core of the data encryption technology for Exchange 2007 are Secure Sockets Layer (SSL) and Transport Layer Security (TLS). By default, Exchange 2007 installs a self-signed certificate on itself during setup to use for data transmissions to other Exchange servers.

By default, Outlook 2007, when used with an Exchange 2007 Server, will encrypt the data stream between client and server. Exchange 2007 uses opportunistic TLS to establish secure relationships between itself and other SMTP servers. This can be configured to happen automatically or it can be configured to occur on a manual basis for each individual host.

Domain security can also be enabled by installing certificates on Edge Transport servers to encrypt email transmission between Exchange 2007 organizations. Both organizations will need to have Edge transport servers and certificates in place to complete the configuration. The configuration of Domain Security requires the following steps to be completed:

1. Create certificates for each of the Edge transport servers.
2. Bind the certificates to SMTP service on each of the Edge transport servers.
3. Configure outbound security by running `Set-TransportConfig -TLSSendDomainSecureList` with a list of all of the email domains that domain security should be used when email is sent to that domain.
4. Enable domain security on the send connector by running `Set-SendConnector Internet -DomainSecurity:$True`.
5. Configure inbound security by running `Set-TransportConfig -TLSRecieveDomainSecureList` with a list of all of the email domains that domain security should be used when receiving email from that domain.
6. Enable domain security on the send connector by running `Set-RecieveConnector Inet -DomainSecurity:$True -AuthMechanism TLS`.

To be able to be sure that TLS negotiation is successful between the two Exchange organizations verbose protocol logging needs to be enabled on the Edge transport connectors.

Summary

As you plan an Exchange Server 2007 deployment, you must consider numerous factors that depend on the systems that are currently in place and that Exchange is working with. Exchange 2007 supports connectivity and coexistence with Exchange 2003, Exchange 2000, federated partners, and Lotus Domino via first-party tools. This chapter walked through some of the interoperability and coexistence scenarios that Exchange 2007 supports.

Because all Exchange 2000 or Exchange 2003 upgrades have a period of coexistence, this chapter covered the requirements for that coexistence and which of the roles and services can coexist. Separate Exchange organization interoperability of address lists and availability also were covered.

Exam Essentials

Understand which legacy features have been replaced. Because Exchange 2007 took on a new role-based architecture, several features and functions have been replaced, moved, or deprecated in Exchange 2007. Functions such as front ends have been replaced with Client Access and Hub Transport servers. Third-party messaging connectors for systems like cc:Mail and Microsoft Mail have been removed completely. Know how to work around these limitations for the exam.

Understand the interoperability options. When working with multiple organizations, it's important to know what needs to be done to get the Availability service working across the forest boundaries. Also, understand the components of the Transporter Suite and how they operate.

Review Questions

1. With which versions of Exchange can Exchange 2007 coexist?
   - **A.** Exchange Server 5.5
   - **B.** Exchange 2000 Server
   - **C.** Exchange Server 2003
   - **D.** Exchange Server 5.0
2. Which of the following is not true when talking about Exchange management tools in an Exchange coexistence environment?
   - **A.** Outlook Mobile Access components can be managed only from the Exchange System Manager.
   - **B.** In the EMC, Exchange 2000 and 2007 mailbox properties can be edited.
   - **C.** Legacy Exchange routing groups can be created in the Exchange Management Console.
   - **D.** To work with Exchange 2007 recipient objects, you must use the Exchange Management Shell.
3. Which foreign mail system connectors are included with Exchange 2007?
   - **A.** Lotus Notes
   - **B.** Lotus cc:Mail
   - **C.** Novell GroupWise
   - **D.** Generic SMTP
4. Which of the following needs to be configured to provide coexistence between Exchange 2003 and Exchange 2007 in the same organization?
   - **A.** Availability service
   - **B.** Client Access
   - **C.** Routing-group connector
   - **D.** Transporter Suite
5. Which server role should you install first in an Exchange 2003 coexistence plan?
   - **A.** Client Access server
   - **B.** Hub Transport server
   - **C.** Mailbox server
   - **D.** Edge Transport server
6. To configure the Availability service to retrieve availability information from a remote Exchange 2007 organization, which cmdlet would you use?
   - **A.** `Add-AvailablityAddressSpace`
   - **B.** `Add-PublicFolderDatabase`
   - **C.** `Set-AvailabilityConfig`
   - **D.** `Set-AdSite`

7. For which functions would you need to use the Exchange 2003 administration tools in a mixed environment? (Choose all that apply.)

   A. Delegating administrative control

   B. Modifying Intelligent Message Filter Gateway settings

   C. Modifying the Recipient Update Service server

   D. Modifying Offline Address Book

8. When coexisting with a Lotus Domino server, which of the following provides mail transport between the systems?

   A. X.400 connector

   B. Lotus Notes connector

   C. SMTP connector

   D. None of the above

9. Which of the following versions of capabilities are supported with Lotus Transporter Suite with Lotus Domino 6.x? (Choose all that apply.)

   A. Directory synchronization

   B. Availability information

   C. Messaging

   D. Unified Messaging

10. Which three components provide free/busy information between Lotus Notes 6.x and higher and Exchange 2007?

    A. Free Busy Connector add-in (`excalcon.exe`)

    B. Free/Busy Connector service

    C. SMTP Gateway

    D. Exchange Server 2007 Availability service

11. When using MIIS or the Windows 2003 Identity Integration Feature Pack what must you have in the Exchange 2007 organization to have a successful directory synchronization?

    A. A legacy Exchange Recipient Update server

    B. A public-folder server

    C. An Edge server role

    D. A Client Access server role

12. Which of the following roles can access data on Exchange 2003 Mailbox servers?

    A. Unified Messaging server role

    B. Client Access server role

    C. Hub Transport server role

    D. Edge Transport server role

13. Which of the following does not to be done before the first Exchange 2007 server is installed in an Exchange 2003 organization with multiple routing groups?
    A. Run setup with `/PrepareAD`.
    B. Remove all Exchange 5.5 servers.
    C. Create a dedicated Active Directory site for the Exchange 2007 servers.
    D. Disable minor link-state updates.

14. Which options allow Exchange 2007 users in a mixed organization to use public-folder data stored on Exchange 2003 servers? (Choose all that apply.)
    A. Add replicas of the public folders on an Exchange 2007 server.
    B. Use the Inter-Organization Replication tool.
    C. Allow public-folder referrals over the routing-group connector.
    D. None of the above

15. In a coexistence environment with multiple connected routing groups, where must minor link-state updates be suppressed?
    A. On all Exchange 2007 servers
    B. On all Exchange 2003 Bridgehead servers
    C. On all Exchange 2003 servers
    D. None of the above

16. Which of the following require keeping a legacy version of Exchange around to support coexistence? (Choose all that apply.)
    A. MS Mail
    B. Lotus Domino
    C. GroupWise
    D. cc:Mail

17. Which of the following services can be provided by a Client Access server for an Exchange 2003 mailbox?
    A. POP3
    B. Outlook Web Access 2003
    C. RPC over HTTP (Outlook Anywhere)
    D. All of the above

18. To track a message that is sent between Exchange 2003 and Exchange 2007 servers in the same organization, what is the minimum number of queries that would need to be made?
    A. One from the Exchange 2007 message-tracking tool
    B. One from the Exchange 2007 message-tracking tool and one from the Exchange 2003 message-tracking tool
    C. One from the Exchange 2003 message-tracking tool
    D. None of the above

19. When replacing the Exchange 2003 front-end servers with Client Access servers, which statement is true when the mailbox is stored on an Exchange 2003 server?

A. Custom setting will not be retained.

B. The user will need to connect to `http://server/owa` to access OWA.

C. The user will not be able to use RPC over HTTP.

D. The user will need to upgrade to Outlook 2007.

20. To use per-user free/busy settings in a cross-forest Exchange 2007 configuration, which of the following must be in place?

A. Public-folder databases in each organization

B. A cross-forest trust

C. Edge Transport servers

D. Inter-Organization Replication tool

Answers to Review Questions

1. B, C. Exchange Server 2007 can coexist only with Exchange Server 2003 and Exchange 2000 Server. Older versions, such as Exchange Server 5.0 and Exchange Server 5.5, are not supported for coexistence.

2. D. The Exchange System manager must be used to manage the Outlook Mobile Access settings and is true. The other tools do not have the ability to manage OMA.

3. D. The only connector that is included with Exchange 2007 is the SMTP connector. You can download the Transporter Suite that provides directory synchronization for Lotus Notes; however, it is not included in the Exchange product.

4. C. To provide coexistence between Exchange 2003 and Exchange 2007, you must configure a routing-group connector. The Availability service and Client Access server role do not require any configuration to work properly. The Transporter Suite is not required to provide coexistence for Exchange 2003 and Exchange 2007 in the same organization.

5. A. The Client Access server role is always the recommended first role to deploy in any site.

6. A. `Add-AvailabilityAddressSpace` is used to create an entry for the Availability service to be able to retrieve availability information from a remote service.

7. A, B, C. Delegating administrative control, modifying Intelligent Message Filter Gateway settings, and modifying the Recipient Update Service server all must be done from the Exchange 2003 ESM. The Offline Address Book can be managed from the Exchange 2007 tools.

8. C. The SMTP connector provides mail transport between the Exchange 2007 and Lotus Domino servers. X.400 and the Lotus Notes connector are not available on Exchange 2007.

9. A, B, C. Lotus Notes 6.x supports all of the coexistence features of the Transporter Suite. Those features are messaging, directory synchronization, and free/busy sharing. Unified Messaging is not available.

10. A, B, D. `Excalcon.exe` is the add-in on the Domino server that provides the service for exporting free/busy information to and receiving it from Exchange. The Exchange Free/Busy Connector service provides the interface for `Excalcon.exe` on the Exchange server. The Availability service provides the public-folder data to the client.

11. A. To support MIIS and IIFP, a legacy Exchange server running the RUS must be in place to stamp the objects that the synchronization creates.

12. B. The Client Access server can be used as a front end for Exchange 2003 mailboxes. The Unified Messaging role cannot be used against Exchange 2003 mailboxes. Edge transport and Hub transport require SMTP servers to be able to deliver messages to Exchange 2003 servers.

13. C. A dedicated Active Directory site does not need to be created to support Exchange 2007. Setup does need to be run with `/PrepareAD` to set appropriate permissions and to extend the schema.

14. A, C. Either public-folder replicas can be created on the Exchange 2007 server or public-folder referrals can be enabled over the routing-group connector. Using the Inter-Organization Replication tool is not supported in the same Exchange organization.

15. C. Minor link-state updates should be disabled on all Exchange servers in a multiple-routing-group environment.

16. A, C, D. Exchange 2007 does not support cc:Mail, MS Mail, or Novell GroupWise with connectors or Transporter Suite tools. To coexist with these systems, legacy Exchange servers would need to be maintained.

17. D. A Client Access server can act as a front-end server for an Exchange 2003 mailbox for POP3, OWA, and RPC over HTTP.

18. B. The message-tracking formats between Exchange 2003 and Exchange 2007 are very different and are incompatible. One query will need to be made using the Exchange 2007 tool, and one will need to be made with the Exchange 2003 tool.

19. A. The custom settings that were made on the front end don't get migrated to the new Client Access server roles, but will need to be re-created. RPC over HTTP can be used, older versions of Outlook can continue to be used, and users will continue to use `http://server/exchange` to access OWA.

20. B. A cross-forest trust must be in place to implement a per-user free/busy configuration.

Chapter 9

Planning a Highly Available Exchange Server 2007 Implementation

---

MICROSOFT EXAM OBJECTIVES COVERED IN THIS CHAPTER:

- ✓ **Plan the service's high availability implementation**
- ✓ **Plan a data redundancy implementation**

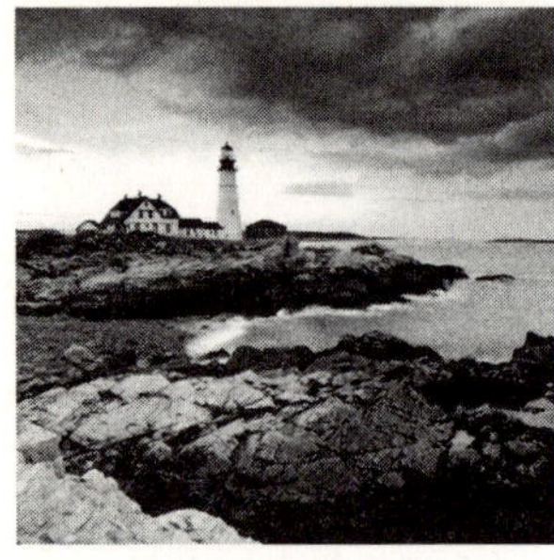

Since email is such an important aspect of today's business, planning your Exchange organization so that it is highly available is often a requirement. In this chapter we will consider the options of various server roles and recovery techniques, as follows.

- Implementing load balancing
- Implementing single-copy clustering (SCC)
- Implementing DNS round-robin
- Implementing multiple Mail Exchanger (MX) records
- Planning data-redundancy implementation
- Implementing local continuous replication (LCR)
- Implementing cluster continuous replication (CCR)
- Using Dial Tone recovery
- Implementing database portability

Planning the Service's High-Availability Implementation

Messaging-service availably can be affected in a large number of ways. Being aware of these factors and how to mitigate them is important when designing a plan for high availability. Adopting good patching and maintenance procedures will go a long way in keeping your messaging platform stable. (You can find more information on patching in Chapter 17 of this book.) No matter how many procedures you adopt, a flawed design can still cause undue frustration. It is important to be aware of any single point of failures in your environment. Care should be taken to choose hardware that best meets the availability requirements. Having redundant power supplies and hot-swappable disk drives in a RAID (redundant array of independent disks) set are important considerations. Also, improperly sized hardware can cause service outages when load exceeds the capacity of the server. Exceeding load can happen when the processors or memory aren't sufficient to handle load. Load can also exceed the space and I/O requirements of the storage. When designing the storage configuration, be sure to not only take into account the space required, but also the I/O requirements. Choosing the RAID type for the log and database disks is important as it affects the redundancy, space, and I/O throughput of the solution. The following list is a review of how RAID drives affect Exchange performance.

RAID 0 is a *stripe*, or a method of writing sequential data across multiple disks. There is no fault tolerance, but performance and space are maximized.

RAID 10 is a mirror of stripes. Fault tolerance is maximized; however, space is minimized because half of the disk space is taken up for redundancy. Writes to the RAID set are slower than they are with a RAID 0 set.

RAID 5 is a striped set with parity. Space available is greater than with a RAID 10 set; however, the fault tolerance is not as high as with a RAID 10 set. Writes to the RAID set are slower than they are with both RAID 0 and RAID 10 sets.

RAID 6 is a striped set with double parity, allowing for failure of two disks for each set. Space available is less than with a RAID 5 set. Write performance is lower than with a RAID 5.

Be sure to select the RAID configuration that fits the solution that you are trying to reach for high availability. Each Exchange Server–related service has a different way of being made highly available. In previous versions of Exchange there were only front-end and back-end server roles. This limited the flexibility of a high-availability solution, especially since all the Exchange services were installed on every type of Exchange 2000 and 2003 server. Now that we can install discrete roles, we can create a tailored high-availability solution. Some of the Exchange roles just need multiple instances installed, while others require special configurations and hardware to provide high availability.

Let's consider the configurations to Mailbox high availability and the other server roles, as shown in Table 9.1.

TABLE 9.1 Methods for Providing High Availability with each Exchange Server Role

Exchange Server Role	Methods for Providing High Availability
Hub Transport (when used at the edge)	Multiple servers with DNS round-robin. Multiple servers with multiple MX records.
Hub Transport (as internal mail transport)	Multiple servers.
Client Access	Multiple servers with Network Load Balancing.
Edge Transport	Multiple servers with network load balancing. Multiple servers with DNS round-robin. Multiple servers with multiple MX records.
Mailbox	Local continuous replication. Cluster continuous replication. Single-copy cluster.
Unified Messaging	Add multiple Servers to a dial plan and use the VoIP gateway or gateways to round-robin connections between the servers.

Although the Unified Messaging role is mentioned here, deployments are typically handled by a Microsoft Certified Partner. To view a list of these partners visit `http://www.microsoft.com/exchange/partners/2007/um.mspx`.

Implementing High Availability for Non-Mailbox Server Roles

Load balancing is the process of spreading network traffic across multiple servers. Each service has a different method for balancing load. In this section we will discuss the various methods of improving availability for each on the non-Mailbox roles.

Table 9.2 lists the supported methods of availability for each non-Mailbox server role.

TABLE 9.2 Availability Options for Non-Mailbox Servers

Availability	Hub Transport (Internal) Server Role	Hub Transport (at Edge) Server Role	Edge Transport Server Role	Client Access Server Role
Multiple servers installed	X			
Multiple servers with Network Load Balancing			X	X
Multiple servers with DNS round-robin		X	X	X
Multiple servers with multiple MX records		X	X	

When using a Hub Transport server internally, there is nothing required other than to install multiple server roles in a site to improve availability. Using a Hub Transport server at the edge to receive inbound SMTP mail does require additional configuration.

Although it is supported, Microsoft does not recommend using a Hub Transport server at the edge.

Implementing Network Load Balancing (NLB)

Network Load Balancing is the use of single network IP and MAC address that is shared by multiple servers. This can be done with either a hardware load-balancing device or by using the Network Load Balancing feature built into Windows Server. The only Exchange Server 2007 roles that are supported with NLB are the Client Access and Edge Transport roles. As you recall, the Client Access server role handles Autodiscover, Outlook Web Access (OWA), Exchange ActiveSync, POP3, IMAP3, Outlook Anywhere, Availability, and the other web services. The Edge Transport role provides SMTP mail services at the edge of the network while providing advanced antispam and message routing.

Choosing between Hardware- and Software-Based Load Balancing

According to a Microsoft TechNet webcast with several of the Microsoft operations teams, Microsoft uses Windows-based load balancing heavily in their production environments. This would lead you to believe that this is a perfect solution for everyone's network load balancing needs. If it works for Microsoft it must work for everyone else. Well, unfortunately that is not really the case. There are a few subtle differences between using Windows network load balancing and a third-party hardware network load balancer. Figure 9.1 shows the logical configuration of a Windows-based load-balanced solution.

What was previously called Windows Load Balancing is now officially called Network Load Balancing (NLB). In this book, in order to avoid confusion with *other* types of network load balancing, we are still calling it *Windows load balancing* or *Windows-based Network Load Balancing.*

FIGURE 9.1 Windows-based Network Load Balancing

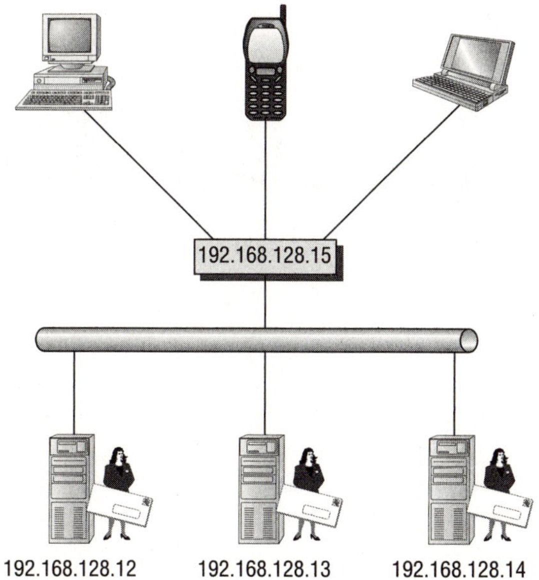

Hardware load balancers (Figure 9.2) often have built-in capabilities for checking the availability and health of the server before sending traffic to it. For example, if a server is responding to pings, it doesn't mean that the Office Outlook Web Access is working properly. In a basic software network load balanced scenario using Windows-based Network Load Balancing, there are no built-in methods to automatically remove or disable a node from the load-balanced cluster to keep it from receiving new connections. With many hardware load balancers, checks can be done to make sure that the service is not only running, but that it is responding properly.

FIGURE 9.2 Hardware load balancing

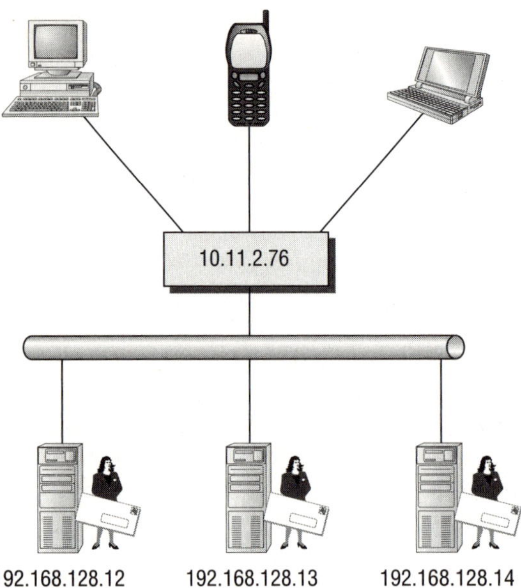

It isn't all positive for hardware load balancing, as it is going to cost more and will require more expertise to properly configure and maintain a hardware solution. Whether you choose a software or hardware load-balancing solution, there are specific issues that will need to be addressed. Let us look at the considerations for both the Client Access and the Edge Transport roles.

Using Network Load Balancing for the Client Access Role

When you use network load balancing to distribute the load across your Client Access servers, you are going to assign a unique load-balanced IP address. You will then instruct the users to connect to a DNS entry that is assigned to the load-balanced IP address. You will now be asking the users to connect to `owa.domain.com`; because of this you will need to modify the ExternalURL property to match the name of the load-balanced name. You will also require an SSL certificate that matches this shared name so that clients will be able to access the web services with a valid certificate.

To be used in a network load balanced configuration, the web services need to be configured. You will need to set the ExternalURL properties to the URL that will be used to access the service. You will also need to set the ExternalURL property for all of the Exchange web services, which include Office Outlook Web Access, offline address book, and ActiveSync on each of the load-balanced servers.

To set the web services (which include the Availability service) virtual directory to use the load-balanced computers, you will need to run the following:

```
Set-WebServicesVirtualDirectory -Identity "Server Name\EWS(default web site)" -
ExternalUrl https://mail.domain.com/EWS/exchange.asmx
```

To set the Outlook Web Access virtual directory to use the load-balanced computers, you will need to run this:

```
Set-OWAVirtualDirectory -Identity "Server Name\OWA(default web site)" -
ExternalUrl https://mail.domain.com/OWA
```

To set the offline address book virtual directory to use the load-balanced computers, you will need to run the following:

```
Set-OABVirtualDirectory -Identity "Server Name\OAB (Default Web Site)" -
ExternalURL "https://mail.domain.com/OAB"
```

To set the ActiveSync virtual directory to use the load-balanced computers, you will need to run this code:

```
Set-ActiveSyncVirtualDirectory -Identity "Server Name\microsoft-server-
activesync" -ExternalURL "https://mail.domain.com/microsoft-server-activesync"
```

Once each of these properties has been set and IIS has been restarted, the load-balanced servers will operate properly for client connections. To verify that the settings have been configured as you expected, you can run the following commands to retrieve the settings:

- `Get-ActiveSyncVirtualDirectory`
- `Get-OABVirtualDirectory`
- `Get-OWAVirtualDirectory`
- `Get-WebServicesVirtualDirector`

Using Network Load Balancing for the Edge Transport Role

It is possible to use network load balancing for Edge Transport servers to provide high availability and load balancing for mail services. In the "Implementing Multiple MX Records" section of this chapter we discuss using multiple MX records, which provides both high availability and load balancing as well; however, it doesn't require the configuration of network load balancing.

The Edge Transport server can be used in a network load balanced cluster to receive email from the Internet. The Edge servers can be put behind a single IP address where all mail is delivered. This would help to provide load balancing and redundant services for inbound email processing. Using network load balancing for the Edge Transport servers is common in high-utilization situations when adding an MX record for every inbound mail server becomes an administrative burden. Also, using a load-balanced Edge Transport server is useful when scheduled maintenance is being performed. During maintenance tasks one server can gracefully be taken out of the network load balanced cluster, patched, and added back in without affecting any inbound mail. Figure 9.3 shows how a server failure can be overcome with network load balancing.

FIGURE 9.3 Using a network load balanced Edge Transport server for failure resilience

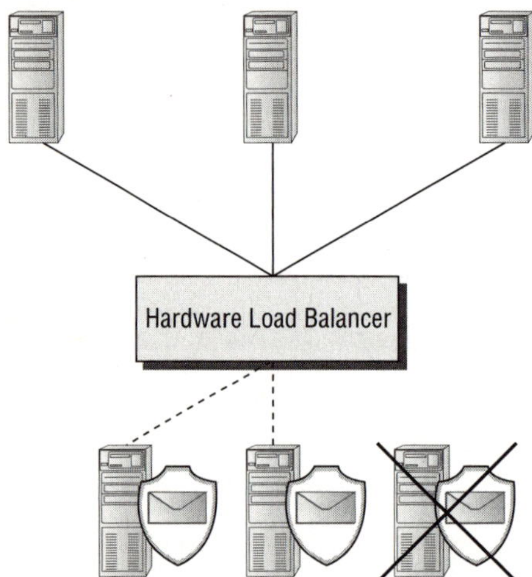

Implementing DNS Round-Robin

DNS round-robin is configuring DNS to return a different primary IP address in a list every time the fully qualified domain name (FQDN) is requested. Each time a client or a client's local DNS server requests the IP address for the FQDN, the DNS server will return the next IP address as the primary address that is in the list. If you have two A (host) records with the FQDN name of `mail.domain.com` has an IP address of 192.168.128.11, and the other has an IP address of 192.168.128.76, the first time a client requests the IP address of `mail.domain.com`, the DNS server would return 192.168.128.76. The second client requesting the IP address would be returned 192.168.128.11. After that the process continues, alternating IP addresses in response to each request. Figure 9.4 illustrates the round-robin DNS process.

Round-robin DNS can be disabled on Windows Server 2003 DNS servers. If you are using Windows Server 2003 for your DNS solution and you are planning on using round-robin, it is important to verify that it is enabled in the server properties.

FIGURE 9.4 How DNS round-robin functions

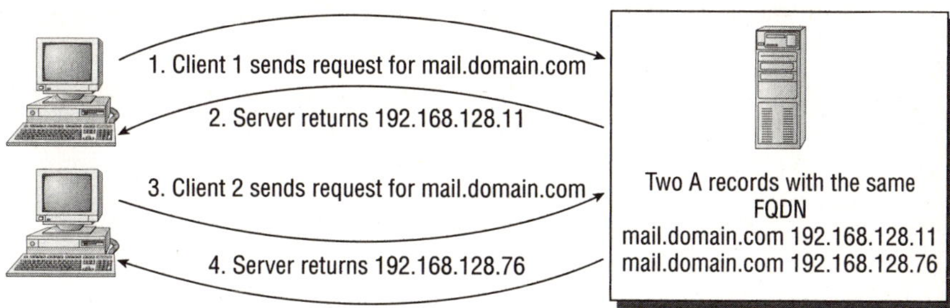

When network load balancing is not used and session preservation is not required, DNS round-robin can be used. It may be beneficial to use DNS round-robin to load-balance Edge Transport and Hub Transport connections, and it is even possible to use this for Client Access connections. In an environment where an administrator controls the end user's DNS resolution, it may also be beneficial to improve availability.

There are several drawbacks to DNS round-robin, however. First, there is no built-in method to ensure that the servers are operating properly before DNS gives out the server IP. Even if one of the servers is unavailable, DNS is still going to hand out the IP addresses. If a user were using Internet Explorer or even Outlook Express to view their email, these clients would not try to retrieve another IP address if the original one retrieved were not responding; the client would not be able to connect. The client would most likely not be able to connect until either the server is restored to service or until the DNS cache expires. At that point it would hopefully be returned the IP address of a functional server from the round-robin DNS entry.

Second, there is little control over how the client will cache the information provided. Granted, there are standards and rules about defining how long a client should cache data; however, the way the client actually uses this time out (time to live or TTL) is out of the authoritative DNS provider's control. The client computer and the client's DNS server all have a cache that would need to be updated. Going back to our example, suppose a user is at home using his ISP and then visits `http://mail.domain.com/owa`. The local ISP DNS server returns 192.168.128.76 as the IP address of the server. The next days the server that corresponds to 192.168.128.76 fails and the entry is removed from the DNS. When the user goes back to check his email he is unable to connect. Why? Because his ISP's DNS server still has 192.168.128.76 cached even though that entry was removed. This is because either the TTL wasn't exceeded (the TTL's expiration would cause the server to expire the cache and recheck the authoritative DNS) or the ISP's DNS server isn't honoring the TTL. True, this can cause a problem even when not using round-robin DNS; however, it is important to have realistic expectations when using round-robin DNS. Round-robin DNS works much more predictably when an administrator has control over how the clients use the DNS for resolution.

Implementing Multiple MX Records

A method similar to DNS round-robin is using multiple MX records. A *Mail Exchanger (MX) record* is an entry in DNS that points to the fully qualified domain name host (A) records of the servers responsible for receiving email for a particular domain. The standard does not allow MX records to point to alias (CNAME) records. Internet mail traffic based on the SMTP protocol was built to be connection-resilient and deals well with server problems as long as the DNS is configured properly. Whether you are using a Hub Transport or an Edge Transport server, using multiple MX records to load-balance works the same.

When you are looking to add redundancy to your inbound SMTP processing, it is as simple as installing another Exchange server role (either another Edge Transport or Hub Transport server) and adding an MX record with the correct preference. Using the data in Table 9.3, let's consider an example to help understand how preferences are used.

TABLE 9.3 Example of MX Record Preference

Host	Preference
`smtp1.domain.com`	50
`smtp2.domain.com`	50
`smtp3.domain.com`	100

If this is your first time learning about MX records, you might assume that the sending server would try `smtp1.domain.com` and `smtp2.domain.com` two times for every one time you would try `smtp3.domain.com`. That assumption is incorrect. The only time that a higher-preference MX record will be tried is if all MX record hosts are unavailable. When you add multiple MX records with the same preference, the sending server will round-robin the connection attempts to the remote servers. Also, the MX records with the lowest priority are used first. If you want to equally load-balance inbound SMTP traffic across these servers, you would assign them all the same preference weight in the MX record. Of note is the fact that the preference weight numbers aren't assigned specifically; the number significance is important only when comparing it against the other MX records for the domain.

If you wanted to set up a disaster recovery site that would receive email in the case of a failure of your primary site, you could use the configuration shown in Table 9.4, assuming that `smtp4.domain.com` and `smtp5.domain.com` are located at the disaster-recovery site.

TABLE 9.4 Using MX Records to Provide for Site Failure

Host	Preference
`smtp1.domain.com`	50
`smtp2.domain.com`	50
`smtp3.domain.com`	50

TABLE 9.4 Using MX Records to Provide for Site Failure *(continued)*

Host	Preference
smtp4.domain.com	100
smtp5.domain.com	100

To have this recovery-site configuration work properly, it would be important to have `smtp4.domain.com` and `smtp5.domain.com` configured to be able to not only receives email for your domain, but also to configure the server to properly deliver the email to the end users.

More information about how MX records work can be found in Internet Engineering Task Force Request for Comment (RFC) 2821. The text of this RFC is available at `http://www.ietf.org/rfc/rfc2821.txt`.

Implementing High Availability for Mailbox Server Roles by Using a Single-Copy Cluster (SCC)

Clusters provide for failures of hardware or even software. The different availability options for the Mailbox role are as follows; each solution solves for a slightly different set of criteria.

Single-copy clusters (SCC). A single-copy cluster (SCC) is a clustered solution similar to the clusters that are available for previous versions of Exchange Server. SCC uses a single copy of the mailbox data that is shared by each cluster node. Only the Mailbox role is supported on the cluster nodes.

Local continuous replication (LCR). LCR is a single-server solution that uses log shipping to create a second copy of the mailbox data.

Cluster continuous replication (CCR). CCR is a clustered solution that uses log shipping to create a copy of mailbox data on a second server. Only the Mailbox role is supported on the cluster nodes.

Clustering and replication apply to only Mailbox server roles.

A single-copy cluster (SCC) is similar to the clusters that are available for previous versions of Exchange Server. The main difference with the Exchange Server 2007 single-copy cluster is that there are no other services besides the Mailbox role installed. To be able to deliver mail, at least one more server is required. This provides a much less complicated cluster since it no longer has to fail over the SMTP and IIS instances to the other node, since they are now running on the Hub Transport and Client Access server roles.

Why is this called a *single-copy cluster*? Because it has a single copy of each database on a shared disk system available to all cluster nodes. (It will become more clear why it is named this when we discuss the other Mailbox role availability options under "Planning a Data-Redundancy Implementation" later in this chapter.)

A single-copy cluster, as pictured in Figure 9.5, leverages Microsoft Clustering Services (MSCS) to handle clustering operations. This includes providing the ability to fail over or hand off services to passive servers.

FIGURE 9.5 A single-copy cluster

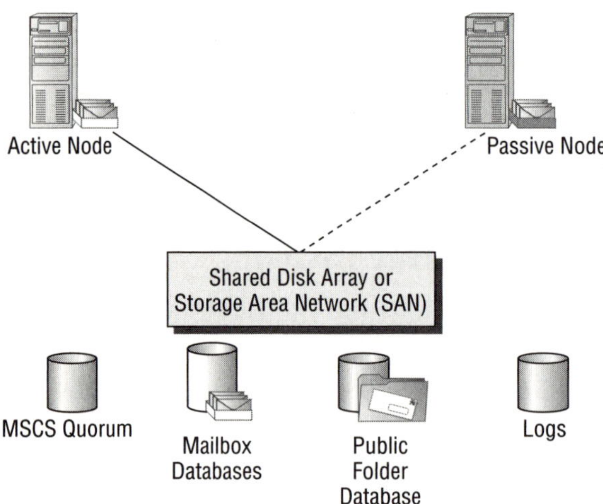

What do you need for a single-copy cluster? You need at least a two-server cluster solution from the Microsoft Windows Catalog of Tested Products under the Cluster Solutions section. This solution will include two identical servers and a storage system that allows at least two servers to share access to the disk. It is important that the entire solution be listed in the catalog in order to be eligible for support from Microsoft. These solutions not only include hardware specifics; the solutions also often include driver and firmware versions that have been tested.

You can view the Windows Catalog of Tested Products at `http://www.windowsservercatalog.com/`.

The cluster shares an IP address and the rest of the resources between each of the nodes. The Exchange services running on the cluster nodes are known as the *clustered Mailbox server*.

The clustering service allows for the clustered Mailbox server to be transferred between cluster nodes. During the transfer process, known as a *failover*, the mail services are temporarily unavailable as the appropriate resources are transferred to the passive node. End users, especially web and Office Outlook in cached mode, rarely will know about a failover event. You can run up to eight nodes in a single cluster to support an Active/Active/Active/Active/Active/Active/Active/Passive Exchange cluster. Since Exchange Server 2007 single-copy clusters rely on MSCS, Windows Server 2003 Enterprise x64 is required. Other important factors that should be considered when deploying a single-copy cluster are as follows:

- Make sure to have the DNS properly configured, and all nodes of the cluster using the same DNS servers.
- Be sure that all cluster nodes are properly registered in the DNS with the fully qualified names.
- All cluster nodes must be in the same domain.
- All cluster nodes must have at least one public and one private IP address, both of which should have separate network adapters.
- Each server in the cluster must have at least one public and one private interface on separate LANs. Each server in the cluster must have these interfaces on the same LAN segments without any routing devices separating them.
- Network latency between the cluster nodes must be less than 500 milliseconds.
- Cluster nodes cannot be Active Directory domain controllers.
- The MSCS cluster must already have been created before the Exchange Server 2007 install is attempted.
- The server node and the Exchange clustered Mailbox server must have a NetBIOS name of less than 15 characters.
- Running Exchange 2007 in a cluster that contains Exchange Server 2003, Exchange 2000 Server, or any version of Microsoft SQL Server is not supported.
- The folder that Exchange Server is going to be installed into should be empty, but cannot be installed in the root of the drive.
- You must install the same version of Exchange 2007 on all nodes in the cluster that are configured as hosts of a clustered Mailbox server.
- The operating system and the Exchange files must be installed on the same paths and drives on all nodes in the cluster.

The Microsoft Clustering Services Cluster Administrator tool can be used to manage the failover of a single-copy cluster, as shown in Figure 9.6. A failover is the process of taking the active resources on one cluster node and moving them to another node. The preferred method of managing the clustered Mailbox server is by using the `Move-ClusteredMailboxServer` cmdlet in the Exchange Management Shell, as shown in Figure 9.7. Using the cmdlet allows for an administrator to provide a documented reason for moving the clustered Mailbox server.

During a manual failover with either the Exchange Management Shell or Cluster Administrator, the Exchange services will be unavailable for a brief period of time.

FIGURE 9.6 Using the Cluster Administrator tool

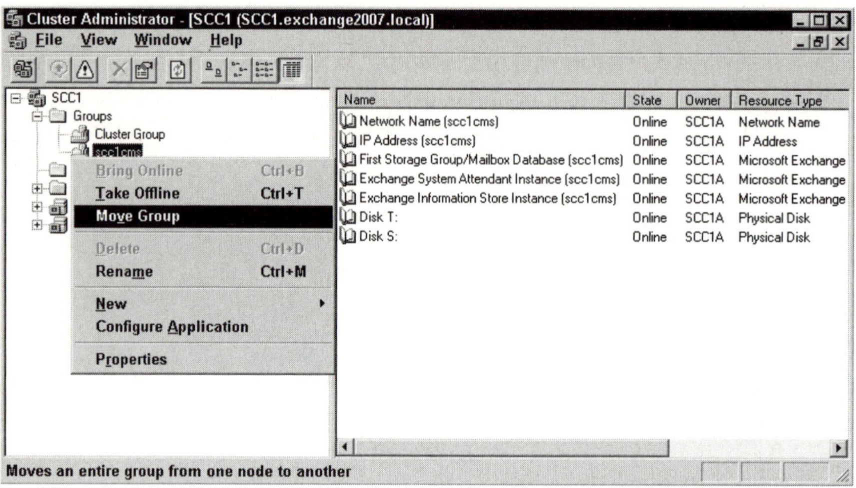

FIGURE 9.7 Using the Move-ClusteredMailboxServer cmdlet

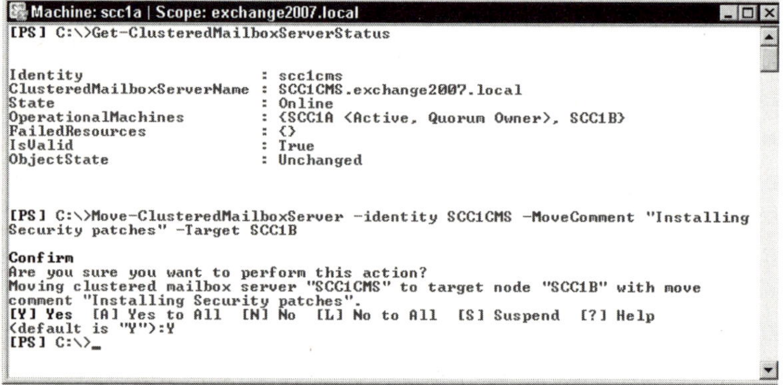

During SCC configuration, keep in mind the following:

- You can have up to five databases in each storage group.
- You can have up to 50 databases on each clustered Mailbox server.
- You may have a public-folder database on an SCC server.

Logs and databases for each storage group should be on separate disks and can be on the same storage system.

In handling your Mailbox server roles, SCR isn't the only strategy available to you. Local continuous replication (LCR) and cluster continuous replication (CCR) provide other ways to implement high availability. Both of these are discussed as part of the following section.

Planning a Data-Redundancy Implementation

A single-copy cluster with the appropriate hardware can withstand many server, software, and storage failures; however, it does not provide redundancy of the database files since it is stored only once. Many companies have recovery-time objectives (RTOs) that dictate the maximum amount of time it would take to restore service in the event of an outage. If a data-loss event were to occur, retrieving data from a backup could take a significant amount of time, making it difficult to achieve set RTOs in many cases.

If a restore is required, there is a very real possibility of data loss. Data loss can also occur if the active log files are lost during the failure event or if the restore is unsuccessful. These scenarios need to be considered when planning a deployment of a highly available Exchange solution.

To provide for not only server-component failure but also data corruption due to component failure, data redundancy can be used. At its release, Exchange Server 2007 provides two options for data redundancy. The first is a single server with multiple disk sets that can be used in a local continuous replication configuration. The second uses a pair of servers with independent storage devices and can be deployed as a cluster with cluster continuous replication.

The key technology that makes data redundancy possible is the way that Exchange uses transaction log files. Although Exchange is not unique in its use of transaction logs, it is important to review how transaction logs work. A transaction log is not a list of email messages that have been delivered, calendar appointments, or task lists. These logs contain the changes that are going to be made to the database at a physical level. For instance, if a user just received a new message, the transaction log would contain entries that include writing the new message to pages in the database. Receipt of a single email message can easily cause more than 10 changes to the database. If a user were to mark this newly received email message in their inbox as having been read, the transaction log would include a change to the database page that contains the read status of the message (changed from unread to read). You can see that ensuring that all transaction logs are applied (and applied in the correct order) is very important. If for some reason we were missing the log file that recorded that we received the email message, and then we tried to apply the log file that changes the read status of that nonexistent message, we would have some serious database problems. This whole logging process enables a single server to be able to recover from a power outage or operating-system crash without losing any data. When Exchange is restarted, a database recovery runs to confirm that each of the transaction log files have been successfully committed to the database.

If we were able to take the concept of database recovery and apply it to two separate copies of the database, we could take the log files that were written on the live database and then apply them to the second copy. If you start with two exact copies of the database and apply the same transactions to them, they should continue to be identical. Both local continuous replication and cluster continuous replication rely on this process, but each works a little differently and thus each is suitable for different environments. The process of establishing the database copy that the log files are to be copied to is called *seeding*. If both copies of the database have diverged or have become out of sync to the point that log files cannot be applied to the passive copy, then you may need to reseed the database. To manually seed or reseed, use the `Update-StorageGroupCopy` cmdlet.

Both local continuous replication and cluster continuous replication depend on the Microsoft Exchange Replication service. This service is responsible for monitoring, copying, verifying, and replaying the active log files to the passive database. After the active log file is completed and closed on the active storage group, the Replication service copies the file to the inspector, which is located in a passive storage group directory, where it is verified for consistency and, if validated, it is moved to the passive database log directory. If the log file is not able to be verified it is recopied from the original location. After the log file is copied to the passive database log directory, it is committed to the passive database. The replication process is shown in Figure 9.8.

FIGURE 9.8 How continuous replication works

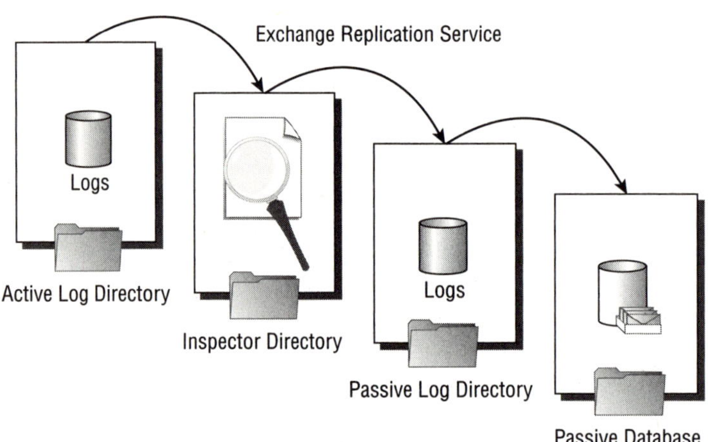

Because we have two copies of the data, the possibility that we would need to restore from a backup is now reduced considerably. Since we are able to rely less on restores, which is often the limiting factor of database size, we can now increase our maximum database size. Microsoft recommends a maximum size of 200 GB on databases protected with LCR or CCR. With larger database sizes being supportable, larger mailboxes can now be supported as well. This is a maximum size; if you choose to use a database of this size, be sure that you will be able to meet your availability requirements in the event of a failure.

Let us look at the both local continuous replication and cluster continuous replication to see the differences and the information needed to create a successful design.

Implementing Local Continuous Replication (LCR)

Local continuous replication, as pictured in Figure 9.9, is a single-server data-redundancy solution. Because this requires only one server, this is a viable solution for limited budgets or those who don't have experience with Microsoft clusters. This solution uses log-file replication with replay to maintain two separate copies of the database. The recommended configuration places the active and passive copies of the data on separate storage devices attached to independent storage controllers. The reason behind this is that if you have a storage device or a controller failure, you can enable the secondary data copy and take the server offline to repair the failed hardware at a more convenient time. Another reason to have separate storage devices is that you separate I/O load across the device, making sure that the replication I/O impacts the active database only minimally.

FIGURE 9.9 A local continuous replication server

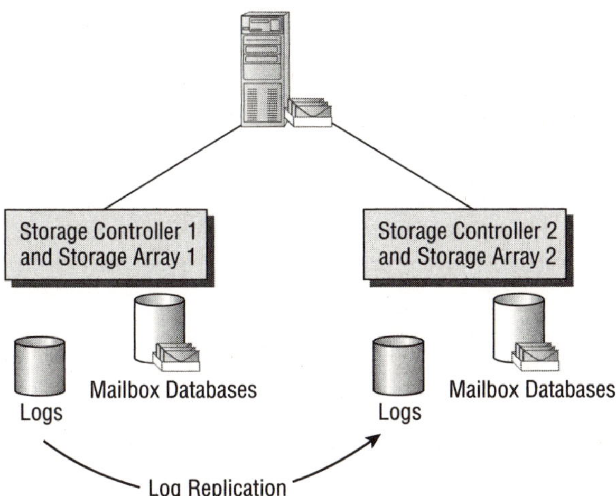

Why is this called *local continuous replication*? This is because as log files are generated they are replicated and then applied to the database on the same server. In the initial release of Exchange Server 2007, there is no way to stagger or delay the log files from being applied to the database. So the passive copy of the database is usually less than a couple of transaction logs behind the active database. Unlike the other forms of mailbox high availability, an administrator can choose specific storage groups to enable LCR on; not all storage groups have to be enabled. Figure 9.10 shows how this process works.

FIGURE 9.10 LCR overview

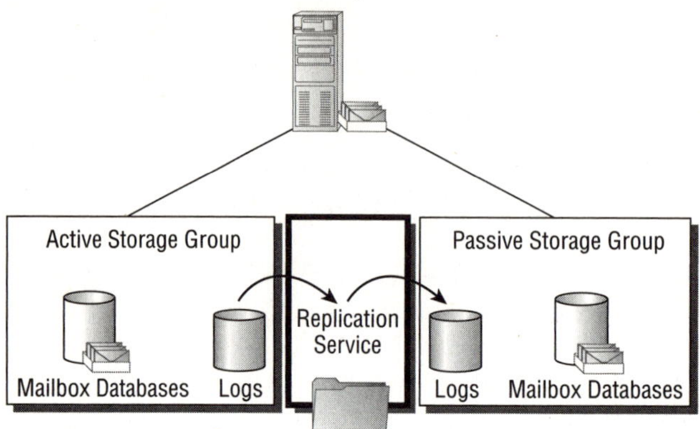

Unlike the other availability options for the Mailbox role, LCR provides only the ability to fail over to the data copy manually. If a failure of the primary database or underlying hardware is detected, an administrator must reconfigure the server manually. In the initial release of Exchange Server 2007, there is no method to perform a failover in the Exchange Management Console. An LCR failover process would follow the following outline.

1. Verify that the server is in a state to failover.
2. Dismount the active database, if applicable.
3. Run the `Restore-StorageGroupCopy` cmdlet to either fail over or fail over and make the copy primary (see Figure 9.11). If you plan on manually moving the file or switching drive letters on the active and passive databases, the `Restore-StorageGroupCopy` cmdlet can be used without the `-ReplaceLocations` switch.

FIGURE 9.11 Failing over to the passive storage group in PowerShell

```
Machine: LCR1 | Scope: exchange2007.local
[PS] C:\>dismount-database -identity "LCR1\First Storage Group\mailbox database"

Confirm
Are you sure you want to perform this action?
Dismounting database "LCR1\First Storage Group\mailbox database".
[Y] Yes  [A] Yes to All  [N] No  [L] No to All  [S] Suspend  [?] Help
(default is "Y"):y
[PS] C:\>Restore-StorageGroupCopy -identity "LCR1\First Storage Group"
        Base name: e00
        Log file: L:\MDBDATA\First Storage Group\E0000000040.log
        Csv file: M:\MDBDATA\First Storage Group\IgnoredLogs\ne5lp2uq.zzc

        Base name: e00
        Log file: M:\MDBDATA\First Storage Group\E0000000040.log
        Csv file: M:\MDBDATA\First Storage Group\IgnoredLogs\ilele2du.icy

Integrity check passed for log file: M:\MDBDATA\First Storage Group\inspector\E0
0.log
WARNING: Restore-StorageGroupCopy on First Storage Group was successful. All
logs were successfully copied.
[PS] C:\>_
```

What do you need for an LCR server? You need a single server capable of running Exchange 2007 as follows:

- You must have only one database for each storage group that is replicated.
- You cannot use LCR on a storage group that contains a public folder if the Exchange organization has any other public-folder databases.
- You can have up to 50 databases on a LCR server.

The following recommendations apply to LCR configuration:

- Logs and databases for each storage group should be on separate disks; however, they can be on the same storage system.
- Active and passive logs for each storage group should be on separate storage devices attached to separate storage controllers.
- Add an additional 1 GB of RAM over a standard Mailbox server for LCR processing overhead.
- Plan for about 20 percent greater CPU usage over a standard Mailbox server for LCR processing overhead.

Implementing Cluster Continuous Replication (CCR)

Cluster continuous replication, as pictured in Figure 9.12, is a two-server clustered data-redundancy solution. One of the servers acts a primary node and the other a passive node. The storage does not fail over with the clustered mailbox instance; it stays with the cluster node. There can be only two nodes participating in a CCR cluster. There is a one-to-one relationship between these servers. Because a CCR cluster does not require a shared disk system, there is no way to have a disk-based quorum drive to ensure that only one server in the cluster has control over the cluster resources. Often a third server is configured as a *file-share witness*. A file-share witness is a server that acts as an arbitrator or a voter in the cluster to maintain a quorum. Microsoft recommends using a Hub Transport server as the file-share witness node. Because this requires two clustered servers and two sets of disks, this is a viable solution only for less constrained budgets and administrators who have experience managing Microsoft clusters. This solution uses log-file replication with replay to maintain two separate copies of the database. As with the single-copy cluster, it is important that the entire solution be listed in the Microsoft Solutions Catalog in order to be eligible for support from Microsoft. These solutions include not only hardware specifics, but also often include driver and firmware versions that have been tested.

Although the removal of the requirement for shared storage makes it easier to build a CCR cluster that spans data centers (also known as a *geo-cluster*) the complexity of the network configuration that would be needed to meet the cluster requirements will keep all but the elite from being able to deploy a geo-cluster.

Why is this called a *cluster continuous replication cluster*? Because the data is continuously replicated between two nodes in a Microsoft cluster. Figure 9.13 shows the data-replication process in a CCR cluster.

FIGURE 9.12 A cluster continuous replication cluster

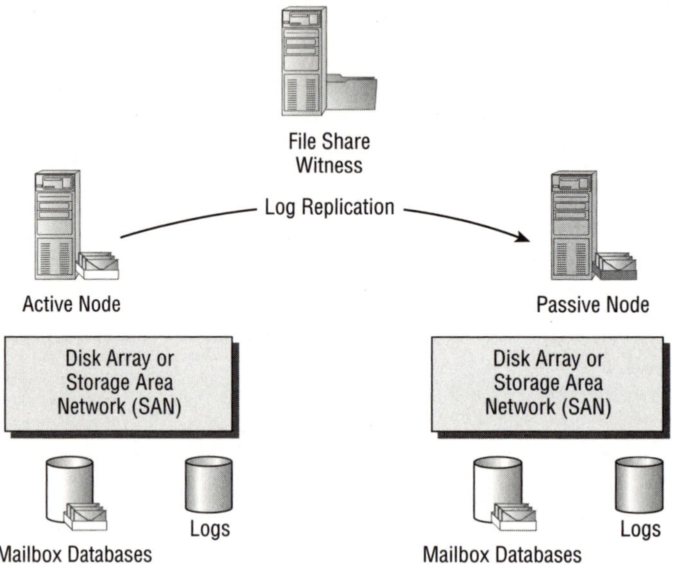

FIGURE 9.13 CCR overview

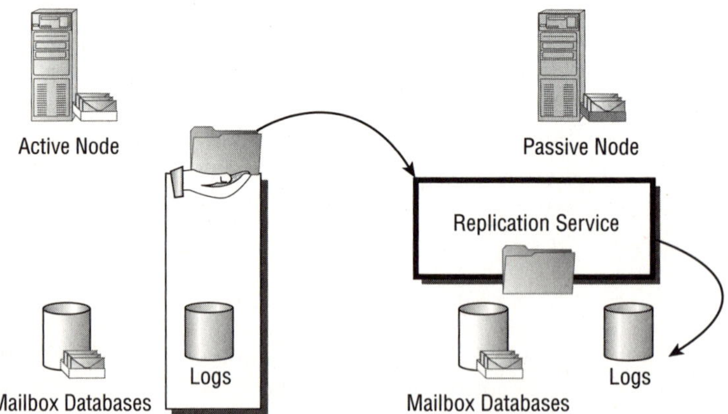

Since Exchange Server 2007 continuous copy replication clusters rely on Microsoft Clustering Services (MSCS), Windows Server 2003 Enterprise x64 is required. Please note the following configuration requirements, as well:

- Make sure to have DNS properly configured and all nodes of the cluster using the same DNS servers.
- Be sure that all cluster nodes are properly registered in DNS with the fully qualified names.
- All cluster nodes must be in the same domain.
- All cluster nodes must have at least one public and one private IP address, both of which should have separate network adapters.
- Each server in the cluster must have at least one public and one private interface on separate LANs. Each server in the cluster must have these interfaces on the same LAN segments without any routing devices separating them.
- Network latency between servers must be less than 500 milliseconds.
- Cluster nodes cannot be Active Directory domain controllers.
- The Microsoft Clustering Service cluster must already have been created before the Exchange Server 2007 install is attempted.
- The server node and the Exchange clustered Mailbox servers must have a NetBIOS name of less than 15 characters.
- Running Exchange 2007 in a cluster that contains Exchange Server 2003, Exchange 2000 Server, or any version of Microsoft SQL Server is not supported.
- The folder that Exchange Server is going to be installed into should be empty; however, it cannot be installed in the root of the drive.
- You must install the same version of Exchange 2007 on all nodes in the cluster that are configured as hosts of a clustered Mailbox server.

The operating system and the Exchange files must be installed on the same paths and drives on all nodes in the cluster. Continuous-copy clusters have specific limitations as well:

- You must have only one database for each storage group.
- You can have a public-folder database on a CCR server only if the CCR clustered Mailbox server is the only copy of the public folder in the Exchange organization.
- You can have up to 50 databases on a CCR clustered Mailbox server.

Note the following deployment recommendations for CCR:

- Logs and databases for each storage group should be on separate disks; however, they can be on the same storage system.
- Use another existing Exchange server in the same site, such as a Hub Transport server as the cluster file-share witness node.

When configuring the CCR cluster, it is important to take into account the automatic database mount settings. You can configure the server by using the `Set-MailboxServer` cmdlet and setting AutoDatabaseMountDial property with one of the following values:

- Lossless: The databases will not automatically mount on the passive node until all of the logs have been copied to the passive node. If the active node goes offline, the databases will not be mounted until the logs are able to be recovered from the failed node.
- GoodAvailability: The databases will mount on the passive node as long as the copy queue length is less than or equal to two. Exchange will continue to copy the remaining logs from the failed node and attempt to mount the database.
- BestAvailability: The databases will mount on the passive node as long as the copy queue length is less than or equal to five. Exchange will continue to copy the remaining logs from the failed node and attempt to mount the database.

These settings affect the automatic mounting of the databases in a CCR cluster; an administrator can choose to force a database mount in case a failover occurs with data loss. Figure 9.14 shows an example of using `Set-MailboxServer` to modify the AutoDatabaseMountDial setting from the default of BestAvailability to Lossless.

FIGURE 9.14 Using Set-MailboxServer to modify the AutoDatabaseMountDial setting

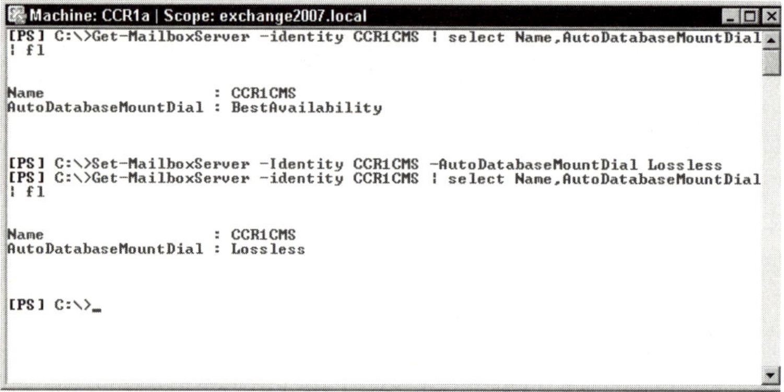

Because CCR uses log-file replication to provide data redundancy, it is possible during a hard failover to the second node that log files are damaged on the second node. This may cause email to be lost. A feature that reduces this possibility is the transport dumpster. The transport dumpster is enabled automatically on Hub Transport servers only for CCR clusters. The Hub Transport servers will maintain a queue of recently delivered email messages to mailboxes that reside on a CCR clustered Mailbox server. If a hard failover occurs that has the possibility of lost data, the clustered Mailbox server will notify the Hub Transport servers to redeliver email messages from the transport dumpster. The clustered Mailbox server will then reprocess the messages and deliver the non-duplicated items. Unfortunately, the transport dumpster will not assist in recovering the following:

- Appointments (not meeting requests)
- Property updates (i.e., flagging, mark as read, etc.)
- Tasks
- Draft email messages created in Office Outlook in online mode

Although the Microsoft Clustering Services Cluster Administrator tool can be used to manage the failover of a CCR cluster, it is not recommended because it does not contain logic to check the health of the replication status before it transfers the clustered Mailbox server. Using the Cluster Administrator can lead to damaged databases. The preferred method of managing the clustered mailbox is to use the `Move-ClusteredMailboxServer` cmdlet in the Exchange Management Shell as pictured in Figure 9.15. Using the cmdlet allows for an administrator to provide a documented reason for moving the clustered Mailbox server, and it properly checks the health of the server before performing the failover.

FIGURE 9.15 Using Move-ClusteredMailboxServer on a CCR server

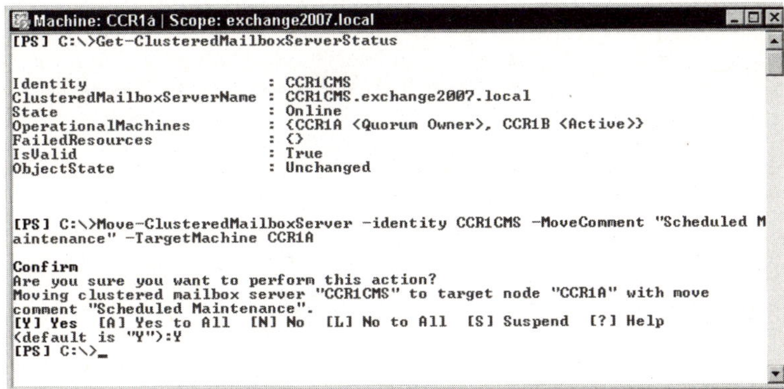

Deciding Which Mailbox-Availability Strategy to Adopt

With so many options, it can be difficult to decide which mailbox-availability strategy to use in a specific situation. Table 9.5 can help you to determine which availability strategy has specific features or limitations.

TABLE 9.5 Mailbox Availability Strategy Features

Feature	LCR	CCR	SCC
Can have only one database per storage group	X	X	
Can run other roles	X		

TABLE 9.5 Mailbox Availability Strategy Features *(continued)*

Feature	LCR	CCR	SCC
Can host public-folder replicas			X
Can span data centers		X	X
Simplest, least expensive	X		
Requires shared storage			X
Provides data redundancy	X	X	
Provides server redundancy		X	X

Using Dial-Tone Recovery

Dial-tone recovery has been a recommend fast recovery method since Exchange Server 2003. When a database has failed and cannot be mounted, dial-tone recovery can be done. Dial-tone recovery moves the damaged database out of the original database location, and then a blank database is mounted. This database has no data in it, but it allows the end users to be able to connect to a mailbox and to send and receive new email while the old data is recovered. The old data could be recovered by either repairing the database or by performing a restore to the recovery storage group. Once the data is recovered, there are two options:

- The data can be merged back into the production mailboxes using the Recover Mailbox Data feature of the recovery storage group.
- The data can be swapped into the location of the dial-tone database so that the dial-tone information can be merged into the recovered database.

Because mounting dial-tone databases loses mailbox rules, delegate data, and offline folder store encryption keys, administrators will often swap the original database back into the production storage group and merge the dial-tone database in using the Recover Mailbox Data feature of the recovery storage group.

Now that Exchange Server 2007 allows for database portability, these dial-tone recovery tasks can be done on a standby server rather than having to complete the recovery on the server where the original failure occurred.

More information about problems that can arise when performing a dial-tone recovery can be found at `http://support.microsoft.com/?kbid=282496`.

Real World Scenario

Managing Employee Relations During an Email Outage

In real-world environments, emails are a very critical piece of business. So when email is down, tempers are up. If a failure occurs and the database needs to be repaired using the Extensible Storage Engine Utility (ESEUTIL) or recovered from a tape, there is usually a better end-user perception of the outage if the users are restored to service using a dial-tone recovery.

It is often difficult for Exchange administrators to admit that restores and repairs have a tendency to fail the first time, especially when you're dealing with the executives' email and your job is at stake. A good way to not fall into this trap is to limit the length of time that you spend on trying to repair or restore the database, so that the end users are not left in the lurch without any access to Exchange services. You should make it standard practice to mount a dial-tone database if you aren't able to repair or restore the database within 30 minutes. After mounting the dial-tone database, send an email to the users describing the reason of the absence of their old mailbox content and what steps are being taken to restore that data.

Following this procedure should reduce the number of times your manager has to come to you with sweat running down his brow and scream at you that he is under a lot of pressure so you need to get Exchange working!

Implementing Database Portability

One of the most painful aspects in previous versions of Exchange Server is the fact that moving a database between servers wasn't a supported way of moving users or of recovering from a server failure. Exchange Server provides for mounting databases on different servers in the same Exchange organization and then modifying the mailbox objects so that they are associated with the location of the new database. To allow for database portability, Exchange 2007 allows any mailbox database to be mounted on any other Exchange 2007 Mailbox server in the organization.

Database portability does not work with public-folder databases.

There are a number of scenarios in which you would use database portability:

- Recovering mailbox data between geographical sites.
- Recovering a clustered Mailbox server to another operational server.
- Using a portable dial-tone recovery. (You can do this by mounting empty databases on a new server while database restores are being done.)

Database portability requires only a few steps that need to be followed when moving a database from one server to another. The overview of the process is as follows:

1. Make sure the database was shut down cleanly or perform a soft recovery if the database isn't in a clean state.
2. Use either the Exchange Management Shell or Exchange Management Console to create a new database with the same name on the new server; however, do not try to mount the new database. Set the new database to allow a restore to overwrite the database. Figure 9.16 shows using the Exchange Management Shell to create the new database and setting it to allow a restore.

FIGURE 9.16 Using the Exchange Management Shell to create a new database

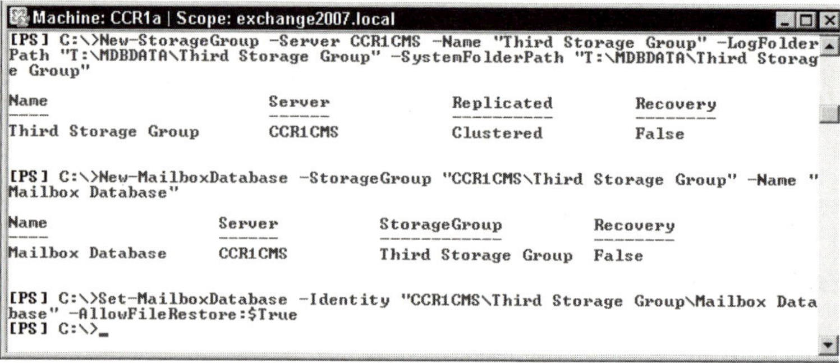

```
Machine: CCR1a | Scope: exchange2007.local
[PS] C:\>New-StorageGroup -Server CCR1CMS -Name "Third Storage Group" -LogFolder
Path "T:\MDBDATA\Third Storage Group" -SystemFolderPath "T:\MDBDATA\Third Storag
e Group"

Name                     Server           Replicated          Recovery
----                     ------           ----------          --------
Third Storage Group      CCR1CMS          Clustered           False

[PS] C:\>New-MailboxDatabase -StorageGroup "CCR1CMS\Third Storage Group" -Name "
Mailbox Database"

Name                 Server         StorageGroup           Recovery
----                 ------         ------------           --------
Mailbox Database     CCR1CMS        Third Storage Group    False

[PS] C:\>Set-MailboxDatabase -Identity "CCR1CMS\Third Storage Group\Mailbox Data
base" -AllowFileRestore:$True
[PS] C:\>_
```

3. Move the database files to the new server in the location you specified for the new database.
4. Mount the new database with the Exchange Management Shell or Exchange Management Console.
5. Use the `MoveMailbox` cmdlet with the `ConfigurationOnly` option to point the mailbox configuration to the new location. Figure 9.17 shows an example of running `Get-Mailbox` to gather the mailboxes from the old database and piping the output to the `Movemailbox` cmdlet with the `-ConfigurationOnly` option.

FIGURE 9.17 Using MoveMailbox with the ConfigurationOnly switch

```
Machine: CCR1a | Scope: exchange2007.local
[PS] C:\>Get-Mailbox -Database "SCC1CMS\First Storage Group\Mailbox Database" |
Move-Mailbox -TargetDatabase "CCR1CMS\Third Storage Group\Mailbox Database" -Con
figurationOnly:$True

Confirm
Are you sure you want to perform this action?
Moving mailbox: Administrator (Administrator@exchange2007.local) to database:
CCR1CMS\Third Storage Group\Mailbox Database. This operation will only modify
the mailbox's Active Directory configuration. Mailbox content can be
potentially lost, and this mailbox will be inaccessible until the changes are
completed.
[Y] Yes  [A] Yes to All  [N] No  [L] No to All  [S] Suspend  [?] Help
(default is "Y"):A_
```

It is important to know how using database portability affects your user base. Since the user's mailbox is now on a server with a different name, the user's client will need to be able to locate where the mailbox has been moved to without the original server being available. As you can see in Table 9.6, both Office Outlook 2007 and Office Outlook Web Access are automatically redirected to the new location. Problems may occur when older clients are in use. These clients will need to be manually reconfigured, or an administrative script can be run on each of the users' computers to reconfigure the older versions of Outlook.

TABLE 9.6 Client Redirection Methods

Client	Redirection	Method
Office Outlook 2007	Automatic	Uses Autodiscover
Outlook 2002 and 2003	Manual	Needs to be reconfigured manually
Office Outlook Web Access	Automatic	Uses Active Directory

Summary

In this chapter we talked about availability options for each of the Exchange server roles. You saw how use of network load balancing as well as DNS round-robin and multiple MX records can provide high availability for most of the Exchange roles. Then you learned how Mailbox roles can use LCR, CCR, and SCC to improve availability. We also discussed the specific requirements for each of the availability options. Last you learned how to leverage database portability and dial-tone recovery to provide rapid recovery during failure situations, even when a server is unrecoverable or if recovery will take longer than the permitted recovery window.

Exam Essentials

Know the differences between the Mailbox role availability types. In the exam you will most likely be asked to differentiate between the ways to make your Mailbox servers more available. You need to know which server types provide data redundancy and which provide server redundancy only. Remember that the single-copy cluster requires shared hardware and that local continuous replication and cluster continuous replication use server-attached storage devices. Remember which servers can have public-folder stores in an enterprise environment and which ones require that only one database be in each storage group.

Know how to make all roles redundant. Each role can be made redundant by adding multiple servers. Most roles, however, require additional hardware or configuration to make the solution failure-resilient. Be sure to understand the pros and cons for each of the redundancy options and what is required to configure each of them.

Know how database portability opens new methods of recovery. Database portability is the new feature that allows a database to be mounted on any Exchange server in the organization. Tools have been created to allow mailbox configuration to be modified so that the mailboxes are pointed to the new location. New features in Microsoft Office Outlook 2007 also allow for the client computers to locate the new server the mailbox is hosted on.

Review Questions

1. You have been asked to design a redundant Mailbox server design. The business requires that the design allow for a single server failure. Which server solutions could you design to meet this requirement?
   - **A.** LCR.
   - **B.** CCR.
   - **C.** SCC.
   - **D.** Add two RAID arrays with a mirror set to a server.
2. The standard remote office deployment consists of two servers: one that has the Hub Transport and Client Access roles installed, and one that has the Mailbox role installed. When the Hub Transport server is offline, internal email message delivery is impacted to the remote office mailboxes. What can be done to reduce this effect?
   - **A.** Add an Edge Transport server at the remote office and create an MX record in the domain for it.
   - **B.** Add a second Client Access server at the remote office and create a round-robin DNS entry for both.
   - **C.** Create an MX record for the Mailbox server at the remote office.
   - **D.** Add a second Hub Transport server at the remote site.
3. You have been asked to design a new redundant Mailbox server design. The business requires that you allow for data redundancy and server redundancy. Which solution could you use to meet the business requirements?
   - **A.** LCR.
   - **B.** CCR.
   - **C.** SCC.
   - **D.** Add two RAID arrays with a mirror set to a server.
4. You have been asked to design a new redundant design for users to access Outlook Web Access. The business requires that you allow for server redundancy and automatic failover. Which solutions could you use to meet the business requirements?
   - **A.** Software network load balancing
   - **B.** Hardware network load balancing
   - **C.** Round-robin DNS entries
   - **D.** Multiple MX records

5. One of your Mailbox servers has had a database failure. The database may take hours to restore or repair. The business requires that you allow users to be able to send and receive email as quickly as possible. Which option will provide for the business requirement?
   A. A dial-tone database
   B. A recovery storage group
   C. Database portability
   D. Streaming database restores

6. Your company plans to deploy standard Mailbox server roles with 5 storage groups and 10 databases to each of the remote offices. The servers were purchased with a single storage device. What would need to be done to optimally reconfigure these servers to support LCR? (Choose all that apply.)
   A. Create five additional storage groups and distribute the mailbox databases evenly.
   B. Add a second server.
   C. Add a second storage controller.
   D. Add a second storage device.

7. Your company plans to deploy centralized Mailbox servers. The servers need to be redundant and minimize data storage on the SAN due to budgetary constraints. What configuration would meet the business needs?
   A. LCR
   B. SCC
   C. CCR
   D. Network load balanced servers

8. You need to deploy an SCC cluster with the fewest servers as well as provide redundancy for Hub Transport servers. What is the lowest number of servers required to meet the requirements?
   A. 2
   B. 3
   C. 4
   D. 6

9. You need to provide redundancy for your company's three Edge Transport servers. You need to have each server used equally. Which of the following are supported options? (Choose all that apply.)
   A. Create MX records with the same preference weight for the host name of each server.
   B. Create MX records with the sequential preference weights for the host name of each server.
   C. Create a network load balanced cluster with each server with a single MX record pointing to the host name of the cluster.
   D. Create MX records with the same preference weights for an alias record of each server.

10. Which tool should you use to manage the failover process on a CCR cluster?

A. Exchange Management Shell

B. Exchange Management Console

C. Cluster Administrator

D. Server Manager

11. Which of the following is not a requirement for a supported CCR cluster?

A. A shared disk system

B. A public and private network interface

C. Server hardware listed on the Microsoft website

D. Windows 2003 Server Enterprise or later

12. Which of the following commands would you use when moving a database between servers?

A. `Move-StorageGroupPath`

B. `Move-DatabasePath`

C. `Move-ClusteredMailboxServer`

D. `MoveMailbox`

13. On an Exchange server with high disk I/O utilization that also requires redundancy, which RAID type would you select?

A. RAID 0

B. RAID 5

C. RAID 10

D. RAID 6

14. When using network load balancing for web services, which property should be set to the load-balanced fully qualified domain name?

A. ExternalURL

B. InternalURL

C. ExternalAuthenticationMethods

D. Instance

15. You added two MX records (`smtp1.domain.com` and `smtp2.domain.com`) with a preference weight of 20 for `domain.com`. You have added another server (`smtp3.domain.com`) at another location with a preference of 40. What behavior will this cause?

A. The `smtp3.domain.com` will be used first; if it is unavailable the others will be load-balanced.

B. All three servers will be load-balanced, `smtp3.domain.com` will be used only one-third of the time.

C. The `smtp1.domain.com` and `smtp2.domain.com` will be load-balanced first; if both are unavailable `smtp3.domain.com` will be used.

D. All three servers will be load-balanced; `smtp3.domain.com` will be used two-thirds of the time.

16. On a continuous-replication server, after a log file is closed it is copied by the replication service into which directory?
    - A. The inspector directory for the storage group on the active node
    - B. The storage-group log directory on the passive node
    - C. The inspector directory for the storage group on the passive node
    - D. The storage-group log directory on the active node

17. A CCR storage-group replication has failed and needs to be reseeded. What cmdlet would you used to reseed the database?
    - A. `Update-StorageGroupCopy`
    - B. `Restore-StorageGroupCopy`
    - C. `Move-ClusteredMailboxServer`
    - D. `Resume-StorageGroupCopy`

18. Which of the following resources need to be considered when sizing an LCR server?
    - A. 20 percent greater CPU load
    - B. 50 percent greater CPU load
    - C. 5 percent greater CPU load
    - D. 100 percent greater CPU load

19. Which of the following failover options will automatically mount a database after a failover if two or fewer log files are missing from the failed node?
    - A. Lossless
    - B. GoodAvailability
    - C. BestAvailability

20. The Transport dumpster does not help recover which of the following? (Choose all that apply.)
    - A. Draft email
    - B. Tasks
    - C. New email received
    - D. New email sent

Answers to Review Questions

1. B, C. Both CCR and SCC will require a minimum of two clustered servers. Both solutions meet the requirement for providing for a server failure. LCR and RAID arrays do not provide for server failure.

2. D. Adding a second Hub Transport server is the only step required to be able to provide redundancy. Internal routing is automatically redundant. Edge transport servers are for email going to and from outside the Exchange organization. The Client Access server does not participate in the delivery of email.

3. B. CCR provides redundancy for servers and data. There are two servers, each with a separate copy of data. LCR, SCC, and RAID arrays may have data protection but do not have server and data redundancy together.

4. A, B. Neither software nor hardware load balancing relies on the client to fail over. The load balancing would be able to remove the failed server from the cluster so that the client can connect to a functional server.

5. A. A dial-tone database will provide the ability for the users to send and receive email messages while restores or repairs are done for the historical data. Recovery storage groups and streaming database restores both require additional downtime to complete. Database portability would require a valid, consistent database to mount, which in this case is unavailable.

6. A, C, D. To properly configure an LCR server you would need to make sure there is a 1:1 storage group–to-database ratio, as well as a second storage controller and storage device for redundancy. Adding a second server is not required to be able to use LCR.

7. B. SCC provides server redundancy and has only one copy of the data so it minimizes the amount of storage used. LCR and CCR both require double the disk space of a SCC clusters and would not meet the criteria. Network load balancing is not supported for mailbox servers.

8. C. SCC clusters cannot run any other role; above the two-node cluster you will also need two servers for redundant Hub Transport servers.

9. A, C. To equally balance load between the servers, create a MX record for each of the server's host records. Another supportable option is to use network load balancing with a single MX record. Creating an MX record for an alias record is not supported and creating sequential weights will cause only the lowest preference to be used.

10. A. The only utility that should be used for CCR failover is the Exchange Management Shell; using Cluster Administrator could lead to data loss. Server Manage and Exchange Management Console do not provide an interface to perform a CCR failover.

11. A. A CCR cluster does not require the use of a shared disk system. Each server can have dedicated storage. The remaining options are requirements for the deploying a supported cluster.

12. D. MoveMailbox with the ConfigurationOnly switch allows an administrator to modify the mailbox objects to point to the new location of the database. Move-StorageGroupPath and Move-DatabasePath are used to move the files for the storage group and the database; they are not used when moving these files between servers. The Move-ClusteredMailboxServer is used to move the clustered resources between cluster nodes.

13. C. RAID 10 is the second best choice for utilization and provides disk-drive redundancy. RAID 0 provides no data redundancy at all. RAID 5 provides more space but has a higher I/O overhead which leads it to not provide as much throughput. RAID 6 provides an even higher redundancy than RAID 5 but has an even higher throughput penalty.

14. A. It is important to set the ExternalURL on each of the Exchange web services so that they can be accessed from the Internet. InternalURL and ExternalAuthenicationMethods should also be set, but they are not specific to configuring load balancing.

15. C. The lower the preference weight, the higher the priority. MX records with higher preference numbers will not be used unless the lower-numbered records are unavailable.

16. C. The log file is copied to the inspector directory on the passive node and checked for consistency before being applied to the passive database copy.

17. A. Update-StorageGroupCopy is able to be used to manually reseed the database. Move-ClusteredMailboxServer is used to move the clustered resource between nodes. Restore-StorageGroupCopy is used prior to mounting the passive copy of a database and is not used to reseed. Resume-StorageGroupCopy is used resume replications if the previous copy has been suspended.

18. A. The standard recommendation is to size for an additional 20 percent CPU load on an LCR Exchange server.

19. B. GoodAvailability requires that two or fewer transaction log files be missing before automatically mounting the database. Lossless allows for zero transaction logs and Best-Availability allows for up to five missing transaction logs.

20. A, B. Tasks and emails saved to the Drafts folder do not traverse the Hub Transport server, so the Transport dumpster does not help in recovering these items. The remaining items do transverse the local Hub Transport servers thus will be retained in the transport dumpster.

Planning a Backup and Recovery Solution for Exchange Server 2007

MICROSOFT EXAM OBJECTIVES COVERED IN THIS CHAPTER:

- ✓ Plan a backup solution implementation.
- ✓ Plan a recovery solution implementation.

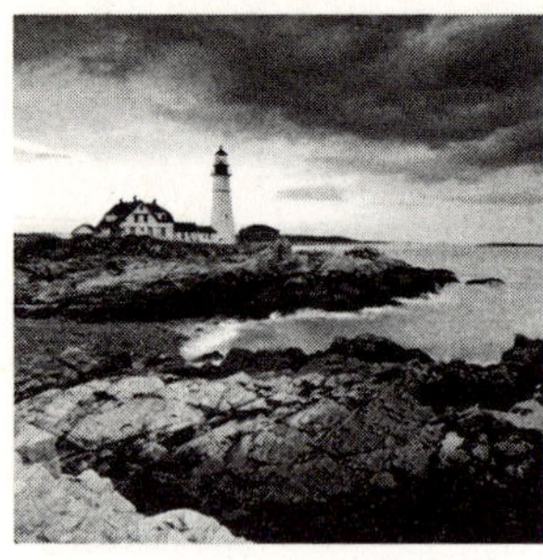

Planning Backup and Recovery

I was once told that backups are not important and that the only important thing was recovery. Although the statement may be considered absurd it highlights the idea that if you cannot restore there is no sense in doing backups. It is essential to completely understand the backup and recovery process to be a successful Exchange professional. In this chapter we will cover the variety of backup options for both Mailbox and non-Mailbox servers as well as methods to recover from each of them.

When determining what type of backups meet your restore needs, it's important to first know what your business requirements are. Once the needs have been documented it will be much easier to determine what backup solution to use and it will be much easier to justify the cost of the solution to the business.

To determine your needs it's good to start with a list of questions:

- How long can it take to restore each group of users and still meet the Service Level Agreements?
- How long can it take before service is restored?
- What services are essential to restore, and in what order?
- How long can it take before all email is restored?
- What is the maximum amount of data that can be lost?
- How long can backups take to complete without affecting end user and other processes?
- What budget has been allocated for backup and recovery?

This list can be summarized into three industry-standard acronyms: SLA, RPO, and RTO. The *Service Level Agreement* or *SLA* will determine how long a mail service can be down before it has to be restored. The *recovery-point objective* or *RPO* will determine how much data can be lost. The *recovery-time objective* or *RTO* will determine the maximum times allowed for recovering each service. Each business will decide upon each of these metrics. Sometimes different business units within an enterprise may have different requirements for each of these, making it even more difficult to come up with a good solution. Often these standards are devised by the business using financial analysis of the effects of these services being offline to see how much it costs the company. These standards are covered in an entire set of courses and books that cross many business disciplines.

Once these standards have been set, a messaging professional can begin to determine the best design that meets these needs.

Planning and Implementing Backup Solutions for Mailbox Server Roles

The Mailbox server role has to be the most important Exchange role. Without the Mailbox role no one is able to read email. There are several options when it comes to backing up the mailbox data; however there are a few other things that need to be backed up in order to be fully protected. The Mailbox server should have a system-state backup completed periodically to be recovered from a backup. Also, a file-system backup of the [Install Directory]\ExchangeOAB should be backed up on the Mailbox server that is set to generate the offline address book to keep the organization from having to rebuild it. Much of the Exchange configuration is stored in Active Directory. It is important to properly back up the domain controllers regularly to be able to recover from corruption and user error. Table 10.1 shows the main components that need to be backed up on a Mailbox server.

TABLE 10.1 Backup Components for the Mailbox Server Role

Data Type	Backup Type
Exchange and service configuration in the registry	System state of the Mailbox server and system state of the Active Directory
Exchange offline address book	File-system backup of [Install Directory]\Exchange OAB
Mailbox	Exchange-aware backup
Public Folder	Exchange-aware backup or replication to other public-folder servers

Another key component for recovery is to avoid having a disaster in the first place. Having redundant hardware, proper patching procedures, change control, and all of the other Microsoft Operations Framework components in place will go a long way toward reducing the need to enact a recovery procedure. Another key way to avoid restoring data needlessly is to set the deleted item and deleted mailbox retention times. Properly configuring deleted item retention will allow items to be recovered after being hard-deleted by the users. The user will have the ability to recover hard-deleted items from within Office Outlook's deleted item recovery feature without having to restore any data from a backup. The deleted mailbox retention time will allow deleted mailboxes to be retained for a period of time before being purged from the database. This will allow an administrator to reconnect a mailbox to a user account during that retention period to recover the entire mailbox. It is important to set the retention period for both mailbox items and mailboxes for a period long enough to minimize the number of times restores would need to be completed. You might think that setting the retention period for both the mailbox and the mailbox items to 999 days might be the answer (so that the only time a restore would be necessary is in the event of corruption). Be aware, however, that a longer retention period will consume more disk space, which will also increase the amount of space that backups will consume.

A problem with Microsoft Office Outlook 2003 when used with Outlook Anywhere may keep hard-deleted items from being restorable. A registry setting on the client computers is required to work around this issue. For more information on the change, please see the Microsoft Knowledge Base article 886205 at `http://support.microsoft.com/kb/886205/`.

Implementing Streaming Backups

Streaming Exchange backups have been available for Exchange since its initial release. The Microsoft Exchange Server 2007 documentation officially calls these backups "legacy streaming backups." Over the years improvements in speed, flexibility, and the number of features have been introduced. Software-based backups use the streaming backup API to back up the online Exchange databases and copy them to either disk or a tape drive.

It is important to remember that you can have only a single simultaneous backup or restore operation in each storage group. To be able to perform backups or restores on multiple databases, the databases need to be separated into multiple storage groups. After splitting up the databases into separate storage groups, you'll be able to perform multiple operations simultaneously (as shown in Figure 10.1). Where possible, put only one database in each storage group, as this simplifies and streamlines both the backup and the restore procedures. Be aware that performing multiple operations simultaneously may have a significant performance impact on the server CPU, memory, and disk systems. It would be good to determine the effects of both single operations and multiple operations before attempting to schedule backups and before performing multiple restores, especially during production hours. Streaming backups can be done against all types of Mailbox servers. Performing a backup of the active copy on both clustered and nonclustered Mailbox servers is supported. Streaming backups can never be done against the passive copies of the databases, such as those that exist on an local continuous replication (LCR) or cluster continuous replication (CCR) Mailbox server.

A streaming backup can be done using NTBackup from a machine with the Exchange management tools installed or by using an agent installed on the Exchange server with a third-party backup application.

A number of types of backups can be completed. The available types of legacy streaming backups are full, copy, incremental, and differential, as shown in Table 10.2. It is essential to understand each of these types of backups and how they affect transaction log files.

FIGURE 10.1 Only one backup can be done for each storage group

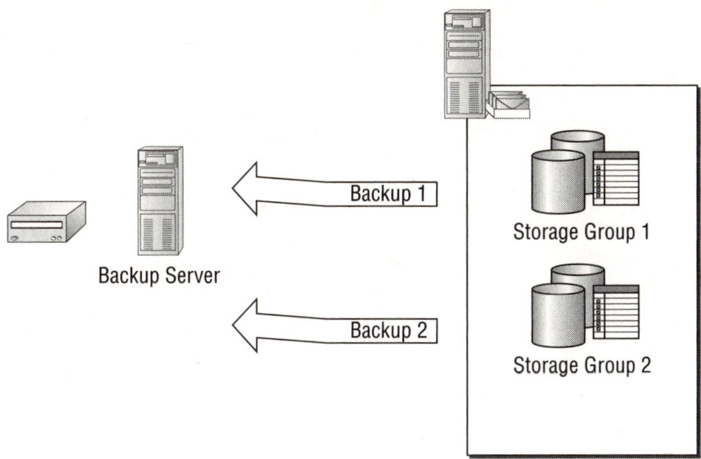

TABLE 10.2 Available Types of Legacy Streaming Backups

Type of Backup	Description
Full	Complete database backup that purges all committed transaction logs.
Copy	Complete database backup and does not purge any transaction logs.
Differential	Transaction logs are not purged.
Incremental	All available transaction logs are purged.

Full Streaming Backups

A full streaming backup will copy the entire database and the required log files to the backup media and then will purge all of the committed transaction logs. The advantage of a full backup is that you can use this backup to restore the database to a consistent state and not need any additional backup sets. The main disadvantages of this backup type are that it can take a long time to complete and that the entire database is backed up to tape including the white space within the database.

When would you use a full backup? If possible, you should always do a full backup. With ever-shrinking backup windows and increasing amounts of data, however, it is often not practical to complete a full backup each time.

Copy Streaming Backups

A copy streaming backup will back up the entire database and will not purge any of the transaction logs. The advantage of a copy backup is that you can use this backup to restore the database to a consistent state and not need any additional backup sets. The main disadvantages of this backup type are that it can take a long time to complete and that the entire database is backed up to tape including the white space within the database. The other disadvantage is that it does not purge the committed transaction logs.

When would you use a streaming copy backup? An excellent use of streaming copy backup is when you need to make an additional backup for archival without affecting the standard backup rotation. As an example, the standard schedule for backups includes a full backup once a week and a differential backup on the remaining days. In the middle of the week you need to create a backup that will be sent offsite to your disaster-recovery site. Running a copy backup to create the backup set to be sent offsite will not affect your ability to use the media onsite to restore service in the case of an outage, since the transaction logs will still be intact.

Differential Streaming Backups

A differential streaming backup will back up the transaction logs that have been generated since the last full or incremental backup. This form of backup does not delete any of the committed transaction logs. Using differential backups minimizes the number of backup sets that would be required for a restore since the last differential backup set would include all of the transaction logs generated. Differential backups cannot be run against storage groups that have circular logging enabled.

When would you use a differential backup? You could use it if you are not able to perform a full backup every day. This would keep all of the log files until the next full backup. You would use differential backup if the server had enough space to hold the log files between full backups.

Incremental Streaming Backups

An incremental streaming backup will back up the logs and then purge them. This form of backup deletes all of the committed transaction logs. Using incremental backups minimizes the number of transaction logs that are kept on the server. It also increases the number of backup sets that would be required for a restore since all the incremental backup sets would need to be restored to recover all of the transaction logs generated. Incremental backups cannot be run against storage groups that have circular logging enabled.

When would you use an incremental backup? When there is not enough space to keep all of the transaction logs between full backup jobs.

Implementing Restores Using Streaming Backups

Legacy streaming restores are fairly straightforward. Restores can be executed back to the original location of the database while it is dismounted, or to a recovery storage group.

Restoring a Streaming Backup

A streaming restore is the simplest restore and does not differ greatly from the process in previous versions of Exchange. You would restore to the original location if a database has been damaged to the point that it cannot be mounted.

Although the actual process will vary slightly depending on your backup software, the procedure to restore to the original location is basically as follows:

1. Dismount the current database.
2. Mark the database able to allow for restore.
3. Perform the full restore.
4. Perform any differential or incremental restores.
5. Perform a hard recovery to apply restored transaction logs.

You can also restore the database to a different server. To complete that process you would follow these steps:

1. Create the new database on the new server.
2. Mark the database able to allow for restore.
3. Perform the full restore to the alternate location.
4. Perform any differential or incremental restores.
5. Perform a hard recovery to apply restored transaction logs.
6. Use database portability to update user objects to the new database location. (More information about database portability can be found in Chapter 8, "Planning a Highly Available Exchange Server 2007 Implementation.")

Hard recovery can be triggered by choosing Last Backup Set in the restore options of the last restore set that you plan to restore, or can be done manually with `ESEUTIL /C`. Performing a hard recovery can take a long time depending on the number of transaction log files that need to be applied. It is important to consider this amount of time in the recovery schedule. Once a hard recovery has been performed, no other log files can be applied to the database.

Streaming backups can also be used to restore public folders to their original location. Public folders rely on having replicas stored on multiple servers to reduce the requirement for restores. To perform single-item or folder restores for a public folder for items that have passed the deleted item retention period, the data restore would need to be done in an alternate forest. After restoring the public-folder data to the alternate forest, Office Outlook would need to be used to export the public-folder data to a personal folders (`.pst`) file that would be used to import the data back into the production public folders.

Restoring to a Recovery Storage Group

Recovery storage groups provide for a very flexible recovery process. They can be used to restore individual mailboxes or specific mailbox items, or for dial-tone recoveries. A recovery storage group can be on any Mailbox server in the Exchange organization and can be used to recover Exchange 2007, Exchange 2003 Service Pack 1 or later, or Exchange 2003 Service Pack 3 or later databases.

Dial-tone recoveries are covered in detail in Chapter 8 of this book.

To perform a restore to a recovery storage group and recover a specific mailbox, the procedure is as follows:

1. Create a recovery storage group.
2. Add the database that you will be recovering to the storage group.
3. Set the database to allow it to be overwritten by a restore.
4. Restore the database and all transaction log files.
5. Mount the recovered database.
6. Use the `restore-mailbox` cmdlet to merge data into mailboxes.

The `restore-mailbox` cmdlet is a very powerful tool, it also provides the ability to recover mail to alternate mailboxes and recover only items selected by date, keyword, or location in the original mailbox.

Implementing Volume Shadow Copy Service (VSS) for Backups

VSS-based backups were first introduced in Microsoft Exchange Server 2003. The Volume Shadow Copy Service (VSS) provides an interface for specialized hardware to be able to create a consistent copy of the database. A consistent copy can be created only if all database writes are *quiesced*, which means *quieted*. The VSS process includes quiescing the writes to the database. As indicated by its name, VSS is volume-based, meaning it does not back up individual files. This means that storage-group placement and database placement are extremely important in an environment that is being planned to implement VSS backups.

You cannot mix VSS and legacy streaming backup types against the same storage group.

What sort of hardware is required to complete VSS backups? As mentioned, specialized hardware is required, as a standard SCSI or SATA RAID controller is not supported. Typically a Fibre Channel or iSCSI Storage Area Network (SAN) is required to deliver this functionality. The hardware needs to be able to support the ability to create two copies of the data rapidly. Creating these copies is typically handled in two different ways even if the hardware manufacturer uses different names and methodologies.

The two basic methods are *clones* or *snapshots*. The clones start out as two synchronized copies of the data and that are split at the point the backup is taken. This leaves one copy inactive as a backup and the other copy continues to be used in production. The snapshot method uses fewer disks and essentially stores a map of the disk data and only keeps track of data that has changed since the snapshot was taken. Although VSS does take less time to complete than streaming backups, the amount of work that goes on at the disk level can be significant. When using clones it could be that the two sets of disk have to synchronize. This synchronization can be likened to the rebuilding of a RAID set and can take a considerable amount of time and resources on the storage hardware. The load that these processes take should be considered when scheduling backups, especially during production hours.

The clone process will vary with each technology vendor and with each VSS hardware provider, but the four main steps typically taken during a clone process are as follows:

1. The two volumes are synchronized during normal database operations, as shown in Figure 10.2.

FIGURE 10.2 Synchronization

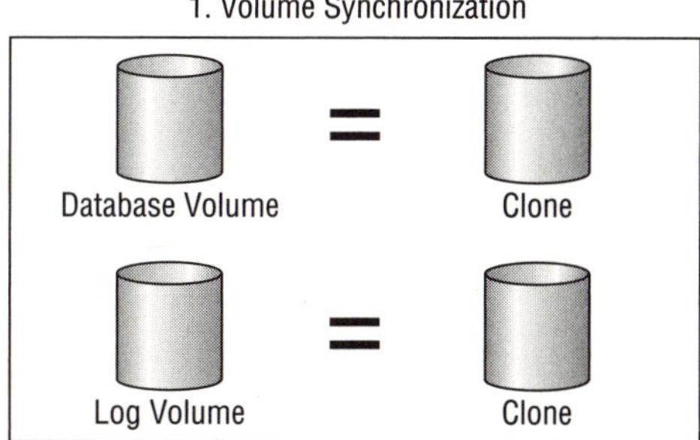

2. Database writes are quiesced and the two volumes are fractured to create a backup, as shown in Figure 10.3.

FIGURE 10.3 Pausing the database writes and fracturing the volumes

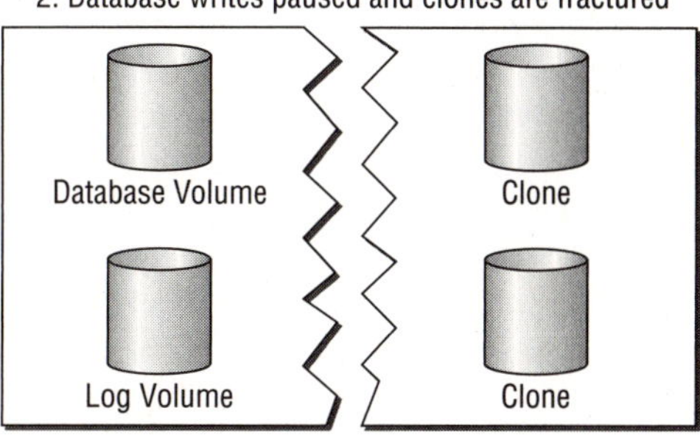

3. The checksum is verified on the copy and is completed by the requestor, as shown in Figure 10.4.

FIGURE 10.4 The checksum is verified and copy is completed

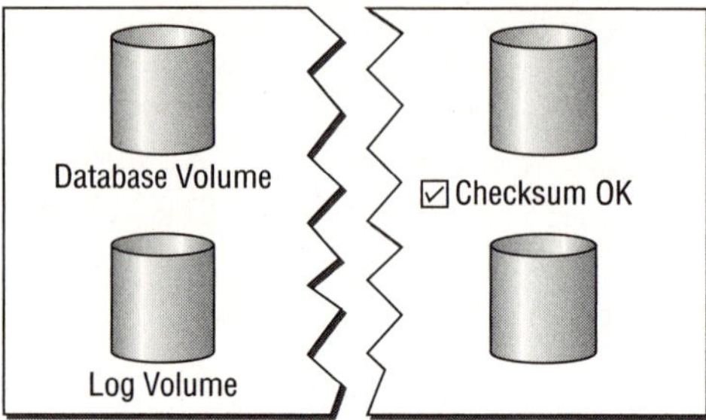

4. The transaction logs are truncated when applicable, as shown in Figure 10.5.

FIGURE 10.5 Transaction logs are truncated

4. Transaction log truncation and writes resume on active volumes

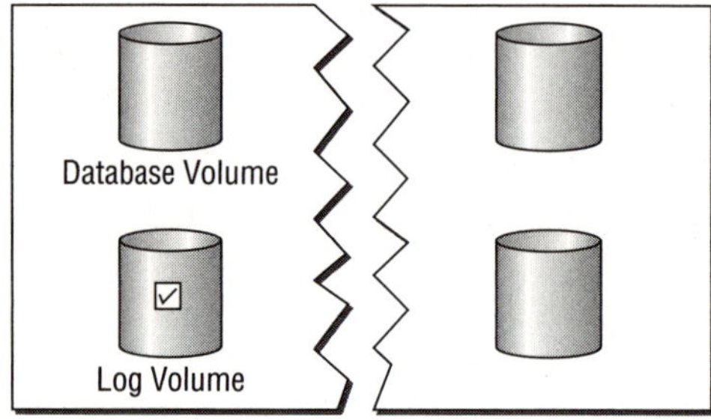

The snapshot process is slightly different from the clone process. Rather than making a full second copy of the data, the snapshot contains only pointers to the data. When data is changed on the active volume, the original data is copied into the snapshot and the changed data is written to the active volume. The benefit of using snapshots is that they don't require the synchronization step. The drawback of using snapshots is that activity done against the snapshot will affect the active volume, since all of the unchanged data is still located on the active volume disks. When streaming backups or other I/O-intensive actions are performed against a snapshot, it can affect the performance of the active volume. Figure 10.6 shows how a snapshot is just a pointer to the original data plus a copy of the original data that has been changed since the snapshot.

The process for creating a VSS snapshot generally follows these three steps:

1. Database is quiesced and writes are paused on the database; a snapshot map is created.
2. Verification of the checksum on the copy is completed by the requestor.
3. The transaction logs are truncated when applicable and writes are resumed to the active database.

FIGURE 10.6 A logical view of a snapshot backup

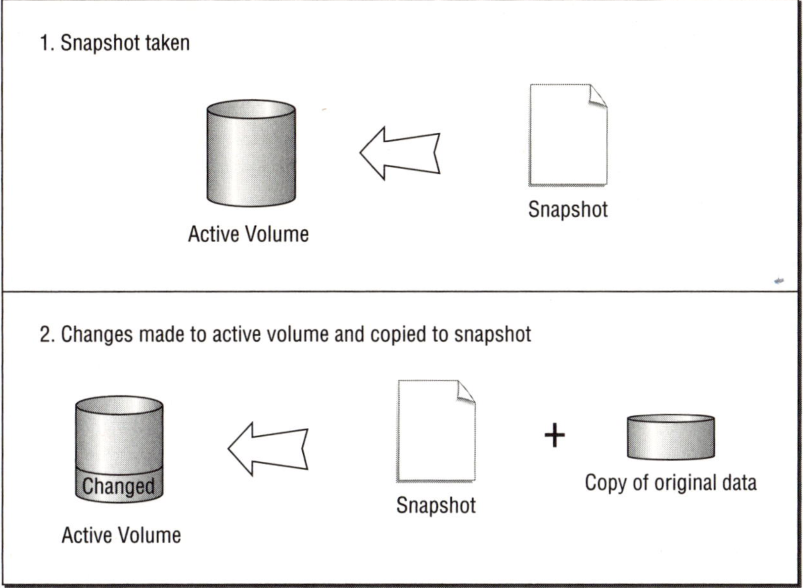

Real World Scenario

Configuring the VSS Volumes for Restores

In order for VSS backups to provide value, one of the following would need to be true:

- VSS backups are able to have multiple copies made.
- Copies are saved to other media.

Many companies will keep several VSS backups on disk. After several days, they will copy the backups to tape media. Because backups and restores are done at a storage-group level, it would make sense that each storage group should have separate volumes as a VSS backup and will include all data on the volume. To provide smooth incremental and differential backups (and more importantly, restores) the database and transaction logs would also need to be on separate volumes.

With many storage solutions, the snapshot and clone volumes also need to be either licensed or at a minimum pre-allocated. This means that for each full backup, a second copy of the volume will be needed. Most companies will choose to keep at least one backup copy online at all times.

But what happens if one of the backup snapshots is corrupt and is unusable? Would you want to have to pull the backup from a tape? Many companies work around this pitfall by assigning two or three sets of backups or volumes so that there will be two full backup copies on disk at all times. They then rotate out each backup set successively.

Here's an example:

- On Monday backup set #1 is used.
- On Tuesday backup set #2 is used. Meanwhile, during business hours on Tuesday backup set #1 can have a file-level backup run to tape.

This system has two advantages:

- If the backup on Tuesday is unsuccessful for any reason, then the backup located on the first set can still be used should it be needed.
- The Tuesday backup set volumes can be synchronizing to the production volumes well before the backup needs to be started.

In all, VSS backups allow for an extremely flexible backup solution. When designing the volume layout be sure to configure them in a way that will meet the backup and restore requirements.

Table 10.3 describes the components in a VSS backup.

TABLE 10.3 Components in a VSS Backup

Component	Description
Requestor	This is typically the backup software.
Writer	Makes sure that Exchange has been quiesced and that the database is in a consistent state.
Provider	Manages communication between the operating system, the backup writer, and the VSS-enabled hardware.

There are four steps for completing a VSS backup:

1. The requestor starts the backup by initiating the writer.
2. When the writer has completed its tasks, it notifies the requestor it can back up the data set.
3. The requestor instructs the provider to notify the hardware to complete the backup.
4. Once the backup has completed, the requestor will notify the writer so that the writer can allow database activity to resume and then the VSS backup process completes.

Just like streaming backups, there are four types of backups that can be done with VSS. Also like streaming backups, they can be done against the active copy of the database. Unlike streaming backups, however, VSS allows for backups to be made against the passive copy of the database, such as those that exist in an LCR or CCR server. VSS backups are disk-based and will usually need to be copied to tape or another medium that can be archived. A simple file-level backup of the VSS snapshot volumes can be made to the offline media.

Now let's discuss the four types of backups and how they work when used with a VSS backup.

Full VSS Backups

A full VSS backup will copy the entire database and the required log files to the backup media and then will purge all of the committed transaction logs. The advantage of a full backup is that you can use this backup to restore the database to a consistent state and not need any additional backup sets. The main disadvantage of this backup type is that it can take a long period of time to complete and it takes the entire volume that the database is located on.

When would you use a full backup? If possible, always. However, with ever-shrinking backup windows and increasing amounts of data it is often not practical to complete a full backup each time.

Copy VSS Backups

A copy VSS backup will back up the entire database and will not purge any of the transaction logs. The advantage of a copy backup is that you can use this backup to restore the database to a consistent state and not need any additional backup sets. The main disadvantage of this backup type is that it takes the entire size of the database volume on disk. The other disadvantage is that it does not purge the committed transaction logs.

When would you use a VSS copy backup? An excellent use of the streaming copy backup is when you need to make an additional backup for archival purposes without affecting the standard backup rotation.

Differential VSS Backups

A differential VSS backup will back up the transaction logs that have been generated since the last full or incremental backup. This form of backup does not delete any of the committed transaction logs. Using differential backups minimizes the number of backup sets that would be required for a restore, since the last differential backup set would include all of the transaction logs generated. Differential backups cannot be run against storage groups that have circular logging enabled.

When would you use a differential backup? You could use a differential backup if you are not able to perform a full backup every day. This will keep all of the log files until the next full backup. You would use the differential backup if the server had enough space to hold the log files between full backups.

Incremental VSS Backups

An incremental VSS backup will back up the logs and then purge them. This form of backup deletes all of the committed transaction logs. Using incremental backups minimizes the number of transaction logs that are kept on the server. This will increase the number of backup sets that would be required for a restore since the all incremental backup sets would need to be restored to recover all of the transaction logs generated. Incremental backups cannot be run against storage groups that have circular logging enabled.

When would you use an incremental backup? You could use an incremental backup if there is not enough space to keep all of the transaction logs between full backup jobs. Table 10.4 has a list and description of the different types of VSS backups.

TABLE 10.4 VSS Backup Types

Type of Backup	Description
Full	Complete database backup that purges all committed transaction logs.
Copy	Complete database backup that does not purge any transaction logs.
Differential	All available transaction logs are not purged.
Incremental	All available transaction logs are purged.

Restoring a VSS Backup

A VSS restore is the simplest restore and does not differ greatly from previous versions of Exchange. Restoring to the original location would be used if a database has been damaged to the point where it cannot be mounted.

Often the backup software will manage the entire restore process. The general process of the restore would have the following key components:

1. Dismount all databases in the storage group.
2. Present or copy the VSS snapshot with the original drive and directory names. This would either be both the database and the transaction logs or just the transaction logs if this were a differential or incremental restore.
3. Mark the database able to allow for restore.
4. Perform a soft recovery to apply restored transaction logs.

You can also restore the database to a different server. To restore to another server a few steps would need to be completed in addition to restoring the data:

1. Create the new database on the new server.
2. Set the database so that it can be overwritten by a restore.
3. Restore the data to the new database location.
4. Use database portability to update user objects to the new database location.

More information about database portability can be found in Chapter 8.

Restoring Backups to a Recovery Storage Group

Typically the Exchange VSS-aware backup software will perform all of the tasks of a restore automatically. The procedure for restoring to a recovery storage group and recovering a specific mailbox has the following main tasks:

1. Restore the database and all required transaction log files by presenting or copying the clone to the location of the recovery storage group.
2. Create a recovery storage group.
3. Add the database that you will be recovering to the storage group.
4. Set the database to allow it to be overwritten by a restore.
5. Mount the recovered database.
6. Use the `restore-mailbox` cmdlet to merge data into mailboxes.

The `restore-mailbox` cmdlet is a very powerful tool; it also provides the ability to recover mail to alternate mailboxes and recover only items selected by date, keyword, or location in the original mailbox.

Implementing Backup Schedules

After determining how long you have to perform restores based on your RTO, RPO, and your SLA, you now need to determine when to schedule your backups.

The first question you need to answer is how long backups are going to take. This can vary greatly and will depend on the type of backups that you are doing as well as how much data will be backed up. Also, you will need to keep in mind the type of load your particular backup solution will put on the server. You would not want to perform a full backup on a heavily loaded Mailbox server during peak usage times (causing end users' performance to suffer) unless there was no alternative.

As mentioned earlier, it is recommended that a full database backup be completed whenever possible. This, of course, has to be balanced against the business's RPO, RTO, and SLAs. If the RPO for a particular server is only four hours, a backup will need to be done during business hours assuming a typical eight-hour workday to allow for recovery of data. In many instances, it will not be possible to run a full backup every night on all of the storage groups. This makes completing a full backup every four hours during the day even more unlikely due to both server load and the amount of space each full backup will consume. To reduce server load and space requirements, a differential or incremental backup can be done every four hours during the day.

When you schedule backups it is important to note that all database maintenance is halted during backup and restore procedures. Since it is essential to complete online maintenance tasks for defragmentation and deleted-item cleanup, it is important to schedule each of these tasks during different time periods. The rule of thumb is that you should schedule enough online maintenance time during the week to allow for a complete defragmentation cycle to complete on each of the databases.

Once you've determined the length of time backups will take and how long database maintenance will need to run, a schedule can be created. Often companies that are unable to fit in full backups every night due to backup-window contention will perform full backups on a select number of storage groups each night while scheduling differential backups on the remaining storage groups.

After completing your backup schedule it is recommended that you also schedule periodic recovery tests. Completing recoveries will continue to validate your recovery plan, validate that your backup hardware is functioning, and improve your recovery skills. After each restore test, it is important to generate an action plan for how to improve the current plan so that any issues that arise can be ironed out for the next test.

Planning and Implementing Backup and Recovery Solutions for Non-Mailbox Server Roles

To recover non-Mailbox server roles, different methods have to be used for each of the server role types. Let us discuss the methods for backup and recovery for each role.

Backup and Recovery for Edge Transport Servers

Edge Transport servers provide external email messaging service for companies that choose to deploy it. A cloned configuration file can be obtained by running the `ExportEdgeConfig.ps1` PowerShell script to export the user-modified configuration from each Edge Transport server. This xml-based configuration file that was exported can be imported on the recovered server to set the user-customized settings. If message tracking or SMTP transport logs need to be recovered they will need to be restored from tape or from the original server and placed in the \TransportRoles\Logs folder.

Certain configuration settings are not exported using the cloned configuration process and must be reset manually or with a custom-written PowerShell script. Certain settings are not exported, such as the servers exempt from connection filtering and maximum send and receive size. Table 10.5 shows the key data types and methods for backing up each Edge Transport server.

TABLE 10.5 Edge Transport Data Protection

Data Type	Backup Type
Active Directory Application Mode data	Use `ExportEdgeConfig.ps1` script
Message queues	Databases must be offline to back up, so backup is not feasible. To recover data, mount the databases on the recovered server.
Message logs	File-system backup of [Install]\TransportRoles\Logs.
Content-filtering database	Use `ExportEdgeConfig.ps1` script.
Service configuration	System state or registry key export.

Performing a recovery requires that the data listed in Table 10.5 has been backed up and includes the following steps:

1. Perform a new install of the Edge Transport server on a new server with the same name as the original.
2. Validate and import the XML-based cloned configuration exported from the original server.
3. Run the EdgeSync process to configure the recovered server to establish configuration replication.
4. Restore logs and message queue if required.
5. Reset any customizations that are not included in the XML-based cloned configuration file.

Backup and Recovery for Hub Transport Servers

Hub Transport servers are probably the second most important server role in the environment since they provide mail-delivery services. As far as recovery order, one of these servers should be recovered early in the process.

To enable you to recover from server failures, specific items will need to be backed up. Much of the configuration of the Hub Transport role is stored in Active Directory, so recovery of the server is fairly straightforward. A recovery can be completed in a very short period of time. Table 10.6 shows the key data types and methods for backing up each Hub Transport server.

TABLE 10.6 Hub Transport Data Protection

Data Type	Backup Type
Message queues	Databases must be offline to back up, so backup is not feasible. To recover, mount the databases from the failed server on a recovered server.
Message logs	File-system backup of [Install]\TransportRoles\Logs.
Service configuration	System state or registry key export.

Performing a recovery for a Hub Transport server includes the following steps, assuming all the appropriate information has been backed up:

1. Run `setup.com /mode:RecoverServer` on a server with the same name as the server that is being recovered.
2. Restore message logs and queues, if required.

More information on recovering message queues from failed severs can be found at the Microsoft TechNet website: `http://technet.microsoft.com/en-us/library/b6904662-d1f1-4ad5-bbc1-5a7791aa2d75.aspx`.

Backup and Recovery for Client Access Servers

To provide for recovery, specific things need to be saved for each function that the Client Access server provides.

The Office Outlook Web Access website has configuration information stored in the ClientAccess\Owa directory. The Client Access directory should be backed up with a file-system backup to retain any customizations. This directory can be restored after the server is recovered to reapply customizations.

The IMAP4 and POP3 protocol settings are stored in the \ClientAccess\PopImap directory. This directory should be backed up using a file-system backup to retain configuration settings. Most of the configuration settings are stored in Active Directory, so regular backups of Active Directory are also recommended.

The Availability service configuration is primarily stored in Active Directory as well; however, it is also important to perform a backup of the \ClientAccess\exchweb\ews directory to capture user-customized configuration settings that would be stored in the `web.config` file.

The Autodiscover virtual directory settings are stored in the IIS metabase, and the service configuration settings (such as the service connection point) are stored in Active Directory. It is important to back up or export the IIS metabase information as well as perform a backup of Active Directory.

Exchange ActiveSync has configuration information stored in Active Directory, in the IIS metabase as well as the `web.config` file in the \ClientAccess\Sync directory. Table 10.7 shows the key data types and methods for backing up each Client Access server.

TABLE 10.7 Client Access Data Protection

Data Type	Backup Type
Office Outlook Web Access	File-system backup of [Install]\ClientAccess\OWA
IMAP4 and POP3	File-system backup of [Install]\ClientAccess\PopImap
Availability	Active Directory backup and file-system backup of [Install]\ClientAccess\exchweb\ews
Autodiscover	System-state backup or export of the IIS metabase
Exchange ActiveSync	File-system backup of [Install]\ClientAccess\Sync and backup or export of the IIS metabase
SSL certificates	System-state backup or export of the SSL certificates and private keys

You can recover a Client Access server in two ways. The server can be recovered by restoring the server with the same name and running `setup.com /mode:RecoverServer` and then restoring the customized settings for each service. The second method of recovering a Client Access server is by installing a new server with a new name and installing the Client Access role. After the role is installed, the customized settings and certificates can either be restored or reconfigured.

Real World Scenario

Doing a Reality Check

In the real world it is usually easier to rebuild an Edge Transport, Hub Transport, or Client Access server provided any customization is documented and stored elsewhere rather than to restore it from a backup. If during your planning and testing it takes about an hour to rebuild a server with all of its customizations and it takes two hours to rebuild the server and then restore from tape, it would seem to make more sense to just go ahead and rebuild the server from scratch. It is always important to do a reality check when developing a recovery strategy; and ask yourself, "Does it really make sense to spend all these resources configuring backups when I can spend less time just documenting or even scripting the original install steps?"

So, how can you shorten your time to deploy, restore, or rebuild an Exchange server? Easy. Windows PowerShell.

The new Exchange Server 2007 command shell built on top of PowerShell provides features that will allow you to script out the installation and configuration of new and rebuilt servers. We have seen an engineer use a PowerShell script that will, with a little base preparation, rebuild an entire SCC cluster.

Why else is automation a great idea? One reason is that especially when servers are down, administrators tend to miss critical steps, which is the last thing that needs to be done when messaging services are already in a degraded state. Another reason is that if the scripts are properly written they can be executed by lower-level engineers that are following a standard operating procedure without having to be concerned that they are going to miss a step. This will also reduce the likelihood of your getting a frantic call to help figure out why the server is not working.

So be sure when designing your recovery plan to weigh the costs of backups and restores, and the troubleshooting work that leads up to the restores. Then look for ways to reduce the complexity and time involved to rebuild the servers.

Backup and Recovery for Unified Messaging Servers

Performing backups to quickly recover Unified Messaging servers is important so that configuration of Outlook Voice Access and of auto-attendants can be restored quickly. Table 10.8 shows the key data types and methods for backing up each Unified Messaging server.

TABLE 10.8 Unified Messaging Data Protection

Data Type	Backup Type
Custom auto-attendant and Outlook Voice Access files	File-system backup of [Install]\UnifiedMessaging\Prompts if servers is a distribution point.
Server configuration	Active Directory backup.
Service configuration	System-state backup or export of the registry.
Incoming call email	Cannot be backed up; must be salvaged from failed server.
Outlook Voice Access Global Address List (GAL) grammar	File-system backup [Install]\UnifiedMessaging\Grammars; if backup is not completed, the GAL Grammar configuration will be rebuilt automatically.

The process for recovering a Unified Messaging server includes these steps:

1. Run `setup.com /mode:RecoverServer` on a server with the same name as the server that is being recovered.
2. Restore custom prompts and audio files back to \UnifiedMessaging\Prompt if required.
3. Restore the GAL grammar configuration files back to \UnifiedMessaging\Grammars.

Summary

Much work goes into planning a backup and recovery solution for your messaging environment. After having the RPO, RTO, and SLAs defined, the ability to design the recovery solution for each of the Mailbox roles begins.

With Mailbox server roles there are two main options for backups: legacy streaming and VSS. These two differ greatly in the technology that enables them, and quite often in complexity in how they are configured and administered. Both types of backups offer the ability to leverage recovery storage groups that facilitate dial-tone recovery as well as mailbox and item recovery. Each non-Mailbox server requires a slightly different backup process to be successful.

Once each service has a defined method of backup and recovery that meets the RPO, RTO, and SLA, it is important to document and test this process at regular intervals to validate the process and keep the administrative staff familiar with the process.

Exam Essentials

Know the keys for designing a backup and recovery solution. Backup and recovery solutions are driven by business requirements. Business requirements will typically fall into one of three categories: recovery-point objective (RPO), recovery-time objective (RTO), and Service Level Agreement (SLA). Each of these requirements will need to be fully defined in order to scope backup schedule and types.

Know the difference between full, copy, incremental, and differential backups. You must be able to differentiate between the types of backups and know when you would use each. Always remember that both full and incremental backups purge log files, and that copy and differential backups do not. It is also important to know the reasons you would use each type of backup.

Each server role has different requirements. Each of the Exchange server roles has different requirements for what needs to be backed up, what will need to be restored, and what will need to be configured manually. Be sure to review the different methods for backing up specific role configurations.

Review Questions

1. You have been asked to design a backup solution. The business requires that the design tolerate only eight hours of lost data with a minimal number of restore sets. Which schedule would meet this need?

    A. Full backup nightly and incremental backups every four hours

    B. Full backup nightly and differential backups every four hours

    C. Copy backup nightly and incremental backups every four hours

    D. Copy backup nightly and differential backups every four hours

2. You have been asked to design a backup solution. The business requires that a backup be created during the middle of the week to be shipped to the disaster-recovery site for a test restore. Only one full backup is currently scheduled each week. What type of backup should be done to test a restore and not affect the local backup rotation?

    A. A full backup

    B. An incremental backup

    C. A copy backup

    D. A differential backup

3. Which of the following business requirements defines for how long a service must be available during a given time?

    A. Recovery-point objective

    B. Service Level Agreement

    C. Recovery-time Objective

    D. Standard operating procedure

4. Which of the following can be recovered using a recovery storage group? (Choose all that apply.)

    A. Mailbox data

    B. Mailbox items

    C. Public-folder items

    D. Unified Messaging data

5. Which of the following is not a component of an Exchange-aware VSS solution?

    A. Writer

    B. Provider

    C. Requestor

    D. Coordinator

6. Which of the following would you need to do to complete a restore of an Edge Transport server? (Choose all that apply.)

   A. Run `setup.com /mode:RecoverServer` on a server with the original name.

   B. Import an XML-based configuration file.

   C. Re-establish the EdgeSync.

   D. Set up a fresh install of the Edge Transport role on a server with the original name.

7. You have been asked to design a VSS backup solution. You need to be able to restore each storage group individually with both differential and full backups. The server will have 10 storage groups. What is the minimum number of volumes that will be required to support the storage groups?

   A. 2

   B. 5

   C. 10

   D. 20

8. A user deleted a critical contact two hours ago and requires it to be restored. What options are available?

   A. Use deleted mailbox retention to restore the mailbox with Exchange Management Console.

   B. Use deleted item retention to restore the item with Outlook.

   C. Restore the last differential backup to the production database.

   D. Restore the last full backup to a recovery storage group and restore the missing item.

9. Your server has three different business units that have mailboxes hosted on one Mailbox server. You need to maintain separate SLAs for each of the business units. Assuming that the restore speed is not a problem, what is the minimum number of storage groups and databases should your design include?

   A. 1

   B. 2

   C. 3

   D. 4

10. To be able to recover a failed Edge Transport server, at a minimum which of the following things would need to be done?

    A. System-state backup of the Edge Transport server

    B. File-system backup of the message queues

    C. Manual export of the Edge Transport configuration to an XML-based file

    D. Backup of the IIS metabase

11. To be able to recover a failed Hub Transport server, at a minimum which of the following things would need to be done?
    - A. Backup or export of the IIS metabase
    - B. System-state backup of the Hub Transport server
    - C. File-system backup of the message queues
    - D. Backup of the \TransportRoles\logs directory
12. To be able to recover a failed Client Access server, at a minimum which of the following things would you need to do?
    - A. File-system backup of \ClientAccess\OWA
    - B. File-system backup of \ClientAccess\exchweb\ews
    - C. File-system backup of \ClientAccess\Sync
    - D. Backup or export of the metabase
13. To be able to recover a Unified Messaging server, at a minimum which of the following things would need to be done?
    - A. Backup of \UnifiedMessaging\Prompts
    - B. File-system backup of the temporary messages
    - C. Backup of \UnifiedMessaging\Grammars
    - D. Backup of \UnifiedMessaging\Config
14. You can use a recovery storage group to recover which of the following?
    - A. Email messages in a mailbox
    - B. Calendar items in a mailbox
    - C. Email messages in a public folder
    - D. Contact items in a public folder
15. Which of the following backup strategies will result in a lowest RPO?
    - A. Full backup nightly, and incremental backups every four hours
    - B. Full backup nightly, and differential backups every eight hours
    - C. Copy backup nightly and incremental backups every two hours
    - D. Copy backup nightly and differential backups every eight hours
16. To ensure that user mailbox configurations were backed up, which of the servers would need to be backed up?
    - A. Mailbox server
    - B. Active Directory server
    - C. Client Access server
    - D. Hub Transport server

17. Which of the following will result in the lowest RTO?
    - **A.** Full nightly backup and incremental backups every four hours
    - **B.** Full nightly backup and differential backups every five hours
    - **C.** Copy backup nightly and incremental backups every eight hours
    - **D.** Copy backup nightly and differential backups every two hours

18. You restored your last full backup and accidentally left the Last Full Backup Set option enabled. You have a differential backup that also needs to be restored. What steps would you need to take to restore the differential backup?
    - **A.** Restore the full backup again without the Last Full Backup Set option enabled.
    - **B.** Use ESEUTIL to perform a hard recovery.
    - **C.** Use ESEUTIL to perform a soft recovery.
    - **D.** Dismount the mailbox store, check the Allow Database to Be Overwritten by Restore box.

19. When planning for disaster recovery of a Mailbox server role that is configured with LCR, which of the following are viable options for backup? (Choose all that apply.)
    - **A.** Streaming backup of the active databases
    - **B.** Streaming backup of the passive databases
    - **C.** VSS backup of the active databases
    - **D.** VSS backup of the passive databases

20. When planning for disaster recovery for a Mailbox server role configured as a cluster continuous replication cluster, which are viable options for restore? (Choose all that apply.)
    - **A.** Streaming restore of the active databases
    - **B.** Streaming restore of the passive databases
    - **C.** VSS restore of the active databases
    - **D.** VSS restore of the passive databases

Answers to Review Questions

1. B. A full backup every night will purge the logs and then the differential backup every four hours will capture the changes since the full backup. The restore would require two backup sets: the full backup and the last differential backup that was made. A full backup nightly with incremental backups every four hours will result in a minimum of three restore sets. Copy backups do not truncate transaction logs so a copy backup with incremental backups requires the last full backup as well as all of the incremental backups since that point. Even when differential backups are used a full backup would still be required.

2. C. A copy backup will create a backup that can be restored at the remote site and it will not purge any logs, leaving the current backup schedule unchanged. Both incremental and differential backups are not able to be used to do a restore without providing a full backup as well. If a full backup were completed, this would truncate the logs and modify the backup schedule already in place.

3. C. A Service Level Agreement defines for how much time a service must be available during a period of time. A Recovery Point Objective defines how much data can be lost in a failure incident. A Recovery Time Objective defines how long the recovery should take to complete and a Standard operating procedure defines the steps a process would take.

4. A, B, D. A recovery storage group can be used to recover all mailbox data—either the entire mailbox or specific mailbox items, including voicemail messages. Recovery storage groups cannot be used to recover any public-folder data.

5. D. The coordinator is not a part of the VSS backup process, but the Writer, Provider, and Requester are all VSS components

6. B, C, D. To recover an Edge Transport server the process is to complete a fresh install of Exchange Edge Transport role, and then import the XML-based configuration file, and then re-establishing the EdgeSync process. Running `setup.com` with the `/mode:recoverserver` is not a supported way to restore an Edge Transport server.

7. D. Each storage group will require two volumes: one for transaction logs and one for databases. None of the other options have enough volumes to allow restoring the databases individually.

8. A, D. The deleted item retention feature will have kept the deleted items until the retention period has expired. Messages are purged from the deleted item retention only after maintenance is run. Also, it would be possible to use the recovery storage group to retrieve the item; however, it is a considerable amount of work.

9. C. Three storage groups would need to be created so that backups and restores for each of the business groups would not affect any of the other storage-group activities.

10. A, C. A system-state backup will be beneficial in restoring service after a failure. An export of the Edge Transport configuration is required to recover most of the customizations of Edge Transport role. Performing a file system backup of the message queues is not possible, as the message queues will be in use and the IIS metabase is not used by the Edge Transport server.

11. B, D. A system-state backup and a backup of the transport logs will allow for a restore of the server. The Hub Transport does not use IIS, thus a backup is not required. It is not possible to backup the message queues with a file system backup.

12. A, B, C, D. Each of the directories under the Client Access is needed to restore customizations. Since much of the customizations are stored in the IIS metabase, this too should be backed up.

13. A. The only item that needs to be backed up is \UnifiedMessaging\Prompts. The \UnifiedMessaging\Grammars can be backed up; however, it can be rebuilt after the Unified Messaging server is rebuilt. The temporary messages cannot be backed up and the \UnifiedMessaging\Config folder does not need to be backed up.

14. A, B. A recovery storage group can be used for recovering only data from within mailboxes. Public folders must be recovered in whole, with deleted item retention or by using a recovery forest.

15. A. A full backup on a nightly basis with incremental backups every four hours will allow the server to be recovered to a point within four hours of a failure. Doing a full backup nightly with differential backups every eight hours would result in a restore point of up to eight hours from a failure. Copy backups cannot be used incremental or differential backups.

16. B. Active Directory contains the configuration of each of the users' mailboxes. Performing backups on Active Directory is essential for any Exchange recovery plan. None of the other servers types store mailbox configuration data.

17. B. Differential backups reduce the number of backup sets that would need to be applied, as they are cumulative since the last full backup. After restoring the full backup only one differential would need to be restored. Even though the incremental backups are run more often, more of them would need to be restored, which would lengthen the RTO. The copy backups never truncate the transaction logs, so all backups since the last full backup would need to be restored.

18. A. After a hard recovery is performed, no additional transaction logs will be able to be applied to the database. To apply the additional differential backup, the full backup would need to be restored again before the differential backup could be used.

19. A, C, D. Any of these three options can be valid as VSS backups can be done against either the active or passive database in both LCR and CCR solutions. Streaming backups can be done only against the active databases.

20. A, C. Restores can be done only to active databases or to a recovery storage group.

Planning the Exchange Server 2007 Storage Group Deployment

MICROSOFT EXAM OBJECTIVE COVERED IN THIS CHAPTER:

✓ Plan the storage group deployment

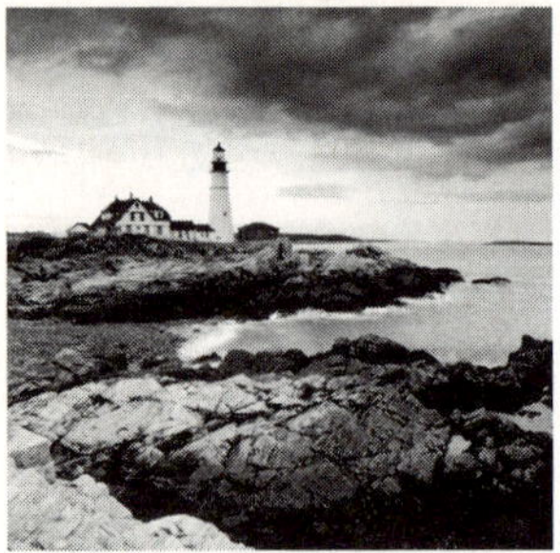

Before deploying the Mailbox roles, it is important to weigh all of the factors that go into designing the storage group placement. Although we will discuss these factors, details about the contributing factors may be found elsewhere in the book. In this chapter, we will cover the following subjects:

- Planning storage group quantities and layout
- Planning the number of the databases to use
- Planning the maximum database size
- Planning the disk volume size and configuration
- Planning for I/O requirements
- Planning for recovery storage groups

Planning the Storage Group Quantities and Layout

The very heart of the Exchange Mailbox server is the database. Exchange 2007 uses the extensible storage engine (ESE) or Jet database, the same engine used by previous versions of Exchange. However, there have been notable improvements in both performance and features.

First let's briefly discuss what types of files we need to place and how they interact in Exchange Server 2007. A storage group is a segregation of data and processes in Exchange. Each database in a storage group shares a common set of transaction logs. In Exchange, transaction logs provide a record of the physical changes that are made to the database. The three types of files in a storage group are the following:

Transaction logs. These logs provide a record of the changes made to the database. In case of a failure, the changes can be reapplied to the database.

System files. These include the checkpoint file and the temporary database for the storage group.

- The checkpoint file marks which transaction logs have been applied to each of the databases in the storage group. The checkpoint file is always 8 Kb.

- The temporary database is used as temporary space for transactions that are being applied. The temporary file is named `tmp.edb` and rarely grows over a couple of megabytes.

Database files. The last type of file used in a storage group is the database files. These files contain the data in each mailbox or public folder.

The system files and the transaction logs are usually stored on the same volume. The database should be stored on a separate volume from the transaction logs. This way if either volume is filled due to an error the other files are not affected. The database and transaction logs should be stored not only on separate volumes but also on separate physical disks. Separate physical disks are recommended because the database and transaction logs have different read and write patterns that could cause disk contention if they were located on the same physical disks.

Another good reason for storing the database and transaction logs on separate physical disks is that only one set of the data needs to be recovered should a problem occur with those physical disks. As long as performance and capacity requirements are met for the transaction logs and the database files, multiple storage groups can be stored on the same volume. However, if the Volume Shadow Copy Service (VSS) is going to be used for backups and individual backup and restores are required, each storage group should be on a separate volume. (See Chapter 9, "Planning a Backup and Recovery Solution for Exchange Server 2007," for more information about volume configuration for VSS.) As discussed in Chapter 8, "Planning a Highly Available Exchange Server 2007 Implementation" the active and passive copies used in local continuous replications and cluster continuous replications also should be on physically separate volumes.

If you plan on placing each storage-group database and transaction log on separate disks and you have more than 11 storage groups, you will run out of drive letters for each of the volumes because there are only 26 letters available. The solution is to use volume mount points. You can create two drive letters, one for transaction logs and one for databases, and mount each volume as a folder.

The three main factors that need to be taken into account are the size to which the databases should be allowed to grow, the number of storage groups and databases that will be used, and the I/O requirements to support the level of service.

Planning the Number of Databases to Use

Depending on the edition and configuration of the server, you can have from one to five databases per storage group. In Table 11.1 we see a how the Standard and Enterprise editions limit the number and size of storage groups and databases that can be configured differently.

TABLE 11.1 Limitations of Different Exchange Server Editions

Limit	Standard	Enterprise
Number of storage groups	5	50
Number of databases	5	50
Size of databases	16 TB	16 TB

The edition of Exchange is not the only factor that plays into the number of databases and storage groups that can be configured. When using both local continuous replication (LCR) and cluster continuous replication (CCR), you can configure only one database in each storage group. Single-copy clusters (SCCs) are limited to five databases per storage group.

Table 11.2 summarizes the number of databases per storage group that each Mailbox role type can have.

TABLE 11.2 Maximum Number of Databases per Storage Group for Different Mailbox Server Configurations

Server Configuration	Databases per Storage Group
Stand-alone	5
LCR	1
CCR	1
SCC	5

Microsoft recommends a single database in each storage group.

Planning the Maximum Database Size

Now that we have determined the maximum number of storage groups and databases, we need to determine the number we need for a specific deployment. There are several main factors that determine how many databases are needed and how large they should be. This is also where sizing Exchange servers becomes more like high-school algebra and less like working with computers. We are going to go over several formulas and the assumptions that are made. The following are three important factors in determining database sizing:

- The size that can be backed up and restored within the Service Level Agreement (SLA) for the specific mailboxes. If your backup infrastructure can reliably restore only 25 gigabytes (GB) an hour and you have an SLA that requires you to have a storage group restored in four hours, you couldn't have a 150 GB database and expect to meet your SLA if the database fails.
- Microsoft's recommendation that databases that are not continuously replicated should not exceed 100 GB in size. Databases that are hosted on either LCR or CCR servers have a recommended maximum of 200 GB. These are not hard limits, but rather recommendations from Microsoft. Once you determine the size that the database should be at its maximum, you can determine the number of mailboxes you can place in each database. To accomplish this, limits or quotas will need to be placed on all mailboxes.
- The length of time to run maintenance on a given database. The larger the database, the longer it will take. Because the maintenance takes longer, the maintenance window will need to be expanded, which leaves less time for backups to take place. Maintenance should be able to run a complete pass on each database each week. Running database maintenance keeps the white space defragmented within the database as deleted items are purged after the retention period.

Be sure to schedule enough time outside the backup window so that each database can complete an online defragmentation pass each week. To determine how often a full defragmentation takes place on each database, look in the event viewer in the application log and filter for Event ID 701 or 703. Event ID 701 will show if the maintenance was completed within the maintenance window, and Event ID 703 will be logged if the maintenance is resumed after being interrupted and then completed. You will see an entry similar to Figure 11.1 for each database at least one time each week.

If you do not see an entry for each of the databases, the maintenance window may need to be extended or moved to a time that backups are not being run. Alternatively, the database may be too large, and you may need to move mailboxes to another database.

To determine what mailboxes should be put into each database, single-instance storage should be considered. When an email message is sent to 100 people in the same database it is only stored once; however, if the mailboxes are spread into a number of databases, then the message is stored once in each database.

To leverage single-instance storage, users who send email to each other should have their mailboxes located in the same database. Many times, arranging the mailboxes so that similar geographic areas are on the same mailbox databases or arranging mailboxes in the same or cooperating departments will provide the best results.

FIGURE 11.1 Event entry for a completed online defragmentation of a database

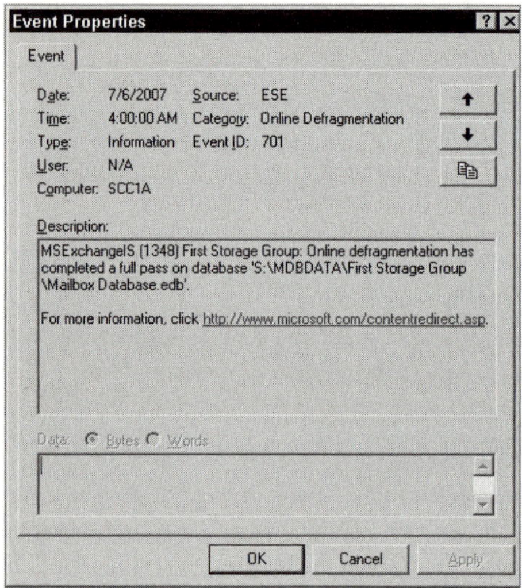

Leveraging single-instance storage will reduce the size of the database and reduce the amount of data to be backed up; however, the primary benefit from planning properly for single-instance storage is that message delivery is improved because the message needs to be delivered only once to each database. To determine the ratio of each of the databases in Performance Monitor, view the single-instance ratio counter for each of the databases in both the MSExchangeIS mailbox and the MSExchangeIS public objects.

One of the easiest ways to set mailbox limits is at the database level. When determining which users go in each database, the limits set for each mailbox will be a factor. It makes sense to keep specific classes of user mailboxes in the same databases to reduce the number of manual changes that need to happen on the user mailboxes. The other benefit of keeping the different user classes in different databases is that, in many instances, the users with higher mailbox quotas also have a higher SLA and require faster restore times. You should consider putting mailboxes with the same SLA in the same database so that they can be restored to service at the same time.

There are very few hard-and-fast rules for determining the number of databases and which mailboxes will be put in each. To best determine what is right for your Exchange organization, it is important to weigh the maximum size that you can support for each database. When determining which mailboxes to place in each database, factors that should be considered are mailbox limits, SLAs for different user classes, and single-instance storage.

Real World Scenario

Determining Where to Place User Mailboxes

It is important to put thought into where mailboxes are placed. Often, messaging professionals will create one or two databases, fill them, and create several more to repeat the process. This may work fine in smaller, dynamic environments; however, in an enterprise environment, there are real benefits of proper planning, including a simplified recovery process, improved ability to meet SLAs, simplified limits administration, or improved single-instance storage.

Although there is not a one-size-fits-all solution for laying out where mailboxes should be placed, you should take the time to weigh the pros and cons of each of the solutions.

Let's go through one example:

Suppose that you have a single server that must host 5,000 mailboxes. The company has a group of 50 executives who have 10 GB mailbox limits, and the rest of the users are capped at a limit of 300 MB. The executives have a higher SLA than the general user population. There are five main departments that contain just fewer than 1,000 mailboxes each. Each department tends to send emails primarily within the department.

In this case, it makes sense to create a single storage group for the executives. Then, for each department, create enough storage groups to handle the mailboxes while keeping within the recommended database size. If each department can be broken into small groups geographically or perhaps by function, it may make sense to group these mailboxes together in the same storage group even though multiple databases will need to be created for each main department.

Planning the Disk Volume Size and Configuration

So far we have discussed the sizing and number of databases. We now need to drill a little farther into what makes up the size of a database and how much disk space we need to allocate for each database. First, we need to know the limits that have been set for each user group.

Even though it would be easy to assume that the size of a mailbox database is simply a cumulative sum of all the mailboxes in the database, it isn't the full story. Also included in database size are deleted item and mailbox retention, white space, and the rest of the database structure, such as table information.

The main variables in determining disk sizing are as follows:

Mailbox limit. Sometimes called the mailbox quota, this is the limit set for the size of the mailbox that, once reached, prevents the user from sending and receiving email messages.

Real World Scenario

Take It to the Limits

Mailbox limits can become a very heated political problem in many organizations, but they are the fundamental building blocks of Exchange storage groups. Once limits have been established, it is important to stick to them or at least have a process in place to re-evaluate the storage-group design when the limits are adjusted to ensure that you can maintain proper disk space and SLAs. Although this may be a difficult feat, it will show that you take your job seriously if you provide a messaging system that performs within business requirements. When it comes down to it, you shouldn't care *what* the agreed-upon limit is, but just that the limit has been factored into server and backup sizing and that the limits are being complied with.

What, though, do you do when a vice president of the organization calls in to the help desk and demands an increase in their mailbox storage limit? A policy should be put in place to avoid anyone being able to call and get a non-standard mailbox size. Also, each approved mailboxe size should have a set of rules applied so that only authorized users can request mailbox size changes, preferably through an automated system that enforces the policy. To compliment this, the help desk and the administrators should not be given authority to change any person's limit. Second, an exceptions report should be run at least once a day to see which users, if any, are not within the standards set for the company. Automating reports of this type is now fairly simple with PowerShell. Third, a corporate policy that has been signed off by all the needed stakeholders must define the limits and what should happen if a request is made to increase the limits for a particular user.

White space. This is the space in the Exchange database that is freed up when email items are removed from the database. Microsoft suggests that white space when database maintenance is running regularly should be about equal to the average amount of email sent and received each day by each user.

Database dumpster. After email messages are hard-deleted from a user's mailbox by being emptied from the deleted items folder or Shift-deleted, the items stay in the database for a period of time in the database dumpster. The default length of time is set to 14 days; however, the retention period can be set to a different length of time. The longer the retention period, the more space is needed to keep these items. To estimate the amount of data in the database dumpster for each user, add the amount of data sent and received for each user for each day deleted items are retained.

If we put these numbers together, we can come up with a simple formula for estimating the size each mailbox will consume on disk:

Mailbox size = mailbox limit + white space + database dumpster size

For example, you have a set of users who have a 300 MB limit and on average they send and receive 10 MB of email each day. The deleted item retention for the mailboxes is 21 days. Plugging this into the formula, we get the following:

520 MB = 300 MB + 10 MB + (21 days × 10 MB)

If we have 175 mailboxes in each database, we would have an estimated database size of about 91 GB. Now that we can determine the size on disk of the database, we also need to add in space for content indexing, which is enabled by default in Exchange Server 2007. The Microsoft recommendation for content indexing is to add an additional five percent of space. Adding the content indexing space to the database size, we have an estimated 95 MB of space required for the database.

The content index files cannot be moved to another directory or volume. The files have to be located with the database files.

How do you size the disk volume that will hold an estimated 95 GB of data? To be able to do any sort of maintenance on the database, you need 110 percent of the size of the database. This brings us to a total volume size of 200 GB just for the allocated number of mailboxes and the set limit. To be safe, let's add a 20 percent overhead to our number to allow for marginal growth and for the possibility of underestimating one of our numbers:

240 GB = 200 GB + 20 percent

So for 175 mailboxes with a 300 MB limit and 21 days of deleted item retention, you need about 240 GB of disk storage. How do we use these numbers to size the transaction logs?

In Exchange Server 2007, the transaction log files have been reduced from 5 MB down to just 1 MB. This means more transaction logs for the same amount of data. To estimate the number of transaction logs that will be generated per mailbox, we can use a range from a very light user who generates about 7 MB of logs each day to a very heavy user who might generate 42 MB of logs each day. In many organizations, we will have a mixture of users, some very heavy, some very light, and a group in between. For our purposes, we are going to guess that our user mailboxes average around 25 MB of transaction logs each day.

In the previous example we had 175 mailboxes in each storage group. If each of these mailboxes generates 30 MB of transaction logs daily, we have just over 5 GB of space required each day. Another large factor in how many transaction logs are generated is the number of mailboxes that are moved. Additional space about equal to the cumulative size of the mailboxes being moved should be included in the log-file size estimate.

The total amount of transaction log space required depends on how often backups are run. If full backups are to be run each night and the transaction logs purged, it is prudent to allow for backup failures that would cause the transaction logs not to be purged correctly. If full backups are going to be done only once a week, enough space will need to be allocated.

Continuing with the scenario, if we have 5 GB of transaction logs generated by normal use, plus an additional 5 GB to handle unscheduled mailbox moves, plus an additional 20 percent overhead for safety, we get 12 GB of log files each day. To plan for a backup failure, we should allocate enough room for about 3 days of usage on the transaction log volume:

Transaction log volume size = total transaction usage between full backups × 3 days

In our case, the formula looks like this:

36 GB = 12 GB × 3

We need about 36 GB of space on our transaction log volume to handle our space requirements.

When creating disk partitions, it is important to use the Diskpart utility in Windows Server. This utility aligns the disk sectors to the disk tracks and can improve Exchange performance. Please see Chapter 12, "Planning the Exchange Server 2007 Server Role Deployment," for more details on using Diskpart.

Planning for I/O Requirements

We now know the sizes of the disk volumes for both the database and the transaction logs. We now must determine the performance we need out of the disk. It is true that, with the appropriate amount of memory, Exchange Server 2007 has a much lower I/O profile than previous versions of Exchange. However, you will still need to give some thought to the I/O requirements for Exchange.

There are a couple rules of thumb for the I/O requirements. One is that the transaction log volumes need about half the number of writes that the database volumes require. In Exchange Server 2003, the I/O required for each user would easily approach one I/O for each active user on highly utilized servers. With Exchange Server 2007 being a 64-bit application, it has opened the way to leveraging a great deal more memory for caching data. This means that the I/O requirements for Exchange Server 2007 computers can be anywhere from 50 to 70 percent lower. A recommended range of I/O per user per second for Exchange Server 2007 with the appropriate amount of memory is anywhere from 0.11 I/O per second on the lower end to 0.50 per second on the very high end.

One way to verify whether a storage system will perform as well as needed for particular profile of users is to use Jetstress. This tool will approximate the disk I/O load generated by Exchange with a specific number of users, mailbox size, and I/O operations generated each second. All of this can be done without having to install Exchange on the server. Jetstress is available in both 32-bit and 64-bit varieties, depending on the host OS. You also will require files from a matching version of Exchange Server.

You can download the 32-bit version of Jetstress at `http://www.microsoft.com/downloads/details.aspx?familyid=94b9810b-670e-433a-b5ef-b47054595e9c&displaylang=en`. The 64-bit version can be downloaded at `http://www.microsoft.com/downloads/details.aspx?FamilyID=73dfe056-0900-4dbb-b14a-0932338cecac&displaylang=en`.

The three main factors in providing disk performance are RAID type, disk speed, and the number of disk spindles. A disk spindle is a physical disk drive. We discussed RAID types in Chapter 8, "A Highly Available Exchange Server 2007 Implementation," and how different configurations will affect performance and available space. Table 11.3 summarizes this data again for your reference.

TABLE 11.3 Summary of RAID Performance

RAID Type	Capacity	Fault Tolerance	I/O Performance
RAID 0	Best	None	Best
RAID 5	Best	Good	Poor
RAID 6	Good	Better	Poor
RAID 10	Poor	Best	Good

As you can see, the best performance and the best capacity are not achieved by the same configuration. Performance limitations for the slower RAID types can usually be overcome with the right number of disk spindles. The more disk spindles added to an array, the more I/Os it can handle. One way to estimate your server's I/O requirements is to use Jetstress. This tool is provided by Microsoft to simulate the I/O that Exchange will place on your disk configuration without having to install Exchange. Jetstress allows you to provide a profile of the I/O that will run against the storage, or it will try to try to maximize the amount of throughput to the disk subsystem. The three types of I/O pattern tests that Jetstress will run are as follows:

Performance. This test simulates normal I/O load of the database with the provided parameters.

Streaming backup. This test simulates the I/O load of a streaming backup to the backup device. This can be done only to a file share.

Soft recovery. This test simulates the I/O load during a replay of transaction logs.

Exercise 11.1 outlines the steps for running Jetstress to simulate a 5,000-user, 300 MB-limit, heavy-usage Exchange server.

EXERCISE 11.1

Using Jetstress to Determine I/O Requirements

Jetstress is an important tool for sizing and testing Exchange data storage systems. This exercise demonstrates how to set up Jetstress on a test server. The server is configured with the disk subsystem that we think is going to handle our 5,000-user configuration with 300 MB mailbox limits. Let's get started.

EXERCISE 11.1 *(continued)*

1. First, download the appropriate version of Jetstress for your processor type. The machine used in this example is a Windows Server 2003 R2 x64 machine. We also have Microsoft .NET Framework 2.0 installed. If you do not have Microsoft .NET Framework 2.0 installed on your test machine, install it now.
2. Double-click on the `Jetstress.msi` file that you downloaded.
3. Click Next on the screen shown here.

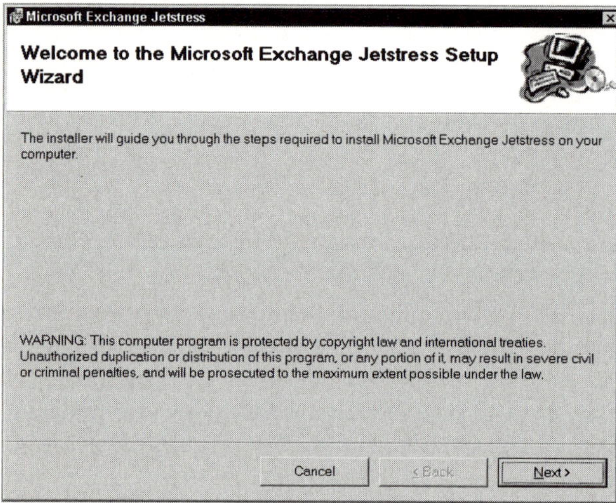

4. On the next screen shown here, accept the terms of the license agreement and click Next.

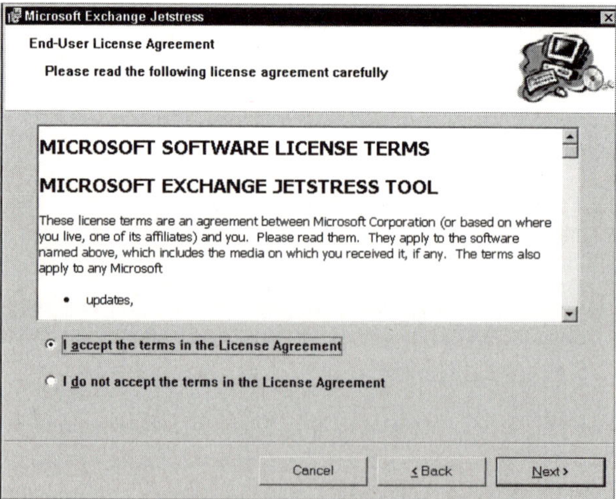

EXERCISE 11.1 *(continued)*

5. On the Select Installation Folder screen, choose the location where you would like Jetstress installed, and then click Next.

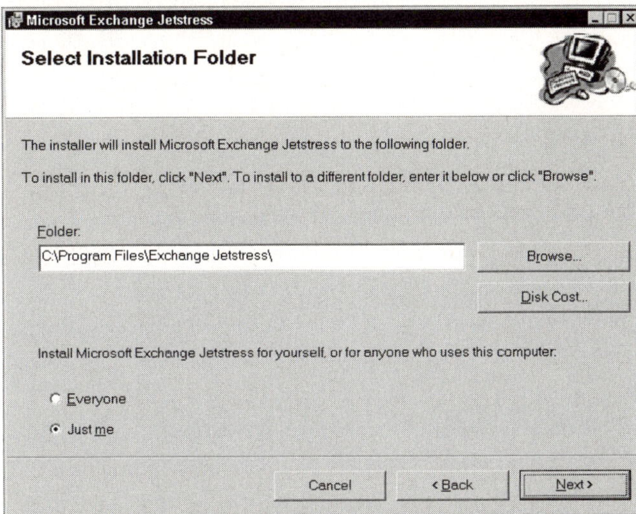

6. On the Confirm Installation screen, click Next.

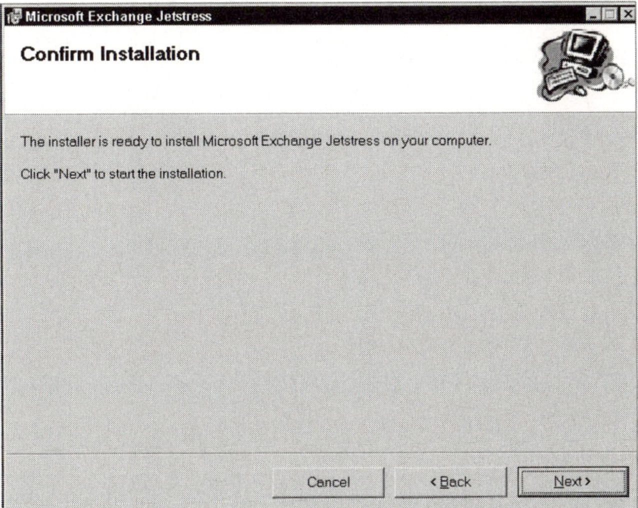

EXERCISE 11.1 *(continued)*

7. On the Installation Complete screen, click Close.

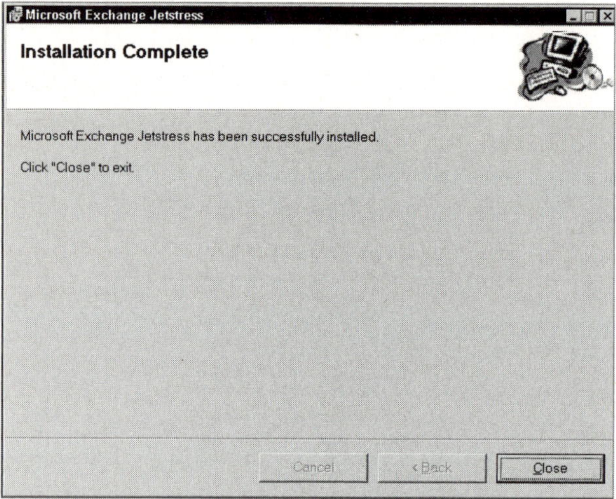

Since we are using a computer running Windows Server 2003 R2 x64 for the test, we will need a couple of files from the Exchange Server 2007 installation media. If we were using a 32-bit operating system, we would need to get these files from the trial 32-bit version of Exchange Server 2007.

8. Copy the following files from the Exchange Server 2007 installation media to the C:\Program Files\Exchange Jetstress folder:

```
ESE.DLL
ESEPERF.DLL
ESEPERF.INI
ESEPERF.HXX
```

Configuring Jetstress is just half the battle. Being able to use Jetstress to properly test a configuration is an art in and of itself.

EXERCISE 11.2

Configuring Jetstress for Testing

1. Now that Jetstress is configured and ready to use, we can start it up and configure it for our test.
2. Click Start ➢ Programs ➢ Microsoft Exchange and then select Exchange Jetstress.

EXERCISE 11.2 *(continued)*

3. On the welcome screen, select Start New Test. (The first time you choose Start New Test, you may need to exit Jetstress and restart it, because the first time Jetstress loads it will install the required performance counters.)

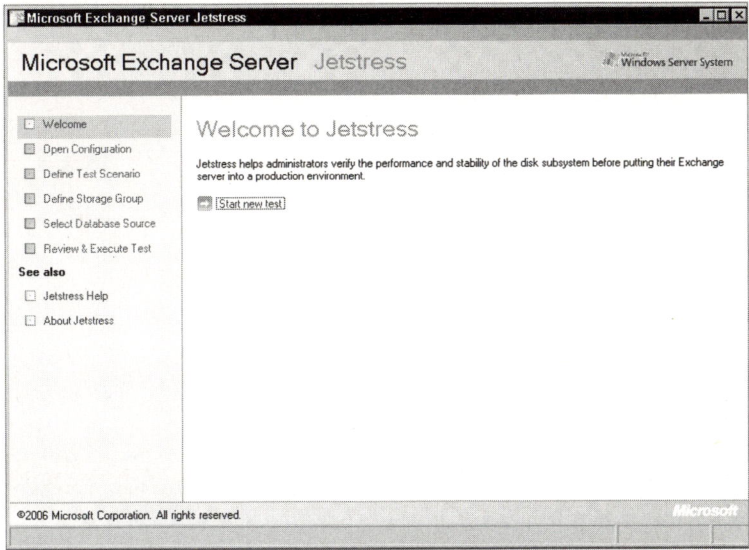

4. After Jetstress completes the system tests, click Next on the Checking Test System screen.

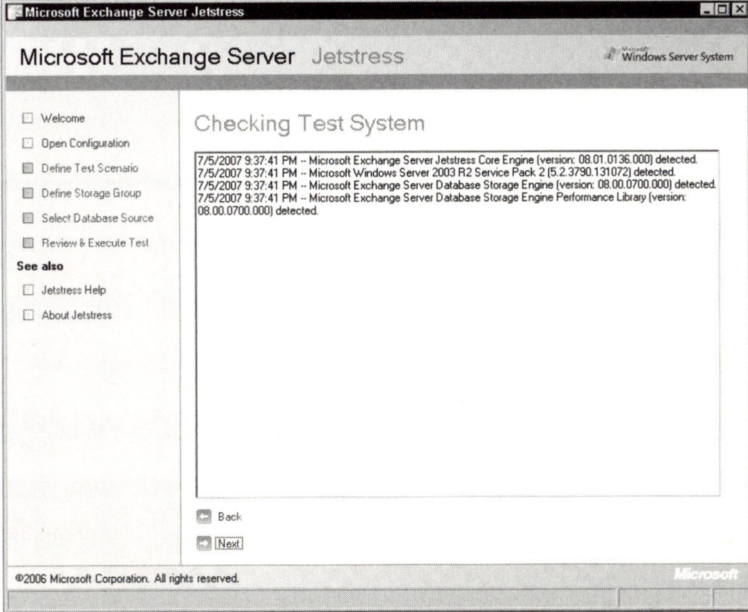

EXERCISE 11.2 *(continued)*

5. On the Open Configuration screen, select Create a New Test Configuration, and select a location to store the test configuration XML-based file. Click Next.

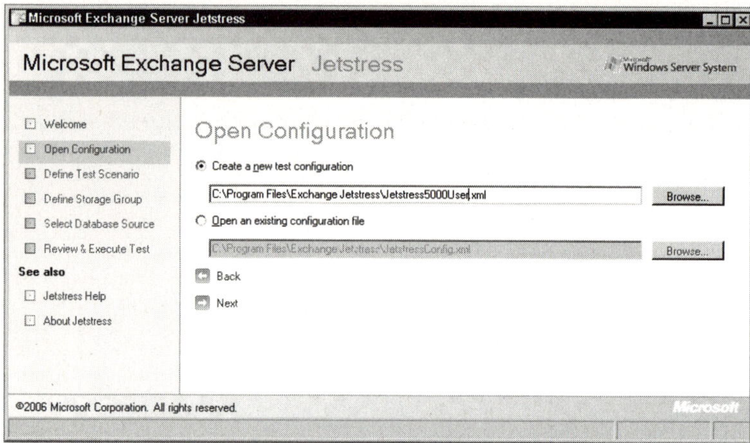

6. Next you'll need to define the parameters of the test. As shown on the Define Test Scenario screen, select Test an Exchange Mailbox Profile. If you like, you can type in a description of the test in the Describe Test Scenario text box. Click Next.

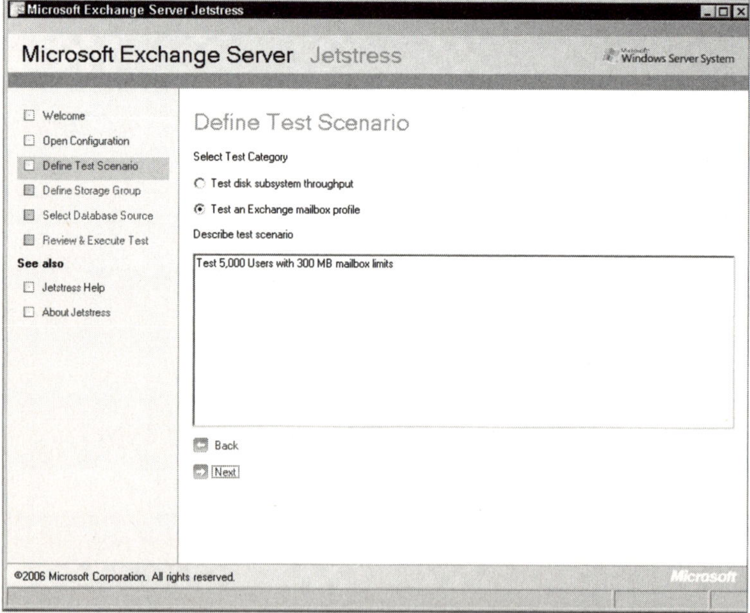

EXERCISE 11.2 *(continued)*

7. In the Exchange Mailbox Profile screen, type **5000** in the Number of Mailboxes box.

8. In the IOPS/Mailbox box, type in **.50** (a very heavy user for an Exchange Server 2007 computer with the correct amount of memory).

9. In the Mailbox Size (MB) box, type in **300**, then click Next.

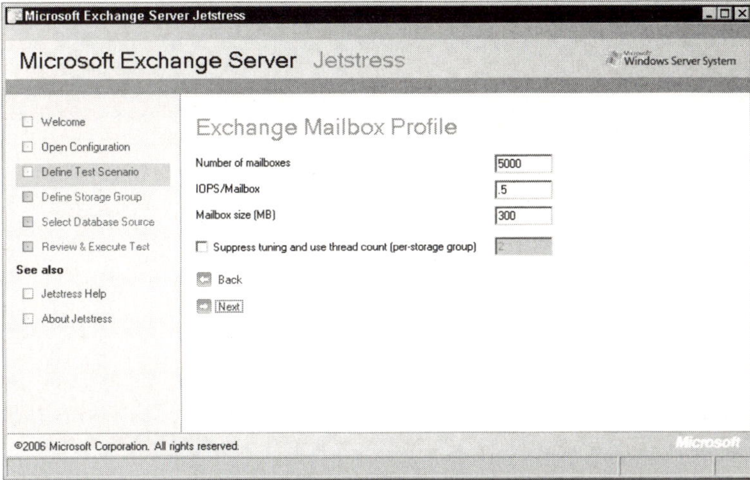

10. On the Select Test Type screen, choose Performance and then click Next. This will allow us to gather performance metrics for how the selected values will react to simulated normal use.

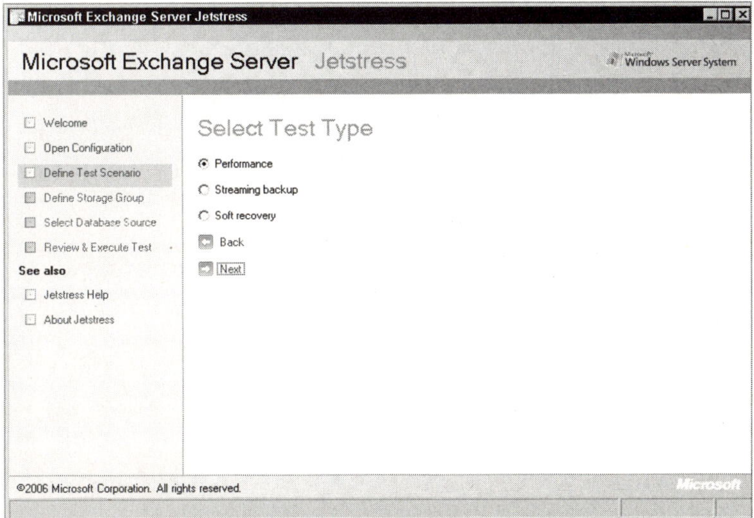

EXERCISE 11.2 *(continued)*

11. On the Define Test Run screen, choose the duration of the Jetstress test and the location where the Performance Monitor files should be stored. In the Output Path for Test Results field, choose the location where you want the Performance Monitor files to be stored for review after the test. Also, set the duration of the test to eight hours by using the Test Duration (Hours) drop-down. Choosing a full work day's length will give an opportunity for the storage to react to the load. Click Next.

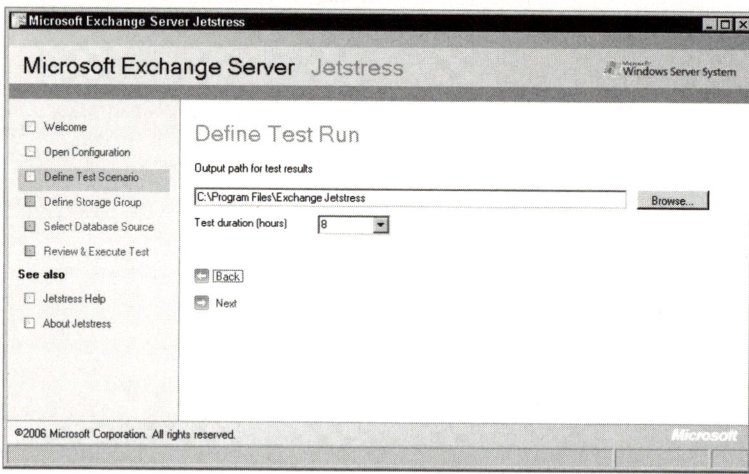

12. Next we need to select the number of storage groups and databases. On the bottom half of the screen, we need to select the volumes where we want each of the storage groups stored. For simplicity, we are going to select only one database and one storage group, then choose the locations for the storage group database and logs. We need to create folders for each storage group on the storage system that we are testing. Click Next.

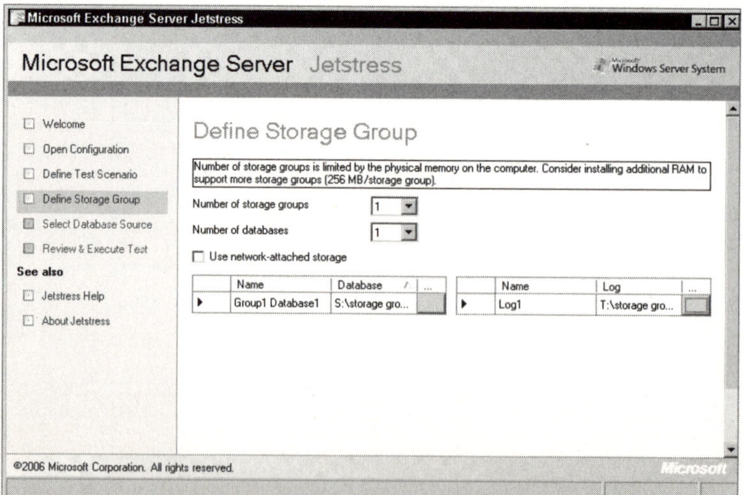

EXERCISE 11.2 *(continued)*

13. On the Select Database Source screen, choose Create New Databases and click Next.

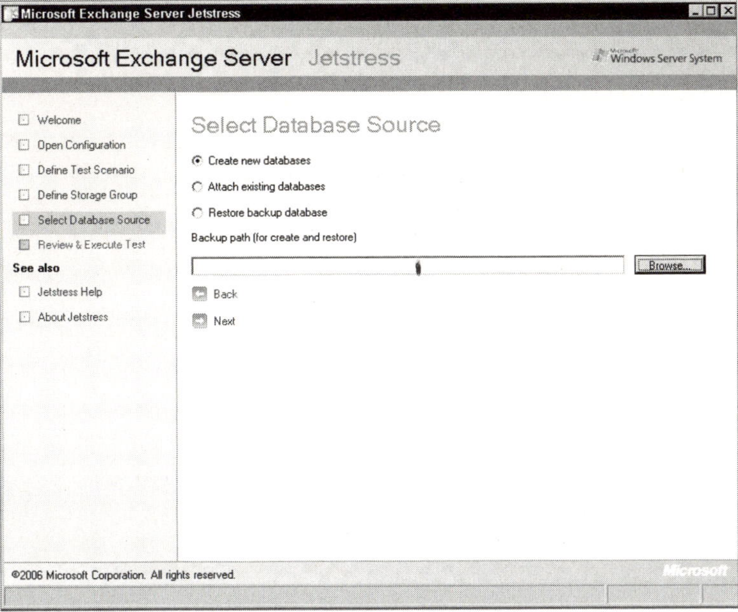

14. On the Review & Execute Test screen, choose Execute Test. The test will begin with the creation of the database and log files. Upon completion of the file creation, the actual test begins automatically.

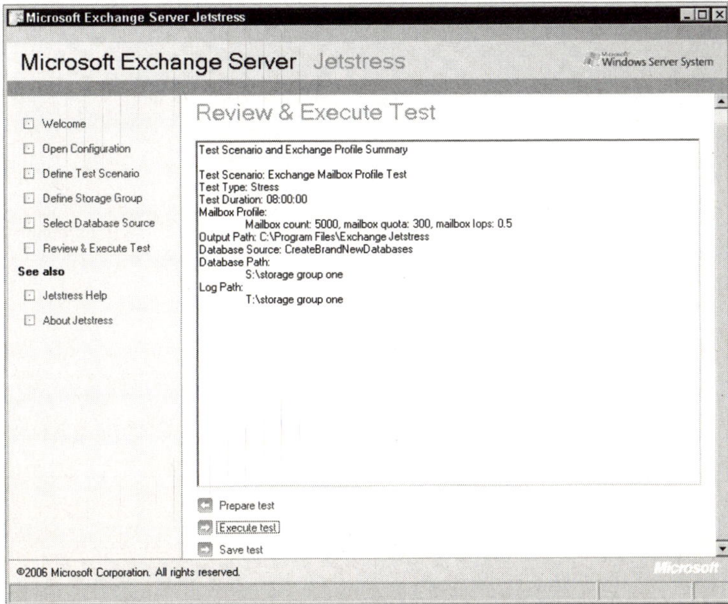

Jetstress generates a number of files that can be used to analyze the test results. The results are summarized in a HTML file; however, detailed results can be analyzed using Performance Monitor.

EXERCISE 11.3

Analyzing the Test Results

At the end of the test, Jetstress will generate a couple of files. One will be an HTML file that summarizes the data from the test.

1. Open the test file from the directory you selected for saving the test.
2. Locate the information on the page that says whether the test passed or failed.
3. Now open Performance Monitor (`perfmon.exe`) and open the saved Performance Monitor data.

You can use the saved data to generate graphs and other meaningful data to help tweak the storage.

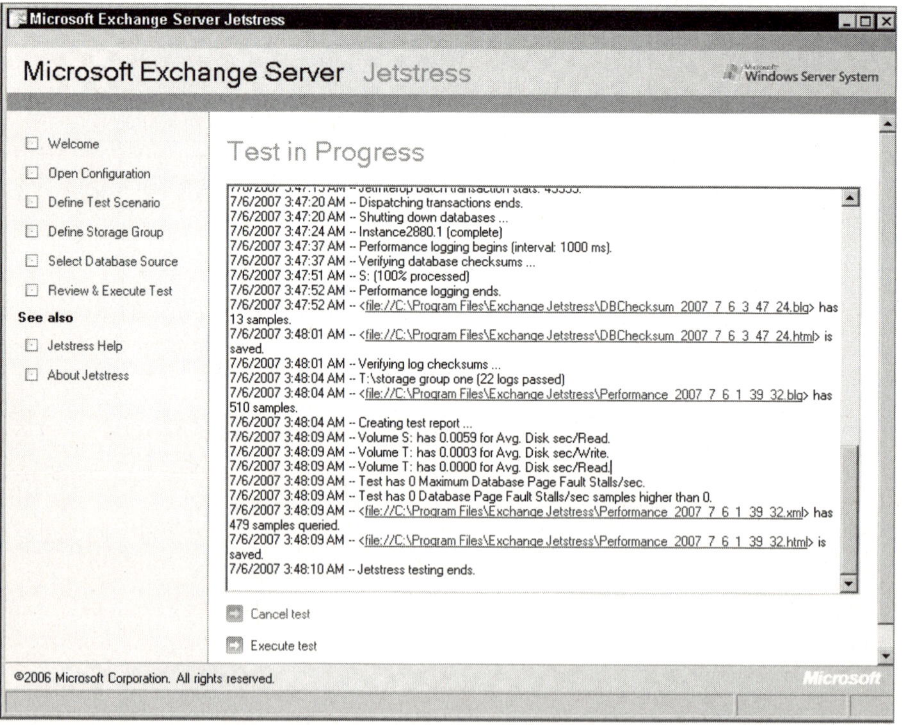

After running Jetstress, you can tweak the test by changing the disk configuration, modifying the I/O parameters, or even adding memory. Be sure to keep good notes on the hardware configuration and changes that are made so that you can compare the results after each test.

Adding memory to the Exchange server will often reduce the amount of disk I/O required because the server will be able to cache more data in memory. To determine the amount of RAM needed for a server, the recommendation is to calculate 2 GB + 5 MB for each mailbox. For a server with 5,000 mailboxes, we will need 2 GB + 5 MB × 5,000 mailboxes, which amounts to 27 GB of RAM. Using this rule of thumb doesn't guarantee performance, but is an excellent place to start.

Planning for Recovery Storage Groups

A recovery storage group can be used to restore single items, entire mailboxes, or even the entire storage group of data. Recovery storage groups are also instrumental in the dial-tone recovery process. A recovery storage group provides a method of redirecting restores of currently active mailbox stores so that they can be mounted and data can be extracted without affecting the active production databases.

Dial-tone recovery is covered in more detail in Chapter 8.

Where should recovery storage groups be placed? If possible, they should be placed on the volumes that will ultimately house the data. This allows you to move the data rather than copying it from volume to volume, which is time-consuming. If a recovery storage group is being used in a dial-tone recovery, the recovery storage group can be placed on the same volumes as the dial-tone database provided the disk can sustain the I/O for both the restore process and the production usage. If the data is restored to the same volume, when the time comes to swap the recovery storage group with the dial-tone database, the files can simply be renamed or moved without having to wait for a file copy to complete.

Summary

Storage-group design is a critical part of the Mailbox server roles. A poorly designed layout can lead to poor performance and the inability to recover data within the assigned SLA. This chapter covered how to determine the number of storage groups and databases we should have. Standard editions of Exchange are limited to five databases and five storage groups. Enterprise editions of

Exchange are limited to 50 databases and 50 storage groups. Any time continuous replication is used with either LCR or CCR, each storage group is limited to one database.

Also, we shared two detailed formulas for estimating database size:

- Mailbox size = mailbox limit + white space + database dumpster size
- Transaction log volume size = total transaction usage between full backups × 3

We concluded the chapter by walking through using the Microsoft Jetstress utility to verify that our storage design meets the requirements set out by our Exchange configuration.

Exam Essentials

Know the keys for estimating required space. Mailbox limits, deleted item retention, and white space all play a large part in sizing the database volumes. Know what these are and how to estimate space required for a storage group when given these variables.

Know the product parameters. Specific versions and configurations require specific storage-group limitations. Review the number of storage groups that Standard and Enterprise editions of Exchange allow. Also, be sure to know that both continuous replication configurations only allow one database in each storage group, even though a single-copy cluster allows up to five.

Review Questions

1. What tool will simulate database I/O load without your needing to have Exchange installed?
   - **A.** Exchange Load Simulator
   - **B.** Jetstress
   - **C.** Exchange Server Stress and Performance
   - **D.** NTBackup
2. Which of the following factors should be considered when determining the amount of space a database will require? (Choose all that apply.)
   - **A.** Mailbox limit
   - **B.** White space
   - **C.** Deleted item retention
   - **D.** Number of emails received
3. Which of the following is a valid configuration of a stand-alone Exchange Mailbox server running Exchange Server 2007 Standard Edition? (Choose all that apply.)
   - **A.** One storage group with four databases
   - **B.** Fifty storage groups and one database in each
   - **C.** Two storage groups and two databases in each
   - **D.** One storage group with five databases
4. Which of the following is a valid configuration of a CCR cluster?
   - **A.** One storage group and four databases
   - **B.** Fifty storage groups and one database in each
   - **C.** Two storage groups and two databases in each
   - **D.** One storage group and five databases
5. When determining placement of the transaction logs, which of the following meets recommendations for a non–VSS-capable server? (Choose all that apply.)
   - **A.** A dedicated, physically separate volume for each set of transaction logs
   - **B.** A dedicated, physically separate volume for all of the transaction logs
   - **C.** A shared volume for both the database files and transaction logs
   - **D.** A second partition on the same physical disks that host the database files
6. What are the three types of files that make up a storage group?
   - **A.** System
   - **B.** Transaction log
   - **C.** Database
   - **D.** Index

7. When installing Jetstress, which of the following files is not required?
   A. `ESE.DLL`
   B. `STORE.EXE`
   C. `ESEPERF.HXX`
   D. `ESEPERF.INI`
   E. `ESEPERF.DLL`

8. Which of the following is not a valid test scenario that Jetstress can accommodate?
   A. Database performance
   B. Streaming backup
   C. Soft database recovery
   D. Streaming restore

9. Which of the following event IDs will provide information on the number of times maintenance has been able to complete on a database? (Choose all that apply.)
   A. 701
   B. 9518
   C. 18159519
   D. 703

10. What are some of the benefits of single-instance storage?
    A. Quicker message delivery
    B. Attachment compression
    C. Smaller database size
    D. Reduced mailbox limits

11. After running Jetstress, you determine that your six-disk RAID 5 set does not perform well enough to meet your I/O requirements. What are possible ways to improve your performance? (Choose all that apply.)
    A. Change the RAID 5 set to a RAID 6 set.
    B. Add additional disks to the RAID 5 set.
    C. Change the RAID 5 set to a RAID 10 set.
    D. Use Diskpart to sector-align the partition.

12. After running Jetstress, you determine that your four-disk RAID 10 set performs very well; however, there is not enough free space to achieve 110 percent available for offline maintenance. Which of the following changes would allow more space and protect against a disk failure? (Choose all that apply.)
    A. Change the RAID 10 set to RAID 5
    B. Change the RAID 10 set to RAID 0
    C. Add additional disks to the RAID 10 set
    D. Use Diskpart to sector align the partition

13. When sizing a transaction-log volume, which key factors determine the size? (Choose all that apply.)
   A. Number of transaction logs generated each day
   B. Database white space
   C. Deleted item retention
   D. How often full backups are scheduled to run

14. Which are valid options of reducing the potential of database growth without affecting the end users?
   A. Move the content index to another disk.
   B. Reduce the deleted item retention time.
   C. Increase the amount of time for which database maintenance runs.
   D. Perform an offline database defragmentation.

15. How can you determine how well single-instance storage is working on a specific database?
   A. Run a full backup.
   B. Use Performance Monitor.
   C. Check for Event ID 701 in the application log.
   D. Check for Event ID 703 in the application log.

16. When you are deciding which mailboxes to deploy into databases, which of the following may work to preserve single-instance storage? (Choose all that apply.)
   A. Arrange users by department.
   B. Arrange users by geographic region.
   C. Arrange users by last name.
   D. Arrange users by mailbox size.

17. After running Jetstress, you want to create a graph of the disk activity during the test. How would you do this?
   A. Run Jetstress again with Performance Monitor in logging mode.
   B. Use the data exported by Jetstress in Performance Monitor.
   C. Run Exchange Load Simulator.
   D. Install Microsoft Office Excel to generate a graph.

18. When a server has more than 26 volumes for which you need to store data, what is the only way to present the data to the server?
   A. Concatenate the volumes into larger logical volumes.
   B. Nothing; you have to limit the number of volumes to 26.
   C. Use mount points to aggregate volumes.
   D. Use network shares to store data.

19. When planning for transaction-log I/O, what ratio should be used as a rule of thumb?

    A. Two database writes for every transaction log write

    B. Four database writes for every transaction log write

    C. Two transaction log writes for every database write

    D. Four transaction log writes for every database write

20. When planning for disaster recovery for a Mailbox server role configured as a local continuous replication and one storage group, what is the minimum number of volumes needed to meet the recommended configuration?

    A. 2

    B. 4

    C. 6

    D. 8

Answers to Review Questions

1. B. Jetstress is used to simulate database I/O without having to install Exchange. Exchange Load Simulator and Exchange Server Stress and Performance requires Exchange to be installed and configured to be used. NTBackup is used to perform backup and restore functions.

2. A, B, C. The mailbox limits, the white space in the database, and the amount of time deleted items are retained are all important factors that affect the size of the database. The number of emails received is not relevant when determining the database size.

3. A, C, D. When a stand-alone Mailbox server has Exchange Server 2007 Standard Edition installed, the total database and storage group count cannot exceed five.

4. B. A CCR cluster can have only storage groups with a single database in each. No other configuration is valid.

5. A, B. The physically separate disks and volumes from the database files meet the recommendations. The other configurations are on the same physical disks and do not meet the requirements.

6. A, B, C. The three types of files that need to be placed in a storage group are database, system, and transaction logs. An index is an object in a database but is not a file type.

7. B. `STORE.EXE` is not required to run Jetstress. However, `ESE.DLL`, `ESEPERF.INI`, `ESEPERF.HXX`, and `ESEPERF.DLL` are all required.

8. D. You cannot use Jetstress to test the performance of a streaming restore. Database performance, streaming backups, and soft database recovery are all valid tests.

9. A, D. Event IDs 701 and 703 denote that maintenance has completed on a specific mailbox. Event IDs 9518 and 9519 are database mounting errors that can occur.

10. A, C. Single-instance storage allows for quicker mail delivery because it only has to be delivered once to each database. Initially, it also reduces the amount of data stored in the database.

11. B, C, D. Adding disks, switching to a RAID 10 set, and using Diskpart to sector-align are all valid ways to improve disk performance.

12. A, C. The RAID 10 set can be changed to a RAID 5 to provide more space. Also, adding additional disks to the existing RAID 10 set would provide more space. RAID 0 does not allow any disk failures and using Diskpart can improve performance but does not increase space.

13. A, D. When sizing the transaction-log volumes, it is important to determine the number of transaction logs that are generated each day. The other factor is how often the logs are purged with a full backup. If incremental backups are done, the transaction-log volume must be able to contain all of the restore sets between full backups, as they will need to be replayed.

14. B, C. The longer the deleted item retention period, the more data will be kept in the database. The content index cannot be moved from the database disk. Ensuring that database maintenance is running long enough will perform online defragmentation so that the database won't needlessly grow. Performing offline defragmentation will not keep the database from growing if there is no free space.

15. B. The single-instance ratio for each of the database instances is a Performance Monitor counter that tracks the single-instance storage ratio. Event IDs 701 and 703 show the results of online maintenance and this does not report on single instance storage.

16. A, B. Arranging the mailboxes into databases based upon who they communicate the most with is the best for single-instance storage and message delivery. Typically users in the same department and geographical area communicate. Arranging users by last name or mailbox size does not typically denote how often they communicate with each other.

17. B. The performance data that is created automatically when you run Jetstress can be used in Performance Monitor to graph the test data.

18. C. Mount points can be used to mount separate volumes as folders on other volumes. Storing data on a network share is not supported.

19. A. Transaction log volumes require about half as many writes as does a database volume.

20. B. To keep the transaction logs and database files separate, two volumes would be required. To keep both the active and passive copies separate, two more volumes would be required (for a total of four).

Planning the Exchange Server 2007 Server Role Deployment

MICROSOFT EXAM OBJECTIVE COVERED IN THIS CHAPTER:

- ✓ Plan server role deployment

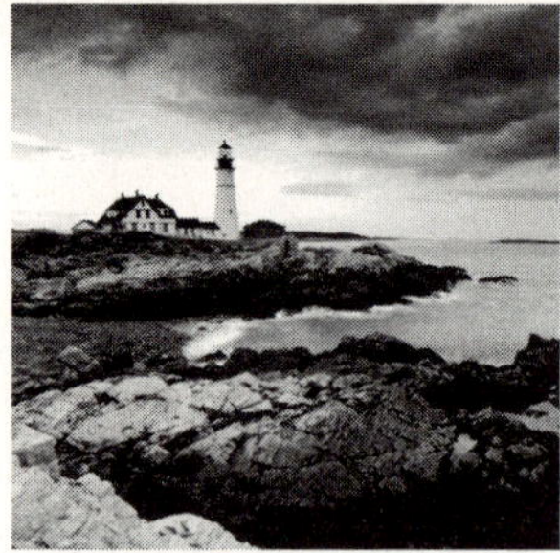

When planning an Exchange Server 2007 deployment many factors play into which roles are deployed at each location and in what sequence they are deployed. Dependencies on specific roles for mail services will either require or cause specific roles to be deployed and dictate in what order. We will look at the recommended deployment process for a variety of different scenarios and why these processes work. Then we will talk about hardware and related service configurations.

This chapter covers the following:

- Defining the server role implementation sequence
- Defining server configurations based on roles
- Verifying that dependent services meet requirements
- Client Access server role
- Edge Transport server role
- Hub Transport server role
- Mailbox server roles
- Unified Messaging server role

Defining the Server Role Implementation Sequence

Deploying or upgrading to Exchange Server 2007 requires a great deal of planning and design. You must keep in mind several basic rules while determining the sequence of deploying server roles. The first guideline to remember is the order in which server roles should be deployed:

- Client Access
- Edge Transport
- Hub Transport
- Mailbox
- Unified Messaging

This does not mean that all deployments will be in this order; however, most of the time it will follow this pattern not only for the initial deployment but for each location. There are a couple ways to remember this order. One is by remembering the acronym C.E.H.M.U. Another easy way is to remember that the first letter of each of the roles is in alphabetical order. Since Client Access starts with a C it is the first role that should be deployed and the Unified Messaging role, which starts with a U, is the last role that should be deployed.

The site deployment order is defined to preserve mail functions. To provide Autodiscover and other Web-based functions a Client Access server will need to be present, so this role should be deployed first. The next role that should be deployed is the Edge Transport server since it will provide inbound and outbound mail services; however, delivery of email won't occur until a connection agreement is created with a deployed Hub Transport server. This means that the next role that should be deployed is the Hub Transport so that mail can be delivered to mailboxes in the site or delivered through this site. At this time the Mailbox role can be deployed into the site and function properly. If you were to install the Mailbox role in a site first, the server would not be able to send or receive email, even to/from other mailboxes on the same server. Lastly, the Unified Messaging role can be deployed. Since the Mailbox, Hub Transport, and Client Access roles are already deployed, the dependent services for Unified Messaging will allow it to function properly.

If the Mailbox role is deployed into a new Active Directory site (despite the warnings given during the setup process) the Mailbox server will not function properly. Since there is no Hub Transport server in the site no email will be able to be sent from, to, or even between mailboxes on the Mailbox server. Also, with no Client Access servers present, any time a web service needs to be queried a Client Access server in another site would need to be accessed.

Defining Server Configurations Based on Roles

When determining how to deploy roles in this order it is important to keep in mind that multiple roles can be installed on a single non-clustered server, with the exception of the Edge Transport role. The Edge Transport role should be installed on a non-domain-joined computer. This means that you can install a single server with Client Access, Hub Transport, Mailbox, and Unified Messaging roles to satisfy the deployment order and to provide a functional email organization. When deploying multiple roles on a single server, you must take care in sizing the server to handle the multiple server-load types. Let's discuss specific configuration issues for each of the roles and what is required for combining the roles.

Exchange Server 2007, as mentioned earlier, is now supported only running on a 64-bit Windows Server operating system. This means that the processor architecture chosen for the Exchange server must be able to run 64-bit applications, which includes the AMD Opteron processor family with AMD64, as well as the Intel processors with Extended Memory 64

Technology (EM64T). Intel Itanium (IA64) processors are not supported. With the requirement of a 64-bit operating system comes the ability to leverage memory space much more efficiently on the server. Another fairly recent development in processors is multiple processor cores on a single installed chip. Each vendor implements multi-cores differently, but they all have the advantage of more processing power in the same amount of space and usually at a cheaper price than the same number of physical processor cores. This opens more configuration options than the maximum of 4 GB of memory that Exchange 2003 was able to use.

Another factor in determining server configuration is disk I/O. Both transactional and non-transactional I/O need to be identified and calculated. An example of transactional I/O is the I/O generated by an email message being received. This would include the data being written to the message-tracking logs, transaction logs being written, and data being written to disk. Examples of non-transactional I/O are generated actions like backup and restore processes, messaging records management, and content indexing. One way to improve disk I/O performance is to utilize the Diskpart utility to sector-align all of the disk partitions.

Real World Scenario

Using Diskpart.exe on Exchange Server Disks

As an Exchange Server administrator you have no doubt had to monitor the disk I/O on your server. Also, with mailbox sizes continually increasing, disk space needs top be closely monitored. The good news is that Diskpart can help reduce disk latency and help increase drive size. This is an invaluable tool that every Exchange engineer needs to be aware of and know how to use—it can make you job a lot easier.

Diskpart is a utility created to enable storage configuration from a command line and from scripts. Why is this of concern to Exchange administrators?

Performance

Modern disks drives have 64 sectors on each track. For some strange reason the built-in Windows tools will format a partition starting at sector 64, the last sector on the track. This means that the partition starts at the end of a track, thus causing the possibility of a single I/O spanning two tracks on a disk. Since the hard-drive heads have to switch tracks to get all the data for a single I/O, this leads to a reduction performance and an additional I/O. When you use Diskpart to create and format the partition, you are sector-aligning the data to optimize performance. The Exchange Server 2007 store process now writes in 8 KB I/O operations, so the starting offset for the partition needs to be a multiple of 8. The offset usually chosen is 64, since this will start the partition on the first sector of the second track for standard disks. Be sure to check with your storage vendor to determine the optimal offset to choose. From my testing with Jetstress I have seen 20 percent performance gains when using Diskpart to sector-align the partitions; however, this varies under differing loads and disk systems.

To use Diskpart to sector-align a partition, all data must be removed from the disk. Diskpart is data-destructive; do not try to run it against a disk that has data on it. It is intended to be run *before* Exchange is installed.

The overall process for running Diskpart is as follows:

1. Open a command prompt.
2. Run Diskpart.
3. Select the disk you want to sector-align.
4. Create a primary partition with an offset of 64.
5. Assign a drive letter to the newly created partition.
6. Format the partition using another tool, such as the Disk Management MMC snap-in.

Expanding Partitions

Another great use for Diskpart is to expand partitions. Diskpart cannot be used to expand system partitions nor partitions on dynamic disks; however it can be used for Exchange installation and data partitions as long as they are stored on basic disks.

When would you use this? When there is more contiguous space on the drive to expand the partition to. If you have a 50 GB partition and you need to provide more space to it, you could expand the partition as long as there is more free space on the disk drive. This sounds limiting, but most disk subsystems and SANs allow an administrator to give more space to a volume. After the drive space has been expanded, Diskpart can be used. This partition-expansion process can be done online and in clustered environments; however good sense dictates that you do perform a full backup for making this change during a scheduled outage window.

What process should be followed to expand a partition?

1. Make additional contiguous physical disk space available.
2. Open a command prompt.
3. Run Diskpart.
4. Select the disk and then the partition that you want to expand.
5. Use the Extend command to extend the partition.

Clearly, Diskpart is an important tool for Exchange administrators to know about and to be able to use. It is able to help reduce disk latency and extend volumes, saving work and frustration.

When defining the configuration or server roles, disk sizing is also a factor; we will discuss in detail in the next section how the space varies for each server role. However, all of the Exchange roles require 1.2 GB of disk space on an NTFS-formatted volume that Exchange is installed to, and an additional 200 MB of space on the system partition.

We are now going to discuss the configuration of each of the roles and see how to create a configuration using standard guidelines. The processor-core configuration recommendations are summarized in Table 12.1 and the memory configuration recommendations are summarized in Table 12.2.

TABLE 12.1 Summary of Server Processor Configuration

Server Role	Recommended Number of Processor Cores	Recommended Maximum Number of Processor Cores
Client Access	2	4
Edge Transport	2	4
Hub Transport	4	8
Mailbox	4	8
Unified Messaging	4	4
Multiple server roles	4	4

TABLE 12.2 Summary of Server Memory Configuration

Server Role	Recommended Amount of RAM	Recommended Maximum Amount of RAM
Client Access	2 GB or 1 GB/core	8 GB
Edge Transport	2 GB or 1 GB/core	16 GB
Hub Transport	2 GB or 1 GB/core	16 GB
Mailbox	2 GB + 2–5 MB/mailbox	32 GB
Unified Messaging	2 GB or 1 GB/processor	4 GB
Multiple server roles	4 GB + 2–5 MB/mailbox	8 GB

Configuring the Client Access Server Role

If you are familiar with previous versions of Exchange Server you may immediately think that sizing a Client Access server would fall into your previous front-end server sizing guidelines. The two previous versions of Exchange ran most of its processes within the `STORE.EXE` process on the back-end server; however Exchange Server 2007 processing has now been split into several individual roles. The Client Access role is now responsible for converting content for IMAP4 and POP3 clients. Since the Streaming Store file (`.stm`) is not present in Exchange Server 2007, all data presented to non-MAPI clients will need to be converted. The Client Access server is now also responsible for rendering all of the web content. This is done in a worker process in IIS that makes MAPI calls to the proper Mailbox server roles to render mailbox data.

A Client Access server role's main services are as follows:

- Outlook Web Access
- Exchange ActiveSync
- Outlook Anywhere
- Exchange Web Services
- Autodiscover
- Offline address book distribution
- POP3
- IMAP4

The Client Access server role is an important role indeed.

The minimum hardware configuration for a Client Access server role is one processor core; however, four processor cores are suggested for servers with moderate to heavy utilization. The current sizing guidelines show that anything above four processors cores provides little benefit.

In a standard environment the suggestion is 1 GB of RAM for each processor core to be used. If the Client Access server is under high utilization or is primarily used for Outlook Anywhere, 2 GB for each processor core should be used.

The disk I/O processing done on a Client Access server is negligible; most modern SCSI- or SAS-based disk subsystems should be able to handle the amount of disk I/O for a Client Access server.

Configuring the Edge Transport Server Role

The Edge Transport role is a new role meant to be deployed in a perimeter network to route email traffic from the Internet into the Hub Transport servers inside the corporate network. The Edge Transport server will send and receive SMTP messages as well as perform antispam tasks and antivirus scanning and apply customized rules on transported email messages. The server can also maintain SMTP message queues for both inbound and outbound email.

The minimum configuration required is only a single processor core; however two processor cores are recommended for most Edge Transport implementations, with a maximum recommended number of processors being four. Only 1 GB of memory for each processor core is recommend to support email services; however, in very high-utilization environments 2 GB per processor can be used if additional Edge Transport servers cannot be deployed.

Disk size is one of the important factors to consider for Edge Transport server roles. First you must determine the amount of disk space required. To make a reasonable estimate on disk sizing it is helpful to determine the number of email messages that the Edge Transport server will receive in a given period of time and the amount of time that would be required for the Edge Transport server to queue messages in both standard operation and in the possibility of a messaging-system failure. If, for example, the Edge Transport server averages receiving 100,000 email messages each day and needs to be able to queue messages for up to 24 hours with an average size of 40 KB of each message, the queue could consume 4 GB of disk space in just 24 hours. Of course, there are other items that must be stored on disk, such as the protocol, message-tracking, agent, and connectivity logs, as well as the antivirus quarantine. These logs, if kept for seven days, can easily consume 8 GB of additional space using our example. Also, by default the Edge Transport server requires 4 GB of free disk space before it initiates back pressure, an internal process that prevents the system from being overwhelmed by new messages so that it will be able to deliver the already received messages. The result of the back pressure process is that the Exchange server will refuse new connections. If the total required is 16 GB (4 GB for the queue, 8 GB for logs and quarantine, and 4 GB for free space) it is suggested that you add at least 20 percent for future growth and for variance.

Disk I/O is the last factor that needs to be considered for an Edge Transport server role. If the server has enough memory installed, the message queue should stay cached in memory. The actual number of disk I/O per second (IOPS) required varies greatly from environment to environment and may need to be observed in production before accurate sizing can be done.

Configuring the Hub Transport Server Role

The Hub Transport role handles delivery of email within the Exchange organization. These servers handle virus scanning, transport rules, and message routing. At least one Hub Transport server must exist in each Active Directory site that has an Exchange Mailbox role. Since they both provide similar services, the Hub Transport role has similar configuration parameters to the Edge Transport role. All email sent by any Exchange user must go through at least one Hub Transport server even if the mail recipient and sender have mailboxes located on the same Mailbox server. This means that the Hub Transport role is a critical piece in the Exchange organization, and if it is improperly sized, email-delivery speed can be affected and end users may notice.

The minimum configuration required is only a single processor core; however, four processor cores are recommended for most Hub Transport implementations, with a maximum of eight recommended. Only 1 GB of memory for each processor core is recommend to support email services, but in very high-utilization environments 2 GB per processor can be used if additional Hub Transport servers cannot be deployed.

When Edge Transport servers are used, disk sizing is fairly easy since only locally bound mail will ever need to be queued. Just like with the Edge Transport role, it is necessary to know how much email will need to be queued; this is a function of the number and size of email messages received over a period of time and how long that the queue would need to be sustained. Add to that number space for message tracking and protocol logs. Disk I/O can also be a factor for a Hub Transport server; however, if the server has enough memory installed the message queue should stay cached in memory. The actual number of I/Os required varies greatly from environment to environment. Obtaining the actual requirements would require evaluating a production server in your environment.

Configuring the Mailbox Server Role

The Mailbox role provides the database services for mailboxes and public folders. This server role is the most important and the most difficult to get configured properly. If the Mailbox server is not configured to handle user load, the end users will be affected. When end users are affected, it usually translates into help-desk calls and an overall bad end-user perception of the messaging system.

For a detailed discussion on what goes into determining disk I/O requirements for the Mailbox role, see Chapter 11, "Planning the Exchange Server 2007 Storage Group Deployment."

The minimum memory configuration for a Mailbox server is 2 GB; however, the recommendation is to have an additional 2 to 5 MB for each user mailbox. The amount of RAM installed will also limit the number of storage groups that should be configured. For every four storage groups, 2 GB of RAM needs to be added. The maximum recommendation is 32 GB of RAM since at this point for the increased cost of the more dense RAM DIMMs there are diminishing returns. Table 12.3 lists the minimum memory requirements based on the number of storage groups. Note that these are just the minimum requirements and that if you follow the "2 GB plus 5 MB per user" rule, you won't have any problems meeting these requirements.

This table can also be used to determine the number of storage groups that should be created based on the amount of memory your server has configured.

As an example if you were to have a Mailbox server that needs to support 2,000 user mailboxes with a heavy usage profile, you would need 12 GB of RAM (2 GB + 2000 × 5 MB = 12 GB). If you have 12 GB of memory you can have a maximum of 24 storage groups configured.

TABLE 12.3 Minimum Amount of Memory Required Based on the Number of Storage Groups

Number of Storage Groups	Minimum Amount of Memory
1–4	2 GB
5–8	4 GB
9–12	6 GB
13–16	8 GB
17–20	10 GB
21–24	12 GB
25–28	14 GB
29–32	16 GB
33–36	18 GB
37–40	20 GB
41–44	22 GB
45–48	24 GB
49 or 50	26 GB

See Chapter 11 for a detailed discussion on determining disk design for Mailbox server roles.

Real World Scenario

When I Was a Kid All I Had Was 640 KB of RAM!

You may wonder why so much memory is required to run Exchange Server 2007, when Exchange Server 2003 and earlier were pretty much capped at 4 GB of RAM. In the real world does Exchange really need so much memory?

We have touched on this a few times in this book; the memory requirement is actually an improvement. This has to do with Exchange Server 2007 running on a 64-bit operating system. This gives the Exchange process a larger amount of memory that it can address. Again you may ask, just because you can does it mean that you have to or that you should? You may even say that this is all because of sloppy programming and "code bloat."

We can understand your frustration, as you have to try to justify ordering 32 GB of RAM for your new Exchange server to the CIO of your company. You just know he is going to ask why he needs to order four times more memory for this new version than he had to for the previous version.

Here are some reasoning points to use to convince your CIO to sign on the dotted line for your Exchange Server 2007 project:

More Memory, Lower Disk I/O Requirements

Adding memory to the Exchange server allows the information store to cache more data in memory, which reduces the number of times it must read and write from disk. As we mentioned elsewhere in this book, this increased cache enabled by running on a 64-bit operating system can reduce disk I/O by up to 70 percent. If your company is having disk I/O problems running Exchange 2003 servers now you may be able to use the same configuration and still add more users. The other possibility is that you can deploy the Exchange Server 2007 servers with direct-attached SAS or SATA disks or even iSCSI systems rather than using an expensive Fibre Channel–attached SAN.

More Features, Fewer Complaints

Adding memory and upgrading processors also adds new features such a messaging records management, content indexing that works (previous versions were rarely used since they slowed down the server too much to be useful), built-in Unified Messaging, and complex transport rules, just to name a few. Do some research on what the top 10 problems are with messaging at your company, and map how Exchange Server 2007 addresses those issues.

Configuring the Unified Messaging Server Role

The Unified Messaging role provides a new feature of Exchange Server 2007: a telephone interface called Outlook Voice Access (OVA). This interface allows for storing of voice mail messages in users' mailboxes as well as the ability for them to use the telephone to access the contents of their mailboxes. To use Unified Messaging, specialized hardware is required to interface the Private Branch eXchange (PBX) to the Unified Messaging server. This hardware is attached to the PBX and communicates with the Exchange Unified Messaging server with Voice over IP (VoIP). The Unified Messaging role is responsible for converting `.WAV` voicemail files to `.WMA` for storage in the mailboxes, which is very processor-intensive. This means the minimum number of recommended processors cores for a Unified Messaging server is four; however, adding more than four processor cores is not recommended due to minimal returns.

The recommended amount of RAM is 2 GB or 1 GB of RAM for each processors core, up to a maximum of 4 GB. Other than for the Exchange installation files, little storage is required. If you need to support multiple languages with the Unified Messaging server you will need to add a language pack, however, which will consume 500 MB of additional disk space. A small amount of additional space will be required for temporary files and protocol logs.

Configuring Multiple Server Roles

As mentioned earlier, multiple server roles can be installed on the same server with some rules. The Edge Transport role cannot be installed on a server with any other Exchange role and should also be on a server that is not a member of the same Active Directory forest as the other Exchange servers. Only the Mailbox role can run on a cluster node, so there is no way to install any other role when you are using a cluster. You can, however, install other roles on a Mailbox server using local continuous replication (LCR).

In many scenarios, for small or remote offices it makes sense to combine server roles. In a remote office, rather than deploying five servers you may deploy only three: one Mailbox server with LCR and two combined Client Access and Hub Transport servers. The basic guidance for multiple role deployments is that processor and memory configuration is additive. If you have a Client Access and Hub Transport combined server you would start off with 4 GB of RAM (2 GB + 2 GB base memory configuration). In smaller sites it may even make sense to combine the Client Access, Hub Transport, and Mailbox server roles on a single server. If some redundancy is needed, you can use local continuous replication to protect the data and provide the needed Client Access and Hub Transport services.

Verifying that Dependent Services Meet Requirements

After getting the server configuration defined, the dependent services and server role prerequisites need to be met. We will now consider the requirements that must be met in Active Directory and the Exchange Organization. Then we will discuss the specific server roles and the software requirements that must be met before Exchange can be installed on them.

Although Exchange has its own requirements, it also requires certain elements from other services. Having an improperly configured Active Directory domain or underpowered server domain controllers can cause severe messaging issues. The domain must meet some basic requirements, as follows:

- Active Directory functional level must be Windows 2000 native or higher. If cross-forest trust is necessary or if availability information is required across forests, the forest functional level must be set to Windows 2003 native mode.
- Active Directory Schema Master must be Windows Server 2003 with Service Pack 1 or higher.
- A domain controller that is also a global catalog server in each Active Directory site that will have an Exchange server must be Windows Server 2003 Service Pack 1 or higher.
- Domain controllers that are non-English must have the hotfix from Microsoft Knowledge Base article KB919166 (`http://support.microsoft.com/kb/919166`) or have Windows Server 2003 Service Pack 2 installed.

If you are installing Exchange Server 2007 into a new Exchange organization it is good to remember that you will not be able to install an Exchange 2003 server at a later date. If you require an Exchange 2003 server in the future you will need to install it before installing Exchange Server 2007. If you have previous versions of Exchange installed, notice the following requirements:

- No Exchange 5.5 or older servers can exist in the Exchange organization.
- All Exchange Server 2000 computers must have Service Pack 3 installed plus the post–Service Pack 3 rollup found in Microsoft's Knowledge Base article KB870540 (`http://support.microsoft.com/kb/870540`).
- All Exchange Server 2003 computers must have Service Pack 2 installed.

After all of these requirements have been satisfied the schema and forest preparation can be run. When previous versions of Exchange are present the `PrepareLegacyExchangePermissions` switch must be used when installing the first Exchange server. This option maintains permissions required for the Exchange 2000/2003 Recipient Update Service to function properly. When this step is complete the forest schema can be updated with the `PrepareSchema` setup switch. This will add the schema attributes to the Active Directory forest. Then setup can be run with the `PrepareAD` switch so that the permission groups are created and permissions are applied. Last, if there are multiple domains, setup can be run with the `PrepareDomain` or the `PrepareAllDomains` switch. This will make sure that the proper groups and permissions are created in other domains in the forest so that Exchange can function properly.

Now that the schema and directory are prepared, the individual Exchange servers can be prepared for installation. Each Exchange server must meet the following requirements before setup can be successful:

- Microsoft .NET Framework Version 2.0 installed
- Microsoft Management Console (MMC) 3.0 installed
- Windows PowerShell installed
- Membership in the same Active Directory forest; applies to all server roles except for Edge Transport
- Active Directory Application Mode (ADAM) SP1 installed; applies to Edge Transport server role

If all of the required components are not installed when the Exchange install is run, the installer will prompt you to install them.

All Exchange server roles besides the Edge Transport role must be a member of the domain. It is important that DNS name resolution is working properly for the Exchange servers. The servers should also be properly registered in DNS so that other servers will be able to resolve their IP addresses. To facilitate domain lookups, the default DNS suffix should be the same as the domain you have joined. If the computer's domain suffix does not match the Active Directory domain that the machine is joined to, the Active Directory domain suffix should be added to the domain search order on the network adapters.

Requirements for the Client Access Server Role

The Client Access server role has some specific software requirements. If the requirements are not met, the installation will not be able to complete. To successfully install the Client Access server role, you must also install the following components:

- Internet Information Service (IIS) 6.0, World Wide Web Service
- Remote procedure call (RPC) over Hypertext Transfer Protocol (HTTP) proxy
- ASP.NET version 2.0

If you are using Windows Server 2003 R2 or later, all of the aforementioned components can be installed using the Add/Remove Windows Components wizard available in the Control Panel.

You need to install the RPC over HTTP Proxy only on Client Access servers that will provide Microsoft Outlook Anywhere access.

Requirements for the Edge Transport Server Role

It is important for all server roles to have proper internal DNS name resolution. This is more difficult for an Edge Transport server than for other server roles since it is not joined to the domain and is typically located in a perimeter network.

When using Microsoft terminology, a *perimeter network* is the same as a *demilitarized zone* (*DMZ*). This is a network segment that is exposed to the Internet and has limited to no access to the internal network. The networks are typically segmented with a firewall.

The SMTP protocol is heavily reliant on DNS for delivery of email messages. Having DNS configured properly is thus crucial for a successful install of the Edge Transport role. To start with, the server must have a DNS suffix defined; otherwise setup will fail. This may sound strange; however, the machine's DNS suffix is usually set when the machine is joined to a domain. Since the Edge Transport server should not be part of a domain, it will not by default have a DNS suffix set.

The server should also be able to resolve the Hub Transport servers that it needs to communicate with directly. This can be done in the following ways:

- Create A records, or host records, for the Hub Transport servers in the external DNS servers that the Edge Transport servers use.
- Modify the Hosts file on the Edge Transport server to include the records for the Hub Transport servers. The hosts file is stored in the X:\Windows\System32\Drivers\Etc folder.

The Hub Transport servers should also be able to resolve the names of the Edge Transport servers. This can be accomplished using the same methods as for the Hub Transport servers:

- Create A records for the Edge Transport servers in the external DNS servers that the Hub Transport servers use.
- Modify the Hosts file on the Hub Transport server to include the records for the Edge Transport servers. The hosts file is stored in the X:\Windows\System32\Drivers\Etc folder.

There are also a few software requirements specific to the Edge Transport role. Since the Edge Transport server provides its own SMTP service and no longer relies on the Internet Information Services (IIS) version of SMTP, you cannot have the SMTP service or the NNTP service installed.

You must, however, install Active Directory Application Mode (ADAM) on the Edge Transport server role. No customization is required during the installation of ADAM. When the Edge Transport role is installed it will complete the configuration of ADAM.

Requirements for the Hub Transport Server Role

The Hub Transport role has most of its requirement met with the base Exchange requirements. However, you cannot have the Internet Information Services (IIS) 6.0 SMTP services or the NNTP service installed. That's because Exchange Server 2007 no longer relies on IIS to provide the base SMTP services, as SMTP has been completely rewritten. If the IIS version of SMTP were installed during the installation of the Hub Transport server, binding conflicts would keep the Exchange SMTP service from functioning properly—therefore the Exchange installation requires the service to be removed before installation will continue.

Requirements for the Mailbox Server Role

In addition to the base Exchange requirements, the Mailbox server role requires the installation of a couple of hotfixes that address issues with Windows Server 2003 x64 if Windows Server 2003 Service Pack 2 has not been installed:

- Hotfix available from Microsoft Knowledge Base Article KB904639 (`http://support.microsoft.com/kb/904639`)
- Hotfix available from Microsoft Knowledge Base Article KB918980 (`http://support.microsoft.com/kb/918980`)

The Mailbox server role requires several Windows components from Internet Information Services to be installed. (You might think the Mailbox role would not require these since the Client Access role has been removed from the mailbox functions.)

- Network COM+ access
- World Wide Web Service

Requirements for the Unified Messaging Server Role

To successfully install the Unified Messaging server role, the following components must be installed prior to running setup:

- Microsoft Exchange Speech Engine service (installed automatically if the setup is run from a command prompt)
- Microsoft Windows Media Encoder
- Microsoft Windows Media Audio Voice codec
- Microsoft Core XML Services (MSXML) 6.0

You cannot install the Unified Messaging role on a computer that has Microsoft Speech Server installed since at its core the Unified Messaging role relies on a customized version of Speech Server. You must remove any version of Speech Server and is components installed on the server before attempting to install the Unified Messaging role.

Summary

In this chapter you learned that the order of deployment and the configuration of the server roles must be planned properly to have a successful Exchange deployment. Always remember the acronym C.E.H.M.U. to determine the order in which to deploy the Exchange roles.

After discussing order, we covered the recommended hardware configurations for each of the server roles and for combined server roles. We then covered the Active Directory and Exchange organization requirements, and finished up the chapter talking about the software requirements for each of the Exchange server roles.

Exam Essentials

Know the recommended order for deploying Exchange roles. Remember that the recommended order of deployment is Client Access, Edge Transport, Hub Transport, Mailbox, Unified Messaging (C.E.H.M.U.). When you are taking the test you may be asked to validate a plan or to build a plan for deploying the server roles; order will be important for such questions.

Know the required and recommended hardware configurations for each Exchange server role. Most Exchange roles have specific hardware requirements for deployment. Familiarize yourself with the hardware requirements.

Know the software requirements for each Exchange server role. Each of the Exchange roles requires basic components to be installed, such as Windows PowerShell and Microsoft Management Console 3.0. Be aware of these requirements as well as the ones specific to each of the roles. Also be aware of the software that cannot be installed on the same server, such as Internet Information Services (IIS) SMTP and NNTP on Hub Transport and Edge Transport servers.

Know Active Directory requirements. Know the Active Directory functional-level requirements along with the operating-system requirements for domain controllers, global catalog servers, and Schema Master servers. Be sure you know the rules about the number and placement of these roles as well.

Understand the Exchange organization requirements. Exchange 2000 and higher servers are supported in the same organization as Exchange Server 2007 servers; however, specific patch levels must be attained on the legacy servers.

Review Questions

1. What forest functional level must the forest be in before Exchange Server 2007 is installed where trusts will not be maintained with other forests?

   A. Windows 2000 native

   B. Windows 2000 mixed

   C. Windows 2003 interim

   D. Windows 2003

2. Which of the following Windows components cannot be installed on a Hub Transport server? (Choose all that apply.)

   A. Internet Information Services (IIS) SMTP

   B. Internet Information Services (IIS) NNTP

   C. RPC/HTTP Proxy

   D. ASP.NET 2.0

3. When planning a configuration for a Mailbox role for 5,000 heavy-profile users, what would be the minimum recommended amount of memory?

   A. 2 GB

   B. 25 GB

   C. 27 GB

   D. 30 GB

4. When deploying a new site, in which order would you deploy the following server roles?

   A. Unified Messaging

   B. Client Access

   C. Mailbox

   D. Hub Transport

5. Why do you need to deploy a Hub Transport server before deploying a Mailbox server? (Choose all that apply.)

   A. Email will not be able to be scanned for viruses.

   B. No email will be able to be sent from the Exchange Mailbox server.

   C. No email will be able to be received from the Exchange Mailbox server.

   D. Users will not be able to access their email with Outlook Web Access.

6. Which of the following processor types are supported to run Exchange in production? (Choose all that apply.)

   A. Intel Itanium

   B. Intel Xeon with EM64T

   C. AMD K6

   D. AMD Opteron with AMD64

7. If you need to install an Exchange Server 2003 computer in an environment to support a specific application, when must you install it?
   A. After all of the Exchange Server 2007 computers are deployed
   B. After the Exchange Server 2007 schema has been applied
   C. Before the Exchange Server 20007 schema has been applied
   D. After the first Exchange Server 2007 server is installed
8. Which of the following roles can be installed on a CCR cluster?
   A. Hub Transport
   B. Edge Transport
   C. Client Access
   D. None of the above
9. Diskpart can be used for which two of the following tasks?
   A. Sector-aligning new partitions
   B. Compressing files
   C. Expanding existing partitions
   D. Sector-aligning existing partitions
10. When using Edge Transport servers, which of the following can to be done for the Edge Transport servers to have proper name resolution? (Choose all that apply.)
    A. Add an MX record for the Hub Transport server.
    B. Add the names of the Hub Transport servers to the Edge Transport servers' Host file.
    C. Add the names of the Hub Transport servers to the external DNS.
    D. Add the names of the Hub Transport servers to the Hub Transport servers' Hosts file.
11. If you have a mixed Exchange 5.5 with Service Pack 4 and Exchange 2000 with Service Pack 3 environment and you want to install Exchange Server 2007, what would you need to do before installing the first Exchange 2007 computer? (Choose all that apply.)
    A. Apply a hotfix to the Exchange 5.5 servers
    B. Remove all of the Exchange 5.5 servers
    C. Apply a hotfix to the Exchange 2000 servers
    D. Remove all of the Exchange 2000 servers
12. Which of the following pieces of software cannot be installed on a server before Unified Messaging role is installed?
    A. Internet Information Services (IIS) 6.0 World Wide Web Services
    B. Microsoft Speech Server
    C. Microsoft .NET Framework 2.0
    D. Windows PowerShell

13. When you have a Mailbox server with 10 GB of RAM, what is the maximum number of storage groups that you can create on an Exchange Mailbox server running Exchange Server 2007 Enterprise edition?

    A. 2

    B. 14

    C. 20

    D. 25

14. Which of the following objects require disk space on an Edge Transport server? (Choose all that apply.)

    A. Message queues

    B. Message-tracking logs

    C. Protocol logs

    D. Agent logs

15. Which of the following need to be installed prior to installing the Exchange Edge Transport role? (Choose all that apply.)

    A. Internet Information Services (IIS) SMTP

    B. Active Directory Application Mode (ADAM)

    C. Internet Information Services (IIS) BITS

    D. Windows PowerShell

16. Which of the following roles can be installed on a Mailbox server using LCR? (Choose all that apply.)

    A. Hub Transport

    B. Edge Transport

    C. Client Access

    D. Unified Messaging

17. Which of the following Windows components cannot be installed on an Edge Transport server? (Choose all that apply.)

    A. Internet Information Services (IIS) SMTP

    B. Internet Information Services (IIS) NNTP

    C. RPC/HTTP Proxy

    D. ASP.NET 2.0

18. If you are planning on using a specific Client Access server for Outlook Anywhere, which of the following components would you need to install on the server before attempting an install? (Choose all that apply.)

    A. Internet Information Service (IIS) 6.0 World Wide Web Service

    B. RPC over HTTP Proxy

    C. ASP.NET Version 2.0

    D. Microsoft Office Outlook 2007

19. Which of the following are benefits of having more system memory? (Choose all that apply.)

    A. Increased database cache

    B. Increased number of disk I/O

    C. Decreased number of disk I/O

    D. Decreased processor cache

20. When you have a Mailbox server with 16 GB of RAM, what is the maximum number of storage groups that you can create on an Exchange Mailbox server running Exchange Server 2007 Enterprise edition?

    A. 2

    B. 14

    C. 32

    D. 45

Answers to Review Questions

1. A. If no trusts will be maintained with other Windows 2003 domains for sharing free/busy information, Windows 2000 native mode is the minimum forest level that Exchange Server 2007 needs.

2. A, B. Neither SMTP nor NNTP can be installed, as they will conflict with the Exchange services. RPC/HTLP Proxy and ASP.NET 2.0 can both be installed on a Hub Transport server.

3. C. For a heavy-profile user it is recommended to add 5 MB for each user on top of the base 2 GB. This means that this configuration would require 27 GB (2 GB + 5000 × 5 MB).

4. B, D, C, A. The recommended order is Client Access, Hub Transport, Mailbox, and Unified Messaging.

5. B, C. No email will be able to be sent or received from the Mailbox server. If the Mailbox server had antivirus software installed it could be scanned for viruses. If the Hub Transport server is not installed, the mailbox server can have antivirus software installed to scan for virus. The Client access provides the Outlook Web Access client not the Hub Transport.

6. B, D. The only types of processors that Exchange Server 2007 is supported on are the Intel processors with EM64T and the AMD Opterons with AMD64.

7. C. Once an Exchange 2007 server is deployed there is no way to deploy an Exchange 2003 computer. The server must be deployed first.

8. D. No other roles besides the mailbox role can be installed on an Exchange CCR cluster.

9. A, C. Diskpart can be used to sector-align new partitions; existing partitions cannot be sector aligned. Diskpart can also be used to expand existing partitions. Diskpart cannot be used to compress files and sector alignment must be done with new partitions.

10. B, C. To ensure host resolution of the Hub Transport servers from the Edge Transport servers you can add the names of the Hub Transport servers either to the Edge Transports Hosts file or to external DNS. Edge Transport servers do not find the Hub Transport servers by MX records so adding an MX record will not work. Adding the Hub Transport server names to the Hub Transport servers host file will not help the Edge Transport servers to resolve the Hub Transport names.

11. B, C. To be prepared for Exchange Server 2007, all Exchange 5.5 servers must be removed from the Exchange organization. Also, all of the Exchange 2000 servers need to have the hotfix available in Knowledge Base article KB870540 (`http://support.microsoft.com/kb/870540.`)

12. B. You need to have both.NET Framework 2.0 and Windows PowerShell installed to be able to install the Unified Messaging role; however you cannot have Microsoft Speech Server installed. IIS can be installed on a server that the Unified Messaging role will be installed.

13. C. You can create only 20 storage groups if the server has only 10 GB of RAM.

14. A, B, C, D. The Edge Transport role needs to store the message queue and tracking, protocol, and agent logs. Care must be taken to properly account for this amount of data storage.

15. B, D. ADAM must be installed but not configured before the Edge Transport role is installed. Also, as with any of the of the Exchange roles, Windows PowerShell must be installed.

16. A, C, D. An LCR-enabled Mailbox server can host all of the roles except for the Edge Transport role.

17. A, B. Neither SMTP nor NNTP can be installed, as they will conflict with the Exchange services. RPC/HTTP Proxy and ASP.NET 2.0 can both be installed as there are no rules against installing them.

18. A, B, C. You would need to install IIS, the RPC over HTTP Proxy service, and ASP.NET 2.0. Installing Microsoft Office Outlook 2007 is not required.

19. A, C. Adding memory to the server gives more memory to the database cache, which will improve performance and reduce the number of disk I/O. Adding memory does not increase the number of disk I/O nor does it decrease the process cache.

20. C. You can create only 32 storage groups if the server has only 16 GB of RAM.

Planning the Deployment of Exchange Server 2007 Services

MICROSOFT EXAM OBJECTIVES COVERED IN THIS CHAPTER:

- ✓ Plan the deployment of required Exchange services
- ✓ Plan the deployment of optional Exchange services

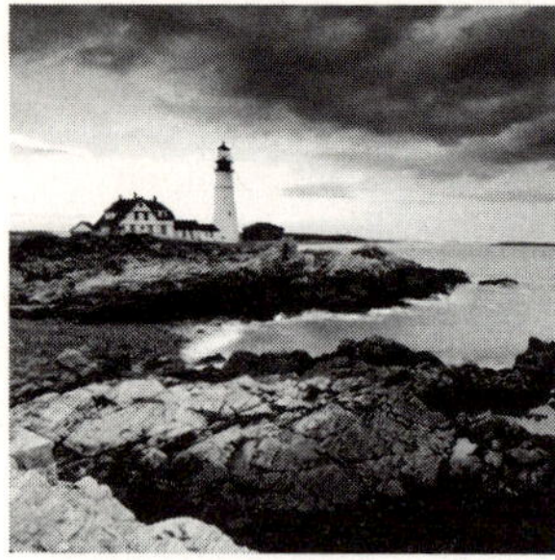

Exchange Server 2007 not only includes new ways of installation, configuration, and administration, but it also offers several new and enhanced services compared to its previous versions that will provide users with the access they need.

In this chapter we will look at how to plan the deployment of those Exchange Server 2007 services. We will dive into the requirements that are set for implementing both required and some optional Exchange services. We also will cover the deployment process itself to highlight the procedures to successfully configure your Exchange 2007 organization.

The main subjects in this chapter are as follows:

- Implementing Autodiscover
- Implementing Availability service
- Implementing mobile devices
- Implementing Microsoft Outlook Web Access (OWA)
- Implementing Outlook Anywhere
- Implementing POP3/IMAP4
- Implementing public folders
- Implementing connectors
- Implementing content indexing
- Implementing DSAccess

Implementing Autodiscover

Microsoft Exchange Server 2007 introduces Autodiscover, a new service that allows Microsoft Office Outlook 2007 to automatically discover the configuration information needed to successfully access Exchange Server 2007 features such as Offline Address Book, Unified Messaging, Out-of-Office, and Availability. The Autodiscover service also can provide the same functionality for supported mobile devices, but this depends on the mobile device operating system that you are using.

To find out if your mobile device that supports synchronization with Exchange Server also can take advantage of the Autodiscover service, contact the manufacturer of your mobile device.

The Autodiscover service is installed automatically when you deploy a Client Access server in your Exchange 2007 organization. Additionally, the Autodiscover service will be configured during deployment:

- An Autodiscover virtual directory is created under the Default Web Site, as shown in Figure 13.1.

FIGURE 13.1 Autodiscover virtual directory

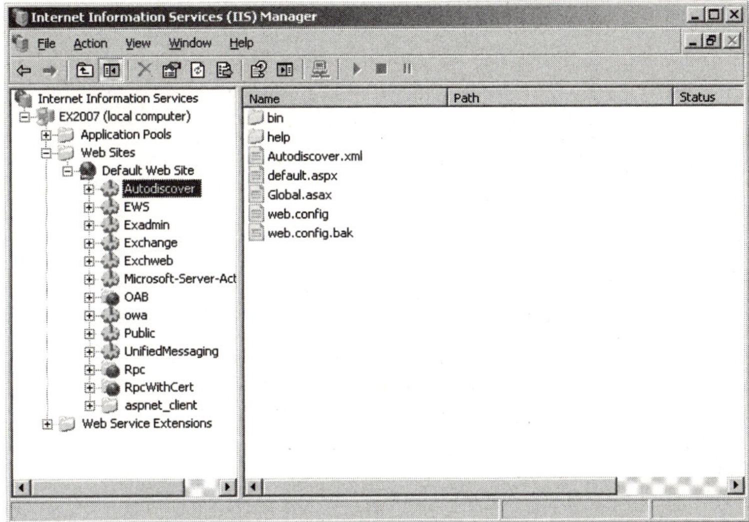

- A Service Connection Point (SCP) is created in Active Directory.

You can update the SCP object by using the `Set-ClientAccessServer` cmdlet.

The Autodiscover agent will provide Microsoft Office Outlook 2007 clients with the following configuration settings:

- Mailbox server name
- Unified Messaging URL
- Offline Address Book download location (public folders or URL)
- Availability service URL
- Out-of-Office URL
- Outlook Anywhere configuration details
- Authentication method

You need to deploy and configure the Autodiscover service to make sure that your Microsoft Exchange services, such as the Availability service, can be accessed by Outlook 2007 clients. These services also must be deployed and configured for clients to receive the correct profile configuration information from the Autodiscover service.

How Do Clients Find the Autodiscover Agent?

The way clients are able to find and take advantage of the Autodiscover service depends on the client. In this part of the chapter, we will cover the differences between domain-joined and non–domain-joined (or clients who are unable to directly access the domain) clients in reference to the Autodiscover service.

Domain-Joined

When you start Microsoft Office Outlook 2007 on a domain-joined client, Outlook will try to find the Autodiscover agent by using your user credentials to authenticate against Active Directory and will look for a Service Connection Point within Active Directory. The Service Connection Point contains the URL to the Autodiscover service, and that will be returned to the client as location of the Autodiscover agent. Outlook will use the URL to connect to the Client Access server and retrieve the configuration information necessary to gain access to the Exchange features.

By default, the Service Connection Point will return the URL to the Autodiscover service in the format `https://FQDN Client Access Server/Autodiscover/Autodiscover.xml`.

Exercise 13.1 outlines the steps a user needs to follow to take advantage of the Autodiscover service when logged on to a domain-joined computer.

EXERCISE 13.1

Autodiscovery with a Domain-Joined Computer

This exercise gives an overview of how the Autodiscover service in Exchange Server 2007 can be used by Microsoft Office Outlook 2007 to configure a new mail profile when joined to a domain.

1. Start Microsoft Office Outlook 2007 for the first time, and click Next to proceed with the wizard to configure Outlook 2007.

2. Select Yes when prompted if you would like to configure an email account.

EXERCISE 13.1 *(continued)*

3. Outlook retrieves the information for your username and email address from Active Directory, as shown here. Click Next to continue.

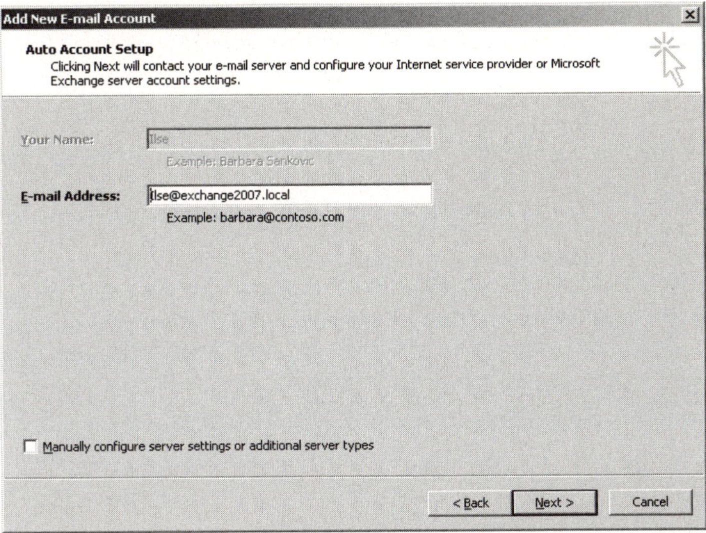

4. When Outlook has finished retrieving Exchange Server settings, you can finish the configuration wizard, as seen here, and Outlook will start successfully.

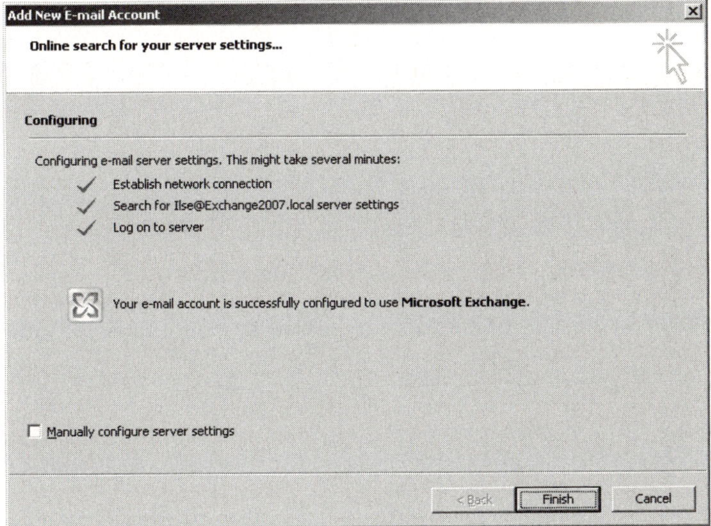

Non–Domain-Joined

When you start Microsoft Office Outlook 2007 on a non–domain-joined client, Outlook will not be able to locate a Service Connection Point within Active Directory, nor will this be possible if you are using a domain-joined computer without access to Active Directory. Microsoft Office Outlook 2007 is programmed to locate the Autodiscover service via DNS. Outlook will use the suffix of your SMTP address, and will perform connection attempts against the following hard-coded URLs:

- `https://suffix_SMTP_ address/autodiscover/autodiscover.xml`
- `https://autodiscover.suffix_SMTP_ address/autodiscover/autodiscover.xml`

To successfully enable clients that are not located in the domain, or not domain joined, you have to make sure that clients can connect to the Autodiscover service via DNS, by adding either an `A` record or a `CNAME` record for Autodiscover, as shown in Figure 13.2.

FIGURE 13.2 Autodiscover CNAME record in DNS

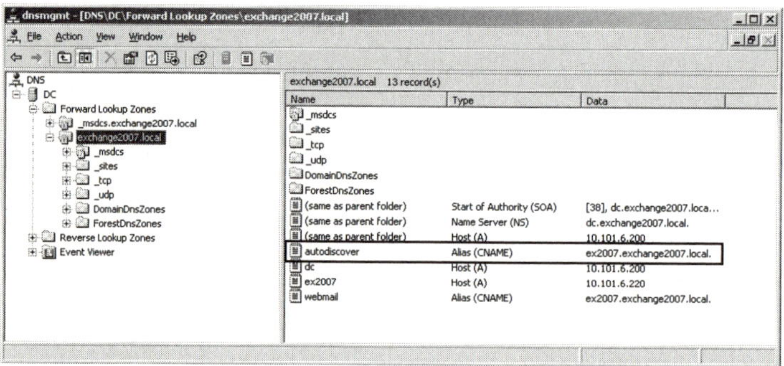

Exercise 13.2 outlines the steps a user needs to follow to take advantage of the Autodiscover service when logged on to a non–domain-joined computer.

EXERCISE 13.2

Autodiscovery with a Non–Domain-Joined Computer

This exercise provides an overview of how the Autodiscover service in Exchange Server 2007 can be used by Microsoft Office Outlook 2007 to configure a new mail profile when not joined to a domain.

1. Start Microsoft Office Outlook 2007 for the first time and click Next to proceed with the wizard to configure Outlook 2007.
2. Select Yes when prompted if you would like to configure an email account.

EXERCISE 13.2 *(continued)*

3. Fill in your name, your email address, and your password, as shown here. Click Next to let Outlook search for the Autodiscover Agent, and discover all Exchange Server feature settings.

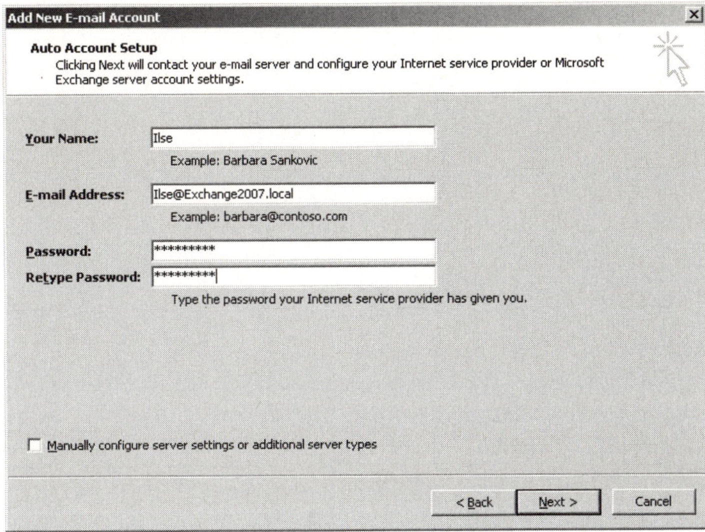

4. When Outlook has finished retrieving Exchange Server settings, you can finish the configuration wizard, as shown here, and Outlook will start successfully.

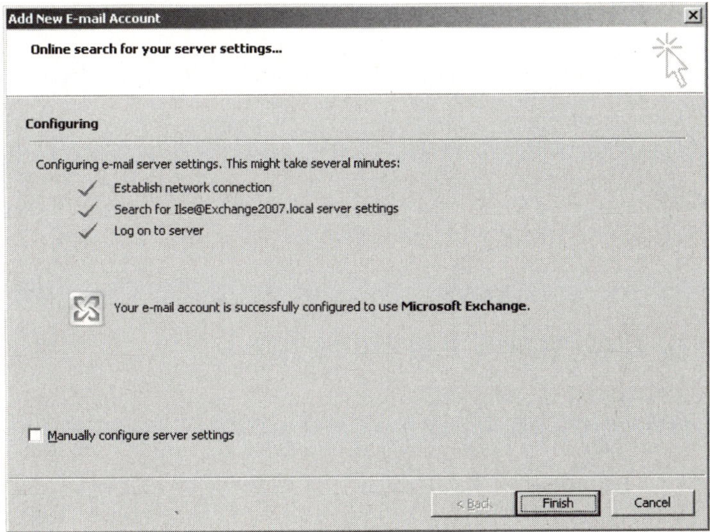

Test Email Autoconfiguration Tool

You can always test if your Autodiscover service is configured correctly by running the Test Email Autoconfiguration tool that is included when you deploy Microsoft Office Outlook 2007. To start the test, just press CTRL and right-click the Outlook icon in the System tray, and select Test Email Autoconfiguration, as shown below.

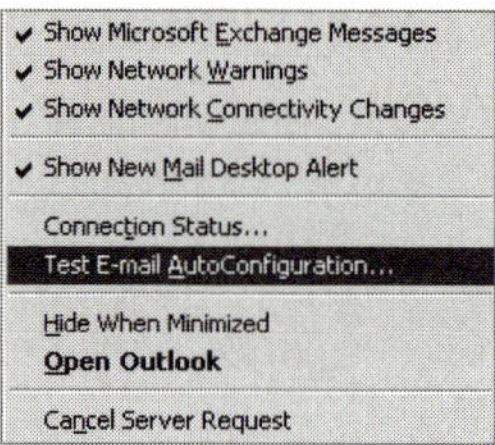

The results from this test, shown in Figure 13.3, will help you troubleshoot or fine-tune your configuration of the Autodiscover service.

FIGURE 13.3 Test Email Autoconfiguration

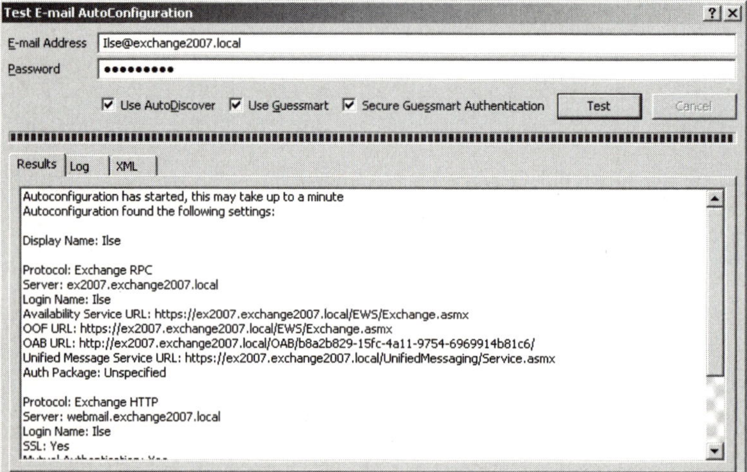

Configuring Exchange Services for the Autodiscover Service

You will need to configure the external URL for Out-of-Office functionality, the Availability service, Unified Messaging, and offline address book downloads by using the Exchange Management Shell. In addition, if you want to enable Outlook Anywhere, you must also configure external access to this Microsoft Exchange service for the Autodiscover service, using the Exchange Management Console or Exchange Management Shell.

The internal URL is generally configured by Microsoft Exchange Setup. You can also change the internal URL by using the Exchange Management Shell.

To perform the following procedures, you must use an account that has been delegated at least the Exchange Server Administrator role and has been made a member of the local Administrators group for the target server.

Configuring the External Host Name for Outlook Anywhere for the Autodiscover Service

You can configure the external host name for Outlook Anywhere when you enable Outlook Anywhere on an Exchange 2007 Client Access server. You can enable Outlook Anywhere using the Exchange Management Console or the Exchange Management Shell. We will cover enabling and configuring Outlook Anywhere later in this chapter.

To change the external host name for Outlook Anywhere, you can use the Exchange Management Console or the Exchange Management Shell, as shown in Figure 13.4.

FIGURE 13.4 Configuring the external host name for Outlook Anywhere using the Exchange Management Shell

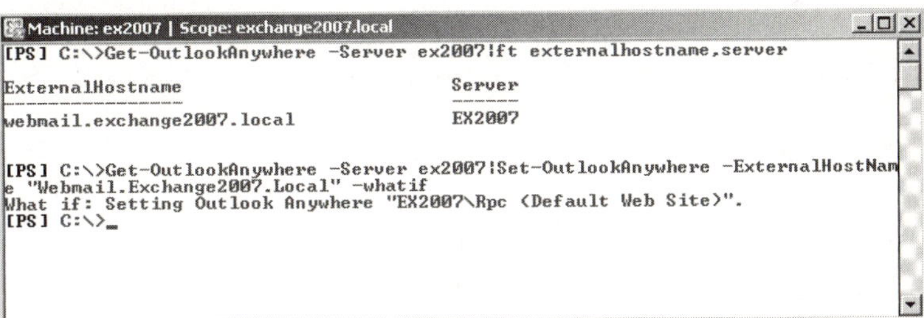

Configuring an External URL for the Offline Address Book for the Autodiscover Service

Exchange Server 2007 allows Microsoft Office Outlook 2007 clients to download the Offline Address Book (OAB) data from the Client Access server, eliminating the need to publish the OAB via a system public folder. Outlook 2007 is still able to download the OAB from a system public folder if required. Outlook 2007 will determine which OAB download method to use via the information it receives from the Autodiscover agent.

If you want your users to be able to download the OAB when they are not connected to your network, you will need to configure an external URL for the OAB for the Autodiscover service. You need to use the Exchange Management Shell cmdlet `Set-OABVirtualDirectory` to configure the external URL, shown in Figure 13.5.

FIGURE 13.5 Configuring an external URL for the offline address book

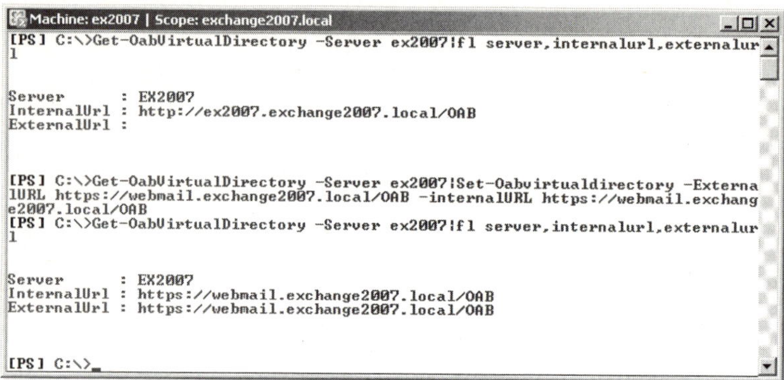

Configuring an External URL for Unified Messaging for the Autodiscover Service

When you configure an external URL for Unified Messaging for the Autodiscover service, users will be able to view and change the settings of Unified Messaging when they open Outlook, and go to `Tools`, `Options`, and select the property page `Voice Mail`, as shown in Figure 13.6.

FIGURE 13.6 Voicemail settings

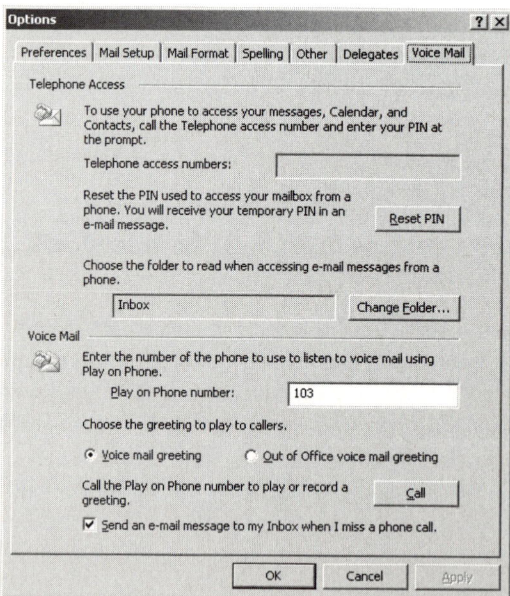

To configure an external URL for Unified Messaging for the Autodiscover service, you need to use the Exchange Management Shell, and use the cmdlet `Set-UMVirtualDirectory` as shown in Figure 13.7.

FIGURE 13.7 Configuring an external URL for Unified Messaging

Configuring an External URL for Exchange Web Services for the Autodiscover Service

The new Out-of-Office features in Exchange Server 2007 that are available when you use Microsoft Office Outlook 2007, and the new Availability service that we will cover later in this chapter, are available via the Exchange Web Services. Microsoft Office Outlook 2007 will receive the location of these Exchange Web Services from the Autodiscover agent.

To configure an external URL for Exchange Web Services for the Autodiscover service, you need to use the Exchange Management Shell cmdlet `Set-WebServicesVirtualDirectory`, as shown in Figure 13.8.

FIGURE 13.8 Configuring an external URL for Exchange Web Services

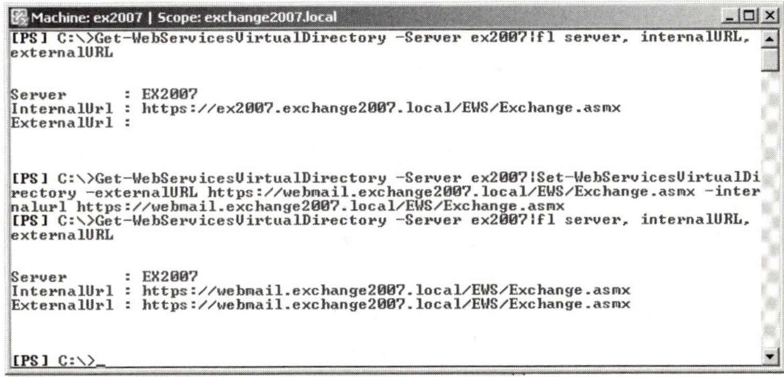

Configuring ActiveSync Autodiscover Settings

If you have a mobile device that supports the Autodiscover service, you can configure the Exchange Server 2007 Autodiscover agent to provide a valid Microsoft-Server-ActiveSync external URL when requested by the mobile device.

To configure the external URL for the Microsoft-Server-ActiveSync virtual directory, you can use the Exchange Management Console, as shown in Figure 13.9, or the Exchange Management Shell.

FIGURE 13.9 External URL for the Microsoft-Server-ActiveSync

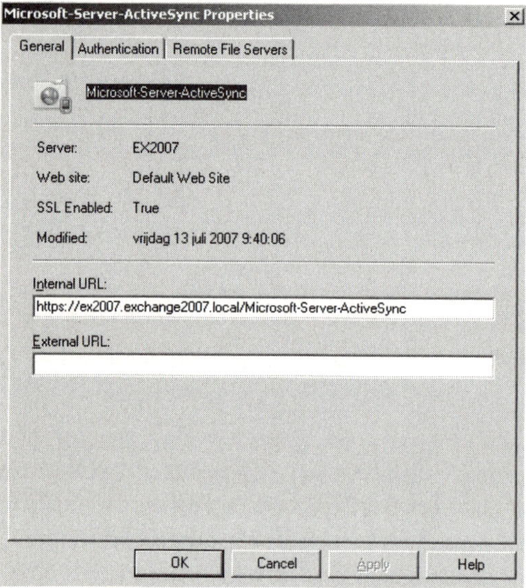

If you are providing external access to Microsoft Exchange by using Outlook Anywhere and you want your Outlook 2007 clients to be automatically configured by using the Autodiscover service, you must install a valid Secure Sockets Layer (SSL) certificate on the Client Access server that includes both the common name (for example, `webmail.matisse.edu`) and a Subject Alternative Name for `autodiscover.matisse.edu`.

Additional Considerations when Deploying the Autodiscover Service

If you want to deploy and configure the Autodiscover service, you need to make sure that your Exchange organization contains at least one Client Access server. However, more deployment considerations should be carefully investigated when you decide to allow external access to your Exchange organization by taking advantage of the Autodiscover service.

In addition to configuring an adequate external URL for all Exchange Server features, you can fine-tune the configuration of the Autodiscover service by doing the following:

- Using separate IIS websites for Internet access to the Autodiscover service
- Using multiple sites for Internet access to the Autodiscover service
- Configuring the Autodiscover service to use site affinity

It is also possible to configure the Autodiscover service for multiple forests.

Implementing the Availability Service

The Microsoft Exchange Server 2007 Availability service provides access to free and busy information and Out-of-Office information for clients running Microsoft Office Outlook 2007. Outlook 2007 will receive this Exchange Web Service URL from the Autodiscover service as noted earlier. The Availability service is part of the Exchange 2007 programming interface, built on top of the Availability API, enabling developers to write custom tools for company-specific purposes.

Outlook Web Access does not use the Availability service; it calls directly into the Availability API.

Process Flow for the Availability Service

To clarify the process flow for the Availability service, we will go through all steps that are taken when a user, Ilse, requests free and busy information from two other users, Joel and Andy.

Client Side

Ilse opens Microsoft Office Outlook 2007 and opens her calendar. She decides to create a new Meeting Request to get together with her manager Joel and her colleague Andy. Ilse uses the Scheduling Assistant to help her pick the most suitable time. She invites both Joel and Andy to the meeting. She selects Calendar Details for all attendees and only available time slots during her working hours. Outlook will retrieve the information using the Availability service and will return the retrieved information to the user, as shown in Figure 13.10.

Server Side

In the example, the Availability service first discovers Ilse's own free and busy information and then requests the calendar information for the invited attendees Joel and Andy.

The Availability service checks the permissions that are granted by the invited attendees to the inviting user with regards their free and busy information. Table 13.1 lists the possible rights that can be granted to another user.

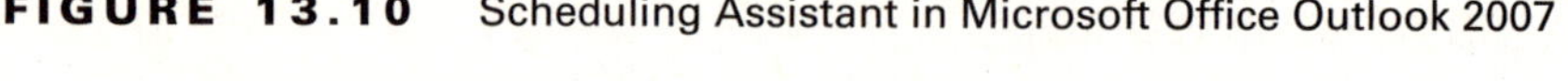

FIGURE 13.10 Scheduling Assistant in Microsoft Office Outlook 2007

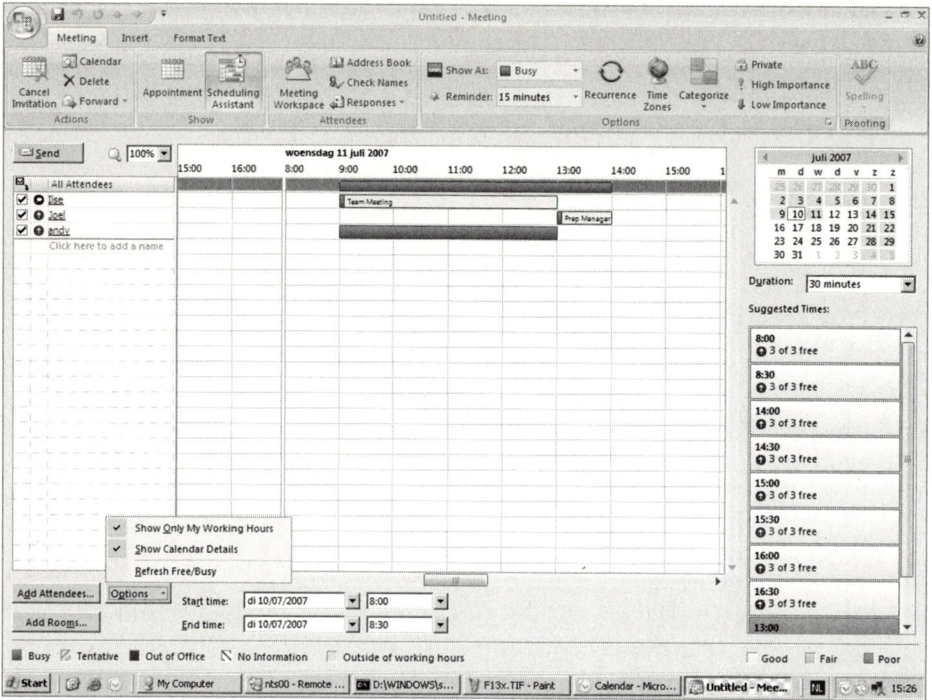

TABLE 13.1 Possible Permissions Level for Free and Busy Information

Permission Level	Information returned to User
None	None
Free/busy time	Status and start/end time for a status
Free/busy, subject, location	Status, start/end time for a status, subject, location
Full details	Status, start/end time, subject, location, and importance

In our example, Ilse has been granted the Full Details permission level for Joel, and free/busy time permission level for Andy.

Out-of-Office Information

The Availability service also provides access to Out of Office (OOF) messages for OOF appointments and global OOF information. The OOF feature in Outlook 2007 is available via the OOF Web service, whose URL is identical to the Availability service URL, as shown in Figure 13.11.

FIGURE 13.11 Out-of-Office information via Exchange Web Services Availability service

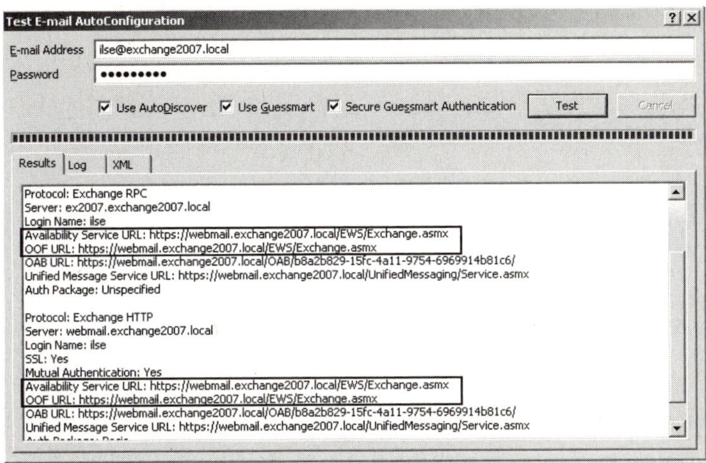

With Exchange 2007 and Microsoft Office Outlook 2007 or Outlook Web Access, you can do the following:

- Schedule when your OOF message is sent
- Use rich edition controls to create your OOF message
- Create different OOF messages to be sent internally and externally
- Select who will receive the OOF messages outside the organization, only your contacts, or anyone outside the organization

As an Exchange administrator, you can configure four OOF settings for one or more domains:

- No OOF messages are sent to the domain
- Allow only external OOF messages
- Allow external OOF messages and OOF messages set by Microsoft Office Outlook 2003 or earlier clients or sent by Exchange Server 2003 or earlier servers
- Allow internal OOF messages and OOF messages set by Outlook 2003 or earlier clients or sent by Exchange 2003 or earlier servers

You can configure these settings by using the Exchange Management Console or the Exchange Management Shell. In Microsoft Exchange Server 2007, you also can configure the OOF feature on a per-user basis, as shown in Figure 13.12, by using the Exchange Management Shell cmdlet `Set-Mailbox`.

Additional Considerations When Deploying the Availability Service

When you start deploying the Availability service, remember the following:

- Use Performance Monitor to collect information about the Availability service.
- The Availability service can show free and busy data for a distribution group up to a maximum of 100 members.

FIGURE 13.12 OOF settings by user and by domain

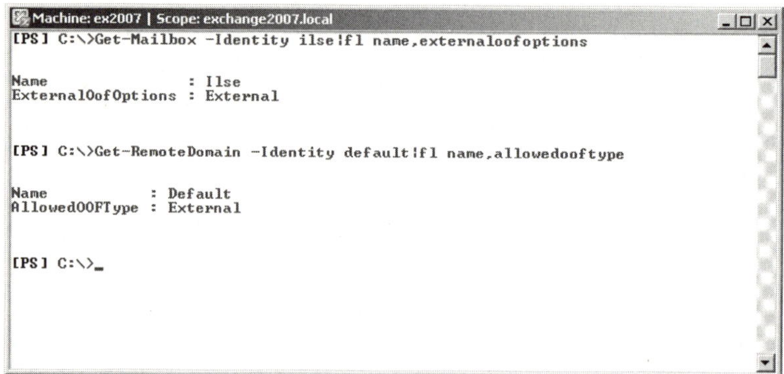

Implementing Mobile Devices

When you deploy the Microsoft Exchange 2007 Client Access server role inside your Exchange organization, you will be able to configure access to your Exchange 2007 Mailbox server by clients using a mobile device that is running Windows Mobile 5.0 or Windows Mobile 6.0.

Windows Mobile Version Feature Matrix

You need to have a Windows Mobile device with Windows Mobile 5.0 or Windows Mobile 6.0 installed. Table 13.2 lists the features that are available when you use Windows Mobile 5.0, with Messaging and Security Feature Pack (MSFP) installed, and Windows Mobile 6.0. The table also lists the features that are only available if you use Windows Mobile 6.0. Depending on the features you require in your organization, you need to get your users the appropriate Windows Mobile version.

TABLE 13.2 Features Supported by Windows Mobile 5.0 (with MSFP) and Windows Mobile 6.0

Feature	Windows Mobile 5.0 (with MSFP)	Windows Mobile 6.0
Direct push	Yes	Yes
Calendar synchronization	Yes	Yes
Contact synchronization	Yes	Yes
Email synchronization	Yes	Yes
Task synchronization	Yes	Yes
Exchange ActiveSync policy support	Yes	Yes
Remote wipe device support	Yes	Yes
SSL encryption	Yes	Yes
HTML email support	No	Yes
Message-flags support	No	Yes
Free and busy information attendees	No	Yes
Out-of-Office management	No	Yes
Exchange search	No	Yes
Windows SharePoint Services and Windows file-share document access	No	Yes
Inline message fetch	No	Yes
Device certificate for authentication management	No	Yes
Recovery password	No	Yes

Exchange ActiveSync Mailbox Policies

Exchange Server 2007 allows you as an Exchange administrator to create and apply Exchange ActiveSync mailbox policies to your users. You can create multiple Exchange ActiveSync policies, but you can only apply one Exchange ActiveSync mailbox policy to a user. You can create and apply Exchange ActiveSync mailbox policies by using the Exchange Management Console or the Exchange Management Shell.

You can use an Exchange ActiveSync mailbox policy to configure password policies, attachment download settings, Windows SharePoint Services and Windows file share document access, and if a user is allowed to connect to his or her mailbox by using a mobile device that cannot be provisioned automatically with the necessary Exchange server settings, as shown in Figure 13.13.

FIGURE 13.13 Exchange ActiveSync mailbox policy settings

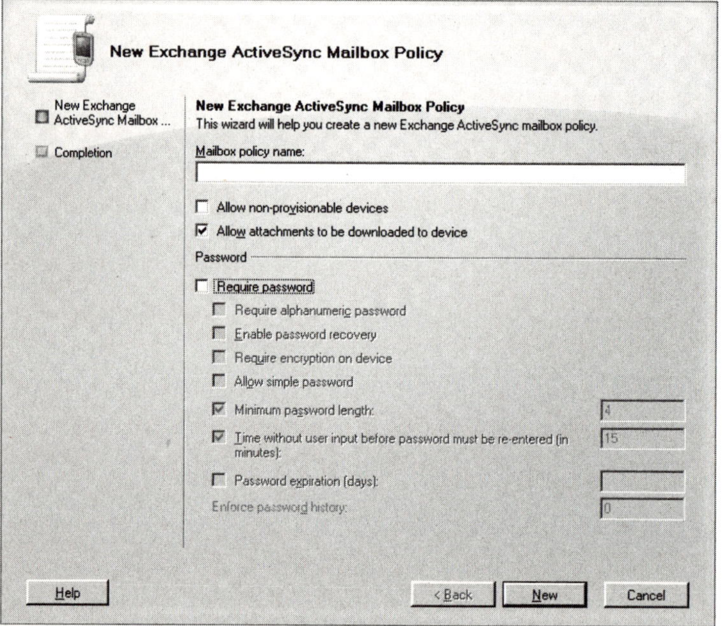

Exercise 13.3 outlines the steps to create and apply an Exchange ActiveSync mailbox policy to a user in your Exchange organization.

EXERCISE 13.3

Create and Apply an Exchange ActiveSync Mailbox Policy to a User

This exercise shows how you can create an Exchange ActiveSync mailbox policy and apply it to a mailbox-enabled user.

1. Open the Exchange Management Console, right-click Client Access under Organization Configuration, and select New Exchange ActiveSync Mailbox Policy, as shown here.

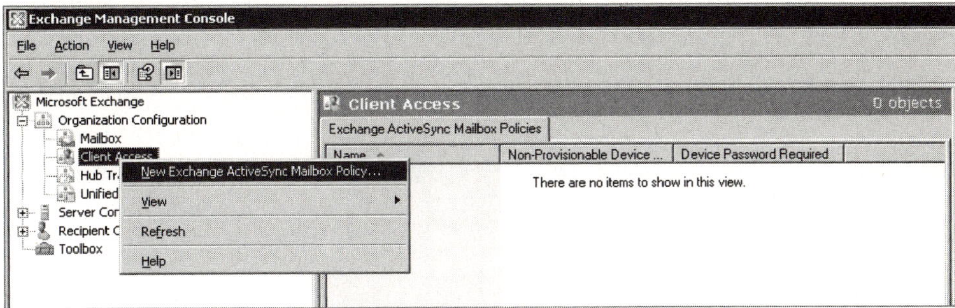

2. Specify a name for the Exchange ActiveSync mailbox policy, including the required settings, as shown here.

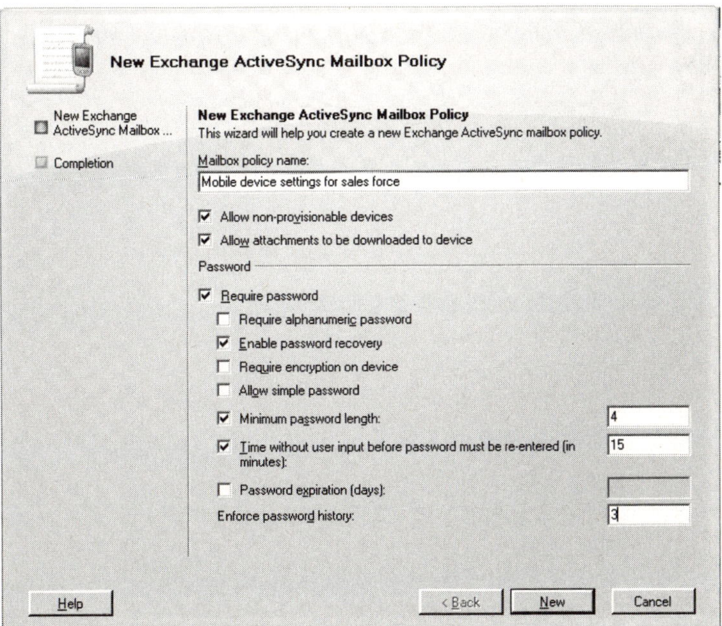

EXERCISE 13.3 *(continued)*

3. Click New to create the new Exchange ActiveSync Mailbox Policy, and Finish to complete the wizard.

4. To configure both attachment download settings and Windows SharePoint Services or Windows file-share document access, right-click on the Exchange ActiveSync mailbox policy, and select Properties, as shown here.

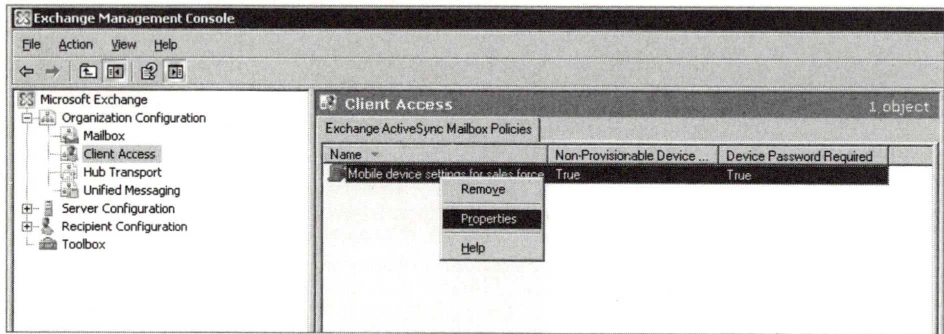

5. To apply this policy to one or more users, open the properties of the user object in Exchange Management Console, and select the property page Mailbox Features. Get the properties of Exchange ActiveSync, and select the policy you want to apply, as shown here. You also can use the Exchange Management Shell cmdlet `Set-CASMailbox`.

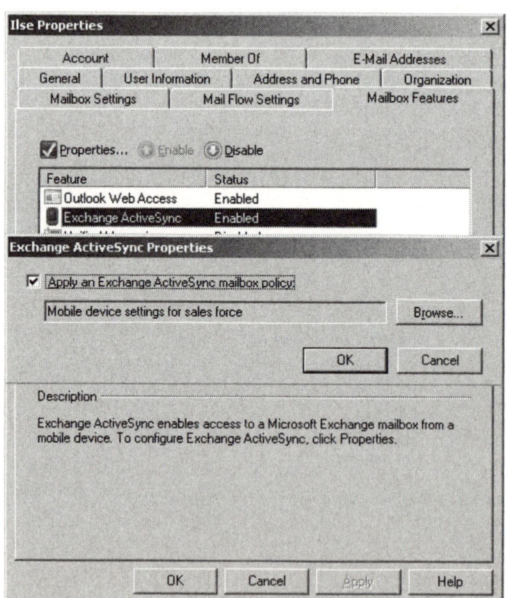

EXERCISE 13.3 *(continued)*

6. The first time the user tries to sync his device with the Exchange Server 2007 server, he will be prompted that the Exchange server must enforce security policies on his device to continue synchronizing, as shown here.

Managing Mobile Devices

The first time a user opens her mailbox by using a Windows Mobile device, a Mobile Device partnership is created between your Exchange Server 2007 and the Windows Mobile device. As an Exchange administrator, you can manage from that point forward the Mobile Device settings for that user with the Exchange Management Console and the Exchange Management Shell. The user also can manage some of her own mobile device settings via Outlook Web Access.

Mobile Device Management Using the Exchange Management Console

To manage a mobile device used by a user to connect to his or her mailbox via the Exchange Management Console, you need to right-click the user in the Exchange Management Console and select Manage Mobile Device, as shown below.

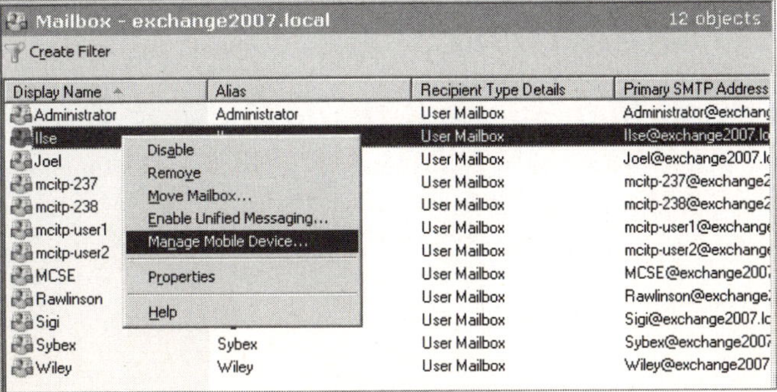

The Manage Mobile Device wizard allows you to remove a mobile device partnership for a specific device, or you can use the wizard to remotely wipe the mobile device you want. Deleting a mobile device partnership will not delete any data on the mobile device itself. The next time the user tries to synchronize the same device with his or her mailbox, a new partnership will be established. You also will be given some additional device information, like the first synchronization time, and the last policy update time, as shown in Figure 13.14.

FIGURE 13.14 Manage Mobile Device wizard

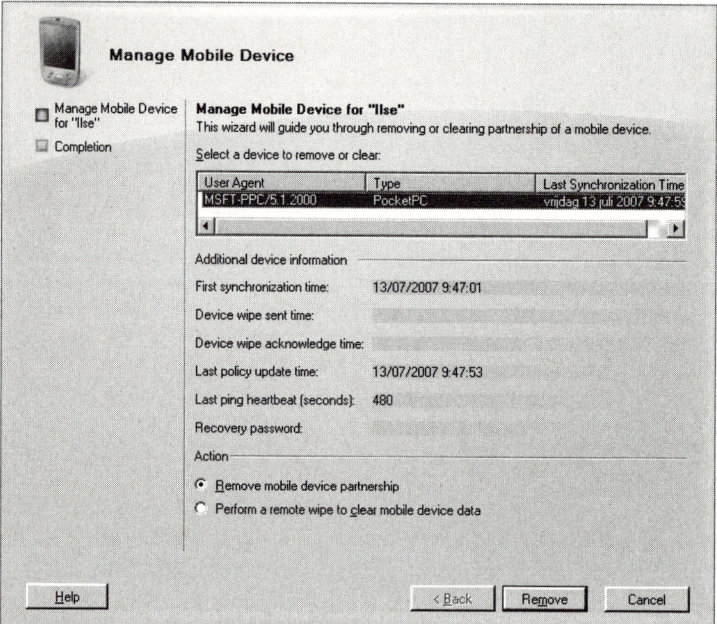

Mobile Device Management Using the Exchange Management Shell

You can use the Exchange Management Shell to do the following:

- Remotely Wipe a Mobile Device, using the cmdlet `Clear-ActiveSyncDevice`
- View mobile device and Exchange ActiveSync statistics for a user, using the cmdlet `Get-ActiveSyncDeviceStatistics`

Mobile Device Self-Management Using Outlook Web Access

In Exchange Server 2007, a user can manage his or her own mobile device partnerships, via Outlook Web Access, as shown in Figure 13.15.

FIGURE 13.15 Mobile device self-management

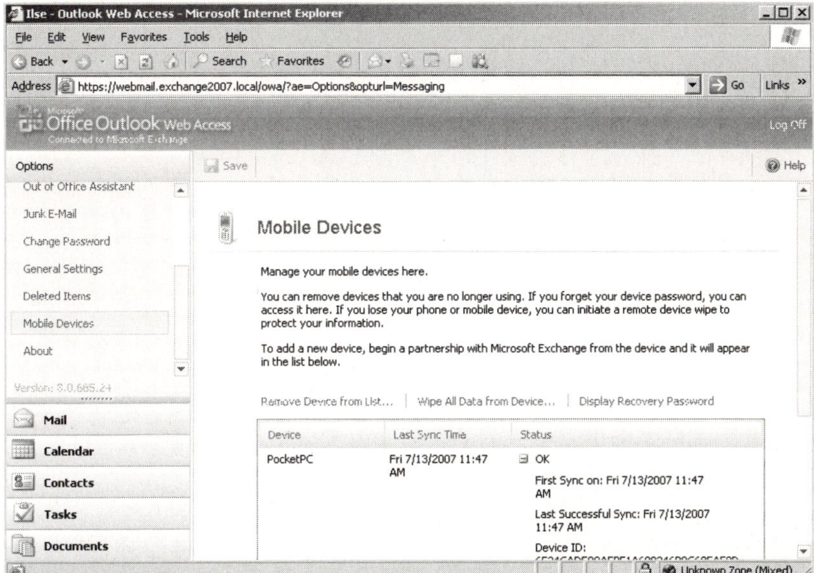

Managing Microsoft-Server-ActiveSync Virtual Directory

You can configure Exchange ActiveSync by changing settings on the Microsoft-Server-ActiveSync virtual directory that is created by default when you deploy an Exchange 2007 Client Access server.

You can make changes to the Remote File Server settings to control which file shares and Windows SharePoint Services document libraries are accessible for mobile devices, as shown in Figure 13.16. You can configure Basic Authentication or Client Certificate Authentication. If you want to disable the requirement of SSL, you need to use IIS. An internal URL is configured during installation, but you can change it and add an external URL. All these settings can be configured using both the Exchange Management Console and the Exchange Management Shell.

Implementing Microsoft Outlook Web Access

When you install the Exchange 2007 Client Access server, you can enable and configure Outlook Web Access (OWA) for mailboxes housed in your Exchange organization. Outlook Web Access is a feature that enables users to gain access to their mailbox using an Internet browser such as Internet Explorer.

FIGURE 13.16 Remote file servers settings Microsoft-Server-ActiveSync virtual directory

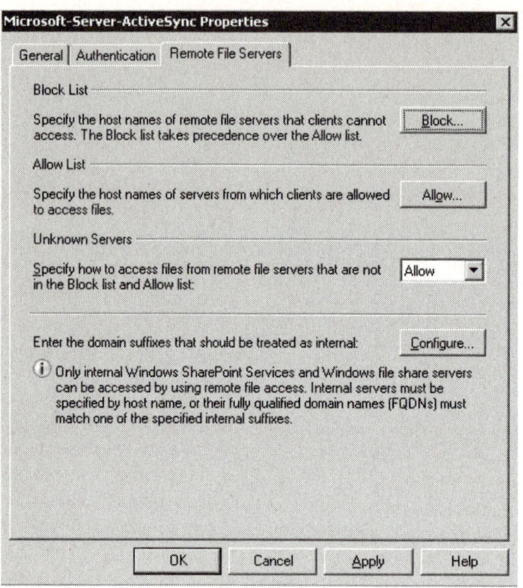

Managing Outlook Web Access Virtual Directories

When you install the Exchange 2007 Client Access server, you will see that Exchange will create and configure five OWA virtual directories in the default Internet Information Services Website on your Exchange server, as shown in Figure 13.17.

FIGURE 13.17 Default OWA virtual directories

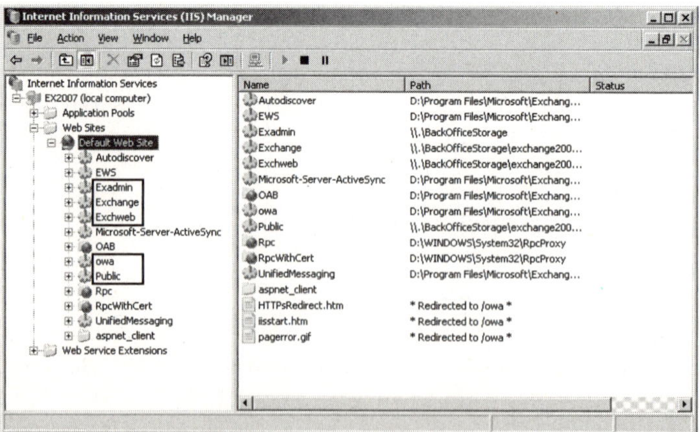

You can view, configure, and change settings of these virtual directories by using the Exchange Management Console, the Exchange Management Shell, and Internet Information Services Manager. Table 13.3 lists the default OWA virtual directories that are created by Exchange during installation of the Client Access server role.

TABLE 13.3 OWA Virtual Directories

Name	Usage
OWA	Used to gain access to mailboxes housed on Exchange Server 2007 Mailbox servers
Public	Used to gain access to public folders that are housed on Exchange 2000 Servers or Exchange Server 2003
Exchweb	Used with the Outlook Web Access application for mailboxes on computers that are running Exchange 2003 or Exchange 2000
Exchange	Used by Outlook Web Access when accessing mailboxes on computers housed on Exchange 2003 or Exchange 2000
ExAdmin	Used to change administrative settings and properties

As Exchange Organization Administrator, you can always choose to create your own new OWA virtual directory using the Exchange Management Shell cmdlet `New-OWAVirtualDirectory`.

You can use the Exchange Management Console or the Exchange Management Shell to view and modify OWA Virtual Directory Settings. If you want to use the Exchange Management Console, you have to select Server Configuration, and then select Client Access. On the Outlook Web Access tab, open the properties of the virtual directory that you want to modify.

Click the appropriate tab, and make the changes that you want. Click OK to save your changes and close the properties window. You also can use the Exchange Management Shell to view and make configuration changes to the OWA virtual directories using cmdlets `Get-OWAVirtualDirectory` and `Set-OWAVirtualDirectory`, as shown in Figure 13.18.

Managing Outlook Web Access URLs

You can configure quite a few things when it comes to Outlook Web Access URLs. You can make some changes to ensure that when a user connects to your Client Access server using `HTTP://`, they will be redirected by default to `HTTPS://`. You also can configure a default redirection from the default website to the virtual directory OWA. As an Exchange administrator, you also can change the internal URL or add an external URL to your Exchange Outlook Web Access URL.

FIGURE 13.18 OWA Virtual Directory Settings in the Exchange Management Shell

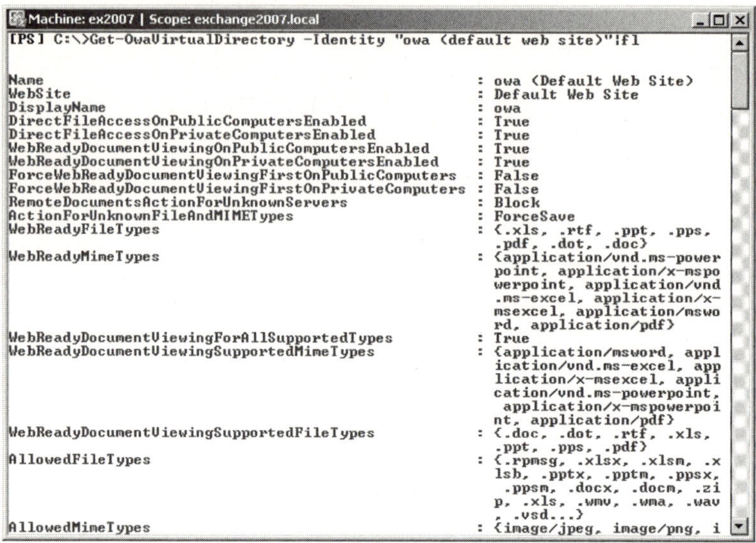

Redirection of Requests to the Outlook Web Access URL

Exercise 13.4 outlines the steps you will need to use to simplify the Outlook Web Access URL.

EXERCISE 13.4

Simplify Outlook Web Access URL

This exercise shows how to simplify the Outlook Web Access URL users have to enter to gain access to their mailbox.

1. Log on to the Exchange Client Access server with a user account that has at least the Exchange Server Administrator role delegated and has Local Administrator rights on the server.
2. Open IIS Manager, navigate to Web Sites/Default Web Site. Right-click Default Web Site, and then click Properties.
3. Click the Home Directory tab, and then click the A Redirection to a URL option.
4. In Redirect To, type **/owa** if all the mailboxes that will be accessed by using Outlook Web Access are located on Exchange 2007 servers. If some are located on Exchange 2000 or Exchange 2003 you will need to specify **/exchange**.

EXERCISE 13.4 *(continued)*

5. In the The Client Will Be Sent To: list, select a directory below the URL entered, as shown here.

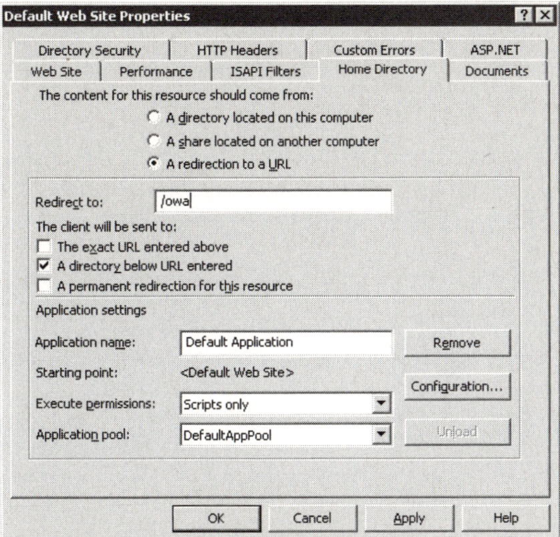

Redirection to HTTPS

Exercise 13.5 outlines the steps you can use to configure an automatic redirection to HTTPS using IIS Manager.

EXERCISE 13.5

Redirection from HTTP to HTTPS

This exercise shows how to simplify the Outlook Web Access URL users have to enter to gain access to their mailbox using HTTPS.

1. Log on to the Exchange Client Access server with a user account that has at least the Exchange Server Administrator role delegated and has local administrator rights on the server.

2. Create a new file in Notepad, and save it to your system drive under the directory \inetpub\wwwroot as an `htm` file. You could name it `HTTPSRedirect.htm`.

3. Enter the following lines in the file; replace `<servername>` with your server name.

EXERCISE 13.5 *(continued)*

4. `<html> <head> <title>HTML Redirection to https:</title> <META HTTP-EQUIV="Refresh" CONTENT="1; URL=https://<servername>/owa"> </head> <body> This page is attempting to redirect you to <a href="https:// <servername>/owa/ ">https:// <servername>/owa</a>
 If you are not redirected within a few seconds, please click the link above to access Outlook Web Access. </body> </html>`

5. Use `https://<servername> /owa` if all the mailboxes that will be accessed by using Outlook Web Access are located on Exchange 2007 servers. If some are located on Exchange 2000 or Exchange 2003 you will need to specify `https://<servername>/exchange`.

6. Open IIS Manager and navigate to Web Sites/Default Web Site. Right-click Default Web Site and then click Properties.

7. Click the Home Directory tab and then click the A Redirection to a URL option.

8. In Redirect To, type **/owa** if all the mailboxes that will be accessed by using Outlook Web Access are located on Exchange 2007 servers. If some are located on Exchange 2000 or Exchange 2003 you will need to specify **/exchange**.

9. In the The Client Will Be Sent To: list, select a directory below URL entered, as seen before.

10. Click the tab Custom Errors, and select HTTP Error 403;4 in the table, then click Edit.

11. Locate the file `HTTPSRedirect.htm` you just created, as shown here, and click OK to save the new configuration.

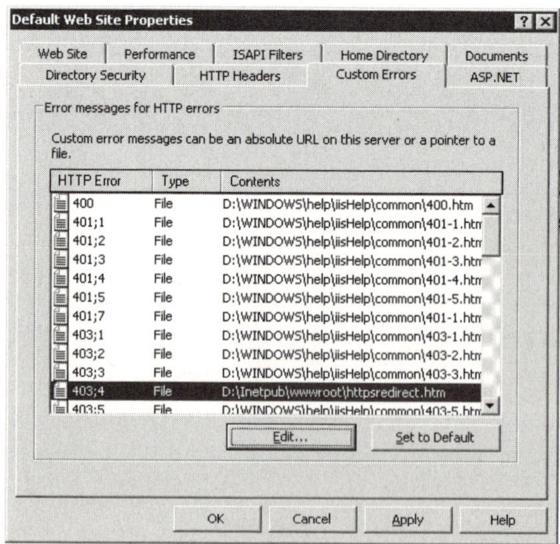

EXERCISE 13.5 *(continued)*

12. Restart IIS by opening a command-prompt window and typing **iisreset /noforce**.

13. Test the configuration by opening a browser window, and enter the URL `http://<servername>`; you will see that you will be redirected automatically to `https://<servername>/owa`.

Configuring Internal and External Outlook Web Access URLs

Internal and external Outlook Web Access URLS for your Outlook Web Access virtual directory OWA, can be done using the Exchange Management Console, as shown in Figure 13.19, or by using the Exchange Management Shell cmdlet `Set-OWAVirtualDirectory`.

For more information about the reason why you would configure an External Outlook Web Access URL, please refer to Chapter 12 that covers the deployment of Client Access servers.

FIGURE 13.19 Configuring internal and external Outlook Web Access URLs using the Exchange Management Console

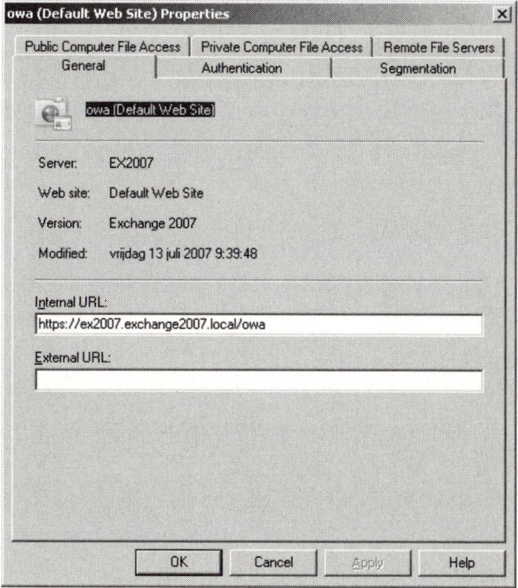

Additional Considerations for Outlook Web Access

When deploying OWA, you can choose to allow remote access to Windows File Share and/or Windows SharePoint services. You also can choose to enable or disable certain OWA features for some users in your organization.

Managing File and Data Access

In Exchange Server 2007, you can configure several settings to provide protection for your Exchange organization while allowing users to connect to their mailbox information from outside your network.

Configuring Public and Private Computer File Access

Using the Exchange Management Console or the Exchange Management Shell, you can define file access and viewing options for a user depending on the kind of computer option he or she chose when logging on, as shown in Figure 13.20.

FIGURE 13.20 Public computer file access

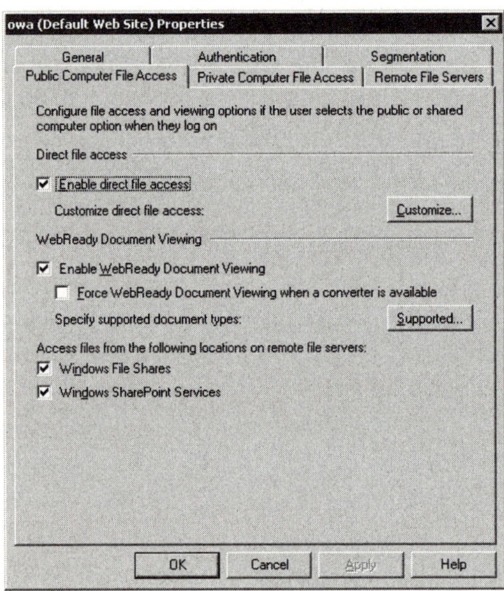

Table 13.4 lists the different configuration options, including descriptions.

TABLE 13.4 Public and Private Computer File Access Settings

Feature	Description
Direct file access	Allows users to open files directly from Outlook Web Access. Files can be attached to email messages, located in a Windows SharePoint Document Library, or a file share. You can customize the file types that can be accessed directly.

TABLE 13.4 Public and Private Computer File Access Settings *(continued)*

Feature	Description
WebReady document viewing	Allows users to convert a file into html and open the file in a browser. As an administrator, you can customize which file types can be converted or if they should be converted if a converter is available.
Remote file server access	Allows users to gain access to files that are located on remote file servers. As an Exchange administrator, you can control whether Windows SharePoint services and Windows file shares are available or not.

Configuring Windows SharePoint Services and Windows File Share Integration for Outlook Web Access

The Windows SharePoint services and Windows file share integration feature is a new feature that is only available in the Exchange 2007 Outlook Web Access Premium client and when either Basic or forms-based authentication is used.

As an Exchange administrator, you can configure settings like the following:

- Allow or block access to Windows SharePoint services and Windows file share documents on specific servers or for all Unknown Servers
- Allow or block access to Windows SharePoint services and Windows file share documents from public and private computers.
- Create a list of host names to be treated as internal. Only documents on internal hosts can be accessed from OWA.
- Enable or disable document access to Windows SharePoint services and Windows file shares by using segmentation, as we will cover later in this chapter.

You can configure these settings by using the Exchange Management Console, as shown in Figure 13.21, or you can use the Exchange Management Shell cmdlets `Set-OWAVirtualDirectory` and `Set-CASMailbox`.

Managing Outlook Web Access Segmentation

You can choose to enable or disable certain OWA features for a virtual directory, or you can choose to enable or disable certain OWA features for one or more users. You can use the Exchange Management Console or the Exchange Management Shell for the virtual directory segmentation settings, as shown in Figure 13.22.

However, you have to use the Exchange Management Shell for getting an overview of the user settings or to make changes.

FIGURE 13.21 Configuring remote file server settings

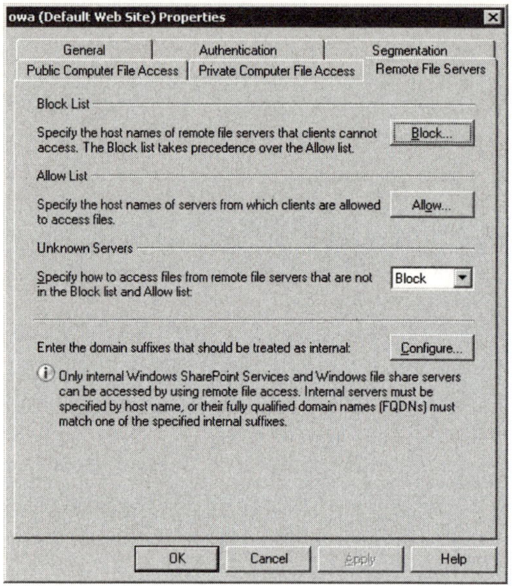

FIGURE 13.22 OWA segmentation settings per virtual directory

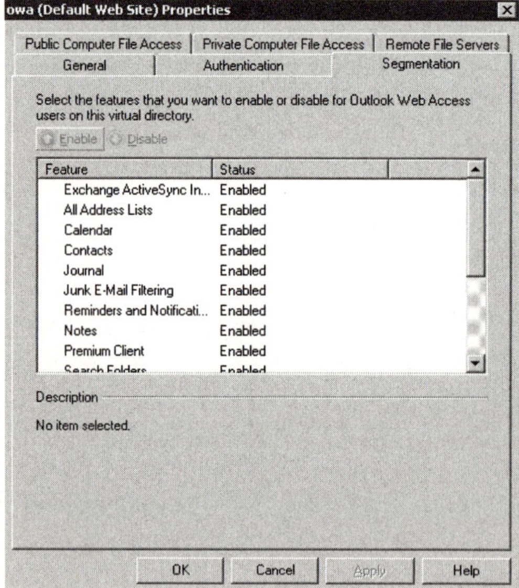

Implementing Outlook Anywhere

Outlook Anywhere is a new name for a feature that was introduced with Exchange Server 2003, RPC over HTTP. Outlook Anywhere enables Microsoft Office Outlook 2003 and 2007 to connect from anywhere to the Exchange mailbox store, using HTTP(s), without requiring the configuration of a Virtual Private Network or opening a massive amount of ports on your firewall.

Exchange Server 2007 has simplified the deployment process of Outlook Anywhere by introducing an Enabling Outlook Anywhere wizard, which you need to run on a Client Access server in your Exchange organization.

Deploying Outlook Anywhere

Deploying Outlook Anywhere is made very easy and straightforward by adding the Enabling Outlook Anywhere wizard to Exchange 2007. To deploy Outlook Anywhere, you need to follow three steps:

- Install a valid Secure Sockets Layer (SSL) certificate
- Install the Windows RPC over HTTP Proxy component
- Enable Outlook Anywhere

Here's how you do it:

1. Install a valid Secure Sockets Layer (SSL) certificate from a certification authority (CA) that the client trusts. This certificate can be the same as the one you use for OWA and Exchange ActiveSync.
2. To install the Windows RPC over HTTP Proxy component on your Client Access server, log on to your Exchange server with an account that has local administrator permissions, and go to Control Panel, Add or Remove Programs, Add/Remove Windows Components, and select under Network Components, RPC over HTTP Proxy, as shown in Figure 13.23.

FIGURE 13.23 Installation RPC over HTTP Proxy component

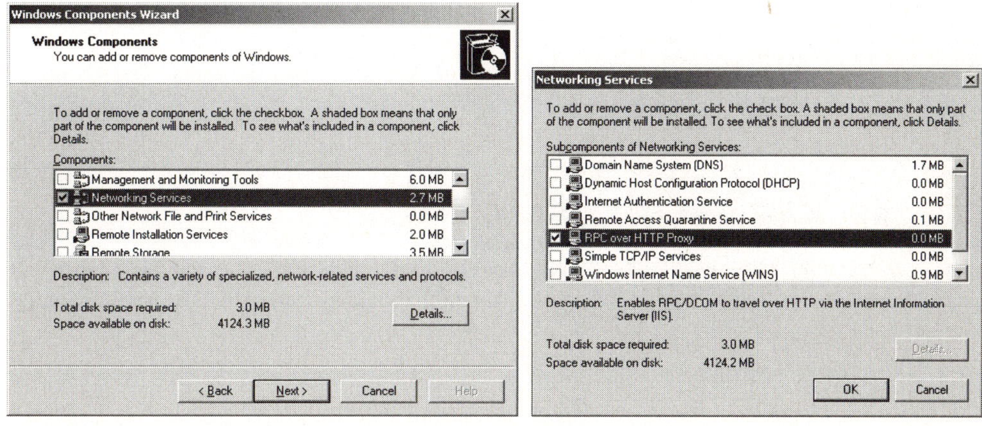

3. Enable Outlook Anywhere on a computer that has the Exchange Server 2007 Client Access server role installed. You need to log on to your Exchange Client Access server with an account that has been delegated at least the Exchange Server Administrator role and local administrator rights. Open Exchange Management Console, go to Server Configuration, Client Access, and select your Client Access Server from the servers listed. Choose the Action Enable Outlook Anywhere in the Action pane. The Enable Outlook Anywhere wizard will start, as shown in Figure 13.24. Fill in the External host name and change the authentication method if required. You also can choose to enable SSL offloading.

FIGURE 13.24 Enable Outlook Anywhere wizard

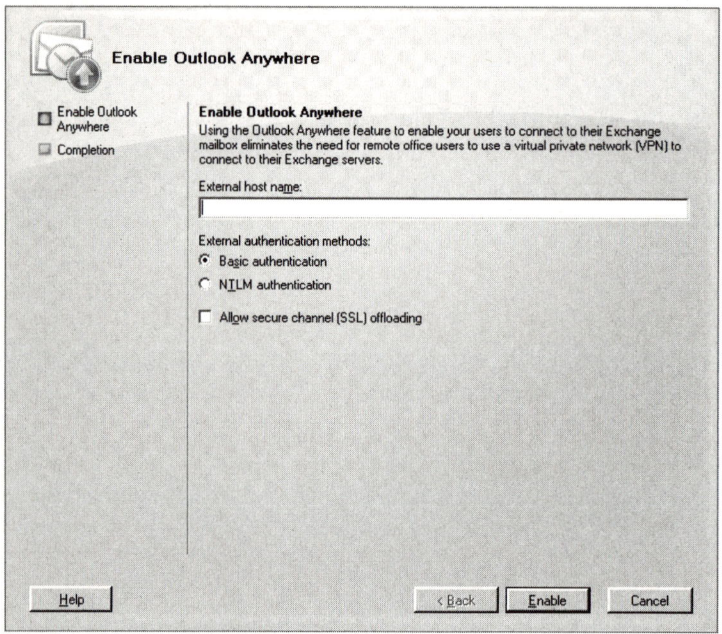

It is also possible to enable Outlook Anywhere using the Exchange Management Shell cmdlet `Set-OutlookAnywhere`.

Managing Outlook Anywhere

If you want to view or make changes to authentication settings, external host name, or the SSL offloading setting, you can use the Exchange Management Console or the Exchange Management Shell, as shown in Figure 13.25.

FIGURE 13.25 Outlook Anywhere settings in the Exchange Management Shell

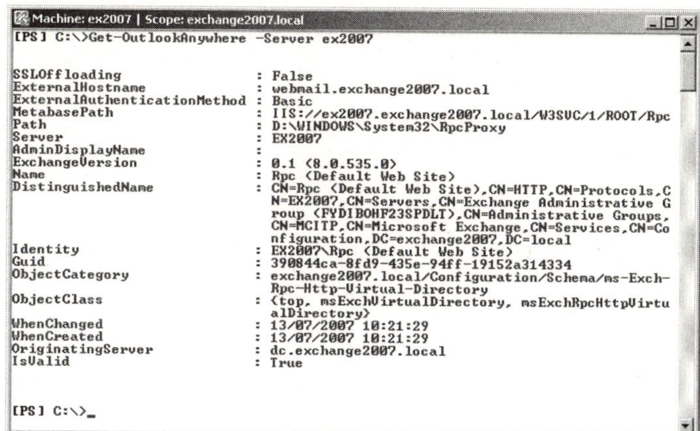

As noted earlier, the Exchange 2007 Autodiscover service will allow Microsoft Office Outlook 2007 clients to receive the Outlook Anywhere settings automatically.

Real World Scenario

Autodiscover and Outlook Anywhere

Suppose you are an Exchange administrator and you have recently transitioned your Exchange 2000 organization to Exchange 2007. You have a lot of users on the road visiting clients and traveling to develop your business. Currently, they are using OWA to gain access to their mailboxes. However, some of the users would like to be able to work offline, while they are on a plane, or waiting at a customer's site. During the migration, all your users received the latest version of Microsoft Office Outlook.

You decide to enable Outlook Anywhere, and you configure the external URL to point to the Client Access server with Outlook Anywhere enabled. You instruct your users to start Outlook when they are connected to the Internet, and you notice that all your users receive the Outlook Anywhere settings via the Autodiscover agent you have configured correctly.

Implementing POP3/IMAP4

Post Office Protocol version 3 (POP3) and Internet Message Access Protocol Version 4rev1 (IMAP4) are supported in Exchange Server 2007 and are installed by default when you deploy the Exchange Client Access server. However, the services are set to manual and not started by default. To manage POP3 and/or IMAP4 settings, you need to use the Exchange Management Shell.

Microsoft plans to make it possible to manage POP3 and IMAP4 using the Exchange Management Console with Exchange Server 2007 Service Pack 1.

You can use the Exchange Management Shell to manage POP3 and/or IMAP4 service settings or to manage POP3 and/or IMAP4 user settings.

POP3 and IMAP4 are retrieve-only protocols. For those clients to send emails, you need to configure a Receive Connector on your Exchange Hub Transport server, as we will cover later in this chapter.

You can manage POP3 and IMAP4 service in the Exchange Management Shell. Using the Exchange Management Shell cmdlets `Get-ImapSettings` and `Get-PopSettings`, you will retrieve the current settings for these Internet protocol services.

Table 13.5 lists the settings you can change using the Exchange Management Shell.

TABLE 13.5 Configuration Options for IMAP and POP

IMAP	POP
Maximum Command Size	Maximum Command Size
Show Hidden Folders	Message Retrieval Sort order
Port Number unencrypted	Port Number unencrypted
SSL Port Number	SSL Port Number
Banner	Banner
LoginType	LoginType
Authentication Timeout	Authentication Timeout
Pre-Authentication Timeout	Pre-Authentication Timeout
Maximum number of connections	Maximum number of connections
Maximum number of connections from a single IP	Maximum number of connections from a single IP
Proxy Target Port	Proxy Target Port
Message Retrieval Mime Format	Message Retrieval Mime Format

TABLE 13.5 Configuration Options for IMAP and POP *(continued)*

IMAP	POP
Calendar Retrieval Item Option	Calendar Retrieval Item Option
OWA Server URL	OWA Server URL

To change any of these settings, you need to use the Exchange Management Shell cmdlets `Set-PopSettings` and `Set-ImapSettings`, as shown in Figure 13.26.

Here's how to manage the user settings: Using the Exchange Management Shell cmdlet `Get-CASMailbox`, you will retrieve the current POP3 and IMAP4 settings for these Internet protocol services for a particular user. You can use the `Set-CASMailbox` cmdlet to make changes to these settings, as shown in Figure 13.27.

FIGURE 13.26 Changing IMAP4 settings using the Exchange Management Shell

```
Machine: ex2007 | Scope: exchange2007.local
[PS] C:\>Get-ImapSettings -Server ex2007|fl name,owaserverURL,Banner

Name          : 1
OwaServerUrl  :
Banner        : Microsoft Exchange Server 2007 IMAP4 service ready


[PS] C:\>Get-ImapSettings -Server ex2007|Set-ImapSettings -OwaServerURL "https://webmail.exchange2007.local/owa" -Banner "This IMAP4 server is ready to rock"
[PS] C:\>Get-ImapSettings -Server ex2007|fl name,owaserverURL,Banner

Name          : 1
OwaServerUrl  : https://webmail.exchange2007.local/owa
Banner        : This IMAP4 server is ready to rock


[PS] C:\>_
```

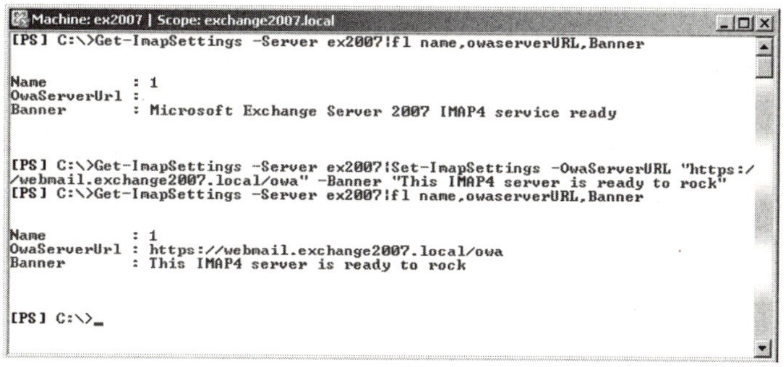

FIGURE 13.27 Changing POP3 settings for a user using the Exchange Management Shell

```
Machine: ex2007 | Scope: exchange2007.local
[PS] C:\>Get-CASMailbox -Identity ilse|fl name,pop*,imap*

Name                                : Ilse
PopEnabled                          : True
PopUseProtocolDefaults              : True
PopMessagesRetrievalMimeFormat      : BestBodyFormat
ImapEnabled                         : True
ImapUseProtocolDefaults             : True
ImapMessagesRetrievalMimeFormat     : BestBodyFormat


[PS] C:\>Get-CASMailbox -Identity ilse|Set-CASMailbox -PopEnabled:$False
[PS] C:\>Get-CASMailbox -Identity ilse|fl name,pop*,imap*

Name                                : Ilse
PopEnabled                          : False
PopUseProtocolDefaults              : True
PopMessagesRetrievalMimeFormat      : BestBodyFormat
ImapEnabled                         : True
ImapUseProtocolDefaults             : True
ImapMessagesRetrievalMimeFormat     : BestBodyFormat


[PS] C:\>
```

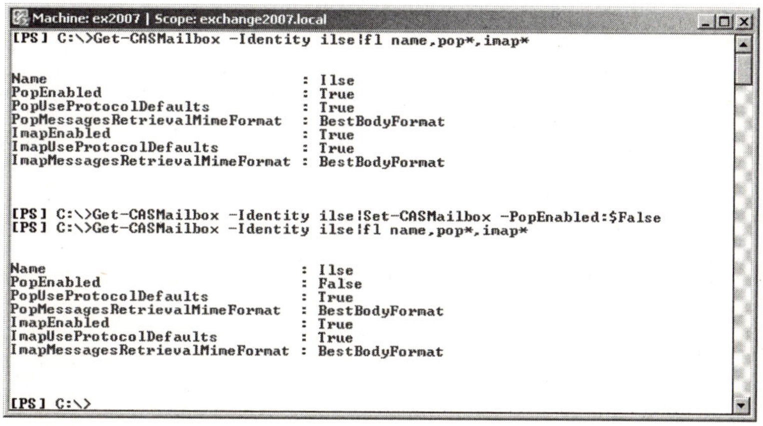

Implementing Public Folders

Even though public folders are supported in Exchange Server 2007, they are de-emphasized in Exchange Server 2007. When you transition an existing Exchange 2003 or Exchange 2000 organization to Exchange 2007, Exchange will create a public folder database by default on the first Exchange 2007 Mailbox server you deploy. However, when you install your first Exchange Server 2007 in a new environment, Exchange will prompt you if you want to allow support for clients older than Outlook 2007. If you choose no, then Exchange will not create a public-folder database for you. You are always able to create one yourself afterwards.

Exchange Server 2007 only supports one public-folder hierarchy and does not provide the ability to create new application public-folder trees like Exchange 2000 and Exchange 2003 did.

You cannot manage public folders only by using the Exchange Management Console, you will need to use the Exchange Management Shell from time to time.

Microsoft plans to include a Public Folder Management Snap-In and public-folder access in OWA in Exchange Server 2007 Service Pack 1.

Creating and Configuring the Public Folder Databases

You can create a public-folder database by using the Exchange Management Console or by using the Exchange Management Shell cmdlet `New-PublicFolderDatabase`, as shown in Figure 13.28.

As noted earlier in this chapter, you cannot configure everything using the Exchange Management Console. For certain settings, you will need to use the Exchange Management Shell cmdlet `Set-PublicFolderDatabase.` Table 13.6 lists the settings you can configure using the Exchange Management Console and/or using the Exchange Management Shell.

FIGURE 13.28 Creating a new public-folder database

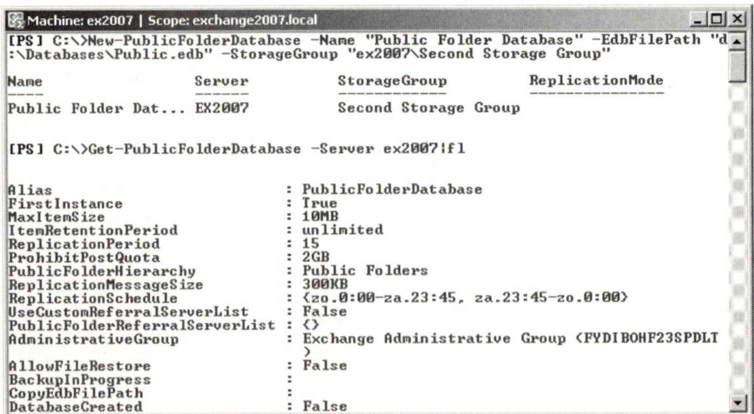

TABLE 13.6 Configuring Public-Folder Database Settings Using the Exchange Management Shell and the Exchange Management Console

Setting	Exchange Management Console	Exchange Management Shell
Maintenance Schedule	Yes	Yes
This Database Can Be Overwritten by a Restore	Yes	Yes
Mount at Startup	Yes	Yes
Replication Interval	Yes	Yes
Replication Interval for "Always Run"	Yes	Yes
Replication Message Size Limit	Yes	Yes
Storage Limits	Yes	Yes
Warning Message Interval	Yes	Yes
Maximum Item Size	Yes	Yes
Deleted Item Retention Time	Yes	Yes
Age Limit	Yes	Yes
Public Folder Referrals	No	Yes

Creating and Configuring Public Folders

You cannot create and configure public folders using the Exchange Management Console. You cannot create or change settings to public folders using OWA. You can create and configure public folders using the Exchange Management Shell, and you can create and configure some public-folder settings using Microsoft Office Outlook.

Within Exchange Server 2007, you may still need to maintain so-called system public folders. System public folders are required by Outlook to gain access to free and busy information, Offline Address Books, and Form libraries. Microsoft Office Outlook 2007 can use the new Exchange 2007 Web Services to get this information, as we have covered before in this chapter. System public folders can only be created and configured using the Exchange Management Shell.

Table 13.7 lists all cmdlets that are available by default to manage public folders within Exchange Server 2007.

TABLE 13.7 Public-Folder Exchange Management Shell Cmdlets

Cmdlet	Description
`Add-PublicFolderAdministrativePermission`	Allows you to give one or more users administrative permissions on a public folder, like the ability to change the access control list of a public folder
`Add-PublicFolderClientPermission`	Allows you to give a user access to a public folder
`Disable-MailPublicFolder`	Removes the email properties of a mail-enabled public folder
`Enable-MailPublicFolder`	Mail-enables a public folder
`Get-MailPublicFolder`	Provides you with an overview of email properties set of a mail-enabled public folder
`Get-PublicFolder`	Provides you with an overview of public-folder properties
`Get-PublicFolderAdministrativePermission`	Provides you with an overview of who has which administrative permissions on a public folder
`Get-PublicFolderClientPermission`	Provides you with an overview of who has which client permissions on a public folder
`Get-PublicFolderDatabase`	Provides you with an overview of general settings of a public-folder database
`Get-PublicFolderStatistics`	Provides you with an overview of statistics of a particular public folder
`New-PublicFolder`	Allows you to create a new public folder
`New-PublicFolderDatabase`	Allows you to create a new public folder database
`Remove-PublicFolder`	Removes a public folder
`Remove-PublicFolderAdministrativePermission`	Can be used to remove a user's administrative permission

TABLE 13.7 Public-Folder Exchange Management Shell Cmdlets *(continued)*

Cmdlet	Description
`Remove-PublicFolderClientPermission`	Can be used to remove a user's client permission
`Remove-PublicFolderDatabase`	Can be used to remove a public-folder database
`Resume-PublicFolderReplication`	Can be used to resume public-folder replication
`Set-MailPublicFolder`	Can be used to change email settings for a public folder
`Set-PublicFolder`	Can be used to change public-folder settings
`Set-PublicFolderDatabase`	Can be used to change public-folder database settings
`Suspend-PublicFolderReplication`	Can be used to suspend public-folder replication
`Update-PublicFolder`	Can be used to start content synchronization of a public folder
`Update-PublicFolderHierarchy`	Can be used to start public folder hierarchy replication

Implementing Connectors

Connectors in Exchange Server 2007 are deployed and configured to enable connectivity between Exchange 2007 Hub Transport servers and other messaging systems. In Exchange Server 2007, there are different kinds of connectors that enable the following:

- Connectivity between Exchange 2007 Hub Transport servers
- Connectivity between Exchange Server 2007 and Exchange Server 2003 or Exchange 2000 Server
- Connectivity between Exchange 2007 servers and foreign mail environments
- Connectivity between Exchange 2007 and the Internet

In this part of the chapter, we will cover the different kinds of connectors, which can be classified as Send connectors, Receive connectors, or Foreign connectors.

Send Connectors

Send connectors use the Simple Mail Transfer Protocol (SMTP) to transport messages to the Internet, or you can configure a Send connector to send mail to a non-SMTP address space, like Lotus Notes.

Creating Send Connectors

Send connectors can be created using the Exchange Management Console or the Exchange Management Shell cmdlet `New-SendConnector`. You need to be logged on with an account that has been delegated the Exchange Organization Administrator role. Send connectors can be only be created on Exchange servers deployed with the Hub Transport server role or Edge Transport server role.

When you create a new Send connector, you need to define the intended use of the connector. Table 13.8 lists those and their descriptions.

TABLE 13.8 Send Connector Intended Use

Type	Description
Custom	Used to connect with systems that are not Exchange servers
Internal	Used to configure the connector to route email to your internal Exchange servers as smart hosts
Internet	Used to send email to the Internet
Partner	Used to configure the connector to only allow connections to servers that authenticate with Transport Layer Security (TLS) certificates for SMTP domains that are included in the list of domain-secured domains

Exercise 13.6 outlines the steps necessary to create a new Send connector to the Internet using the Exchange Management Console.

EXERCISE 13.6

Creating a New Send Connector Using the Exchange Management Console

This exercise shows how you can create a Send connector using the Exchange Management Console.

1. Log on to the Exchange server with an account that has been delegated the Exchange Organization Administrator role.

EXERCISE 13.6 *(continued)*

2. Open the Exchange Management Console, expand the organization configuration, select Hub Transport, and click the Send Connectors tab in the work pane.
3. Choose New Send Connector in the action pane, and the New SMTP Send Connector wizard will start.
4. Fill out the name and intended use on the Introduction page, and click Next.
5. On the Address Space page, enter all domain names this connector will send mail to, as shown here.

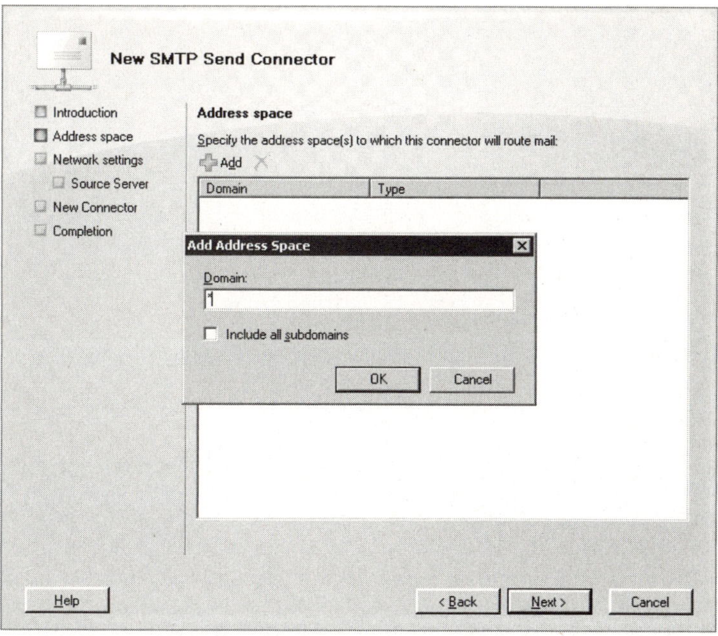

6. On the Network Settings page, select how to send email with the Send connector, by using domain name system (DNS) MX records to route mail automatically, or by routing all mail through a smart host. When selecting a smart host, you can add authentication settings if needed.
7. On the Hub Transport server, you will also receive a Source Server page where you need to define the Bridgehead servers for this connector.

EXERCISE 13.6 *(continued)*

8. Review the configuration summary for the connector, and click New to create the new Send connector, as shown here.

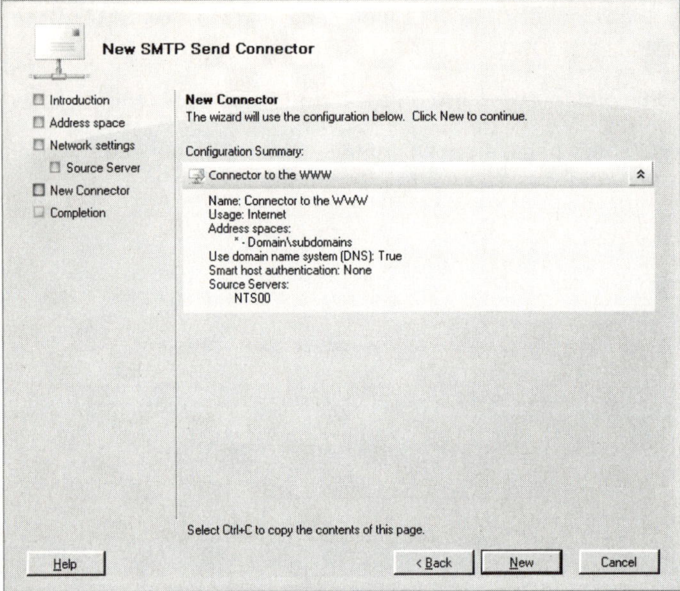

Configuring, Disabling, and Removing Send Connectors

You can always change the configuration of an existing Send connector by using the Exchange Management Console or by using the Exchange Management Shell cmdlet `Set-SendConnector`.

You also can disable a Send connector temporarily if needed. To disable a Send connector, you can use the Exchange Management Console or the Exchange Management Shell, as shown in Figure 13.29. If you choose to disable a Send connector, you need to be aware of the following:

- If you are running previous versions of Exchange in the same organization, they will not know the connector is disabled and they will continue using it.
- If you are running previous versions of Exchange in the same organization, you might have message loops occurring.

You can remove a Send connector by using the Exchange Management Console or by using the Exchange Management Shell cmdlet `Remove-SendConnector`.

Linked Connectors

You can create or configure an existing Send connector as a so-called linked connector only by using the Exchange Management Shell, as shown in Figure 13.30. By configuring a Send connector as a linked connector, you actually configure that connector to forward every mail that is received by the linked Receive connector to a specified smart host.

FIGURE 13.29 Disable Send connector using the Exchange Management Shell

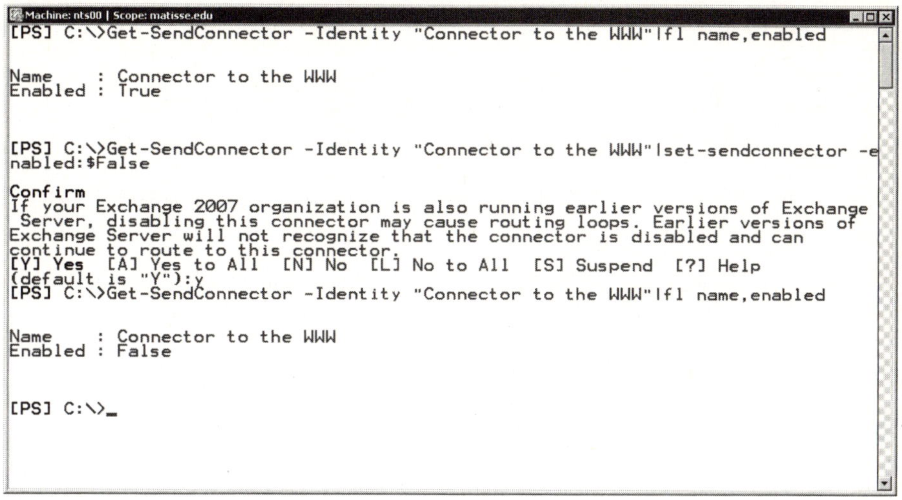

```
Machine: nts00 | Scope: matisse.edu
[PS] C:\>Get-SendConnector -Identity "Connector to the WWW"|fl name,enabled

Name    : Connector to the WWW
Enabled : True


[PS] C:\>Get-SendConnector -Identity "Connector to the WWW"|set-sendconnector -e
nabled:$False

Confirm
If your Exchange 2007 organization is also running earlier versions of Exchange
 Server, disabling this connector may cause routing loops. Earlier versions of
Exchange Server will not recognize that the connector is disabled and can
continue to route to this connector.
[Y] Yes  [A] Yes to All  [N] No  [L] No to All  [S] Suspend  [?] Help
(default is "Y"):y
[PS] C:\>Get-SendConnector -Identity "Connector to the WWW"|fl name,enabled

Name    : Connector to the WWW
Enabled : False


[PS] C:\>_
```

FIGURE 13.30 Creating a linked Send connector

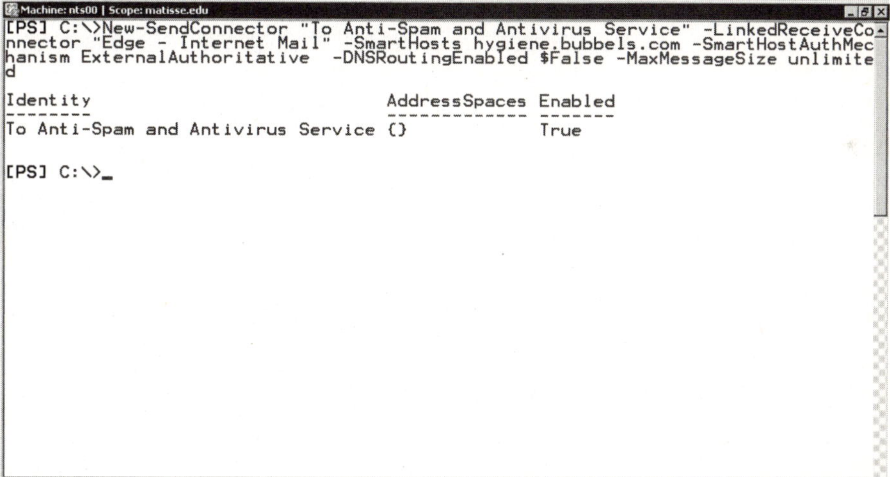

Linked connectors are often used to make sure that every mail that is received from the Internet is forwarded by Exchange first to an anti-spam and antivirus device, before it is delivered back to Exchange and delivered in the mailbox store.

Receive Connectors

All Receive connectors use SMTP to transport messages and can be configured to accept mail only from SMTP address spaces.

An SMTP Receive connector is required for an Exchange 2007 Hub Transport server or Exchange 2007 Edge Transport server to be able to accept any SMTP email. You can configure additional SMTP Receive connectors with different parameters on a single Exchange Hub Transport or Edge Transport server. But every SMTP Receive connector on a Hub Transport server or Edge Transport server must use a unique combination of port number, listening IP address, and accepted remote IP addresses.

Default Receive Connectors

By default, when you deploy a Hub Transport server, two SMTP Receive connectors are already created and configured, as shown in Figure 13.31.

FIGURE 13.31 Default Receive connectors on a Hub Transport server

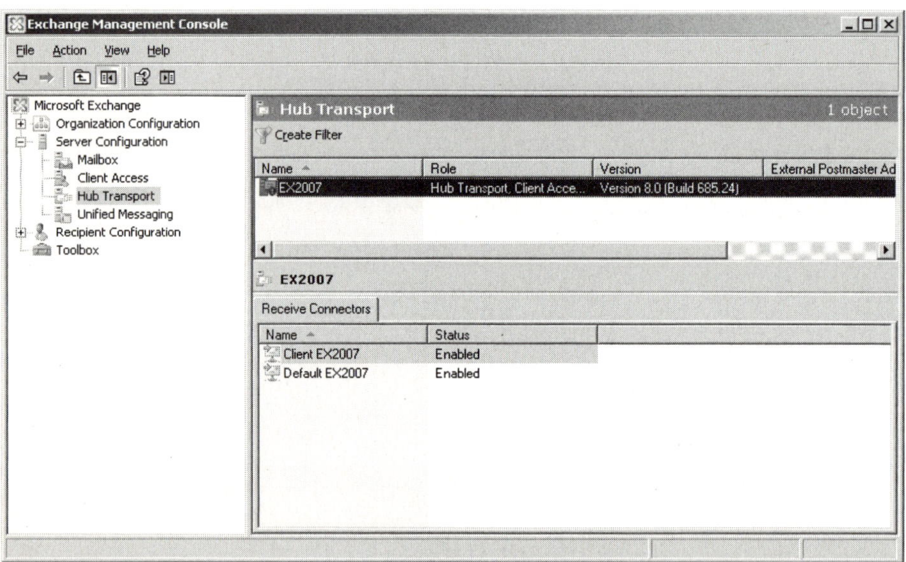

The `Client` *<Servername>* connector is configured to listen on port 587, whereas the `Default` *<Servername>* connector is configured to listen on port 25. Port 587 has been proposed in RFC 2476 as the one that should be used for message submission from email clients that require message relay, like POP and IMAP clients.

Also different are the permission groups that are allowed to use the connector or that are able to send mails to the Exchange server, as shown in Figure 13.32.

FIGURE 13.32 Permission groups on a Receive connectors

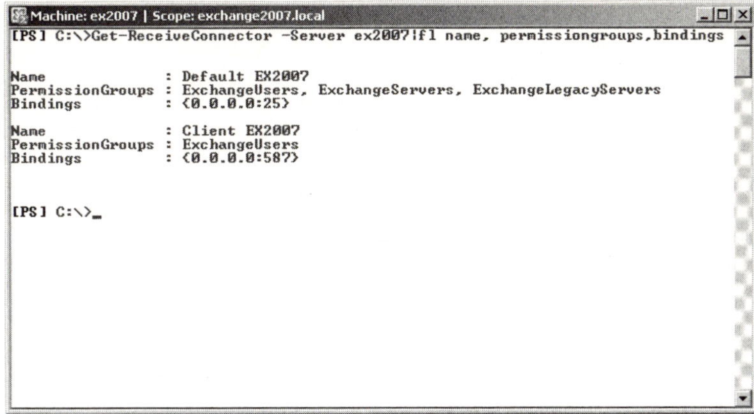

By default, anonymous users are not allowed to relay messages, as shown in Figure 13.33. To allow anonymous users to relay, you could choose to configure an existing or a new Receive connector to grant relay permission to anonymous connections or by configuring a new or existing Receive connector as externally secured.

FIGURE 13.33 Anonymous users

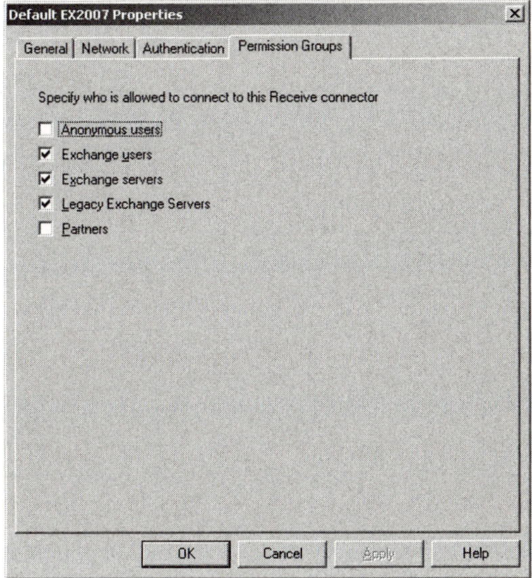

Configuration Options for Receive Connectors

You can use the Exchange Management Console and the Exchange Management Shell to configure SMTP Receive connectors. Figure 13.34 shows some settings you can configure for the `Default` *<ServerName>* Receive connector using the Exchange Management Shell cmdlet `Set-ReceiveConnector`.

FIGURE 13.34 Configuring the Receive connector

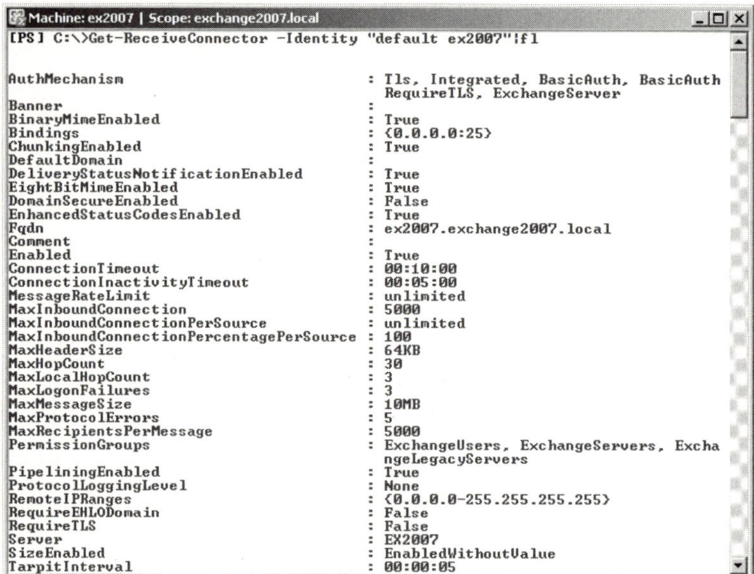

Foreign Connectors

Foreign connectors transport messages from Hub Transport servers to local messaging servers that do not use SMTP to transport messages. Foreign connectors can be configured to send mail to SMTP or non-SMTP address spaces, such as X.400. Foreign connectors are most commonly used to connect with Lotus Notes messaging environments.

A Foreign connector controls outbound connections from the Hub Transport to the foreign gateway server. The outbound messages are put in a Drop directory on the Hub Transport server or in a network file share on a remote server. Each Foreign connector uses its own Drop directory. The foreign gateway server must be configured to obtain messages from the Drop directory that is specified for that Foreign connector.

To create a Foreign Connector, you need to use the Exchange Management Shell cmdlet `New-ForeignConnector`.

Implementing Content Indexing

Exchange Server 2007 provides a new way of content indexing that is enabled by default for every mailbox database in your Exchange organization, as shown in Figure 13.35.

FIGURE 13.35 Mailbox database is index enabled by default

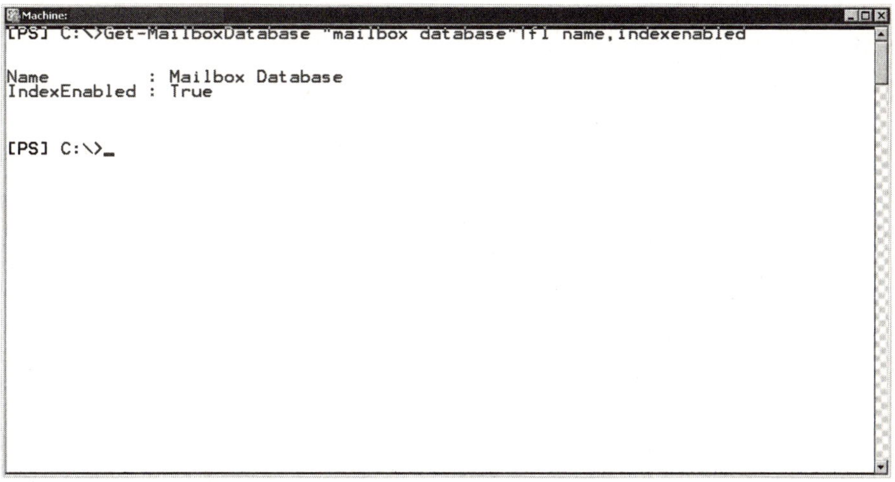

```
[PS] C:\>Get-MailboxDatabase "mailbox database"|fl name,indexenabled

Name         : Mailbox Database
IndexEnabled : True


[PS] C:\>_
```

Exchange Server 2007 uses the same search technology as Microsoft SQL Server 2005. Indexing uses a notification-based mechanism that allows new messages to be indexed within a minute or two after being delivered or created. Using this new search technology has decreased the server resources that are needed to maintain the content index and has also led to a search index that is significantly smaller than in Exchange Server 2003 and Exchange 2000 Server. You should keep in mind that the search index will be about five percent of the size of the mailbox database.

The search index is available for OWA clients, and Microsoft Office Outlook clients in online mode. When you run a mailbox search against a Microsoft Office Outlook configured in cached mode, the search will run against the content indexing of the offline copy of the mailbox.

As noted earlier, it is not necessary or recommended to back up and restore the indexes. Indexes are not unique data and can be easily re-created after restoring the mailbox or Public Folder database.

Implementing DSAccess

Directory Service Access, DSAccess, runs inside the System Attendant and is responsible for building a topology of the domain controllers (DCs) available to the Exchange server, enabling

Exchange to determine the destination of an email for example, and maintaining the DSAccess cache. In Exchange Server 2007, DSAccess consists of two parts: Ad Provider and Ad Driver. Ad Provider is responsible for maintaining the DSAccess cache and for passing LDAP queries to AD. Ad Driver is a sub-component of the Ad Provider and builds and maintains the DC topology.

By default, DSAccess chooses the primary domain controller (PDC) emulator operations master role computer to handle its requests. If you want to, you can change the default behavior by defining the following:

- A static list of domain controllers
- A static list of global catalogs
- A static list of configuration domain controllers
- A list of domain controllers that have to be excluded

For example, you can use the Exchange Management Shell cmdlet `Set-ExchangeServer` to specify a static list of domain controllers. Exchange will check your requested changes before applying them, as shown in Figure 13.36.

FIGURE 13.36 Get-ExchangeServer

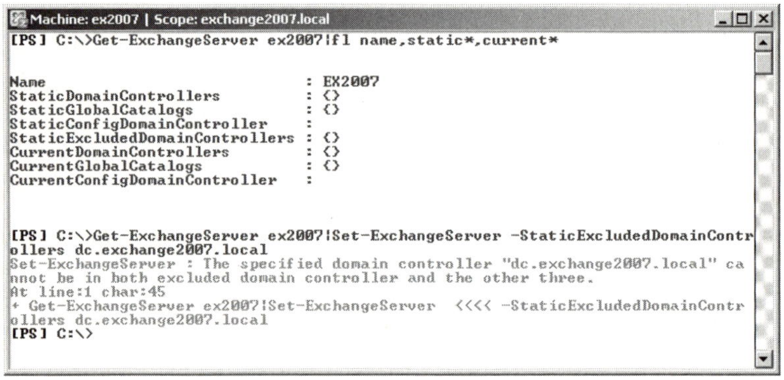

```
Machine: ex2007 | Scope: exchange2007.local
[PS] C:\>Get-ExchangeServer ex2007|fl name,static*,current*


Name                              : EX2007
StaticDomainControllers           : {}
StaticGlobalCatalogs              : {}
StaticConfigDomainController      :
StaticExcludedDomainControllers   : {}
CurrentDomainControllers          : {}
CurrentGlobalCatalogs             : {}
CurrentConfigDomainController     :



[PS] C:\>Get-ExchangeServer ex2007|Set-ExchangeServer -StaticExcludedDomainContr
ollers dc.exchange2007.local
Set-ExchangeServer : The specified domain controller "dc.exchange2007.local" ca
nnot be in both excluded domain controller and the other three.
At line:1 char:45
+ Get-ExchangeServer ex2007|Set-ExchangeServer  <<<< -StaticExcludedDomainContr
ollers dc.exchange2007.local
[PS] C:\>
```

Summary

In this chapter, we looked at planning the deployment of Exchange Server 2007 Services. First, we took a look at the Autodiscover service. We defined the features this service offers for Microsoft Office Outlook 2007 and some Windows Mobile devices, and then we covered in detail the way the Autodiscover service provides its services. We also looked at how you can configure some other Exchange Web Services to make sure the Autodiscover service can provision non–domain-joined clients.

Next, we investigated the Availability service that enables Microsoft Office Outlook 2007 clients to gain access to free and busy information and OOF configuration settings. Then we dug into how we can implement mobile devices in our Exchange organization. We covered the differences between Windows Mobile 5.0 and Windows Mobile 6.0, and we looked at the different Exchange ActiveSync Mailbox Policy settings we can set for a user. We also covered how to deploy and configure Outlook Web Access in Exchange Server 2007, followed by the deployment and configuration options for Outlook Anywhere, POP3, and IMAP4.

We also briefly touched the different ways to manage public-folder databases and public folders, followed by a more in-depth look at the different kind of connectors you can create and configure in Exchange Server 2007. We covered the Send connector, Receive connector, and the Foreign connector. To conclude the chapter, we looked at content indexing and how we can manage the Directory Service Access component in Exchange Server 2007, DSAccess.

Exam Essentials

Implementing Autodiscover For the exam, it is important to know which clients can use the Autodiscover service to automatically configure Exchange features. A lot of questions will cover the Exchange Web Services that you need to configure for external access.

Implementing Availability Service You should know that the Availability service is used by Microsoft Office Outlook 2007 and no other version. You have to know that Microsoft Office Outlook 2007 can get the free and busy information from a system public folder as well if the client's mailbox is housed on Exchange Server 2003. You also have to know that, in case of transitioning, the Exchange Client Access server will give the client every user's free and busy information, regardless of where the user's mailbox is housed.

Implementing Mobile Devices Make sure that you know that in Exchange Server 2007 a user can now remotely wipe his or her own mobile device partnership and that you can create an Exchange ActiveSync Mailbox policy for a user or a group of users.

Implementing Microsoft Outlook Web Access (OWA) For the exam, you need to know that it is just the OWA virtual directory that is used for Outlook Web Access Exchange 2007 and that the Exchange virtual directory is only there to provide the ability for Exchange 2003–housed mailbox users to gain access to their mailbox via the Exchange Server 2007 Client Access server.

Implementing Outlook Anywhere Concerning Outlook Anywhere, you need to know that it is a straightforward process in Exchange Server 2007 to enable Outlook Anywhere and that you need to ensure that you have a valid certificate for Outlook Anywhere.

Implementing POP3/IMAP4/Public Folders For POP, IMAP, and public folders, you need to know that you cannot manage them using the Exchange Management Console. If you want to change any setting for a particular public folder, you can only use the Exchange Management Shell.

Implementing Connectors Make sure you know that you need to create a Send connector in Exchange Server 2007 before you can send an email to the Internet and that you can use Send connectors to connect to other messaging environments. You need to know that there are two Receive connectors created during the installation of the Exchange 2007 Hub Transport server role and that anonymous mail relay is by default disabled.

Implementing Content Indexing For the exam, you need to know that content indexing is enabled by default and that you shouldn't include the search index in your backup schedule.

Implementing DSAccess Last but not least, you should remember when you take the exam that you can specify which domain controllers and global catalogs your Exchange server will use when needed.

Review Questions

1. You are an Exchange administrator who is responsible for an Exchange 2007 organization that contains two Exchange 2007 Mailbox servers, one Client Access server, and one Hub Transport server. Your users use either Microsoft Office Outlook 2000 or Microsoft Office Outlook XP to open their mailboxes. All client workstations are running Windows XP Professional SP2. Your management has heard about the new Autodiscover feature and they want you to make sure that all your users can use this new feature. What should you do?

   A. Upgrade the client workstations to Windows Vista Home.

   B. Upgrade the client workstations to Windows Vista Business.

   C. Upgrade Microsoft Office Outlook to Microsoft Office Outlook 2007.

   D. Wait for Exchange Server 2007 Service Pack 1.

2. You are an Exchange administrator with a single Exchange Server 2007 that houses 300 mailboxes. You have given every sales person a new laptop, including Microsoft Office Outlook 2007, and you have enabled and configured Outlook Anywhere. However, almost every member of the sales force calls you to complain they are unable to get free and busy information for their colleagues they invite to a meeting. What should you check?

   A. Check if the external URL for the offline address book is configured correctly.

   B. Check if the external URL for Unified Messaging is configured correctly.

   C. Check if the external URL for Outlook Anywhere is configured correctly.

   D. Check if the external URL for the Exchange Web Services is configured correctly.

3. You are an Exchange administrator who is in the process of transitioning from Exchange Server 2003 to Exchange 2007. You have just decommissioned your Exchange Server 2003 front-end server after deploying a new Exchange 2007 Client Access server. You are now in the process of configuring an automatic redirection to make sure that when users connect to the root of your Client Access server, they will be redirected without a problem to the logon page of Outlook Web Access. To what URL should you redirect the default website?

   A. `/Owa`

   B. `/Exchange`

   C. `/ExAdmin`

   D. `/Exchweb`

4. You are an Exchange administrator with a single Exchange Server 2007 that houses 300 mailboxes. You did not choose to enable support for Outlook clients before 2007 when you deployed your Exchange Server 2007. You have given every sales person a new laptop, including Microsoft Office Outlook 2007, and you have enabled and configured Outlook Anywhere. However, every member of the sales force calls you to complain they are unable to gain access to the address when they are offline. What should you check?

   A. Whether the external URL for the offline address book is configured correctly

   B. Whether the external URL for Unified Messaging is configured correctly

   C. Whether the external URL for Outlook Anywhere is configured correctly

   D. Whether the external URL for Exchange Web Services is configured correctly

5. You are an Exchange administrator with a single Exchange Server 2007 that houses 300 mailboxes. You did not choose to enable support for Outlook clients before 2007 when you deployed your Exchange Server 2007. You have given every sales person a new laptop, including Microsoft Office Outlook 2007, and you have enabled and configured Outlook Anywhere. However, every member of the sales force calls you to complain they are unable to gain access review their Unified Messaging settings. What should you check?

   A. Whether the external URL for the offline address book is configured correctly

   B. Whether the external URL for Unified Messaging is configured correctly

   C. Whether the external URL for Outlook Anywhere is configured correctly

   D. Whether the external URL for Exchange Web Services is configured correctly

6. You are an Exchange administrator who just finished the transition from Exchange Server 2003 to Exchange 2007. You have just decommissioned your last Exchange Server 2003 back-end server. You are now in the process of configuring an automatic redirection to make sure that when users connect to the root of your Client Access server, they will be redirected without a problem to the logon page of Outlook Web Access. To what URL should you redirect the default website?

   A. `/Owa`

   B. `/Exchange`

   C. `/ExAdmin`

   D. `/Exchweb`

7. You are an Exchange Administrator who is responsible for an Exchange 2007 organization that contains two Exchange 2007 Mailbox servers: one Client Access server, and one Hub Transport server. Your users use either Microsoft Office Outlook 2003 or Microsoft Office Outlook 2007 to open their mailboxes. All client workstations are running Windows XP Professional SP2. You would like to enable clients to gain access to a file share located on Server2 in your network when they use Outlook Web Access. What should you do?

   A. Upgrade all Microsoft Outlook versions to Outlook 2007.

   B. Configure direct file access for Outlook Web Access.

   C. Deploy Windows SharePoint Services.

   D. Configure VPN.

8. You are an Exchange administrator with two Exchange 2007 servers: one Mailbox server, and one Hub Transport/Client Access server. You did not choose to enable support for Outlook clients before 2007 when you deployed your Exchange Server 2007. You have given every sales person a new laptop, including Microsoft Office Outlook 2007, and now you would like to enable Outlook Anywhere. What should you do? (Choose all that apply.)

   A. Install a valid SSL certificate for Outlook Anywhere.

   B. Install the Windows RPC over HTTP Proxy component.

   C. Install the Exchange RPC over HTTP Proxy component.

   D. Enable Outlook Anywhere on the Client Access server.

   E. Enable Outlook Anywhere on the Mailbox server.

9. You are an Exchange administrator with two Exchange 2007 servers: one Mailbox server, and one Hub Transport/Client Access server. You did not choose to enable support for Outlook clients before 2007 when you deployed your Exchange Server 2007. Now you would like to disable the use of calendars in Outlook Web Access for some users. What should you do?

   A. Use the Exchange Management Console to disable the Calendar for those users

   B. Use the Exchange Management Shell to disable the Calendar for those users

   C. Create Public Folders

   D. Wait for Exchange Server 2007 Service Pack 1

10. You are an Exchange administrator with two Exchange 2007 servers: one Mailbox server, and one Hub Transport/Client Access server. You have enabled POP and IMAP on your Client Access server, and now you would like to change the banner for POP and IMAP. What tool should you use?

   A. Exchange Management Console

   B. Exchange Management Shell

   C. Registry Editor

   D. ADSI Edit

11. You are an Exchange administrator with two Exchange 2007 servers: one Mailbox server, and one Hub Transport/Client Access server. You have enabled POP and IMAP on your Client Access server, CAS1, now you would like to change the banner for POP. Which Management Shell cmdlet would you use?

   A. `Get-PopSettings -server CAS1|Set-PopSettings -banner` *`new banner`*

   B. `Get-PopSettings -server CAS1 -banner` *`new banner`*

   C. `Change-PopSettings -server CAS1 -banner` *`new banner`*

   D. `Change-PopSettings -server CAS1|Set-PopSettings -banner` *`new banner`*

12. You are an Exchange administrator with two Exchange 2007 servers: one Mailbox server, and one Hub Transport/Client Access server. Which tools can you use to create new public folders? (Choose all that apply.)

   A. Exchange Management Console

   B. Exchange Management Shell

   C. Microsoft Office Outlook

   D. Outlook Web Access

13. You are an Exchange administrator with two Exchange 2007 servers: one Mailbox server, and one Hub Transport/Client Access server. You would like to configure the Age Limit for the public-folder store. Which tool(s) can you use? (Choose all that apply.)

   A. Exchange Management Console

   B. Exchange Management Shell

   C. Microsoft Office Outlook

   D. Outlook Web Access

14. You are an Exchange administrator with two Exchange 2007 servers: one Mailbox server, and one Hub Transport/Client Access server. You would like to configure the Age Limit for one particular public folder. Which tool(s) can you use? (Choose all that apply).
    - **A.** Exchange Management Console
    - **B.** Exchange Management Shell
    - **C.** Microsoft Office Outlook
    - **D.** Outlook Web Access

15. You are an Exchange administrator with two Exchange 2007 servers: one Mailbox server, and one Hub Transport/Client Access server. You would like to enable your users to send mail to the Internet by using the services of your ISP mail provider that can be used as a smart host. What kind of connector should you configure?
    - **A.** Send connector
    - **B.** Receive connector
    - **C.** Foreign connector
    - **D.** Linked connector

16. You are an Exchange administrator with two Exchange 2007 servers: one Mailbox server, and one Hub Transport/Client Access server. You would like to enable your users to send mail to a fax gateway you have configured recently. What kind of connector should you configure?
    - **A.** Send connector
    - **B.** Receive connector
    - **C.** Foreign connector
    - **D.** Linked connector

17. You are an Exchange administrator with two Exchange 2007 servers: one Mailbox server, and one Hub Transport/Client Access server. You would like to allow anonymous users to connect to your Exchange Server 2007 Hub Transport server and submit messages for any of your accepted domains. What kind of connector should you configure to make this possible?
    - **A.** Send connector
    - **B.** Receive connector
    - **C.** Foreign connector
    - **D.** Linked connector

18. You are an Exchange administrator with two Exchange 2007 servers: one Mailbox server, and one Hub Transport/Client Access server. You would like to determine if your mailbox database files are index enabled or not. What tool can you use to check this?
    - **A.** Exchange Management Console
    - **B.** Exchange Management Shell
    - **C.** Registry Editor
    - **D.** IIS Manager

19. You are an Exchange administrator with two Exchange 2007 servers: one Mailbox server, and one Hub Transport/Client Access server. You have checked that your mailbox database files are index-enabled. What backup type should you consider for your search index?

    A. Online backup

    B. Offline backup

    C. VSS

    D. None

20. You are an Exchange Administrator who is responsible for an Exchange 2007 organization that contains two Exchange 2007 Mailbox servers: one Client Access server, and one Hub Transport server. You would like to configure a specific list of global catalogs your Exchange Servers are allowed to query when needed. Which tool can you use to configure this?

    A. Exchange Management Console

    B. Exchange Management Shell

    C. Registry Editor

    D. IIS Manager

Answers to Review Questions

1. C. You need at least Microsoft Office Outlook 2007 to be able to take advantage of the new Autodiscover service. Autodiscover service is included with Exchange Server 2007 RTM so you don't need to wait for Service Pack 1. There is no need to upgrade the client operating system to be able to take advantage of the Autodiscover feature.

2. D. To provide remote users using Outlook Anywhere with access to free and busy information, the external URL for the Exchange Web Services has to be configured correctly. You don't need to configure an external URL for the offline address book, either for Unified Messaging or Outlook Anywhere, since they are not used to retrieve free and busy information.

3. B. When you are in the middle of a transitioning process, some mailboxes will still be located on Exchange 2003, so you will need to specify `https://<servername>/exchange`. You don't need to configure an external URL for the offline address book, either for Unified Messaging or Outlook Anywhere, since they are not used to retrieve free and busy information.

4. A. If you want your users to be able to download the offline address book when they are not connected to your network, you will need to configure an external URL for the offline address book for the Autodiscover service. You don't need to configure an external URL for the offline address book, either for Unified Messaging or Outlook Anywhere, since they are not used to retrieve free and busy information.

5. B. You need to configure an external URL for Unified Messaging for the Autodiscover service if you want users to be able to view and change the settings of Unified Messaging when they open Outlook. You don't need to configure an external URL for the offline address book, either for Unified Messaging or Outlook Anywhere, since they are not used to retrieve free and busy information.

6. A. If you only have mailboxes housed on Exchange Server 2007, you should specify `/Owa`, since that is the virtual directory used to gain access to a user's mailbox housed on Exchange Server 2007 using Outlook Web Access. You don't need to configure an external URL for the offline address book, either for Unified Messaging or Outlook Anywhere, since they are not used to retrieve free and busy information.

7. B. Configuring the file share to be accessible via Outlook Web Access will allow users to read files from that file share. You don't need to configure an external URL for the offline address book either for Unified Messaging or Outlook Anywhere, since they are not used to retrieve free and busy information.

8. A, B, D. If you want to enable Outlook Anywhere you need to install a valid SSL certificate, you need to install the Windows RPC over HTTP Proxy component, and you need to enable Outlook Anywhere on the Client Access server. You don't need to configure an external URL for the offline address book either for Unified Messaging or Outlook Anywhere, since they are not used to retrieve free and busy information.

9. B. If you want to specify Outlook Web Access segmentation settings for one or more users, you have to use the Exchange Management Shell.

10. B. You can use only the Exchange Management Shell to change the banner. The other listed tools cannot be used to change the banner.

11. A. There's only one correct answer in the list. `Change-PopSettings` doesn't exist, and `Get-PopSettings` will only show you an overview of settings. To change settings, you will need to use the cmdlet `Set-PopSettings`.

12. B and C. You can create public folders only using the Exchange Management Shell or Microsoft Office Outlook. You cannot use the Exchange Management Console or Outlook Web Access to create and manage public folders.

13. A and B. You can configure an Age Limit using both the Exchange Management Console and the Exchange Management Shell. You cannot configure an Age Limit using Microsoft Office Outlook or Outlook Web Access.

14. B. You can only use the Exchange Management Shell to configure public folder specific settings, such as Age Limit. The other listed tools can not be used to configure public folder specific settings like Age Limit.

15. A. Send connectors use SMTP to transport messages to the Internet. Receive connectors are used to receive messages. Foreign and linked connectors cannot be used for the specified purpose.

16. C. Foreign connectors transport messages from Hub Transport servers to local messaging servers that do not use SMTP to transport messages. Foreign connectors can be configured to send mail to SMTP or non-SMTP address spaces, such as X.400. Foreign connectors are most commonly used to connect with Lotus Notes messaging environments or fax gateways. A Foreign connector controls outbound connections from the Hub Transport to the foreign gateway server. Receive connectors are used to receive messages. Send and linked connectors cannot be used for the specified purpose.

17. B. By default, anonymous users are not allowed to relay messages. To allow anonymous users to relay, you could choose to configure an existing or a new Receive connector to grant relay permission to anonymous connections or by configuring a new or existing Receive connector as externally secured. Send, Foreign, and linked connectors cannot be configured for the specified purpose.

18. B. You have to use the Exchange Management Shell cmdlet `Get-MailboxDatabase` to check if a mailbox database is index enabled. You cannot use the Exchange Management Console, the IIS Manager, or the Registry Editor to check if a mailbox database is index-enabled.

19. D. It is not necessary or recommended to back up and restore the indexes. Indexes are not unique data and can be easily re-created after restoring the mailbox or public folder database. Since you don't need to consider the files for backup, you don't need to consider online, offline, or VSS types of backup.

20. B. You can use only the Exchange Management Shell cmdlet `Set-ExchangeServer` to specify a static list of global catalogs. The other listed tools cannot be used to configure a static list of global catalogs.

Planning Antivirus and Antispam for Exchange Server 2007

MICROSOFT EXAM OBJECTIVES COVERED IN THIS CHAPTER:

- ✓ Plan the antivirus and antispam implementation

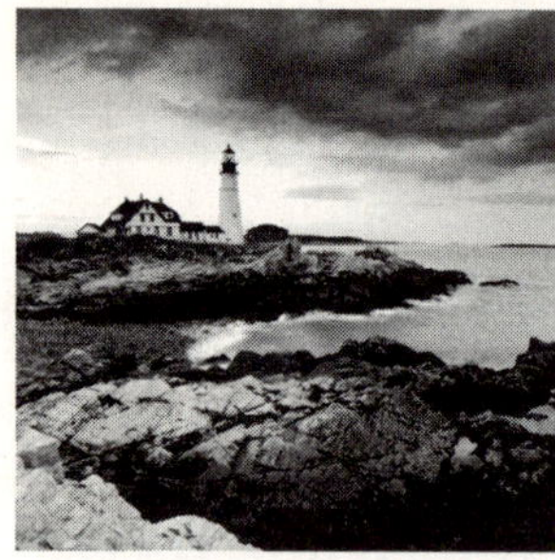

Over the last few years, email has become an important business application for most organizations, being used for internal and external communications, appointments, addresses, schedules, notes, and more. If not properly secured, your messaging server can be attacked by viruses, hoaxes, spam, and phishing. To secure your messaging environment, you should follow a defense-in-depth approach, deploying defenses on several levels in your organization. This approach means that you not only secure your environment by deploying multiple firewalls, but also secure your client, client OS, messaging application, servers, and messaging server.

Exchange 2007 offers several new features to protect your organization from viruses and spam. With Microsoft Exchange Server 2007, you can have the Exchange Server 2007 Edge Transport server role in your environment, which protects your Exchange organization at your network perimeter. Alternatively, you can choose Microsoft Exchange Hosted Services, which protects your messaging environment in the cloud. Microsoft also offers Forefront Security for Exchange Server 2007 to protect Exchange servers within your local area network (LAN).

This chapter offers several step-by-step exercises to configure and implement Exchange security in your environment. The main subjects of this chapter are as follows:

- Understanding Microsoft Exchange Hosted Services
- Planning and implementing Exchange Server 2007 antispam features
- Understanding Microsoft Exchange Forefront Security
- Planning and implementing Exchange Server 2007 antivirus features

Understanding Microsoft Exchange Hosted Services

Electronic messaging is a mission-critical application for any organization. Over the last few years, the messaging environment has been subject to a growing array of threats, including viruses, spam, phishing, denial-of-service attacks, and worms. At the same time, governments are introducing regulations regarding messaging security, archiving, and business continuity to protect individuals' privacy.

In Exchange Server 2007, Microsoft has integrated several built-in features to stop threats before they affect your organization and your users. Microsoft also has introduced Microsoft Exchange Hosted Services. In 2005 and 2006, Microsoft made several messaging- and security-related acquisitions, including FrontBridge Technologies, a managed-services provider. The former FrontBridge services are now offered under the brand of Microsoft Exchange Hosted Services.

Microsoft Exchange Hosted Services is a suite of four distinct services. These services help organizations protect themselves from email-borne malware, satisfy retention requirements, provide email continuity to preserve access to email during and after emergency situations, and encrypt email to preserve confidentiality.

These services help organizations protect themselves from email-borne malware, satisfy retention requirements, provide email continuity to preserve access to email during and after emergency situations, and encrypt email to preserve confidentiality. These services have not changed since the FrontBridge acquisition; however, Microsoft is continuously improving performance and expanding the security and services.

Figure 14.1 offers an overview of Microsoft Exchange Hosted Services.

With Microsoft Exchange Hosted Services, you can transfer key security functions to a hosted solution outside your organization without making changes to your messaging infrastructure.

FIGURE 14.1 Microsoft Exchange Hosted Services

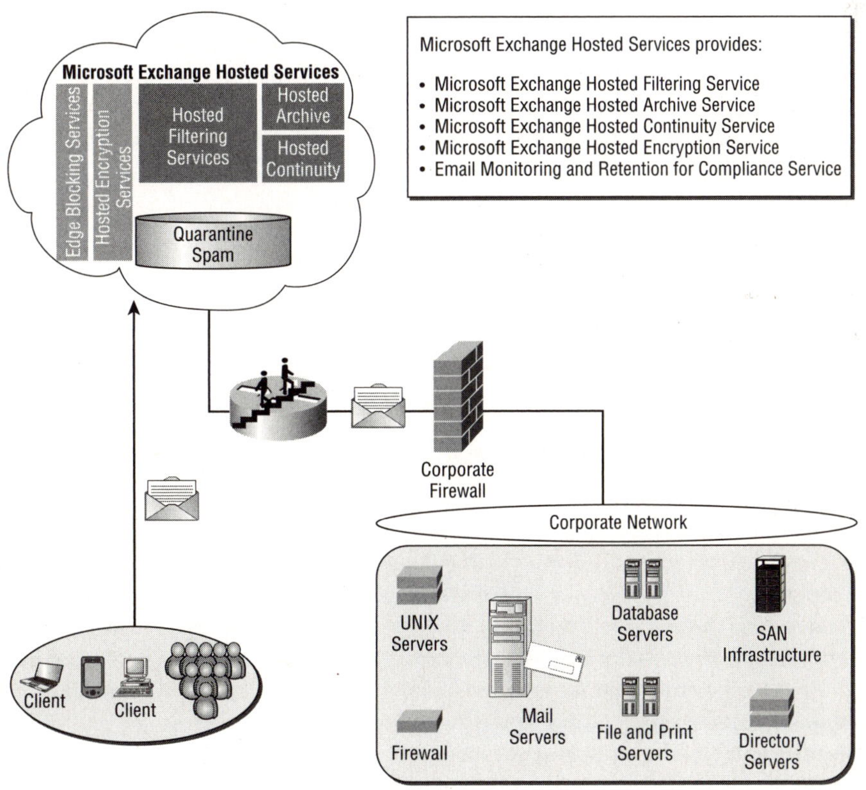

Together, these services eliminate upfront capital investment, free up IT resources, and empower companies to concentrate on their business.

To integrate Hosted Services into your messaging infrastructure, you need only to update the existing Mail Exchanger record. You don't need to introduce new components into the messaging infrastructure or buy additional hardware and software.

Microsoft Exchange Hosted Filtering

Multipronged message filtering in the perimeter network is available through the Edge Transport server role. However, for small or medium organizations, Microsoft offers "cloud" filtering (as an Internet-based service) through Exchange Hosted Filtering Services.

Microsoft Exchange Hosted Filtering services help to protect client emails from viruses, spyware, spam, and other forms of malware. Microsoft Exchange Hosted Filtering uses a defense-in-depth approach protects your Exchange organization from email spam, viruses, phishing scams, and email-policy violations. It provides antivirus scanning using your choice of four engines (Trend Micro, Symantec, Sophos, and Kaspersky Lab) to protect against viruses. The service also provides tools to queue emails for delivery in the event of an email-server outage at the client's environment. Exchange Hosted Filtering also works with other email platforms, including Lotus Notes.

Microsoft Exchange Hosted Archiving

Many organizations have begun treating and preserving email in the same manner as paper records. At the same time, to protect individual privacy, governments have begun passing different laws or implementing regulations that dictate how companies must secure, manage, and retain individual information. To comply with these regulations, your organization may have to develop certain processes, procedures, and practices to secure individual information, and find methods to secure and retain emails for certain period of time, which increases the need for a centralized repository.

Microsoft now offers "cloud" archiving (as an Internet-based service) through the Exchange Hosted Archiving solution, which is an add-on service of Microsoft Exchange Hosted Services.

As messages pass through the cloud, they are filtered and scanned by antivirus software and antispam filtering rules to make sure that the email is not infected. Next, a copy of each message is stored in a repository that is managed by an intelligent archiving system. The archiving system assigns a unique serial number and time stamp to a message. Messages can be retrieved later by header, subject line, attachment type, and message body. The archiving service also provides a backup system in case of network and email service outages. You pay only small amount per user, per month to get not only archiving but also an online backup system, which allow your users to access, read, compose, search, send and reply to emails in real time without any downtime to email.

Microsoft Exchange Hosted Continuity

One of the most significant issues in managing a messaging environment is how to provide email continuity to your users and business. Email outages cost organizations a significant amount of money. For many companies, uninterrupted email service is the most important business application for generating revenue and for communicating with partners, customers, vendors, and employees.

It is common to find that your business team expects rapid connectivity and continuity of email service when the email system is disrupted by natural disaster, server failure, technical errors, network interruption, human errors, software or hardware issues, or other crises. Most administrators use hot-standby servers to handle these kinds of issues, which may not be an appropriate choice in your situation because of hardware, software, administration, and maintenance costs.

The Microsoft Exchange Hosted Continuity service is another subscription-based service that is sold as an add-on. Whether your email outages are planned or unplanned, the Hosted Continuity service allows you to continuously provide email services to your employees and business, and can help you minimize the financial impacts of an outage. Some organizations may choose this as a backup service in case of network disruptions and email-service outages.

Like Exchange Hosted Archiving, the Hosted Continuity service takes full advantage of in-stream spam and protection against spam, viruses, and phishing attacks. As messages pass through the cloud, they are filtered and scanned by virus-scan software and antispam filtering rules to make sure that the email is not infected. Then a copy of each message is stored in a 30-day rolling message repository, which is managed by an archiving system. If your primary email system is not available, your users will be able to access the password-protected, offsite message repository at any time to read, compose, and reply to messages. After you restore the primary messaging system, you also will have the option to restore the messages that your users sent and received by means of the web-based interface while the primary messaging system was down. The only drawback of this service is that users will have access to only the past 30 days of email messages during the absence of their primary messaging system. You pay only a small amount, per month to get email continuity, which allows your users to continue their business communication in real time while your primary messaging system is down for maintenance.

Microsoft Exchange Hosted Encryption

The typical email messages travel in plain-text format and pass through many different servers and networks. Some of these servers and networks are secure, while others are not secure and are unmonitored, which means those emails are unprotected. In short, pretty much anyone with access to any of those servers or who is sniffing packets anywhere along the way can read your plain-text "private" email messages and see what you're sending. Messages also can be modified in transit, even before they reach their destination.

It is not surprising that information security and integrity are becoming more important for business communications with customers, partners, and vendors. Many organizations have started encrypting messages to protect individuals' confidential information and comply with corporate policies. For most organizations, existing solutions such as public key infrastructure

(PKI) and server-to-server-level encryption can be expensive and complicated to deploy. Moreover, these solutions do not provide the flexibility and ease of use that corporate users need to deploy email encryption for external communications.

Microsoft Exchange Hosted Encryption services are one of the four distinct managed services that make up Microsoft Exchange Hosted Services. As with other services in the Microsoft Exchange Hosted Services portfolio, Microsoft offers cloud-based encryption. The Exchange Hosted Encryption service can help organizations meet government regulations such as the Health Insurance Portability and Accountability Act and the Gramm-Leach-Bliley Act.

The Microsoft Exchange Hosted Encryption service protects private, sensitive, and valuable information communicated via email, and addresses many security problems such as eavesdropping, identity theft, invasion of privacy, message modification, false messages, message replay, unprotected backups, and repudiation.

Exchange Hosted Encryption is a convenient, easy-to-use email encryption service that provides policy-based encryption from sender to recipient. It is a solution that is easy to use for organizations that communicate sensitive or regulated information via email with external business partners and customers. Email encryption provides assurance to senders and recipients of email that their messages will not be read by others. Users can send and receive secure emails directly from their desktops as easily as regular email without involvement of any hardware, software, configuration, training, or maintenance. The encryption process is so transparent to the sender that they don't need to do anything other than write and send the message as usual. Upon receiving an encrypted message, the recipient completes an easy two-step authentication process through email answerback to verify the recipient's identity. The recipient will then be able to decrypt, view, and read the message using the Voltage Zero Download Messenger.

Real World Scenario

Microsoft Exchange Hosted Services

As email has become a key business tool, many small to medium companies are facing challenges to maintain their email environments and protect their users from external threats and viruses. A lot of businesses have started using the Microsoft Exchange Hosted Filtering to protect their users from spam and email outages and to improve user productivity.

I recently implemented Microsoft Exchange Hosted Filtering Services for a small company that wanted security against viruses and spam. Initially, the client was hesitant to use the Hosted Filtering services because they were concerned about email privacy. However, based on my recommendation the client agreed to implement Microsoft Exchange Hosted Services for a short time.

The client's messaging administrator recently told me my recommendation and solution helped him to minimize virus threats and spam and increase the security of the company's email environment. He verified that none of their users had received any spam email or viruses within the last several months. The client found that Exchange Hosted Filtering provides accurate and reliable spam filtering and virtually no false positives by stopping email-borne threats at the network perimeter.

I have recommended that this firm use the other features of Microsoft Exchange Hosted Services, including continuity, archiving, and encryption. These services will help them to continual access to functionality of anyone of their enterprise's most critical and valuable communication tools.

Planning and Implementing Exchange Server 2007 Antispam Features

Spam is Internet slang that often refers to unwanted commercial email messages. According to recent surveys, spam can account for 80 to 90 percent of the message traffic on the Internet. Some organizations receive more spam than legitimate emails. Spam costs the sender very little to send because advertisers have no operating costs beyond the management of their mailing lists; however, spam costs organizations a significant amount of money and resources in terms of lost productivity and time.

Securing your organization and eliminating spam are not easy tasks. As the messaging environment has become more vulnerable to security threats, many administrators find it an ongoing responsibility to protect their users from spam emails. Fortunately, Exchange 2007 offers antivirus and antispam features that are especially effective when coupled with Microsoft Outlook 2007. By implementing these features, you can significantly decrease the amount of spam that your organization receives.

Several of these features are integrated in Exchange 2007's Edge Transport server role, allowing you to protect messages from spam and viruses at the perimeter network without installing any third-party solutions. By eliminating spam at the perimeter network, you save lots of processing power, network bandwidth, and storage along the mail flow path. The antispam features on the Edge Transport server are known as *filtering agents*, which are frequently updated. These built-in filtering agents in the Edge Transport server protect your internal network by filtering out spam messages before they reach your internal network.

Table 14.1 lists all the built-in antispam filtering agents and features in Exchange 2007. These filters are applied in the order in which they appear in the table. In the next section, we'll look at the configuration of these filters.

TABLE 14.1 Built-in Antispam Filtering Agents and Features in Exchange 2007

Agent/Feature	Details
Connection filtering	Connection filtering checks the IP address of the remote SMTP server, and then uses a variety of IP Block lists, IP Allow lists, IP Block providers, and IP Allow provider services to block or allow connection from the specific IP address.
Sender filtering	Sender filtering uses an administrator-defined list of senders or sender domains to screen inbound messages. The filter compares the sender's MAIL FROM: SMTP command to the administrator-defined list and, based on the result, it will allow, drop, block, delete, or quarantine the message.
Recipient filtering	Recipient filtering compares the recipients' RCPT TO: SMTP command with an administrator-defined list. If the result is true, it will block the message. It also compares recipients with the local recipient directory to determine if the message is addressed to valid recipients. If there is no valid recipient in the local directory, the message can be rejected at the organization's network perimeter.
Sender ID filtering	Sender ID filtering checks whether the sender is spoofed or not by using the IP address of the sending server and the purported responsible address (PRA) of the sender.
Attachment filtering	Attachment filtering allows you to block, drop, or reject a message and its attachment or strip the attachment and allow the message.
Sender reputation	Sender reputation relies on persisted data about the IP address of the sending server to determine what action, if any, to take on an inbound message. This agent collects analytical data from SMTP sessions, message content, Sender ID verification, and general sender behavior and creates a history of sender characteristics. It uses all this knowledge along with sender reputation level (SRL) to determine if the message is coming from spammers or malicious senders. You also can define a threshold period and, based on your configuration and threshold, senders whose SRL exceeds the threshold will be blocked for 48 hours.
IP Reputation Service	The Microsoft IP Reputation Service is an IP Block list that allows administrators to implement and use IP Reputation Service in addition to other real-time block list services. This IP Block list service is offered exclusively to Exchange 2007 customers.

The filtering agents are enabled by default on the Edge Transport server. You also can enable these agents on the Hub Transport server if it is directly accessible from the Internet and you don't want to deploy an Edge Transport server in your environment.

Exercise 14.1 demonstrates how to enable filtering agents on the Hub Transport server.

EXERCISE 14.1

Enabling Filtering Agents on the Hub Transport Server

Follow these steps to enable filtering agents on the Hub Transport server:

1. Log on to the server on which you want to run this command.
2. Click Start ➤ All Programs ➤ Microsoft Exchange Server 2007, and then click on Exchange Management Shell.
3. In the Exchange Management Shell window, navigate to the script folder where you have Exchange Server 2007 scripts by typing **CD C:\Program Files\Microsoft\Exchange Server\Scripts** and then pressing Enter.
4. Install the filtering agents by typing **.\Install-AntispamAgents.ps1**.
5. An information message will indicate that the agents have been installed successfully. Restart Microsoft Exchange Transport Services for the change to take effect.
6. Type **Exit** to close the Exchange Management Shell.

When the script has finished, you can control the antispam agent settings from the Exchange Management Console.

7. Open the Exchange Management Console by clicking on Start ➤ All Programs ➤ Microsoft Exchange Server 2007, and then click on Exchange Management Console.
8. Click on Organization Configuration, and then click on Hub Transport.
9. To see the list of antispam agents, click on the Antispam tab in the Exchange Management Console. Once you verify that all agents are enabled, close the Exchange Management Console.

Connection Filtering

Connection filtering is the first antispam agent that applies to remote SMTP servers when they initiate a connection with the Exchange Server 2007 server. Connection filtering combats spam by determining the IP address of the remote SMTP server, and then comparing the

IP address with the list of IP addresses defined in the IP Allow/Block lists. An IP Allow list is a list of trusted servers for which email communication cannot be disrupted. The IP Allow list contains the servers and domains/IP addresses identified as "good and trustworthy" servers that send legitimate email messages. Conversely, the IP Block list covers servers and domains/IP addresses that are considered "bad and risky" and that propagate spam and viruses that can harm your users and Exchange organization. If the IP address of a remote SMTP server is in the IP Allow list, then the message will be accepted and forwarded to its destination. On the other hand, if the remote SMTP server's IP address is on the IP Block list, the connection from the remote SMTP server will be dropped after `RCPT TO` headers are processed or before Exchange Server 2007 accepts the contents of the message. On the Edge Transport server, IP Allow/Block lists are enabled by default and can be configured using the Exchange Management Shell (EMS) or Exchange Management Console (EMC).

The IP Allow/Block lists are manually configured by administrators. You can either include individual IP addresses or define an IP range to block a network or portion of any network. Alternatively, you can use subscription-based services to get an IP Allow/Block list from a list provider. If the IP address of the SMTP server isn't listed on either the IP Allow list or the IP Block list, the connection-filtering agent will check with the list provider before taking further action.

Subscribing to the IP Allow/Block List services can save you enormous effort, time, resources, and energy, and you won't have to manually configure your lists. (More details about IP Block/Allow list providers are given in the next section.)

You can add an IP address to the IP Block list temporarily by setting an expiration time. This feature is useful if, for example, you begin receiving viruses or spam messages from a partner organization. You know that your partner's messaging server has been compromised, but you don't want to permanently block their messages. This feature allows you to block messages for a specific duration until they resolve the problem. Note that entries on the IP Allow list cannot be scheduled to expire.

IP Allow and IP Block

The following sections describe the steps for configuring IP Allow lists and IP Block lists. First we'll walk you through the steps for performing each of these tasks in the Exchange Management Console. Then we'll show you how to do it in Exchange Managed Shell.

Configuring an IP Allow List

As explained before, the IP Allow list contains the list of trusted servers for which email communication cannot be disrupted. The IP Allow list ensures that a message from specific source servers is not blocked by the Edge Transport server and the Hub Transport server. You can add single IP addresses, IP addresses and subnet masks, and IP ranges from which to allow email messages; however, before adding any IP address to the list, you must obtain the IP address or address ranges of the servers that are allowed to send legitimate email messages.

Exercise 14.2 outlines the instructions to configure an IP Allow list on the Exchange Server 2007 server.

EXERCISE 14.2

Configuring an IP Allow List

Follow these steps to add an IP address to the IP Allow list:

1. Log on to the server on which you want to run this command.
2. Click Start ➢ All Programs ➢ Microsoft Exchange Server 2007, and then click on Exchange Management Console.
3. Click on the Edge Transport server in the Console tree.
4. Click on the Anti-spam tab, right-click on the IP Allow List agent, and then click on Properties.
5. The General tab of the Agent Properties window displays its current status (Enabled or Disabled), the last time the agent's settings were modified, and a brief description of the agent. To add the IP addresses of the SMTP servers that are identified as "good and trustworthy" servers, click the Allowed Addresses tab in the Properties of IP Allow List window.
6. Select the down arrow next to Add, and click on IP Address to add an IP address of an SMTP server that is allowed to send email messages.
7. Type in the IP Address of SMTP server in the IP Address field, as shown below. Note that you can either type in the IP address of a single SMTP server or use the CIDR format to add the IP addresses (for example, 10.10.1.5/24). Click OK to continue.

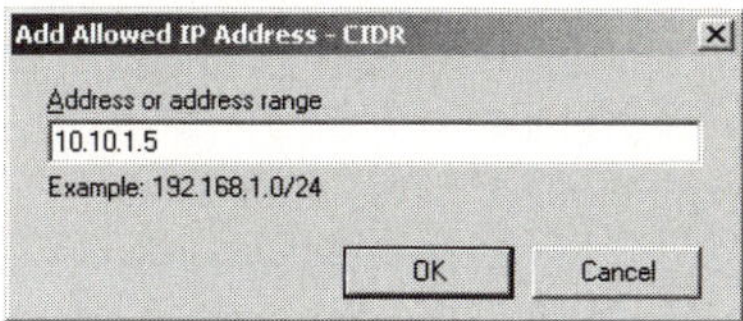

8. The IP address is now shown in the Remote IP Address(es) section of the Allowed Addresses tab in the IP Allow List Properties window, as shown here.

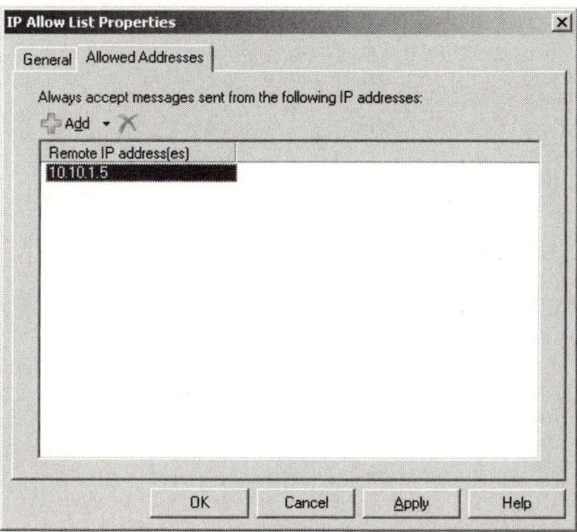

EXERCISE 14.2 *(continued)*

9. Click Apply to save the changes, or click OK to save the changes and close the window.

10. Close the Exchange Management Console.

Follow these steps to add an IP Address and subnet mask to the IP Allow list:

11. Log on to the server on which you want to run this command.

12. Click Start ➢ All Programs ➢ Microsoft Exchange Server 2007, and then click on Exchange Management Console.

13. Click on the Edge Transport in the Console tree.

14. Click on the Antispam tab, right-click on the IP Allow List agent, and then click on Properties.

15. The General tab of the Agent Properties window displays its current status (Enabled or Disabled), the last time the agent's settings were modified, and a brief description of the agent. To add the IP addresses of the SMTP servers that are identified as "good and trustworthy" servers, click the Allowed Addresses tab in the properties of IP Allow List window.

16. Select the down arrow next to Add, and then click on IP and Mask to add the IP address and subnet mask of SMTP servers that are allowed to send email messages, as shown below.

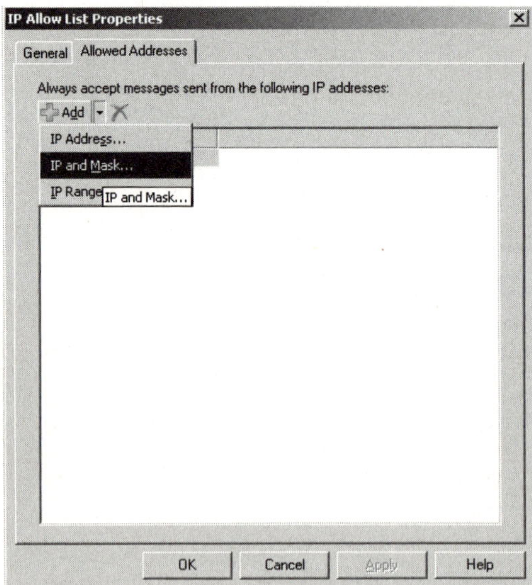

EXERCISE 14.2 *(continued)*

17. Type in the IP Address of SMTP servers in the IP Address field, and then type in the subnet mask information in the IP Mask field to define the range, as shown below. Click OK to continue.

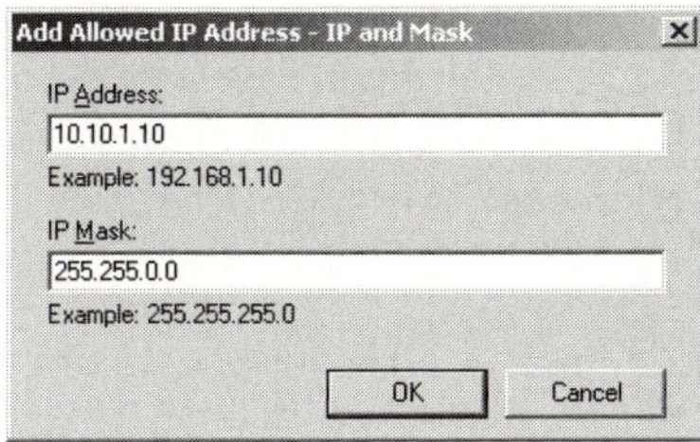

18. The IP address is now shown in the Remote IP Address(es) section of the Allowed Addresses tab in the IP Allow List Properties window, as follows.

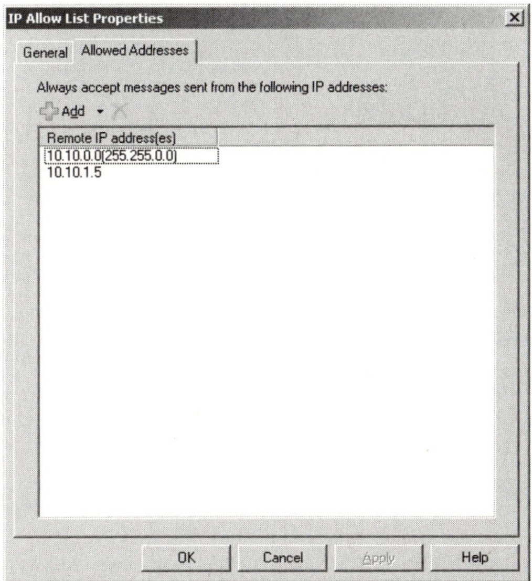

19. Click Apply to save changes, or click OK to save changes and close the window.

20. Close the Exchange Management Console.

Follow these steps to add an IP address range to the IP Allow list:

21. Log on to the server on which you want to run this command.

22. Click Start ➤ All Programs ➤ Microsoft Exchange Server 2007 ➤ Exchange Management Console.

EXERCISE 14.2 *(continued)*

23. Click on the Edge Transport in the Console tree.

24. Click on the Antispam tab, right-click on the IP Allow List agent, and then click on Properties.

25. The General tab of the Agent Properties window displays its current status (Enabled or Disabled), the last time the agent's settings were modified, and a brief description of the agent. To add the IP addresses of the SMTP servers that are identified as "good and trustworthy" servers, click the Allowed Addresses tab in the properties of IP Allow List window.

26. Select the down arrow next to Add, and then click on IP Range to add the IP address range of multiple SMTP servers that are allowed to send email messages, as shown below.

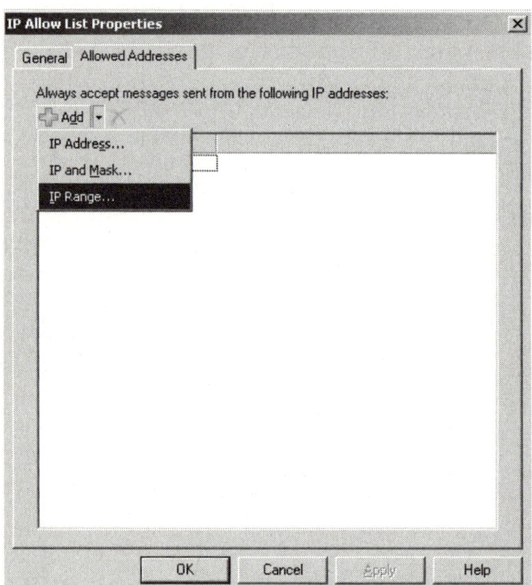

27. Type in the starting and ending IP address range, as shown below. Click OK to continue.

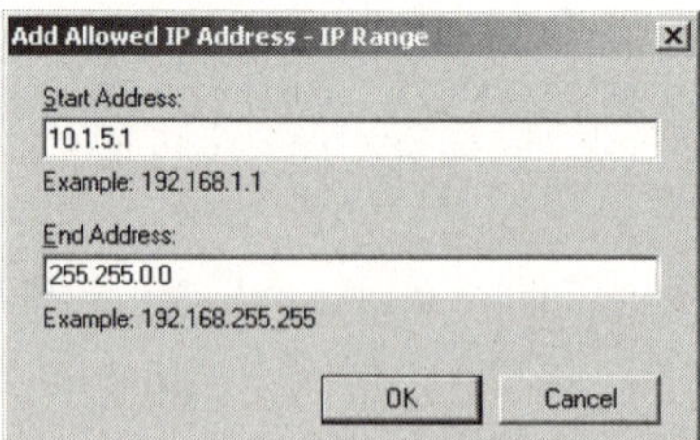

EXERCISE 14.2 *(continued)*

28. The network IP address range is now shown in the Remote IP Address(es) section of the Allowed Addresses tab in the IP Allow List Properties window as follows.

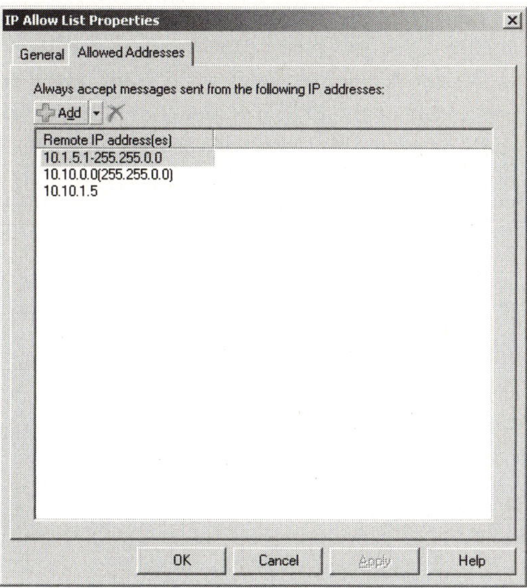

29. Click Apply to save changes, or click OK to save changes and close the window.

30. Close the Exchange Management Console.

Configuring an IP Block List

As explained before, an IP Block list contains the IP addresses of servers and domains/IP addresses that propagate spam and viruses. The servers in the IP Block list are identified as "bad and risky" servers that can harm your users and Exchange organization.

Exercise 14.3 outlines the instructions to configure the IP Block list on the Exchange Server 2007 server.

EXERCISE 14.3

Configuring the IP Block List

To add an IP address to the IP Block list, do the following:

1. Log on to the server on which you want to run this command.

2. Click Start ➢ All Programs ➢ Microsoft Exchange Server 2007, and then click on Exchange Management Console.

EXERCISE 14.3 *(continued)*

3. Click on the Edge Transport in the Console tree.
4. Click on the Anti-spam tab, right-click on the IP Block List agent, and then click on Properties.
5. The General tab of the Agent Properties window displays its current status (Enabled or Disabled), the last time the agent's settings were modified, and a brief description of the agent. To add the IP addresses of the SMTP server that is identified as "bad and risky" server, click the Blocked Addresses tab in the properties of IP Block List window.
6. Select the down arrow next to Add, and click on IP Address to add the IP address of a single SMTP server.
7. In the screen shown below, type in the IP address of an SMTP server in the IP Address field. Note that you can either add the IP address of a single SMTP server or use the CIDR format to add the IP address (for instance, 192.168.1.0/24). In addition to permanently adding an IP address, you can choose to block the IP address only until a specific date and time. Select the expiration settings according to your requirements. Click OK to continue.

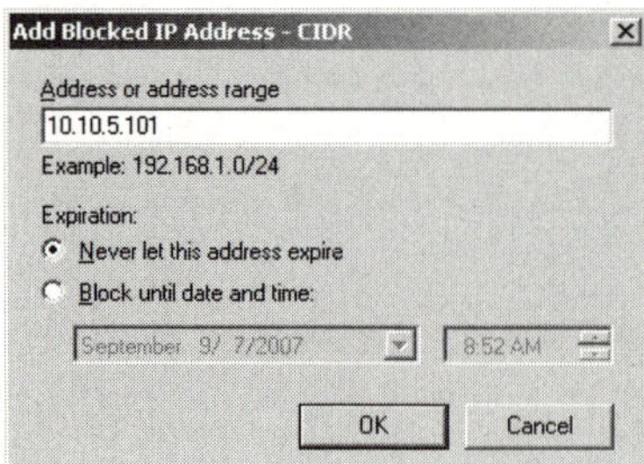

8. The IP address is now shown in the Remote IP Address(es) section of the Blocked Addresses tab in the IP Block List Properties window, as shown below.

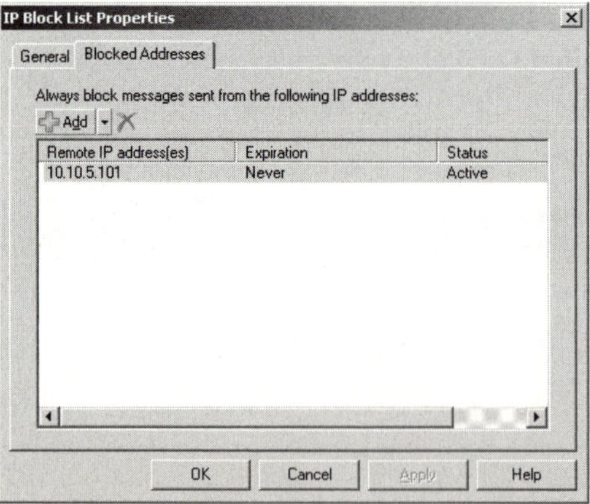

EXERCISE 14.3 *(continued)*

9. Click Apply to save changes, or click OK to save changes and close the window.
10. Close the Exchange Management Console.

Follow these steps to add an IP address and subnet mask in the IP Block list:

11. Log on to the server on which you want to run this command.
12. Click Start ➢ All Programs ➢ Microsoft Exchange Server 2007, and then click on Exchange Management Console.
13. Click on the Edge Transport server in the Console tree.
14. Click on the Anti-spam tab, right-click on the IP Block List agent, and then click on Properties.
15. The General tab of the Agent Properties window displays its current status (Enabled or Disabled), the last time the agent's settings were modified, and a brief description of the agent. To add the IP addresses of the SMTP servers that are identified as "bad and risky" servers, click the Blocked Addresses tab in the Properties of the IP Block List window.
16. Select the down arrow next to Add, and then click on IP and Mask to add the IP address and subnet mask, as shown below.

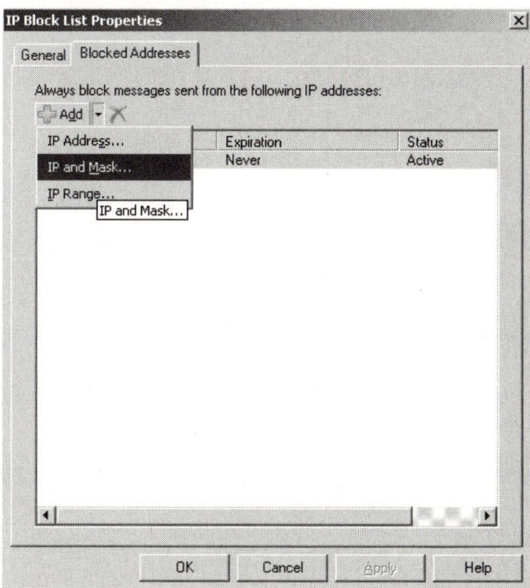

EXERCISE 14.3 *(continued)*

17. Type in the IP address of the SMTP servers in the IP Address field, and then type in the subnet mask information in the IP Mask field to define the range, as shown below. In addition to permanently adding an IP address and subnet mask, you can choose to block the IP address until a specific date and time. Select the expiration settings according to your requirements. Click OK to continue.

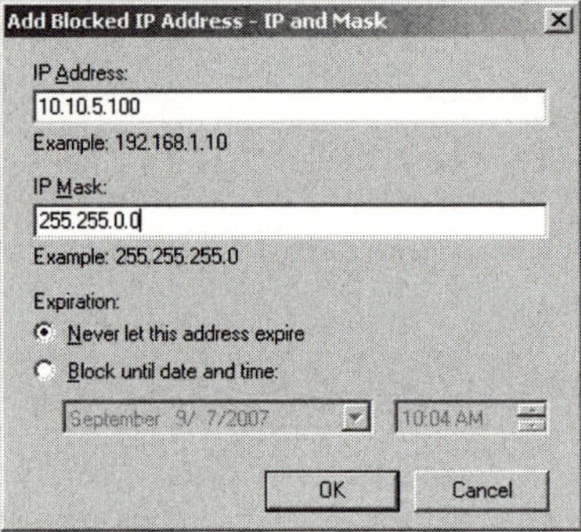

18. The IP address is now shown in the Remote IP Address(es) section of the Blocked Addresses tab in the IP Block List Properties window. Click Apply to save changes, or click OK to save changes and close the window.
19. Close the Exchange Management Console.

Follow these steps to add an IP address range to the IP Block list:

20. Log on to the server on which you want to run this command.
21. Click Start ➤ All Programs ➤ Microsoft Exchange Server 2007, and then click on Exchange Management Console.
22. Select Edge Transport in the Console tree.
23. Click on the Anti-spam tab, right-click on the IP Block List agent, and then click on Properties.
24. The General tab of the Agent Properties window displays its current status (Enabled or Disabled), the last time the agent's settings were modified, and a brief description of the agent. To add the IP addresses of the SMTP servers that are identified as "bad and risky" servers, click the Blocked Addresses tab in the Properties of the IP Block List window.

EXERCISE 14.3 *(continued)*

25. Select the down arrow next to Add, and then click on IP Range to add the IP address range of multiple SMTP servers, as shown below.

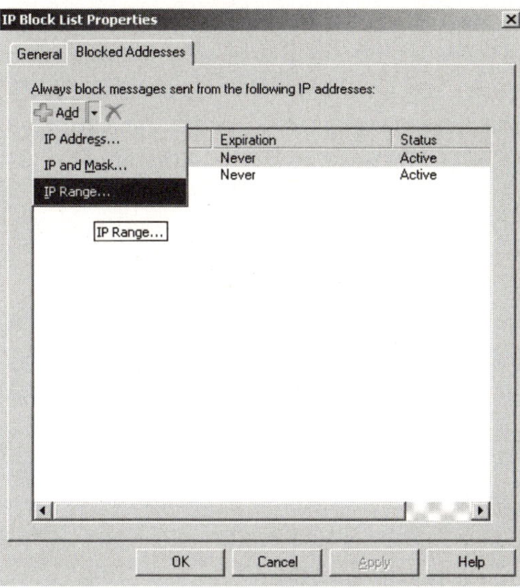

26. Type in the starting and ending IP address range. In addition to permanently adding an IP address range, you can choose to block the range until a specific date and time. Select the expiration settings according to your requirements. Click OK to continue.

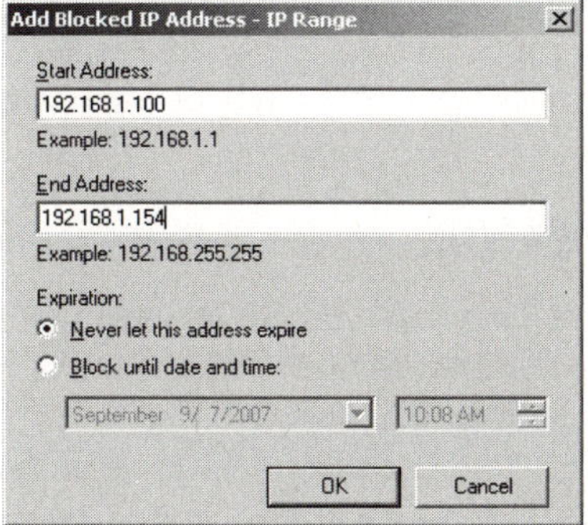

27. The IP address is now shown in the Remote IP Address(es) section of the Blocked Addresses tab in the IP Block List Properties window. Click Apply to save changes, or click OK to save changes and close the window.

28. Close the Exchange Management Console.

Configuring IP Allow and Block Lists from the Exchange Management Shell

As explained in earlier chapters, each task that you do from the Exchange System Console can be done using the Exchange Management Shell. The Exchange Management Shell is extremely powerful, allowing administrators to do almost every single administrative task with an interactive command line. The EMS can use the power of scripting to automate all of the administrator's frequent operations. The EMS and PowerShell replace VBScript, ADSI, and WMI. The EMS enables you to write secure automation scripts that can run locally or remotely. Each shell command in the EMS has its own parameters. To configure IP Allow/Block lists, you can use one of four commands in the EMS (i.e., `Get`, `Add`, `Remove`, and `Set`).

To organize your IP Allow list and IP Block list operations from cmdlet, you can use the `Get`, `Add`, `Remove`, and `Set` cmdlets with the following syntax:

```
Get-IPAllowListConfig
Add-IPAllowListEntry -IPRange 192.168.0.1
Add-IPAllowListEntry -IPRange 192.168.0.1/16 -ExpirationTime 01/24/2007
10:55:00
Remove-IPAllowListEntry -Identity
Set-IPBlockListConfig -InternalMailEnabled $true
```

Real-Time Allow/Block Lists

Spammers invest considerable energy, time, resources, and creativity in finding ways to penetrate our defense mechanisms. No single product, service, tool, or process can eliminate all spam; however, you can use a combination of different products and features to minimize spam and viruses through a multifaceted approach. Most viruses use spam-like tactics to destroy your defense mechanisms by sending legitimate-looking email designed to trick users into opening it. If you can filter out most spam at the perimeter network, you have a better chance of quarantining viruses before they get into your organization.

Using a Real-Time Block List

System administrators often use a real-time Block list (RBL) to catch and delete spam before it reaches the internal network. RBLs contain the IP addresses of SMTP servers that are considered "bad and risky." Because spammers use a variety of techniques to send spam to your organization, it is difficult and time-consuming to maintain an up-to-date RBL by yourself. To save time and energy, you may want to subscribe to an RBL service through Microsoft or your Internet service provider.

When choosing RBL providers, remember that their criteria for adding IP addresses to their databases differ. They also update their databases at different intervals (for instance, Microsoft provides updates twice per week, while other service providers may update more frequently). Do your research before subscribing to an RBL.

Once you subscribe to an RBL, you can configure the RBL provider for Exchange Server 2007 following the instructions in Exercise 14.4.

EXERCISE 14.4

Configuring an Real-Time IP Block List Provider

Here's how to configure the RBL provider:

1. Log on to the server on which you want to run this command.
2. Click Start ➢ All Programs ➢ Microsoft Exchange Server 2007, and then click on Exchange Management Console.
3. Select Edge Transport in the Console tree.
4. Click on the Anti-spam tab, right-click on the IP Block List Providers agent, and then click on Properties.
5. The General tab of the Agent Properties window displays its current status (Enabled or Disabled), the last time the agent's settings were modified, and a brief description of the agent. Click on the Providers tab. Here you can add, edit, or delete entries in the IP Block list providers. Click on Add to add the name of IP Block list provider.
6. Type in the name of the real-time IP Block list provider in the Provider Name field, and then type in the IP address or fully qualified domain name (FQDN) in the Lookup Domain field, as shown below.

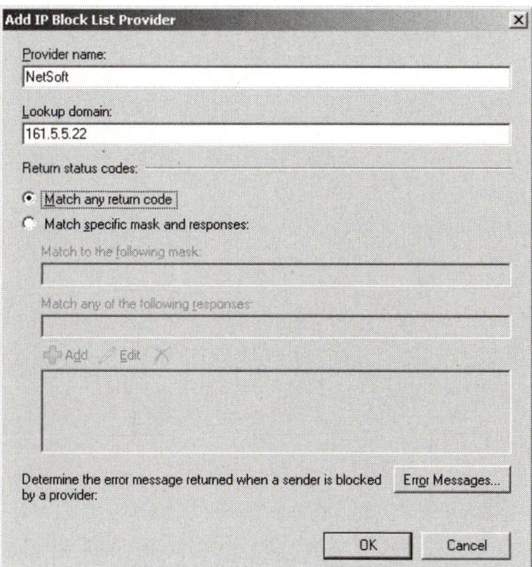

EXERCISE 14.4 *(continued)*

7. Choose Match Any Return Code to identify all delivery status notifications (DSNs) and respond to them accordingly.

8. Choose Match Specific Mask and Responses, and then click on Match to the Following Mask to specify an IP address or subnet mask. To list multiple IP addresses or subnet masks and respond accordingly, choose Match Any of the Following Responses.

9. You can configure a custom error message to blocked senders in the Return Status Codes section. Click on Error Messages, and then click on Custom Error Message, as shown below. Click OK to save the custom error message and close the window.

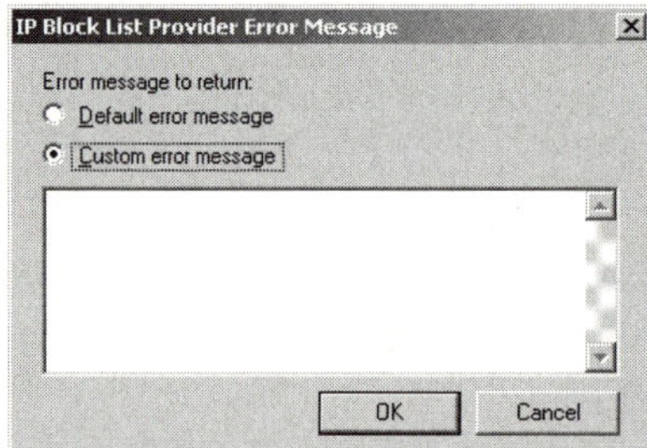

10. The newly created provider entry will be displayed in the IP Block List Providers Properties window shown below. Click Apply to save changes, or click OK to save changes and close the window.

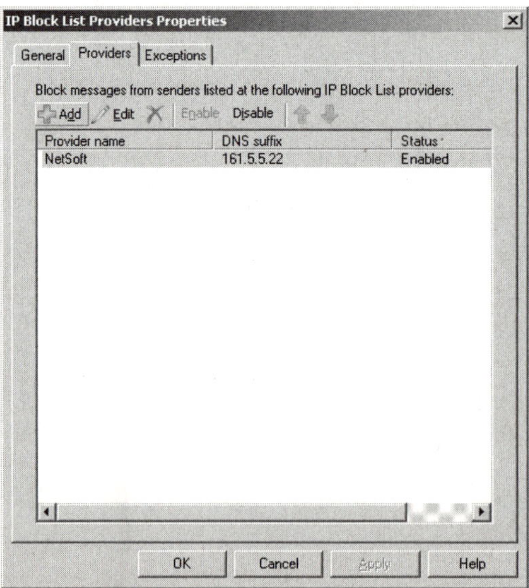

11. Close the Exchange Management Console.

There are few limitations and considerations when it comes to RBLs:

- RBLs cannot completely secure your messaging environment from spam because spammers use a variety of techniques and tools to bypass RBL lists, including spoofing, using open relays, using third-party and offshore servers, and using subject headers. Even with all the tools available to detect these bypassing techniques, it is difficult to eliminate all spam without losing any legitimate emails.
- Some domains/IP addresses may be incorrectly listed on an RBL, blocking legitimate emails. If legitimate domains/IP addresses are mistakenly listed on an RBL, then the organization must contact the RBL provider to be removed from the RBL. Processing such requests can take anywhere from 24 to 72 hours. The list provider also may request that you check the security settings of your SMTP/mail servers because they may be relaying unauthorized emails from other systems.

You can use the Exceptions tab in the RBL Provider screen to define exceptions to the database. Simply add the email addresses of senders to the Do Not Block Messages from the Following E-mail Addresses list.

If a legitimate company is listed in the RBL, you can bypass the RBL by adding the company's IP address to an IP Allow list.

An RBL can significantly reduce spam, but it also can affect the performance of your Edge/Hub Transport servers because they must query and communicate with the RBL provider for each incoming connection. If your organization receives a high volume of emails, you may want to spend some time testing and designing your architecture so that performance of your Edge/Hub Transport server is not negatively affected.

Using a Real-Time Allow List

Real-time IP Allow list providers maintain lists of trusted and legitimate servers for which email communication cannot be disrupted. Exercise 14.5 outlines the instructions to configure real-time IP Allow list providers on Exchange Server 2007.

EXERCISE 14.5

Configuring a Real-Time IP Allow List Provider

To configure a real-time IP Allow List provider, follow these steps:

1. Log on to the server on which you want to run this command.
2. Click Start ➢ All Programs ➢ Microsoft Exchange Server 2007, and then click on Exchange Management Console.

EXERCISE 14.5 *(continued)*

3. Select Edge Transport in the Console tree.
4. Click on the Anti-spam tab, right-click on the IP Allow List Providers agent, and then click on Properties.
5. The General tab of the Agent Properties window displays its current status (Enabled or Disabled), the last time the agent's settings were modified, and a brief description of the agent. Click on the Providers tab to add, edit, or delete entries in the IP Allow List Providers list. Click on Add to add the name of IP Allow List provider.
6. As shown below, type in the name of the IP Allow list provider in the Provider Name field, and then type in the IP address or fully qualified domain name (FQDN) in the Lookup Domain field.

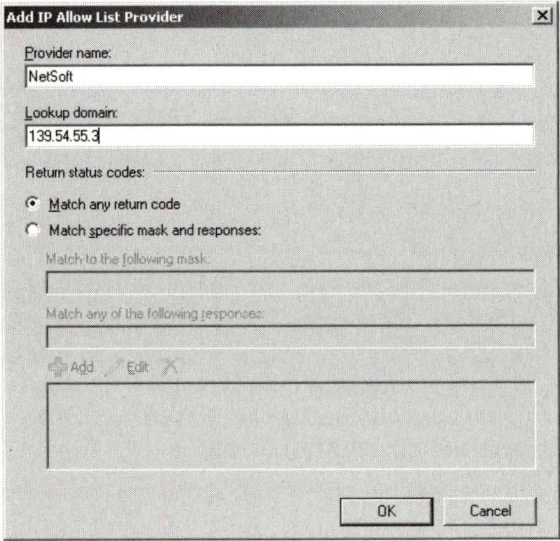

7. Choose Match Any Return Code to identify all delivery status notifications (DSNs) and respond to them accordingly.
8. Choose Match Specific Mask and Responses, and then click on Match to the Following Mask to specify an IP address or subnet mask. To list multiple IP addresses or subnet masks and respond accordingly, choose Match Any of the Following Responses. Click OK to save the custom error message and close the window.
9. The newly created provider entry will be displayed in the IP Allow List Providers window. Click Apply to save changes, or click OK to save changes and close the window.
10. Close the Exchange Management Console.

Configuring Real-Time Allow and Block Lists from the Exchange Management Shell

To configure your real-time Allow list and real-time Block list providers via cmdlet, you can use the `Get`, `Add`, `Test`, `Remove`, and `Set` cmdlets with the following syntax:

```
Get-IPAllowListProvider
Get-IPBlockListProvider
Add-IPAllowListProvider -Identity Providername
Add-IPBlockListProvider -Identity Providername
Test-IPAllowListProvider -Identity Providername -Server Servername
Test-IPBlockListProvider -Identity Providername -Server Servername
Remove-IPAllowListProvider -Identity Providername
Remove-IPBlockListProvider -Identity Providername
```

Sender and Recipient Filtering

Sender- and recipient-filtering agents apply to remote email messages once they pass through the connection-filtering agent. These agents check the spam confidence level (SCL) of the message and, if allowed, the message will be passed on to the Sender ID Filtering agent. By default both agents are enabled on the Edge Transport server and can be configured using the Exchange Management Shell or Exchange Management Console.

Sender Filtering

Sender filtering is the second antispam agent that compares remote servers or the email address of a sender against the list of email addresses and domains you have specified under the Sender Filtering properties.

Because it is common to find that your recipients are being attacked by some specific external user or domain, sender filtering, is very helpful if you want to block email from specific email addresses, domains, and subdomains. When the agent on your Edge/Hub Transport server receives messages from a blocked email address or domain, the sender-filtering agent returns the default response of "554 5.1.0 Sender Denied" to the sender. Sender filtering also applies to email messages received from the Internet for delivery to your Exchange recipient.

Sender filtering also allows you to stamp messages instead of rejecting them. If you decide to do so, the metadata of the email message will be updated to reflect your decision, indicating that the message was sent by a sender/domain on the block list. During email-message processing, the content filter will use the stamp to calculate the SCL of the message. The sender reputation filter agent will use the SCL rating during the development of the sender reputation level.

The sender-filtering agent is enabled by default and can be configured using the EMC or EMS. If you decide to disable sender filtering, you can do so using the EMC and the EMS. Disabling sender filtering using the EMC is simple. You can just right-click on the agent icon and then select Disable in the Action pane. To disable sender filtering using the EMS, run the `set-SenderFilterConfig -Enabled $false` command.

Exercise 14.5 outlines the instructions to configure sender filtering on the Exchange Server 2007 server. Note that the procedure described is applied only to the local system. If you are running more than one Edge Transport server in your organization, then follow the procedure on your other Edge Transport servers to maintain consistency.

EXERCISE 14.6

Configuring Sender Filtering

Use the following steps to configure sender filtering:

1. Log on to the server on which you want to run this command.
2. Click Start ➢ All Programs ➢ Microsoft Exchange Server 2007, and then click on Exchange Management Console.
3. Select Edge Transport in the Console tree.
4. Click on the Anti-spam tab, right-click on the sender-filtering agent, and then click on Properties.
5. The General tab of the Agent Properties window displays its current status (Enabled or Disabled), the last time the agent's settings were modified, and a brief description of the agent. Click on the Blocked Senders tab to add, edit, or delete entries in the Blocked Senders list.
6. At the bottom of the window shown below, choose the Block Messages from Blank Senders option. This option blocks messages that do not specify the sender's email address. (A common technique of spammers is to hide the sender address or not specify an email address in the sender field.) Click on Add.

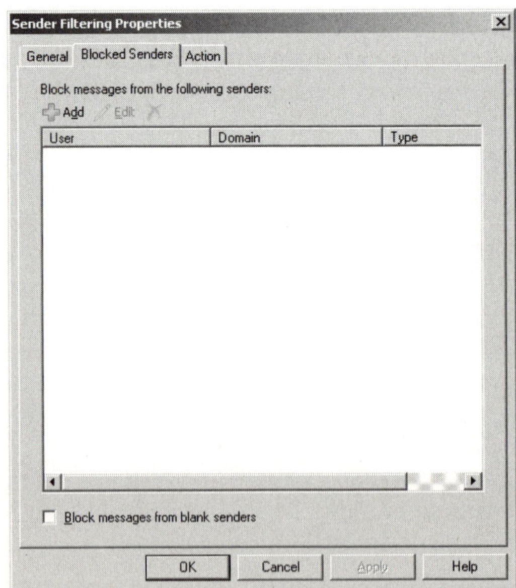

EXERCISE 14.6 *(continued)*

7. In the Add Blocked Senders dialog box, under Individual E-mail Address, type in the email address of a sender (`rawlinson@externaldomain.com` in this example), as shown below, and then click OK to continue. You also can choose Domain to block particular domains and subdomains.

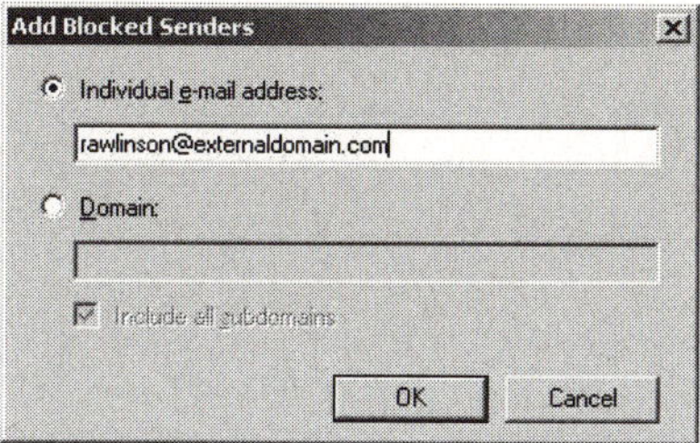

8. On the Action tab, ensure that Reject Message is selected. Alternatively, you can choose to stamp messages with "Blocked Sender" and continue processing instead of rejecting the messages.

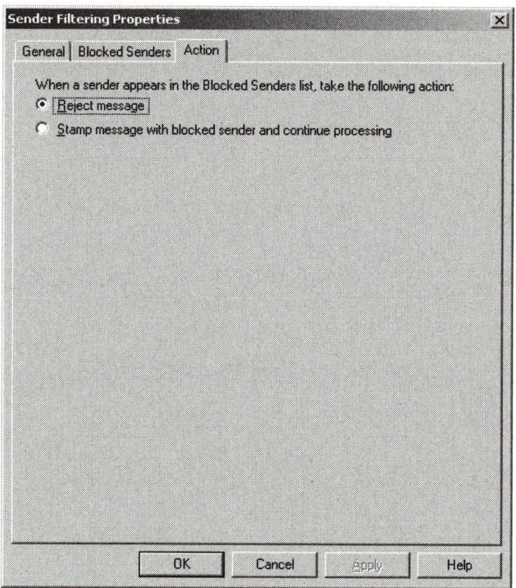

9. Click Apply to save changes, or click OK to save changes and close the window.

10. Close the Exchange Management Console.

Sender filtering allows you to use the asterisk (*) wildcard to block multiple email addresses. For example, you can add `*@externalcompany.com` to the Individual Email Address field to block all emails from `externalcompany.com`. You can get the same result by adding `externalcompany.com` to the Domain field.

Sender filtering overrides the Outlook Safe Senders list, which means that your Edge Server will reject/stamp the message even if your users/recipients have included the sender on an Outlook Safe Senders list.

Once you configure sender filtering, the next step is to test your changes. Exercise 14.7 outlines the steps to test sender filtering on the Exchange Server 2007.

EXERCISE 14.7

Testing Sender Filtering

To test sender filtering, follow these steps:

1. Log on to the server on which you want to run this command.
2. Click Start ➤ Run, type **cmd.exe**, then press Enter or click OK.
3. In the command-prompt windows, type **telnet YourExchangeServername 25,** and then press Enter.
4. Type **EHLO**, and then press Enter.
5. Type **Mail From: mcitp.user2@externaldomain.com**, and then press Enter. Confirm that you receive a "sender denied" message.
6. Type **Quit** to exit, and then press Enter.
7. Type **Exit** to close the command prompt and return to the Windows Shell.

Recipient Filtering

Emails that are not rejected by sender filtering are handed over to the recipient-filtering agent. Recipient filtering is similar to sender filtering, except it is designed for your Exchange organization and is based on the recipient address instead of sender address. With recipient filtering you can block email messages from the Internet to specific internal email addresses. This option is extremely helpful in stopping spam to specific email accounts, such as those that are no longer active in your organization, or commonly named email accounts (such as `info@mycompany.com` or `sales@mycompany.com`).

Recipient filtering checks the recipient of the email against the Blocked Recipient list. If the recipient is not listed, the email is handed over to the next agent. If the Edge Transport server receives an email message addressed to a recipient that is either listed on the Blocked Recipient list or not present in the Global Address List, a "550 5.1.1 User unknown SMTP" session error will be returned to the sender of the message.

Recipient filtering is enabled by default and can be configured using the Exchange Management Console or Exchange Management Shell. If you decide to disable recipient filtering, you can do so by using the EMC and the EMS. Disabling recipient filtering using the EMC is simple. Right-click on the agent icon in the Action pane and select Disable. To disable recipient filtering using the EMS, run the `set-RecipientFilterConfig -Enabled $false` command.

Exercise 14.8 outlines the instructions to configure recipient filtering on the Exchange Server 2007 server. Note that the procedure described in the exercise applies only to the local system. If you are running more than one Edge Transport server in your organization, follow the procedure on your other Edge Transport servers to maintain consistency.

EXERCISE 14.8

Configuring Recipient Filtering

Use the following steps to configure recipient filtering:

1. Log on to the server on which you want to run this command.
2. Click Start ➢ All Programs ➢ Microsoft Exchange Server 2007, and then click on Exchange Management Console.
3. Select Edge Transport in the Console tree.
4. Click on the Anti-spam tab, right-click on the recipient-filtering agent, and then click on Properties.
5. The General tab of the Agent Properties window displays its current status (Enabled or Disabled), the last time the agent's settings were modified, and a brief description of the agent. Click on the Blocked Recipient tab to add, edit, or delete entries in the Blocked Recipient list.

EXERCISE 14.8 *(continued)*

6. Click on Block the Following Recipients. In the Block the Following Recipients text box, type **mcitp.baduser@exchange2007.com** and then click Add to continue. Click Add again to add more recipients. Spammers often send emails to common names (such as Michelle, Cindy, Lisa, John, Jason, James, etc.). To address the "common recipient" spamming technique, you can block messages that are sent to recipients not listed in your Global Address List. As shown below, simply check the box to block messages sent to recipients not listed in the Global Address List.

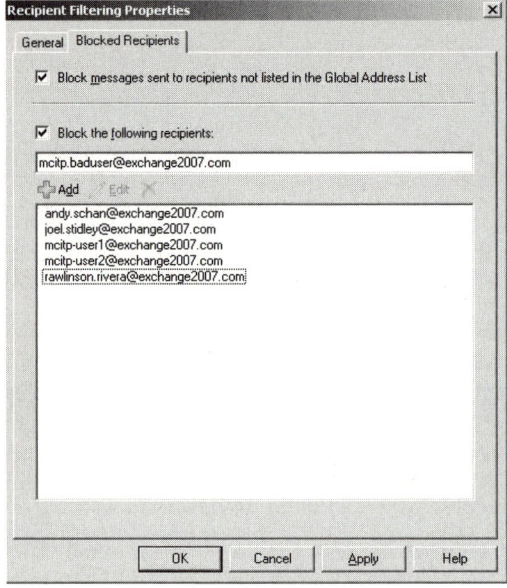

7. Click Apply to save changes, or click OK to save changes and close the window.
8. Close the Exchange Management Console.

Any email addresses entered on the Blocked Recipients list will be blocked only for senders who are located outside of your organization or who are sending emails from the Internet. Internal users will still be able to send messages to recipients listed in the Blocked Recipient list. Recipient filtering allows you to enter up to 800 email addresses.

Once you configure recipient filtering, the next step is to test your changes. Exercise 14.9 outlines the steps to test recipient filtering on the Exchange Server 2007.

EXERCISE 14.9

Testing Recipient Filtering

Follow these steps to test your recipient filtering:

1. Log on to the server on which you want to run this command.
2. Click Start ➢ Run then type **cmd.exe**. Press Enter or click OK.
3. In the command-prompt window, type **telnet YourExchangeServername 25,** and then press Enter.
4. Type **EHLO** and then press Enter.
5. Type **Mail From: mcitp.user1@externaldomain.com** and then press Enter.
6. Type **Rcpt To: mcitp.user2@yourdomain.com** and then press Enter. Confirm that you receive a "user unknown" message.
7. Type **Quit** to exit, and then press Enter.
8. Type **Exit** to close the command prompt and return to the Windows shell.

The Edge Transport server receives the recipient list from the Active Directory. Because recipient filtering can only check recipients in the Global Address List, you must configure the EdgeSync process between the Active Directory Application Mode (ADAM) and Active Directory forest for recipient lookup.

Sender ID Filtering

If an email message has not been rejected by sender filtering and recipient filtering, it goes to sender ID filtering. Sender ID filtering counters domain spoofing and phishing schemes by ensuring that an email message is sent from an SMTP server that is authorized to send email messages for a specific domain. Recipient servers accomplish this by extracting the email address in the From field of the message headers and checking the address of the sending email server against a list of registered servers that the domain owner has authorized to send emails. When configured correctly, sender ID filtering can help you accurately eliminate malicious email without additional analysis of its content. All verification is performed automatically by the Edge Transport server or Hub Transport server before the message is delivered to the recipient. Once the sender ID has been recognized and authenticated, the email message is delivered to other filters for additional processing.

Sender Policy Framework (SPF) Records

To configure sender ID filtering, you must first understand the Sender Policy Framework (SPF) records. SPF records work with sender ID filtering to stop malicious emails. The SPF record is a piece of information on the DNS servers that is required by sender ID filtering to determine whether the email message was sent by an authorized server for the specified domain. In simple terms, an SPF record is a listing of authorized SMTP servers for a particular domain or set of domains in the DNS database. Publishing an SPF record in the public DNS allows the recipient SMTP servers to perform a reverse Mail Exchanger (MX) lookup by cross-referencing the IP addresses of the authorized SMTP servers against that organization's DNS entry for their domain.

SPF records can be in different formats. Here are few examples:

mcitpdomain.com IN TXT "v=spf1 mx -all" This indicates that all servers identified by an MX record for the mcitpdomain.com domain are allowed to send email for that domain.

v=spf1 mx ip4:192.168.10.10 –all This SPF record indicates that server 192.168.10.10 identified by an MX record is allowed to send email for your domain.

MAIL IN TXT "v=spf1 a -all" This SPF record indicates that server MAIL is allowed to send email for your domain.

mcitpdomain.com IN TXT "v=spf1 ip4:192.168.10.10 -all" This SPF record indicates that a server with IP address 192.168.10.10 is allowed to send email for the `mcitpdomain.com` domain.

v=spf1 mx mx:mail1.mcitpdomain.com mx:mail2.mcitpdomain.com mx:mail3.mcitpdomain .com -all This SPF record for `mcitpdomain.com` uses an MX record to identify three mail servers (mail1, mail2, and mail3) that are authorized to send emails from the `mcitpdomain .com` domain.

Creating a Sender Policy Framework (SPF) Record

To create SPF records, you can use Microsoft's four-step wizard. If you want to use the advanced features of SPF format, you may need to manually edit the SPF record created by the wizard.

Exercise 14.10 outlines the steps to create an SPF record.

EXERCISE 14.10

Creating an SPF Record

1. The wizard is found online at `http://www.microsoft.com/mscorp/safety/content/technologies/senderid/wizard/`.
2. At Identify Your Domain, enter the domain name for which you want to create a new SPF record (in this example, `mcitpdomain.com`).
3. At Display Published DNS Records, you'll see that the wizard checked the DNS for information about `mcitpdomain.com`, including existing SPF, MX, and A records. If an SPF record was found, you can verify its contents and use the remaining steps of the wizard to modify the record. If no SPF record was found, you can use information from the domain's MX and A records to create a new SPF record.

EXERCISE 14.10

4. At Create SPF Record, the wizard prompts you to choose proper options to create SPF records. This step is divided into different sections. Your choices are as follows:

   No Mail Is Sent from Domain: Choose this option if the domain does not send email.

   Domain's Inbound Servers May Send Mail: Choose this option if your inbound mail servers are also used to send outbound mail.

   All Addresses Listed in A Records May Send Mail: If all the IP addresses listed in A records for your domain in DNS are outbound mail servers, you should include this option in your new SPF record. You also can enter any additional IP addresses you wish to add to your SPF record.

   All PTR Records Resolve to Outbound Email Servers: Choose this option if all reverse DNS Pointer records (PTR) resolve to the domain's outbound email servers.

   Outsourced Domains: Choose this option if domain's outbound email is routed through another domain (outsourced).

   Does Your Domain Send Email from Any IP Addresses That Are Not Identified in the Above Sections? Choose appropriate settings for your environment.

5. At Generate SPF Record, the wizard will provide you with the generated SPF records.

The record example for `mcitpdomain.com` looks like this:

```
v=spf1 mx mx:mail1.mcitpdomain.com mx:mail2.mcitpdomain.com
mx:mail3.mcitpdomain.com -all
```

Where:

`v=spf1` designates that this is an SPF record and it is version 1.

`mx mx:mail1.mcitpdomain.com mx:mail2.mcitpdomain.com mx:mail3.mcitpdomain.com` signifies that mail1, mail2, and mail3 are authorized to send and receive email for `mcitpdomain.com`.

`-all` designates that no one besides the IP addresses in `mcitpdomain.com`'s MX records are authorized to send email.

Configuring Sender ID Filtering

Sender ID filtering is enabled by default and can be configured using the Exchange Management Console or Exchange Management Shell. You also can disable sender ID filtering by using the EMC and the EMS. Disabling sender ID filtering using the EMC is simple. Right-click on the agent icon in the Action pane, and then select Disable. To disable sender ID filtering using the EMS, run the `set-SenderIDFilterConfig -Enabled $false` command.

The following exercise outlines the steps to configure sender ID filtering on the Exchange Server 2007 server. Note that the procedure described in the following section applies only to the local system. If you are running more than one Edge Transport server in your organization, follow the procedure on your other Edge Transport servers to maintain consistency.

EXERCISE 14.11

Configuring the Sender ID Filtering Agent

To configure the sender ID filtering agent, follow these steps:

1. Log on to the server on which you want to run this command.
2. Click Start ➢ All Programs ➢ Microsoft Exchange Server 2007, and then click on Exchange Management Console.
3. Select Edge Transport in the Console tree.
4. Click on the Antispam tab, right-click on the Sender ID agent, and then click on Properties.
5. Click on the Action tab. As shown below, you can configure sender ID filtering to reject a message, delete a message, or stamp a message with the sender ID result and continue processing.

   Choose Reject Message if you want to reject the message and send an error response to the sending server.

   Choose Delete Message if you want to delete the message without notifying the sender.

   Choose Stamp Message with Sender ID Result and Continue Processing if you are planning to append certain information to the message headers for the content-filtering agent. This information, often referred to as metadata, is used by the content filter to create the SCL.

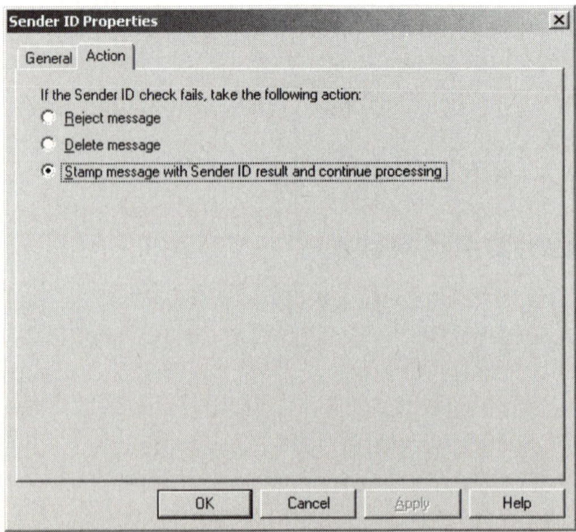

EXERCISE 14.11 *(continued)*

6. Click OK to continue.
7. Close the Exchange Management Console.

How Sender ID Filtering Works

To use sender ID filtering, the sender organization must create a Sender Policy Framework records and publish it as a DNS host record on the sender's public DNS servers. The published SPF record is a single TXT record in the public DNS database that holds the IP address information of the SMTP servers that are allowed to send emails for that domain. The receiving Exchange servers check the SPF records to confirm that the sending SMTP server is on the list of authorized servers for that particular domain. If the sending SMTP server is not listed, then the receiving Exchange server will assume the email is coming from an unauthorized server and either drop the message or forward it with additional header information.

In general, sender ID filtering works as follows:

1. The message is received by the Exchange Edge Transport server.
2. The Edge Transport server checks the IP address of the sending SMTP server and queries the DNS for the SPF record.
3. If the SPF record matches the sender SMTP server, the Edge Transport server forwards the message to the next filter for additional processing or sends it to the recipient, depending on how your environment is configured.
4. If the SPF record does not match the sender SMTP server, the Edge Transport server will drop the message or forward it with additional header information.

We highly recommend that you create an SPF record for your domain. Doing so helps protect your domain and makes it difficult for spammers to forge your domain name and use it to spam to other organizations.

Content Filtering

Content filtering is another antispam agent that blocks or quarantines messages based on their content, regardless of the originating SMTP servers. Content filtering analyzes the content of all the emails received by your Edge Transport server to evaluate whether the messages are spam. It is useful for identifying messages containing content deemed unacceptable to your organization, such as advertisements or sexually explicit remarks.

Content filtering checks emails for specific content and keywords. Depending on your organizational requirements, the filter can block the email message or send it to quarantine. In either case, when the Edge/Hub Transport server receives messages with content or phrases included on a list of blocked keywords, the content-filtering agent returns a default response message of "550 5.7.1 Message rejected due to content restrictions" to the sender. You can customize this message by using the `Set-ContentFilterConfig` command in the Exchange Management Shell.

Content filtering is considered the next generation of the Intelligent Message Filter (IMF, version 3), which is based on Microsoft's SmartScreen Filter technology (a proprietary message-analyzing filter). The content filter, developed based on evaluations of millions of messages, can distinguish between spam and legitimate email. The filter is updated periodically through Microsoft Software Update Services.

When the Edge Transport server with content filtering enabled receives an email, it evaluates the content of the email and assigns it an overall rating based on the probability that the message is spam. This rating is generally referred to as the SCL, and it is stored as an email message property (actually a MAPI property). Because the rating is saved as a property of the email message, it will persist with the email message when it is sent to other Exchange servers. The SCL rating is a numerical value between zero and nine (with zero indicating that the message is highly unlikely to be spam and nine meaning that the message is very likely to be spam). Depending on how you configure your environment and the threshold value of the SCL, you can silently delete, reject, or quarantine the message to a specified mailbox.

Content filtering includes the following options:

Block or Allow Messages: Allows you to define a list of customized words and phrases and block or allow messages based on that list. You can create a list of words or phrases that will not be blocked no matter what the SCL rating of the particular message is. You also can create a list of words or phrases that will be blocked no matter what the message's SCL rating is.

Allow Exceptions: You can define an exceptional recipient list so that the content-filtering agent excludes the recipients in the list and delivers messages to the recipients.

Specify Actions: You can configure the SCL threshold and threshold actions. You can choose to delete, reject, or quarantine messages for which the SCL value is higher than your specified settings.

If an email's SCL rating is equal to the SCL delete threshold, the message will be deleted without notifying the sending server. If an email's SCL is equal to the SCL reject threshold, the message will be deleted and a rejection response of "550 5.7.1 Message rejected due to content restrictions" will be returned to the sending server. If an email's SCL rating is equal to the SCL quarantine threshold, the message will be sent to the email address specified in the Quarantine mailbox email address field.

In general, configuring the content filter on an Edge Transport server involves seven steps:

1. Enable the content-filtering agent.
2. Create a mailbox for quarantined messages.
3. Designate a quarantine mailbox.
4. Configure allow and block keywords and phrases.
5. Configure the exceptional recipient list.
6. Specify actions and configure SCL threshold values.
7. Specify recipient and sender exceptions.

These steps are detailed in the following sections.

Step 1: Enabling the Content-Filtering Agent

The content-filtering agent is enabled by default and can be configured using the Exchange Management Console or Exchange Management Shell. As noted earlier, you can disable content filtering using the EMC and EMS.

The following exercise outlines the steps to configure content filtering on Exchange Server 2007 servers. Note that the procedure described in the following section is applied only to the local system. If you are running more than one Edge Transport server in your organization, follow the procedure on your other Edge Transport servers to maintain consistency.

EXERCISE 14.12

Configuring the Content-Filtering Agent

Use the following steps to configure the content-filtering agent:

1. Log on to the server on which you want to run this command.
2. Click Start ➤ All Programs ➤ Microsoft Exchange Server 2007, and then click on Exchange Management Console.
3. Select Edge Transport in the Console tree.
4. Click on the Anti-spam tab, right-click on the content-filtering agent, and then click on Enable or Disable.
5. Close the Exchange Management Console.

To disable the content-filtering agent using the Exchange Management Shell, run the `set-ContentFilterConfig -Enabled $false` command.

Step 2: Creating a Quarantine Mailbox

The second step in the process is to create a mailbox called Quarantined Messages and a corresponding Active Directory user account. This mailbox will store messages on which an action of "quarantine" was taken. You may want to consider creating multiple quarantine mailboxes solely for each individual Edge Transport server. Generally, it is recommended to have one quarantine mailbox per Edge Transport server. Although this may create more work for Exchange system administrators, it will decrease the load on one Mailbox server. It's also extremely helpful if you have to troubleshoot configurations and quarantine issues between the Edge Transport servers. Depending on how many messages are received by your Exchange organization and how many recipients you have in your Exchange organization, configure a reasonable quota (designate a quota based on your organization's policies, practices, and email volume) for this mailbox because the spam quarantine can grow substantially. You also may want to set up delegation if you're going to open the mailbox as an additional mailbox by using your primary mailbox account.

The following exercise outlines the steps to create and configure the quarantine mailbox.

EXERCISE 14.13

Creating a Quarantine Mailbox

Follow these steps to create and configure the quarantine mailbox:

1. Log on to the server on which you want to run this command.
2. Click Start ➢ All Programs ➢ Microsoft Exchange Server 2007, and then click on Exchange Management Console.
3. In the Console tree, expand Recipient Configuration, and then click Mailbox.
4. Right-click on the mailbox, and then click New Mailbox.
5. Click Next to accept the default option of User Mailbox.
6. Click Next to accept the default option of New User.
7. Beside Organizational Unit, click Browse. In the Select Organizational Unit dialog box, expand an appropriate OU where you would like to keep this mailbox. Click OK.
8. Enter the following information for the new user, and then click OK:

   First name: Quarantine

   Last name: Mailbox

   User logon name (User Principal Name): Quarantine

   Password: Pa$$w0rd
9. Click Next.

EXERCISE 14.13 *(continued)*

10. Click Next again to accept the default mailbox settings.
11. Read the summary, and then click New to create the Active Directory user and mailbox.
12. Click Finish to continue.
13. Close the Exchange Management Console.

Step 3: Designating the Quarantine Mailbox

The third step in the process is to designate the quarantine mailbox that will store the messages that exceed the SCL quarantine threshold value of the content filter. You must designate and define the quarantine mailbox before you configure content filtering in your environment, so that the messages marked for quarantine are sent to a quarantine mailbox where they can be reviewed later. You can configure the quarantine mailbox only in the EMS on an Edge Transport server using the `Set-ContentFilterConfig` command.

The following exercise outlines the steps to designate the quarantine mailbox.

EXERCISE 14.14

Designating the Quarantine Mailbox

Follow these steps to designate the quarantine mailbox:

1. Log on to the Edge Transport server on which you want to run this command.
2. Click Start ➢ All Programs ➢ Microsoft Exchange Server 2007, and then click on Exchange Management Shell.
3. Type **Set-ContentFilterConfig –QuarantineMailbox quarantine@mycompany.com**, as shown below.

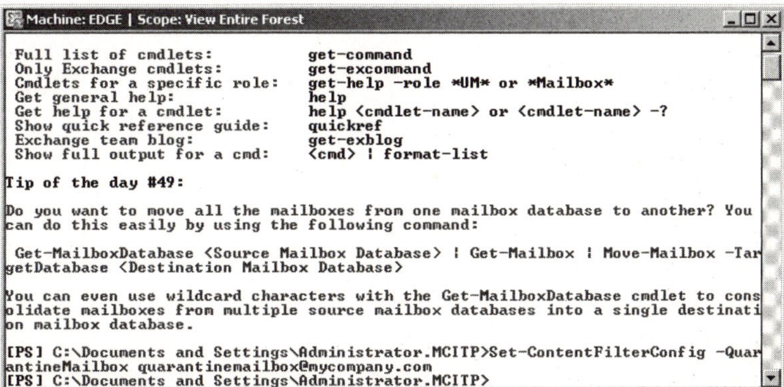

4. Type **Exit** to exit the EMS.

Step 4: Configuring Allow and Block for Keywords and Phrases

Content filtering allows you to define keywords or phrases that must not be blocked on the Exchange 2007 Edge Transport server. These are commonly used words specific to certain professions and industries.

Exercise 14.15 outlines the steps to create and configure content filtering to allow keywords and phrases.

EXERCISE 14.15

Configuring to Allow Keywords and Phrases

Follow these steps to allow keywords and phrases:

1. Log on to the server on which you want to run this command.
2. Click Start ➢ All Programs ➢ Microsoft Exchange Server 2007, and then click on Exchange Management Console.
3. Select Edge Transport in the Console tree.
4. Click on the Anti-spam tab, right-click on the content-filtering agent, and then click on Properties.
5. The General tab of the Agent Properties window displays its current status (Enabled or Disabled), the last time the agent's settings were modified, and a brief description of the agent. Click on the Custom Words tab to add, edit, or delete entries. On the Custom Words tab, in the Message Containing These Words or Phrases Will Not Be Blocked box, type **Information Technology** and then click Add, as shown below. Repeat the procedure to add more words that are common to your business.

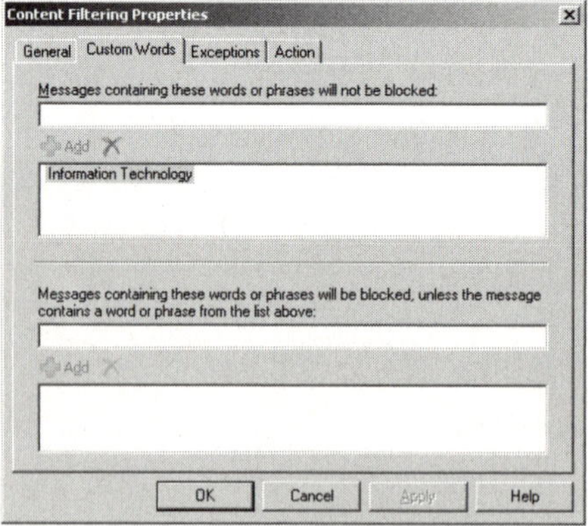

6. To remove an entry, highlight it and click Delete.
7. Click Apply to save your changes or OK to save changes and close the Content Filtering dialog box.
8. Close the EMC.

Content filtering also allows you to define keywords or phrases to be blocked on the Exchange 2007 Edge Transport server. For example, you may want to include commonly used words that are specific to "adult" industries or other forms of spam. Messages containing a blocked word or phrase are given an SCL score of nine, and they will either be deleted or quarantined.

The following exercise outlines the instructions to create and configure content filtering to block keywords and phrases.

EXERCISE 14.16

Configuring to Block Keywords and Phrases

Use the following steps to block keywords and phrases:

1. Log on to the server on which you want to run this command.
2. Click Start ➤ All Programs ➤ Microsoft Exchange Server 2007, and then click on Exchange Management Console.
3. Select Edge Transport in the Console tree.
4. Click on the Anti-spam tab, right-click on the content-filtering agent, and then click on Properties.
5. The General tab of the Agent Properties window displays its current status (Enabled or Disabled), the last time the agent's settings were modified, and a brief description of the agent. Click on the Custom Words tab to add, edit, or delete entries. On the Custom Words tab, in the Message Containing These Words or Phrases Will be Blocked, Unless the Message Contains a Word or Phrase from the List Above box, type **Sex** and then click Add, as shown below. Repeat the procedure to add more words to the list.

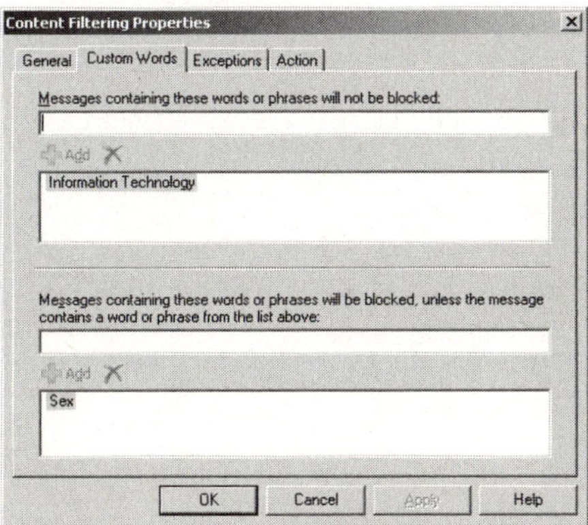

6. To remove an entry, highlight it and click Delete.
7. Click Apply to save your changes, or OK to save changes and close the Content Filtering dialog box.
8. Close the EMC.

Step 5: Configuring the Exceptional List

The next step is to configure the Exceptional list. In the Content Filtering Properties window, the Exceptions tab defines exceptions so that messages to certain recipients are excluded from content filtering. For example, a company might include the IT, Sales, Help Desk, and Information mailboxes because employees in those departments might need to view these messages to perform their duties. The only drawback to the Exceptional list is that it is restricted to a maximum of 100 entries.

The following exercise outlines the steps to define the Exceptional list.

EXERCISE 14.17

Defining the Exceptional List

Follow these steps to define the Exceptional list:

1. Log on to the server on which you want to run this command.
2. Click Start ➢ All Programs ➢ Microsoft Exchange Server 2007, and then click on Exchange Management Console.
3. Select Edge Transport in the Console tree.
4. Click on the Anti-spam tab, right-click on the content-filtering agent, and then click on Properties.
5. The General tab of the Agent Properties window displays its current status (Enabled or Disabled), the last time the agent's settings were modified, and a brief description of the agent. On the Exceptions tab, in the Do Not Filter content in Messages Addressed to the Following Recipients Box, click Add to include the new entry. Type **mcitp.user1@yourcompany.com**, as shown below, and then click Add.

   To add more email addresses to the list, repeat the procedure. To remove an entry, highlight it, and click Delete. To edit the email address of an entry, highlight it, and click Edit.

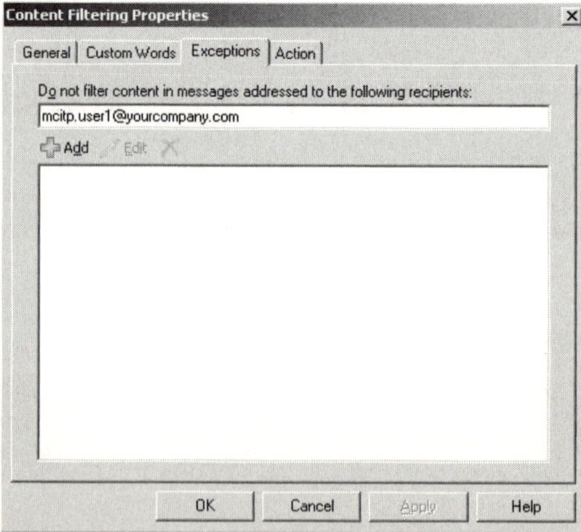

EXERCISE 14.17 *(continued)*

6. Click Apply to save your changes, or OK to save changes and close the Content Filtering dialog box.
7. Close the Exchange Management Console.

Step 6: Configuring the SCL Threshold Values

The next step is to configure the SCL threshold values. The Edge Transport server assigns an SCL rating to messages, based on the probability that the messages are spam. The SCL is stored as an email message property.

When defining an action, it is important to remember that Delete takes precedence over Reject, which takes precedence over Quarantine. For example, if you set your threshold to Delete if the SCL is eight or higher, Reject if the SCL is five or higher, and Quarantine if the SCL is three or higher, then a message with an SCL of nine would be deleted, a message with an SCL of six would be rejected, and a message with an SCL of four would be quarantined.

The following exercise outlines the steps to specify actions and configure SCL threshold values.

EXERCISE 14.18

Configuring the SCL Threshold Values

Follow these steps to configure the SCL threshold values:

1. Log on to the server on which you want to run this command.
2. Click Start ➢ All Programs ➢ Microsoft Exchange Server 2007, and then click on Exchange Management Console.
3. Select Edge Transport in the Console tree.
4. Click on the Anti-spam tab, right-click on the content-filtering agent, and click on Properties.
5. On the Action tab, and choose appropriate settings for your Exchange organization, as shown below.

   Choose the Delete Messages That Have a SCL Rating Greater Than or Equal To option, and set the threshold appropriately. All messages with the respective SCL or higher would be deleted.

   Choose the Reject Messages That Have a SCL Rating Greater Than or Equal To option, and set the threshold appropriately. All messages with the respective SCL or higher would be rejected.

EXERCISE 14.18 *(continued)*

Choose the Quarantine Messages That Have a SCL Rating Greater Than or Equal To option, and set the threshold appropriately. All messages with the respective SCL or higher would be quarantined.

To disable any action, uncheck the box next to it.

To change the SCL threshold of an action, either type in a new number in the box or use the up and down arrow keys to change the value.

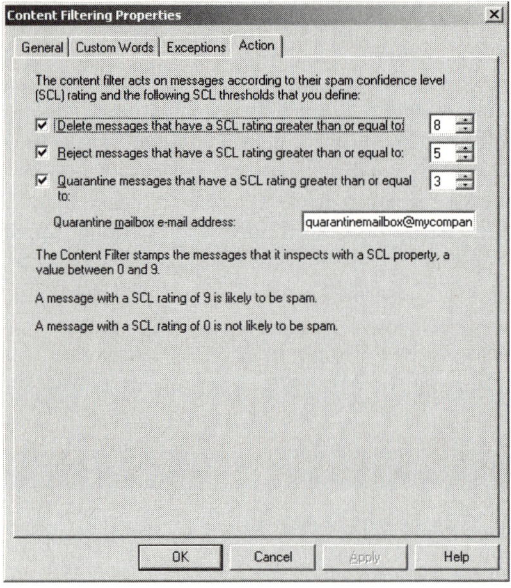

6. Click Apply to save your changes, or OK to save changes and close the content filtering Properties dialog box.
7. Close the EMC.

Step 7: Specifying Recipient and Sender Actions

The final step is to exclude specific senders and sending domains from content filtering. You must use the EMS to define an exclusion list to exclude specific senders and sending domains.

Exercise 14.19 outlines the steps to exclude specific senders and sending domains from the EMS.

EXERCISE 14.19

Excluding Specific Senders and Sending Domains

Follow these steps to exclude specific senders:

1. Log on to the Edge Transport server on which you want to run this command.
2. Click Start ➢ All Programs ➢ Microsoft Exchange Server 2007, and then click on Exchange Management Shell.
3. Type **Set-ContentFilterConfig –BypassedSenders ilse.vancriekinge@mcitpdomain.com, joel.stidley@mcitpdomain.com, rawlinson.rivera@mcitpdomain.com, andy.schan@mcitpdomain.com**. (Note: The BypassedSenders parameter allows you to specify up to 100 external email addresses.)
4. Type **Exit** to exit the Exchange Management Shell.

To exclude specific domains, use the following steps:

5. Log on to the Edge Transport server on which you want to run this command.
6. Click Start ➢ All Programs ➢ Microsoft Exchange Server 2007, and then click on Exchange Management Shell.
7. Type **Set-ContentFilterConfig –BypassedSenderDomains *.companyabc.com, companyxyz.com, *.companyasd.com**. (Note: The BypassSenderDomains parameter works similarly to the BypassedSenders parameter, but it is used to exclude the whole domain instead of individual email addresses. This saves time and will consume fewer entries in your list. BypassedSenderDomains parameter allows you to specify up to 100 external domains.)
8. Type **Exit** to exit from the Exchange Management Shell.

Attachment Filtering

Attachment filtering allows you to filter content in messages to prevent malicious or offensive content from being transmitted via attachments. It allows you to filter out both the message and attachment or just the attachment. Moreover, it allows you to "silently" delete both the message and the attachment, or just delete the attachment without notifying the sender.

Attachment filtering is a powerful tool that allows you to filter out specific attached files, file names, extensions, or file MIME content types. It can be applied to incoming and outgoing email, which gives flexibility to Exchange system administrators to prevent the distribution of unacceptable contents and files. You also can use this feature to define certain levels of security to protect your organization's proprietary data.

Before configuring attachment filtering, you must make a few decisions, including the following:

- Determine what attachments and types of attachments you want to block.
- Determine attached files, file names, extensions, or file MIME content types to block.
- Determine whether you want to configure attachment filtering for inbound or outbound messages, or both.
- Determine what you want to do with messages containing the unwanted attachments.

Based on your organizational requirements, you can choose one of the following default actions:

Reject: Reject the message by stopping delivery of the message and attachments to the recipient and send an "undeliverable" response to the sender. Neither the message nor the attachment will be delivered to the recipient.

Strip: Strip the attachment in the message, and then deliver the email to the recipient with a notification that the attachment has been removed.

SilentDelete: Reject the message by stopping delivery of the message and attachment to the recipient without sending an "undeliverable" response to the sender. Neither the message nor the attachment will be delivered to the recipient.

Table 14.2 lists all file name extensions and content types on which attachment filtering can be used.

TABLE 14.2 File Name and Content Types to Use with Attachment Filtering

Type	Name	Identity
ContentType	Application/x-msdownload	ContentType:application/xmsdownload
ContentType	Message/partial	ContentType:message/partial
ContentType	Text/scriptlet	ContentType:text/scriptlet
ContentType	Application/prg	ContentType:application/prg
ContentType	Application/msaccess	ContentType:application/msaccess
ContentType	Text/javascript	ContentType:text/javascript
ContentType	Application/x-javascript	ContentType:application/xjavascript
ContentType	Application/javascript	ContentType:application/javascript
ContentType	x-internet-signup	ContentType:x-internet-signup

TABLE 14.2 File Name and Content Types to Use with Attachment Filtering *(continued)*

Type	Name	Identity
ContentType	Application/hta	ContentType:application/hta
FileName	*.ade	FileName:*.ade
FileName	*.adp	FileName:*.adp
FileName	*.app	FileName:*.app
FileName	*.asx	FileName:*.asx
FileName	*.bas	FileName:*.bas
FileName	*.bat	FileName:*.bat
FileName	*.chm	FileName:*.chm
FileName	*.cmd	FileName:*.cmd
FileName	*.com	FileName:*.com
FileName	*.cpl	FileName:*.cpl
FileName	*.crt	FileName:*.crt
FileName	*.csh	FileName:*.csh
FileName	*.exe	FileName:*.exe
FileName	*.fxp	FileName:*.fxp
FileName	*.hlp	FileName:*.hlp
FileName	*.hta	FileName:*.hta
FileName	*.inf	FileName:*.inf
FileName	*.ins	FileName:*.ins
FileName	*.isp	FileName:*.isp
FileName	*.js	FileName:*.js

TABLE 14.2 File Name and Content Types to Use with Attachment Filtering *(continued)*

Type	Name	Identity
FileName	*.jse	FileName:*.jse
FileName	*.ksh	FileName:*.ksh
FileName	*.lnk	FileName:*.lnk
FileName	*.mda	FileName:*.mda
FileName	*.mdb	FileName:*.mdb
FileName	*.mde	FileName:*.mde
FileName	*.mdt	FileName:*.mdt
FileName	*.mdw	FileName:*.mdw
FileName	*.mdz	FileName:*.mdz
FileName	*.msc	FileName:*.msc
FileName	*.msi	FileName:*.msi
FileName	*.msp	FileName:*.msp
FileName	*.mst	FileName:*.mst
FileName	*.ops	FileName:*.ops
FileName	*.pcd	FileName:*.pcd
FileName	*.prf	FileName:*.prf
FileName	*.prg	FileName:*.prg
FileName	*.ps1	FileName:*.ps1
FileName	*.ps11	FileName:*.ps11
FileName	*.ps11xml	FileName:*.ps11xml
FileName	*.ps1xml	FileName:*.ps1xml

TABLE 14.2 File Name and Content Types to Use with Attachment Filtering *(continued)*

Type	Name	Identity
FileName	*.reg	FileName:*.reg
FileName	*.scf	FileName:*.scf
FileName	*.scr	FileName:*.scr
FileName	*.sct	FileName:*.sct
FileName	*.shs	FileName:*.shs
FileName	*.shs	FileName:*.shb
FileName	*.url	FileName:*.url
FileName	*.vb	FileName:*.vb
FileName	*.vbe	FileName:*.vbe
FileName	*.vbs	FileName:*.vbs
FileName	*.wsc	FileName:*.wsc
FileName	*.wsf	FileName:*.wsf
FileName	*.wsh	FileName:*.wsh

To add file extensions or file names to the list, you can use the `Add-AttachmentFilterEntry` cmdlet. For example, if you want to filter out `.rar` files, you need to run the `Add-AttachmentFilterEntry -Name *.rar -Type FileName` cmdlet. If you later decide to remove the file from the list, use the `Remove-AttachmentFilterEntry –Identity filename:*.rar` cmdlet.

The attachment-filtering agent is enabled by default and can be configured using only the EMS. If attachment filtering is disabled, you can enable it using the `Enable-TransportAgent -Identity "Attachment Filtering Agent"` cmdlet and pressing Enter.

Attachment filtering can be configured only through the `Get`, `Add`, `Remove`, and `Set` commands in the EMS. Each shell command has its own parameters to perform certain actions. For example, you can use the following commands:

- To display a list of the current settings for AttachmentFilterListConfig, use `Get-AttachmentFilterListConfig` cmdlet.
- To add a file name to the attachment-filtering agent, use the `Add-AttachmentFilterEntry -name filename.exe -type FileName` cmdlet.

- To remove an attachment filter entry, use the `Remove-AttachmentFilterEntry -Identity filename:filename.exe` cmdlet.
- To change the values and modify the configuration of the attachment filter, use the `Set-` command. For example, to configure a custom response message that is returned to the sender when a message and an attached file are blocked, use the `Set-AttachmentFilterListConfig -Action Reject -RejectResponse "The Attachment type is not allowed in this organization."` cmdlet.
- To filter out messages that contain a specific attachment, use the `Add-AttachmentFilterEntry -Name specificfilename -Type FileName` cmdlet.

All attachment filter entries on the Edge Transport server use the same filtering behavior. For example, when you use the command `Set-AttachmentFilterConfigList -Action SilentDelete` to silently delete both a message and an attachment, the command applies to all attachments rather than to one particular attachment.

For additional help and information on configuring attachment filtering, use `Get-Help Set-AttachmentFilterListConfig` in the EMS or see the Exchange Server 2007 Help file.

Sender Reputation Filtering

Sender reputation filtering is another antispam feature in Exchange 2007 that helps reduce unwanted email. This filtering agent uses dynamic data to block inbound messages according to the sender's reputation, which is a collection of dynamic values collected by Exchange server based on real-time data about messages sent from a specific sender. These dynamic values determine if the source of the messages is legitimate or if it is sending spam. By default, sender reputation filtering is enabled only for incoming messages from the Internet.

How Sender Reputation Filtering Works

Based on the email messages received from senders, the Sender Reputation agent analyzes various information and statistics about the sender and then assigns an overall rating based on the probability that the message is spam. This rating is generally known as Sender Reputation Level (SRL), which is very similar to the SCL. The SRL rating is a numerical value between zero and nine. A zero rating indicates that there is less than a one percent chance that the sender is a spammer, whereas a rating of nine indicates a higher than 99 percent chance that the email message is coming from a spammer. Depending on your organizational requirements, you can configure an SRL threshold. When the threshold is exceeded because the sender appears to be a source of spam, the sender is automatically added to the IP Block list for a specified number of hours. The default is 24 hours, but you can configure the duration from 0 to 48 hours.

When the Edge Transport server receives the first message from the specific sender, it assigns the SRL value of zero. As it receives more messages from the same source, it will then evaluate the messages and adjust the SRL value accordingly. The SRL is derived from the following four criteria:

Sender open-proxy test: This test is generally referred as an open relay test. If the Edge Transport server can communicate back to itself through the network on which the sending IP address resides through known open-proxy ports and protocols, the sending server is considered an open proxy. Open proxies and open relays are very common in the messaging world and are used by spammers to hide the identity of the sending email server. When email messages are received from an open proxy, the Sender Reputation agent takes that information into an account and updates the sender's open-proxy test statistics.

HELO/EHLO analysis: The `HELO/EHLO` SMTP commands are intended to provide the domain name and IP address of the sending SMTP server from which the message originated and are often forged by spammers. Spammers often modify the `HELO/EHLO` SMTP commands to spoof the sending domain and the SMTP IP address information from the actual domain name and the IP address. If the sender uses a different domain name and IP address information in the `HELO/EHLO` statements, the Sender Reputation agent will consider the sender a spammer.

Reverse DNS lookup: When an external SMTP server establishes an SMTP session, the Sender Reputation agent also performs a reverse DNS lookup by verifying that the IP address of the SMTP server matches the registered domain name. The Sender Reputation agent performs a reverse DNS query by submitting an originating IP address of the sender to DNS. If the IP address doesn't match the resolved domain name, there's a good chance that the sender is a spammer, and the overall SCL rating of the sender is adjusted accordingly.

Analysis of SCL ratings: As noted earlier, when the content-filtering agent processes an inbound message, it assigns an SCL rating to the message. The Sender Reputation agent takes the SCL rating into account when calculating the SRL for a particular IP address by analyzing the high and low message ratings from that sender.

Over time, the Sender Reputation agent uses the cumulative results of these four items to calculate the SRL of each message received from the sending IP address. When the SRL rating exceeds the set threshold, the IP address of the sending SMTP server is automatically added to the IP Block list for a period of time.

Configuring Sender Reputation Filtering

The Sender Reputation agent is enabled by default and can be configured using the EMC or EMS. If you decide to disable the sender-filtering agent, you can do so by using the EMC and the EMS. Disabling the Sender Reputation agent using the EMC is simple. Right-click on the agent icon in the Action pane, and then select Disable. To disable the sender-filtering agent using the EMS, run the `set-SenderReputationConfig -Enabled $false` command.

The following exercise outlines the steps to configure sender filtering on the Exchange Server 2007. Note that the procedure described is applied only to the local system. If you are running more than one Edge Transport server in your organization, then follow the procedure on your other Edge Transport servers to maintain consistency.

EXERCISE 14.20

Configuring Sender Reputation Filtering

Use the following steps to configure sender reputation filtering:

1. Log on to the server on which you want to run this command.
2. Click Start ➢ All Programs ➢ Microsoft Exchange Server 2007, and then click on Exchange Management Console.
3. Select Edge Transport in the Console tree.
4. Click on the Anti-spam tab, right-click on the Sender Reputation agent, and then click on Properties. The General tab provides a quick overview of the agent along with its current status (Enabled or Disabled), the last time the agent's settings were modified, and a brief description of the agent.
5. The Sender Confidence tab allows you to enable (default) or disable the open proxy test, as follows.

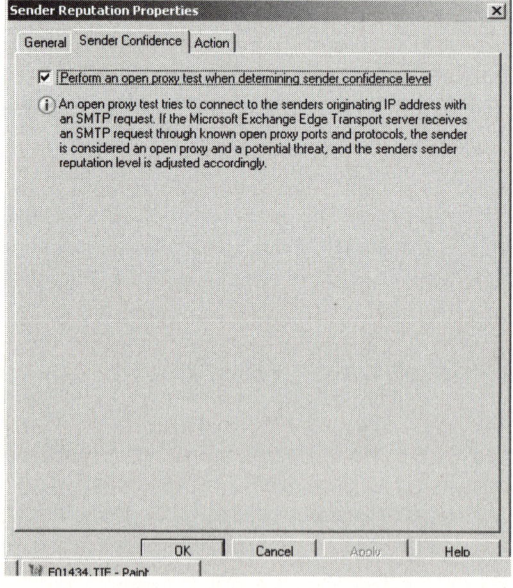

EXERCISE 14.20 *(continued)*

6. The Action tab allows you to set the block threshold for SRL on a scale of zero to nine. (The default setting is nine, the maximum.) You also can use the Action tab to configure how long (0 to 48 hours) the IP address should remain on the Edge Transport server's IP Block list (the default is 24 hours), as shown below.

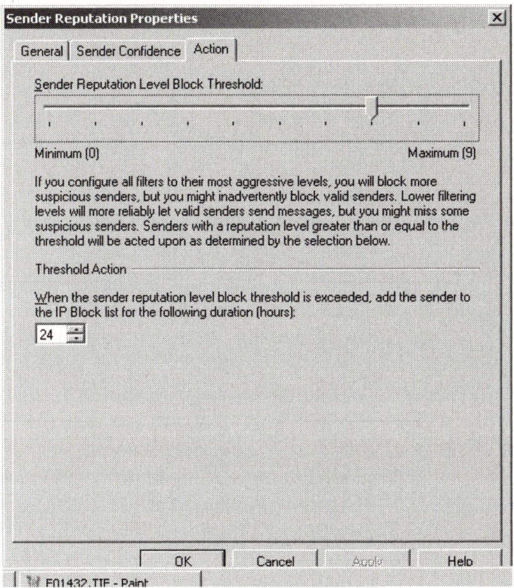

7. Click Apply to save changes, or click OK to save changes and close the window.

8. Close the Exchange Management Console.

Understanding Microsoft Exchange Forefront Security

Microsoft has introduced several new antivirus features for messaging environments. In 2005 Microsoft acquired Sybari and its Antigen products. The former Antigen antivirus is now integrated in Exchange Server 2007 as Microsoft Exchange Forefront Security. The license for Forefront Security for Exchange Server is included in the Exchange Enterprise CAL. Microsoft also recently introduced Forefront Client Security (for business desktops, laptops, and server operating systems) and Forefront Security for SharePoint.

Forefront Security for Exchange provides improved protection and performance, and centralized management features. Table 14.3 shows these features.

TABLE 14.3 Forefront Security for Exchange Server 2007

Feature	Description
Multiple antivirus scan engines	Up to five antivirus solutions protect your messaging infrastructure against viruses, phishing, worms, and other threats. Getting antivirus updates quickly is important for messaging administrators. By using five antivirus engines, you increase the chances of getting an update before a virus can affect your environment. Also, if one engine goes offline or fails, the other engines continue to protect your messaging environment without delaying mail delivery.
Centralized management	Allows for remote installation, engine and signature updating, reporting, and alerts through the centralized Forefront Server Security Management Console.
Antivirus stamping	Provides coordinated scanning across Edge Transport, Hub Transport, and Mail servers. The email scanned at the Edge and/or Hub Transport server will not be scanned again at the Mail server, saving time and server resources. Supports in-memory scanning rather than using more-traditional techniques such as spooling to disk. Multithreaded scanning analyzes multiple messages simultaneously.
Filtering	Allows filtering by file name, extension, or size. Can also scan or block high-compression `.zip` files and `.rar` archives.
Notification	Provides comprehensive notifications for senders, recipients, and the messaging administrator.
Monitoring	Allows IT administrator to monitor the health of Forefront Security for Exchange Server by using a management pack for Microsoft Operations Manager.
Multilanguage support	Supports 11 languages, including English, German, French, Japanese, Italian, Spanish, Korean, Chinese, Traditional Chinese, Portuguese (Brazilian), and Russian.
Centralized web management	Works with the Microsoft Forefront Server Security Server Management Console, which allows administrator to manage Forefront on multiple Exchange servers from a single console instead of using many different consoles.

TABLE 14.3 Forefront Security for Exchange Server 2007 *(continued)*

Feature	Description
Migration support	Customers who purchase Forefront Security for Exchange Server also will be licensed to use Microsoft Antigen for Exchange, Microsoft Antigen for SMTP Gateways, and Antigen Spam Manager to protect Microsoft Exchange 2000 Server and Microsoft Exchange Server 2003 environments.
Mail cluster support	Supports Exchange Server 2007 cluster continuous replication (CCR), ensuring that both active and passive nodes have up-to-date signatures and configuration.

Table 14.4 shows the minimum system configuration to evaluate Forefront Security for Exchange Server.

TABLE 14.4 System Requirements for Forefront Security for Exchange Server

Item	Minimum Configuration Required
Processor	32-bit trial 64-bit trial (Intel Xeon processor and AMD processor)
Operating system	Microsoft Windows Server 2003
Microsoft Exchange	Microsoft Exchange Server 2007
Hard disk	300 MB of available disk space
Memory	512 MB RAM—1 GB recommended
Number of processors	1 Intel processor (1 GHz or higher)

More information about Microsoft Exchange Forefront Security is available on the Microsoft Web site `http://www.microsoft.com/technet/antigen/default.mspx`.

Implementing Antivirus Software

Microsoft has enhanced the Virus Scanning Application Programming Interface (VSAPI) that was introduced in Exchange 2000 and Exchange 2003 and has integrated several built-in features in Exchange Server 2007 to stop threats before they affect your organization and users. Exchange Server 2007 supports Forefront Security for Exchange Server 2007, which is included in the Exchange 2007 Enterprise CAL, and it also supports third-party products such as McAfee, Symantec, and others.

It is important to understand that email viruses are different from file-level viruses because they tend to spread infection as soon as an attachment is opened. Before you know it, your whole organization is infected. To protect your environment from viruses, strong antivirus and antispam measures must be implemented in a layered configuration.

The Edge Transport server role acts like a hygiene gateway by providing antivirus and antispam message protection for the Exchange infrastructure. You should maintain and use an Exchange-aware server-side antivirus solution. The Exchange aware server-side virus scanner continuously scans incoming and outgoing emails. Based on your configuration, virus-scan software can detect infected messages and attachments, and clean them up for you by deleting those messages or quarantining them before they harm your environment.

Once you protect your Edge/Hub Transport server, the next step in the process is to protect your Mailbox server. The enhanced VSAPI engine on Exchange Server 2007 allows you to integrate third-party products with Exchange Server 2007, which will allow you to run Exchange 2007 database-level scans and scan for viruses in real time before any message is written to the database.

The last checkpoint for your virus protection is installing file- and email-aware virus-scan software on users' workstations. By implementing a separate antivirus solution on the desktop, you can minimize your exposure to viruses.

Summary

We've covered a lot of ground in this chapter; all of it focused on protecting your Exchange organization from viruses, email threats, spam, and phishing attacks. We discussed Microsoft Hosted Services, which include filtering, archiving, continuity, and encryption. These services help organizations protect themselves from email-borne malware, satisfy retention requirements, provide email continuity to preserve access to email during and after emergency situations, and provide email encryption to preserve confidentiality. We also discussed how to configure and implement antispam agents on the Edge Transport and Hub Transport servers, and covered Connection Filtering, Sender Filtering, Recipient Filtering, Attachment Filtering, Sender Reputation and IP Reputation agents that can significantly decrease the amount of spam your organization receives. These built-in filtering agents in the Edge Transport server protect your internal network by filtering out unsolicited email messages and spam messages at the perimeter network.

Exam Essentials

Understand the purpose and use of Microsoft Exchange Hosted Services. Over the last few years, the messaging environment has become vulnerable to a growing array of threats such as viruses, spam, phishing attacks, denial-of-service attacks, and worms. To respond to these challenges, Microsoft integrated several built-in features in Exchange Server 2007 and introduced Microsoft Exchange Hosted Services.

Understand the use of antispam agents. Exchange Server 2007 has several built-in antispam agents. You must understand the differences between them, and the usage and configuration of these antispam agents for the exam.

Know where to go. The exam is likely to ask you what configuration is needed to produce a required result. Take the time as you review the material and content in this book to think about what types of configuration and management tasks you find yourself performing in each antispam agent setting of the Exchange Management Console.

Review Questions

1. You have been asked to choose Microsoft Exchange Hosted Services. The business requires protecting their users' email from viruses. Which of the following Microsoft Exchange Hosted Services will help you to achieve this?
   - **A.** Microsoft Exchange Hosted filtering (known as FrontBridge)
   - **B.** Microsoft Exchange Hosted archive
   - **C.** Microsoft Exchange Hosted continuity
   - **D.** Microsoft Exchange Hosted encryption
   - **E.** None of the above

2. Which of the following is not a component of Microsoft Exchange Hosted Services?
   - **A.** Microsoft Exchange Hosted filtering (known as FrontBridge)
   - **B.** Microsoft Exchange Hosted archive
   - **C.** Microsoft Exchange Hosted continuity
   - **D.** Microsoft Exchange Hosted encryption
   - **E.** Microsoft Exchange Hosted backup and archiving solution

3. Microsoft Exchange Hosted Filtering provides antivirus scanning using your choice of ________________ engines.
   - **A.** Two (Trend Micro and Symantec)
   - **B.** Three (Trend Micro, Symantec, and Sophos)
   - **C.** Four (Trend Micro, Symantec, Sophos, and Kaspersky Lab)
   - **D.** Five (Trend Micro, Symantec, Sophos, Kaspersky Lab, and McAfee)

4. Microsoft Exchange Hosted continuity service stores a copy of each massage in a managed ________________-day message repository. In case of any disaster, your users will be able to access the off-site message repository through ______________ at any time to read, compose, and reply to messages.
   - **A.** 14 and Outlook and Outlook Express
   - **B.** 14 and a password-protected web-based interface
   - **C.** 30 and Outlook and Outlook Express
   - **D.** 30 and and a password-protected web-based interface

5. Which of the following agents will check the IP address of the remote SMTP server and then use a variety of IP Block lists, IP Allow lists, IP Block provider, and IP Allow provider services to block or allow a connection from the specific IP address?
   - **A.** Sender ID filtering
   - **B.** Sender reputation filtering
   - **C.** IP reputation service
   - **D.** Connection filtering

6. Which of the following agents will compare the sender's `MAIL FROM:` SMTP command to an administrator-defined list of senders or sender domains to block, delete, drop, or quarantine an inbound message, and based on the result, will allow, drop, block, delete, or quarantine the message?

   A. Sender filtering

   B. Recipient filtering

   C. Sender reputation filtering

   D. Sender ID filtering

7. Which of the following agents will check whether the sender is spoofed by using the IP address of the sending server and the purported responsible address (PRA) of the sender?

   A. Sender filtering

   B. Recipient filtering

   C. Sender reputation filtering

   D. Sender ID filtering

8. Which of the following agents will collect analytical data from SMTP sessions, message content, sender ID verification, and general sender behavior to create a history of sender characteristics, and then uses all this knowledge along with sender reputation level (SRL) to determine whether the message is coming from spammers or malicious senders?

   A. Sender ID filtering

   B. Attachment filtering

   C. Sender reputation filtering

   D. IP reputation service

9. Which of the following agents will compare a recipient's `RCPT TO:` SMTP command with the administrator-defined list and, if the result is a match, will block the message? It also compares recipients with the local recipient directory to determine if the message is addressed to valid recipients. If there is no valid recipient in the local directory, the message can be rejected at the organization's network perimeter.

   A. Sender filtering

   B. Recipient filtering

   C. Sender reputation filtering

   D. Sender ID filtering

10. Which of the following agents filters messages based on the attachment, and allows you to block, drop, and reject a message and its attachment or strip the attachment and allow the message?

    A. Sender ID filtering

    B. Attachment filtering

    C. Sender reputation filtering

    D. IP reputation service

11. Which of the following PowerShell commands allows you to disable the sender-filtering agent using the EMS?
    - A. `Set-SenderFilterConfig -Enabled $false`
    - B. `Set-SenderFilterConfig -Enabled $true`
    - C. `Set-SenderFilterConfig -Enabled`
    - D. `Set-SenderFilterConfig -Disabled`
12. The content-filtering agent uses the default response of "550 5.7.1 Message rejected due to content restrictions" and returns the message to the sender. Which of the following commands will allow you to customize this message?
    - A. `Set-ContentFilterConfig`
    - B. `Get-ContentFilterConfig`
    - C. `Modify-ContentFilterConfig`
    - D. `Change-ContentFilterConfig`
13. Content filtering uses a quarantine mailbox to store quarantined messages. Which of the following commands allows you to designate this mailbox?
    - A. `Set-ContentFilterConfig -Quarantine`
    - B. `Get-ContentFilterConfig -QuarantineMailbox`
    - C. `Modify-ContentFilterConfig -QuarantineMailbox`
    - D. `Set-ContentFilterConfig -QuarantineMailbox quarantine@mycompany.com`
14. Content filtering allows you to exclude specific senders and sending domains from content filtering. Which of the following commands allows you to exclude a specific sender instead of a whole domain?
    - A. `Set-ContentFilterConfig -BypassedSenders mcitp.user1@mcitpdomain.com`
    - B. `Get-ContentFilterConfig -BypassedSenders mcitp.user1@mcitpdomain.com`
    - C. `Modify-ContentFilterConfig -BypassedSenders mcitp.user1@mcitpdomain.com`
    - D. `Set-ConfigFilter -BypassedSenders mcitp.user1@mcitpdomain.com`
15. Content filtering allows you to exclude specific senders and sending domains from content filtering. Which of the following commands allows you to exclude a whole domain instead of an individual sender?
    - A. `Set-ContentFilterConfig -BypassedSenderDomains *.companyabc.com`
    - B. `Get-ContentFilterConfig -BypassedSenderDomains *.companyabc.com`
    - C. `Modify-ContentFilterConfig -BypassedSenderDomains *.companyabc.com`
    - D. `Set-ConfigFilter -BypassedSenderDomains *.companyabc.com`

16. Attachment filtering allows you to filter out content in messages to prevent malicious or offensive contents being stored in the attachment. You can choose the following actions for attachments containing malicious or offensive contents: (Choose all that apply.)

    A. Reject

    B. Strip

    C. SilentDelete

    D. Quarantine

    E. All of the above.

17. The sender reputation filtering agent uses dynamic data to assess whether the source of a message is legitimate or if it is sending junk emails. Based on the information and statistics about the sender, the agent then assigns an overall score to the message, generally referred to as Sender Reputation Level (SRL), which is very similar to the SCL. The SRL rating is a numerical value between

    A. 0 and 1

    B. 0 and 5

    C. 0 and 10

    D. 0 and 9

18. The Sender Reputation Level (SRL) value is derived from which of the following?

    A. Sender open proxy test

    B. HELO/EHLO analysis

    C. Reverse DNS lookup

    D. Analysis of SCL ratings

    E. All of the above.

19. The former ________________ antivirus is now integrated in Exchange Server 2007 as Microsoft Exchange Forefront Security.

    A. McAfee

    B. Norton Antivirus

    C. Antigen

    D. All of the above.

20. Microsoft Exchange Forefront Security uses up to ________________ antivirus solutions to protect your messaging infrastructure against viruses, phishing, worms, and other threats.

    A. three

    B. four

    C. five

    D. six

    E. seven

Answers to Review Questions

1. A. Multipronged message filtering in the perimeter network is available through the Edge Transport server role; however, for small to medium organizations, Microsoft now offers the "cloud" filtering (as an Internet-based service) through Exchange Hosted filtering. Microsoft Exchange Hosted filtering helps to protect client emails from viruses, spyware, spam and other forms of malware. Microsoft Exchange Hosted filtering services block unwanted email messages from entering your organization. The Exchange Hosted filtering services are an ideal solution for any organization that is looking to enhance their protection against spam, virus, and phishing attacks.

2. E. Microsoft Exchange Hosted Services include all of the choices in the question except E.

3. C. Exchange Hosted Filtering provides antivirus scanning using your choice of four engines (Trend Micro, Symantec, Sophos, and Kaspersky Lab).

4. D. Microsoft Exchange Hosted continuity service stores a copy of each massage in a 30-day message repository. In case of disaster, your users will be able to access email in an offsite message repository through a password-protected web-based interface at any time to read, compose, and reply to messages.

5. D. Connection filtering checks the IP address of the remote SMTP server and then uses a variety of IP Block lists, IP Allow lists, IP Block provider, and IP Allow provider services to block or allow a connection from a specific IP address.

6. A. Sender filtering uses an administrator-defined list of senders or sender domains to block, delete, drop, or quarantine an inbound message. Sender filtering compares the sender's `MAIL FROM:` SMTP command to this customized list and responds accordingly.

7. D. Sender ID filtering checks whether the sender is spoofed by using the IP address of the sending server and the purported responsible address (PRA) of the sender.

8. C. Sender reputation filtering relies on persisted data about the IP address of the sending server to determine what action, if any, to take on an inbound message. This agent collects analytical data from SMTP sessions, message content, sender ID verification, and general sender behavior and creates a history of sender characteristics. It uses all this knowledge along with sender reputation level (SRL) to determine whether the message is coming from spammers or malicious senders. You also can define a threshold. Based on your configuration and threshold, senders whose SRL exceeds the threshold will be temporarily blocked for 48 hours.

9. B. Recipient filtering is very similar to sender filtering. It compares the recipient's `RCPT TO:` SMTP command to the administrator-defined list. If the result is true, it will block the message. It also compares recipients to the local recipient directory to determine if the message is addressed to valid recipients. If there is no valid recipient in the local directory, the message can be rejected at the organization's network perimeter.

10. B. Attachment filtering filters messages based on the attachment. You can block, drop, and reject a message and its attachment or strip the attachment and allow the message.

11. A. To disable the sender-filtering agent using the EMS, run the `set-SenderFilterConfig -Enabled $false` command.

12. A. You can customize the message using `the Set-ContentFilterConfig` command in the EMS (EMS).

13. D. `Set-ContentFilterConfig -QuarantineMailbox quarantine@mycompany.com` allows you to designate the quarantine mailbox.

14. A. `Set-ContentFilterConfig -BypassedSenders mcitp.user1@mcitpdomain.com` allows you to exclude a specific email address instead of a whole domain.

15. A. `Set-ContentFilterConfig -BypassedSenderDomains *.companyabc.com` allows you to exclude the whole domain instead of entering the email address of each and every individual. This saves time as it will consume fewer entries in your list. The BypassedSenderDomains parameter allows you to specify up to 100 external domains.

16. A, B, and C. Attachment filtering allows you to filter out content in messages. It allows you to filter out both the message and attachment or just the attachment. You can choose from three options: rejecting the message to stop delivery of the message and attachments to the recipient and sends an undeliverable response to the sender, stripping the attachment from the message and then delivering the email to the recipient with a notification that the attachment in the message has been removed, or using SilentDelete on the message to stop delivery of the message and attachments to the recipient without sending any undeliverable response to the sender.

17. D. The SRL rating is a numerical value between zero and nine. Zero indicates that there is less than a one percent chance that the sender is a spammer. Nine indicates that there is more than a 99 percent chance that the sending is a spammer.

18. E. The Sender Reputation Level (SRL) value is derived from all four of the characteristics noted.

19. C. The former Antigen antivirus is now integrated in Exchange Server 2007 as Microsoft Exchange Forefront Security. McAfee and Norton are different antivirus manufacturers, and operate independently from Microsoft.

20. C. Forefront Security for Exchange uses up to five antivirus solutions to protect your messaging infrastructure against viruses, phishing, worms, and other threats. By using five antivirus engines, you increase the chances of getting an update quickly before the virus affects your environment. Also, if one engine goes offline or fails, other engines continue to protect your messaging environment without delaying mail delivery.

Planning Exchange Server 2007 Security

MICROSOFT EXAM OBJECTIVES COVERED IN THIS CHAPTER:

- ✓ Plan the network layer security implementation
- ✓ Plan the transport rules implementation

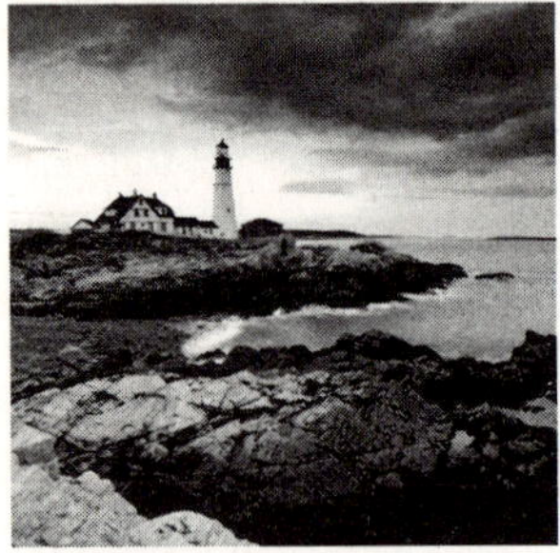

Planning Exchange security is becoming more of a requirement in an Exchange 2007 messaging professional's life. To plan a secure messaging environment for a larger organization, you need to understand the security concepts. This chapter introduces you to many of the security concepts of Exchange 2007, such as network-based protection, email encryption, and transport rules. It also includes a discussion about the role of Internet Security and Acceleration (ISA) Server 2006.

In-depth understanding is not required in every area, but it is important to understand how these concepts work on Exchange Server 2007 and what to configure where.

The main subjects of this chapter are as follows:

- Defining firewall rules for every Exchange server role
- Network-based secure communication using Internet Protocol Security (IPSec) or Virtual Private Network (VPN)
- Session-based secure communication using Transport Layer Security (TLS)
- Implementing transport rules and edge rules
- Implementing Secure Multipurpose Internet Mail Extensions (S/MIME)
- Implementing message journaling
- Protecting Exchange Server 2007 with ISA Server 2006

Planning the Network Layer Security Implementation

This section covers the requirements for planning the network layer security for an Exchange Server 2007 implementation. We'll start with firewall rules and then continue with an overview of secure communications solutions using IPSec, VPN, and TLS.

Defining Firewall Rules

When the first versions of Exchange came out, security was not a major consideration. Obviously, this has changed in recent years and a firewall became part of the base system of a Windows 2003 server. This section covers what's important when defining firewall rules and which ports and protocols must be allowed to enable certain types of services between servers and clients.

When defining your firewall ports, you should always consider the concept of "less is more." The fewer ports you allow to open, the more secure your system will be.

To provide an easy overview of the masses of ports, this section is organized according to the Exchange server roles. The tables are sorted according the required ports so you can recognize what ports are used for what services or data paths.

The most important ports are always the ones frequently used. You should remember the key services for each server role and what ports they require.

Mailbox Server

The Mailbox server role hosts the mailbox and public-folder databases and, therefore, must be accessible to the clients. Table 15.1 shows which ports are required for services or data paths from and to the Mailbox server role. It's important to understand that Remote Procedure Call (RPC) traffic is always encrypted.

TABLE 15.1 Mailbox Server Ports

Data Path	Required Ports	Encrypted by default?
Messaging application programming interface (MAPI) access, Availability web service, Content indexing, Recipient Update Service RPC access, Microsoft Exchange Active Directory Topology Service access, Microsoft Exchange System Attendant service legacy access (MAPI client), Offline address book (OAB) accessing Active Directory	135/TCP (RPC)	Yes
Clustering, mailbox assistants, Admin remote access (remote registry), Microsoft Exchange System Attendant service (listen)	135/TCP (RPC)	No

TABLE 15.1 Mailbox Server Ports *(continued)*

Data Path	Required Ports	Encrypted by default?
Active Directory access	389/TCP/UDP (LDAP), 3268/TCP (LDAP GC), 88/TCP/UDP (Kerberos), 53/TCP/UDP (DNS), 135/TCP (RPC Netlogon)	Yes
Microsoft Exchange System Attendant service legacy access to Active Directory, Recipient update to Active Directory, DSAccess to Active Directory	389/TCP/UDP (LDAP), 3268/TCP (LDAP GC), 88/TCP/UDP (Kerberos), 53/TCP/UDP (DNS), 135/TCP (RPC Netlogon)	Yes
Admin remote access (SMB/File)	445/TCP (SMB)	No
Cluster nodes communication (intranode)	3343/UDP + randomly high TCP ports	No

Transport Servers

The Hub Transport server takes care of messages that are routed within an organization; the Edge Transport server role routes messages inside and outside of the organization. Table 15.2 explains which ports are required for services or data paths from and to the Hub Transport and the Edge Transport server roles.

TABLE 15.2 Hub and Edge Transport Server Ports

Data Path	Required Ports	Encrypted by default?
Hub Transport server to Hub Transport server	25/TCP (SSL), 587/TCP (SSL)	Yes
Hub Transport to Edge Transport and vice versa	25/TCP (SSL)	Yes
Active Directory access from Hub Transport server	389/TCP/UDP (LDAP), 3268/TCP (LDAP GC), 88/TCP/UDP (Kerberos), 53/TCP/UDP (DNS), 135/TCP (RPC Netlogon)	Yes

TABLE 15.2 Hub and Edge Transport Server Ports *(continued)*

Data Path	Required Ports	Encrypted by default?
Edge Transport to Edge Transport server	25/TCP (SSL), 389/TCP/UDP, 80/TCP (certificate authentication)	No
Microsoft Exchange EdgeSync service	50636/TCP (SSL)	Yes
Active Directory Application Mode (ADAM) local access on Edge Transport server	50389/TCP (No SSL)	No
Mailbox server to Hub Transport Hub Transport to Mailbox server via MAPI	135/TCP (RPC)	Yes

As the table shows, encryption is the default in many situations. Hub Transport to Hub Transport is encrypted by default using Exchange 2007's certificates. If there are no machine certificates available for your Exchange 2007 server, the system will use self-signed certificates for encrypting the communication. This is the same for Hub Transport to Edge Transport communication.

Traffic between Edge Transport servers in two different organizations is opportunistic Transport Layer Security (TLS). This means that if both servers offer a valid server certificate, traffic will be encrypted. If only their self-signed certificate is available, traffic will not be encrypted. (Additional security can be added using a feature called Domain Security, as discussed in the "Implementing Domain Security" section of this chapter.)

As the Edge Transport server is designed to be located in the perimeter network or demilitarized zone (DMZ), it is assumed that only the communication between Hub Transport and Edge Transport needs to be protected by firewalls. Of course, Edge Transport communication to the Internet also should be protected if the Edge Transport server is located in the perimeter network.

Client Access Server

Table 15.3 describes which ports are required for services or data paths from and to the Client Access server (CAS) role.

TABLE 15.3 Client Access Server Ports

Data Path	Required Ports	Encrypted by default?
Autodiscover service, Availability service, Outlook Web Access (OWA), Outlook Anywhere (formerly known as RPC over HTTP), Exchange ActiveSync application, Client Access server to a Mailbox server that is running an earlier version of Exchange Server, CAS to CAS for Exchange ActiveSync and OWA, WebDAV	80/TCP, 443/TCP (SSL)	Yes
POP3	110/TCP (TLS), 995/TCP (SSL)	Yes
IMAP4	143/TCP (TLS), 993/TCP (SSL)	Yes
CAS to Unified Messaging server	5060/TCP, 5061/TCP, 5062/TCP, One dynamic port	Yes
CAS to Exchange 2007 Mailbox server	RPC with many ports	Yes

When your Exchange 2007 Client Access server is communicating with an Exchange 2003 server, it is a best practice to use Kerberos authentication and disable NTLM and basic authentication.

Unified Messaging

Table 15.4 explains which ports are required for services or data paths from and to the Unified Messaging server role.

TABLE 15.4 Unified Messaging Server Ports

Data Path	Required Ports	Encrypted by default?
Unified Messaging to Hub Transport	25/TCP (SSL)	Yes
Unified Messaging server to Mailbox server	135/TCP (RPC)	Yes

TABLE 15.4 Unified Messaging Server Ports *(continued)*

Data Path	Required Ports	Encrypted by default?
Unified Messaging Web Service	80/TCP, 443/TCP (SSL)	Yes
Unified Messaging fax, Unified Messaging private branch exchange (PBX)	5060/TCP, 5061/TCP, 5062/TCP, One dynamic port	Yes

Defining Secure Communication Solutions Using IPSec, VPN, and TLS

Secure messaging in Exchange 2007 can be separated into three categories: network-based, SMTP-based, and client-based.

In the first part of this section, you will read about the network-based approach using IPSec or VPN protocol. The second part covers the session-based approach using TLS for authentication and encryption. This section also introduces a new concept called Domain Security that is based on mutual TLS as the protocol.

Client-based security using Secure MIME (S/MIME) is covered in the "Implementing S/MIME" section later in this chapter.

Network-Based Secure Communication Using IPSec or VPN

IPSec provides a set of extensions to the basic IP protocol and is used to encrypt server-to-server communication. It can be used to tunnel traffic or peer-to-peer to secure all IP communications natively. Because it operates on the transport layer, applications like Exchange 2007 don't need to be aware of IPSec. The same applies to VPN, which also operates on the transport layer and very often uses IPSec as the underlying protocol.

You use IPSec normally to secure server-to-server or client-to-server communication. VPN is used to connect site to site or client to site. Both operate as mentioned on the transport layer, which can be an advantage over application-layer protocols such as S/MIME because they do not require the application on both ends to know about the protocol.

Because Exchange 2007 by default encrypts its network traffic using TLS and self-signed certificates (if you do not by default roll out server certificates), the requirements for network-based security are less. In Exchange 2003 for example, you wanted to implement IPSec for communication between Exchange 2003 front-end and back-end servers. Front-end servers were often placed in the perimeter network or directly in the Internet, but needed to communicate with the back-end servers quite heavily (they were members of the domain). Having this traffic encrypted provides more protection.

Of course, Exchange 2007 also has an advantage if you have already implemented network-based secure communication. You don't need to do anything to make Exchange 2007 work; however, to optimize performance, you should consider a few points when you have network-based security in place.

Let's assume that you configured IPSec for all the Exchange servers in your organization. (Configuring IPSec is beyond the scope of this book and of the exam, so this section focuses only on the settings you need to configure in Exchange 2007.) You now need to access the Receive connectors of your Hub Transport server and enable Externally Secured on the Authentication tab as shown in Figure 15.1. Externally Secured means that the connection is considered secured by a security mechanism that is external to Exchange 2007. In the Exchange Management Shell (EMS), External Secured is referred to as `ExternalAuthoritative`.

FIGURE 15.1 The Receive connector's Authentication tab

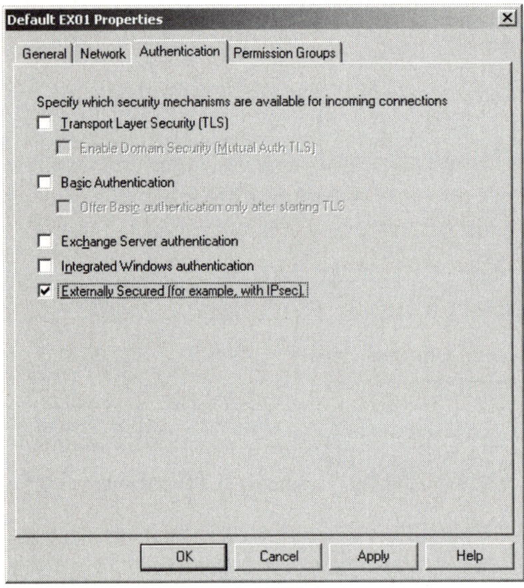

Normally you don't need any other authentication method. You're able to add Transport Layer Security (TLS) only on top of your network security, but this will decrease the performance of message transfers, since the communication gets encrypted several times. Other options like Exchange Server authentication do not work with Externally Secured and, therefore, should be disabled.

Additionally, you need to configure Exchange Servers on the Permission Groups tab of the Receive connector because this group is used to permit a connection to the server. You can see the configuration in Figure 15.2.

Using network-based security is a work-intensive solution. Unless you have already implemented IPSec or other network-based protocols, you may want to consider other options for Exchange 2007.

FIGURE 15.2 The Receive connector's Permission Groups tab

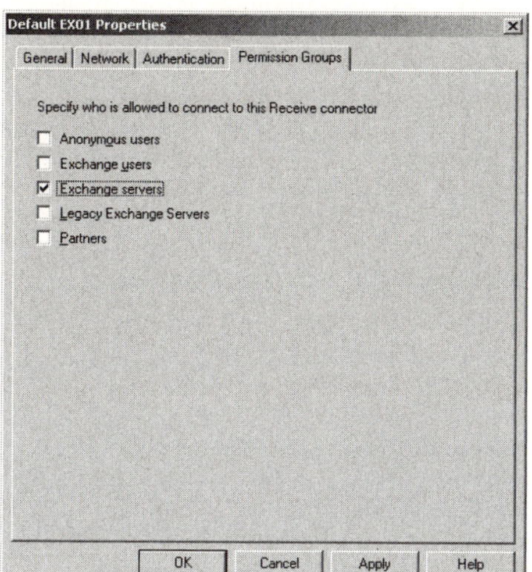

Session-Based Secure Communication Using TLS

The TLS protocol is the default protocol used in an Exchange 2007 organization to encrypt server communication. It uses Exchange 2007 self-signed certificates that are created during the setup for encryption.

This means self-signed certificates provide novice or lazy Exchange 2007 administrators a way to have OWA or other services automatically secured. Also, self-signed certificates are used to automatically encrypt messages between Hub Transport and Edge Transport servers to encrypt traffic. They also are used to encrypt traffic between two Edge Transport servers located in different organizations.

If you're planning to implement Exchange 2007 Domain Security to provide secured message paths between Exchange 2007 Edge Transport servers over the Internet, you need a more thorough certificate implementation. Self-signed certificates do not work when you want to implement Domain Security.

Domain Security uses TLS with mutual authentication (mutual TLS) to provide session-based authentication and encryption. Standard TLS is used to provide confidentiality by encrypting but not authenticating the communication partners. This is typical of Secure Sockets Layer (SSL), which is the HTTP implementation of TLS.

We'll start by taking a look at the different types of certificates. Then we'll cover the obstacles you must consider when requesting a certificate. Finally, we'll discuss implementing Domain Security for Exchange 2007.

Types of Certificates

Three different types of certificates are available: self-signed certificates, Windows public key infrastructure (PKI)–generated certificates, and third-party certificates. Table 15.5 provides you with an overview of these types of certificates and their uses.

TABLE 15.5 Types of Certificates

Certificate Type	Description
Self-signed certificates	When Exchange 2007 is installed, a new certificate is generated automatically. This certificate is used by default to encrypt all communication inside and outside the Exchange organization. If you access your OWA using a web browser, you need to confirm the server's certificate is correct because you do not trust this certificate by default.
Windows PKI–generated certificates	These certificates are issued by a Windows certificate authority (e.g., Windows Server 2003), and you can request them at no extra cost and install them immediately. They are not trusted publicly, so you need to make sure that the root certificate is imported at every server, client, and device that does not belong to your Active Directory. In your Active Directory, the information is distributed automatically.
Third-party certificates	This type of certificate is automatically trusted within the Internet and can be purchased by a third-party certificate authority (CA) such as VeriSign. It is the easiest and least time-consuming way to implement certificates, but you need to buy them. Thus, you probably won't have an official certificate for every Exchange server in your environment.

You cannot use self-signed certificates for mutual TLS or Domain Security communication to and from the Internet in Exchange 2007—only Windows PKI–generated certificates or third-party certificates are supported there.

If you decided to use Windows PKI–generated certificates for your external traffic, you have to make sure that your partners' servers trust your root CA (by importing your root certificate).

Exchange 2007 certificates need to have a certain format to work correctly with the TLS protocol. Because the Exchange servers in the perimeter network, namely your Edge Transport servers, have multiple domain names or service connection points (SCPs), you have two options:

- Use a single certificate on your server(s) with Subject Alternative Names (SAN Certificate) support, also known as Unified Communications Certificates.
- Use individual certificates.

Microsoft recommends using a SAN certification because it's simpler to administer on the servers. Unfortunately, it is also more expensive than a normal certificate if purchased from a third-party CA.

For example, if you have a domain called Exchange2007.com and an Edge Transport server called ED01, you should configure at least the following domains as Subject Alternative Names on which TLS works correctly:

- ED01.Exchange2007.com
- Exchange2007.com

Requesting and Installing a Certificate

To request a SAN certificate, you can use the Exchange Management Shell (EMS) to create a request. Use the following cmdlet to issue a request that you then can send to your Windows CA or a third-party CA to receive a certificate for your TLS communication in Exchange 2007:

```
Net-ExchangeCertificate -GenerateRequest -FriendlyName "Internet" -Path
c:\edge.req -SubjectName "DC=com,DC=Exchange2007,CN=ed01.exchange2007.net" -
DomainName exchange2007.com
```

The name of the server is ED01 and it is part of the domain Exchange2007.com and is the Edge Transport server for the inbound domain Exchange2007.com.

Once you receive the certificate, you can use the following cmdlet to import the certificate and enable it for the Service SMTP. It imports the certificate that is available at `c:\certnew.cer` and enables it automatically for SMTP.

```
Import-ExchangeCertificate -Path c:\certnew.cer | Enable-ExchangeCertificate -
Services SMTP
```

Once you receive the certificate, you can use the certificates snap-in in Microsoft Management Console to verify that all SAN domains have been included accordingly. Figure 15.3 shows the SAN configuration for the certificate that we requested.

As you see, the SAN includes Exchange2007.com, for which this server can receive mutual TLS connections. The server FQDN is part of the normal subject, and so is not shown as a SAN.

Implementing Domain Security

Domain Security in Exchange 2007 is a new feature that provides a relatively low-cost alternative to S/MIME or other message-encryption solutions. It uses mutual TLS, where each server verifies the identity of the other server by validating the certificate that is provided by the other server. It is an easy way for administrators to manage secured message paths between domains over the Internet.

Domain Security is manually enabled for every domain by an Exchange organization administrator, so you must coordinate with the communication partner to make it work. It cannot be enabled just on one side, but must be configured in domains.

FIGURE 15.3 The Subject Alternative Name configuration

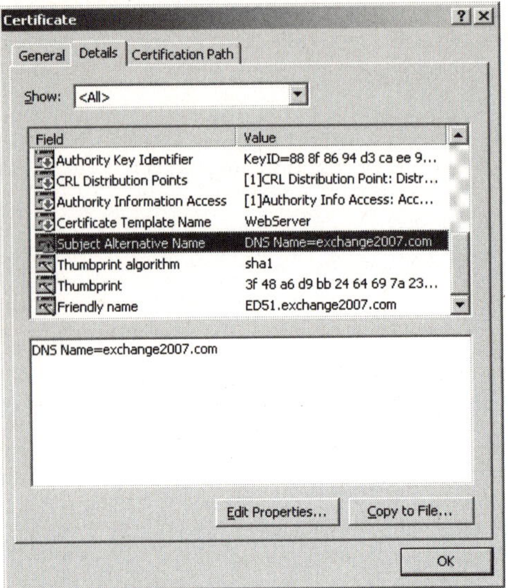

Typically, Domain Security is enabled only on an Edge Transport server because the server needs to reside in the perimeter network or directly on the Internet to communicate with the other domains. However, you also can enable Domain Security on a Hub Transport server if needed.

The high-level steps to implement Domain Security are as follows:

- Request and install a SAN certificate on the Edge Transport server(s) where you want to enable mutual TLS.
- Configure outbound and inbound Domain Security.
- Test mailflow.

The tricky part in this configuration is understanding where to configure the settings. The certificate is directly installed on the Edge Transport server; the outbound and inbound Domain Security is configured on the Hub Transport server in your Exchange organization.

REQUESTING AND INSTALLING A SAN CERTIFICATE

As noted earlier, the requirements for the certificate are as follows:

- It must be a certificate that was either issued by a trusted party (by importing their root certificate) or by a third-party CA.
- The certificate must be valid.

- The certificate must match the domain. For example, if you're sending an email from Exchange2007.com, the certificate must include the domain name Exchange2007.com as the subject or SAN.
- The certificate must be enabled for SMTP on the Edge server(s).

Verify that the certificates are enabled by using the following command in the EMS: `Get-ExchangeCertificate |fl`.

To verify that your Edge Transport server is ready to serve mutual TLS requests, you should use the command `TELNET <servername> SMTP` and verify that when you enter the command `EHLO` you see `STARTTLS` listed (see Figure 15.4). If it is not listed, check your Event Viewer's application log to find out what is wrong.

FIGURE 15.4 Edge Transport server that supports mutual TLS

```
Telnet ed01
220 ED01.exchange2007.com Microsoft ESMTP MAIL Service ready at Thu, 9 Aug 2007
18:59:48 +0200
250-ED01.exchange2007.com Hello [192.168.48.192]
250-SIZE 10485760
250-PIPELINING
250-DSN
250-ENHANCEDSTATUSCODES
250-STARTTLS
250-X-ANONYMOUSTLS
250-AUTH
250-X-EXPS NTLM
250-8BITMIME
250-BINARYMIME
250-CHUNKING
250 XEXCH50
```

Don't forget to check your partner's domain to verify that it supports mutual TLS before configuring outbound and inbound Domain Security. It will stop all message traffic if a mutual TLS connection cannot be made.

CONFIGURING OUTBOUND AND INBOUND DOMAIN SECURITY

After you ensure that the certificate is working correctly, the next step is to implement Domain Security for your business partners by specifying their domains. You can decide whether you want to enable it for one way (e.g., sending to your partner domain) or both directions.

Make sure you understand the impact of this decision. If Domain Security is not correctly enabled on both your side and the partner side, you may stop all message traffic between your domains. For example, if your partner domain's administrator forgets to configure the domain security but you already configured it, no messages can flow between the domains until either you remove the domain from the list or the other administrator configures your domain as secure.

To configure domain security, you need to connect to a Hub Transport server and run the following commands in the EMS:

- To enforce domain security on an outbound connection, use the following command:

  ```
  Set-TransportConfig -TLSSendDomainSecureList <DomainList>
  ```

- To enforce domain security on an inbound connection, run this command:

  ```
  Set-TransportConfig -TLSReceiveDomainSecureList <DomainList>
  ```

You need to configure this on a per-domain level. The domain list is not additive, so new domains are not automatically added, but replaced. You have to separate the domains using a comma. For example, you can use the following command to configure outbound domain security for the domains `partner.net` and `acme.net`:

```
Set-TransportConfig -TLSSendDomainSecureList acme.net, partner.net
```

Your last task is to make sure that the Send connectors and Receive connectors are enabled for Domain Security (Mutual Auth TLS). This is the default configuration, which is enabled if you do not change anything. The Send connector must be configured on the Hub Transport server; the Receive connector must be configured directly on the Edge Transport server.

As you are performing this configuration on your Hub Transport servers, it takes a cycle before your Edge servers will recognize it. To speed up this process, you can use the `Start-EdgeSynchronization` cmdlet in Exchange Management Shell.

TESTING MAIL FLOW

Testing the mail flow between your Exchange organization and your partner domain might be obvious, but it is the only way to find out if domain security is working correctly.

To test, you must use an Outlook 2007 client because OWA does not yet display the Domain Secured icon. Send a message to your partner and let them respond if you configured in both directions. If you receive a message that was sent over a domain-secured path, you should see a green check icon on the top right side of the message. Double-click to see the information, as shown in Figure 15.5.

FIGURE 15.5 Domain Security information in Outlook 2007

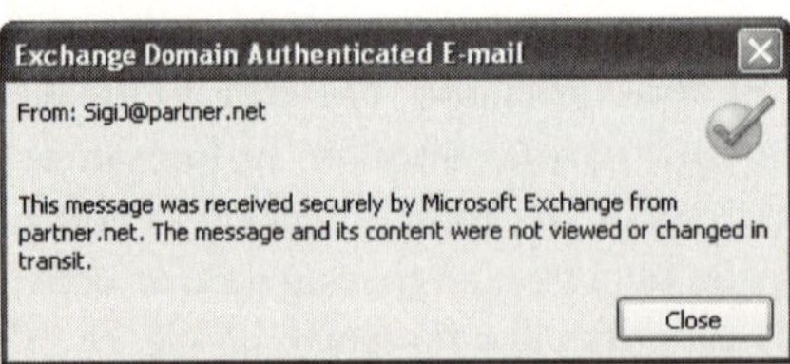

If the test does not work correctly, check the following on your Edge Transport server to find the problem:

- Event Viewer's application log
- The Queue Viewer in the Exchange Management Console's toolbox
- Protocol logging (if enabled)

Planning the Transport Rules Implementation

Exchange Server 2007 makes it easy to apply certain message policies to email messages flowing through your Exchange organization by using transport rules. You can think of transport rules as similar to Microsoft Outlook's email rules. Using a wizard, you can define what happens to an email that meets certain conditions.

This is an improvement over earlier Exchange versions, in which you had to programmatically create transport sinks that few programmers had experience writing code for. In Exchange 2007, you also can write custom code using the Exchange 2007 software development kit (SDK). However, for the most common scenarios, using the SDK is unnecessary because you can use the Transport Rule wizard to configure Exchange 2007.

As mentioned before, every message inside the Exchange organization must pass a Hub Transport server, so this is the place where the Hub Transport rules (or transport rules) are processed. Transport rules also can be applied to Edge Transport servers. The differences between them are as follows:

Hub Transport rules are used to apply compliance and policy-based rules to all messages in your Exchange organization. For example, they are used to add a disclaimer to the body of every message.

Edge rules are used to manage antispam and antivirus protection for your organization. For example, you can use them to easily prevent a certain message from entering the Exchange organization.

For the exam, it is important to understand the difference between a transport rule and an edge rule. You must understand when you use a transport rule and why you do not use an edge rule in the same situation. For example, if you add a disclaimer, you always use a transport rule but never an edge rule. For more information, see Table 15.6, "Examples of Differences between Transport Rules and Edge Rules."

The EMC and EMS do not differ between transport rules and edge rules. You configure them either as a transport rule directly on the Hub Transport server or directly on the Edge Transport server. We use the terms to differentiate between these two types of rules, as they have a different scope for usage.

Using Transport Rules

Transport rules on Hub Transport servers are important for applying message policies for your Exchange organization. In general, they are used to apply compliance and policy-based rules to messages. Many organizations require message policies because they are forced by law, regulatory requirements, or company policies to limit the interaction between certain departments or people. For example, certain workers may be allowed to communicate with their colleagues, but not with external recipients on the Internet. In general, you can use transport rules to perform the following tasks:

- Filtering confidential information
- Preventing confidential/company-sensitive information from leaving the organization
- Redirecting messages for inspection or preventing receipt of inbound and outbound messages
- Adding disclaimers to messages
- Applying an ethical firewall where people are not allowed to communicate with each other

The transport rules on the Hub Transport servers are managed centrally using the EMC. They are stored in Active Directory and are applied to every Hub Transport server once Active Directory replication takes place. Therefore, you only can apply a transport rule globally to all Hub Transport servers. Applying it to a single server is not possible.

Using Edge Rules

You use edge rules to prevent unwanted messages (such as spam or viruses) from entering or leaving your Exchange organization. Think about the last virus attack you had from the Internet, especially when message storms were generated. Edge rules can identify and screen out these messages by using the subject of the message) before they enter the organization. Edge rules would have prevented some disasters when the Melissa virus showed up years ago.

Some examples of situations in which you should consider using edge rules are as follows:

Virus outbreaks. You can react to an email virus even before the antivirus software can provide updates.

Spam attacks. Similar to virus outbreaks, but spam attacks are probably harder to identify. You can identify such messages and prevent them from entering the organization.

Denial of service attacks. If your organization experiences a denial of service (DoS) attack, you may be able to identify a way to drop the SMTP connections immediately so you're able to lower the attack's impact.

Because the Edge Transport server is not part of your Active Directory infrastructure, edge rules are stored in the Active Directory Application Mode (ADAM) instance on each server.

The drawback is that edge rules cannot be managed centrally but must be managed separately on every Edge Transport server.

Applying edge rules to each Edge Transport server separately allows you to define a granular approach to rules for your servers. For example, if you want to set rules based on the Edge Transport server's address, you can do so. On the other hand, you can distribute edge rules easily by using the EMS's cmdlet `Export-TransportRuleCollection` and `Import-TransportRuleCollection`.

Implementing Transport Rules

Now that you know the key differences between transport rules on a Hub Transport server and on an Edge Transport server, let's take a look at how these rules are implemented.

Each transport rule consists of the following components:

Conditions. Conditions are used to select the messages that will be subject to the transport rule action. If you do not select any condition, it will be applied to all messages.

Exceptions. Exceptions are used to identify messages to which the transport rule action should not be applied. You don't need to configure exceptions if you don't require them.

Actions. Actions are what will happen to the mail you specified using conditions and exceptions. You must have at least one action configured for every rule.

Additionally, when you create multiple rules, each rule will receive a priority. Using these priorities, you can control which rule will act on a message first. Rules with a lower priority will be processed first. For example, say you have two rules that apply for the same recipient; one rule is priority zero and the other rule is priority one. The priority-zero rule will first process the message, then the priority-one rule will process that same message. You may want to modify this if there are two rules that contradict or influence each other.

The transport rules differ from the edge rules in the areas of conditions, exceptions, and actions used: the transport rules are focused on organizational policy and compliance, whereas the edge rules are focused on protecting your organization from unwanted or harmful messages.

Table 15.6 provides an overview of how the transport rules differ from the edge rules. Not every condition, exception, or action is included, but it provides examples to give you an overview of the differences.

TABLE 15.6 Examples of Differences between Transport Rules and Edge Rules

Area	Transport Rules	Edge Rules
Examples of common conditions	From people From a member of distribution list Sent to users inside or outside the organization Marked with classification	When a subject field contains specific words When a message header contains specific words When any recipient address contains specific words
Examples of common actions	Apply message classification Append disclaimer text using font, size color, with separator and fall-back to action if unable to apply	Drop connection Put message in spam quarantine mailbox Reject the message with status code and response
Examples of common exceptions	Except when the message is from member of distribution list Except when the message is marked as classification Except when the message is marked as important	Except when the from address contains text patterns Except when text-specific words appears in any recipient address Except when text patterns appear in any recipient address

Rules can be applied to all messages apart from signed or encrypted messages. Signed or encrypted messages (e.g., S/MIME) are not changed because Exchange 2007 would break the digital signature or encryption. Only rules based on the client side are capable of applying rules to signed or encrypted messages.

In Exercise 15.1, you will use the EMC to configure a company disclaimer for every message that is sent outside the Exchange organization. Also, you will configure an exclusion rule to define users who do not have a disclaimer automatically added to their messages.

EXERCISE 15.1

Implementing a Company Disclaimer

To configure a company disclaimer, follow these steps:

1. Open the EMC on one of your Hub Transport servers.
2. Expand Organization Configuration and click on Hub Transport.
3. Select New Transport Rule on the Actions pane (right side).

EXERCISE 15.1 *(continued)*

4. Fill in the transport rules name and a comment (provide some information about when and why this rule was created). Click Next.

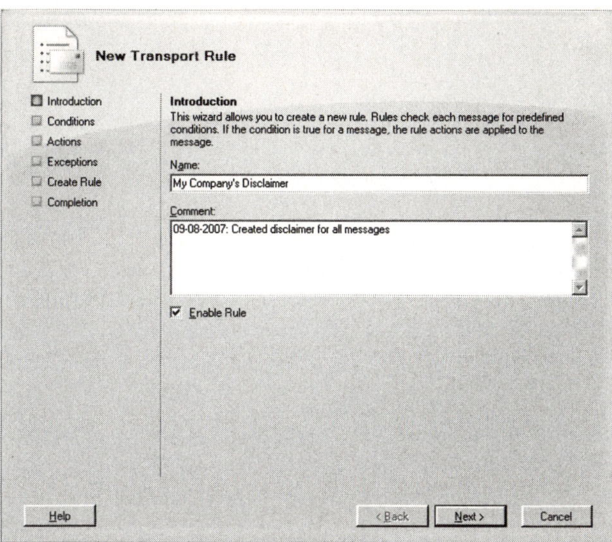

5. On the Conditions window, select Sent to Users Inside or Outside the Organization and choose Outside in the Edit the rule pane. Click Next.

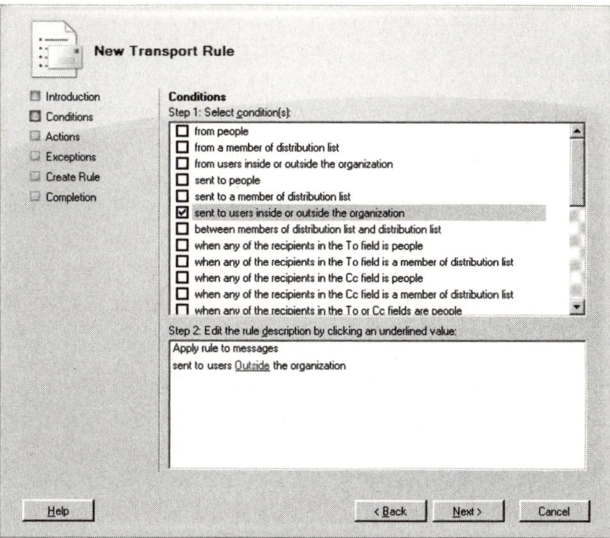

6. In the Actions window, select Append Disclaimer Text Using Font, Size, Color, with Separator and Fallback to Action If Unable to Apply.

EXERCISE 15.1 *(continued)*

7. In the Edit rule, you can add a disclaimer text and select other options, such as font. For this exercise, simply add some disclaimer text and then click Next.

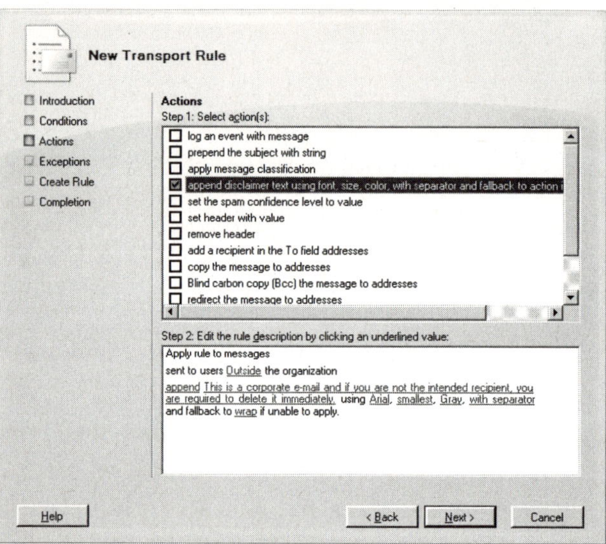

8. In the Exceptions window, select Except When the Message Is from People. You can now define which people you want to exclude from this rule, meaning that no disclaimer will be added for them. Click Next.

9. The next window shows the configuration summary. Click Next.

10. The completion window will be displayed. Click Finish to end the wizard.

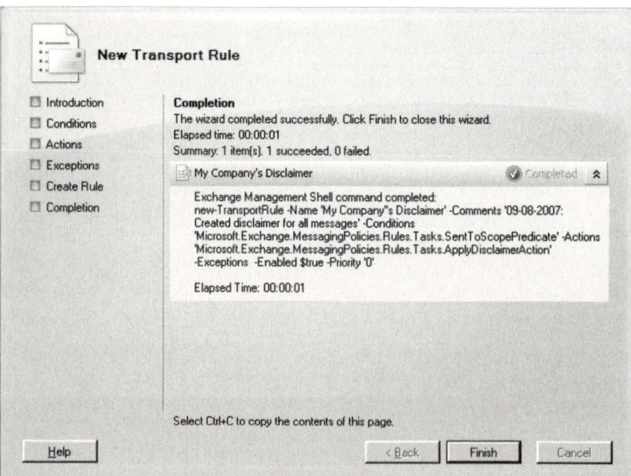

EXERCISE 15.1 *(continued)*

11. You will see the new transport rule that is part of the Transport Rules tab in your organization configuration. If you have multiple rules, you also can apply priorities. Remember that this rule is first stored to the Active Directory, so it takes some time until the Hub Transport servers will act on it.

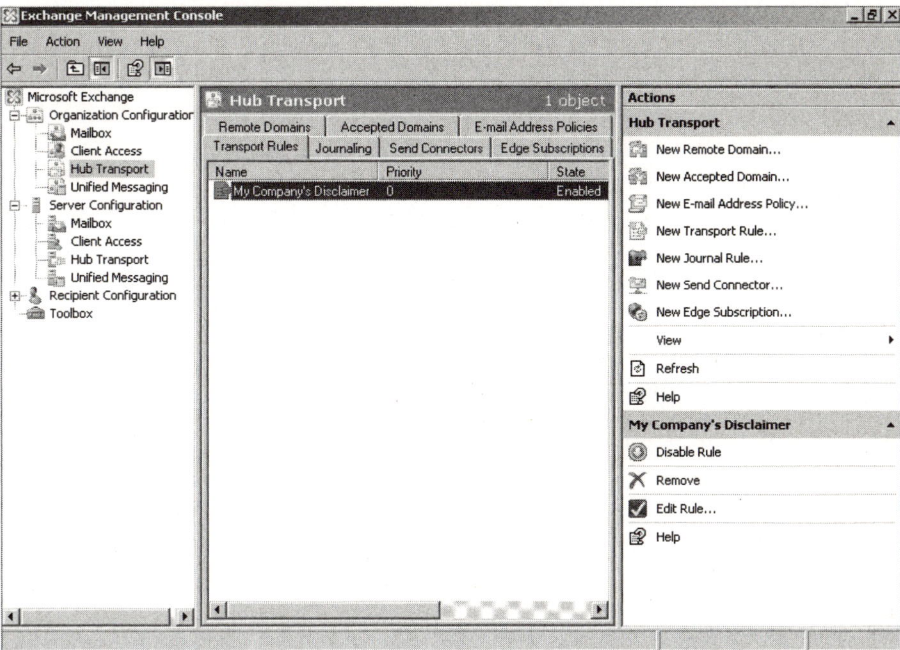

Implementing S/MIME

S/MIME is a standard for public-key encryption and signatures of email messages. Encryption is used to protect the content of a message so only the intended recipients can read it. Signing a message means that the recipient can verify whether the message has been changed on the way from the sender to the recipient.

S/MIME is an important security topic in Exchange Server 2007 and is included here to provide a complete discussion of message security. However, it's *not* a part of the Microsoft exam.

S/MIME is a client-based encryption and signing protocol that provides end-to-end security, from the sending mailbox to the receiving mailbox. Unlike other encryption protocols that are session-based on the transport layer (like TLS), the message also remains encrypted and signed within the mailbox. Even administrators cannot decrypt it if their digital certificate does not allow them to do so. Implementing S/MIME offers the following abilities:

- Use digital signatures as a way to prove to your communication partners that the content was not altered.
- Authenticate messages (especially for crucial functions such as when your boss approves your travel requests).
- Encrypt messages to prevent accidental disclosure of the content.

By default, Exchange Server 2007 fully supports S/MIME for message encryption and signatures. Unlike in previous versions, where you had to configure every mailbox database, you do not need to configure any server-side setting to support S/MIME.

Because S/MIME provides end-to-end security, it is important that the email application you use to read and write S/MIME messages meets the following two requirements:

- It must support S/MIME encryption and signatures.
- The digital signature must be configured in the email application.

Table 15.7 provides an overview of the email access S/MIME included in Exchange Server 2007.

TABLE 15.7 S/MIME Support in Exchange 2007

Email Access	S/MIME Support
Outlook 2003	Yes
Outlook 2007	Yes
OWA in Exchange 2007	No
Mobile devices using Exchange ActiveSync	No

OWA will support S/MIME encryption when Exchange Server Service Pack 1, is applied. This feature is not available in the release version of Exchange Server 2007.

To implement S/MIME in your Exchange organization, you need to follow these steps:

1. Set up a CA that issues certificates for your users or buy user certificates from a third-party CA such as VeriSign. If you set up your own CA, make sure that the communication partner of your company trusts your root CA, and have your users' public keys available, either stored in their contacts or in the directory.
2. Provide the certificates to your users either manually or automatically by publishing the certificate to the Active Directory.
3. Install certificates on your users' workstations.
4. Enable certificates in Outlook. You must select the correct certificate in the security settings to be able to use them.

Signing and encrypting messages also means that your antivirus or spam protection will not act upon these messages because they might destroy the digital signature. Also, Exchange 2007 transport rules ignore S/MIME messages.

In your S/MIME implementation plan, you also should consider these business questions:

- Should everybody in the organization be allowed to encrypt messages? Especially in compliance areas where archiving is a mandatory requirement, you should discuss this with your legal department.
- Are encrypted messages allowed to leave the organization? If so, confidential information could be sent to an unauthorized recipient, including a competitor, and no evidence will be available.

Exercise 15.2 shows you how to enable S/MIME in Outlook 2007 for the user Carola Mechelke who installed a certificate to her workstation using Internet Explorer. You can verify whether the certificate was installed correctly using the Internet Explorer options Content tab and clicking on Certificates. You should see at least one certificate for the local user.

EXERCISE 15.2

Manually Enable S/MIME Encryption in Outlook 2007

To manually enable S/MIME encryption in your Outlook 2007 client, follow these steps:

1. Click Start ➢ All Programs ➢ Microsoft Office ➢ Microsoft Office Outlook 2007.
2. Click Tools ➢ Trust Center.
3. On the left pane, select Email Security.
4. Click on Settings.

EXERCISE 15.2 *(continued)*

5. If your certificate is the only one installed on the local computer, you should have all the configuration options preconfigured. You just need to confirm the settings by clicking on OK.

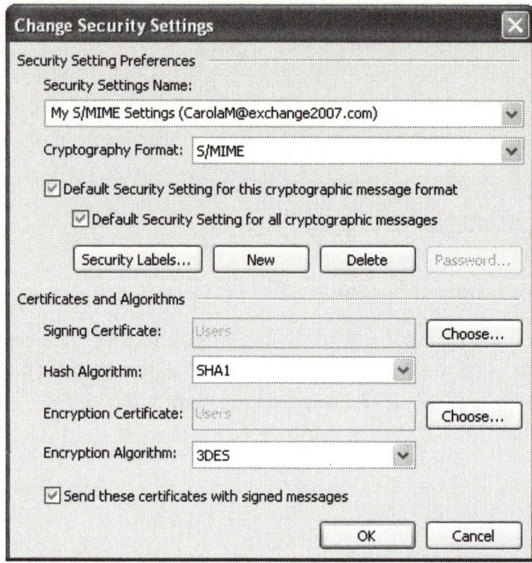

6. Confirm your default settings by clicking OK.

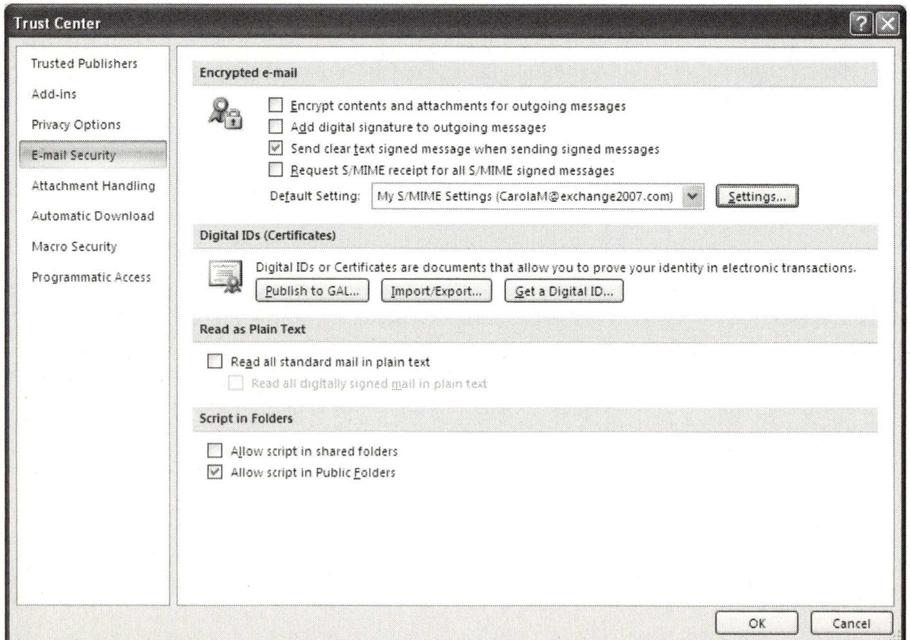

EXERCISE 15.2 *(continued)*

7. Once you compose a new message, you the encryption buttons will be available in Outlook 2007. Confirm your default settings by clicking OK.

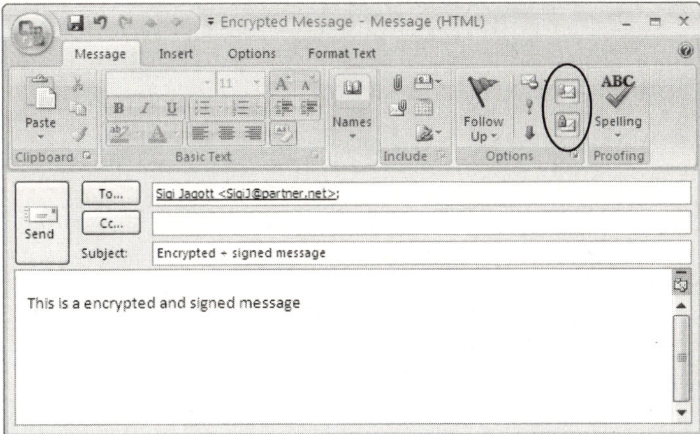

Implementing Message Journaling

Message journaling is becoming more important for companies. Whereas archiving refers to reducing the amount of data by moving it to other (usually cheaper) storage, *journaling* means recording all communications in an organization for use in the organization's archival strategy. Journaling is a part of security because it enables you to satisfy company or governmental policies about storing and keeping sensitive information for later lookup.

Journaling is required in certain industries or regions because of governmental regulations such as the Sarbanes-Oxley Act of 2002 (SOX), Securities and Exchange Commission Rule 17a-4 (SEC Rule 17a-4), and the European Union Data Protection Directive (EUDPD). It is important to talk to your company's compliance or security people to determine the journaling requirements for the messaging system you're planning.

Exchange 2007 provides two different options for journaling: standard and premium. But before we jump into the details of these two options, we will first explore some basics about journaling—journal reports and journaling mailboxes.

Journal Reports

When journaling is enabled, any message that is stored to a journaling mailbox is called a journal report. In Exchange 2003, a journal message was a copy of the message, the results being similar to adding the journal mailbox as BCC (blind carbon copy) to every email. In Exchange 2007 this changed to the envelope journaling format.

A journal report using the envelope journaling format includes the following:

- The original message is included unaltered as an attachment in Transport Neutral Encapsulation Format (TNEF). TNEF is a richer format that maintains higher fidelity of the original message. For example, information such as voting buttons or read receipts is retained.
- The body of the journal report contains the sender email address, subject, message ID, and recipient email addresses from the original message.

Figure 15.6 shows an example of a journal report message.

FIGURE 15.6 A journal report message

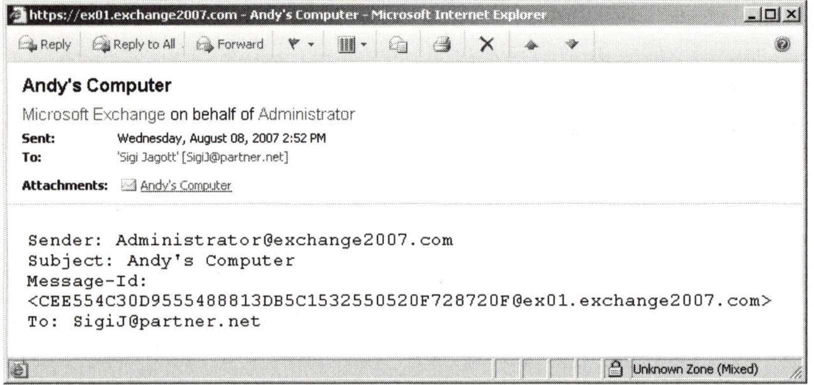

When you move from Exchange 2003 to Exchange 2007, make sure your archiving software supports journal report envelopes. If not, you need to wait until you get Exchange 2007 SP1 because it will include functionality to down-convert journal reports to the old format.

Journaling Mailboxes

Journaling mailboxes are used to store journal reports. You can create a single mailbox for all your company and journal rules or create a mailbox for each rule. How you configure it depends on your special requirements.

Because journaling mailboxes contain company-sensitive information, you should clearly define who will be able to access them. You should limit access to only those individuals who have a direct need to access the journal mailboxes. Directly add each user account to the mailbox, and make sure that you closely monitor who accesses that mailbox.

Many laws require that messages remain tamer-free (meaning nobody is allowed to log in and modify the messages), but how can you prevent the journaling mailbox from being mistakenly addressed by others? The best practice is to limit access to itself only. You can achieve this by using the following EMS command on a mailbox ("Journal" is used here as an example mailbox name):

```
Set-Mailbox "Journal" -AcceptMessagesOnlyFrom "Journal" -
RequireSenderAuthenticationEnabled $True
```

Standard Journaling

Standard journaling in Exchange 2007 refers to the journaling concept of Exchange 2003. That is, you can define a journal mailbox on every mailbox database that saves every message sent from or received by recipients from this mailbox database.

This means that you can configure journaling based on a mailbox database. All messages that flow through this store are copied to the journal mailbox. You can control journaling by moving mailboxes between certain mailbox stores on an Exchange server or between Exchange servers.

It is easy to implement standard journaling. Just open your Mailbox server in Server Configuration of the Exchange Management Console, and click on Properties in your mailbox database. You'll see a window that is similar to the one shown in Figure 15.7, where you can define the journal recipient for this specific mailbox database.

FIGURE 15.7 Server properties for journaling

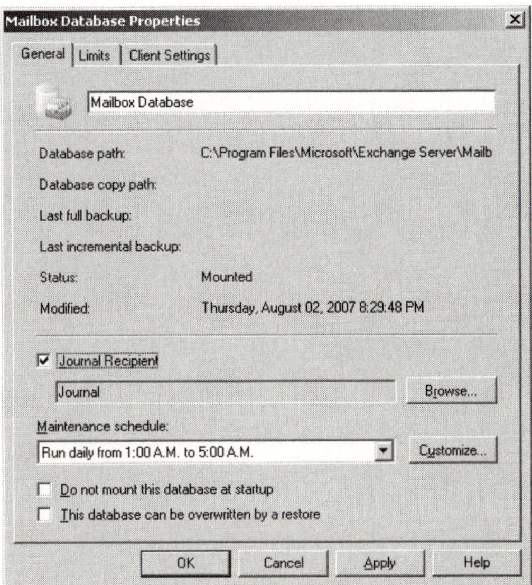

To enable or disable journaling on a mailbox database, you need to be either an Exchange Server Administrator for that server or an Exchange Organization Administrator.

Premium Journaling

Standard journaling is sufficient for small to medium companies that do not have hundreds of databases on their Exchange servers. However, in large companies with many Exchange Mailbox servers hosting multiple databases each, it can be difficult to configure and maintain each and every database. Remember—if compliance requires archiving all the messages for a specific person or group, you better make sure it is happening!

For that reason Microsoft added a feature called premium journaling or journal rules to Exchange 2007. Using this feature you can create one or more rules that match your specific journaling needs. Journal rules can be defined on the following parameters:

- Journal messages for recipient
- Journal rule scope
- Journal Unified Messaging

Journal Messages for Recipient

New in Exchange 2007 is the journal feature that allows you to select specific mailboxes, contacts, or distribution lists to journal. This object must belong to your Exchange organization, so you cannot use an SMTP address without creating a contact for journaling. However, distribution lists are a very flexible way to control journaling.

For example, you can create a company-wide journal distribution group to which you add all mailboxes that you need to journal because they may be subject to the regulatory requirements. Management is simplified because you can simply assign permission for this distribution list to your company's compliance department so they can manage it themselves.

If you do not select any recipient or disable Journal Message for Recipient, all messages sent to or from your Exchange organization are considered by journaling.

Because every Hub Transport server maintains a recipient cache to look up recipient and distribution group information, changes to journal rule recipients might take up to four hours (when the recipient cache is refreshed on a Hub Transport server).

Journal Rule Scope

You also can define journaling based on a scope that you can set for each journal rule. This is especially important if you need to control the message flow in a certain way, outbound or internal. You can select one of the following three scopes:

Global. All messages that pass through Hub Transport servers

Internal. Messages that are sent or received by recipients inside your Exchange organization

External. Messages that are sent to recipients or from senders outside your Exchange organization

For example, a journal rule scope could be used to journal all messages for all stock traders that are sent to or received from external recipients. Another example is to journal all internal message traffic for a specified period of time when the audit department requires it.

Journal Unified Messaging

Journaling by default also includes any Unified Messaging message like voicemail and missed-call notifications. You may decide not to journal such messages in your Exchange organization (for example, to preserve hard disk space). You can enable or disable journaling for voicemail by using the following command in the EMS:

```
Set-TransportConfig -VoicemailJournalingEnabled $False
```

This command will disable journaling for voicemails and missed-call notifications for your entire Exchange organization. Unfortunately, there is no way to define this on a per-server or per-user scope; you can only enable or disable it globally.

When you decide to disable voicemail journaling, remember that this only applies to voice messages and missed-call notifications, but not to faxes or messages received from the Unified Messaging server—they will always be part of journaling.

Managing Premium Journaling

Because all journal rules are configured in the Organization Configuration section of the Exchange Management Console, you need to be an Exchange Organization Administrator to create and modify them. As you know, the Organization Configuration is automatically replicated to all Exchange servers within your Exchange organization. This makes it easy to configure journal rules on your Hub Transport servers: Just configure them once, and they are applied to all servers automatically using replication.

If you create multiple journal rules that include the same mailbox, you will end up journaling multiple copies of the journal reports. For example, if you created a journal rule that includes all mailboxes and journals all internal messages and you create a journal rule for a mailbox called Trader; all messages from and to the mailbox Trader will be send to both the first and the second journal mailbox. To prevent message journaling redundancy, you should plan your journaling rules clearly.

Premium journaling requires an Exchange 2007 Enterprise Client Access License (CAL). If you're planning to use this feature, don't forget to mention it when buying the licenses for your company. Otherwise you should only use standard journaling.

To practice premium journaling, you will now create a journal rule that will journal all messages (scope: Global) for `Administrator@exchange2007.com` to the journal mailbox called Journal. Exercise 15.3 takes you through the steps.

EXERCISE 15.3

Configuring a Journal Rule

To configure a journal rule to journal all messages for the Administrator mailbox, follow these steps:

1. Open the Exchange Management Console.
2. Expand Organization Configuration.
3. Select Hub Transport and click on the Journal tab.
4. On the Action pane, click New Journal Rule to bring up the New Journal Rule window.
5. Configure all settings as shown below, then click New to create the rule.

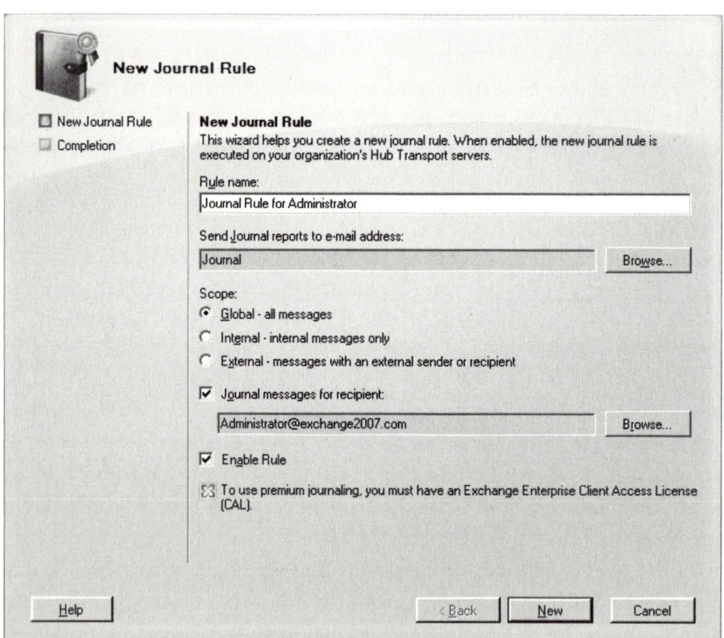

Don't forget that the rules are first stored in the Configuration partition of the Active Directory and will not immediately be applied to your Hub Transport servers.

Real World Scenario

The Practical Case for Journaling

Financial institutions such banks are required to journal all the communications of their stockbrokers. Imagine if you were an administrator using Exchange 2003 at such an institution. You'd have to put these mailboxes on a specific mailbox database and enable journaling for that database. If the brokers were spread throughout your organization on a global basis, this would be quite some effort to implement. Either you'd end up with many mailbox databases just for the purpose of journaling, or you'd enable journaling for too many mailboxes. This, of course, would increase your hard-disk space requirements tremendously.

Now imagine using Exchange 2007 instead. In Exchange 2007, implementation of such a rule is made quite easy for the messaging professional. You just create a distribution list that includes all your stockbrokers and apply this to a journal rule. Only the messages from mailboxes on the distribution list would be journaled. This way, you would optimize your archiving volume immediately with just a few steps.

Your finance department will be happy about that!

Protecting Exchange Server 2007 with ISA 2006

Internet Security and Acceleration (ISA) Server 2006 is a security gateway that helps to protect your applications from Internet-based threats. You can think of ISA Server 2006 as an enhanced firewall system for your perimeter network. It is not part of Exchange 2007 and has to be purchased separately from Microsoft if you want to use it.

ISA 2006 is not a part of the exam. We've included this information because it will be useful to you as an Exchange Server administrator.

ISA Server 2006 and Microsoft Exchange Server 2007 are designed to work together to provide you with a secure messaging environment. Microsoft lists the following new features for ISA Server 2006, which are designed specifically for Exchange 2007:

Web publishing load balancing. ISA Server 2006 balances the request from the client to an array of published servers. This eliminates the need to deploy Network Load Balancing (NLB) on the published array.

Link translation. Some published web sites may include references to internal names of computers. Because only the ISA Server 2006 firewall and external namespaces are available to external clients, these references appear as broken links. ISA Server 2006 includes a link-translation feature that you can use to create a dictionary of definitions for internal computer names that map to publicly known names.

Secure Sockets Layer (SSL) bridging support. For authenticated and encrypted client access, ISA Server 2006 provides end-to-end security and application layer filtering by using SSL-to-SSL bridging.

Client Access for Exchange 2007. ISA Server 2006 is designed to work specifically with the client access methods like Outlook Anywhere available in Exchange 2007.

Although ISA Server 2006 offers several other features; this section provides only an overview of the Exchange-related features focused on routing SMTP messages and managing client access.

Routing SMTP Messages

You can configure an ISA Server 2006 to route SMTP messages before they reach an Exchange server. In previous versions of Exchange, this functionality was more important, but with the introduction of the Exchange server role concept, especially with the Edge Transport server role, you might want to consider directly routing messages to your Edge Transport server rather than using the ISA Server 2006 for that task.

However, you can still configure it, and this section explains the steps you need to consider when you want to route your inbound and outbound SMTP email traffic through your ISA Server 2006. Namely, for ISA Server 2006, you publish your SMTP mail server.

You have to meet the following DNS requirements before you can publish your SMTP server:

- You need to have an A record pointing to the external IP address of your ISA Server 2006.
- Your mail domain's public Mail Exchanger (MX) record must point to that A record.

Don't forget to verify that the MX record only includes the A record of your ISA Server 2006; otherwise the message might skip ISA Server and go directly to an Exchange server.

Additionally, you must take the following steps to configure the ISA Server 2006 to route messages to and from your Exchange organization correctly. You have to perform the following steps in Firewall Policy using the Microsoft ISA Server 2006 snap-in:

1. Publish mail servers to configure inbound email communication to be forwarded from the ISA server to your Edge Transport server.
2. Create a computer object for all your sending Edge Transport servers.
3. Create an access rule and add all the created computer objects to configure outbound communication so your Edge Transport servers are able to send emails to the Internet.

After you've configured all the steps, you should verify that the message flow to and from the Internet is working correctly. Don't forget to check the message paths and connections to verify that the message communication is passing the ISA Server 2006.

Configuring Client Access

One of the key benefits of the ISA Server 2006 is to provide Internet-based client access. It does not support placing a Client Access Server in the perimeter or on the Internet. But many companies still want to provide their users with access to their mailboxes when they are outside their corporate LAN. You need to use an advanced firewall server to securely publish client access. ISA Server 2006 provides you with an easy way to publish client access because it includes a new Exchange Publishing Rule wizard (found in the ISA Server under Firewall Policy tasks). The wizard helps you to configure the ISA Server 2006 for access to the following features:

- Outlook Web Access
- Exchange ActiveSync
- Outlook Anywhere
- POP3 and IMAP4 access

To understand the complete process, the following sections will walk you through the requirements for configuring client access, including installing a certificate on your server, choosing your client authentication, configuring your Client Access server, and implementing publishing rules.

Installing a Certificate on the ISA Server

You should start by installing a server certificate on the ISA Server 2006. The differences between the various certificates are described in the "Types of Certificates" section earlier in this chapter.

One of the basic requirements for the ISA Server 2006 is to have a certificate from a CA that is trusted by your clients. Therefore, you either should get a third-party CA or install your root certificate on all of the devices that will use your ISA Server 2006 to access their Exchange mailboxes. If you forget this task, your clients will receive a message to confirm the certificate of your ISA Server 2006 every time they access it.

Deciding Which Client Authentication to Use

Before configuring your ISA Server 2006, you need to decide how clients will authenticate. The following table provides you with a list of the most common and recommended client-authentication methods.

TABLE 15.8 Client Authentication for ISA Server 2006

Client Authentication Method	Authentication Validation	Authentication Delegation	Access Methods
HTML forms-based authentication	Windows (AD) LDAP RADIUS	Basic Negotiate (Kerberos / NTLM)	OWA (see the important note below) Outlook Anywhere Microsoft ActiveSync (only basic)

TABLE 15.8 Client Authentication for ISA Server 2006 *(continued)*

Client Authentication Method	Authentication Validation	Authentication Delegation	Access Methods
HTML forms-based authentication	RSA SecurID	RSA SecurID	OWA Microsoft ActiveSync (requires RSA SecurID component installed on Exchange servers)
SSL client certificate authentication	Windows (Active Directory)	Kerberos constrained delegation	OWA Microsoft ActiveSync

Configuring Your Client Access Server

Before continuing, make sure that the following steps are configured on your Client Access Server:

1. Make sure that forms-based authentication is not enabled on your CAS and basic authentication is used.
2. Enable Outlook Anywhere.
3. Install a server certificate on your CAS.
4. Configure the default website on your CAS to require secure sockets layer (SSL).

Implementing Exchange Publishing Rules

Before you create Exchange web Client Access publishing rules, you need to create a web listener. You must have Microsoft ISA Server 2006 installed. Remember: ISA 2006 is *not* part of the exam. The following sections simply offer you real-world examples of how to combine the two products.

Creating a Web Listener

The web listener is used to indicate the IP address and port to which a client connects, and then the IP address is assigned to publishing rules. Web listeners can be used by more than one publishing rule. This means if you do not have any business requirements to divide up the IP addresses or ports for your clients, you can use a single web listener for all our Exchange publishing rules.

The following are the web listener properties:

- IP addresses and ports used for listening for web requests
- Server certificates to use with IP addresses
- Authentication method to use
- Number of concurrent connections that are allowed

To create a web listener in your ISA Server 2006, follow these steps:

1. Click Start ➢ All Programs ➢ Microsoft ISA Server ➢ ISA Server Management.
2. Click on Firewall Policy.
3. Click on the right pane access Toolbox tab and select New ➢ Web Listener in Network Objects, as shown in Figure 15.8.

FIGURE 15.8 Selecting New ➢ Web Listener

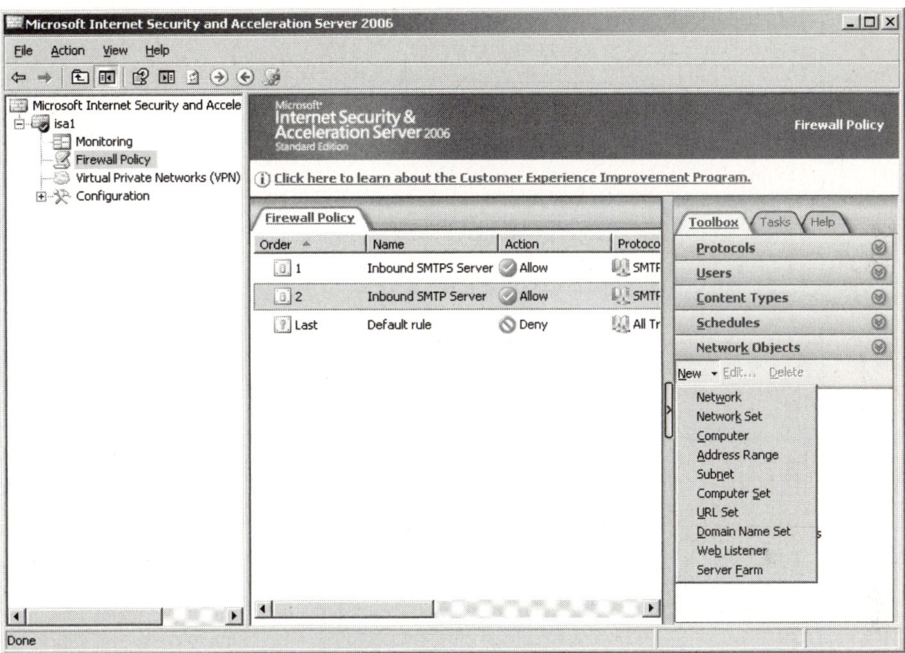

4. On the Welcome page, provide a web listener name (e.g., Exchange Client Access).
5. As shown in Figure 15.9, select Require SSL Secured Connections with Clients and click Next.
6. Select External in the Listen for Incoming Web Requests frame and click on Select IP Addresses.
7. Check Specified IP addresses on the ISA Server, and add your IP address to Selected IP Addresses. Click OK.
8. As shown in Figure 15.10, continue with Next and select Use a Single Certificate for this Web Listener. Select the server certificate you installed on the ISA server using the Select Certificate button, and click Next.

FIGURE 15.9 Client Connection Security page

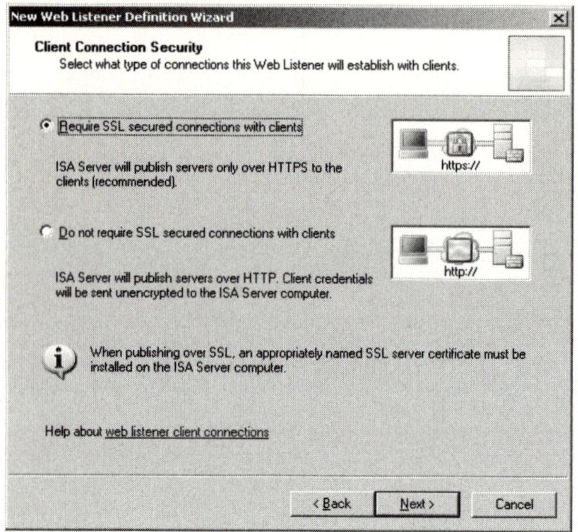

FIGURE 15.10 Listener SSL Certificates page

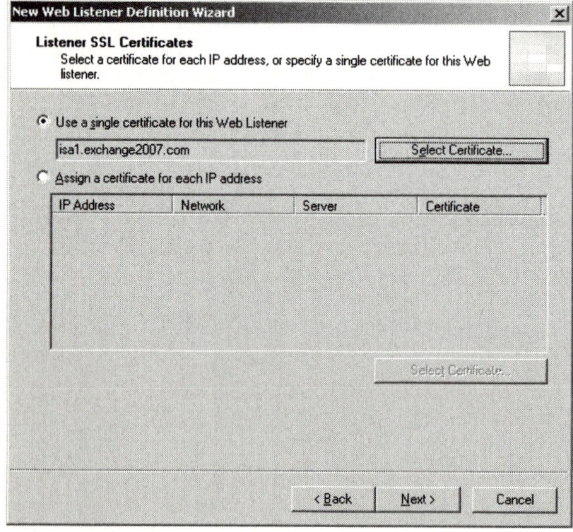

9. On the Authentication Settings page, select HTML Form Authentication to enable forms-based authentication and select which client credentials the ISA server uses. Click Next to continue.
10. On the Single Sign On Settings page (Figure 15.11), add your Active Directory domain name and click Next.
11. On the Summary page, verify your settings and click Finish to create the web listener.

FIGURE 15.11 Single Sign On Settings page

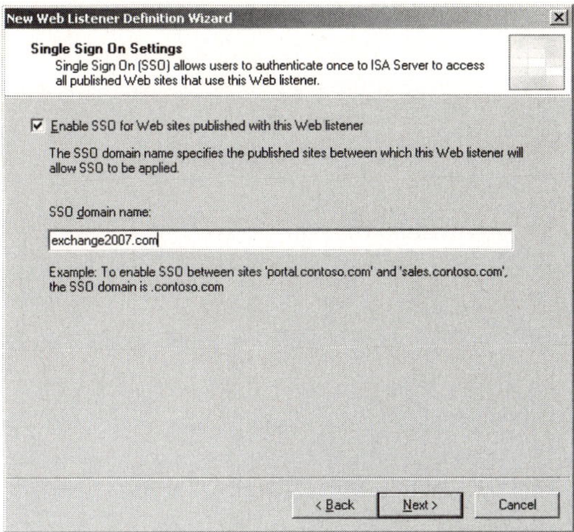

The web listener should be available in the Network Objects area of your toolbox.

Creating Exchange Publishing Rules

An Exchange publishing rule is used to configure your ISA Server 2006 to fully support Exchange client requests from the Internet. There will be no direct connect of a client to your CAS, but all the clients will connect to the ISA Server 2006 first, which then forwards the request to the CAS according to the conditions of your publishing rule.

Because ISA Server 2006 includes an Exchange Publishing Rule wizard that is optimized for Exchange 2007, this task is not very difficult.

You cannot publish multiple access methods at the same time when using the Exchange Publishing Rule wizard; you have to create one rule for every access method, such as OWA or Outlook Anywhere.

To create an Exchange publishing rule for OWA, follow these steps:

1. Click Start ➢ All Programs ➢ Microsoft ISA Server ➢ ISA Server Management.
2. Click on Firewall Policy.
3. On the right pane, access the Tasks tab and click on Publish Exchange Web Client Access.
4. Enter a name for the Exchange publishing rule (e.g., Exchange OWA) and click Next.
5. Select your Exchange version (Exchange Server 2007) and the client access method you want to configure. For this exercise, check Outlook Web Access, as shown in Figure 15.12, and click Next.
6. On the next page, you have to select the publisher type. Select Publish a Single Website or Load Balancer, and continue with Next.
7. Select Use SSL to Connect to the Published Web server or Server Farm, and click Next.

FIGURE 15.12 Select Services page

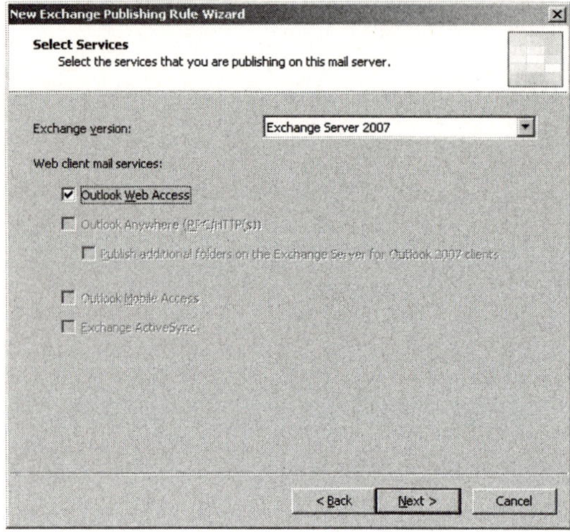

8. On the Internal Publishing Details page, you have to enter the internal site name, which is normally the FQDN of your CAS, and click Next. (See Figure 15.13.)
9. Next add the public name that your users will type to access the ISA server, as shown in Figure 15.14. Remember that this must match the FQDN of the certificate you selected when you created the web listener. Choose Next to continue.
10. Select the web listener for the publishing rule and click Next.
11. On the Authentication Delegation page, select the authentication method ISA Server uses for the published web server. Select Basic authentication, and click Next.

FIGURE 15.13 Internal Publishing Details page

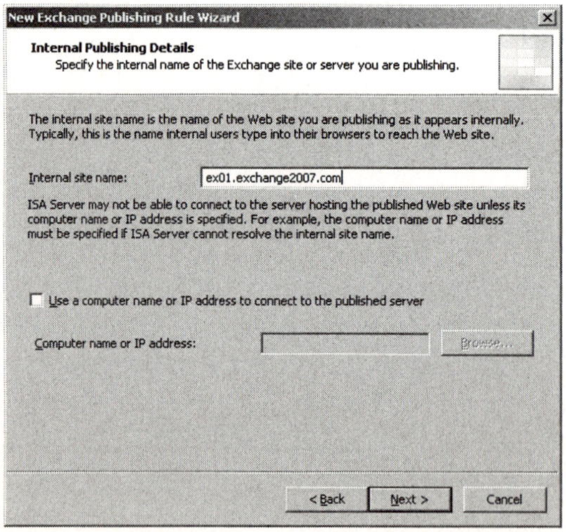

FIGURE 15.14 Public Name Details page

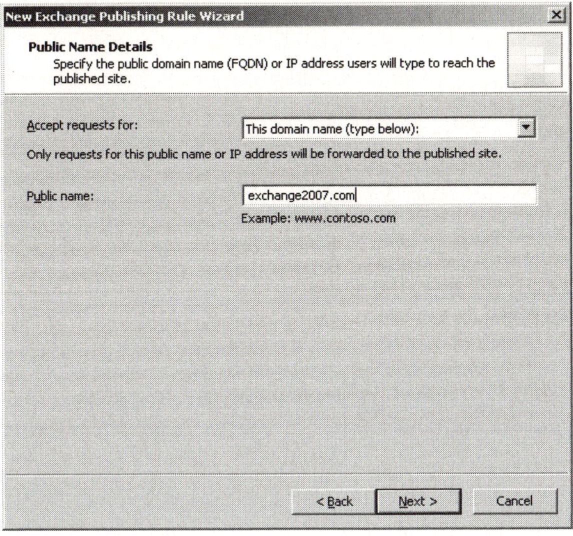

12. Finally, define the user set that this rule applies to. Leave the default (All Authenticated Users), and choose Next to continue.
13. On the summary page, verify your settings and click Finish to create the Exchange publishing rule.
14. Click on Apply in the Details pane to update the configuration.

You have now created a single Exchange publishing rule for OWA. If you want to enable the other access methods, you must create more rules for Outlook Anywhere and Exchange ActiveSync.

ISA Server 2006 attachment blocking with Exchange Server 2007 is not supported. If you want to block attachments, you need to configure attachment blocking on the Exchange 2007 server.

Summary

Planning for security is quite a complex (and, hopefully, interesting) task. It touches many different areas, such as the network, Windows Active Directory, certificates, and transport rules, making it one of the most complex topics in Exchange server design.

By now you should understand the basics of certificates and which protocols to use to achieve certain security results. Good security design also should consider the differences between network-based, session-based, and client-based encryption and when to use each. But communication encryption and authentication are not the only aspects of security. You also need to consider the use of journaling to archive messages and the use of transport rules to act on specific messages.

All these topics together, combined with a solid understanding of what Exchange Server 2007 can offer your company in terms of security, provide a good way to create a thorough plan. And that is exactly what is required of an excellent Exchange Messaging IT professional.

Exam Essentials

Know about firewall rules and what Ports need to be considered. In a secure environment, you need to understand what is required and what can be shut down, especially when considering the firewall ports. Here you should see the interaction between the different server roles and what service requires what ports to be opened at the firewall. Don't forget to recognize when the server communication is encrypted and when it is not.

Understand the different security protocols of Exchange 2007. Exchange 2007 supports various security protocols, but the most important are IPSec, VPN, and TLS. You should understand the differences among these protocols and how Exchange 2007 uses TLS to establish domain security. Mutual TLS is one of the key topics in this chapter that you should be able to describe and configure. Also, you should recognize the different types of certificates to be used and their requirements.

Transport rules make a major difference. Transport rules are another key topic. They provide an easy way to set rules on the message flow. You need to understand the differences between Hub Transport rules and Edge Transport rules and when to configure a rule where. Hub Transport rules are configured once for all Hub Transport servers, but Edge Transport rules have to be configured at every single Edge server.

Understand S/MIME support in Exchange 2007. By default, Exchange Server 2007 supports S/MIME and you do not need to configure anything on the server side. But you need to understand what S/MIME is about, how you can implement it for your organization, and what it requires.

Know about message journaling. You should understand the differences between standard and premium journaling and how to configure journaling. Don't forget about the license requirements for the premium journaling features and the new journal report format that might cause some problems with your existing archiving software.

Review Questions

1. You want to open access on your firewall to a Mailbox server. What ports do you need to open for MAPI access? (Select all that apply.)

   A. 25/TCP (SSL)

   B. 53/TCP/UDP (DNS)

   C. 135/TCP (RPC)

   D. 445/TCP (SMB)

2. On your Edge Transport server, you did not install any other certificates after running Exchange 2007 setup. Your partner in a different Exchange organization that also has also an Edge Transport server in the perimeter network did the same. Will the communication between both Edge Transport servers be encrypted by default?

   A. Yes

   B. No

3. What firewall ports do you need to open to let an ISA Server 2006 sitting in the perimeter network communicate to the CAS role sitting in your LAN for Outlook Web Access or Outlook Anywhere? (Select all that apply.)

   A. 80/TCP (HTTP)

   B. 443/TCP (SSL)

   C. 110/TCP (TLS)

   D. 995/TCP (SSL)

4. Carola is system administrator of a highly secured messaging environment. She has to make sure that server-to-server traffic is fully encrypted even when Exchange is not sending the data. What protocol should Carola use to satisfy her requirements? (Choose one.)

   A. S/MIME

   B. TLS

   C. SSL

   D. IPSec

5. You implemented IPSec as the protocol to encrypt server-to-server traffic as part of your Exchange Server 2007 implementation plan. What configuration steps do you need to consider on the Exchange Server 2007 Receive connector? (Select all that apply.)

   A. Enable Exchange Servers on the Permission Groups tab.

   B. Enable Legacy Exchange Servers on the Permission Groups tab.

   C. Enable Externally Secured on the Authentication tab.

   D. Enable Exchange Server Authentication on the Authentication tab.

6. You want to implement a secured message path over the Internet to some of your partners who also have Exchange 2007 and have Internet-facing Edge Transport servers. What do you need to do to gain the required functionality? (Choose one.)

   A. You have to make sure that all Edge Transport servers from you and your partners have server certificates installed and you configured Domain Security for your partners' domains on your side.

   B. You have to make sure that your Edge Transport server has a server certificate installed and that you and your partners configured Domain Security for your domains.

   C. You have to make sure that your Edge Transport server has a server certificate installed and that you configured Domain Security for your partners' domains on your side.

   D. You have to make sure that all Edge Transport servers from you and your partners have server certificates installed and that you and your partners configured Domain Security for your domains.

7. What types of certificates support Exchange 2007 Domain Security using mutual TLS? (Select all that apply.)

   A. Exchange 2007 self-signed certificates

   B. Third-party certificates such as certificates from VeriSign

   C. Windows PKI–generated certificates

   D. Paper certificates

8. Andy is administrator of a large messaging environment that has the address space `Exchange2007.com`. He set up an Edge Transport server called Edge.Exchange2007.com and now wants to request a server certificate for his Edge Transport server that supports TLS and mutual TLS. What information does he need to provide to the CA? (Select all that apply.)

   A. The server name, Edge.Exchange2007.com, which should be added as the subject name

   B. The domain name, Exchange2007.com, which has to be added as a Subject Alternative Name (SAN) to the certificate

   C. The domain name, Exchange2007.com, which has to be added as an Alternative Name to the certificate

   D. The server name, Edge.Exchange2007.com, which should be added as an Alternative Name (AN) to the certificate

9. You installed a server certificate to your Edge Transport server. After a reboot, you use `TELNET <servername> SMTP` and the command `EHLO` to verify that the TLS is working correctly. Unfortunately, the command `STARTTLS` is not displayed in the command list. What could be the possible reasons for this? (Select all that apply.)

   A. The certificate installed is not valid anymore.

   B. The certificate was not enabled for SMTP.

   C. The certificate does not match to the domain.

   D. The certificate was issued by a third-party CA.

10. Jan is thinking about implementing transport rules for providing a company disclaimer. On what Exchange Server role does he need to configure the rule? (Choose one.)

A. Mailbox server

B. Hub Transport server

C. Client Access server

D. Edge Transport server

11. On Monday morning, you notice an awful lot of emails floating on your Exchange servers from and to the Internet. You realize that it is a mail storm and that all the emails have some words in the subject line in common. What can you do to prevent a further increase in the flow of those emails? (Choose one.)

A. Configure a transport rule on every Edge Transport server to filter the floating messages based on the subject line and delete them before they can be forwarded to the Exchange organization.

B. Configure a transport rule on one Edge Transport server to filter the floating messages based on the subject line and delete them before they can be forwarded to the Exchange organization.

C. Configure a transport rule on one Hub Transport server to filter the floating messages based on the subject line and delete them.

D. Configure a transport rule on every Hub Transport server to filter the floating messages based on the subject line and delete them.

12. You have been informed by the legal department that sensitive information (such as an employee's Social Security number) was sent to the Internet without their knowledge. You must make sure that this does not happen again. How can you do this in Exchange 2007? (Choose one.)

A. Create a rule on an Edge Transport server to filter any information based on keywords.

B. Create a rule on a Hub Transport server to filter any information based on keywords.

C. Send information to all of the users informing them that sensitive information is not allowed to be sent anymore.

D. Create a rule on a Hub Transport server and add a company disclaimer.

13. You want to make sure that edge rules on all Transport servers are the same. How can you make sure? (Select all that apply.)

A. Configure them as Hub Transport rules so they are automatically replicated everywhere.

B. Use the EMS command `Export-TransportRuleCollection` on the Edge Transport server that you use to create edge rules.

C. Configure the Edge Transport rule on one Edge Transport server; they will be applied to all other Edge Transport servers automatically using EdgeSychronization.

D. Use the EMS command `Import-TransportRuleCollection` on all Edge Transport servers to import rules either manually or automatically.

14. Which of the following applications support S/MIME encryption and signatures? (Select all that apply.)

A. Outlook 2003

B. OWA in Exchange 2007

C. Outlook 2007

D. Mobile devices using Exchange ActiveSync

15. What is the best definition of S/MIME? (Choose one.)

A. S/MIME is a network-based security mechanism to provide server-to-server encryption.

B. S/MIME is used to provide end-to-end security for encrypting and signing email messages.

C. S/MIME is a session-based security protocol that is used in Exchange Server 2007.

D. S/MIME is a client-based encryption format in which the Exchange Server 2007 server encrypts all messages automatically.

16. For what features of journaling in Exchange Server 2007 do you need an Exchange Enterprise Client Access License (CAL)? (Select all that apply.)

A. Journal messages for an Exchange database

B. Journal messages for recipients or distribution groups

C. Journal rule scope (e.g., Global)

D. Journal Unified Messaging

17. Robert is planning the archiving solution for messaging. He met with his financial department and the legal department to gather the requirements for the solution. He recognized that the people who are required by law to archive their message communications are spread throughout the Exchange organization. What would be the steps to implement the best journaling solution for his company, providing the least maintenance time? (Select all that apply.)

A. Enable journaling on all message databases where people who need to journal their messages are located.

B. Create a distribution group that includes all people who need to journal their messages.

C. Create a journal rule that includes the distribution group containing all the people who need to journal their messages.

D. Create a mailbox as a target for journaling.

18. When you enabled journaling, you found that all journal messages are in a journal report envelope format that is not supported by your archiving software. What can you do? (Choose one.)

A. Switch from the journal report envelope format to the old format so your archiving software does not have any problems handling it.

B. Upgrade your archiving software to support journal reports.

C. Define a target mailbox on an Exchange 2003 server.

D. Use standard journaling based on Exchange databases.

19. For which of the following areas can you use the ISA Server 2006 to provide you with enhanced security features by protecting and monitoring the network? (Select all that apply.)

    A. Encrypting server-to-server traffic

    B. Routing SMTP messages

    C. Signing messages with a corporate certificate

    D. Client access (e.g., OWA)

20. The ISA Server 2006 can be configured to secure what types of client access methods? (Select all that apply.)

    A. Outlook Anywhere

    B. Outlook Web Access

    C. Outlook MAPI

    D. Exchange ActiveSync

Answers to Review Questions

1. C. The only port that needs to be accessed for MAPI is 135/TCP (RPC) because remote procedure calls are used. The rest refer to server-side protocols such as SMTP, DNS, and SMB that are not used in a MAPI connection.

2. B. On both Edge Transport servers, the local one and the partner one, only self-signed certificates are installed by default. This is enough to support encryption by default between the Hub Transport and the Edge Transport server. However, to support Edge Transport-to-Edge Transport encryption, both machines need to install valid server certificates including their domain names.

3. A, B. You need to open the ports 80/TCP and 443/TCP to enable communication between the ISA Server 2006 located in the perimeter network and the Client Access Server located in your LAN. Because the CAS will forward the request to the appropriate mailbox server, no other ports have to be opened. Ports 110/TCP and 995/TCP belong to POP3 communication and need to be enabled only when you want to use the POP3 protocol.

4. D. S/MIME is end-to-end security that provides authentication and encryption. In this case, server-to-server communication is required to be encrypted, so A is not the correct answer. TLS and SSL can be used to encrypt server-to-server traffic, but they are session-based and therefore initiated in Exchange Server 2007. The only protocol that is server-to-server and independent from the application is IPSec because it is network-based and encrypts any traffic, no matter which application it comes from.

5. A, C. You need to enable Exchange Servers on the Permission Groups tab and Externally Secured on the Authentication tab on your Receive connectors to optimize the configuration for the IPSec protocol. Enabling Legacy Exchange Servers on the Permission Groups tab is not needed because the question did not mention any server other than Exchange 2007. Exchange Server Authentication on the Authentication tab cannot be enabled when you enable Externally Secured.

6. D. A secured message path points to Domain Security in Exchange 2007. Therefore, you need to know the requirements for Domain Security: the Edge Transport server in the local and remote site has a server certificate installed and both sides are configured with Domain Security for your domain. If one side is not configured for Domain Security, you will get TLS but not a secured message path.

7. B, C. Self-signed certificates do not support mutual TLS because a CA must issue the certificate and both sides must verify that the certificate is valid. Only an official (but expansive) third-party certificate or a Windows PKI–generated certificate can be used for mutual TLS. If you use a Windows-generated certificate, you also have to make sure that your partner trusts your root certificate; otherwise it will not work. Paper certificates are useless in this scenario.

8. A, B. A certificate for TLS and mutual TLS must include the domain name of the Edge Transport server and additional information such as domain name added as a Subject Alternative Name (SAN) to the certificate. An Alternative Name (AN) is not available in any certificate.

9. A, B, C. The `STARTTLS` command is only available when a valid certificate is installed on the Exchange server that includes the local domain name and that is enabled for SMTP. Thus, you have to verify if the certificate is expired, if the certificate is enabled for SMTP and if the domain name was added to it as the Subject Alternative Name (SAN). It does not matter where the certificate was issued, as long as it was a trusted third-party CA, thus this must be a wrong option.

10. B. Transport rules on Hub Transport servers are for company policy and compliance rules. Edge Transport rules do not support disclaimers because they are intended for a different purpose. Mailbox servers and Client Access servers do not have message-routing capabilities and, therefore, do not provide any rules. The only possible answer is Hub Transport server.

11. A. This question requires you to understand two perspectives of transport rules: First, you need to use Edge Transport rules to prevent mail storms like the one in this scenario. Second, you have to configure an Edge Transport rule on every Edge Transport server separately because it does not automatically replicate like a Hub Transport rule. Using Hub Transport rules to prevent mail storms is a bad idea because you would be trying to fight the problem inside the Exchange organization.

12. B. Edge rules should not be used for filtering sensitive information out of messages. Informing your users would be good, but does not provide the required result because it already happened and the users probably already had been informed about not including sensitive information in messages. Adding a company disclaimer also does not provide the desired result.

13. B, D. Edge Transport rules do not automatically synchronize with other Edge Transport servers. The only way is to export all edge rules is to the EMS command `Export-TransportRuleCollection` on the Edge Transport server where the rules have been created and then to import them on all Edge Transport servers using the command `Import-TransportRuleCollection`. You cannot configure edge rules on a Hub Transport server.

14. A, C. Currently, only Outlook 2003 and Outlook 2007 support S/MIME encryption. OWA and mobile devices using Exchange ActiveSync cannot read S/MIME using the release version of Exchange Server 2007.

15. B. S/MIME is a client-based protocol that provides end-to-end security by encrypting and signing email messages. It is client-initiated, but fully supported with Exchange 2007.

16. B, C, D. Normal journaling that is based on Exchange databases does not require an Enterprise Client Access License (CAL), but the CAL is required by premium features such as journaling messages based on recipients, scope, or Unified Messaging.

17. B, C, D. Configuring journaling on multiple Exchange databases and journaling every message to and from these databases might be overkill. The best solution is to create a mailbox to store all journal reports, create a distribution group for all the people who need to journal their messages, and then create a journal rule that includes this distribution list. It is easy to manage just using the group membership. Only the required people will journal their messages, which means you preserve hard-disk space.

18. B. Currently, the only way to solve this problem is by upgrading your archiving software to support the journal report envelope format. There is no way to switch to the old format, nor does it help to put the journal mailbox on an Exchange 2003 server. Standard journaling creates journal reports, so it does not help, either.

19. B, D. The ISA Server 2006 can be used as a single entry point to protect Internet-based client access such as OWA and to route SMTP messages. It cannot encrypt server-to-server traffic on systems where it is not involved, nor can it sign messages with a corporate certificate.

20. A, B, D. The ISA Server 2006 can be used to secure OWA, Outlook Anywhere, and Exchange ActiveSync traffic. Outlook MAPI is not supported.

Planning Exchange Server 2007 Compliance

MICROSOFT EXAM OBJECTIVES COVERED IN THIS CHAPTER:

- ✓ **Plan the messaging compliance implementation.**

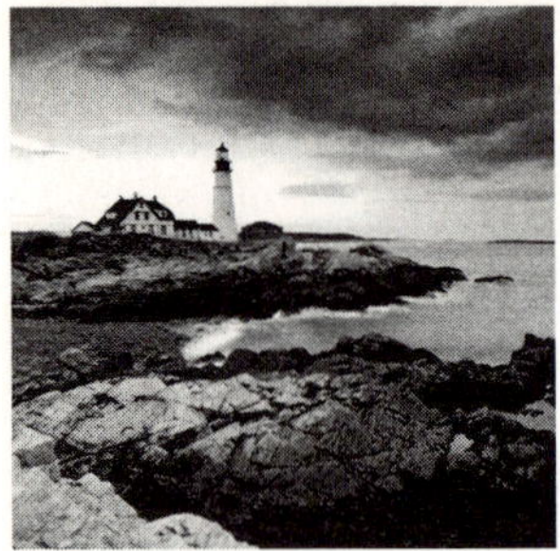

Over the past 10 years there has been a marked increase in government legislation and regulation, with the ever-present possibility of litigation or other legal action with the accompanying legal discoveries as required by these legal actions. These two factors have caused email compliance to become a front-and-center concern for many messaging professionals. Exchange Server 2007 has introduced capabilities and features that allow organizations to meet these challenges in a cost-effective manner without having to integrate third-party solutions.

The main subjects of this chapter are as follows:

- Defining compliance
- Defining messaging records management
- Identifying messaging records management requirements
- Planning messaging records management
- Defining message classification
- Identifying message-classification dependencies
- Deploying message classification
- Understanding message classification and transport rules
- Defining RMS
- Identifying RMS requirements
- Integrating RMS

Email Compliance

The email compliance capabilities that Exchange Server 2007 introduces focus primarily on regulatory compliance and legal discovery (meaning the requirement to produce all relevant email during litigation, usually by subpoena). The three broad categories of compliance are as follows:

Legal (court-ordered). Legal compliance is generally the result of litigation.

Regulatory. Regulatory compliance is typically done in response to government regulations. It is of concern to all private and public sectors, but particularly those in the financial services and healthcare sectors, while public-sector organizations are required to comply with information requests from citizens. In the United States, the regulations of concern in the private sector include Sarbanes-Oxley, SEC Rules 17a-3 and 17a-4 (which require broker-dealers to create and retain certain records), Gramm-Leach-Bliley, and the Health Insurance Portability and Accountability Act (HIPAA). The public sector is subject to the Freedom of Information Act and the Federal Information Security Management Act (FISMA), among others. For public- and private-sector organizations, protection of privacy information is a primary concern, as well.

Internal. Internal compliance is a means of risk mitigation for an organization; examples of risks to be mitigated include corporate liability (criminal or civil), financial loss, privacy breaches, disclosure of intellectual assets, discrimination/harassment, or breach of client/attorney privilege.

By all estimates, the total cost of compliance is steep—a $25 billion price tag in 2005 for the securities industry, according to the Securities Industry Association (SIA)—but the penalties for noncompliance can be much steeper, including stock exchange de-listing, multimillion-dollar fines, and even prison terms. By some estimates, up to 90 percent of the compliance costs are staff-related. The functionality introduced in Exchange Server 2007 reduces the complexity and lowers the effort required for compliance to meet the needs of many organizations of all sizes.

As defined by Microsoft, the primary capabilities required by an email compliance solution are as follows:

Message retention. Also defined as the email life cycle (ELC), this includes not only functionality to automatically retain email for specified time periods based on specified criteria, but the ability to search for and retrieve retained email when required. This capability is particularly important for legal discovery and public-sector access to information requests, as the penalties for noncompliance can be extremely steep. It does no good if the records have been retained but can't be located when required.

Controlled access. Not only must organizations retain specified email as required for compliance purposes, but they also must protect private information and keep data secure from unauthorized access. Organizations need to be able to protect data from unauthorized access or inadvertent disclosure, both in transit and at rest.

Information and process integrity. This capability can include classifying email based on content and processing email according to its classification. It also may include automatically copying compliance personnel on relevant email, as well as creating "ethical firewalls" to prevent conflict-of-interest scenarios, such as communication between stock brokers and market-research personnel in a financial institution.

Corporate email policy is the most important component of any email compliance implementation. This component is not a technical document, but a business policy; it should include compliance measures created by your compliance or risk officers based on the relevant laws and regulations for your industry. The email policy also should address areas of risk and potential liability, particularly in the areas outlined at the beginning of this section.

Real World Scenario

Implementing Compliance Technologies

Organizations implement some technologies to enforce policy and impose certain behavior on end users. For example, your organization may wish to enforce retention periods or delete or restrict messages based on content. The technologies discussed in this chapter can fall into this category, especially messaging records management.

The introduction of a feature set, such as messaging records management or message classification, may not always be well received by users, who may see it as an intrusion or an obstacle to doing their job. In many cases, this resistance is the result of an unclear or non-existent email policy, insufficient communication to end users regarding the purpose of the new features, lack of upper-management sponsorship, or all of those elements. If you design and present your messaging records management deployment as an aid to the organization rather than as an obstacle to be overcome, then you are much more likely to achieve a successful implementation that meets the needs of the organization.

If you don't have a clearly defined corporate email policy endorsed by the upper management of your organization, you're essentially implementing the compliance solutions discussed here by flying by the seat of your pants. As a result, the implementation will likely be a failure in the long run.

With a compliance implementation (and any other technology implementation, for that matter), the technology needs to meet the requirements of the business; the business should not have to adapt to the technology.

Messaging Records Management

Exchange Server 2007 introduces messaging records management (MRM). This feature provides the message-retention capability defined in the previous section of this chapter, giving users and the organization the ability to retain or remove messages as required for company policy compliance, government regulations, or legal needs. When the retention limit for an email is reached, it can be deleted or archived, an event can be logged, or the message can be flagged for user attention. MRM also can be combined with message classification and transport rules to provide a comprehensive email compliance solution.

Messaging records management is composed of the following components:

- Managed folders (default and custom)
- Managed content settings
- Managed folder mailbox policies
- Managed Folder Assistant

Messaging records management is managed through the Exchange Management Console (EMC) mailbox work center, as shown in Figure 16.1.

FIGURE 16.1 Messaging records management through EMC

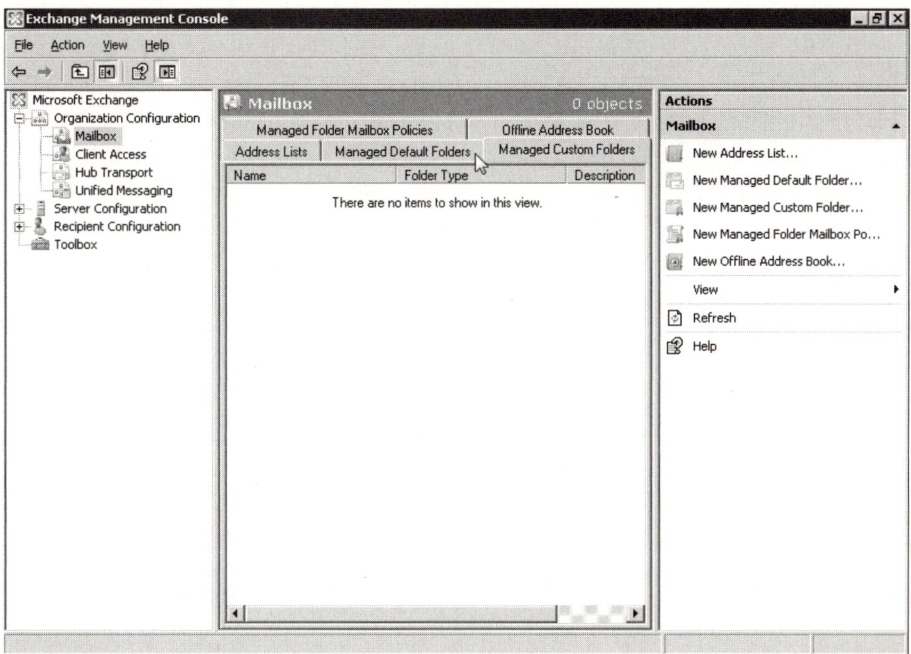

The following cmdlets are available for configuring and managing MRM through the Exchange Management Shell (EMS):

- `Get-ManagedContentSettings`
- `Get-ManagedFolder`
- `Get-ManagedFolderMailboxPolicy`
- `New-ManagedContentSettings`
- `New-ManagedFolder`
- `New-ManagedFolderMailboxPolicy`
- `Remove-ManagedContentSettings`
- `Remove-ManagedFolder`
- `Remove-ManagedFolderMailboxPolicy`
- `Set-ManagedContentSettings`
- `Set-ManagedFolder`
- `Set-Mailbox`

- `Set-MailboxServer`
- `Set-ManagedFolderMailboxPolicy`
- `Start-ManagedFolderAssistant`
- `Stop-ManagedFolderAssistant`

MRM Requirements

To apply a managed folder mailbox policy to a mailbox, that mailbox must reside on an Exchange Server 2007 computer. Mailboxes that have a managed folder mailbox policy applied to them can be accessed via Exchange Server 2007 Outlook Web Access, Outlook 2007, and Outlook 2003 SP2. Outlook 2003 SP2 clients can access the mailbox but will not have access to all the features that are available to Outlook 2007 clients. For example, Outlook 2003 SP2 clients do not see the managed-folder comments as configured in the EMC or EMS.

Accessing mailboxes that have managed folder mailbox policies assigned to them with clients running versions of Outlook older than Outlook 2003 SP2 is not supported.

Planning MRM

Once a corporate email policy is defined, your MRM deployment can be planned, using the policy as a framework. The steps to deploy MRM are as follows:

1. Create managed folders
2. Create managed content settings
3. Define managed folder mailbox policies
4. Apply managed folder mailbox policies
5. Configure the Managed Folder Assistant

Managed Folders

Managed folders are default and custom folders within mailboxes that have MRM enabled. Managed folders are created, then managed content settings are applied to them as required to satisfy corporate email policy. For example, if the corporate email policy states that messages pertaining to client projects are retained for two years and messages containing data covered by a piece of legislation that has been introduced named the Privacy Act are retained for 90 days, you would create managed custom folders for this purpose.

Managed folders are the most visible portion of messaging records management to end users. They can't be moved, deleted, or renamed by end users, and all managed custom folders appear in the user's mailbox under a top-level folder named Managed Folders. The managed folders folder also can't be moved, deleted, or renamed by end users or administrators.

Managed Default Folders

Managed default folders are folders created in a user's mailbox by default with or without MRM implemented. These folders include the Inbox, Sent Items, and Deleted Items folders, among others. A complete list of the default folders in a standard Exchange Server 2007 installation is shown in Figure 16.2.

FIGURE 16.2 Managed default folders

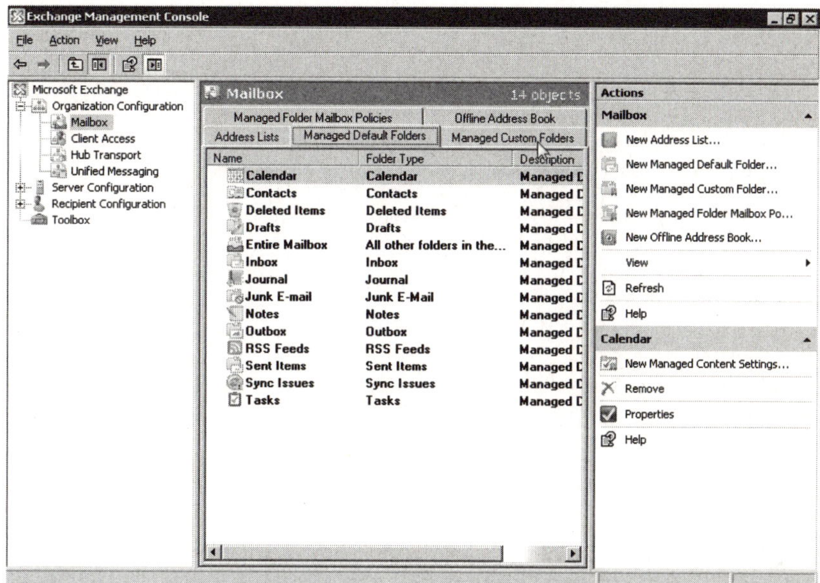

You can create new managed default folders for use in MRM to apply unique settings to certain groups of users. For example, you might want to create a new managed default folder of Inbox type named One-Year Retention with a retention period of one year. The One-Year Retention default folder could then be assigned to users who need those settings rather than the settings assigned to the standard Inbox folder.

New instances of managed default folders always display with the standard default name. For instance, in the example outlined earlier, users with the One-Year Retention folder assigned to them would see the folder in their mailbox as Inbox (as the folder is of the Inbox type) rather than the One-Year Retention name assigned to it on creation.

Only one managed default folder of any type (Inbox, for example) can be assigned to a mailbox. This is because you can't assign more than one managed default folder of any folder type in any one managed folder mailbox policy, and you can assign only one managed folder mailbox policy per mailbox.

Managed Custom Folders

Managed custom folders are created for the express purpose of MRM and appear in a mailbox's folder list separately from default folders, under a special default folder named Managed Folder. They are created through the Exchange Management Console or the Exchange Management Shell and assigned to users or groups of users. These folders are displayed in Outlook 2007 with a special folder icon, as shown in Figure 16.3. The managed folders are displayed similarly in Exchange Server 2007 Outlook Web Access.

FIGURE 16.3 Managed custom folders in Outlook 2007

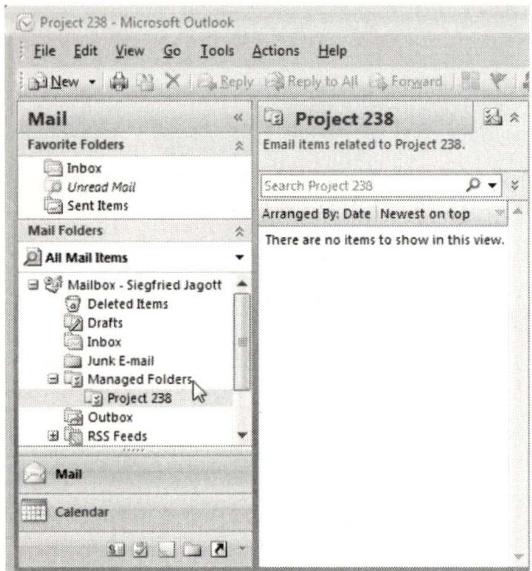

Real World Scenario

Using Managed Folders

With managed folders, as with many other end-user-facing features, less is generally better. Keeping the number of managed folders to a minimum will make your end users happier and simplify ongoing management of your Exchange Server 2007 system. If users have an overwhelming number of managed folders in their mailboxes, they will find them difficult to use and will be more likely to try to find ways to work around them.

However, you need to remember that your users are professionals just like you; they simply have different areas of expertise. Their goal, just like yours, is to do their job; your goal needs to be to design an MRM implementation that allows your end users to do their jobs. They are your customers, after all.

A good approach to take is to determine which managed folders can be used by your entire organization, using your corporate email policy as a guide and keeping this number to an absolute minimum. Then, using these folders as a baseline, design additional folders as required to meet the needs of specific departments or sections in your organization.

And, at all times, you need to keep it lean and mean; just because you can create hundreds of managed folders doesn't mean you should.

Creating Managed Folders

Exercise 16.1 outlines the steps required to create a managed custom folder for a project named Project 237 using the Exchange Management Console and a second managed custom folder for Privacy Act data using the Exchange Management Shell.

EXERCISE 16.1

Creating Managed Custom Folders

Managed custom folders can be created using either the Exchange Management Console GUI or with PowerShell via the Exchange Management Shell. Let's walk through the steps to create folders using both methods.

Using the Exchange Management Console

In this section of the exercise, we will create a managed custom folder using the Exchange Management Console.

1. Select Start ➢ All Programs ➢ Microsoft Exchange Server 2007, and then click on Exchange Management Console. Within the Exchange Management Console, expand the Organization Configuration work center, select the Mailbox subnode, and then select the Managed Custom Folders tab in the result pane, as shown here.

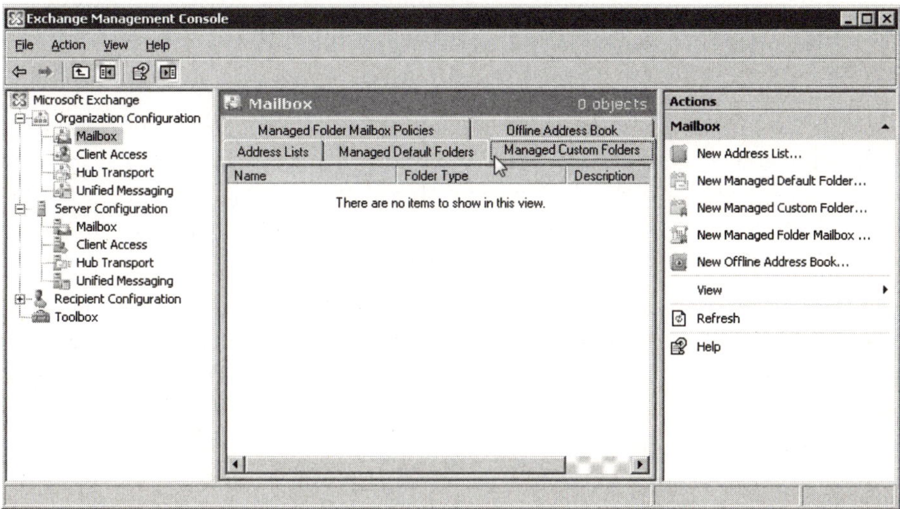

EXERCISE 16.1 *(continued)*

2. In the action pane for the Managed Custom Folders tab, select New Managed Custom Folder to start the New Managed Custom Folder wizard.

3. In the New Managed Custom Folder wizard shown below, enter **Project 237** in the Name field. (Note that the display name for Outlook is set to the same value as the Name field by default; these can be configured differently if required.) In the comment field, enter **Email content related to Project 237; to be retained for two years**. Then click New.

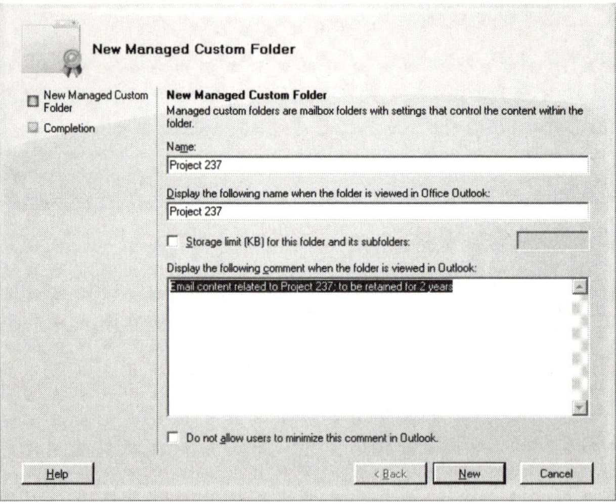

4. On the Completion screen of the New Managed Custom Folder wizard, confirm that the command completed successfully, and click Finish.

5. Back in the Exchange Management Console result pane, verify that the newly created Project 237 folder is listed on the Managed Custom Folders tab as shown here.

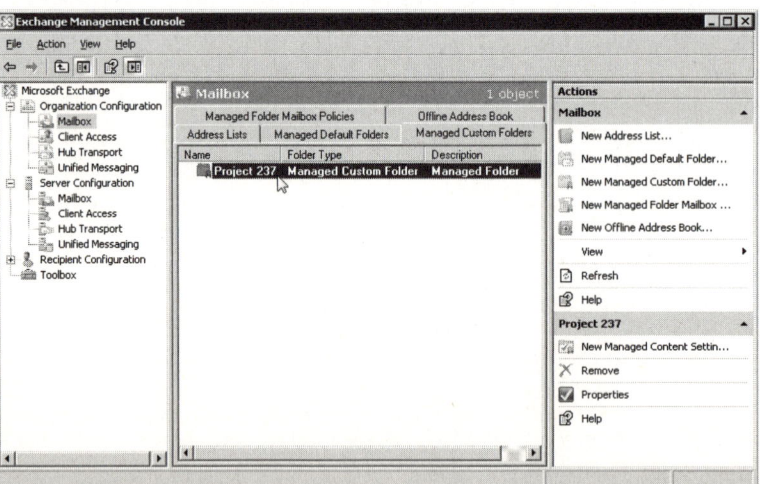

EXERCISE 16.1 *(continued)*

Using the Exchange Management Shell

Now we will create a second managed custom folder, this time using PowerShell.

1. Select Start ➤ All Programs ➤ Microsoft Exchange Server 2007, and then click on Exchange Management Shell. In the Exchange Management Shell, enter the following cmdlet and press Enter:

```
New-ManagedFolder -Name 'Privacy Act' -FolderName 'Privacy Act' -StorageQuota
'unlimited' -Comment 'Email content containing data covered by the Privacy Act;
to be retained for 90 days'
```

2. Verify the output of the cmdlet as shown here.

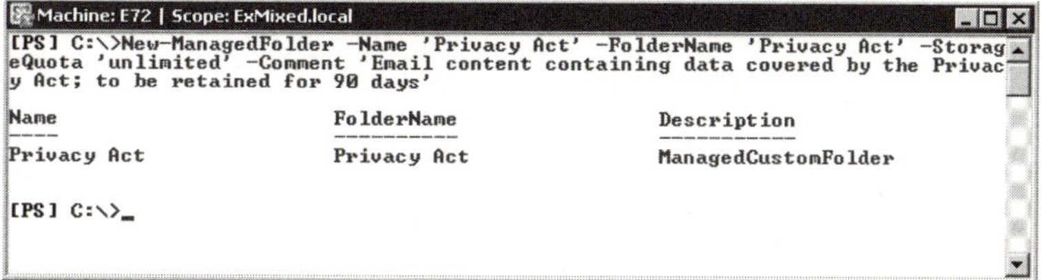

The newly created folder also can be seen in the Exchange Management Console GUI (you may have to refresh the view by pressing F5).

Managed Content Settings

Managed content settings are applied to managed folders to control the life cycle of items in users' mailboxes by controlling retention, applying actions to content no longer needed, and journaling relevant content to a storage location outside the mailbox.

Managed content settings can be defined for either existing default folders or newly created managed folders. Retention settings as well as journaling parameters are defined; all settings are defined per managed folder. Retention settings include the length of retention (in days), the definition of when retention starts, and the action to be taken at the end of retention.

The following settings are available for defining when the retention period starts:

- When delivered, end date for calendar, and recurring tasks
- When item is moved to the folder

In addition, the following actions can be performed at the end of the retention period:

- Move to the Deleted Items folder
- Move to a managed custom folder

- Delete and allow recovery
- Permanently delete
- Mark as past retention limit

Creating Managed Content Settings

Now that we've created some managed custom folders, we can configure content settings for these folders. Content settings define the retention policies for the folder and the actions to be taken at the end of the retention period.

As with all other features of Exchange Server 2007, the Exchange Management Console GUI is derived from and is a subset of PowerShell as provided in the Exchange Management Shell. This means that, although most functions can be performed through the management console, you will almost certainly find it necessary to learn the PowerShell cmdlets that are being invoked. Doing so will enable you to leverage PowerShell to script and automate management tasks, which in many cases is the only practical approach in a typically complex enterprise environment (which is why this book shows you how to perform each task with both the management console and the equivalent PowerShell cmdlets).

We are going to focus on defining managed content settings for custom folders here. The methodology for creating content settings for default folders is essentially identical.

Exercise 16.2 outlines the steps to create managed content settings for the managed folders created in Exercise 16.1. We will create the content settings for the Project 237 folder using the GUI and for the Privacy Act folder using a PowerShell cmdlet.

EXERCISE 16.2

Creating Managed Content Settings

As with managed folders, the managed content settings can be configured with either the Exchange Management Console or the Exchange Management Shell. In this exercise, we will walk through the steps involved in both methods.

Using the Exchange Management Console

1. Start the Exchange Management Console using Start ➢ All Programs ➢ Microsoft Exchange Server 2007. Within the Exchange Management Console, expand the Organization Configuration work center, select the Mailbox subnode, and then select the Managed Custom Folders tab in the result pane. Highlight the Project 237 folder, then select New Managed Content Settings.

EXERCISE 16.2 *(continued)*

2. On the Introduction page of the New Managed Content Settings wizard shown here, enter **Retain for 2 years** as the name of the managed content settings. Select the Length of Retention Period (Days) check box, then enter **730** in the retention field. Select When Item Is Moved to the Folder in the Retention Period Starts pull-down, and set the action to Move to the Deleted Items Folder. Finally, select Next to continue to the wizard's next screen.

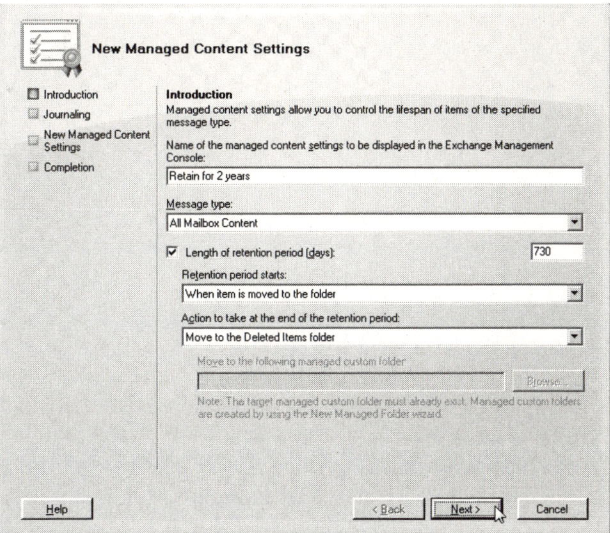

3. On the Journaling page of the wizard, click Next.

4. On the Configuration Summary page of the wizard, verify the configuration and click New.

5. On the Completion page, verify that the operation completed successfully and then click Finish to exit the wizard and return to the Exchange Management Console.

Using the Exchange Management Shell

In this section we will create managed content settings for the Privacy Act folder, in this case using Retain for 90 Days as the name and setting the retention period to 90 days.

1. Start the Exchange Management Shell from Start ➢ All Programs ➢ Microsoft Exchange Server 2007. At the PowerShell prompt, enter the following cmdlet and then press Enter.

```
new-ManagedContentSettings -Name 'Retain for 90 days' -FolderName 'Privacy Act' -
RetentionAction 'MoveToDeletedItems' -AddressForJournaling $null -
AgeLimitForRetention '90.00:00:00' -JournalingEnabled $false -
MessageFormatForJournaling 'UseTnef' -RetentionEnabled $true -LabelForJournaling
'' -MessageClass '*' -MoveToDestinationFolder $null -TriggerForRetention
'WhenMoved'
```

EXERCISE 16.2 *(continued)*

2. Verify the output of the cmdlet as follows:

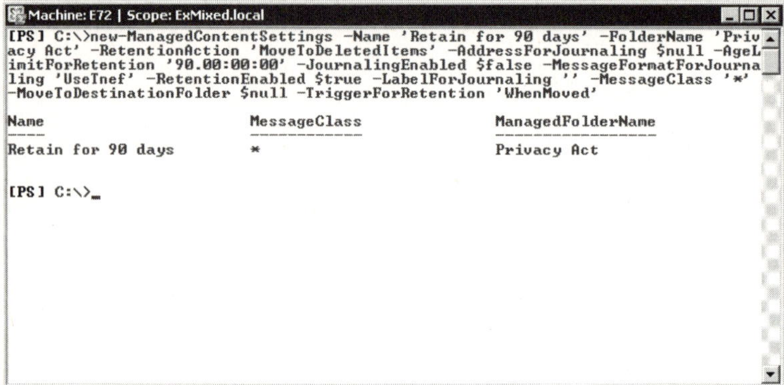

Managed Folder Mailbox Policies

Managed folder mailbox policies define logical groupings for deployment and management. The policies are then applied to users' mailboxes, deploying all the managed folders that are linked to the policy to the applicable mailboxes in a single operation. As many managed folder mailbox policies as necessary can be created, and each policy can contain as many managed folders as required.

Although you can create as many managed folder mailbox policies as you want and have them contain as many managed folders as you want, there is a one-to-one relationship between managed folder mailbox policies and mailboxes; only one managed folder mailbox policy can be assigned to any one mailbox.

Defining Managed Folder Mailbox Policies

An administrator creates managed folder mailbox policies, either via the Exchange Management Console GUI or with PowerShell cmdlets and scripts through the Exchange Management Shell.

Exercise 16.3 outlines the steps to create a managed folder mailbox policy incorporating the managed folders and their content settings created in the previous exercises.

EXERCISE 16.3

Defining Managed Folder Mailbox Policies

In this exercise we will define managed folder mailbox policies using the managed folders you created in the previous exercises.

Using the Exchange Management Console

1. Start the Exchange Management Console from Start ➤ All Programs ➤ Microsoft Exchange Server 2007. Within the Exchange Management Console, expand the Organization Configuration work center, select the Mailbox subnode, then select New Managed Folder Mailbox Policy from the action pane to start the New Managed Folder Mailbox Policy wizard.

2. On the first page of the New Managed Folder Mailbox Policy wizard, enter **Company Standard MRM Policy** as the policy name, then click Add to open the Select Managed Folder dialog.

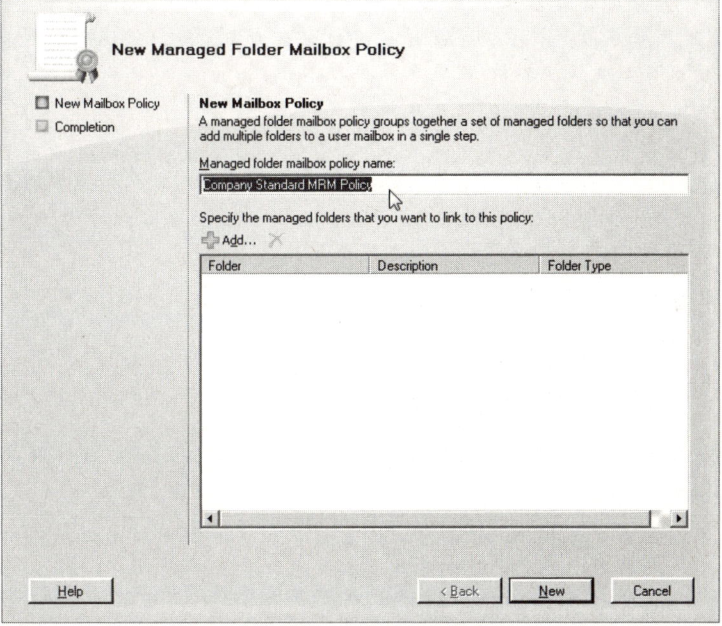

3. In the Select Managed Folder dialog, select the Privacy Act and Project 237 managed folders and click OK to return to the New Managed Folder Mailbox Policy wizard.

4. Back in the New Managed Folder Mailbox Policy wizard, click New to create the policy.

EXERCISE 16.3 *(continued)*

5. On the Completion screen of the wizard, verify that the operation completed successfully with the proper parameters, and then click Finish to exit the wizard and return to the Exchange Management Console.

Using the Exchange Management Shell

In this section of the exercise, we will be creating a second managed folder mailbox policy using the `New-ManagedFolderMailboxPolicy` PowerShell cmdlet. This policy will contain only the Privacy Act managed custom folder.

1. Start the Exchange Management Shell from Start ➢ All Programs ➢ Microsoft Exchange Server 2007. At the PowerShell prompt, enter the following cmdlet and then press Enter:

```
new-ManagedFolderMailboxPolicy -Name 'Privacy Act Compliance Policy' -
ManagedFolderLinks 'Privacy Act'
```

2. Verify that the output of the cmdlet looks as shown in the following image:

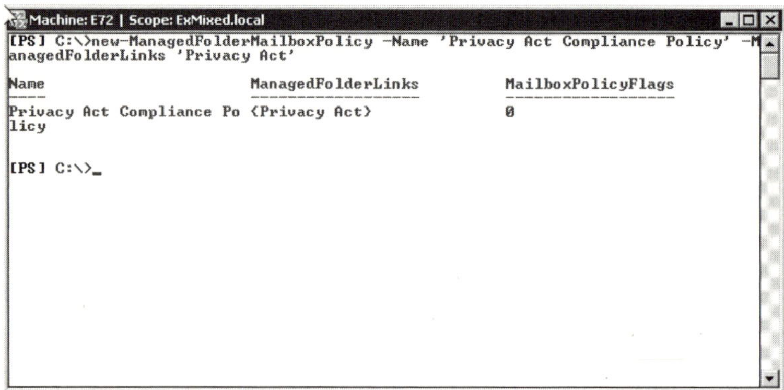

Assigning Managed Folder Mailbox Policies to Users

Once created, managed folder mailbox policies can be assigned to users. The administrator can assign the policies via the management GUI (the EMC). As with all procedures performed in the EMC, you also can assign policies in PowerShell cmdlets and scripts, incorporating powerful filtering and selection criteria for bulk user configurations and modification of particular groupings of users (for example, you can apply a policy to all human resources analysts).

The company-standard MRM policy created in Exercise 16.3 is assigned to a user with the EMC GUI as follows:

1. Start the Exchange Management Console from Start ➢ All Programs ➢ Microsoft Exchange Server 2007. Within the Exchange Management Console, select the Recipient

Configuration work center. Highlight the user the policy that will be assigned to in the Results pane then select Properties from the Action pane.

2. In the Properties dialog of the mailbox, select the Mailbox Settings tab. Highlight Messaging Records Management as shown in Figure 16.4, then click Properties.

FIGURE 16.4 Accessing MRM settings for a user

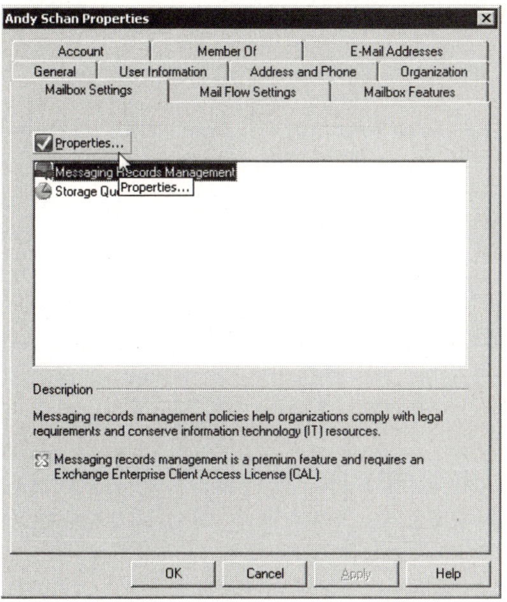

3. In the Messaging Records Management dialog, select the managed folder mailbox policy checkbox, then click Browse to access the Select Managed Folder Mailbox Policy dialog.
4. In the Select Managed Folder Mailbox Policy dialog, select the Company Standard MRM Policy entry, then click OK to return to the Messaging Records management dialog.
5. Once you're back in the Messaging Records Management dialog, click OK to set the policy and return to the mailbox's Properties dialog. Click OK to close the Properties dialog and apply the changes to the mailbox. Click Yes in the warning dialog advising of client support for managed folders as shown in Figure 16.5 to return to the EMC.

Next you can assign the Privacy Act compliance policy to a user with PowerShell using the `Get-User` and `Set-Mailbox` cmdlets. This is accomplished as follows: Start the Exchange Management Shell from Start ➤ All Programs ➤ Microsoft Exchange Server 2007. At the PowerShell prompt, enter the following cmdlet and then press Enter:

```
Get-User | Where-Object {$_.RecipientType -eq "UserMailbox" -and $_.Title -eq
"Human Resources Analyst"} | Set-Mailbox -ManagedFolderMailboxPolicy "Privacy
Act Compliance Policy"
```

FIGURE 16.5 Client version warning when assigning managed folder policies

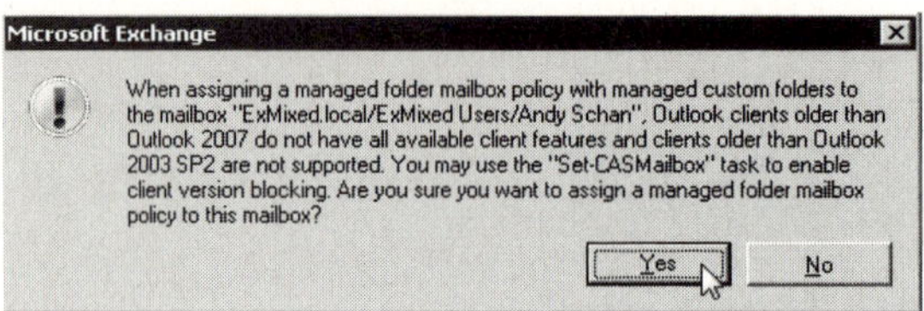

You can confirm the assignment of the policy by typing **Y** at the confirmation prompt as shown in Figure 16.6.

FIGURE 16.6 Assigning a managed folder with PowerShell

```
Machine: E72 | Scope: ExMixed.local
[PS] C:\>Get-User | Where-Object {$_.RecipientType -eq "UserMailbox" -and $_.Tit
le -eq "Human Resources Analyst"} | Set-Mailbox -confirm:$false -ManagedFolderMa
ilboxPolicy "Privacy Act Compliance Policy"

Confirm
When assigning a managed folder mailbox policy with managed custom folders to
the mailbox "ExMixed.local/ExMixed Users/Siegfried Jagott", Outlook clients
older than Outlook 2007 do not have all available client features and clients
older than Outlook 2003 SP2 are not supported. You may use the "Set-CASMailbox"
 task to enable client version blocking. Are you sure you want to assign a
managed folder mailbox policy to this mailbox?
[Y] Yes  [A] Yes to All  [N] No  [L] No to All  [S] Suspend  [?] Help
(default is "Y"):_
```

If the cmdlet is successful, no output is returned. You can confirm the setting of the policy on the mailbox by running the following cmdlet:

```
Get-User | Where-Object {$_.RecipientType -eq "UserMailbox" -and $_.Title -eq
"Human Resources Analyst"} | get-Mailbox | Format-Table Name,
ManagedFolderMailboxPolicy
```

The output of this cmdlet should be similar to that shown in Figure 16.7.

FIGURE 16.7 Verifying managed folder assignments with PowerShell

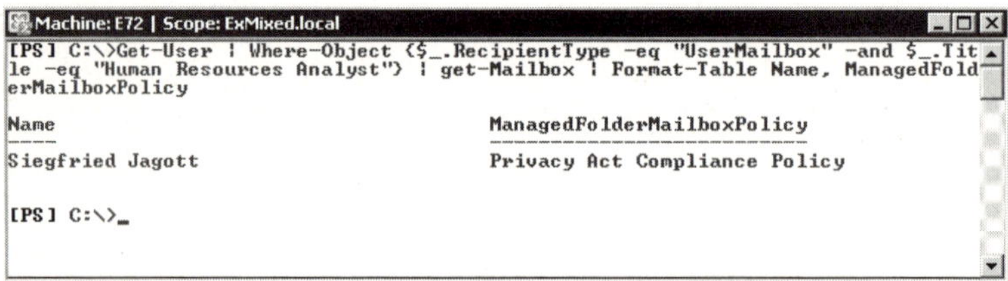

Managed Folder Assistant

The Managed Folder Assistant is the core of the MRM solution and is configured at the mailbox server level. It configures managed folders in users' mailboxes and processes mailbox content based on the MRM configuration created by the administrator. By default, the Managed Folder Assistant is configured to never run; a schedule must be set to enable regular processing of the MRM configuration.

It's best to run the Managed Folder Assistant during off-hours or other times of low server load, as it can be a resource-intensive process, particularly the first time it is run against a mailbox store. Also, Microsoft recommends to not run the Managed Folder Assistant at the same time as backups or online database maintenance.

The Managed Folder Assistant is configured through the MRM tab of the mailbox server's Properties dialog as accessed through the Server Configuration work center. The MRM tab and the folder assistant's Schedule dialog are shown in Figure 16.8.

FIGURE 16.8 Configuring the Managed Folder Assistant through the EMC

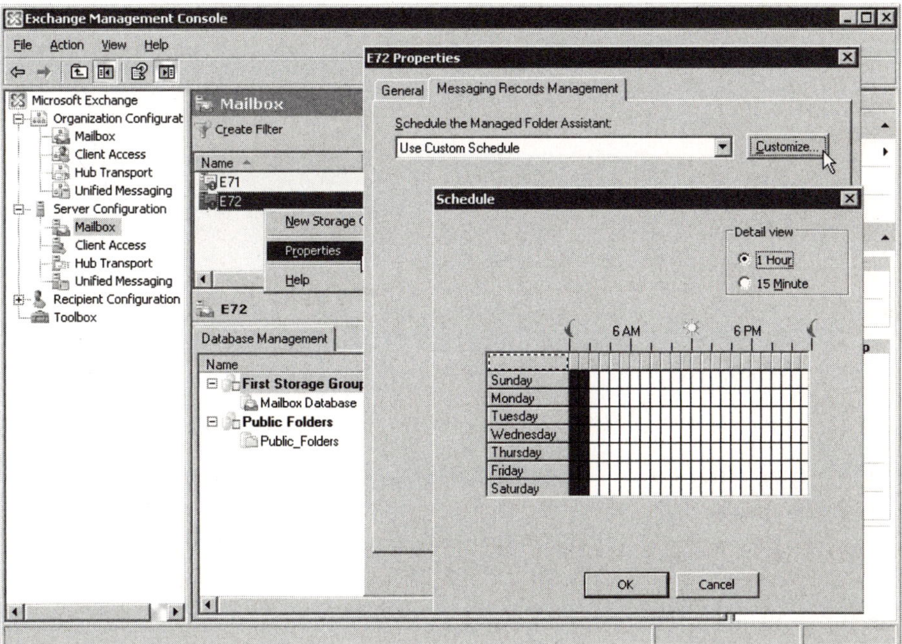

Configuring the Managed Folder Assistant

The Managed Folder Assistant is configured on each mailbox server, either through the EMC GUI or by using the `Set-MailboxServer` PowerShell cmdlet through the EMS. Exercise 16.4 walks you through the steps.

EXERCISE 16.4

Configuring the Managed Folder Assistant

To apply the policies we have assigned to the users, you need to configure the Managed Folder Assistant. Let's walk through the steps to do that, using both the management GUI and PowerShell.

Using the Exchange Management Console

1. Start the Exchange Management Console from Start ➤ All Programs ➤ Microsoft Exchange Server 2007. Within the Exchange Management Console, expand the Server Configuration work center, then select the Mailbox subnode. Highlight the mailbox server to be configured in the Results pane, then select Properties from the server section of the Action pane.

2. In the Properties dialog for the mailbox server, select the Messaging Records Management tab. Select Use Custom Schedule from the schedule drop-down menu, then click Customize.

3. In the Schedule dialog, select the 6 a.m. and 7 a.m. time slots for all days so that the schedule is configured as shown here, then click OK to create the schedule and return to the Properties dialog for the mailbox server.

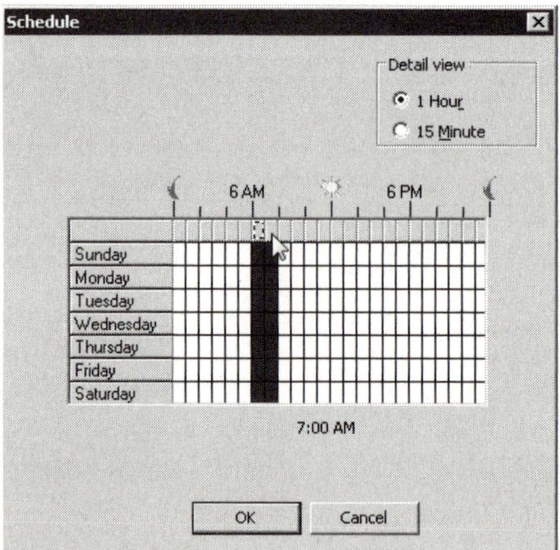

4. Back in the Properties dialog for the mailbox server, click OK to apply the changes and return to the Exchange Management Console.

EXERCISE 16.4 *(continued)*

Using the Exchange Management Shell

In this section of the exercise, we will be setting the Managed Folder Assistant schedule using the `Set-MailboxServer` PowerShell cmdlet against the same mailbox server as we configured previously through the management GUI. We will be changing the schedule from running daily from 6 a.m. to 8 a.m. to running daily from 12 a.m. to 2 a.m.

1. Start the Exchange Management Shell from Start ➤ All Programs ➤ Microsoft Exchange Server 2007. At the PowerShell prompt, enter the following cmdlet and then press Enter:

   ```
   Set-MailboxServer -identity mailbox_server_name -ManagedFolderAssistantSchedule
   "Sun.00:00-Sun.2:00","Mon.00:00-Mon.2:00","Tue.00:00-Tue.2:00","Wed.00:00-
   Wed.2:00","Thu.00:00-Thu.2:00","Fri.00:00-Fri.2:00","Sat.00:00-Sat.2:00"
   ```

   Note that *`mailbox_server_name`* is the name of the mailbox server configured previously through the Exchange Management Console.

2. When the cmdlet is successful, no output is returned. The setting of the policy on the mailbox can be confirmed by running the following cmdlet:

   ```
   Get-MailboxServer -identity mailbox_server_name
   ```

   The output of that cmdlet should be similar to the one shown here:

Message Classification

Although organizations have typically invested heavily in solutions protecting against threats from inbound email such as malware (viruses, worm, Trojans, and phishing, for example) and spam, little thought has been devoted to the compliance and intellectual-property risks of internal and outgoing email. Messaging records management can assist in dealing with these issues for email at rest (residing in mailboxes), but depends to a large extent on end users and, in some cases, administrators making decisions on the content of messages. These decisions are typically focused on the designation of messages, particularly in the context of intended use, audience, retention, etc.

Email classification is a technique for adding metadata and visual labels to email messages to describe the intended use of or audience for a message to enable processes to make decisions based on those designations. Message classifications are typically applied by the message sender as a decision on the content of the email before sending. These classifications can denote the sensitivity, intended distribution, retention periods, or other designations as required by an organization. If message classifications are deployed with some planning, they can offer a crucial piece of an effective strategy for managing and controlling email by maintaining policy and ensuring regulatory compliance.

Some examples of message classifications are Unclassified, Confidential, and Secret, while other organizations may use designations such as Non-Business, Partner Confidential, Mergers and Acquisitions, Privacy Act, etc.

As with managed folders, the number of message classifications should be kept as low as possible. This aids in keeping the interface uncluttered for end users, which will in turn encourage them to adopt the new functionality.

In Outlook 2007 and Exchange Server 2007 Outlook Web Access, the classification metadata can be used to display visual labels in the form of a user-friendly description of the classification for the recipients and the sender of the email.

Exchange Server 2007 message classifications are visible only in Exchange Server 2007 Outlook Web Access and Outlook 2007. Message classifications are visible to Outlook Web Access (OWA) clients by default, while Outlook 2007 requires additional configuration to make them visible.

The classification metadata also can be leveraged to perform actions on messages, through the use of Exchange Server 2007 transport rules, to enforce company policy for compliance purposes. For example, messages classified Company Internal that are sent to users outside your organization can be blocked, with a copy sent to a compliance officer. Transport rules also can be used to apply classifications to messages. For example, messages containing privacy information such as Social Security numbers can have a Privacy Act classification applied to them using a transport rule.

Classifications are created on Exchange Server 2007 using PowerShell cmdlets, although there are some predefined default classifications. The default user-accessible classifications in Exchange Server 2007 Outlook Web Access are A/C Privileged, Company Confidential, and Company Internal; these are shown in Figure 16.9.

FIGURE 16.9 Default message classifications as seen in OWA

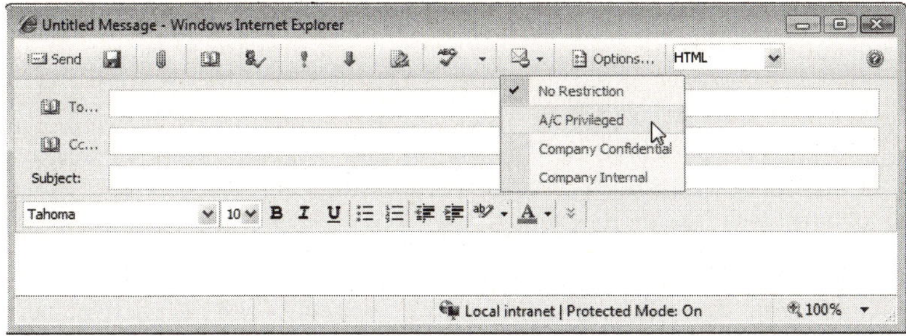

It is worth noting that the message-classification labels seen in Figure 16.9 are just the display names of the classifications. The `Display Name` parameter defines the labels the sender sees from the selection menu (Figure 16.9), while the `SenderDescription` defines the description that is shown to the sender in the composed message, as shown in Figure 16.10. The `RecipientDescription`, as seen in OWA, is shown in Figure 16.11.

FIGURE 16.10 Message-classification sender description

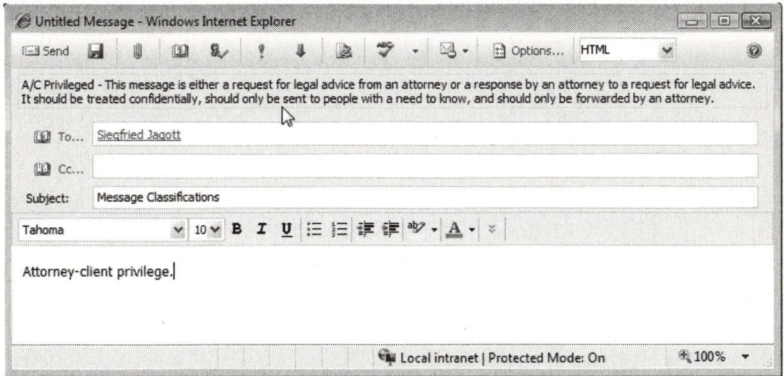

FIGURE 16.11 Message-classification recipient description

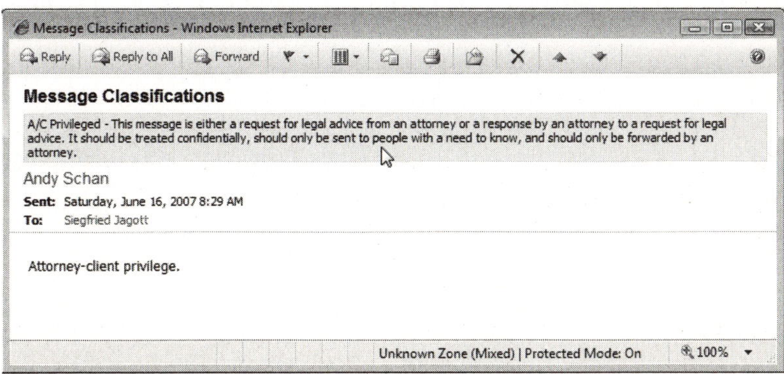

To create a new message classification you use the New-MessageClassification PowerShell cmdlet in the Exchange Management Shell. The three required parameters are Name, DisplayName, and SenderDescription, although RecipientDescription many times is set as well. If the RecipientDescription is not set, the value for SenderDescription is used.

There also are third-party solutions that provide message-classification capability for Outlook. As with any technology, any evaluation of the message-classification functionality in Exchange Server 2007 would be best served by comparing it to other solutions that are available.

All configurable message-classification parameters are shown in Table 16.3, along with their descriptions.

TABLE 16.1 Message-Classification Parameters

Classification Parameter	Parameter Description
Common Parameters	
DisplayName	Specifies the display name for the message-classification instance. The display name appears in Outlook 2007 and Outlook Web Access and is used by the message sender to select the appropriate message classification before they send a message. The DisplayName parameter must contain 64 or fewer characters.
SenderDescription	Explains to the sender what the message classification is intended to achieve and is used by Outlook and Outlook Web Access users to select the appropriate message classification before they send a message. The SenderDescription parameter must contain 1,024 or fewer characters.
RecipientDescription	Explains to the recipient what the message classification is intended to achieve and is viewed by Outlook and Outlook Web Access users when they receive a message with this classification. The RecipientDescription parameter must contain 1,024 or fewer characters. If no value is set for this parameter, the description entered for SenderDescription is used.
Locale	Specifies a culture code to create a locale-specific version of the message classification. You also must specify the Identity parameter of the existing message classification when you create a new locale-specific version. Values for the Locale parameter are the string names listed in the Culture Name column in the Microsoft .NET Class Library class reference that is available at http://go.microsoft.com/fwlink/?LinkId=67222.

TABLE 16.1 Message-Classification Parameters *(continued)*

Classification Parameter	Parameter Description
Other Parameters	
`Identity`	Used to create a translated version of an existing message classification. You also must specify the `Locale` parameter. The `Identity` parameter can take a string value, which is the `Name` value of an existing message classification.
`Name`	Specifies the administrative name for the message classification instance. The name is used to administer the message classification instance. When you specify a name that includes spaces, you must enclose the whole name in quotation marks. The `Name` parameter must contain 256 or fewer characters.
`ClassificationID`	Used to specify a classification ID of an existing message classification that you want to import and use in your Exchange organization. Used if you are configuring message classifications that span two Exchange forests in the same enterprise.
`DomainController`	To specify the fully qualified domain name of the domain controller that writes this configuration change to Active Directory, include the `DomainController` parameter on the command. This parameter is not supported on computers that have the Edge Transport server role installed, as the Edge Transport server role only writes to and reads from the local Active Directory Application Mode (ADAM) instance.
`TemplateInstance`	Uses the configuration of an existing template to create an identical copy of the object on a local or target server.
`UserDisplayEnabled`	Used to specify whether the values that you entered for the `DisplayName` and `RecipientDescription` parameters are displayed in the recipient's Outlook message. If this parameter is set to `$false`, messages sent to recipients that have this classification do not display any classification information.

Dependencies of Message Classification

The primary dependencies of message classification in Exchange Server 2007 are Active Directory and the messaging client used. In the following sections, we'll go over each of these in turn.

Active Directory Configuration Container

Message classifications, like all Exchange Server 2007 configurations, are stored in Active Directory; in particular, in the Configuration container in the path Configuration/Services/

Microsoft Exchange/<Organization>/Transport Settings/Message Classifications/<Locale>. The classifications can be verified using ADSI Edit (`ADSIEdit.msc`), as shown in Figure 16.12.

As you can infer from Figure 16.12, message classifications are locale-specific (language-specific). This means that you can have several locale-specific versions of the same classification, presented to users in their own language as determined by their client locale settings. If a localized version is not available for the locale of the user, the default message classification is used.

Messaging Client

As stated previously, Exchange Server 2007 message classifications are set by the message sender on outgoing messages in Outlook 2007 and Exchange Server 2007 Outlook Web Access.

FIGURE 16.12 Message classifications in Active Directory

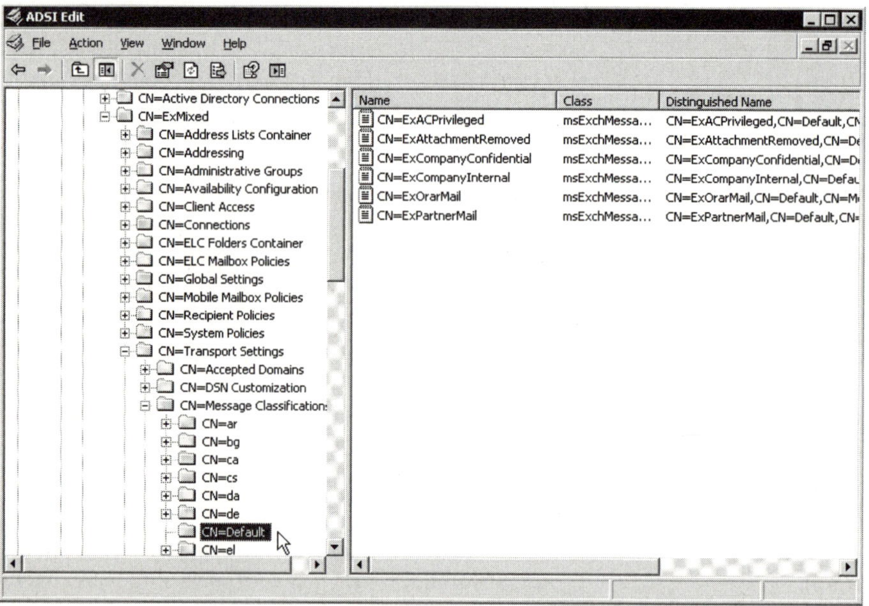

Message classifications are configurable only in Outlook 2007 and Exchange Server 2007 Outlook Web Access, and are visible only to recipients using those same clients; they are not visible or configurable in Outlook 2003 or earlier or in earlier versions of Outlook Web Access.

Figure 16.13 shows the same message that was pictured in Figure 16.11, but from an Outlook 2003 client; as you can see, the message classification metadata is not visible in Outlook 2003.

FIGURE 16.13 Message classifications in Outlook 2003

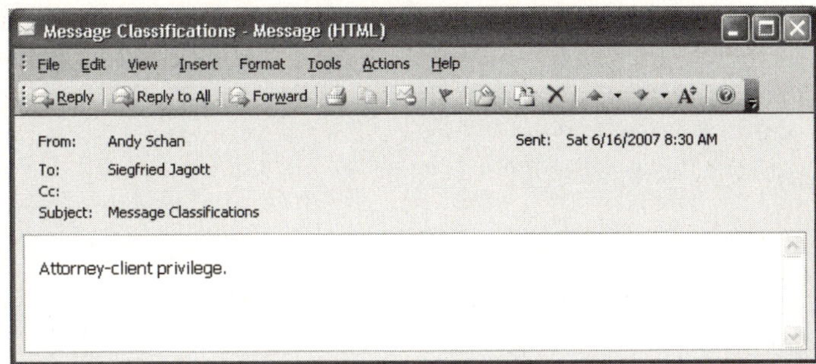

Configuring Message Classifications for Different Locales

You can create localized versions of an existing message classification to accommodate multilingual environments. When a message is classified and sent, Exchange Server 2007 first determines the language of the recipient by examining the recipient's mailbox. If Active Directory contains a message classification in the corresponding language, it attaches that classification to the message. If a language match is not found, Exchange determines the locale of the recipient by examining the recipient mailbox's locale property. If there is no match for the specific locale of the recipient Exchange Server 2007 looks for a culture-neutral version, such as *es* for *es-MX*, (Spanish-Mexico) or *fr* for *fr-CA* (French-Canada). Finally, if no language-specific or culture-neutral match is found, the default message classification is used regardless of its locale.

Localized message classifications are created with the `New-MessageClassification` cmdlet, using the `Identity` parameter to identify the existing classification and the `Locale` parameter to indicate the locale of the new classification. For example, to create a Spanish version of a message classification named Privacy, you would use the following cmdlet:

```
New-MessageClassification -Identity Privacy -Locale es-ES -DisplayName "España
Example" -SenderDescription "Este es el texto de la descripción"
```

To view message classifications in the Exchange Management Shell for locales other than the default, you must use the `Get-MessageClassification` cmdlet with the `IncludeLocales` parameter set to True. For example:

```
Get-MessageClassification -IncludeLocales:$true
```

Configuring Message Classifications for Outlook 2007

For Outlook 2007 users to be able to set message classifications, the classifications must be exported from Active Directory to an XML file, and this file made accessible to Outlook 2007 clients. There is an Exchange Server 2007 PowerShell script named `Export-OutlookClassification.ps1` provided for this purpose; this script is located in the *<install_drive>*:\Program Files\Microsoft\Exchange Server\Scripts directory on the Exchange Server 2007 computer.

Next, to use the classification XML file, Outlook 2007 clients also require message classification to be enabled. This is done through the registry, by creating the three values shown below:

```
[HKEY_CURRENT_USER\Software\Microsoft\Office\12.0\Common\Policy]
"AdminClassificationPath"="c:\\Classifications.xml"
"EnableClassifications"=dword:00000001
"TrustClassifications"=dword:00000001
```

The Policy key is not present by default in Outlook 2007, so it must be created.

The `AdminClassificationPath` string value defines the location where the classification XML file is stored. This can be any location accessible to the Outlook 2007 client, including a network share.

Deploying the message classification XML file to Outlook 2007 clients presents some challenges about where to store the XML file so it is accessible to clients. Storing it in a local path on the client computer ensures message classifications are accessible when the user is offline in cached mode, but requires that the file be copied to and updated on all client computers, especially if classifications are modified or added/removed. Storing the XML file on a network share means it has to be maintained in only one location, but presents challenges for offline users. One approach is to store the file on a network share, and force that network share to be available offline for all connected users (using Windows offline files). This ensures that message classifications are available to end users at all times, while leaving only one file location to maintain.

Exercise 16.5 outlines the steps to create a custom message classification and to enable Outlook 2007 for message classifications.

EXERCISE 16.5

Deploying Message Classifications

In this exercise we will create a custom message classification, then deploy the classification to an Outlook 2007 client.

Creating a Custom Message Classification

First we will create a new message classification named Privacy Act and define the `SenderDescription` and `RecipientDescription` fields appropriately for end users.

1. Start the Exchange Management Shell from Start ➢ All Programs ➢ Microsoft Exchange Server 2007. At the PowerShell prompt, enter the following cmdlet and then press Enter.

EXERCISE 16.5 *(continued)*

```
New-MessageClassification -Name Privacy -DisplayName "Privacy Act" -
SenderDescription "This message contains personal information as described by
the Privacy Act" -RecipientDescription "This message contains private
information of clients as defined in the Privacy Act"
```

The output of the cmdlet should be similar to the following:

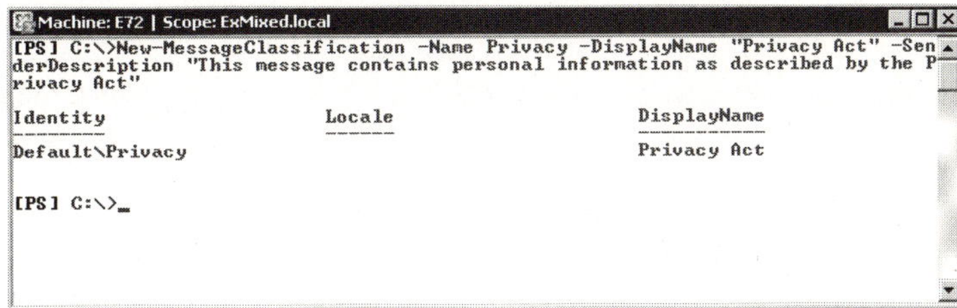

```
Machine: E72 | Scope: ExMixed.local
[PS] C:\>New-MessageClassification -Name Privacy -DisplayName "Privacy Act" -SenderDescription "This message contains personal information as described by the Privacy Act"

Identity                Locale                DisplayName
--------                ------                -----------
Default\Privacy                               Privacy Act

[PS] C:\>_
```

2. To confirm the message classification you just created, open Internet Explorer and log on to Outlook Web Access as a user in the Exchange Server 2007 organization. Start a new message and click the classification icon as shown here to view the newly created message classification:

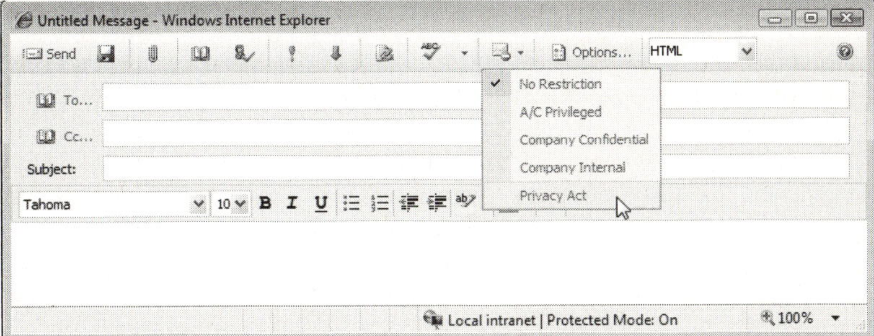

3. Select Privacy Act, and compose a message to another user. The sender description can be seen in the composed message, as shown here. Send the message to the user by clicking Send.

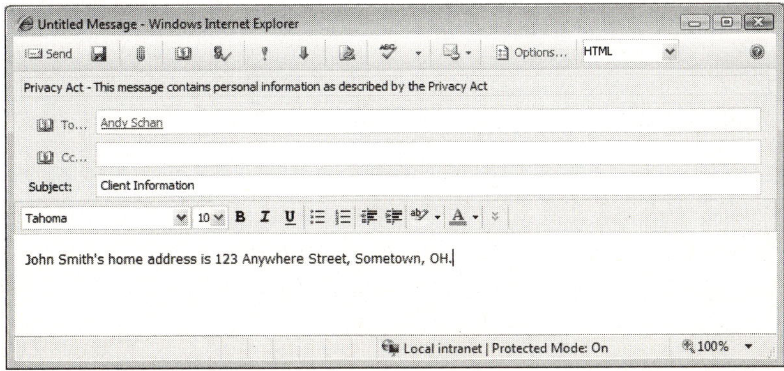

EXERCISE 16.5 *(continued)*

4. Log on to Outlook Web Access as the recipient of the message sent. The message classification assigned by the sender and the recipient description appear in the Preview pane, as shown here:

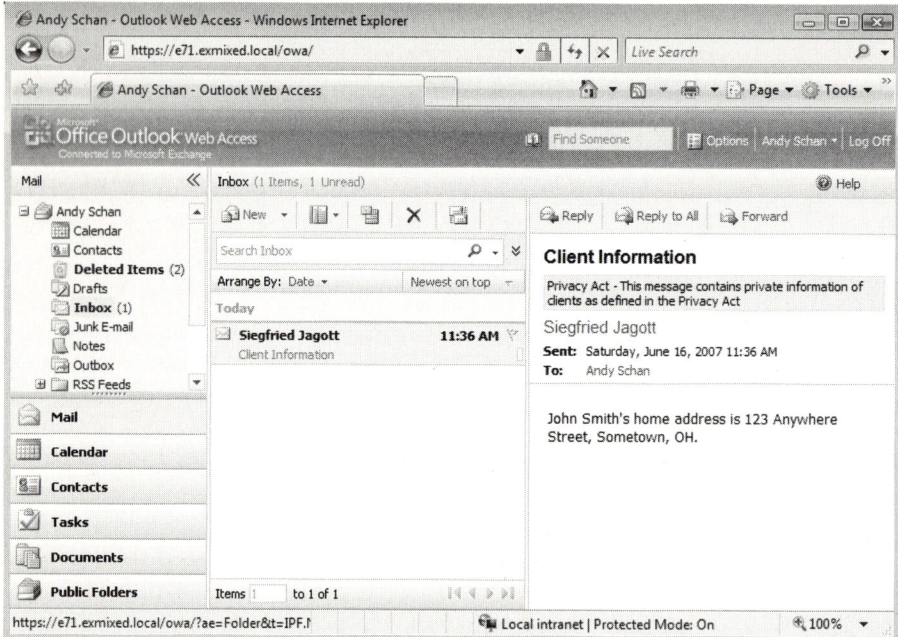

5. Open the received message in Outlook Web Access and note that the message classification and recipient description appear in the message, as shown here. Close the message and log out of Outlook Web Access.

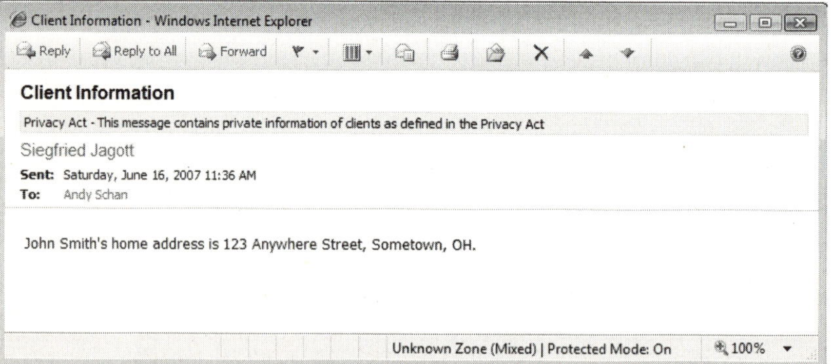

EXERCISE 16.5 *(continued)*

Deploying Message Classifications to Outlook 2007 Clients

In this section of the exercise, we will distribute the message classification XML file to the Outlook 2007 client and enable Outlook 2007 for message classification.

1. Log on to the client computer as the recipient of the Privacy Act classified message sent in the first part of this exercise. Open Outlook 2007, highlight the received message in the inbox, and note that no classification labels are visible in the Preview pane.

2. Double-click on the message in Outlook 2007 to open it. Note that the classification labels are also not visible in the message itself.

3. Log on to the Exchange Server 2007 computer, and create a folder on the C: drive named C:\Export.

4. Start the Exchange Management Shell from Start ➢ All Programs ➢ Microsoft Exchange Server 2007. At the PowerShell prompt, run the following script from the Program Files\Microsoft\Exchange Server\Scripts directory:

   ```
   ./Export-OutlookClassification.ps1 > c:\exports\Classifications.xml
   ```

   If the `Export-OutlookClassification` script is successful, no output will be returned at the PowerShell prompt.

5. Using Windows Explorer, confirm the `Classifications.xml` file was created successfully. Double-click the `Classifications.xml` file to open it in Internet Explorer, then scroll down and note the section defining the Privacy Act classification as shown below, then close Internet Explorer.

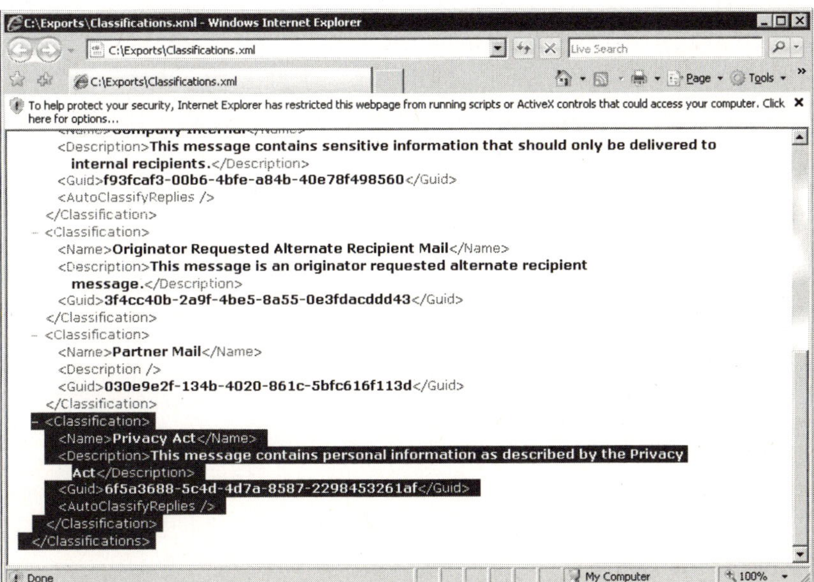

EXERCISE 16.5 *(continued)*

6. Copy the `Classifications.xml` file from the Exchange Server 2007 computer to C:\Classifications.xml on the client computer.

7. Log on to the client computer as the recipient of the previously classified message and create the following registry values (you will have to create the Policy key as well):

```
[HKEY_CURRENT_USER\Software\Microsoft\Office\12.0\Common\Policy]

"AdminClassificationPath"="c:\\Classifications.xml"

"EnableClassifications"=dword:00000001

"TrustClassifications"=dword:00000001
```

8. Close and re-open Outlook 2007. Highlight the received message in the Inbox and note that the classification label is now visible in the Preview pane, as follows:

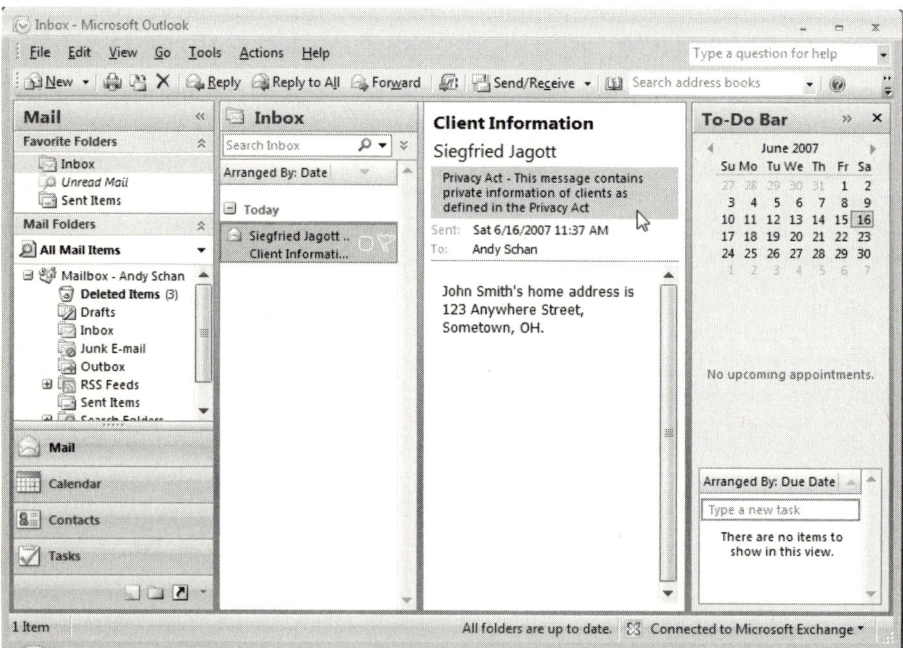

EXERCISE 16.5 *(continued)*

9. Double-click on the message in Outlook 2007 to open it. Note that the classification label is now also visible in the message itself, as shown here. Close the message.

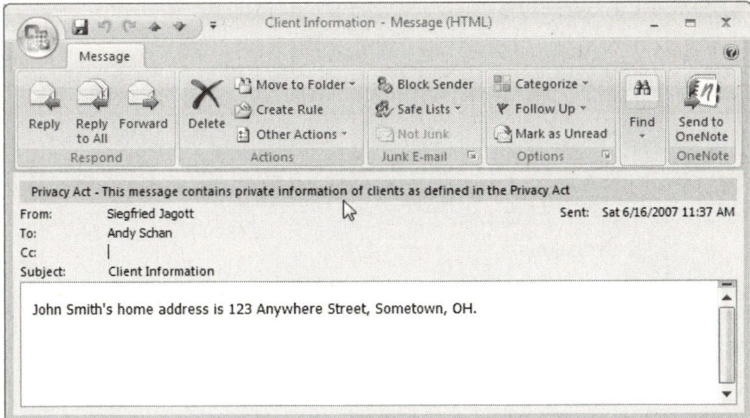

10. Back in the Outlook 2007 main window, start a new message, then click on the drop-down beside the Permission button as shown below. Note that all the default message classifications, as well as the newly created Privacy Act classification, are now accessible as shown here:

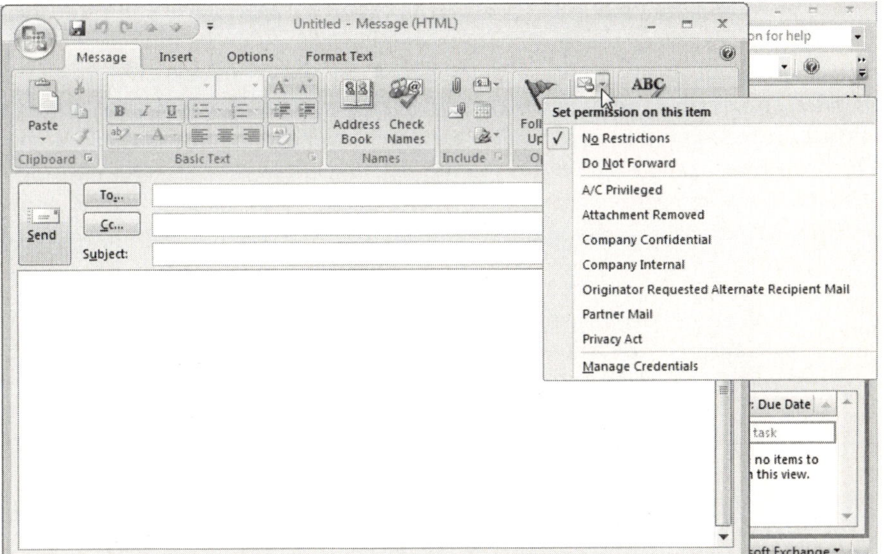

EXERCISE 16.5 *(continued)*

11. Select the Privacy Act classification, then compose a message to another user in the organization. Note that the sender description appears in the message as shown here. Click Send to send the message.

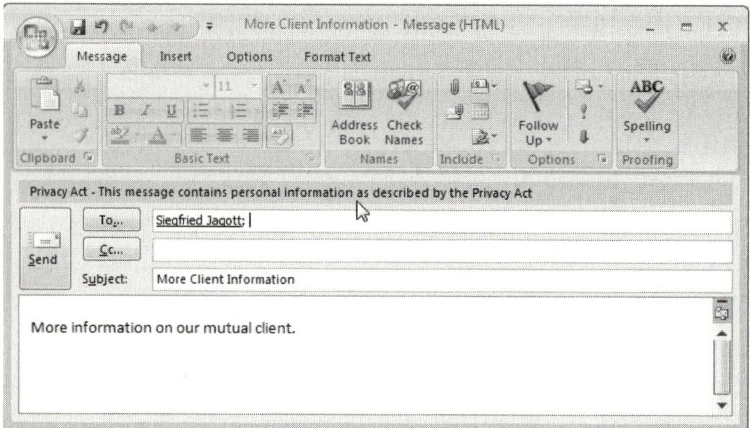

Assigning Message Classifications with Transport Rules

In addition to providing end users with the ability to assign message classifications to messages before they are sent, Exchange Server 2007 can automatically assign message classifications based on specified criteria using transport rules run by the Hub Transport role. As with any transport rules, you define conditions for the rule, then set an action for the rule to take when the conditions are met (in this case, to apply a message classification). For example, a transport rule can be configured to apply the Privacy Act message classification to any message containing a Social Security number to ensure compliance with regulatory and company policies or it could block messages with Social Security numbers in them from being sent to external recipients.

In addition to creating transport rules that assign classifications, you can create transport rules that act on classifications. For example, you could prevent messages classified Company Internal from leaving the organization. Thus, even though message classifications are only visible in Outlook 2007 and Exchange Server 2007 Outlook Web Access, they may still be of use in your organization.

The steps to create a transport rule for the Exchange organization to apply the Privacy Act classification would be as follows:

1. Start the Exchange Management Console from Start ➢ All Programs ➢ Microsoft Exchange Server 2007. Within the Exchange Management Console, expand the Organization Configuration work center, then select the Hub Transport subnode. In the Results pane, select the Transport Rules tab as shown in Figure 16.14, then select New Transport Rule from the Action pane.

FIGURE 16.14 Creating a new transport rule

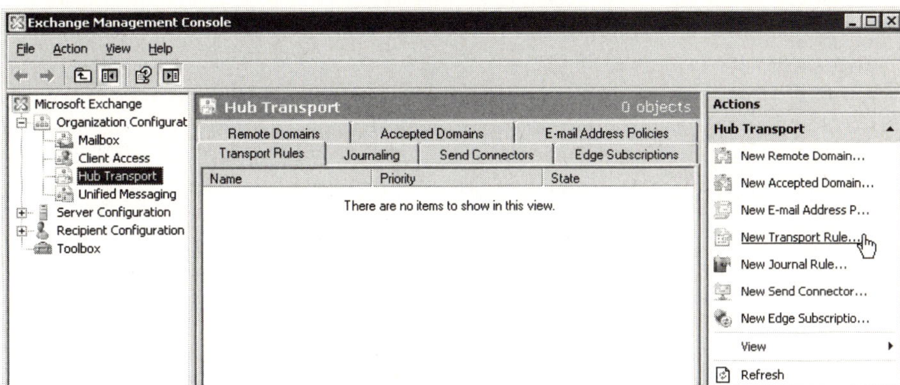

2. On the Introduction screen of the New Transport Rule wizard, enter **Social Security** as the name of the rule and enter the comment **Messages containing private information to be assigned the message classification Privacy Act.** Leave the Enable Rule check box selected, then click Next.
3. On the Conditions page of the wizard, scroll down the conditions list as shown in Figure 16.15 and select When the Subject Field or the Body of the Message Contains Text Patterns, then click the Text Patterns link.

FIGURE 16.15 Configuring a text-pattern condition in a transport rule

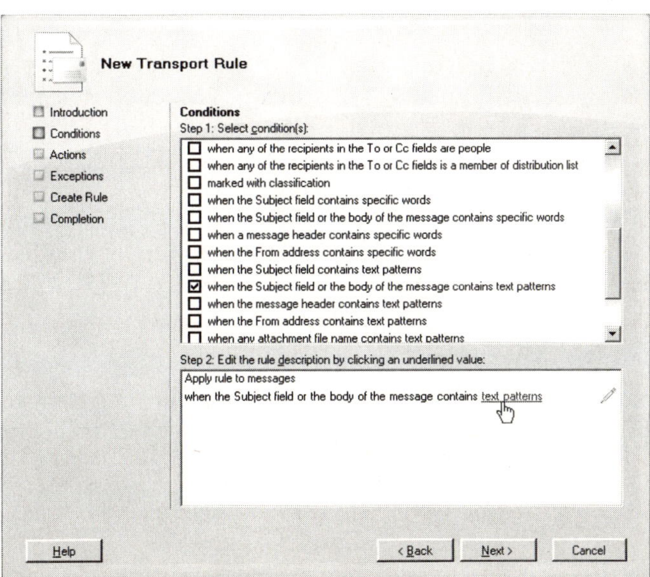

4. In the Specify Text Patterns dialog, enter **\d\d\d-\d\d-\d\d\d\d**, then click Add. Select OK to return to the New Transport Rule wizard.
5. Back on the Conditions screen of the New Transport Rule wizard, click Next to proceed to the Actions screen.
6. On the Actions screen of the wizard, select the Apply Message Classification action as shown in Figure 16.16, then click the Message Classification link.

FIGURE 16.16 Applying a message-classification action

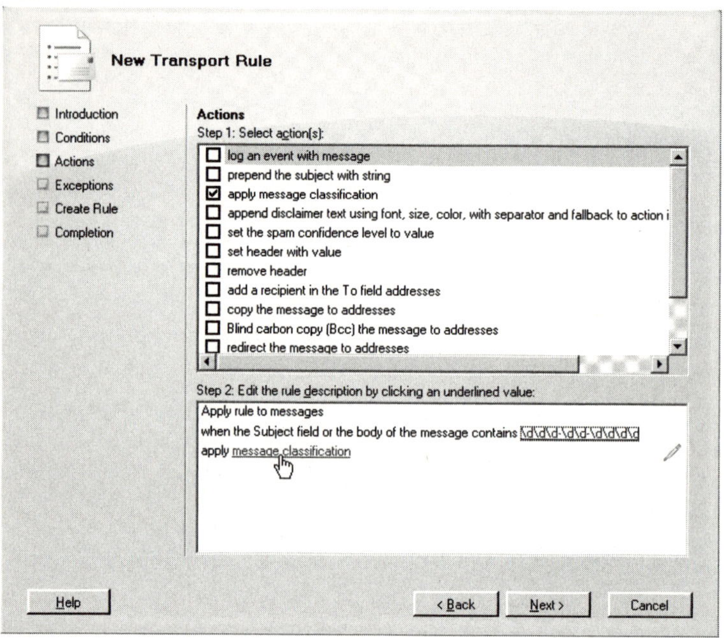

7. In the Select Message Classification dialog, select the Privacy classification, then click OK to return to the Actions screen.
8. Back on the Actions screen of the wizard, select Next to move to the Exceptions screen:
9. On the Exceptions screen of the wizard, leave Exceptions unchecked and click Next.
10. On the Create Rule screen of the wizard, verify the summary of your new rule, and click New to create it.
11. On the Completion screen of the wizard, note the Exchange Management Shell command that was executed to create the rule, and click Finish.
12. Back in the Exchange Management Console, note that the newly created Social Security rule now appears on the Transport Rule tab in the Results pane, as shown in Figure 16.17.

FIGURE 16.17 A newly created Hub Transport rule

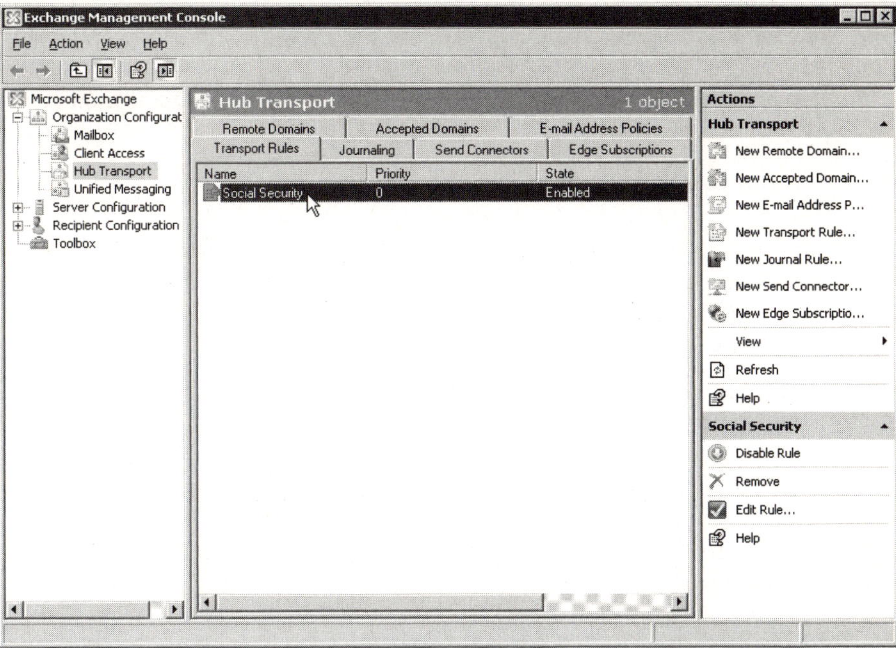

If you create a Hub Transport rule as discussed, you can log on to the client as a user with a mailbox in the Exchange Server 2007 organization, then send a new message addressed to another recipient in the organization. Enter **Client Information** as the subject, then type **John Smith's Social Security Number is 123-45-6789** in the body of the message. Click Send to send the message.

Now if you log on to a client as the recipient of the message sent and start Outlook 2007, you can highlight the received message in the inbox. Note that the message-classification label, including the recipient description, is shown in the Preview pane as illustrated in Figure 16.18.

Opening the message in the Inbox shows that the message classification display name and recipient description appear in the message, as shown in Figure 16.19.

Rights Management Service (RMS) Integration

Windows Rights Management Services is Windows-platform information-protection technology that allows organizations to better safeguard sensitive information by providing a means for publishers of confidential email messages and documents to control who can view their content by applying persistent protection to the email or document. This is done using public key technology using XrML (Extensible Rights Markup Language)-based certificates.

Although RMS is a public/private key technology, it is not a replacement for your X.509 PKI implementation. The two provide different solutions for different problems and are complementary. In the same vein, deploying RMS does not require you to implement a PKI certificate authority (CA).

FIGURE 16.18 A message classification assigned by a Hub Transport rule

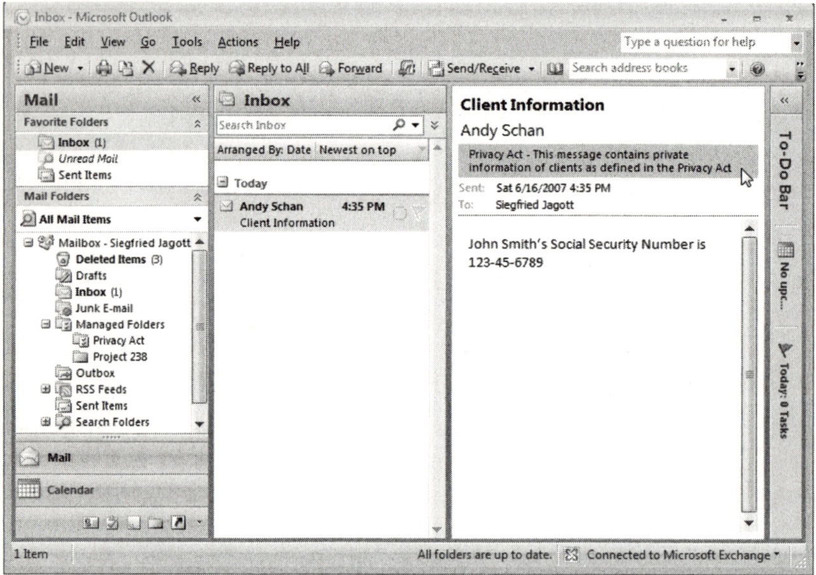

FIGURE 16.19 An assigned message classification displayed in a message

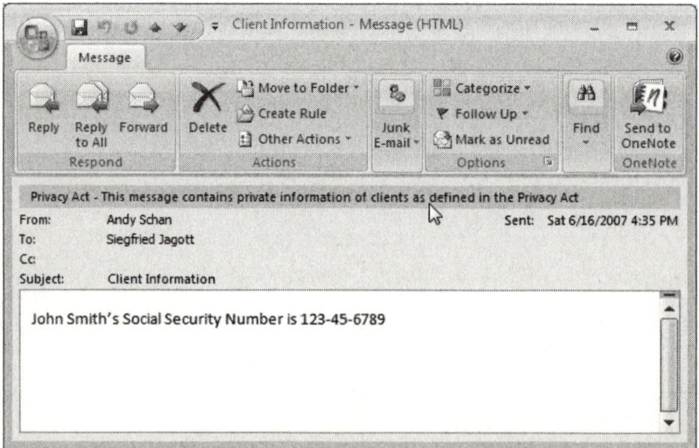

The fundamental difference between RMS and other encryption technologies such as S/MIME or PGP is that RMS provides persistent content protection. With an S/MIME encrypted email, once the recipient has opened the message using their keys, they have complete control over the message: they can forward it, cut/copy/paste the contents, print the message, etc. RMS persistent content protection means that the rights the recipient has over the content have been explicitly defined, are in effect when the message is opened, and persist with the message, whether it is in their Exchange Server 2007 mailbox, in a PST file, or wherever else the message resides. Most importantly, rights are enforced while the message is opened, meaning that unless the explicit rights have been granted, the recipient cannot forward the message, print, cut, copy, or paste it.

Users are granted a *Rights management Account Certificate* (RAC; their RMS credentials) after presenting valid Active Directory credentials to the RMS server. The RMS server also issues a certificate for the client computer; if the user moves to a different client computer, they obtain another instance of their RAC from the RMS server, encrypted for the new client computer.

In addition to their RAC, a user is also issued a *client licensor certificate* (CLC). This is also known as the publishing license and enables the user to protect (encrypt) content offline without having to contact the RMS server. Offline publishing is the default behavior for the RMS client.

When a user receives an RMS-protected email, their rights for that email are granted in the form of a use license issued by the RMS server. Use licenses, like the user's RAC, are encrypted for a specific client computer with that client computer's RMS certificate. RMS-protected content can be encrypted for a single user or for groups (mail-enabled groups defined in Active Directory).

The various certificates issued to users (RACs, CLCs, use licenses, and machine certificates) can be viewed in the user's profile. In Windows XP, this is in the path %userprofile%\Local Settings\Application Data\Microsoft\DRM. In Windows Vista, these are located at %userprofile%\AppData\Local\Microsoft\DRM.

An RMS implementation consists of the following components. All of these components are required, with the exception of RMS templates. While templates facilitate the application of a predefined set of RMS rights and users, they are not required for the base functionality.

Active Directory. RMS requires Active Directory to locate and authenticate users and determine group memberships for content protected for groups; group memberships are cached in SQL to reduce the number of AD queries required.

RMS server. The RMS server hosts the RMS server software, which is a web service for Windows Server 2003 that handles the XrML-based certification of trusted entities, licensing of rights-protected information, enrollment of servers and users, and administration functions. The RMS server software requires the Microsoft Message Queuing service to be installed, along with IIS and ASP.NET.

Database server. The database server is SQL Server 2000 or 2005, or it can be MSDE for a single-server installation.

MSDE is generally used only in a lab or proof-of-concept environment; in a production installation, even an initial pilot, it is recommended to use SQL Server 2000 or, better yet, SQL Server 2005.

RMS client. The RMS client software is a download for Windows XP SP2; Windows Vista has the RMS client built in, so no download is required.

RMS-aware applications. The only applications supported natively for protecting content are Office 2003 or Office 2007 Professional, although Office 2003 Standard Edition can access RMS-protected content (but it cannot RMS-protect content). Outlook email messages and Word, PowerPoint, and Excel files can all be RMS-protected, as can XML Paper Specification (XPS)-based documents. Third-party products exist that extend RMS functionality into other applications and file formats, including PDF, CAD/CAM file formats, and BlackBerry Enterprise Server, among others.

RMS templates. Although RMS rights can be applied to Office documents and Outlook email messages without templates, RMS templates provide a packaged collection of rights and user/group assignments to facilitate consistent application of RMS protection. RMS templates are defined on the RMS server and stored in the RMS SQL database, and they are defined in XML files in a location configured on the RMS server for the use of RMS clients. However, similar to message classifications (discussed earlier in this chapter), to be usable for end users the RMS template XML files must be made available to end users, and that poses the same distribution and management challenges as with message classification XML files for Outlook 2007.

In an RMS infrastructure, templates are best used sparingly to keep the deployment manageable and to make the list of options as short as feasible for end users. Many large, multinational organizations with 100,000 users or more have deployed RMS with less than five templates for the entire organization.

Figure 16.20 illustrates a typical RMS infrastructure.

As of this writing, the current version of RMS is version 1.0 SP2. Version 2.0 will be released with Windows Server 2008 (formerly code-named Windows Server Longhorn), will be renamed Active Directory RMS, and will include new functionality, such as a Microsoft Management Console (MMC)-based administrative interface (the current administrative interface is web-based) and integration with Active Directory Federated Services (ADFS).

FIGURE 16.20 Typical RMS infrastructure

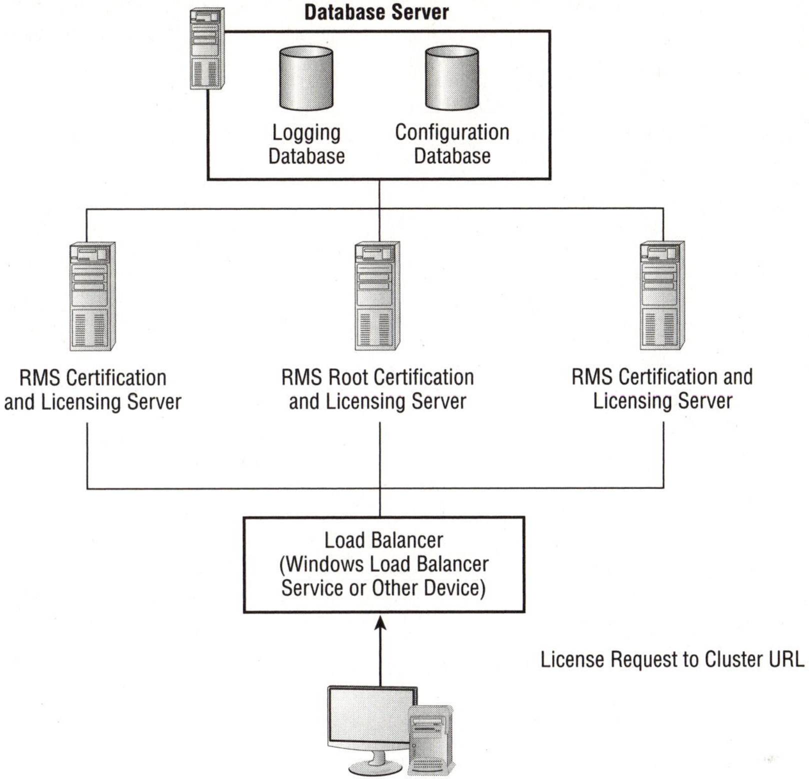

Real World Scenario

RMS Protecting for External Recipients

Similar to Exchange, there is a single RMS infrastructure per Active Directory forest. To RMS-protect messages for recipients outside your Exchange organization, such as partners or customers, you have three alternatives:

- You can establish an RMS trust between your organization and the partner's organization (with RMS deployed in both).

- You can create accounts in your internal Active Directory forest for the external recipients.
- Rather than creating accounts in your internal forest, you can establish a separate Active Directory forest with RMS in a perimeter network accessible by the external users where they can obtain RMS credentials and use licenses for RMS-protected email; an RMS trust is then established between this perimeter RMS and your internal RMS deployment. This is generally preferred from a security point of view.

The last two alternatives can be easier to implement from a legal point of view than establishing an RMS trust between two companies, but requires that you create an account for every external recipient in the perimeter Active Directory forest or your internal forest. This can quickly become a management nightmare. One solution is to establish an automated account provisioning system with appropriate checks in place to ensure the validity of created accounts.

Another option that will be available with Active Directory RMS in Windows Server 2008 is to use ADFS with RMS to accept your partner's or customer's Active Directory credentials for use by RMS. RMS would then issue use licenses for content based on the user's credentials from their organization's Active Directory.

As with establishing an RMS trust, though, implementing ADFS with Windows Server 2008 against a partner's or customer's organization can present significant legal and liability challenges. In many cases, the technology implementation will be straightforward, but establishing the business relationship and accompanying legal requirements can be a significant effort.

RMS and Exchange Server 2007

RMS can be integrated with Exchange Server 2007 through Outlook 2003 and Outlook 2007, assuming an RMS server infrastructure has been established on the network. Once RMS is in place, messages can be encrypted using Outlook 2003 or Outlook 2007. If the client OS is Windows XP, the RMS client has to be installed; if the client OS is Windows Vista, the RMS client is built in. RMS-protected messages can be accessed with Outlook 2003, Outlook 2007, or Outlook Web Access, assuming the recipient has been granted appropriate RMS rights to the message.

Outlook 2003 and Outlook 2007 have the ability to pre-fetch RMS use licenses for received messages as the messages are received, without the user having to open them. This facilitates offline use so that the user can open the messages on an airplane, for example, without having opened the message previously while connected to the organization's intranet. This functionality requires Outlook 2003 or Outlook 2007 to be running and have connectivity to both the Exchange Server 2007 mailbox server and the RMS server when the message is received in order to be able to pre-fetch the RMS use licenses. Use licenses are stored in the user's Windows profile on the client computer.

As of this writing, Exchange Server 2007 SP1 will introduce server-side use license pre-fetching. This will provide the Hub Transport server role the ability to pre-fetch the use license on behalf of the user and include it in the RMS-protected message. This will provide offline access to RMS-protected messages for the user without requiring Outlook connectivity for the pre-fetch operation.

Protecting Messages with RMS

Assuming RMS is deployed in the environment, Outlook 2007 uses the same toolbar button to RMS-protect messages that is used to apply message classifications. Without RMS templates deployed, the standard Do Not Forward RMS permission is available, as shown in Figure 16.21.

FIGURE 16.21 Setting RMS protection in Outlook 2007

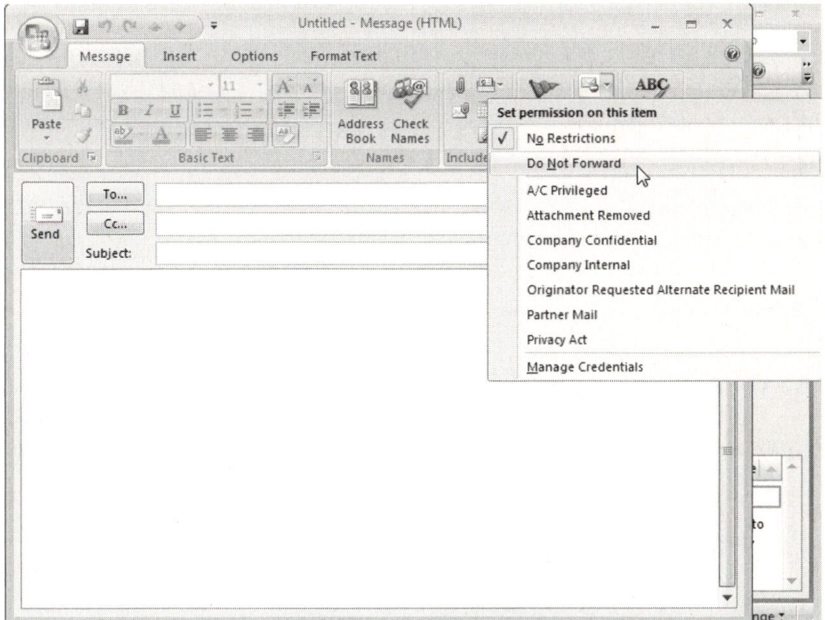

Once the Do Not Forward permission is selected, an information bar is displayed in the message window. As you can see in Figure 16.21, this information bar is very similar to the one displayed when message classifications are set on a message being composed. When Send is clicked, the specified RMS rights are applied and the message is sent to the recipient. Figure 16.22 shows a composed message with RMS set on it, prior to being sent, while Figure 16.23 shows the RMS licenses stored in the user's Windows profile after the message is composed and sent.

Consuming RMS-Protected Messages

Opening (or *consuming*, in RMS terminology) RMS-protected messages you have received is generally a transparent operation; the recipient just has to double-click on the message to confirm their credentials and obtain a use license from the RMS server. Figure 16.24 shows an RMS-protected message in a user's inbox before a use license is obtained. Note that the message has a special icon in the message list, denoting that the message is RMS-protected and that the Preview pane view of the message is unavailable.

FIGURE 16.22 Outlook 2007 composed message with RMS applied

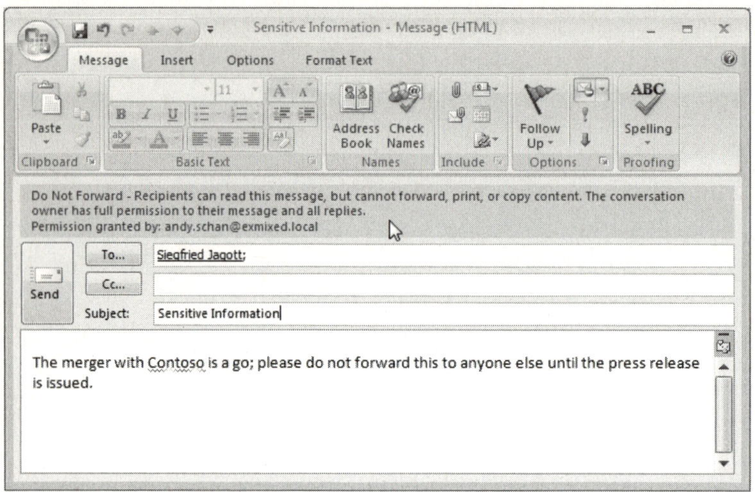

FIGURE 16.23 RMS licenses in a user's profile

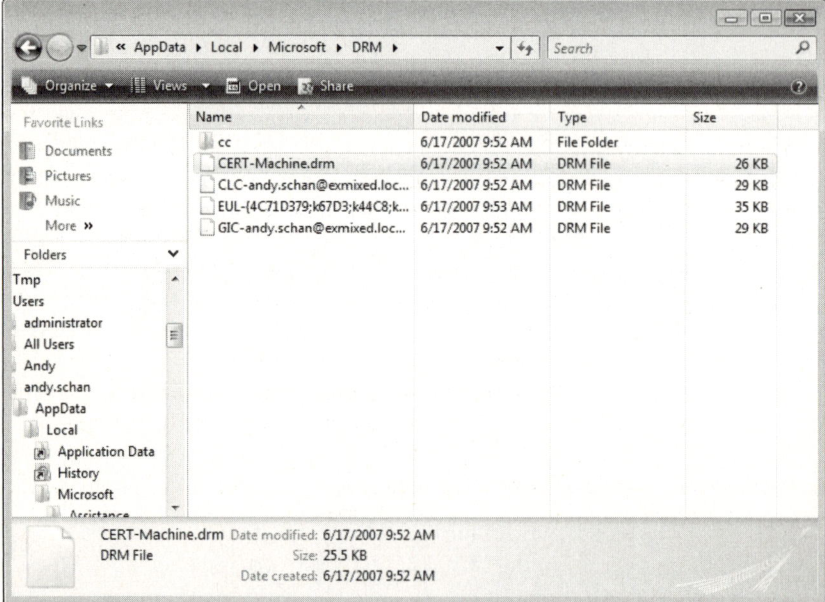

FIGURE 16.24 RMS-protected message in the Inbox

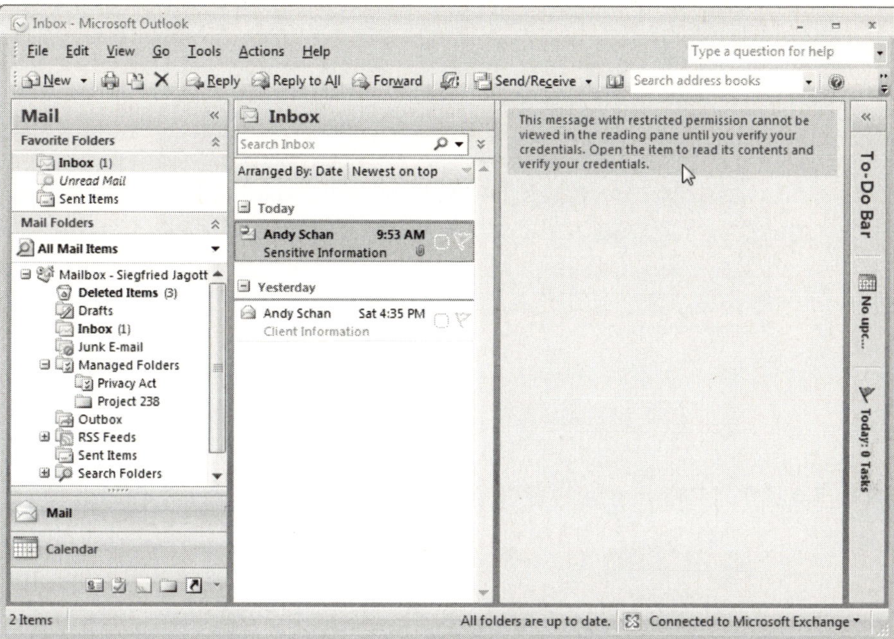

Pre-fetching RMS Use Licenses with Outlook

When the recipient double-clicks on an RMS-protected message for the first time, they are presented with a dialog box asking for confirmation to connect to the RMS server. If desired, the user can select a Don't Show This Message Again check box before clicking OK. In that case, the user will not be presented with the dialog in the future and RMS use licenses will be pre-fetched in the background for later RMS-protected messages. This feature was discussed earlier in this chapter, in the introduction to the "RMS and Exchange Server 2007" section.

Remember that this RMS license pre-fetching is available as a server-side operation in the Hub Transport server role in Exchange Server 2007 SP1.

Figure 16.25 shows an opened RMS-protected message received by a user. Again, note the similarities to message classifications illustrated earlier in Exercise 16.5. A primary difference is the text denoting the conversation owner; the owner is the one who assigned the RMS protection, and the only person who is able to modify that protection.

Choosing Reply or Reply All to an RMS-protected message in Outlook 2007 shows some of the behavior imposed by RMS. As can be seen in Figure 16.26, the To and Cc fields are grayed out and unchangeable and, as the note indicates, you are unable to cut or copy the original text. You also can see in the Quick Launch bar at the top of the message that the print icon is grayed out; you cannot print the message.

FIGURE 16.25 An RMS-protected message

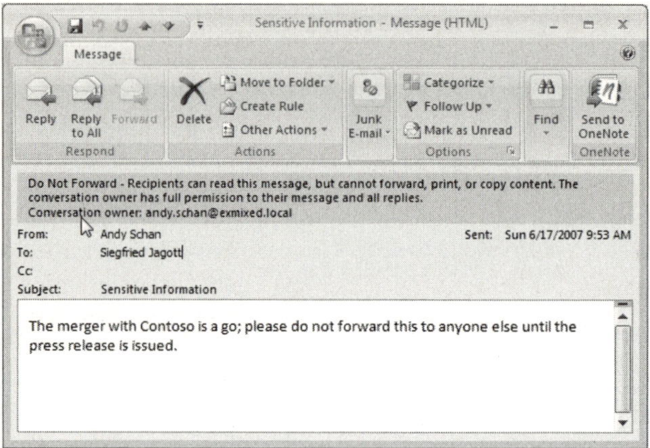

FIGURE 16.26 Replying to an RMS-protected message in Outlook 2007

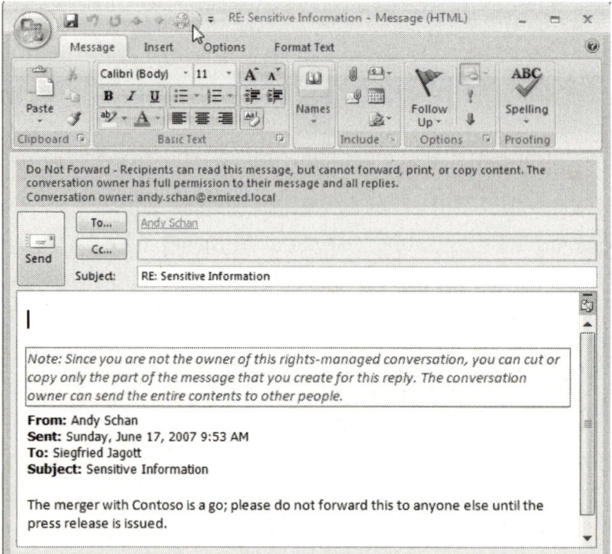

The preservation of the email thread in replies to RMS-protected messages is a feature that was introduced in Outlook 2007; in Outlook 2003, all replies to protected messages excluded the original message. An Outlook 2003 user is presented with a dialog box warning them that the body of the original message will not be included in their reply message.

Summary

In this chapter we covered the solutions provided by Exchange Server 2007 to allow you to plan and deploy an email compliance solution in your environment. Like any other technology, the compliance solutions provided in Exchange Server 2007 are tools. Just as carpentry tools do not make you a carpenter, these compliance tools alone do not make you compliant. The solutions provided in Exchange Server 2007 aid you in implementing your corporate compliance policy, but without that policy defined and in place the tools will not help you.

Messaging records management in Exchange Server 2007 provides the next generation of the Mailbox Manager functionality in Exchange Server 2003, with much greater flexibility for custom policies for different groups of users and enhanced reporting, auditing, and retrieval capabilities.

In Exchange Server 2007, Microsoft has provided a first-generation message classification capability to provide for adding classification metadata and, in some cases, visual labels to email messages. The metadata can be leveraged through transport rules to act on classified messages or apply classifications to messages as desired; the classification metadata also may be leveraged by third-party applications.

RMS (Rights Management Service) can be leveraged in an Exchange Server 2007 organization to provide comprehensive policy management of email, to limit inadvertent or intentional information disclosure, and to ensure messages are protected in transit and at rest wherever they are stored. Although we didn't cover how to implement RMS in your environment, we discussed in detail how RMS interacts with Exchange Server 2007, Outlook 2003, and Outlook 2007.

Exam Essentials

Understand the functions of the different messaging records management components. Messaging records management (MRM) is composed of managed folders (default and custom), managed content settings, managed folder mailbox policies, and the Managed Folder Assistant. Managed content settings are created per managed folder; manager folder mailbox policies are collections of managed folders that can be assigned to users.

Understand managed folder mailbox policies and how they apply to users. There is a one-to-one relationship between managed folder mailbox policies and mailboxes; only one managed folder mailbox policy can be assigned to any user. Also, a managed folder mailbox policy can contain only one instance of any default managed folder (such as the inbox). Assigning a managed folder to a managed folder mailbox policy without defining managed content settings on that folder has no effect.

Understand how message classification is implemented, and its dependencies. Message classification is a new concept to many Exchange professionals. Understanding what it is and how to implement it is a crucial piece of a comprehensive compliance strategy. You should be sure to understand which clients can use and view message classification, from both a sender and recipient point of view. You also should know how to implement message classification for Outlook 2007 clients and how to leverage classification in transport rules.

Understand how RMS interacts with Exchange, Outlook, and Active Directory. Although you won't be expected to know all the intricacies of RMS for the exam, you should understand how RMS interacts in general terms with Exchange Server 2007, Outlook 2003, Outlook 2007, and Active Directory, and how you can exchange RMS-protected messages with users external to your organization.

Review Questions

1. Your company has an email policy stating that all email must be deleted after 90 days. This applies to managers as well, with the exception that specific project-related email must be retained for 180 days. What approach should you plan? (Choose two correct answers.)

   A. Configure a transport rule to drop all project-related email and return a non-delivery report to the sender.

   B. Deploy another storage group and mailbox database. Configure deleted items retention on this database for 180 days, and move all managers' mailboxes to this database.

   C. Configure managed content settings for the Entire Mailbox default managed folder to retain content for 90 days, then permanently delete. Create a managed folder mailbox policy containing the Entire Mailbox folder, and assign this policy to all users except managers.

   D. Create a custom managed folder named Projects. Assign managed content settings to this folder to retain items for 180 days, then permanently delete. Configure managed content settings for the Entire Mailbox default managed folder to retain content for 90 days, then permanently delete. Create a managed folder mailbox policy containing these two folders, and assign the policy to all managers.

2. You need to plan a messaging records management deployment to have different groups of users have unique retention settings on their Inbox folders, and you need to retain the name Inbox for the folder. What should you do?

   A. Design managed content settings for the default Inbox managed folder with the most-restrictive retention settings required for your environment. Assign these settings to the correct users with a managed folder mailbox policy. Instruct all other users to delete email as per the policies that apply to them.

   B. Design a managed custom folder for each group of users with the appropriate retention settings assigned to each folder. Configure managed contents settings appropriately for each managed custom folder. Assign these managed folders to the appropriate users with managed folder mailbox policies.

   C. Design new managed default folders of the Inbox type for each group. Name these folders with the name of the group they will apply to. Configure managed contents settings appropriately for each managed default folder. Assign these managed folders to the appropriate users with managed folder mailbox policies.

   D. Design managed content settings for the default Inbox managed folder with the least-restrictive retention settings required for your environment. Assign these settings to the users with the least-restrictive retention policies with a managed folder mailbox policy. Instruct all other users to delete email as per the policies that apply to them.

3. A new company policy states that the marketing manager should have access to all email discussing specific clients held by certain users in the marketing department. Privacy concerns dictate that the marketing manager should see only client-related email. What should you do?

   A. Design a managed custom folder named Clients. Assign managed content settings to this folder to copy all messages to the marketing manager. Create a managed folder mailbox policy containing this managed folder and assign this policy to all members of the marketing department. Instruct the designated users to move all client-related email to this managed custom folder.

   B. Design a transport rule to copy all email received and sent by the designated users in the marketing department to the marketing manager.

   C. Design a transport rule to copy email received and sent by all users in the marketing department with the client's name in the subject or body to the marketing manager.

   D. Design managed content settings for the Entire Mailbox managed default folder to copy all email to the marketing manager. Design a managed folder mailbox policy containing the Entire Mailbox managed default folder and assign this policy to the designated users.

4. You are designing a messaging records management deployment for your organization. All users are expected to empty their Deleted Items folder at least every 30 days, while managers are expected to retain items in their Inbox for 90 days. What actions should you include in your deployment plan?

   A. Design managed content settings for the Entire Mailbox managed default folder to permanently delete items after 30 days. Design a managed folder mailbox policy containing the Entire Mailbox managed default folder, and assign this policy to all users.

   B. Configure the Managed Folder Assistant to run every day from 2 a.m. to 4 a.m.

   C. Design a managed custom folder named Deletions. Assign managed content settings to this folder to retain items for 30 days then permanently delete. Create a managed folder mailbox policy containing this managed folder and assign this policy to all users.

   D. Design a managed custom folder named Inbox Retention. Assign managed content settings for the Inbox Retention managed custom folder to permanently delete items after 90 days. Design a managed folder mailbox policy containing the Inbox Retention managed custom folder and assign this policy to all users.

5. How many different managed folder mailbox policies can be assigned to a user?

   A. 5

   B. 10

   C. 2

   D. 1

6. What versions of Outlook are supported for mailboxes that have managed folder mailbox policies assigned to them? (Choose all that apply.)

   A. Outlook 2007

   B. Outlook XP

   C. Outlook 2003 RTM

   D. Outlook 2003 SP2

   E. Outlook 2003 SP1

   F. Outlook 2000

7. Which of the following PowerShell cmdlets are used to manage messaging records management in Exchange Server 2007? (Choose all that apply.)

   A. `Set-MailUser`

   B. `New-ManagedFolder`

   C. `New-ManagedFolderMailboxPolicy`

   D. `New-SystemMessage`

   E. `New-JournalRule`

   F. `Set-MailboxServer`

8. You are designing the messaging records management implementation for your company's Exchange Server 2007 deployment. Engineers working on a classified project named Project X must retain messages related to the project for two years, at which time messages should be archived. What should you include in your plan?

   A. Create a new message classification named Project X. Configure a transport rule that will archive messages classified Project X to a separate mailbox.

   B. Create a managed custom folder named Project X. Configure managed content settings for the folder to journal messages to an archive mailbox and retain messages for two years. Create a managed folder mailbox policy containing this folder and assign it to the engineers.

   C. Configure a managed default folder of the type Inbox named Project X. Configure managed content settings for the folder to journal messages to an archive mailbox and retain messages for two years. Create a managed folder mailbox policy containing this folder and assign it to the engineers.

   D. Configure a transport rule that will archive messages containing the words *Project X* to a separate mailbox.

9. In which work center of the Exchange Management Console do you configure messaging records management?

   A. Organization Configuration

   B. Server Configuration

   C. Recipient Configuration

   D. Toolbox

10. You are implementing messaging records management for your organization and have deployed a pilot of mailbox policies to a group of users on one server. The IT group running backups reports that the backup of that server is now taking twice as long as it did before messaging records management was implemented. What should you do?

    A. Modify the managed content settings for the managed folders to reduce the retention periods by 50 percent.

    B. Move 50 percent of the users to a different mailbox server.

    C. Modify the managed folder mailbox policies to reduce the number of managed folders in each policy by 50 percent.

    D. Modify the Managed Folder Assistant schedule to run at a different time than the server backups.

11. You are planning message classification for use by your end users and have deployed a pilot to your environment. Some users report they are unable to see the message classifications. What should you do? (Choose all that apply.)

    A. Implement transport rules to set message classifications as necessary.

    B. Copy the `Classifications.xml` file to all client computers.

    C. Implement RMS to the environment and instruct users to use the Permissions task bar button before sending email.

    D. Modify the registry on all client computers.

    E. Deploy Outlook 2007 to all client computers.

12. Which message classification parameters control what users see in messages? (Choose all that apply.)

    A. `DisplayName`

    B. `SenderDescription`

    C. `Name`

    D. `Identity`

    E. `RecipientDescription`

    F. `TemplateInstance`

    G. `Locale`

13. You are planning your company's Exchange Server 2007 implementation. Company policy dictates that messages containing proprietary material must be designated accordingly and must not leave the organization. What should you include in your deployment plan? (Choose two.)

    A. Implement messaging records management and create a managed custom folder named Proprietary.

    B. Design a transport rule to prevent messages classified Proprietary from leaving the organization.

    C. Implement message classifications and create a message classification named Proprietary. Deploy this message classification to all clients.

    D. Design a managed folder mailbox policy including the Proprietary managed custom folder. Assign this policy to all mailboxes.

14. You are planning the message classification implementation for your organization. You want message classification to provide visual labels to end users. Which clients are supported for this? (Choose all that apply.)

    A. Outlook 2007

    B. Outlook Web Access

    C. Outlook 2003 SP1

    D. Outlook 2003 SP2

    E. Outlook XP

    F. Outlook 2000

    G. Outlook 2003 RTM

15. You are planning the Exchange Server 2007 implementation for your organization. Company policy states that all messages with the word *Confidential* in the subject must be designated Confidential and archived for review. What actions should you include in your plan? (Choose two.)

A. Deploy a custom message `Classifications.xml` file to all client computers and modify the registry to enable message classifications.

B. Upgrade all client computers to Outlook 2007.

C. Create a new message classification named Confidential.

D. Implement a transport rule to set the Confidential message classification on all messages with *Confidential* in the subject line and copy them to an archive mailbox.

16. Which PowerShell cmdlet is used to set locale-specific versions of an existing message classification?

A. `Set-MessageClassification`

B. `Set-DetailsTemplate`

C. `New-MessageClassification`

D. `Get-MessageClassification`

17. You are planning the message classification implementation for your Exchange Server 2007 organizations. What steps must you include in your implementation plan to deploy message classifications to clients?

A. Upgrade all clients to Outlook 2003 SP2 or higher.

B. Run the `Export-OutlookClassification.ps1` script on the Exchange Server 2007 computer.

C. Copy the `Classifications.xml` file to all client computers.

D. Implement a managed default folder of the Outbox type for each message classification.

E. Implement transport rules to set message classifications on designated messages.

F. Upgrade all clients to Outlook 2007.

18. What applications can be used to RMS-protect email messages?

A. Outlook 2003 SP2

B. Outlook 2000

C. Outlook 2007

D. Outlook Web Access

19. You are planning an implementation of Exchange Server 2007 into your environment with RMS already deployed. What steps do you need to take to be able to send and receive RMS-protected email to and from external recipients?

A. Add the SMTP domains of the external users to the partner send connector.

B. Create a partner send connector to implement secure messaging to the external user's SMTP domain.

C. Implement an Active Directory forest in a perimeter network accessible by the external users. Create an Active Directory account in this forest for every external user.

D. Implement RMS in the Active Directory forest and establish an RMS trust to your internal RMS infrastructure.

20. You are planning your company's implementation of Exchange Server 2007 and Outlook 2007. Your company plans to use Windows Rights Management Services to apply policy control to email. What action should you include in your deployment plan to ensure that offline Outlook 2007 clients are able to read RMS-protected email?

A. Implement transport rules to copy classified email to an external address.

B. Instruct users to access email using Outlook Web Access.

C. Instruct users to enable use license pre-fetching in Outlook 2007.

D. Deploy the `Classifications.xml` file to all Outlook 2007 clients.

Answers to Review Questions

1. C, D. Managed content settings that you apply to the special managed default folder named Entire Mailbox apply to all folders that users manually create at the root level of the mailbox folder hierarchy and all managed default folders that are not applied by means of a policy. The Entire Mailbox folder can be assigned to users via managed folder mailbox policies. If another managed custom folder is assigned to a user via the same policy, its managed content settings take precedence over the managed content settings applied to the Entire Mailbox special folder.

2. C. Newly created managed default folders are displayed in the user's mailbox with the name of their type (e.g., Inbox), regardless of the name assigned to them when they are created.

3. A. A managed custom folder assigned to all users will allow the designated users to move email covered under the new policy to this folder, where it will be copied to the marketing manager. A transport rule will act only on mail sent and received after the rule is created; it won't have any effect on mail already held in users' mailboxes.

4. B. By default, the Managed Folder Assistant is set to never run; it must be configured by the administrator and a schedule set on it for managed folder mailbox policies to be applied and maintained.

5. D. There is a one-to-one relationship between managed folder mailbox policies and mailboxes; only one policy can be assigned per mailbox.

6. A, D. Only Outlook 2007 and Outlook 2003 SP2 are supported when the mailbox being accessed has been assigned a managed folder mailbox policy.

7. B, C, F. In addition to `New-ManagedFolder` and `New-ManagedFolderMailboxPolicy`, the `Set-MailboxServer` cmdlet is used to configure the Managed Folder Assistant on mailbox servers.

8. B. To enforce both the retention policy and journaling to a separate mailbox, a managed custom folder must be used; transport rules will apply only to messages in transit.

9. A. Messaging records management is configured in the Organization Configuration work center in the Exchange Management Console.

10. D. It is recommended to schedule the Managed Folder Assistant to run at a different time than the backups and database online maintenance.

11. B, D, E. Message classifications are visible only in Outlook 2007 and OWA, and Outlook 2007 requires access to the `Classifications.xml` file and for registry modifications to be applied.

12. A, B, E, G. `DisplayName` determines what the message sender sees in the Permissions drop-down as they are composing the message. `SenderDescription` and `RecipientDescription` control what the sender and recipient see after the message is composed and sent. The `Locale` parameter is used to create different language versions of an existing message classification.

13. B, C. To designate messages as proprietary, a message classification should be deployed. Messages with this classification assigned can be prevented from leaving the organization with a transport rule.

14. A, B. Outlook 2007 and Outlook Web Access are the only clients that will display the message classification visual labels on messages.

15. C, D. In this case, you need to create the message classification and implement a transport rule to apply the classification to messages meeting the criteria; it is not necessary to enable message classifications for the client computers.

16. C. The `New-MessageClassification` cmdlet is used with the `Identity` and `Locale` parameters to create locale-specific versions of an existing classification.

17. B, C, F. As part of the process to enable message classifications for Outlook clients, you must generate the `Classifications.xml` file with the `Export-OutlookClassification.ps1` script, copy the `Classifications.xml` file to the client computers, and upgrade all clients to Outlook 2007. The registry on the client computers also must be modified to enable message classification and define the path to the `Classifications.xml` file.

18. A, C. Outlook 2003 SP2 and Outlook 2007 are the only applications that can apply RMS protection to email messages.

19. C, D. Deploying an AD forest with RMS in a perimeter network with an RMS trust to your internal RMS infrastructure and creating accounts for external users will provide the ability of exchanging RMS-protected emails with those users.

20. C. The use license pre-fetch feature of Outlook 2007 enables Outlook 2007 to obtain use licenses for RMS-protected messages as they are received, allowing users to read those messages offline at a later time.

Planning for Exchange Server 2007 Messaging Infrastructure Improvements and Maintenance

MICROSOFT EXAM OBJECTIVES COVERED IN THIS CHAPTER:

- ✓ Plan for Exchange infrastructure improvements
- ✓ Plan for configuration changes
- ✓ Plan for change management
- ✓ Plan for patch and service pack implementation
- ✓ Plan for monitoring and reporting

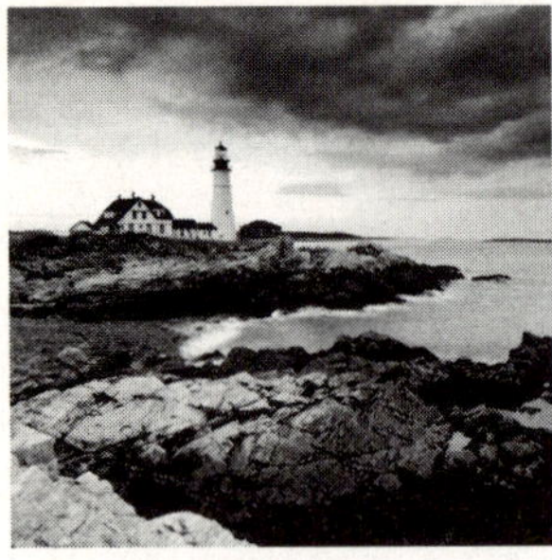

Probably the single most important factor that will influence the stability and availability of your Exchange Server 2007 environment is a well-thought-out change-management strategy. This can mean the difference between managing a messaging environment that meets your organization's business requirements in a cost-effective manner with minimal downtime and being required to update your résumé.

Change management is an all-encompassing term that can mean many things to many people. For the purposes of this chapter, we will consider change management to include planning for infrastructure and configuration changes, as well as the process of analyzing your business requirements and creating your change-management plan based on this analysis. In addition, we will discuss patch management and monitoring/reporting as they relate to the Exchange Server 2007 planning process.

The main subjects of this chapter are as follows:

- Planning for infrastructure or configuration changes
- Documenting your Exchange Server 2007 organization
- Analyzing business requirements
- Defining the issue to be addressed
- Defining the change to be made
- Preparing your change deployment
- Planning change management
- Planning patch management
- Planning monitoring and reporting

Planning for Infrastructure or Configuration Changes

Planning for change in your environment will ensure the ongoing stability and availability of messaging services and allow you to introduce changes with minimal disruption and risk. We will discuss how to go about planning for change in the following sections.

Infrastructure changes include changes to improve performance, availability, and resiliency. Examples of this are adding servers, increasing storage, or adding disaster-recovery sites. Configuration changes encompass adding, removing, or modifying services and functionalities, such as implementing SSL for Outlook Web Access (OWA) or adding another SMTP address space to your list of accepted domains.

Documenting Your Exchange Server 2007 Organization

Before you can deploy any change in your environment, you must determine what that change is going to be. Equally obvious is that if you're changing something, you're changing it for a reason. You also need to know whether your changes are successful. Perhaps more importantly, you need to know whether your changes break anything. It does no good to deploy a new functionality that's used by 10 percent of your users, only to discover afterwards that 100 percent of your users can no longer access their mailboxes using OWA.

What may not be immediately obvious, however, is that if you're changing something, you need to know what state it's in before you change it. Otherwise, how do you know if you've changed it? Knowing what comprises a functioning Exchange Server 2007 organization also forms the basis for functional testing—proving that the system is performing as it should. That allows you to verify that changes applied haven't adversely affected service. Combined with tests performed to verify a new functionality or service is working, it also gives you the basis for deciding when and if a change is successful.

Documenting Your Servers

Arguably the most obvious portion of documenting your environment is documenting your servers and server configurations. This encompasses server-specific information such as hardware, operating system, installed software, and software configurations.

Table 17.1 illustrates some of the hardware parameters that should be recorded for each of your Exchange Server 2007 computers, while Table 17.2 provides an example of an operating system configuration worksheet. Table 17.3 lists software installed on the server and applicable configuration information.

TABLE 17.1 Server Hardware Configuration

Parameter	Description
Make/model	Dell PowerEdge 2950
Serial number	123-ABC-456
Network interface card	Broadcom GigE Ethernet (embedded)
RAM	8 GB

TABLE 17.1 Server Hardware Configuration *(continued)*

Parameter	Description
CPU	Two Quad Core Intel Xeon, 1.6 GHz
Hard-drive controller	PowerEdge RAID Controller 5/i
Hard drives	Drive 0: 160 G SAS Drive 1: 160 G SAS
RAID configuration	Array A configuration: RAID 1 Members: Disk 0, Disk 1
SAN HBA	IBM Fibre Channel

TABLE 17.2 Server Operating System Configuration

Parameter	Description
Base OS	Windows Server 2003
Service pack	SP2
Server name	MB1.company.com
Installed patches	KB925902, KB936782
Drive configuration	C: 160G, local drives D: 160G, SAN E: 1024G, SAN
Pagefile	4094M, drive C:
IP address	192.168.0.20
Subnet mask	255.255.255.0
Gateway	192.168.0.1
DNS servers	192.168.10.10 192.168.10.20

TABLE 17.3 Installed Applications

Installed Application	Version	Configuration
Exchange Server 2007	SP1	Refer to Exchange Server 2007 Mailbox Server build document
Microsoft Forefront	1.0	Refer to Exchange Server 2007 Mailbox Server build document
Microsoft Operations Manager Agent	2005 SP1	Management Packs: Windows Server 2003 and Exchange Server 2007

Documenting Your Exchange Organization Configuration

Keeping current, accurate configuration records of your environment is an essential part of managing Exchange Server 2007. This includes not only server-specific configurations, such as OS configuration, OS and Exchange Server 2007 patches installed, and other applications installed, but configurations performed at an organizational or non-server-specific level.

Examples of organizational configurations that should be documented include the following:

- List of assigned Exchange administrators and their roles (e.g., Exchange Organization Administrator, Exchange Recipient Administrator, Exchange View-Only Administrator, Exchange Server Administrator)
- Managed folders and managed-folder mailbox policies
- Address lists
- Offline address books
- ActiveSync mailbox policies
- Hub Transport rules
- Remote and accepted domains
- Email address policies
- Edge subscriptions
- Send and receive connectors
- Journaling configurations
- Unified Messaging configurations
- Public-folder configurations

Verifying Functionality and Performance Levels

As you may have gathered by now, determining that your Exchange Server 2007 installation is functioning correctly is much more than ensuring there is power to the servers and that they are connected to the network. In addition to documenting server and organizational configurations, you need to verify that the system is providing the functionality it was intended to provide at the performance levels your business requires. To verify these service and performance levels, it's best to document what they are as a starting point. Let's examine each of these topics in detail.

Messaging Services and Functionality

Your organization has Exchange Server 2007 deployed to provide certain services and functionalities to your end users; let's look at what those are.

The most obvious service is sending and receiving email; how much other functionality you need to define will depend on your environment. You may even need to define "send and receive email" more completely. The following are some examples.

- Send and receive email between users on the same Mailbox server.
- Send and receive email between users on different Mailbox servers in the same Active Directory site.
- Send and receive email between users on different Mailbox servers in different Active Directory sites.
- Send email to a distribution group defined in Active Directory.
- Receive email addressed to a distribution group.
- Send email to and receive email from Internet recipients.
- Send email to and receive email from a foreign connector or third-party connectors such as fax gateways.

You also need to define the other functionality your system provides. A partial list is provided here. Note that this is not intended to be all-encompassing, but to give you an idea of what needs to be considered when defining the services and functionality your Exchange Server 2007 organization is expected to deliver. As with "send and receive email," some of these also may need to be further defined.

- Free/busy lookups within your Exchange organization
- Free/busy lookups across Exchange organizations
- Global Address List lookups across your Exchange organization
- Offline address book downloads to Outlook clients
- Outlook Web Access for remote users
- Outlook Anywhere for remote users
- MAPI access for Outlook clients
- Outlook versions supported
- POP3/IMAP/SMTP for non-MAPI messaging clients
- Mailbox access for delegates
- "Send as" functionality
- Message classifications
- Calendaring

Real World Scenario

Introducing New Services or Functionality

The functionality your messaging system provides may already be defined to some extent (or defined completely) in a Service Level Agreement (SLA), or you may need to define it yourself. In any case, clearly defining this functionality is the foundation for successful planning of changes to your environment and for ensuring existing functionality is maintained when new services are introduced.

Imagine that your organization is introducing new functionality in the form of antispam filtering. If antispam filtering is going to be applied on the perimeter—with Exchange Server 2007 Edge Transport servers or Exchange Hosted Services, for example—then you will need to verify the new functionality when it's implemented. You also will need to verify that existing service and functionality have not been compromised at the same time.

For example, when implementing Edge Transport servers or Exchange Hosted Services, you'll need to confirm the following:

- They accept and deliver email for all the address spaces hosted in your environment.
- If you are routing outbound email through the new service or servers, that outbound mail is delivered to the next hop (typically using DNS MX records).
- All firewalls are configured correctly to allow SMTP connections to and from your organization, and they allow SMTP connections only to and from acceptable hosts.
- The solution is designed to handle the amount of SMTP traffic your organization sends and receives.
- Your solution doesn't reduce the level of availability your Exchange Server 2007 organization provides. For example, if you have several Exchange Server 2007 Hub Transport servers in your organization that were originally accepting SMTP from the Internet, but you deploy a single Edge Transport server, you have introduced a single point of failure where before you had redundancy.

- Mobile device access such as Windows Mobile or BlackBerry
- End-user management of distribution groups
- Autodiscover service

Performance Levels

Besides defining the functionality Exchange Server 2007 is providing, you also need to define the performance and service levels you are expected to be providing. In addition, you should determine how your system is actually performing and what level of service is being provided.

These criteria, along with your functional definitions, help you assess changes you introduce into the environment. Monitoring and reporting will be discussed in more detail in the "Planning a Monitoring and Reporting Solution" section of this chapter.

Some examples of performance metrics you want to monitor are as follows:

- CPU utilization
- Memory usage
- Disk performance
- Network utilization
- RPC latency
- Message queue lengths
- Message delivery times

These performance metrics allow you to assess changes to the environment and also form the basis of a performance baseline that you can use to set monitoring thresholds and generate reports. Monitoring and reporting are discussed in more detail later in this chapter.

Figure 17.1 shows the counters available by default in the Exchange Server Performance Monitor. The Exchange Server Performance Monitor is available in the Toolbox work center in the Exchange Management Console.

FIGURE 17.1 The Exchange Server Performance Monitor

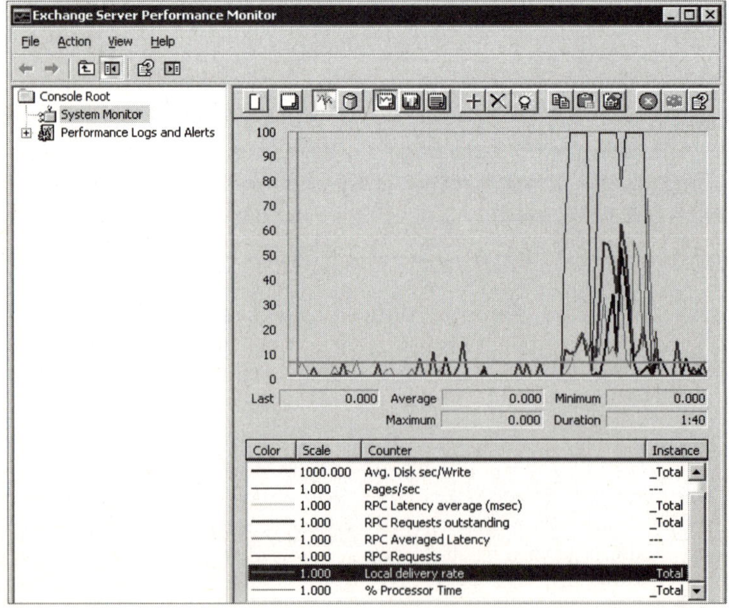

Conducting Functional Tests

Once you have defined what services and performance metrics comprise a working Exchange Server 2007 infrastructure for your environment, you can document functional tests to perform to verify that your Exchange organization is functioning within accepted parameters. These consist not only of the test procedures to perform, but also the pass/fail criteria associated with those tests. These tests provide the framework to consistently assess changes (both infrastructure and configuration changes) and patches and service packs, both prior to deployment and to verify the deployment's success.

For example, a test procedure to verify mailbox and public-folder access could be as follows:

1. Log on to an Exchange Server 2007 mailbox with the standard Outlook 2007 build.
2. Verify that you can open, compose, and send messages.
3. Verify that you can access existing folders within the mailbox and create new folders.
4. Verify that you can access public folders and open items in public folders.
5. Verify that, with appropriate permissions, you can create new public folders.
6. Verify that, with appropriate permissions, you can manage public-folder permissions.

In this example, the pass/fail criteria are obvious (i.e., for step 1, if you can't log on to the mailbox, the test has failed), but it's generally best practice to document all pass/fail criteria anyway because what is obvious to one person may not be to someone else.

Analyzing Business Requirements

Understanding the business requirements your Exchange Server 2007 infrastructure is fulfilling is an important part of planning for Exchange Server 2007 management. A large portion of managing your messaging system is ensuring that you are meeting your SLAs, which involves monitoring the technical aspects of the environment and applying remedial action as necessary (such as introducing a change to the environment or fixing issues that arise). When focusing on the technical aspects, however, it is easy to lose sight of the fact that you are dealing with technical requirements that have been established to fulfill the needs of the business. You have to remember that your Exchange Server 2007 organization is there to serve the requirements of the business, not the other way around.

Business requirements are basically a broad specification of what the business wants. This means that your business requirements should avoid speaking in terms of specific technology or function, and instead define why you need those technologies or functions. Some broad categories that business requirements may fall under include security, disaster recovery and business continuity, mobility, and collaboration. For example, a business requirement may be that your workers need secure access to email data from any computer; to fulfill this business requirement, you may provide Outlook Web Access functionality for mobile workers. The technical requirements for this function are Exchange Server 2007 Client Access servers deployed and encrypted with SSL and Microsoft Internet Security and Acceleration (ISA) server as a reverse proxy to provide secure user access to Outlook Web Access from the Internet.

Separating Business Requirements from Technical Requirements

It is important to keep in mind the difference between business and technical requirements—particularly that your technical requirements are derived from and fulfill your business requirements and not the other way around. Otherwise, you may have a messaging system that is technically rock-solid, but is failing the business.

Example One: POP3 Access to Mailboxes

One example of common confusion is stating the need for a specific technology or function as a business requirement. For instance, suppose that you have defined a business requirement incorrectly stating that POP3 access to mailboxes must be provided. (This should be listed as a technical requirement, not a business need.) This then locks you into providing POP3 access to mailboxes, with all the corresponding limitations:

- Access to Inbox only
- Email stored in `.pst` files and not on the server
- No group calendaring or free/busy functionality
- No access to email except from workstation on which the `.pst` file is stored
- No backups of `.pst` files
- Authentication in clear text

Instead, you can correctly state your business requirement as the need for mobile workers to securely access their messaging data (email, contacts, and calendaring) from company-supplied computers. Doing so allows the technical requirements definition to encompass providing mobile workers with Windows Vista laptops and Outlook 2007, deploying Exchange Server 2007 Client Access servers with SSL, configuring Outlook Anywhere (RPC/HTTPS), and implementing Microsoft ISA as a reverse proxy to provide Outlook Anywhere access from the Internet.

In this way, you have provided a more robust technical solution to the organization that fulfills the needs of the business much better than implementing POP3 access for mobile workers.

Example Two: Limiting Mailbox Quotas

Mailbox quotas are another area where you may be likely to focus on technical aspects not fulfilling the needs of the business. Many Exchange professionals will have strictly enforced mailbox sizes (100 MB, for example) as a technical solution to prevent running out of disk space on their Mailbox servers. Although this addresses the needs of the Exchange professional to keep Mailbox server storage at a predictable level, it likely does not fulfill the messaging needs of the users or the business requirements. The users likely need to save older messaging data, while the business may have a requirement to save messaging data for compliance purposes. The strictly enforced mailbox quotas then result in users exporting from their Exchange mailboxes to `.pst` files, which they store on the organization's file servers. The result is the needs of the Exchange administrators being met, but the storage simply being shifted from the Exchange Mailbox servers (where messages are stored in a robust database with single-instance storage and are easily accessible) to file servers (where the data is stored in easily corruptible and difficult-to-manage `.pst` files). Is disk space and backup/restore really cheaper on your file servers than on your Exchange servers? Also, the compliance requirements of the business are likely not being met because the data you need to preserve is stored on widely scattered file servers across the enterprise and is difficult (if not impossible) to search and retrieve when necessary.

A better approach would be to allow larger mailbox sizes and implement Exchange Server 2007 functionalities, such as messaging records management, journaling, and message classification, to provide a comprehensive solution to address the overall requirements of the business and the users.

These two examples help illustrate how properly defining business requirements and separating them from the technical requirements provide the necessary framework for planning infrastructure improvements and configuration changes.

Defining the Issue and Identifying the Changes Necessary

As a wise man (George Harrison) once said, "If you don't know where you're going, any road will take you there." In this vein, you need to understand what issue you're attempting to address with your proposed change; for example, it is unlikely that you are adding a Client Access server to an Active Directory site simply to keep yourself occupied. The real issue you are addressing may be providing increased capacity (supporting a larger number of concurrent users) for OWA clients, or you may be addressing how users can have access to their mailboxes using OWA if a network link goes down. In the first case, adding a Client Access server to the same Active Directory site may be the answer. For the second example, the issue may be better addressed by placing the new Client Access server in a separate site or by upgrading the network link. At other times you may need to deploy newly issued patches or service packs to address vulnerabilities. In that case, you need to assess those patches and service packs against your environment to determine their necessity and their impact (including how much testing will be required and how quickly they need to be deployed).

Clearly identifying your change's goal also provides you with the information you require to determine when the change is successful or not. In the example of increasing the number of concurrent OWA users you can support, your success criteria isn't that the Client Access server is installed successfully; it's only deemed a success if your Exchange Server 2007 organization can support more concurrent users than before the change was implemented.

Once you have documented your Exchange Server 2007 system, identified the services and performance levels you are to deliver, and determined the issue you are addressing, then you can define the change you are going to perform. Using the example of providing fault tolerance for OWA users, the change to be implemented could be adding a second Exchange Server 2007 computer with the Client Access server role installed on it, then configuring Network Load Balancing (NLB) to provide fault tolerance to OWA users who contact the `https://owa.company.com` URL.

Preparing Your Change Deployment

Preparing for the deployment of the change you have defined involves several steps:

Create a deployment plan. This plan can involve high-level steps, such as determining in which order a certain patch should be deployed to your servers. For example, install the patch on Client Access servers first, followed by Hub Transport servers, and finally Mailbox servers.

Create installation and test procedures. Sometimes known as a build document, this details the steps to take to actually deploy the change. In some cases, the actual installation may be performed by others who will use these procedures to implement the change.

Prepare contingency plans. In the event that the change is not successful, you need to have contingency plans that include back-out procedures that allow you to return the environment to the state it was in before the change was implemented. For example, this plan could involve restoring mailbox databases from backup (and ensuring that backups are performed before the change is implemented), reverting configuration changes to previous values, or uninstalling patches that have been applied.

Test the changes in a lab or pre-production environment. Before implementing any change on production systems, it is highly recommended to test these changes in an environment that will not affect production.

Implement and test the changes. When the change is implemented, it is important to conduct tests to determine that the change was successful and that no other services have been adversely affected. You want to know at the time of the change that it has disabled Outlook Anywhere access to all users, not during the next business day when your CEO calls from a hotel room 2,000 miles away.

Update the appropriate documentation and records. As with anything else, the job isn't over until the paperwork is done.

Case Study: Improving Outlook Web Access Availability

Let's go through a scenario that illustrates some of the concepts we've been discussing. We'll do this by using the example of improving Outlook Web Access availability in the event of a single Exchange Server 2007 computer failure, and we'll follow the steps we've defined for preparing a change deployment.

Step 1: Documenting Your Infrastructure

Your hypothetical Exchange Server 2007 organization consists of one Exchange Server 2007 computer with the Client Access server role installed on it, a second Exchange Server 2007 computer with the Mailbox and Hub Transport roles installed on it, and one Exchange Server 2007 computer with the Edge Transport role installed on it. You have documented all of your Exchange Server 2007 computers and your Exchange organization's configuration. In addition, you have documented all the functionality and service levels Exchange Server 2007 provides and created a performance baseline for monitoring purposes. The layout of the Exchange Server 2007 organization as seen in the Server Configuration work center in the Exchange Management Console is shown in Figure 17.2.

FIGURE 17.2 Exchange server roles

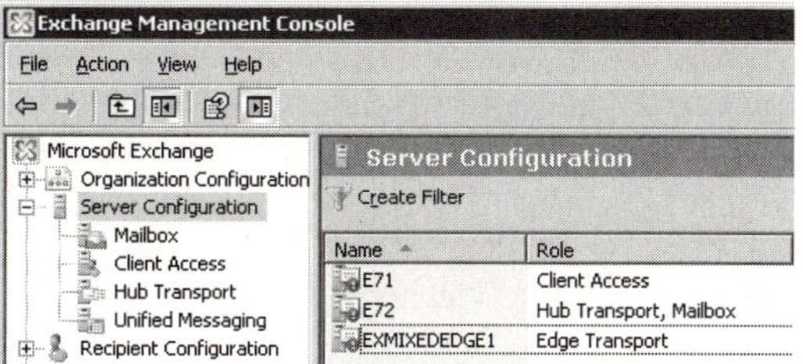

Step 2: Analyzing Business Requirements

Last week the motherboard failed on the Exchange Server 2007 computer holding the Client Access role. During the time it took to obtain a replacement and perform the repair, users reported that they were unable to access their mailboxes using Outlook Web Access.

The effect of this outage was significant productivity losses to the company and lost sales revenue. As a result of this, it has been determined that ensuring uninterrupted OWA access to user's mailboxes is a business requirement for your organization.

Step 3: Defining the Issue and Identifying the Changes Necessary

To maintain Outlook Web Access availability in the future, you determine that the issue to be addressed is that you need to provide fault tolerance for OWA access to mailboxes. You decide that you will introduce an infrastructure change to your environment consisting of two major components. The first component involves adding another Exchange Server 2007 computer holding the Client Access role to the organization. The second component consists of configuring an NLB cluster named owa.*company.tld* (where *tld* is your top-level domain; for example, .com, .net, .local) composed of the new and existing Client Access servers.

Step 4: Creating a Deployment Plan

You determine that your deployment plan will be as follows:

1. Acquire an IP address for the NLB cluster, then create a new A record in DNS for owa.*company*.*tld* pointing to this IP address.
2. Install Windows Server 2003 R2 on the new Client Access server using your standard Windows Server 2003 R2 build procedures.
3. Install the prerequisites for Exchange Server 2007 on the new server: PowerShell Internet Information Services (IIS) with ASP.NET.
4. Install an SSL certificate in the name owa.*company*.*tld* on both Client Access servers.
5. Install Exchange Server 2007 using the custom installation option, choosing only the Client Access server role.
6. Verify the new Client Access server's functionality by accessing a mailbox via OWA with Internet Explorer pointing directly to the server with the URL https://*new_server.company.tld*/owa (not using the NLB cluster URL).
7. Install and configure NLB to create an NLB cluster named owa.*company.tld* consisting of the two Client Access servers.
8. Test the new configuration by shutting down the Client Access servers one at a time and verifying that OWA is accessible via the URL of the NLB cluster (https://owa.*company.tld*/owa).

Step 5: Creating Installation and Test Procedures

Next you create installation and test procedures to be used to deploy and test the new Client Access server and NLB cluster. These procedures outline in detail the steps to take to deploy this change.

The first portion of your implementation procedures consists of assigning an IP address for the NLB cluster, then creating a DNS A for owa.*company.tld* pointing to this IP address. Figure 17.3 shows the New Host dialog in the DNS management console; screenshots such as this would be used as part of your documented installation procedure, assuming you are using Windows Server 2003 DNS.

In most enterprise environments, it is best to implement DNS additions or modifications well in advance of the implementation of the new servers and NLB cluster (for example, 24 hours before). This allows for replication of the DNS changes throughout your environment, and account for your DNS time to live (TTL) and DNS cache values. For example, if your DNS records have a TTL of 86,400 seconds (24 hours) this means that DNS clients (including other DNS servers that have queried for that record) will cache whatever response they get for 24 hours. This means that any changes you make to this record may not be reflected across your environment for up to 24 hours. In addition, Windows Server 2003, Windows XP, and Windows Vista cache negative responses (Record Not Found).

FIGURE 17.3 Creating a DNS A record for an NLB cluster for Outlook Web Access

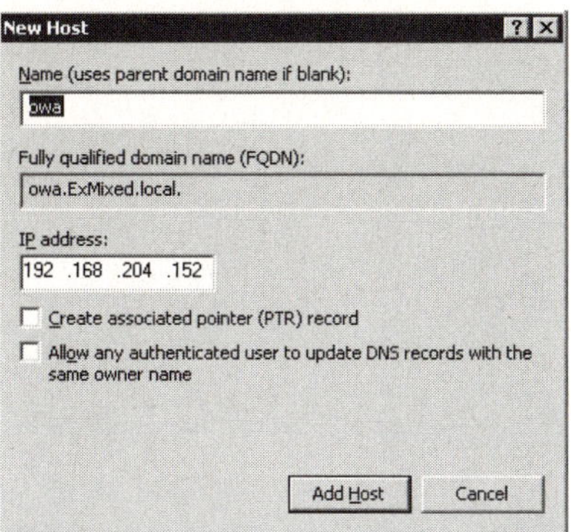

An example of the procedure to install Exchange Server 2007 on the new Client Access server and configure NLB is as follows (assuming that Windows Server 2003 R2 has been installed and configured, and the computer has been joined to Active Directory):

Example Installation Procedures: Installing the SSL Certificate

This procedure assumes that a Windows Server 2003–based PKI certificate authority (CA) is already deployed in the environment.

1. Log on to the new server with an account with local administrative privileges and the Exchange Organization Administrator role assigned to it.
2. Start IIS Manager from Start ➤ Administrative Tools ➤ Internet Information Services (IIS) Manager. Expand the local computer node in the navigation pane, then expand Web Sites and highlight Default Web Site. Right-click the Default Web Site in the navigation pane and select Properties from the context menu.
3. In the Properties dialog of the Default Web Site, select the Directory Security tab, then select Server Certificate from the Secure Communications section as shown in Figure 17.4 to start the Web Server Certificate wizard.
4. On the Welcome page of the Web Server Certificate wizard, click Next. If the website already has an SSL certificate assigned to it (a self-signed certificate, for example), the Modify the Current Certificate Assignment page will appear. Select to remove the current certificate, then click Next. On the Remove a Certificate page, click Next, and then click Finish on the final page of the wizard.
5. Back on the Directory Security tab of the Properties dialog, select Server Certificate to start the Web Server Certificate wizard again, and click Next on the wizard's Welcome screen. On the Server Certificate page, select Create a new certificate, and then click Next.
6. On the Delayed or Immediate Request page of the wizard as shown in Figure 17.5, select to send the request immediately, and click Next.

FIGURE 17.4 Starting the Web Server Certificate wizard

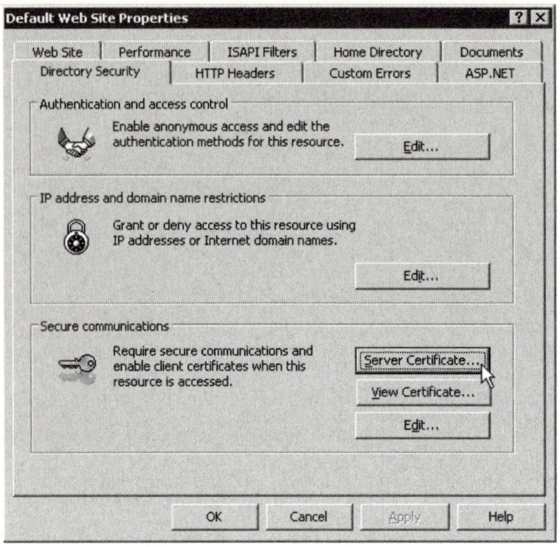

FIGURE 17.5 Sending the certificate request to an online CA

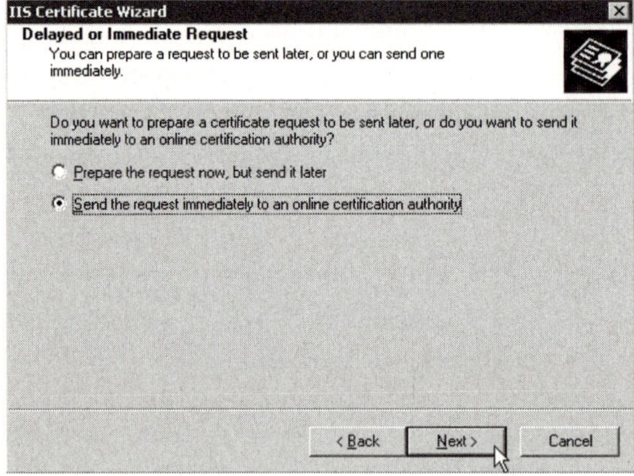

7. On the Name and Security Settings wizard page, select Next.
8. On the Organization Information page of the wizard, enter appropriate values for the Organization and Organizational unit, then click Next.
9. On the wizard's Your Site's Common Name, enter `owa.`*company.tld* as the common name as shown in Figure 17.6 and then click Next.
10. On the Geographical Information wizard page, enter in the Country, State, and City information as appropriate (do not use abbreviations), and click Next.

FIGURE 17.6 Setting the web certificate's common name

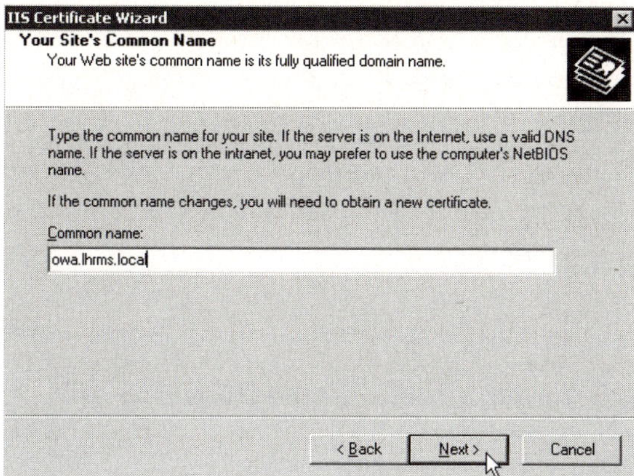

11. In the SSL Port page, ensure the SSL port is set to 443, and click Next.
12. On the Choose a Certification Authority wizard page, ensure that your online CA is selected, and click Next.
13. Click Next on the Certificate Request Submission page to submit the certificate request. On the Completing the Web Server Certificate wizard page indicating the certificate was installed successfully, click Finish to exit the wizard.
14. Back on the Directory Security tab of the Properties dialog, select View Certificate and verify the certificate common name (shown as "Issued to") and that the proper CA issued the certificate (shown as "Issued by"), as illustrated in Figure 17.7.

FIGURE 17.7 Verifying the web server certificate

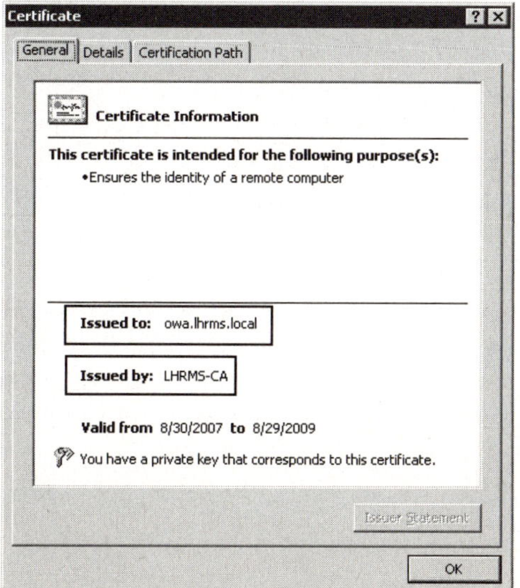

Example Installation Procedures: Installing Exchange Server 2007

To install Exchange Server 2007, follow these steps:

1. Insert the Exchange Server 2007 source CD into the CD drive of the new server.
2. Log on to the new Client Access server with an account with local administrative privileges and the Exchange Organization Administrator role assigned to it.
3. Open a command prompt and enter the following command: `setup.com /mode:Install /roles:CA`. As indicated at the completion of the installation as shown in Figure 17.8, reboot the Exchange Server 2007 computer.

FIGURE 17.8 Installing the Client Access role using setup.com

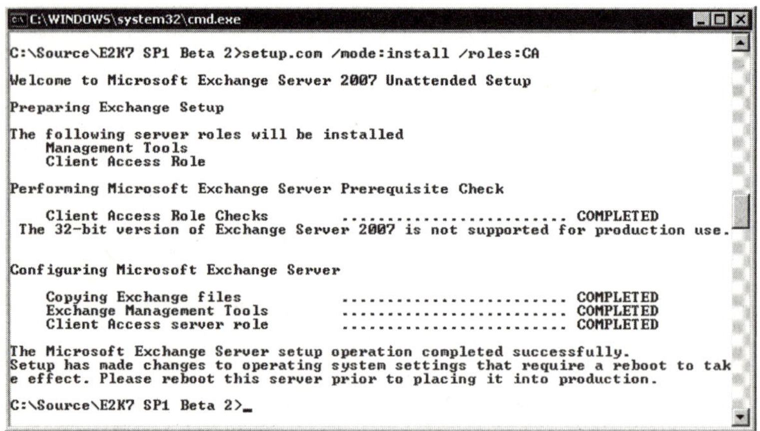

4. In the Shut Down Windows dialog shown in Figure 17.9, select Restart for the action to perform. Select Other for the Option in the Shutdown Event Tracker section, then enter **Reboot after installation of Exchange Server 2007** in the Comments section. Click OK to initiate the reboot.
5. Log back on to the Exchange Server 2007 computer with the same account Exchange Server 2007 was installed under. Start the Exchange Management Console from Start ➤ All Programs ➤ Microsoft Exchange Server 2007 ➤ Exchange Management Console, and select the Server Configuration work center from the console tree. Verify that the newly installed Exchange Server 2007 computer is listed in the results pane, with Client Access as the only role installed, as shown in Figure 17.10.
6. Log on to a Windows Vista computer with a standard user account that has an Exchange Server 2007 mailbox. Open Internet Explorer and browse to the URL `https://`*new_server.company.tld*`/owa`. Log on to OWA, and verify that you see the user's inbox as shown in Figure 17.11.

FIGURE 17.9 Rebooting the computer after installing Exchange Server 2007

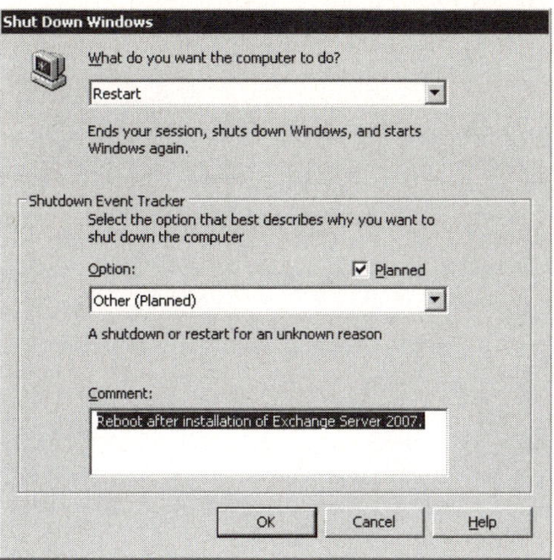

FIGURE 17.10 Verifying the Client Access installation through the EMC

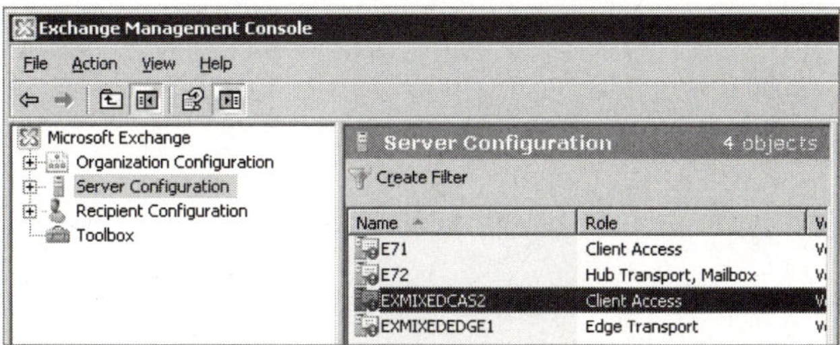

Example Installation Procedures: Installing and Configuring Network Load Balancing

To install and configure NLB, follow these steps:

1. Log on to the original Client Access server and start the NLB Manager from Start ➤ Administrative Tools ➤ Network Load Balancing Manager. In the NLB Manager GUI, right-click Network Load Balancing Clusters in the navigation tree and select New Cluster from the context menu to start the Cluster Parameters wizard.
2. On the first page of the Cluster Parameters wizard as shown in Figure 17.12, enter the IP address, subnet mask, and fully qualified domain name (FQDN) of the cluster in the Cluster IP configuration section. Select Multicast as the cluster operation mode, then click Next.

FIGURE 17.11 Verifying the new CA server from a Windows Vista computer

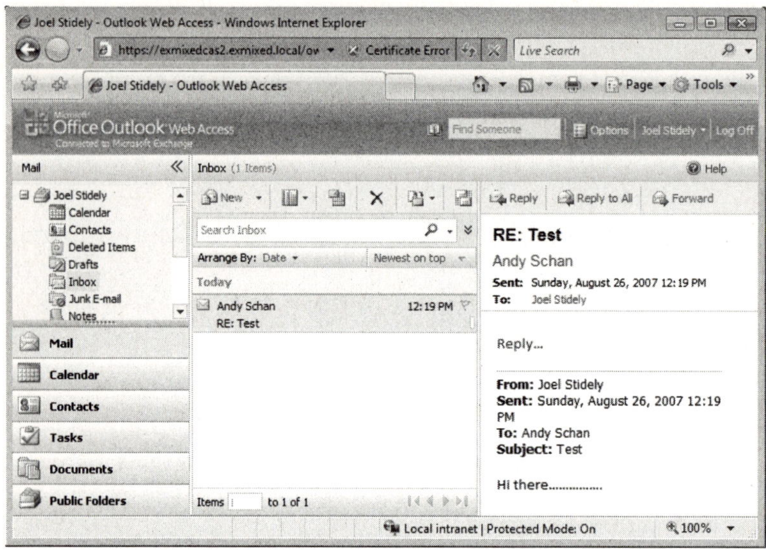

FIGURE 17.12 Configuring IP information for your NLB cluster

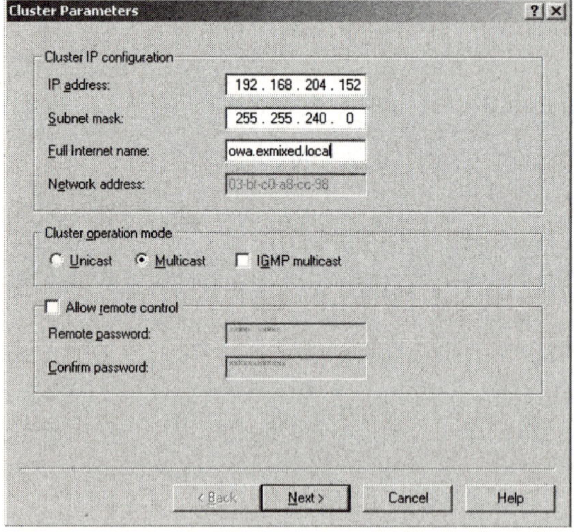

3. On the Cluster IP Addresses screen of the wizard, click Next.
4. On the Port Rules screen of the wizard, select Edit to open the Add/Edit Port Rule dialog. Set both the From and To Port range values to 443 as shown in Figure 17.13, then click OK to return to the Port Rules screen. Click Next to continue.

FIGURE 17.13 Modifying the NLB cluster port rule

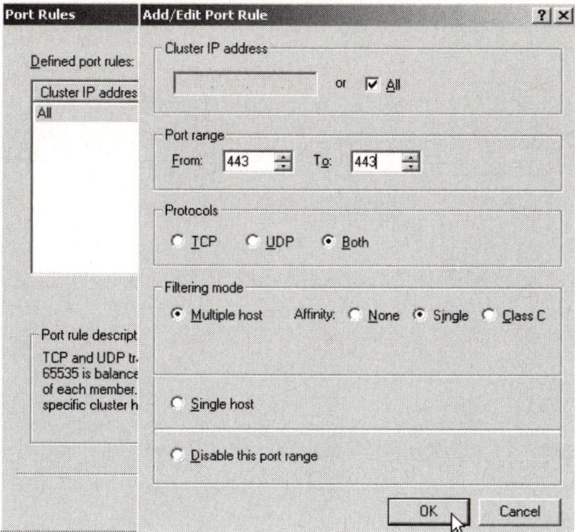

5. On the Connect screen of the wizard, enter the hostname of the original Client Access server as the host, then click Connect to add that server to the Interfaces list. Highlight the Local Area Connection entry as shown in Figure 17.14, then click Next to continue.

FIGURE 17.14 Adding hosts to the NLB cluster

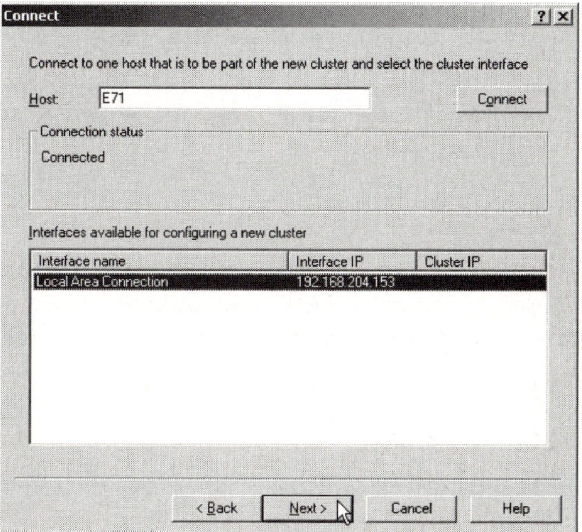

6. Click Finish on the Host Parameters screen to complete the wizard and return to the NLB Manager GUI.
7. Right-click the newly created NLB cluster and select Add Host To Cluster from the context menu to open the Connect dialog.
8. In the Connect dialog, enter the hostname of the new Client Access server as the Host then click Connect. Highlight the Local Area Connection entry for that server, then click Next to continue. Click Finish on the Host Parameters screen to add the server to the cluster and return to the NLB Manager GUI.
9. Back in the NLB Manager GUI, highlight the owa.*company.tld* cluster entry in the navigation tree. Both hosts in the cluster should show a status of Converged, as shown in Figure 17.15.

FIGURE 17.15 Converged hosts in the owa.company.com cluster

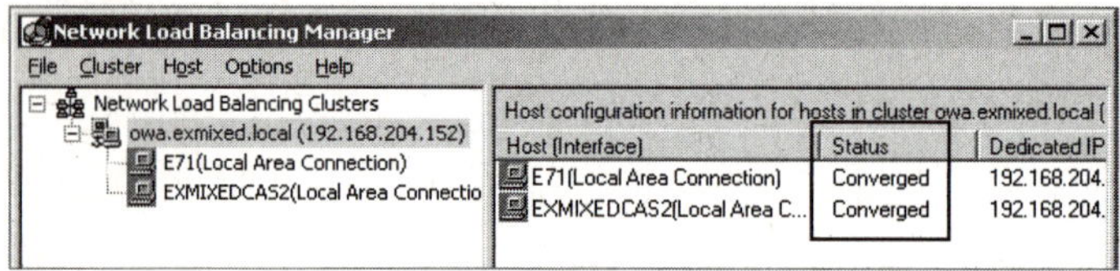

10. Log on to a Windows Vista computer with a standard user account that has an Exchange Server 2007 mailbox. Open Internet Explorer and browse to the URL `https://owa` `.`*company.tld*`/owa`. Log on to OWA, and verify that you see the user's inbox. Log off OWA, then close Internet Explorer.
11. Shut down the original Client Access server, then repeat step 10 to verify that OWA is still accessible.
12. Restart the original Client Access server, then shut down the new server. Repeat step 10 again to verify that OWA is still accessible with the second host in the NLB cluster shut down.
13. Power up all the servers, then log off all servers and workstations.

The preceding examples illustrate the level of installation procedures you would need to design and document to implement a change of this nature. In many cases, you would be preparing these procedures for others (for example, your Messaging Operations group) to implement the change.

Step 6: Preparing Contingency Plans

Contingency plans for a change of this type would likely be composed of the following steps:

1. Ensure there are full backups of the existing Client Access server and Active Directory.
2. Verify your backup media and disaster recovery procedures by restoring to a lab environment.

3. In the event of any part of the change failing, remove the newly installed Exchange Server 2007 Client Access computer from the environment, including removing it from the Exchange Server 2007 configuration in Active Directory.
4. Remove NLB from the original Client Access server (or restore that server from backup).
5. Reverse any DNS additions or modifications.
6. Perform functional tests to ensure the environment is restored to its original condition.

Step 7: Testing the Changes in a Lab

The next part of the process involves testing this change in a lab environment. Doing so allows you to verify that the changes you are making will perform as expected or, if you are deploying software patches, that the patches do not adversely affect the environment.

With the virtualization solutions available today, such as Microsoft Virtual PC/Server or VMWare, there is no good reason for not testing changes in a lab environment before introducing them into production.

When deploying and testing your changes in the lab environment, it is best to use the installation and test procedures you created during your deployment planning. This way, you are not only verifying the changes you are making but also validating that your documentation is accurate and complete. This is especially important if the actual changes to the production Exchange Server 2007 environment will be performed by someone else in your group or in another group entirely.

Step 8: Implementing, Testing, and Documenting the Change

At this point, the new Client Access server can be deployed into the production environment and the NLB cluster can be created and configured.

When the new OWA functionality has been tested and confirmed to be operational, all pertinent documentation should be updated. Documentation that may need to be updated includes the following:

- Visio drawings updated to include the new Client Access server
- Network diagrams and spreadsheets updated to reflect the new NLB cluster and the new Client Access server's IP address
- A new server configuration sheet created to document the new Client Access server's details, such as IP address, patches installed, OS configuration, etc.
- Change management logs updated to reflect the successful completion of the change
- Any firewall changes documented; for example, to modify the external OWA connectivity firewall rule to point to the new NLB cluster

Planning Change Management

In most large enterprises, change management is an established fact of life. Before we discuss change management, though, let's see if we can define it. In essence, the purpose of change management is to introduce required changes into an IT environment in a disciplined manner to ensure minimal disruption to ongoing operations. What this really means is to allow for change, but to avoid breaking anything with your changes. To paraphrase the Hippocratic Oath, "first, do no harm."

Many people may consider change management to be a barrier to doing their jobs, and feel, "I can make this change in five minutes; why should I spend all this time creating a change request, planning, and getting approvals?" A true IT professional, however, will recognize that a well-designed and -enforced change-management process is one of the primary factors in maintaining a high level of service availability and keeping operational disruptions to a minimum.

How this process is implemented can vary widely between enterprises, but the following sections describe the recommended approach (which is also the approach laid out on the Microsoft Operations Framework).

The change-management process includes the following steps:

1. A change is initiated by submitting a Request for Change (RFC).
2. The urgency and impact of the change is assessed, then a category and a priority are assigned to it. How fast the change is addressed and the authorizations the change will require are influenced by these assignments.
3. The change is then submitted to a change manager and the Change Advisory Board (CAB) for approval or rejection (see the section "Seeking Change Approval" for more detail about the CAB).
4. The change is developed; its deployment is planned and then reviewed. How much planning and reviewing are required can vary greatly depending on the change and its impact. The time involved can be a couple of minutes in the case of an emergency change, or it can be months or years in the case of deploying a new software package for the enterprise.
5. The change is released and deployed into the production environment. This step involves the building and testing of the change, preparing for the release into production, and the deployment of the change into production
6. Finally, a post-change review is undertaken to assess the change. This involves determining whether the change has met its goals and the decision whether to keep the change or back out of it.

The flow of the change-management process as discussed is shown in Figure 17.16.

FIGURE 17.16 Change-management process flow

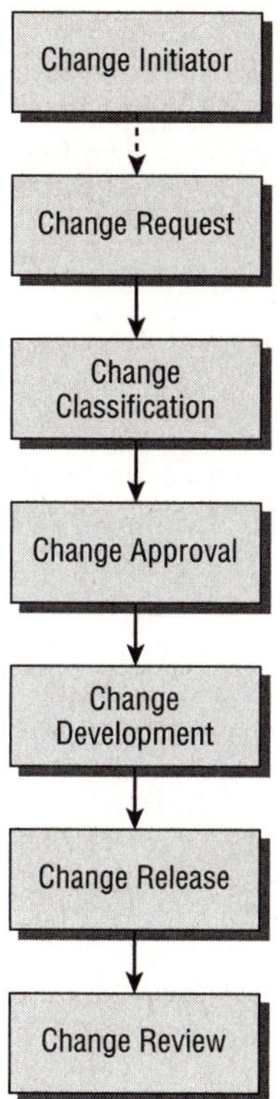

Creating a Request for Change (RFC)

An *RFC* can take on many forms, but in most cases it is a standard document outlining the basics about the change (such as applying a Windows patch to Exchange servers). In most cases, the RFC also contains more-detailed information such as the overall effects of the change (for example, the services that this change could affect or the systems that interact with the affected servers).

The intent of the RFC is to address the "5 Ws" of the change—what, why, who, when, and where—as well as the "how":

What: A description of the change, the effort required, and its impact on the environment.

Why: The purpose of the change.

Who: The initiator of the change and who will be performing the change; these may or may not be the same people.

When: When the change is required, as well as its urgency.

Where: On which systems the change will be implemented.

How: How the change will be implemented, including contingency procedures (back-out plan) and change review plan.

Also, the RFC usually includes supporting information for any or all of the above, such as the cost of the change, its urgency, the configuration items involved, etc. The goal is that the RFC contains enough information for a quick and accurate initial screening of the change and for the official CAB review.

Assessing and Classifying the Change

The first step in this part of the change-management process is to screen the RFC. The intent of screening is not to deny or authorize the change, but to ensure the RFC has enough detail, has been completed correctly, and is relevant to the IT change-management process. A common approach is to have the initial screening performed by the change initiator's manager.

After the initial screening process, the RFC is classified by a change manager for *priority* and impact (*change category*). The priority is determined by the need for the change and the implications of not performing it. For example, a service outage would probably dictate that a change would be assigned an emergency priority. Setting the correct priority is extremely important because the priority has a direct impact on how the change is expedited through the change-management process and determines when the change can be implemented. Although priority levels can be defined uniquely by your organization, Table 17.4 lists standard priority classifications.

TABLE 17.4 Standard Priority Classifications

Priority	Definition
Emergency	Change addresses a loss of service or severe usability problems to a large number of users, a mission-critical system, or some equally serious problem. Immediate action required. Emergency meetings of the CAB or CAB/EC may need to be convened. (See the "Seeking Change Approval" section for more on the CAB/EC.) Resources may need to be immediately allocated to deploy such authorized changes.
High	Change addresses an issue severely affecting some users or having an impact on many users. The change is to be given highest priority for change building, testing, and implementation resources.
Medium	The issue the change addresses does not have a severe impact, but rectification of the issue cannot be deferred until the next scheduled upgrade, for example. Allocated medium priority for resources.
Low	The change is justified and necessary, but can wait until the next scheduled release or upgrade. Resources to be allocated accordingly.

Along with a priority, a change is assigned a change category. The change category classifies the change's impact on users, the IT infrastructure, or the business, and determines the level of approval required for any given change. For example, changes that fall under the Standard category are automatically approved for deployment Examples of changes categorized as Standard could be antivirus signature updates or new Outlook forms; basically, changes that are minor in nature and determined to be routine. As with priorities, an organization can define its own change categories, but Table 17.5 outlines suggested change categories.

TABLE 17.5 Suggested Change Categories

Category	Definition
Major	The change involves potential impact on the highest percentage of users or a business-critical system. The change may be new technology or a configuration change and may involve downtime of the network or a service.
Significant	The change affects a high percentage of users and/or is a nonstandard change, such as a new product, new users, or network changes. It may involve downtime of the network or a service.
Minor	The change affects a smaller percentage of users and risk is less because of the organization's experience level with the proposed change.
Standard	The change affects the smallest percentage of users and has a set release process.

Seeking Change Approval

Once your change has been assigned a priority and change category, it must be approved. The approval process for an RFC is generally determined by its priority and change category; again, this can vary among organizations. Depending on the priority and change category, the approval process can involve the *Change Advisory Board (CAB)*. This cross-functional group evaluates change requests for priority, business need, cost or risk vs. benefit, and potential impact on other systems or processes. The CAB can approve or deny changes brought before it, and also can generate recommendations for implementation, further analysis, deferment, or cancellation.

To accommodate emergency changes, a subset of the CAB called the Emergency Committee (commonly referred to as the *CAB/EC*) can be formed. The purpose of the CAB/EC is to convene on short notice for the authorization (or rejection) of emergency priority changes.

Table 17.6 provides a list of suggested processes for levels of priority and change categories.

TABLE 17.6 Standard Approval Processes

Priority or Classification	Approval Process
Emergency priority	Escalate to the CAB/EC for fast-track approval.
Standard change	Approve automatically; goes directly to the planning and release phases.
Minor change	Can be approved by the change manager without referral to the CAB.
All other changes	Require the approval of the CAB.

Developing the Change

After your change has been approved, it enters the development portion of the change-management process. Change development is composed of the following steps:

- Schedule the change.
- Appoint a change owner based on the scope, technology, category, and priority of the change.
- Develop the change, including the planning, documentation, and testing to prepare for the release (deployment) of the change.

This portion of change development was discussed in detail in the "Preparing Your Change Deployment" section of this chapter.

- Conduct milestone reviews with CAB members as necessary to ensure that each phase of the change development has been successfully completed.
- Ensure that the change developed has met acceptance (pass/fail) criteria before entering the change release portion of the change-management process. This is accomplished through functional testing, which was discussed in detail in the "Conducting Functional Tests" section of this chapter.
- The change development process flow is illustrated in Figure 17.17.

Deploying the Change

Change release, or *change deployment*, is that part of the process where the change is actually deployed into the production environment (you thought we'd never get there, didn't you?). Change release is composed of the following elements:

- Select a team to perform the deployment.
- Train users.

FIGURE 17.17 Change development process

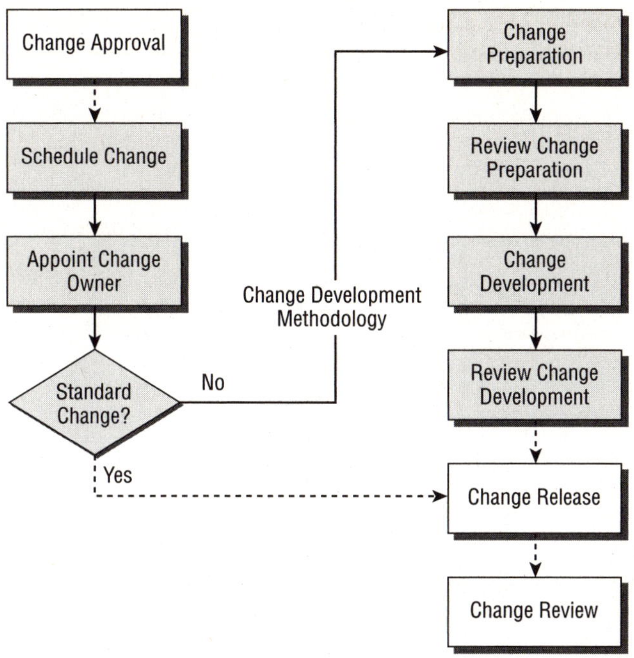

- Deploy the change into the production environment.
- Test the change.
- Pass feedback to the change manager for use in the change review.

The change deployment process flow is illustrated in Figure 17.18. Once a deployment team is selected and users are trained (if necessary), the change is deployed. If successful, the change procedures are revised to reflect the actual deployment experience, and the change is rolled out to other systems as necessary. When the change is successfully completed, the change-review stage is entered. If the deployment is not successful, the failure is analyzed and the deployment is either canceled or the problem is resolved. If the deployment is canceled, the change is backed out of and the change manager is notified. If the problem is resolved or a workaround implemented, the deployment procedures are modified; then, if the rollout is complete, the change-review stage is entered.

Reviewing the Change

Once a change has been deployed into production, it must be reviewed to determine whether it is successful. In particular, you must ensure it has had the expected effect and that the original RFC's requirements have been met.

FIGURE 17.18 Change deployment (release) process

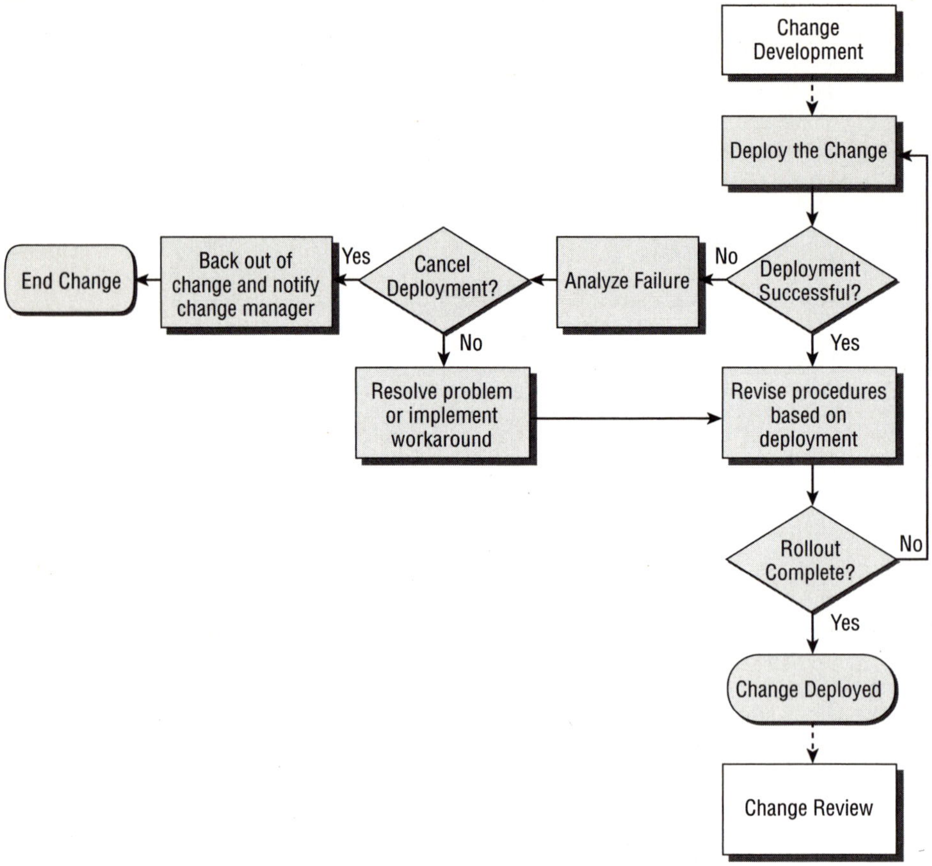

Change Development
Deploy the Change
Deployment Successful?
No
Analyze Failure
Cancel Deployment?
Yes
Back out of change and notify change manager
End Change
No
Resolve problem or implement workaround
Yes
Revise procedures based on deployment
Rollout Complete?
No
Yes
Change Deployed
Change Review

The change-review process, much like the change-approval process, will vary widely for different changes. The process is generally influenced by the same criteria that determined the approval process the change underwent, and in many cases it will be very brief. For example, the review for a standard change that was approved automatically (such as an antivirus signature update or a new Outlook form) could simply consist of verifying that the user sees the expected functionality from the change. Changes that had a wider-reaching impact (such as changes classified major or significant) will necessarily have a more elaborate and stringent review process.

Emergency changes, although they typically do not go through the full change-management process, should be reviewed. In the case of emergency changes, the review process is even more important because they undergo much less stringent testing and planning because of time constraints (a service outage that needs to be resolved as quickly as possible, for example). For that reason, when the dust settles, the emergency change needs to be reviewed to determine whether there were any adverse effects.

The change-review process consists of the following elements:

- Review and monitor the results of the change to ensure the RFC's objectives were met.
- Review lessons learned and incorporate this feedback into the appropriate documents/ processes for the benefit of future changes.
- In the event that the change was unsuccessful, back out of the change, mitigate the failure with corrective action, or accept the issues and move on.
- Close the successful RFC and notify the change initiator.

Planning Patch and Service Pack Implementation

Managing patches and service packs is a critical task for IT professionals. It is one of the cornerstones of your security strategy, playing a key role in maintaining your security posture. In addition to addressing security vulnerabilities, patches and service packs address stability or functionality issues, which can arguably be as important as security concerns. Security issues can result in data theft or data loss, lost credibility with your customers and the public, legal implications, and financial losses from any or all of the above. Lost revenue or productivity, downtime, and potentially lost customers are some of the possible effects of stability issues or functional issues. Because patching is a given, patch management and proper planning are vital.

It is important that patches and service packs be deployed, but it is crucial that the *proper* patches and service packs be deployed; this requires that the patch and the vulnerability be evaluated for your environment. You also need to plan the deployment and test the deployment's and the patch's impact on your environment before introducing it into production. Deploying a patch that causes downtime, instability, or loss of functionality in your environment is counterproductive. This is commonly known as a CLM (career-limiting move).

The four phases of a structured patch and service-pack management process are as follows:

Assess: Assess your production environment.

Identify: Identify new software patches or service packs.

Evaluate and Plan: Evaluate the patch or service pack and plan its deployment.

Deploy: Deploy the patch or service pack into production.

These phases may appear to be a linear progression, starting at assessing and ending when a patch is deployed, but the reality is that this is an iterative process, as illustrated in Figure 17.19.

We will cover each of these phases in more detail in the following sections.

FIGURE 17.19 The patch-management process

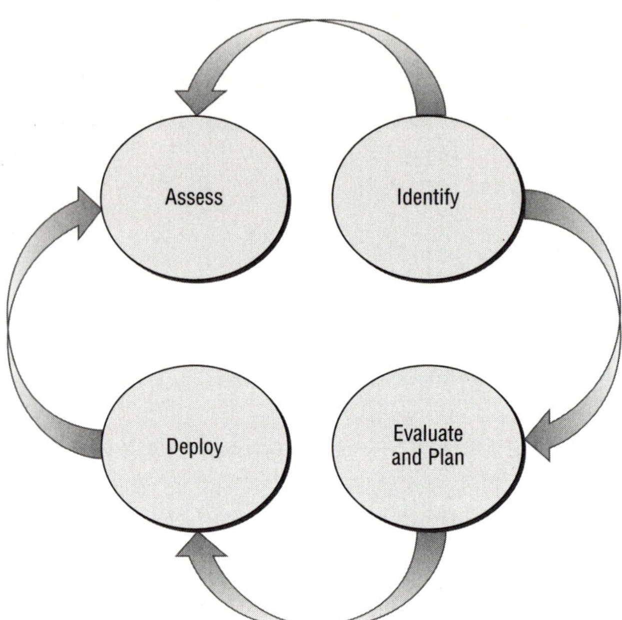

Phase 1: Assess

The first phase of the patch-management process is assessment. We call it the first phase, but it is also an ongoing process that ensures you are aware of the components that comprise your Exchange organization, how they are protected, and whether your software deployment methodology is capable of meeting the needs of patch management in your environment.

Assessing your existing Exchange organizations encompasses gathering information on the following, as well as keeping this information current:

Hardware types and versions: Includes desktops, mobile computers (laptops or Windows Mobile devices), or servers, and the versions of each (for example, a server that is a Dell PowerEdge 2950).

Operating system types and versions: For example, Windows XP SP2, Windows Server 2003 SP2, Windows Vista.

Applications and versions: Includes not only the applications (such as Exchange Server 2007 or Exchange Server 2003 SP2), but also roles (for example, what Exchange Server 2007 roles a server hosts, or what connectors a particular Hub Transport server acts as source server for).

Identifying installed and missing patches: Includes what patches have and have not been installed, and on which assets.

Security threats and vulnerabilities: With the inventory of your existing assets and their details as outlined previously, assess the threats to your environment and analyze system vulnerabilities.

You may have noticed that this phase is very similar to what we discussed in the "Documenting Your Exchange Server 2007 Organization" section of this chapter. In most cases, the assessment phase of patch management will be closely related to overall documentation of your infrastructure that is used for not only patch management but also for change management.

If Microsoft Windows Server Update Services (WSUS) 3.0 is your patch-deployment tool, you can determine what patches are installed and which are missing using the Update Services MMC snap-in. If Microsoft Systems Management Server (SMS) is deployed in your environment as your patch management solution, it can be used for your inventorying and reports needs as well.

Phase 2: Identify

This phase of patch management consists of discovering or being notified of a new patch, determining whether the patch is relevant to your environment, obtaining the patch, and assigning a priority to it.

Discovering new patches can be accomplished through tools such as the Microsoft Baseline Security Analyzer (MBSA), signing up for email security notifications at `http://www.microsoft.com/technet/security/bulletin/notify.mspx`, using the Update Services management console for WSUS, or using the Software Update Management feature of SMS. There are third-party solutions for patch management as well.

The Updates node of the WSUS management console is shown in Figure 17.20.

Once patches have been discovered, you need to determine how relevant those patches are to your environment, and their priority. For example, a patch that addresses a denial of service vulnerability on Exchange Server 2007 may be highly relevant to your environment, but if your Exchange Server 2007 computers are not exposed to the Internet then the priority of these patches may not be as high. If your servers are exposed to the Internet, there may be mitigating factors in place or that can be implemented to reduce the vulnerability.

Obtaining the discovered patches involves not only downloading the installation files but also verifying them. Verification is generally a combination of downloading from trusted locations (the Microsoft website or FTP site, or the Microsoft Update site (`http://www.update.microsoft.com/microsoftupdate`) and verifying the Authenticode digital signature as shown in Figure 17.21.

FIGURE 17.20 Update overview in WSUS console

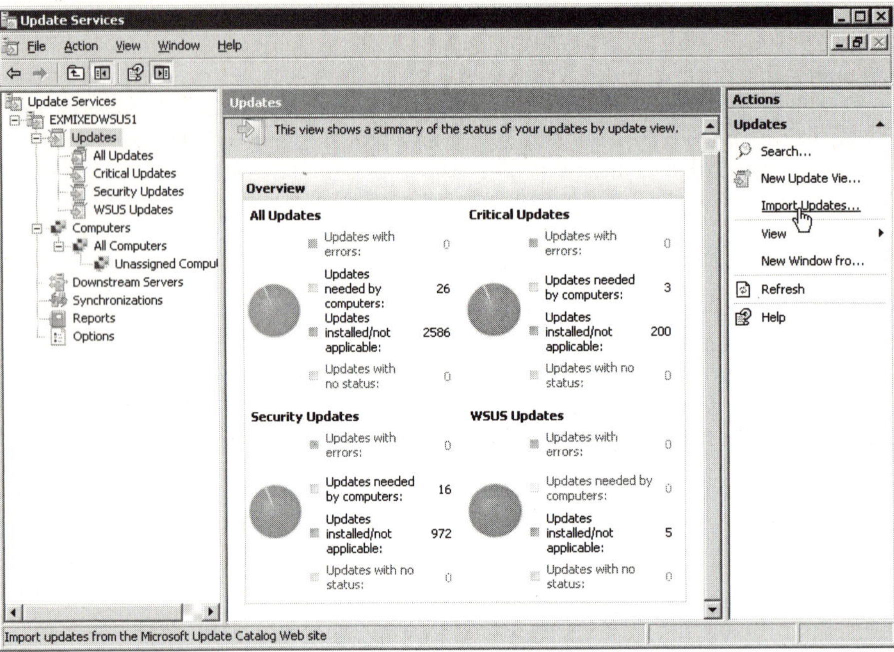

FIGURE 17.21 Authenticode digital signature

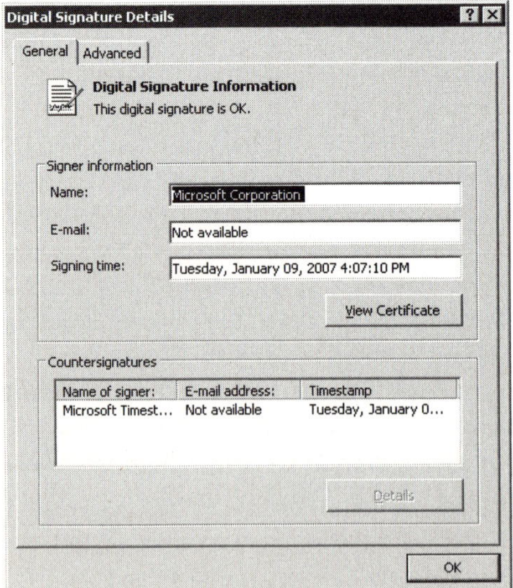

Phase 3: Evaluate and Plan

The next phase in your patch-management strategy is to evaluate and plan. In most cases this phase consists of the change-management process, beginning with the initiation of an RFC and the assignment of the priority and category of the change. Change management is discussed in detail in the "Planning Change Management" section of this chapter. The milestone for the end of this phase and handover to the deployment phase is the patch passing acceptance testing and being approved for deployment into production.

Phase 4: Deploy

The last phase of the patch-management process is reached when the patch is approved for deployment. This phase maps to the change release and change review portions of the change-management process, which we discussed in detail in the "Planning Change Management" section of this chapter. As well as deploying the patch, you are rescanning the environment to verify success, executing back-out procedures if necessary, and performing a review of the patch-management process upon completion.

Microsoft WSUS 3.0 is a cost-effective method of patch and service pack deployment in small- and medium-sized environments. WSUS 3.0 itself is managed through the web-based administrative interface on the server running WSUS 3.0, while your Exchange Server 2007 computers and other clients updated by the WSUS 3.0 server are configured and managed using group policy in Active Directory. A group policy object (GPO) can be configured specifically for your Exchange Server 2007 computers, and then applied to the organizational unit (OU) containing those computers. WSUS client behavior that can be configured and managed with group policy includes the download and installation behavior (whether to prompt for installation, or install on a specified schedule), the computer behavior when restarts are required and whether to allow patches signed by publishers other than Microsoft.

Planning a Monitoring and Reporting Solution

Monitoring your Exchange Server 2007 organization plays a significant role in the world of IT operations. Monitoring provides you with the means to detect and act on issues before they affect your end users, and helps ensure that you are meeting your SLAs. Monitoring also provides a means of establishing a baseline for use as a reference and facilitates estimating future needs based on performance and/or usage patterns.

The following are some best practices for monitoring and reporting on your Exchange Server 2007 environment:

- Document the targets defined in your SLAs (Service Level Agreements) and *OLA*s (Operating Level Agreements) for the messaging system. In addition, capture the monitoring requirements for these targets in this document, which is known as a *service monitoring requirements document*.

- Implement a monitoring solution or solutions based on the targets and requirements outlined in the service monitoring requirements document. There is much monitoring and reporting possible through the Exchange Server 2007 PowerShell, as well as with Exchange Server 2007 and Windows Server 2003 tools. However, Microsoft Operations Manager (MOM) 2005 is the recommended monitoring and reporting solution. MOM provides a comprehensive monitoring and reporting solution for Exchange Server 2007, as well as for the rest of your IT infrastructure.
- Establish and record a baseline of your Exchange Server 2007 messaging environment. This allows you to establish meaningful alert levels and helps you interpret alerts that are generated. These alerts allow you to respond appropriately (and, in many cases, proactively before the event affects your users) when an event is outside established parameters.
- Centralize your Exchange monitoring so that data and reports are stored in one place. This minimizes the administrative overhead involved in maintaining consistent monitoring and reporting across your environment. MOM 2005 with the Exchange Server 2007 Management Pack provides a centralized monitoring approach.
- Regularly generate reports for management and customers (end users), such as availability and service-level reports. Customer-focused reports could be posted on an intranet website, for example.

Using Windows and Exchange Tools for Monitoring and Reporting

Exchange Server 2007 can be monitored using built-in Windows tools, such as Performance Monitor and the Event Viewer. Other Microsoft utilities, such as the MBSA, can be used to monitor security configurations and patch levels.

Exchange Server 2007 also provides Exchange-specific tools for monitoring and reporting. Graphical tools provided include the Exchange Server Performance Monitor and the Queue Viewer. The Exchange Server Performance Monitor, available in the Toolbox work center in the Exchange Management Console, is a customized Performance Monitor console pre-populated with the most significant Exchange-related performance counters.

The Exchange Server Performance Monitor is shown in Figure 17.1.

Aside from graphical tools, PowerShell provides extensive scriptable monitoring and reporting capabilities via cmdlets through the Exchange Management Shell.

Some monitoring-specific PowerShell cmdlets are as follows:

- `Test-ActiveSyncConnectivity`
- `Test-EdgeSynchronization`
- `Test-ExchangeSearch`
- `Test-Mailflow`

- Test-MAPIConnectivity
- Test-OutlookWebServices
- Test-OwaConnectivity
- Test-SenderId
- Test-ServiceHealth
- Test-SystemHealth
- Test-UMConnectivity
- Test-WebServicesConnectivity

In addition, most of the get-* cmdlets can be utilized to generate reports on virtually every aspect of your Exchange Server 2007 environment and can be exported to .csv files by pipelining the output into the export-csv cmdlet.

For example, the following cmdlets retrieve all mailboxes in the Boston office and export the list to a .csv file:

```
$OfficeName = "Boston"
get-mailbox -filter {Office -eq $OfficeName } | select name,office, *quota |
sort name | export-csv export.csv
```

To view mailbox statistics for the current server, including storage size, use the following:

```
get-MailboxStatistics | select DisplayName, TotalItemSize, TotalDeletedItemsize,
DatabaseName | Export-Csv mbstats.csv
```

In larger enterprise environments, it is more likely that you will be using a centralized monitoring and reporting package such as MOM 2005 SP1.

Using MOM 2005 SP1 for Monitoring and Reporting

Deploying the Exchange Server 2007 Management Pack for MOM 2005 SP1 on the full version of MOM gives you the ability to monitor all options centrally on multiple servers and view reports.

The workgroup edition of MOM can monitor only 10 servers and does not provide reporting.

The Exchange Server 2007 Management Pack monitors the following key scenarios:

- All Exchange services are running.
- All databases are mounted and the disk volumes have sufficient free space.
- Outlook 2007 clients can connect with acceptable performance.
- Mail is flowing between servers.
- Exchange Server 2007 is performing reliably and at acceptable service levels.
- Exchange Server 2007 is configured correctly and is secure; for example, backups are being completed regularly.

MOM 2005 SP1 can use SQL Server 2000 or SQL Server 2005 for the report server database. If MOM is configured to use SQL 2000 and Internet Explorer 7 (IE7) is installed, the document map will not display anything (this is in the navigation pane on the left side of the reports). Normally you will see links in the document map that you can click to move to different sections in the reports.

In the Exchange Server 2007 Management Pack, there are 149 performance-data collection rules. These rules start with the word *Collect:* to indicate they only collect data, while rules that collect data for use in reports end with *Report Collection*. This naming convention makes it easier to locate the rules used in performance data collection in the event you want to disable these rules. In the Exchange Server 2003 Management Pack many organizations disabled these performance data collection rules to minimize the MOM reporting database growth and maximize database performance.

Monitoring starts with deploying MOM 2005 SP1 and the Exchange Server 2007 Management Pack, then deploying the agents to your Exchange Server 2007 computers. Once the Exchange Server 2007 Management Pack is implemented, however, you need to adjust the monitoring configuration so that it actually becomes useful to you. Otherwise, you can have a situation where so many meaningless events are generated that significant events are lost in the clutter and people just log on to the Operator Console occasionally and clear all the events. When your monitoring solution is in this state, it is just generating data that is of no use.

On the other hand, configuring the system so that any alerts or warnings generated are legitimate results in a situation where meaningful events are being noted and acted upon. In this case, your monitoring system is generating information—not just data—which makes all the difference in the world.

EXERCISE 17.1

MOM 2005 SP1 Agent Action Account Configuration

When you're deploying the Exchange Server 2007 Management Pack, the Agent Action account on your Exchange Server 2007 computers must be configured to run as the Local System account.

To configure the Agent Action account, do the following:

1. Start the MOM 2005 Administrator Console from Start ➤ All Programs ➤ Microsoft Operations Manager 2005 ➤ Administrator Console.
2. In the navigation pane of the Administrator Console, expand Microsoft Operations Manager ➤ Administration ➤ Computers, then highlight Agent-Managed Computers.
3. In the results pane, right-click the Exchange Server 2007 computer to be configured, and select Update Agent Settings from the context menu.

EXERCISE 17.1 *(continued)*

4. In the Update Agent Settings Task dialog box, select Local System for the Agent Action account, as shown here.

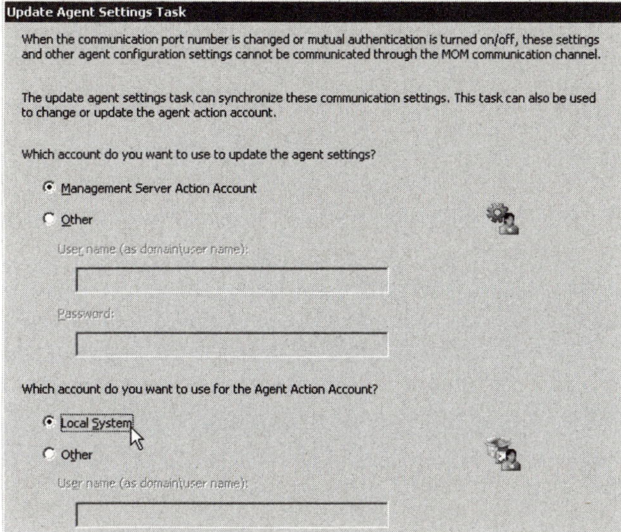

Exchange Server 2007 Management Pack Reporting Services

The management pack for Exchange Server 2007 provides numerous reports for viewing service availability, antispam statistics, and performance and usage metrics. The reporting is accomplished by querying the MOM data warehouse, summarizing the data returned, and formatting the data into a report. Because the MOM data warehouse is used, reporting is available only in the full version of MOM 2005 SP1.

When viewing Exchange reports in MOM 2005, keep in mind that MOM 2005 reports, including the Exchange reports, do not show new data until the Data Transformation Services (DTS) job has run, which is at 01:00 a.m. every day by default. This job transfers data to the MOM data warehouse from the MOM operational database.

Numerous predefined reports are supplied with the Exchange Server 2007 Management Pack, and custom reports can be created as required. All reports have the following information in common:

- Description of the purpose and objectives of the report.
- Report parameters.

- Related rules.
- Calculation method (where appropriate).
- Click-through functionality (click fields to see more detailed information).

Service Availability Reports

The Exchange Server 2007 Management Pack provides several reports to examine the availability of Exchange services, including a general service availability summary:

- Mailbox service availability
- Mailflow local service availability
- Mailflow remote service availability
- Outlook Web Access external service availability
- Outlook Web Access internal service availability
- ActiveSync internal availability
- Unified Messaging local voice service availability
- Unified Messaging local fax service availability
- Unified Messaging remote voice service availability

Generating the service availability reports can be a lengthy process because of the large amount of data. You may want to configure a Snapshot schedule using the Properties tab of the reports or create a subscription for the reports to generate them on a scheduled basis and email them to you.

Metrics Reports

The metrics reports provide detailed information on the following five Exchange Server 2007 components:

- Client performance
- Mailbox count
- RPC and database performance
- Unified Messaging call summary
- Unified Messaging message summary

Antispam Reports

The antispam reports provide information on the following aspects of Exchange Server 2007's antispam functionality:

- Attached file filter
- Connection filter

- Recipient filter
- Sender ID
- Sender filter
- Content filter
- Protocol analysis

Summary

Many IT professionals, while proficient in technical matters, tend to neglect the "softer" aspects of the job. This is especially true when it comes to planning infrastructure and configuration changes, and change management in general. Proper attention to planning in these areas, however, will minimize downtime and ensure that your service levels are being met in the most cost-effective manner. Behind all of this is the recognition of the business requirements of your organization and how your Exchange Server 2007 infrastructure is fulfilling those requirements.

In addition to properly planning and managing change in your environment, a well-thought-out approach to patch management helps ensure you maintain a proper security posture and deploy patches when appropriate. Much of the planning of patch management is intertwined with your change management, especially in the planning and deploying phases. However, assessing and identifying patches is an essential part of the patch-management process and should not be overlooked or minimized.

Finally, the monitoring of and reporting on your Exchange Server 2007 organization provides the means for you to discover and take action on issues that arise, ideally before they affect your end users. Another result of proper monitoring and reporting planning is a performance baseline, which provides you with a means of setting realistic alert levels and predicting future requirements based on current patterns.

Exam Essentials

Understand the different phases of planning for infrastructure and configuration changes. Before introducing change, you need to document what you have, then define functional tests to verify the current state. Next, clarify the business requirements and define the issue at hand. At that point, you can identify what needs to be changed. Finally, plan, test, and implement the change.

Understand the different aspects of change management. Infrastructure and configuration changes fit into the larger change management of the organization, so understanding the overall change-management process is essential to planning change for your Exchange Server 2007 environment.

Know how best to deploy a change into your environment. Once a change has been approved, plan and document the deployment. Test the change in a lab environment; if testing is successful, deploy the change in a controlled manner to minimize downtime and service-level degradation. Finally, test and review the change to ensure the expected results have been obtained, and accept or reject the change on that review.

Understand patch-management methodology. To ensure the right patches are applied to the right systems at the right times, you should understand the various phases of patch management. You also should know how patch management fits into overall change management, and what aspects of patch management are unique.

Know how to plan a monitoring and reporting solution. Understand the best practices for monitoring and reporting on Exchange Server 2007. You also should know the recommended solution for Exchange Server 2007 monitoring and reporting, as well as what to monitor. In addition, you should have a solid understanding of what a performance baseline is and how it's used.

Review Questions

1. You have a single Exchange Server 2007 Edge Transport server that all of your inbound and outbound SMTP traffic is routed through. One day, this computer experienced a system board failure, and email service was degraded until it was repaired. As a result, you need to plan a change to address this issue and avoid interruptions to mail service in the future. What change do you propose?

   A. Implement an additional Hub Transport server.

   B. Implement an additional Client Access server.

   C. Implement an additional Edge Transport server.

   D. Implement an additional network interface card in the existing Edge Transport server.

2. You are a messaging professional responsible for an Exchange Server 2007 organization. You have deployed Exchange Server 2007 Client Access servers to provide access to Outlook Web Access for internal users. Now you need to provide Outlook Web Access connectivity for users from the Internet. As part of your planning, you obtain an SSL certificate from a trusted vendor. Next you plan to replace the self-signed certificate on your Client Access server with the new certificate, then publish this server to the Internet using Microsoft ISA server and create the necessary DNS records in your external DNS. What tests should you include in your deployment plan to verify the implementation was successful? (Choose all that apply.)

   A. Verify that internal users can connect to their mailboxes using Outlook 2007.

   B. Verify that users can log on to their mailboxes with Outlook Web Access from the Internet.

   C. Verify that users can log on to their mailboxes with Outlook Web Access from the internal network.

   D. Verify that email flow to and from the Internet is not affected by the change.

   E. Verify that email flow between users in your Exchange Server 2007 organization is not affected.

3. You are responsible for documenting your Exchange Server 2007 computer configurations. What information should you record for each server? (Choose all that apply.)

   A. TCP/IP configuration

   B. User profile settings

   C. Disk configurations

   D. Distributed File System settings

   E. Installed applications

4. You are documenting the configuration of your Exchange Server 2007 organization; the organization configuration is being recorded separately from the Exchange Server 2007 computer-specific configurations. What values should you record for the organization configuration? (Choose all that apply.)

   A. Storage-group configurations

   B. Mailbox storage limits

   C. Hub Transport rules

   D. Send connectors

   E. Outlook Anywhere authentication methods

   F. Managed-folder mailbox policies

5. You are planning to implement an application on all Exchange Server 2007 Mailbox servers to provide new functionality required by your business. This service must be implemented on all Mailbox servers in your production environment as soon as possible. What should you include in your deployment plan?

   A. Contact the application vendor to verify that there are no known conflicts with Exchange Server 2007, then install the application on all Mailbox servers simultaneously.

   B. Install the application on half of your Exchange Server 2007 Mailbox servers one day, then install it on the rest of the Mailbox servers the following day.

   C. Install the application in your lab environment and complete full testing of the application. Next, deploy the application in a pilot environment with a subset of users. Finally, deploy the application into your production environment on one Mailbox server at a time.

   D. Research the application using the Internet and industry publications. Use this research to create a deployment plan, and then use this deployment plan to implement the application into your production environment.

6. You are planning to implement a change to improve the message retention for policy compliance in your messaging system. What should you include in the implementation plan?

   A. Implement Exchange Hosted encryption services

   B. Configure Outlook Anywhere

   C. Implement new send connectors

   D. Implement Exchange Hosted archive services

7. You are planning to implement Outlook Web Access functionality for your organization for users to connect from the Internet. Until now, the only client connections allowed were Outlook clients from the internal network. What should you include in the implementation plan? (Choose all that apply.)

   A. Deploy a Client Access server on your internal network.

   B. Deploy a Client Access server in your perimeter network.

   C. Deploy an Edge Transport server in your perimeter network.

   D. Deploy an ISA server in your perimeter network.

   E. Configure DNS records for the Autodiscover service.

8. You are planning to implement a lab for testing changes to your production environment before deploying those changes into production. Your Exchange Server 2007 organization consists of four locations. One location is your head office, where the Client Access, Hub Transport, and Mailbox server roles are deployed on separate computers. The other three locations are branch offices with a computer holding the Mailbox role, and a second Exchange Server 2007 computer with the Client Access and Hub Transport roles installed. You need to design a lab with the fewest number of computers possible but still perform valid tests for changes to the Client Access role. You have a single computer deployed in your lab to provide Active Directory and DNS services; no Exchange Server 2007 roles can be installed on this computer. What should you do?

   A. Deploy a single Exchange Server 2007 computer with the Mailbox, Hub Transport, and Client Access roles. Create another Active Directory site, and install a Windows Server 2003 global catalog server in the second site. Implement a single Exchange Server 2007 computer with the Mailbox, Hub Transport, and Client Access roles in the second site.

   B. Deploy an Exchange Server 2007 computer with the Mailbox role, a second Exchange Server 2007 computer with the Hub Transport role, and a third Exchange Server 2007 computer with the Client Access role. Deploy a fourth Exchange Server 2007 computer holding the Hub Transport and Client Access roles.

   C. Deploy a single Exchange Server 2007 computer with the Mailbox, Hub Transport, and Client Access roles.

   D. Deploy an Exchange Server 2007 computer with the Mailbox role, a second Exchange Server 2007 computer with the Hub Transport role, and a third Exchange Server 2007 computer with the Client Access role.

9. What is the first step in the change-management process?

   A. The change is assessed to determine its urgency and impact.

   B. The deployment of the change is planned and then reviewed.

   C. A Request for Change is created.

   D. The change is submitted to the CAB for approval or rejection.

10. You are planning the deployment of antivirus updates to your Exchange Server 2007 environment. Because of the routine nature of these updates, they have been classified as standard changes. What approval process should these changes undergo?

   A. Because of their routine nature, they can be implemented without any formal review.

   B. The CAB/EC reviews them so that you don't have to wait for the full CAB to convene to obtain approval of the changes.

   C. Because of their routine nature, they are approved by the change manager without referral to the CAB.

   D. All changes require the approval of the CAB.

11. You are a messaging professional responsible for your company's Exchange Server 2007 organization. A business-critical, third-party application installed on your Hub Transport servers caused a service outage across your entire company. To correct this outage, a patch supplied by the application vendor needs to be deployed on to the Hub Transport servers immediately. This emergency change is approved by the CAB/EC. When service is restored, what action needs to be taken to close this RFC?

    A. A change review is performed, then the RFC is closed.

    B. Because this was an emergency change pre-approved by the CAB/EC, the RFC is closed without review.

    C. The RFC is sent to the full CAB for formal approval.

    D. The RFC is submitted to the change manager for assessment.

12. You are planning to deploy dedicated Client Access servers to your environment, and you are submitting a plan for approval through your company's change-management process. At what point in the change-management process do you need to outline your back-out procedures to use in the event that the implementation is not successful?

    A. During the change-development phase, when you create your formal deployment documentation

    B. In the Request for Change

    C. When the change is assessed and classified

    D. After the change is developed, but before it is deployed into production

13. You are planning the patch-management strategy for your Exchange Server 2007 organization. You need to document procedures that allow patches to be reviewed to ensure they are relevant, then applied to your Exchange Server 2007 computers. What procedures should you include in your patch-management strategy? (Choose all that apply.)

    A. Implement Windows Server Update Services (WSUS). Review available patches and approve the relevant patches. Configure a Group Policy Object (GPO) to deploy the patches and assign this GPO to the organizational unit (OU) containing your service accounts.

    B. Log on to each Exchange Server 2007 computer. Browse to the Microsoft Update site with Internet Explorer and select the Custom option.

    C. Log on to each Exchange Server 2007 computer. Browse to the Microsoft Update site with Internet Explorer and select the Express option.

    D. Implement Windows Server Update Services (WSUS). Review available patches and approve the relevant patches. Configure a GPO to deploy the patches and assign this GPO to the OU containing your Exchange Server 2007 computers.

14. In what order do the phases of patch management occur?

    Identify

    Evaluate and plan

    Assess

    Deploy

    A. Identify, assess, evaluate and plan, deploy
    B. Evaluate and plan, identify, assess, deploy
    C. Evaluate and plan, identify, deploy, assess
    D. Assess, identify, evaluate and plan, deploy

15. You are planning the patch-management strategy for your company. You need to provide a means to review all patches before they are deployed and minimize the effort required to deploy the patches to your Exchange Server 2007 computers. You also need to deploy the minimum number of services or computers required. What should you include in your deployment plan? (Choose all that apply.)

    A. Configure a GPO to "auto download and notify for install" patches from the Microsoft Update website. Apply this GPO to the OU containing your Exchange Server 2007 computers.
    B. Log on to each Exchange Server 2007 computer. Review the downloaded updates and select the relevant one to install.
    C. Deploy a Windows Server 2003 computer and implement WSUS on this computer. Review available patches and approve the relevant ones.
    D. Configure a GPO to "auto download and schedule the install" patches from the WSUS computer. Apply this GPO to the OU containing your Exchange Server 2007 computers.

16. You are planning the patch-management strategy for your Exchange Server 2007 organization. In what phase of the patch-management process do you determine which patches are relevant to your environment?

    A. Assess
    B. Identify
    C. Evaluate and plan
    D. Deploy

17. You are planning an Exchange Server 2007 monitoring and reporting solution for your organization. Your solution needs to provide centralized storage of monitoring data and customized reports with the minimum configuration effort required. What products or functionalities should you include in your solution? (Choose all that apply.)

    A. Microsoft Systems Management Server
    B. Microsoft Operations Manager 2005 SP1
    C. Exchange Server 2007 Management Pack
    D. Performance Monitor
    E. Event Viewer
    F. Exchange Management Shell

18. You are creating a monitoring and reporting strategy for your Exchange Server 2007 environment. What portion of your monitoring and reporting strategy provides the ability to establish meaningful alert levels for notification?

A. Documenting the targets defined in your Service Level Agreements in a service monitoring requirements document

B. Implementing a monitoring solution based on the targets and requirements outlined in the service monitoring requirements document

C. Establishing and recording a baseline of your Exchange Server 2007 messaging environment

D. Generating reports on service availability, performance, and usage metrics

19. You are planning to implement a monitoring solution for Exchange Server 2007. Your environment consists of six Exchange Server 2007 computers in two sites. You need to provide for centralized storage of monitoring data with minimal configuration and management effort, and your solution also must provide the ability to generate reports on service availability. Because your company is in a competitive market, you need to minimize the costs of the solution by only purchasing the minimum software licenses and versions required. What should you include in your implementation plan?

A. MOM 2005 SP1

B. MOM 2005 SP1 Workgroup Edition

C. Exchange Management Shell

D. Performance Monitor

20. You are planning your monitoring and reporting deployment for Exchange Server 2007. You have decided that you will use MOM 2005 SP1 with the Exchange Server 2007 Management Pack as your solution. There is an existing SQL Server 2000 computer in your Active Directory domain. You need to ensure that you have all reporting functionality, and that you deploy no more software or servers than are required. What should you include in your deployment plan?

A. Install MOM 2005 on a new Windows Server 2003 computer and use the existing SQL Server 2000 computer.

B. Deploy a new Windows Server 2003 computer and install SQL Server 2005 on it. Deploy a second new Windows Server 2003 computer and install MOM 2005 on it. Configure MOM 2005 to use the SQL Server 2005 instance on the first new computer.

C. Install MOM 2005 on the SQL Server 2000 computer. Configure MOM 2005 to use the SQL Server 2000 instance on that computer.

D. Deploy a new Windows Server 2003 computer. Install MOM 2005 and SQL Server 2005 on this computer. Configure MOM 2005 to use the SQL 2005 instance on that computer.

Answers to Review Questions

1. C. As the Edge Transport server is a single point of failure, the change you need to plan for is to implement an additional Edge Transport server to avoid interruptions in mail flow resulting from one Edge Transport server failing.

2. B, C. You need to verify that OWA connectivity is functional for both internal users and users connecting from the Internet because you are not only replacing the self-signed SSL certificate on your Client Access server with a purchased certificate, you also are publishing the Client Access server to the Internet using ISA server and modifying your external DNS. As Client Access servers are not involved in email routing, it is not necessary to verify email flow. Also, because MAPI clients do not connect to the Client Access server, it is not necessary to test Outlook 2007 connectivity for internal users.

3. A, C, E. TCP/IP configuration, disk configurations, and installed applications are all components that should be documented on Exchange Server 2007 servers. User profile settings have no bearing on Exchange Server 2007, so do not need to be documented. Distributed File System is not used for Exchange Server 2007, so it does not need to be documented either.

4. C, D, F. Hub Transport rules, Send connectors, and managed-folder mailbox policies are configured at the organization level, so they should be recorded in this document. Storage-group configurations, mailbox storage limits, and Outlook Anywhere authentication methods are all configured on a per-server basis.

5. C. To add new services or functionality, you must follow established change procedures. These procedures include testing the change in a lab environment, piloting the change into production, implementing the change on one server at a time, and verifying that change before proceeding to the next server.

6. D. To provide message retention, you must implement Exchange Host archive services. Exchange Hosted encryption services provide policy-based encryption from sender to recipient, while Outlook Anywhere allows for RPC/HTTP access to Exchange with Outlook 2003 or Outlook 2007. Send connectors may provide redundancy for message routing, but do not provide message retention capabilities.

7. A, D. A Client Access server needs to be deployed in your internal network, along with an ISA server in the perimeter network to publish OWA to the Internet. Client Access servers should not be deployed in a perimeter network because of the number of ports that need to be open on the firewall, and the Edge Transport role has no bearing on providing Outlook Web Access. Autodiscover DNS records are not required for OWA functionality, either.

8. B. To perform valid tests on changes to the Client Access role, you need to duplicate the production environment that has the Client Access role on both dedicated Exchange Server 2007 computers and on Exchange Server 2007 computers holding both the Client Access and Hub Transport roles. The scenario outlined in answer B is the only one that provides this arrangement.

9. C. As outlined in the Microsoft Operations Framework, the first step in the change-management process is to create a Request for Change.

10. A. All changes classified as standard changes are approved automatically and go directly to the planning and release phases of change management. All other changes undergo varying levels of approval, depending on the classification of the change.

11. A. An emergency change necessarily goes through an abbreviated process. Because it undergoes less-stringent testing and planning, it is even more important that it be reviewed upon completion. After the change is reviewed, the RFC is closed; it does not need to be resubmitted for formal approval.

12. B. The contingency procedures (also known as a back-out plan) are outlined in the Request for Change, at the beginning of the change-management process. The contingency procedures are then assessed as part of the overall change.

13. B, D. Logging on to the Exchange Server 2007 computers, accessing the Microsoft Update site, and selecting the Custom option allows you to review the patches and apply the relevant ones. Deploying WSUS and assigning the appropriate GPO to your Exchange Server 2007 computers also allows you to deploy the appropriate patches after they are approved on the WSUS server. Assigning the WSUS GPO to the OU containing service accounts will not apply the patches to your Exchange Server 2007 computers, and using the Express option on the Microsoft Update site does not give you the option to review patches before applying them.

14. D. The phases of patch management as defined in the Microsoft Operations Framework (MOF) and Microsoft's patch-management process (`https://www.microsoft.com/technet/security/guidance/patchmanagement/secmod193.mspx`) are assess, identify, evaluate and plan, and deploy.

15. C, D. To review patches before they are applied and minimize the deployment effort required, you need to deploy WSUS; this will allow you to review and approve relevant patches. A GPO can then be configured and applied to the Exchange Server 2007 computers to automatically download and apply the patches on a set schedule without administrator intervention. Configuring a GPO to download patches from Microsoft Update and notify for install allows you to review the patches, but requires maximum effort as you need to log on to each Exchange Server 2007 computer and initiate the installation process manually.

16. B. You determine what patches are relevant to your environment in the identify phase of patch management. The assess phase is concerned with assessing your existing environment and vulnerabilities; the evaluate and plan phase deals with the deployment planning and testing for the patch.

17. B, C. MOM 2005 SP1 with the Exchange Server 2007 Management Pack is the recommended monitoring and reporting solution. It provides for consistent and centralized monitoring with minimal configuration effort. Performance Monitor, Event Viewer, and the Exchange Management Shell can be used for monitoring and reporting, but this solution would not be centralized and would require a considerable amount of configuration and scripting effort.

18. C. Establishing a baseline enables you to establish meaningful alert levels and helps you interpret alerts that are generated by providing you with a representation of the Exchange Server 2007 organization's normal running state.

19. A. Although you have only six Exchange Server 2007 computers to monitor, and MOM 2005 SP1 Workgroup Edition can monitor up to 10 computers, the Workgroup Edition does not have reporting capability. A combination of the Exchange Management Shell and Performance Monitor can provide some monitoring and reporting capability, but this solution won't be centralized and will require more configuration and management effort.

20. D. Although installing MOM 2005 on the SQL Server 2000 computer would require the fewest servers and software installations, using SQL Server 2000 for the MOM 2005 reporting database results in reduced functionality when using the reporting web page; the document map will not display anything. Normally, you will see links in the document map that you can click to move to different sections in the reports. Deploying MOM 2005 and SQL Server 2005 on separate servers would require another Windows Server 2003 computer, and you need to minimize the number of servers to be deployed.

About the Companion CD

IN THIS APPENDIX:

- ✓ What you'll find on the CD
- ✓ System requirements
- ✓ Using the CD
- ✓ Troubleshooting

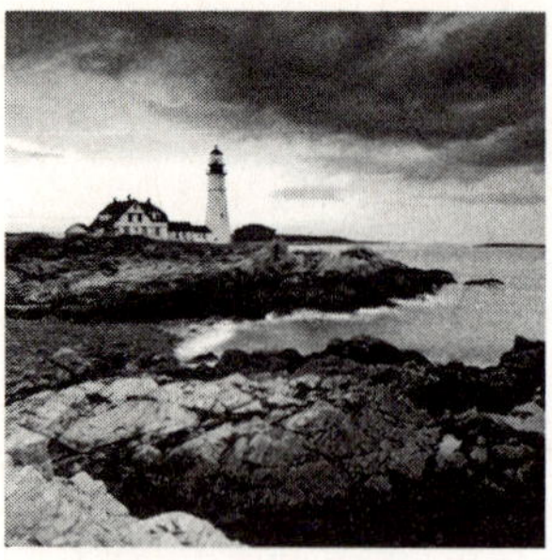

What You'll Find on the CD

The following sections are arranged by category and provide a summary of the software and other goodies you'll find on the CD. If you need help with installing the items provided on the CD, refer to the installation instructions in the "Using the CD" section of this appendix.

Some programs on the CD might fall into one of these categories:

Shareware programs are fully functional, free, trial versions of copyrighted programs. If you like particular programs, register with their authors for a nominal fee and receive licenses, enhanced versions, and technical support.

Freeware programs are free, copyrighted games, applications, and utilities. You can copy them to as many computers as you like—for free—but they offer no technical support.

GNU software is governed by its own license, which is included inside the folder of the GNU software. There are no restrictions on distribution of GNU software. See the GNU license at the root of the CD for more details.

Trial, demo, or *evaluation* versions of software are usually limited either by time or functionality (such as not letting you save a project after you create it).

Sybex Test Engine

For Windows

The CD contains the Sybex Test Engine, which includes all of the Assessment Test and Chapter Review questions in electronic format, as well as four bonus exams located only on the CD.

PDF of the Book

For Windows

We have included an electronic version of the text in `.pdf` format. You can view the electronic version of the book with Adobe Reader.

Adobe Reader

For Windows

We've also included a copy of Adobe Reader, so you can view PDF files that accompany the book's content. For more information on Adobe Reader or to check for a newer version, visit Adobe's website at `http://www.adobe.com/products/reader/`.

Electronic Flashcards

For PC, Pocket PC and Palm

These handy electronic flashcards are just what they sound like. One side contains a question or fill in the blank, and the other side shows the answer.

System Requirements

Make sure that your computer meets the minimum system requirements shown in the following list. If your computer doesn't match up to most of these requirements, you may have problems using the software and files on the companion CD. For the latest and greatest information, please refer to the ReadMe file located at the root of the CD-ROM.

- A PC running Microsoft Windows 98, Windows 2000, Windows NT4 (with SP4 or later), Windows Me, Windows XP, or Windows Vista.
- An Internet connection
- A CD-ROM drive

Using the CD

To install the items from the CD to your hard drive, follow these steps.

1. Insert the CD into your computer's CD-ROM drive. The license agreement appears.

Windows users: The interface won't launch if you have autorun disabled. In that case, click Start ➢ Run (for Windows Vista, Start ➢ All Programs ➢ Accessories ➢ Run). In the dialog box that appears, type **`D:\Start.exe`**. (Replace *D* with the proper letter if your CD drive uses a different letter. If you don't know the letter, see how your CD drive is listed under My Computer.) Click OK.

2. Read through the license agreement, and then click the Accept button if you want to use the CD.

The CD interface appears. The interface allows you to access the content with just one or two clicks.

Troubleshooting

Wiley has attempted to provide programs that work on most computers with the minimum system requirements. Alas, your computer may differ, and some programs may not work properly for some reason.

The two likeliest problems are that you don't have enough memory (RAM) for the programs you want to use, or you have other programs running that are affecting installation or running of a program. If you get an error message such as "Not enough memory" or "Setup cannot continue," try one or more of the following suggestions and then try using the software again:

Turn off any antivirus software running on your computer. Installation programs sometimes mimic virus activity and may make your computer incorrectly believe that it's being infected by a virus.

Close all running programs. The more programs you have running, the less memory is available to other programs. Installation programs typically update files and programs; so if you keep other programs running, installation may not work properly.

Have your local computer store add more RAM to your computer. This is, admittedly, a drastic and somewhat expensive step. However, adding more memory can really help the speed of your computer and allow more programs to run at the same time.

Customer Care

If you have trouble with the book's companion CD-ROM, please call the Wiley Product Technical Support phone number at (800) 762-2974. Outside the United States, call +1(317) 572-3994. You can also contact Wiley Product Technical Support at `http://sybex.custhelp.com`. John Wiley & Sons will provide technical support only for installation and other general quality control items. For technical support on the applications themselves, consult the program's vendor or author.

To place additional orders or to request information about other Wiley products, please call (877) 762-2974.

Glossary

A

accepted domain An email domain that your Exchange servers accept inbound mail for.

Access Control Entries (ACEs) Entries on an Access Control List (ACL) that define a user's permission for an object.

Access Control List (ACL) A list of users and groups allowed to access a resource and the particular permissions each user has been granted or denied.

Active Directory Stores information about objects in a Windows Server 2003 network and makes this information easy for administrators and users to find and use.

address space The set of remote addresses that can be reached through a particular connector. Each connector must have at least one entry in its address space.

administrative group Used to define administrative boundaries within an Exchange 2000/2003 environment.

administrative rights NTFS permissions that determine what administrative tasks a user or group is permitted to perform on a public folder.

age limit A property that specifies the length of time a unit of data may remain in its container (e.g., public folder).

alias An alternative name for an object. In Exchange, an alias is normally generated for a user based on the user's name.

All Public Folders The name for the default public folder tree in an Exchange organization. This tree is accessible by all clients that can access public folders.

Anonymous access Accessing a server by logging in using a Windows account set up for general access.

Anonymous authentication *See* Anonymous access.

Application Programming Interface (API) A collection of programming classes and interfaces that provide services used by a program. Other programs can use a program's API to request services or communicate with that program. For example, Windows 98 contains an API referred to as the win32 API. For an application to request a service from Windows 98, it must issue that request using a win32 API.

architecture The description of the components of a product or system, what they are, what they do, and how they relate to each other.

attribute A characteristic of an object. For example, attributes of a mailbox-enabled user include display name and storage limits. The terms *attribute* and *property* are synonymous.

auditing Windows Server 2003 can be configured to monitor and record certain events. This can help diagnose security events. The audit information is written to the Windows Event Log.

authentication A process whereby the credentials of an object, such as a user, must be validated before the object is allowed to access or use another object, such as a server or a protocol. For instance, the Microsoft Exchange Server POP3 protocol can be configured to allow access only to POP3 clients that use the Integrated Windows authentication method.

B

backfill The process used in public folder replication to fill in messaging data that is missing from a replica.

Bad Mail folder The folder in which SMTP stores undeliverable messages that cannot be returned to the sender.

Basic (Clear-Text) authentication Requires the user to submit a valid Windows username and password. The username and password are sent across the network as unencrypted clear text.

Basic over Secure Sockets Layer (SSL) authentication Extends the Basic (Clear-Text) authentication method by allowing an SSL server to encrypt the username and password before they are sent across the network.

C

cache mode A feature in Outlook 2003 and Outlook 2007 that allows clients to work disconnected from the Exchange server. Outlook will periodically reconnect to the Exchange server and synchronize any changes to the user's mailbox.

Categorizer A component of the Exchange Server 2007 routing engine used to resolve the sender and recipient for a message, expanding any distribution groups as needed. In previous versions of Exchange Server, this task was performed by the MTA.

centralized model An administrative model in which one administrator or group of administrators maintains complete control over an entire Exchange organization.

certificate Allows verification of the claim that a given public key actually belongs to a given individual. This helps prevent someone from using a phony key to impersonate someone else. A certificate is similar to a token.

Certificate Authority (CA) The central authority that distributes, publishes, and validates security keys. The Windows Server 2003 Certificates Services component performs this role. *See also* public key, private key.

Certificate Revocation List (CRL) A list containing all certificates in an organization that have been revoked.

Certificate Store A database created during the installation of a Certificate Authority (CA) that is a repository of certificates issued by the CA.

certificate templates Stored in Active Directory and define the attributes for certificates.

Certificate Trust List (CTL) Holds the set of root CAs whose certificates can be trusted. You can designate CTLs for groups, users, or an entire domain.

challenge/response A general term for a class of security mechanisms, including Microsoft authentication methods, that use Windows Server 2003 network security and an encrypted password.

change number One of the constructs used to keep track of public folder replication throughout an organization and to determine whether a public folder is synchronized. The change number is made up of a globally unique identifier for the Information Store and a change counter that is specific to the server on which a public folder resides.

checkpoint file The file (`EDB.CHK`) that contains the point in a transaction log that is the boundary between data that has been committed and data that has not yet been committed to an Exchange database.

child domain Any domain configured underneath another domain in a domain tree.

circular logging The process of writing new information in transaction log files over information that has already been committed. Instead of repeatedly creating new transaction logs, the Exchange database engine "circles back" and reuses log files that have been fully committed to the database. Circular logging keeps down the number of transaction logs on the disk. These logs cannot be used to re-create a database because the logs do not have a complete set of data. The logs contain only the most recent data not yet committed to a database. Circular logging is disabled by default.

Client Access License (CAL) Gives a user the legal right to access an Exchange server. Any client software that has the ability to be a client to Microsoft Exchange Server is legally required to have a CAL purchased for it.

client access server Non-MAPI clients, such as POP3, IMAP4, mobile, and web-based clients must connect to the Mailbox servers via a Client Access server. In this way, the Client Access server is most like the front-end servers utilized in previous versions of Exchange Server. All requests from these non-MAPI clients are received by the Client Access server and then forwarded to the applicable Mailbox server for action.

cluster A group of servers (also called nodes) that function together as a single unit.

Clustering A Windows service that enables multiple physical servers to be logically grouped together for reasons of fault tolerance.

Cluster Continuous Replication (CCR) This is a new cluster implementation that removes the requirement for a shared disk implementation such as a SAN. This configuration uses a Majority Node Set quorum and log shipping to keep the data synched up between the active and passive nodes.

cluster resource A service or property, such as a storage device, an IP address, or the Exchange System Attendant service, that is defined, monitored, and managed by the cluster service.

cluster service The cluster service is the software service used to manage all of the cluster activity. The cluster service controls access to resources by the individual nodes of the cluster.

committed When a transaction is transferred from a transaction log to an Exchange database, it has been committed.

Computer Management snap-in An administrative tool holding a variety of utilities, including Event Viewer and disk management tools.

contact A recipient object that represents a foreign message recipient. Contacts appear in the Global Address List (GAL) and allow Exchange clients to address messages to foreign mail users. Also referred to as a mail contact.

container object An object in the Exchange or Active Directory hierarchy that contains and groups together other objects. For example, the organization object in System Manager is a container object that contains all other objects in the organization.

contiguous namespace When multiple entities share a common namespace. For example, Windows Server 2003 domain trees share a contiguous namespace; domain forests do not.

continuous availability (CA) The unattainable desire to never have applications unavailable.

convergence The process during which the active nodes in a cluster calculate a new, stable state among themselves after the failure of one or more cluster nodes.

copy backup During a copy backup, all selected files are backed up, regardless of how their archive bit is set. After the backup, the archive bit is not changed in any file.

D

daily backup During this backup, all files that changed on the day of the backup are backed up, and the archive bit is not changed in any file.

Data Encryption Standard (DES) A secret-key encryption method that uses a 56-bit key.

DAVEx An IIS component that passes client requests between W3svc and the Information Store.

database There are two types of databases in Exchange Server 2007: public databases that hold public folders meant to be accessed by groups of users and mailbox databases that hold user mailboxes.

DCDiag A command-line utility that can be used to analyze the state of all domain controllers in a forest and report problems that were found.

decentralized model Typically used to define administrative boundaries along real geographical or departmental boundaries. Each location would have its own administrators and its own administrative group.

decryption Translating encrypted data back to plaintext.

dedicated public folder server An Exchange server whose primary purpose is to hold public folder databases and from which the mailbox databases have been removed.

deleted-item retention time The period that items in a public or private database deleted by users are actually retained on the Exchange server.

demilitarized zone (DMZ) *See* perimeter network.

differential backup A method in which all files that have been changed since the last full backup are backed up. *See also* incremental backup.

digital signature A process of digitally signing data using public and private keys so that the recipient of the data can verify the authenticity of both the sender and the data.

directory A hierarchy that stores information about objects in a system. A Directory Service (DS) manages the directory and makes it available to users on the network.

directory replication The transferring of directory information from one server to another. In Active Directory, directory information is replicated between domain controllers. In previous versions of Exchange, directory information is replicated between Exchange servers.

directory rights Used to configure the NTFS permissions that determine who can perform modifications on the public folder object that is stored in Active Directory.

Disaster Recovery Mode A mode in which you can run Exchange Server 2007 setup that lets you recover an Exchange installation after a failure.

discretionary access control list (DACL) A list of Access Control Entries (ACEs) that give users and groups specific permissions on an object.

dismounting The process of taking a public or mailbox database offline.

distribution group An Active Directory group formed so that a single e-mail message can be sent to the group and then sent automatically to all members of the group. Unlike security groups, distribution groups don't provide any security function.

domain A group of computers and other resources that are part of a Windows Server 2003 network and share a common directory database.

domain controller A computer running Windows Server 2003 that validates user network access and manages Active Directory.

domain forest A group of one or more domain trees that do not necessarily form a contiguous namespace but may share a common schema and Global Catalog.

Domain Name Service (DNS) The primary provider of name resolution within an organization.

domain tree A hierarchical arrangement of one or more Windows Active Directory domains that share a common namespace.

DNS *See* Domain Name Service (DNS).

dynamic distribution group An e-mail enabled distribution group whose group membership is determined by the results of an LDAP query created when the group is configured.

E

edge transport server Designed to be deployed in the DMZ of your network, the Edge Transport server is used to provide a secure SMTP gateway for all messages entering or leaving your Exchange organization. As such, the Edge Transport server is responsible for antivirus and antispam controls, as well as protecting the recipient data held within Active Directory.

EHLO The ESMTP command used by one host to initiate communications with another host.

e-mail Electronic messages sent between users of different computers.

encryption The process of scrambling data to make it unreadable. The intended recipient will decrypt the data into plaintext in order to read it.

Enterprise CA Acts as a Certificate Authority for an enterprise and requires access to the Active Directory. *See also* Certificate Authority (CA).

Enterprise Edition The premier version of Exchange Server 2007 with support for up to fifty storage groups and fifty databases.

Event Log A set of three logs (Application, Security, and System) maintained by Windows Server. The operating system and many applications, such as Exchange Server 2007, write software events to the Event Log.

Exchange Management Console A snap-in for the Microsoft Management Console used to manage an Exchange Server 2007 organization.

expanding a distribution group The process of determining the individual addresses contained within a distribution group. This process is performed by the home server of the user sending the message to the group unless an expansion server is specified for the group.

extended permissions Permissions added to the standard Windows Server 2003 permissions when Exchange Server 2007 is installed.

Extensible Storage Engine (ESE) The database engine used by Exchange Server 2007.

F

failback The process of cluster resources moving back to their preferred node after the preferred node has resumed active membership in the cluster.

failover The process of moving resources off a cluster node that has failed to another cluster node. If any of the cluster resources on an active node becomes unresponsive or unavailable for a period time exceeding the configured threshold, failover will occur.

File Share Witness (FSW) KB921181 describes this new feature. The FSW is nothing more than a file share on another server that is not part of the cluster but can be used to allow for a failure and allow the cluster to still maintain a majority for MNS. The new file share witness feature allows for the creation of another quorum resource that will work with MNS quorum resources to provide more redundancy of the quorum. This new change allows the use of two nodes for the cluster, and a third server of some kind some place on the network to provide another quorum resource to work with MNS. The file share witness is perfect for those clusters that have no need for shared storage for their data, or it can be provided via other methods. Now, you can have two nodes and still have a majority available in the case of a single node failure.

firewall A set of mechanisms that separate and protect your internal network from unauthorized external users and networks. Firewalls can restrict inbound and outbound traffic, as well as analyze all traffic between your network and the outside.

folder-based application An application built within a public folder by customizing properties of the folder, such as permissions, views, rules, and the folder forms library to store and present data to users.

foreign system A non-Exchange messaging system.

forest root domain The first domain installed in a domain forest and the basis for the naming of all domains in the forest.

Forms Registry Stores the Outlook Web Access (OWA) forms rendered by Internet Information Services (IIS) and passed to the client.

frame The unit of information sent by a Data Link protocol, such as Ethernet or Token Ring.

free/busy Terminology used in the Microsoft Schedule+ application to denote an unscheduled period of time (free) or a scheduled period of time (busy).

front-end server *See* back-end server.

full-text indexing A feature that can be enabled for a database in which every word in the database (including those in attachments) is indexed for much faster search results.

Fully Qualified Domain Name (FQDN) The full DNS path of an Internet host. An example is `sales.dept4.widget.com`.

function call An instruction in a program that calls (invokes) a function. For example, MAPIReadMail is a MAPI function call.

G

GAL *See* Global Address List (GAL).

gateway Third-party software that permits Exchange to interoperate with a foreign message system. *See also* connector.

general-purpose trees Public folder trees added to an Exchange organization beyond the default public folder tree. General-purpose trees are not accessible by MAPI clients such as Microsoft Outlook.

Global Address List (GAL) A database of all the recipients in an Exchange organization, such as mailboxes, distribution lists, custom recipients, and public folders.

Global Catalog Used to hold information about all objects in a forest. The Global Catalog enables users and applications to find objects in an Active Directory domain tree if the user or application knows one or more attributes of the target object.

group A collection of users and other groups that may be assigned permissions or made part of an e-mail distribution list.

groupware Any application that allows groups of people to store and share information.

H

heartbeat A special communication among members of a cluster that keeps all members aware of one another's existence (and thus their operational state).

HELO The SMTP command used by one host to initiate communications with another host.

high availability (HA) The combination of well defined, planned, tested, and implemented processes, software, and fault tolerant hardware focused on supplying and maintaining application availability.

hierarchy Any structure or organization that uses class, grade, or rank to arrange objects.

Host Bus Adapter (HBA) This adapter connects the server node to the storage area network using fiber or, potentially, an iSCSI SAN.

HTML *See* HyperText Markup Language (HTML).

HTTP *See* HyperText Transfer Protocol (HTTP).

HTTP Digest authentication An Internet standard that allows authentication of clients to occur using a series of challenges and responses over HTTP.

hub transport server The primary function of the Hub Transport server is to route messages for delivery within the Exchange organization. By moving message routing to another server (other than the Mailbox server), many new and needed features and functions become available. As an example, while messages are being routed through the Hub Transport server, they can have transport rules and filtering policies applied to them that determine where they'll wind up, such as being delivered to a compliance mailbox in addition to the recipient's mailbox, or what they'll look like, such as stamping a disclaimer on every outbound message.

HyperText Markup Language (HTML) The script language used to create content for the World Wide Web (WWW). HTML can create hyperlinks between objects on the Web.

HyperText Transfer Protocol (HTTP) The Internet protocol used to transfer information on the World Wide Web (WWW).

I

IIS metabase The Registry-like database of configuration information maintained by Internet Information Services.

Inbox The storage folder that receives new incoming messages.

Inbox Repair tool A utility (`Scanpst.exe`) that is used to repair corrupt personal folder (PST) files.

incremental backup Method in which all files that have changed since the last normal or incremental backup are backed up.

Information Store *See* `Store.exe`.

inheritance The process through which permissions are passed down from a parent container to objects inside that container (child objects).

Infrastructure master An operations master role server that is responsible for updating references from objects in its domain to objects in other domains.

installer package (MSI file) One of the files generated by Windows Installer; used to control configuration information during installation. The installer package contains a database that describes the configuration information. *See also* installer transform (MST file).

installer transform (MST file) One of the files generated by Windows Installer; used to control configuration information during installation. The transform file contains modifications that are to be made as Windows Installer installs Outlook. *See also* installer package (MSI file).

Integrated Windows authentication Requires the user to provide a valid Windows username and password. However, the user's credentials are never sent across the network. If you are running in the Windows 2000 mixed domain functional level, this method uses the NTLM authentication protocol used by Windows NT 4.0. If your network is running at the Windows 2000 native domain functional level or the Windows Server 2003 domain functional level, this method uses Kerberos v5.

Internet Information Services (IIS) A built-in component of Windows Server 2003 that allows access to resources on the server through various Internet protocols, such as POP3, IMAP4, and HTTP.

Internet Message Access Protocol version 4 (IMAP4) An Internet retrieval protocol that enables clients to access and manipulate messages in their mailbox on a remote server. IMAP4 provides additional functions over POP3, such as access to subfolders (not merely the Inbox folder), and selective downloading of messages.

ipconfig A command-line utility that can be used to display and modify TCP/IP information about all installed network adapters. Common uses include flushing the local DNS resolver cache and releasing and renewing DHCP leases.

K

Kerberos version 5 (v5) The primary form of user authentication used by Windows Server 2003.

key A randomly generated number used to implement advanced security, such as encryption or digital signatures. *See also* key pair, public key, private key.

key pair A key that is divided into two mathematically related halves. One half (the public key) is made public; the other half (the private key) is known by only one user.

L

leaf object An object in a Microsoft Management Console window that does not contain any other objects.

Lightweight Directory Access Protocol (LDAP) An Internet protocol used for client access to an X.500-based directory, such as Active Directory.

Local Continuous Replication (LCR) This is a single server environment where the production storage group is copied to another physical disk on the same server using log shipping.

Local Procedure Call (LPC) When a program issues an instruction that is executed on the same computer as the program executing the instruction. *See also* Remote Procedure Call (RPC).

lockbox The process of using a secret key to encrypt a message and its attachments and then using a public key pair to encrypt and decrypt the secret key.

Logical Unit Number (LUN) The logical unit number is the disk structure as defined on the SAN or NAS device used to provide disk resources to a cluster. For example, on the SAN, there may be ten physical disks combined together in a RAID format. These disks are then exposed from the SAN to the computer as one unit. The Windows computer then sees one large physical disk connected to it. See, now you are really confused.

M

Mail and Directory Management (MADMAN) MIB A specialized version of the base Management Information Base that was created for monitoring messaging systems. *See also* Management Information Base (MIB).

mailbox The generic term referring to a container that holds messages, such as incoming and outgoing messages.

mailbox-enabled user A user who has been assigned an Exchange Server mailbox.

mailbox database A database on an Exchange server that holds mailboxes. *See also* database.

mailbox server The primary function of the Mailbox server role is to provide users' with mailboxes that can be accessed directly from the Outlook client. The Mailbox server also contains the databases that hold public folders if you are still using them in your organization, so, as a point of comparison, the Mailbox server is most like the back-end server from previous versions of Exchange.

mail-enabled user A user who has been given an e-mail address but no mailbox.

Mail Exchanger (MX) Record A record in a DNS database that indicates the SMTP mail host for an organization.

majority node set cluster In Windows Server 2003, Enterprise Edition, Microsoft presented another option to the shared disk environment for the quorum. Instead of selecting a shared physical disk to host the quorum, it is possible to select the Majority Node Set (MNS) option to create a server cluster. From the perspective of Windows, MNS looks just like a single quorum disk, but the quorum data is actually stored on multiple disks across the cluster. MNS is designed and built so that it ensures that the cluster data stored kept consistent across the different disks on different computers.

Management Information Base (MIB) A set of configurable objects defined for management by the SNMP protocol.

MAPI *See* Messaging Application Programming Interface (MAPI).

MAPI client A messaging client that uses the Messaging Application Programming Interface (MAPI) to connect to a messaging server. *See also* Messaging Application Programming Interface (MAPI).

MAPI subsystem The second layer of the MAPI architecture; this component is shared by all applications that require its services and is therefore considered a *subsystem* of the operating system.

message state information Information that identifies the state of a message in a public folder. Message state information is made up of a change number, a time stamp, and a predecessor change list.

Messaging Application Programming Interface (MAPI) An object-oriented programming interface for messaging services, developed by Microsoft.

Microsoft Clustering Service (MSCS) A Windows service that provides for highly available server solutions through a process known as failover. An MSCS cluster consists of two more nodes (members) that are configured such that upon the failure of one node, any of the remaining cluster nodes can transfer the failed node's resources to itself, thus keeping the resources available for client access.

Microsoft Management Console (MMC) A framework application in which snap-ins are loaded to provide the management of various network resources. System Manager is an example of a snap-in.

Microsoft Office Outlook 2007 The premier client application for use with Exchange Server 2007.

Microsoft Search Service The service that performs full-text indexing of mailbox and public databases.

migration Moving resources, such as mailboxes, messages, etc., from one messaging system to another.

mounting The process of bringing a mailbox or public database online. *See also* dismounting.

Multipurpose Internet Mail Extensions (MIME) An Internet protocol that enables the encoding of binary content within mail messages. For example, MIME could be used to encode a graphics file or word processing document as an attachment to a text-based mail message. The recipient of the message would have to be using MIME also to decode the attachment. MIME is newer than UUENCODE and in many systems has replaced it. *See also* Secure/Multipurpose Internet Mail Extensions (S/MIME), UUENCODE.

multimaster replication model A model in which every replica of a public folder is considered a master copy.

multipathing Multipathing is commonly used in Fiber SAN designs. Nodes will have two HBAs (remember, high availability requires redundancy) that are then joined together using software. Some common products that you may have heard of include PowerPath (EMC) and SecurePath (HP). The two HBAs can be bound together and load balanced to improve throughput from 2 GB to 4 GB for a particular node. It is also fairly common, though, that the Fiber Array will also use two HBAs bound together to provide 4GB of throughput which is then shared among all of the servers that attach to the array for storage. 4GB may not be enough. In some cases, organizations will invest and provide 4 fiber connections from the SAN to the fabric thus providing 8 GB of throughput.

MX *See* Mail Exchanger (MX).

N

name resolution The DNS process of mapping a domain name to its IP address.

namespace Any bounded area in which a given name can be resolved.

nbtstat A command-line utility that is used to resolve NetBIOS names to IP addresses.

Network load balancing (NLB) Network Load Balancing is used at the TCP/IP level to provide both horizontal scalability as well as high availability. Horizontal scaling is achieved by the servers sharing the load between them. If the application becomes over subscribed, new servers can be built and added into the NLB web farm to spread the load out even more. High availability is achieved through the NLB web farm in that if a single (or even multiple) server fails, NLB will redistribute the load among the remaining servers.

Network News Transfer Protocol (NNTP) An Internet protocol used to transfer newsgroup information between newsgroup servers and clients (newsreaders) and between newsgroup servers.

NetDiag A command-line utility that is used to troubleshoot and isolate network connectivity problems by performing a number of tests to determine the exact state of a server.

netstat A command-line utility that is used to display TCP/IP connection information and protocol statistics for a computer.

NNTP *See* Network News Transfer Protocol (NNTP).

node In a Microsoft Management Console window, a node is any object that can be configured. In clustering, a node is one of the computers that is part of a cluster.

normal backup During this backup, all selected files are backed up, regardless of how their archive bit is set. After the backup, the archive bit is set to off for all files, indicating that those files have been backed up.

notification Defines the event that is triggered when a service or resource being watched by a server or link monitor fails. Notifications can send e-mail and alerts and even run custom scripts.

nslookup A command-line utility that can be used to gather information about the DNS infrastructure inside and outside an organization and troubleshoot DNS-related problems.

O

object The representation, or abstraction, of an entity. As an object, it contains properties, also called attributes, that can be configured. For example, each Exchange server is represented as an object in System Manager. An Exchange server object can have properties that give certain administrators permission to configure that server.

Object Linking and Embedding version 2 (OLE 2) The Microsoft protocol that specifies how programs can share objects and therefore create compound documents.

Offline Address Book (OAB) A copy stored on a client's computer of part or all of the server-based Global Address List (GAL). An OAB allows a client to address messages while not connected to their server.

offline folder *See* Offline Storage folder (OST).

Offline Storage folder (OST) Folders located on a client's computer that contain replicas of server-based folders. An OST allows a client to access and manipulate copies of server data while not connected to their server. When the client reconnects to their server, they can have their OST resynchronized with the master folders on the server.

OLE 2 *See* Object Linking and Embedding version 2 (OLE 2).

Open Shortest Path First (OSPF) A routing protocol developed for IP networks based on the Shortest Path First or Link State Algorithm.

Organization The highest-level object in the Microsoft Exchange hierarchy.

organizational unit An Active Directory container into which objects can be grouped for permissions management.

Outlook Web Access (OWA) A service that allows users to connect to Exchange Server and access mailboxes and public folders using a web browser.

OWA Light A scaled version of Outlook Web Access that was referred to as *Basic* in the Exchange Server 2003 version of OWA.

Outlook Anywhere A new mode of connecting remote Outlook 2007 clients to an Exchange Server 2007 organization without requiring the use of a Virtual Private Network (VPN) or Outlook Web Access (OWA). RPCs are passed over the HTTP connection and secured with SSL encryption. Basic authentication is used to authenticate the user and is also protected by the SSL. Outlook Anywhere was first introduced in Exchange Server 2003 as RPC over HTTP.

P

patch files Temporary logs that store transactions while a backup is taking place. Transactions in these logs are committed when the backup is finished.

pathping A new command that is a mix of both `ping` and `tracert`. The `pathping` command provides the ability to determine the packet loss along each link in the path and at each router in the path to the destination, which can be particularly helpful when troubleshooting problems where multiple routers and links are involved.

Performance Monitor *See* Performance snap-in.

Performance snap-in A utility used to log and chart the performance of various hardware and software components of a system. In various documentation, the Performance snap-in is also referred to as Performance Monitor, Performance tool, and System Monitor.

Performance tool *See* Performance snap-in.

perimeter network A network formed by using two firewalls to separate an internal network from the Internet and then placing certain servers, such as an Exchange front-end server, between the two firewalls. This is also referred to as a demilitarized zone (DMZ).

permission Provides specific authorization or denial to a user to perform an action on an object.

Personal Address Book (PAB) An address book created by a user and stored on that user's computer or a server.

Personal STore (PST) folder Folder created by a user and used for message storage instead of using their mailbox in the mailbox database. PSTs can be located on a user's computer or on a server.

Pickup folder Used for outbound messages on some SMTP hosts. Exchange Server 2007 creates, but does not normally use, this folder.

PING Packet Internet Groper. The basic network connectivity troubleshooting tool that works by sending a series of ICMP Echo Request datagrams to a destination and waiting for the corresponding ICMP Echo Reply datagrams to come back. The return packets are then used to determine how many datagrams are getting through, the response time, and the TTL (time to live).

plaintext Unencrypted data. Synonymous with clear text.

Point-to-Point Protocol (PPP) An Internet protocol used for direct communication between two nodes. Commonly used by Internet users and their Internet Service Provider on the serial line point-to-point connection over a modem.

polling Process that queries a server-based mailbox for new mail.

POP3 *See* Post Office Protocol version 3 (POP3).

port number A numeric identifier assigned to an application. Transport protocols such as TCP and UDP use the port number to identify to which application to deliver a packet.

postmaster mailbox The postmaster mailbox is required in every messaging infrastructure per RFC 2822 and receives non-delivery reports and delivery status notifications.

Post Office Protocol version 3 (POP3) An Internet protocol used for client retrieval of mail from a server-based mailbox.

Primary Domain Controller (PDC) emulator An operations master role server that is responsible for authenticating non–Active Directory clients, such as Windows 95 or Windows 98 clients. The PDC emulator is responsible for processing password changes from these clients and is also the responsible server for time synchronization within the domain.

private folder *See* mailbox.

private key The half of a key pair that is known by only the pair's user and is used to decrypt data and to digitally sign messages.

property A characteristic of an object. Properties of a mailbox include display name and storage limits. The terms *property* and *attribute* are synonymous.

public folder A folder stored in a public store on an Exchange server and accessible to multiple users.

public folder hierarchy The relative position of all of the folders in a public folder tree.

public folder replication The transferring of public folder data to replicas of that folder on other servers.

public folder referral The process by which a client can locate a requested public folder outside of their home Exchange server.

public folder tree A hierarchy of public folders associated with a particular public database.

public key The half of a key pair that is published for anyone to read and is used when encrypting data and verifying digital signatures.

public-key encryption An encryption method that employs a key pair consisting of a public and a private key.

public key infrastructure (PKI) A system of components working together to verify the identity of users who transfer data on a system and to encrypt that data if needed.

public database A databases that holds public folders on an Exchange server. *See also* database.

public folder A folder used to store data for a group of users. Some of the features of a public folder are permissions, views, and rules.

Q

Queue folder A folder in which messages that have yet to be delivered are stored.

Queue Viewer A part of the Exchange System Manager that lets you view and manipulate the messages in a queue.

quorum disk The disk set that contains definitive cluster configuration data. All members of an MSCS cluster must have continuous, reliable access to the data that is contained on a quorum disk. Information contained on the quorum disk includes data about the nodes that are participating in the cluster, the applications and resources that are defined within the cluster, and the current status of each member, application, and resource.

R

random failover In this cluster operation mode, the clustered resource will be randomly failed over to an available cluster node.

recipient An object that can receive a message. Recipient objects include users, contacts, groups, and public folders.

recovery server A server separate from the organization that is used as a dummy server for recovering individual mailboxes or messages from a backup.

Recovery Storage Group A feature first introduced in Exchange Server 2003 that provides a special storage group on a server that can be used for performing restorations without the need to use an alternative recovery forest or the need to take the database offline for an extended period of time.

Relative Identity (RID) master An operations master role server that is responsible for maintaining the uniqueness of every object within its domain. When a new Active Directory object is created, it is assigned a unique security identifier (SID). The SID consists of a domain specific SID that is the same for all objects created in that domain and a relative identifier (RID), which is unique amongst all objects within that domain

remote domain An email domain outside of your Exchange organization.

replica A copy of a public folder located on an Exchange server.

replication The transferring of a copy of data to another location, such as another server or site. *See also* directory replication, public folder replication.

remote delivery The delivery of a message to a recipient that does not reside on the same server as the sender.

Remote Procedure Call (RPC) A set of protocols for issuing instructions that can be sent over a network for execution. A client computer makes a request to a server computer, and the results are sent to the client computer. The computer issuing the request and the computer performing the request are separated remotely over a network. RPCs are a key ingredient in distributed processing and client/server computing. *See also* Local Procedure Call (LPC).

reserve log files Two transaction log files created by Exchange Server that are reserved for use when the server runs out of disk space.

resolving an address The process of determining where (on which physical server) an object with a particular address resides.

resource group Functions in a cluster that are not bound to a specific computer and can fail over to another node.

Rich-Text Format (RTF) A Microsoft format protocol that includes bolding, highlighting, italics, underlining, and many other format types.

role A group of permissions that define which activities a user or group can perform with regard to an object.

root CA Resides at the top of a Certificate Authority hierarchy; is trusted unconditionally by a client. All certificate chains terminate at a root CA. *See also* Certificate Authority (CA).

root domain The top domain in a domain tree.

routing group A collection of Exchange servers that have full-time, full-mesh, reliable connections between each and every server. Messages sent between any two servers within a routing group are delivered directly from the source server to the destination server.

Routing Group Connector (RGC) The primary connector used to connect routing groups in an organization. The RGC uses SMTP as its default transport mechanism.

Routing Group Master A server that maintains data about all of the servers running Exchange Server 2000/2003 in a routing group.

rule A set of instructions that define how a message is handled when it reaches a folder.

S

scalable The ability of a system to grow to handle greater traffic, volume, usage, etc.

Schedule+ Free Busy public folder A system folder that contains calendaring and synchronization information for Exchange users.

schema The set of rules defining a directory's hierarchy, objects, attributes, etc.

Schema master An operations master role server that controls all updates and changes that are made to the schema.

secret key A security key that can be used to encrypt data and that is known only by the sender and the recipients whom the sender informs.

Secure/Multipurpose Internet Mail Extensions (S/MIME) An Internet protocol that enables mail messages to be digitally signed, encrypted, and decrypted.

Secure Sockets Layer (SSL) An Internet protocol that provides secure and authenticated TCP/IP connections. A client and server establish a "handshake" whereby they agree on a level of security they will use, such as authentication requirements and encryption. SSL can be used to encrypt sensitive data for transmission.

security group A group defined in Active Directory that can be assigned permissions. All members of the group gain the permissions given to the group.

Server License Provides the legal right to install and operate Microsoft Exchange Server 2007 (or another server product) on a single-server machine.

service provider A MAPI program that provides messaging-oriented services to a client. There are three main types of service providers: address book, message store, and message transport.

signing The process of placing a digital signature on a message.

simple display name An alternate name for the mailbox that appears when, for some reason, the full display name cannot.

Simple Mail Transfer Protocol (SMTP) The Internet protocol used to transfer mail messages. It is now the default transport protocol for Exchange 2000 Server.

Simple Network Management Protocol (SNMP) Internet protocol used to manage heterogeneous computers, operating systems, and applications. Because of its wide acceptance and applicability, SNMP is well suited for enterprise-wide management.

Single Copy Cluster (SCC) This is a standard cluster much like previous server cluster implementations for Exchange. This implementation requires use of a shared disk implementation such as a SAN to host the quorum, the storage disks, and the transaction log disks.

single-instance storage Storing only one copy. A message that is sent to multiple recipients homed in the same storage group has only one copy (i.e., instance) stored on that server. Each recipient is given a pointer to that copy of the message.

single-node cluster A cluster model useful for testing and application development that has only one cluster node that uses either local storage or an external storage device.

site A logical grouping of servers in previous versions of Exchange (prior to Exchange 2000 Server) that are connected by a full mesh (every server is directly connected to every other server) and communicate using high-bandwidth RPC. All servers in a site can authenticate one another either because they are homed in the same Windows domain or because of trust relationships configured between separate Windows domains. A site is also a group of Windows servers that are connected with full-time, reliable connections.

smart host An SMTP host designated to receive all outgoing SMTP mail. The smart host then forwards the mail to the relevant destination.

S/MIME *See* Secure/Multipurpose Internet Mail Extensions (S/MIME).

SMTP *See* Simple Mail Transfer Protocol (SMTP).

SMTP Connector Using SMTP as its transport mechanism, the SMTP Connector can be used to connect routing groups to one another and to connect Exchange to a foreign SMTP system.

SMTP virtual server A logical representation of the SMTP protocol on a physical server.

SNMP *See* Simple Network Management Protocol (SNMP).

spooling The process used by SMTP to temporarily store messages that cannot be delivered immediately.

stand-alone CA Used to issue certificates to users who are outside the enterprise and who do not require access to the Active Directory. *See also* Certificate Authority (CA), Enterprise CA.

Standard Edition The basic version of Exchange Server 2007 with support for up to five storage groups and five databases.

standard permissions Permissions that are defined in a standard installation of Windows Server 2003. Extended permissions are created when Exchange Server 2007 is installed.

Storage Area Network (SAN) A SAN is a set of connected devices (e.g., disks and tapes) and servers that are connected to a common infrastructure such as Fiber Channel. The communication and data transfer channel for a given SAN environment is commonly called a storage fabric. The fabric of the SAN enables multiple servers to connect to a pool of storage devices which can include multiple arrays. In a SAN, any server can be configured to access any storage device or part of a storage device. In a SAN environment, management of the environment provides security for the storage units.

storage group A collection of databases (up to five) that all share a common set of transaction logs.

Store.exe The actual process that governs the use of stores on an Exchange server. Often referred to as the Information Store service.

store-and-forward A delivery method that does not require the sender and recipient to have simultaneous interaction. Instead, when a message is sent, it is transferred to the next appropriate location in the network, which temporarily stores it, makes a routing decision, and forwards the message to the next appropriate network location. This process occurs until the message is ultimately delivered to the intended recipient or an error condition causes the message to be returned to the sender.

subordinate CA A CA found underneath the root CA in the CA hierarchy and maybe even under other subordinate CAs. *See also* Certificate Authority (CA), root CA.

subsystem A software component that, when loaded, extends the operating system by providing additional services. The MAPI program, `MAPI32.DLL`, is an example of a subsystem. `MAPI32.DLL` loads on top of the Windows 98 or Windows XP operating system and provides messaging services.

System Monitor *See* Performance snap-in.

system state backup A form of backup that includes the Windows Registry, the IIS metabase, and the Active Directory (if run on a domain controller).

T

Task Manager Displays the programs and processes running on a computer. It also displays various performance information, such as CPU and memory usage.

telnet A text-based command-line tool that allows you to remotely communicate with a host.

template An object, such as a user or group, that contains configuration information that is applicable to multiple users. Objects for each user can be easily created by copying the template and filling in individual information.

TLS encryption Transport Layer Security (TLS) encryption is a generic security protocol similar to Secure Sockets Layer encryption.

token The packet of security information a Certificate Authority sends to a client during advanced security setup. Information in the packet includes the client's public key and its expiration. A token is similar to a certificate.

top-level folders The folders found in the root level of a public folder tree.

tracert A command-line utility that uses ICMP packets to determine the path that an IP datagram takes to reach its final destination.

transaction log A file used to quickly write data. That data is later written to the relevant Exchange database file. It is quicker to write to a transaction log file because the writes are done sequentially (i.e., one right after the other). Transaction log files can also be used to replay transactions from the log when rebuilding an Exchange database. All stores in a single storage group share the same set of transaction logs.

Triple Data Encryption Standard (3DES) A newer, more secure, variant of the DES standard that uses three 56-bit keys, one after another, to produce a 168-bit key.

Typical installation This option installs the Exchange Server software, the basic Messaging and Collaboration components, and the System Manager snap-in program. It does not include the additional connectors.

U

unified messaging server The Unified Messaging server role provides the following functionality to an Exchange Server 2007 organization:

- Fax reception and delivery to Exchange mailboxes
- Voice call answering and delivery of recorded voicemail file to Exchange mailboxes
- Voicemail access via a phone connection
- Message read back via a phone connection, including replying to the message or forwarding it to another recipient
- Calendar access via a phone connection, including meeting request acceptance
- Out-of-office messages in voicemail via a phone connection

Uniform Resource Identifier (URI) A generic term for all types of addresses that refer to objects on the World Wide Web and private networks.

Uniform Resource Locator (URL) An addressing method used to identify Internet servers and documents.

URL *See* Uniform Resource Locator (URL).

Usenet A network within the Internet that is composed of numerous servers containing information on a variety of topics. Each organized topic is called a newsgroup.

user object An object in Active Directory that is associated with a person on the network. Users can be mailbox-enabled or mail-enabled in Exchange Server 2007.

UUENCODE Stands for UNIX-to-UNIX Encode, and is a protocol used to encode binary information within mail messages. UUENCODE is older than MIME. *See also* Multipurpose Internet Mail Extensions (MIME.)

V

virtual server A group of resources that contains an IP Address resource and a Network Name resource. The network name is then published to the network so that others can attach to its name to access resources included within the group. Clients access the resources of a virtual server exactly like they would access the resources of a physical server. Whether the server is a virtual server or a physical server doesn't matter to client computers on the network. They don't know the difference and they just don't care, either.

Virtual Local Area Network (VLAN) A VLAN is an implementation where remote sites can be configured so that they appear to be on the same network segment.

Volume Shadow Copy A new feature in the Windows Server 2003 Backup Utility to back up open files as if they were closed at the moment of the backup event.

W

W3svc The World Wide Web (WWW) publishing service of Internet Information Server (IIS).

Web The World Wide Web (WWW).

WebReady file types Certain file types, such as Microsoft Word documents and Adobe Acrobat PDF documents, can be converted to HTML easily. You can configure OWA to display these file types as HTML documents, thus allowing access to them even on computers that may not have the original applications they were created in installed.

well-known port numbers Numbers that are commonly used as the TCP port numbers for popular applications.

Windows 2000 mixed domain functional level The domain functional level that allows Windows NT 4.0 backup domain controllers to exist and function within a Windows 2003 domain.

Windows 2000 native domain functional level The domain functional level that requires all domain controllers to be Windows 2000 Server or Windows Server 2003 and does not provide support for Windows NT 4.0 backup domain controllers.

Windows Event Log *See* Event Log.

Windows site A group of computers that exist on one or more IP subnets. Computers within a site must be connected by a fast, reliable network connection.

Windows Internet Naming System (WINS) A name resolution service for resolving NetBIOS names on a Windows network.

Windows Server 2003 domain functional level The highest domain functional level in Windows 2003, which implements all the new features of Windows 2003 Active Directory.

World Wide Web (WWW) The collection of computers on the Internet using protocols such as HTML and HTTP.

WWW *See* World Wide Web (WWW).

X

X.400 An International Telecommunications Union (ITU) standard for message exchange.

X.500 An International Telecommunications Union (ITU) standard for directory services.

X.509 certificate The most widely used format for certificates, X.509 certificates contain not only the public key but also information that identifies the user and the organization that issued the certificate.

Index

Note to the Reader: Throughout this index **boldfaced** page numbers indicate primary discussions of a topic. *Italicized* page numbers indicate illustrations.

A

B

E

F

G

I

J

K

L

M

N

O

P

Q

R

S

T

U

V

W

X

Y

The Absolute Best MCITP: Enterprise Messaging Administrator Book/CD Package on the Market!

Get ready for the new Pro: Designing Messaging Solutions with Microsoft Exchange Server 2007 (70-237) and Pro: Deploying Messaging Solutions with Microsoft Exchange Server 2007 (70-238) exams with the most comprehensive and challenging sample tests anywhere!

The Sybex Test Engine features:

- All the review questions, as covered in each chapter of the book
- Challenging questions representative of those you'll find on the real exam
- Four full length bonus exams (two for each of the Exchange Server exams) available only on the CD
- An Assessment Test to narrow your focus to certain objective groups.

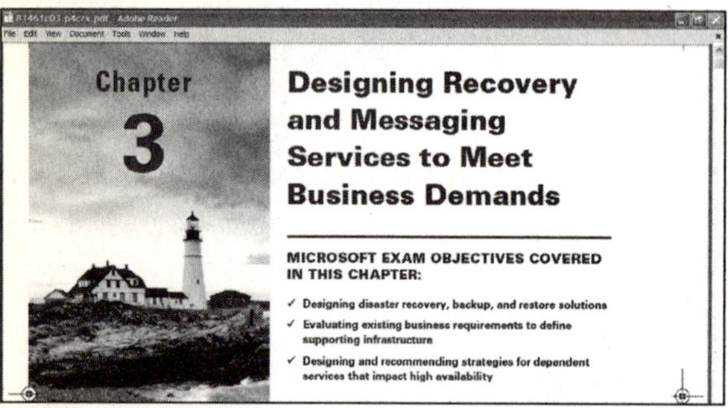

Chapter 3

Designing Recovery and Messaging Services to Meet Business Demands

MICROSOFT EXAM OBJECTIVES COVERED IN THIS CHAPTER:

- ✓ Designing disaster recovery, backup, and restore solutions
- ✓ Evaluating existing business requirements to define supporting infrastructure
- ✓ Designing and recommending strategies for dependent services that impact high availability

Search through the complete book in PDF!

- Access the entire *MCITP: Microsoft Exchange Server 2007 Messaging Design and Deployment Study Guide,* complete with figures and tables, in electronic format.
- Search the *MCITP: Microsoft Exchange Server 2007 Messaging Design and Deployment Study Guide* chapters to find information on any topic in seconds.

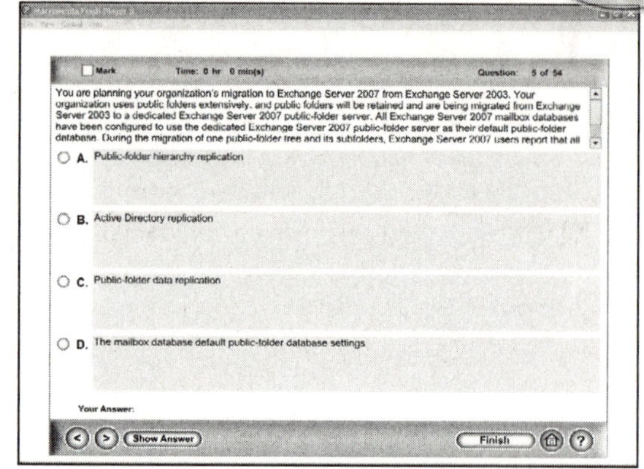

Use the Electronic Flashcards for PCs or Palm devices to jog your memory and prep last-minute for the exam!

- Reinforce your understanding of key concepts with these hardcore flashcard-style questions.
- Download the Flashcards to your Palm device and go on the road. Now you can study for the Pro: Designing Messaging Solutions with Microsoft Exchange Server 2007 and Pro: Deploying Messaging Solutions with Microsoft Exchange Server 2007 exams any time, anywhere.

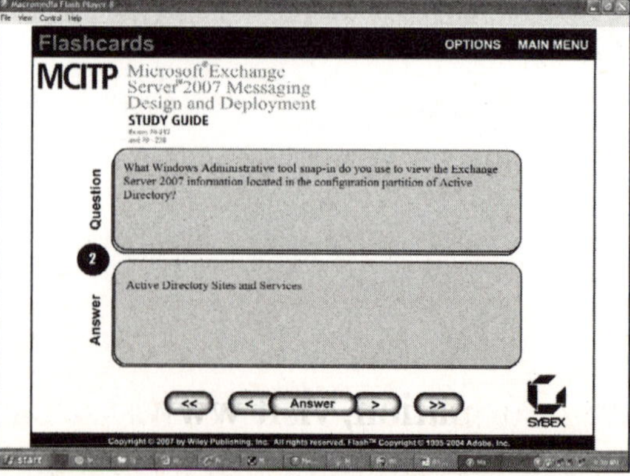

SYBEX | SERIOUS SKILLS.

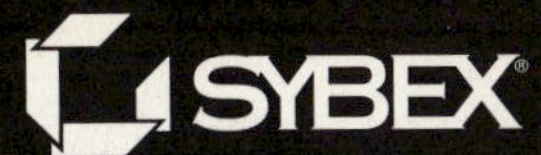

Migrate with us.

Bridge the gap between the old, the new, and the very latest in Microsoft technologies with our practical, in-depth guides at your side. You'll get up to speed and down to business in no time.

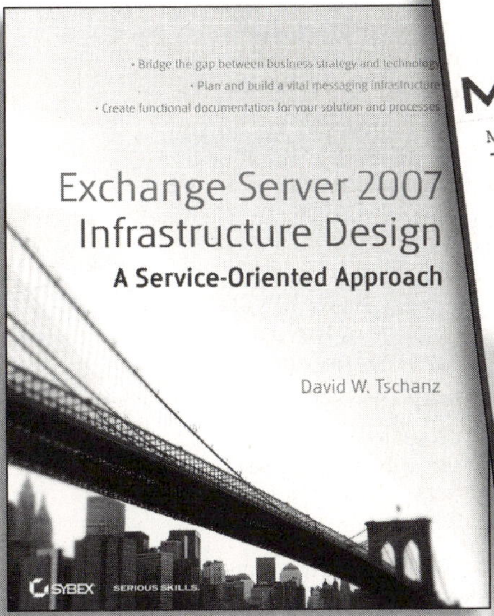

Exchange Server 2007
Infrastructure Design
A Service-Oriented Approach
David W. Tschanz
SYBEX SERIOUS SKILLS.

978-0-470-22446-5

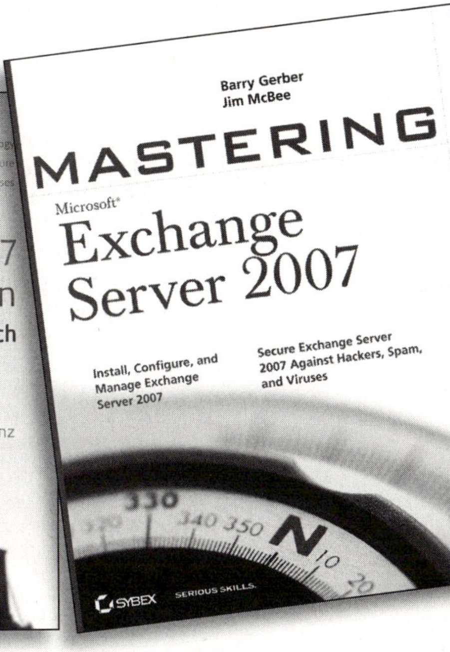

Barry Gerber
Jim McBee
MASTERING
Microsoft®
Exchange Server 2007
Install, Configure, and Manage Exchange Server 2007
Secure Exchange Server 2007 Against Hackers, Spam, and Viruses
SYBEX SERIOUS SKILLS.

978-0-470-04289-2

Microsoft®
Exchange Server 2007
Implementation and Administration
GET UP TO SPEED AND DOWN TO BUSINESS
Jim McBee
SYBEX SERIOUS SKILLS.

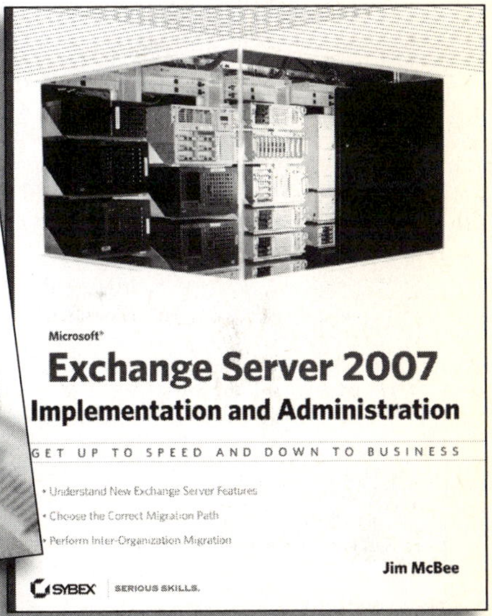

978-0-470-18741-8

For more information, visit www.sybex.com.

Wiley, the Wiley logo, and the Sybex logo are registered trademarks of John Wiley & Sons, Inc. and/or its affiliates. All other trademarks are the property of their respective owners.

SYBEX®
An Imprint of WILEY

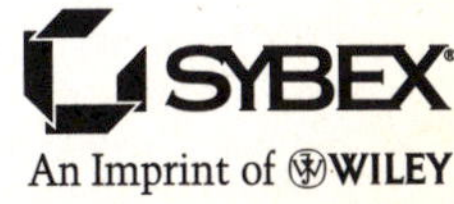

Wiley Publishing, Inc. End-User License Agreement

READ THIS. You should carefully read these terms and conditions before opening the software packet(s) included with this book "Book". This is a license agreement "Agreement" between you and Wiley Publishing, Inc. "WPI". By opening the accompanying software packet(s), you acknowledge that you have read and accept the following terms and conditions. If you do not agree and do not want to be bound by such terms and conditions, promptly return the Book and the unopened software packet(s) to the place you obtained them for a full refund.

1. License Grant. WPI grants to you (either an individual or entity) a nonexclusive license to use one copy of the enclosed software program(s) (collectively, the "Software," solely for your own personal or business purposes on a single computer (whether a standard computer or a workstation component of a multi-user network). The Software is in use on a computer when it is loaded into temporary memory (RAM) or installed into permanent memory (hard disk, CD-ROM, or other storage device). WPI reserves all rights not expressly granted herein.

2. Ownership. WPI is the owner of all right, title, and interest, including copyright, in and to the compilation of the Software recorded on the physical packet included with this Book "Software Media". Copyright to the individual programs recorded on the Software Media is owned by the author or other authorized copyright owner of each program. Ownership of the Software and all proprietary rights relating thereto remain with WPI and its licensers.

3. Restrictions On Use and Transfer.

(a) You may only (i) make one copy of the Software for backup or archival purposes, or (ii) transfer the Software to a single hard disk, provided that you keep the original for backup or archival purposes. You may not (i) rent or lease the Software, (ii) copy or reproduce the Software through a LAN or other network system or through any computer subscriber system or bulletin-board system, or (iii) modify, adapt, or create derivative works based on the Software.

(b) You may not reverse engineer, decompile, or disassemble the Software. You may transfer the Software and user documentation on a permanent basis, provided that the transferee agrees to accept the terms and conditions of this Agreement and you retain no copies. If the Software is an update or has been updated, any transfer must include the most recent update and all prior versions.

4. Restrictions on Use of Individual Programs. You must follow the individual requirements and restrictions detailed for each individual program in the About the CD-ROM appendix of this Book or on the Software Media. These limitations are also contained in the individual license agreements recorded on the Software Media. These limitations may include a requirement that after using the program for a specified period of time, the user must pay a registration fee or discontinue use. By opening the Software packet(s), you will be agreeing to abide by the licenses and restrictions for these individual programs that are detailed in the About the CD-ROM appendix and/or on the Software Media. None of the material on this Software Media or listed in this Book may ever be redistributed, in original or modified form, for commercial purposes.

5. Limited Warranty.

(a) WPI warrants that the Software and Software Media are free from defects in materials and workmanship under normal use for a period of sixty (60) days from the date of purchase of this Book. If WPI receives notification within the warranty period of defects in materials or workmanship, WPI will replace the defective Software Media.

(b) WPI AND THE AUTHOR(S) OF THE BOOK DISCLAIM ALL OTHER WARRANTIES, EXPRESS OR IMPLIED, INCLUDING WITHOUT LIMITATION IMPLIED WARRANTIES OF MERCHANTABILITY AND FITNESS FOR A PARTICULAR PURPOSE, WITH RESPECT TO THE SOFTWARE, THE PROGRAMS, THE SOURCE CODE CONTAINED THEREIN, AND/OR THE TECHNIQUES DESCRIBED IN THIS BOOK. WPI DOES NOT WARRANT THAT THE FUNCTIONS CONTAINED IN THE SOFTWARE WILL MEET YOUR REQUIREMENTS OR THAT THE OPERATION OF THE SOFTWARE WILL BE ERROR FREE.

(c) This limited warranty gives you specific legal rights, and you may have other rights that vary from jurisdiction to jurisdiction.

6. Remedies.

(a) WPI's entire liability and your exclusive remedy for defects in materials and workmanship shall be limited to replacement of the Software Media, which may be returned to WPI with a copy of your receipt at the following address: Software Media Fulfillment Department, Attn.: *MCITP: Microsoft Exchange Server 2007 Messaging Design and Deployment Study Guide,* Wiley Publishing, Inc., 10475 Crosspoint Blvd., Indianapolis, IN 46256, or call 1-800-762-2974. Please allow four to six weeks for delivery. This Limited Warranty is void if failure of the Software Media has resulted from accident, abuse, or misapplication. Any replacement Software Media will be warranted for the remainder of the original warranty period or thirty (30) days, whichever is longer.

(b) In no event shall WPI or the author be liable for any damages whatsoever (including without limitation damages for loss of business profits, business interruption, loss of business information, or any other pecuniary loss) arising from the use of or inability to use the Book or the Software, even if WPI has been advised of the possibility of such damages.

(c) Because some jurisdictions do not allow the exclusion or limitation of liability for consequential or incidental damages, the above limitation or exclusion may not apply to you.

7. U.S. Government Restricted Rights. Use, duplication, or disclosure of the Software for or on behalf of the United States of America, its agencies and/or instrumentalities "U.S. Government" is subject to restrictions as stated in paragraph (c)(1)(ii) of the Rights in Technical Data and Computer Software clause of DFARS 252.227-7013, or subparagraphs (c) (1) and (2) of the Commercial Computer Software - Restricted Rights clause at FAR 52.227-19, and in similar clauses in the NASA FAR supplement, as applicable.

8. General. This Agreement constitutes the entire understanding of the parties and revokes and supersedes all prior agreements, oral or written, between them and may not be modified or amended except in a writing signed by both parties hereto that specifically refers to this Agreement. This Agreement shall take precedence over any other documents that may be in conflict herewith. If any one or more provisions contained in this Agreement are held by any court or tribunal to be invalid, illegal, or otherwise unenforceable, each and every other provision shall remain in full force and effect.